ADO.NET:
The Complete Reference

About the Authors

Michael Otey is Senior Technical Editor for
Windows & .NET Magazine and SQL Server
Magazine. He is also President of TECA, Inc.
(www.teca.com), a software development
and consulting company that specializes in
network and database applications. Michael
is the co-author of the SQL Server 2000
Developer's Guide published by Osborne
McGraw Hill.

Denielle Otey is the Vice President of TECA,
Inc., as well as a software consultant who has
extensive experience designing, implementing,
testing, and debugging software in C, VC++,
VB, and Visual Studio.NET. She also is the
developer of several SQL Server utilities.

ADO.NET:
The Complete Reference

Michael Otey
Denielle Otey

McGraw-Hill/Osborne

New York Chicago San Francisco
Lisbon London Madrid Mexico City
Milan New Delhi San Juan
Seoul Singapore Sydney Toronto

The McGraw·Hill Companies

McGraw-Hill/Osborne
2600 Tenth Street
Berkeley, California 94710
U.S.A.

To arrange bulk purchase discounts for sales promotions, premiums, or fund-raisers, please contact **McGraw-Hill/Osborne** at the above address. For information on translations or book distributors outside the U.S.A., please see the International Contact Information page immediately following the index of this book.

ADO.NET: The Complete Reference

1234567890 DOC DOC 019876543
ISBN 0-07-222898-9

Publisher
   Brandon A. Nordin

Vice President & Associate Publisher
   Scott Rogers

Editorial Director
   Wendy Rinaldi

Project Editor
   Julie M. Smith

Acquisitions Coordinator
   Athena Honore

Technical Editor
   Mark Goedert

Copy Editor
   Nancy Rapoport

Proofreader
   Linda Medoff

Computer Designers
   Apollo Publishing Services,
   Lucie Ericksen

Illustrators
   Lyssa Wald, Melinda Moore Lytle,
   Michael Mueller

Series Design
   Peter F. Hancik

This book was composed with Corel VENTURA™ Publisher.

Contents

Part I

ADO.NET Fundamental Concepts

Part II

The ADO.NET Connection Object

Part III

The ADO.NET Command Object

Part IV

The ADO.NET DataReader Object

Part V

The ADO.NET DataSet Object

Acknowledgments

This book involved the help of many people without which the book would not have been possible. First, we'd like to thank Wendy Rinaldi at Osborne for her involvement with this project and for giving this book a life. Thank-yous also go out to Athena Honore, Julie Smith, and Tim Madrid for their roles managing in the whole book making process and for keeping everything flowing smoothly. Thank you to Mark Goedert for providing technical reviews of the material, which helped us to deliver accurate and understandable explanations and greatly improved the book. We'd also like to thank and copyeditor Nancy Rapoport for adding so much value to the material with her thorough and insightful editing work. And thank you to everyone at Osborne-McGraw Hill who has played a role in getting this book onto the shelves.

Introduction

Whether you are new to ADO.NET or have had some experience with it, this book will address many essential data access practices. New ADO.NET developers will find that the fundamental concepts section lays a solid foundation for building into the more complex aspects of accessing data, while the advanced topics and complete ADO.NET class reference are invaluable for the more experienced developers.

This book is divided into sections that describe the core features and data objects found in ADO.NET. The book starts with a section on ADO.NET basics that give you a history of data access technologies and how ADO.NET addresses some of the problem issues of older methods of accessing data. The next four sections take an in-depth look at the central ADO.NET objects and how to really put them into practice. These sections guide you through using the visual ADO.NET objects in the Visual Studio .NET development environment for quick and simple data manipulation. They also delve into using the ADO.NET classes in your program code to give your applications expanded flexibility and tackle the complicated scenarios that often require more advanced data accessing techniques. Section six explains XML and ADO data integration and the appendices give you a complete reference to the namespaces that are part of ADO.NET. Brief descriptions of the book sections are given here.

Part I—ADO.NET Fundamental Concepts   Part I gives you a general history of data access technologies and a synopsis of ADO.NET, then moves into understanding the .NET Framework and an overview of the complete ADO.NET architecture. Chapter 1 reviews the predecessors to ADO.NET, like DAO, RDO, ODBC, and ADO. Realizing how ADO.NET has addressed some of the limits to these other methods of data access will help you utilize the features of ADO.NET in the most effective way. An understanding of system requirements is essential in writing robust applications and this is presented in Chapter 2. Here, also the .NET Architecture and .NET Framework Class Library, the platform of managed code that ADO.NET is built on, are explained. The ADO.NET Architecture itself is laid out in Chapter 3, and gives you an overview of the classes used in ADO.NET. This chapter shows which ADO.NET classes are provided by the .NET Data Providers to allow access to the specific backend data source you are using. The chapter also outlines the common ADO.NET classes that work with your data independently of any specific database.

Part II—The ADO.NET Connection Object   This section focuses on the ADO.NET Connection object that is included by each of the .NET Data Providers. The Connection object is the main link to opening a data source and each of the .NET Data Providers includes a Connection object that optimizes the link to their specific database. Each chapter uses a different .NET Data Provider's Connection object which shows the unique connection technologies used by each provider. This section explores opening trusted connections, connecting to a database using a UDL file, DSN-less connections, and enabling connection pooling. These methods for connecting to a data source may be used for any of the Connection objects. For example, Chapter 4 shows opening a trusted connection using the SqlConnection object, but you may also open a trusted connection using the OracleConnection object, the OleDbConnection object, or the OdbcConnection object. We elected to separate each .NET Data Provider's objects to give you thorough examples that point out any syntax differences you may need to be aware of when connecting to the different data sources.

Part III—The ADO.NET Command Object   Like the ADO.NET Connection object, each .NET Data Provider includes their own Command object. One of the most common database actions that are required by applications are executing SQL statements and stored procedures. The chapters in this section demonstrate not only dynamic SQL queries, but also parameterized queries using the .NET Data Provider's Command objects. Stored procedures with return values and stored procedures with output parameters using the Command object are also explained, showing the use of the .NET Data Provider's Parameter classes and the data source specific parameter marker symbols. Transactions that enable you to group together multiple operations to performed as a single unit of work exhibited in this section. You'll see how the .NET Data Provider's Transaction classes are used in conjunction with the Command classes to help ensure database integrity. The Command class, Parameter class, and

Transaction class methods shown in this section may be used with any of the .NET Data Provider's Command, Parameter, or Transaction classes.

Part IV—The ADO.NET DataReader Object   Part IV covers the ADO.NET DataReader object. A DataReader is an object that retrieves a fast, forward-only result set. Again, each .NET Data Provider supplies their own DataReader and the methods described in each chapter may be used with the other .NET Data Provider's DataReader objects. This section shows examples of returning forward-only result sets, multiple results sets, and hierarchical results sets. When detailed table schema information is needed, the DataReader may be used to retrieve schema-only information. Populating a DataSet and retrieving Binary Large Objects (BLOBs) are useful actions that are also described in this section.

Part V—The ADO.NET DataSet Object   The ADO.NET DataSet object is the core object in an ADO.NET application. The DataSet class is essentially an in-memory database. Chapter 16 of this section, discusses building a DataSet and the common .NET Framework classes that make up the elements of the DataSet object, including the DataTable, DataColumn and DataRow, DataRelation, DataView, and Unique and ForeignKey constraints. The next chapters move into working with the important DataAdapter class. The DataAdapter is the mechanism by which data from your data source is loaded to the DataSet and then posted back to your database when changes are made to the DataSet information. The DataAdapter interacts with the different data sources and so each .NET Framework Data Provider supplies their own DataAdapter class. Chapters 17 through 21 show populating the DataSet from the different data sources using the DataAdapter from each of the .NET Framework Data Providers, but the methods used throughout the chapters may be used with any of the DataAdapter classes. Loading data to the DataSet using the DataAdapter and SQL statements or stored procedures is exhibited, as well as using multiple DataAdapters to fill a DataSet from multiple data sources. Once the data is in your DataSet, you may browse, search, sort, or select records for updating. These navigating methods and features are described in Chapter 22 through Chapter 24. After working with the information in your DataSet, the changes you've made will need to be sent back to the data source. Chapters 25 through 28 show updating the database with the DataSet data using the DataAdapter class. Here again, each chapter uses the DataAdapter that is supplied by each of the .NET Framework Data Providers, but the techniques for updating your database may be used by any of the DataAdapter classes. These chapters demonstrate updating your data source using custom update commands and also how to use the CommandBuilder class to automatically generate the update commands. The DataForm Wizard is explained that allows creating quick and simple data-bound Windows forms. Using parameters and stored procedures is illustrated, as well as selecting rows that have a certain update type, for example selecting only inserted records, for control over updating the database in a particular order. Chapter 29 rounds out this section with some advanced updating tips and methods. Merging DataSets, working with

AutoIncrement fields, and checking the DataSet for errors and then Accepting or Rejecting the DataSet rows before being sent to the database are covered.

Part VI—ADO.NET Data Integration   Part VI explains using ADO.NET and mapping data to XML and ADO and ADO.NET coexistence. In Chapter 30, you'll see an overview of XML terminology and XML documents and elements and then how XML is used by the ADO.NET Framework. Described are the XMLReader class, XML DiffGrams, the XPath query language, and XSLT/L. Chapter 31 discusses importing the COM-based ADO objects into the .NET Framework. There you'll see how to use ADO recordset from ADO.NET, and covers some coexistence issues when working with both ADO and ADO.NET.

Part VII—Appendixes   Appendix A through Appendix F are included in Part VII of the book. Each appendix provides a thorough reference for each of the ADO.NET namespaces. They show explanations of the classes, delegates, enumerations, and interfaces supplied in each of the namespaces, as well as, code examples for use. These namespace references are focused specifically on ADO.NET objects and are compiled in a format that is efficient and easy to use. Complete code examples in C# are provided for each of the class objects constructors, giving you one point of reference and helping you to produce error free program code quickly.

On the Web   All of the application code presented in this book can be downloaded from Osborne/McGraw-Hill's web site. The executable application and its source code can also be accessed directly off the web. You can download this code at www.osborne.com by searching for *ADO.NET: The Complete Reference*. In addition, cutting and pasting from the sample can give you a head start in developing your own ADO.NET applications.

The
Complete
Reference

ADO.NET

Part I

ADO.NET Fundamental Concepts

The
Complete
Reference

Chapter 1

Introduction to
ADO.NET

ADO.NET is the latest evolutionary step in the development of Microsoft's data access technologies. In this chapter, you'll get an introduction to Microsoft's new ADO.NET data access framework. First, to get some perspective on the why's and wherefore's concerning ADO.NET, you'll get a brief look back at some of the history leading up to ADO.NET. Here, you'll be able to see the progression of Microsoft's data access strategy, as well as how each new technology addresses the problems and technological challenges faced by each of its predecessors leading up to the development of ADO.NET. You'll see how ADO.NET more effectively addresses today's data access issues than any of its predecessors. Next, we dive into the .NET Framework. In this section, you'll get a high-level summary of the architecture of the .NET Framework, and you'll see exactly how ADO.NET fits within the .NET Framework. If you want to jump ahead, you can find more detailed information about the .NET Framework in Chapter 2. This chapter wraps up by providing a high-level overview of the different .NET namespaces and classes that comprise ADO.NET. You can find specific in-depth reference materials covering the ADO.NET classes in the appendixes of this book.

Microsoft Data Access Technologies

Microsoft first began working on standard database access mechanisms back in 1992 with the original release of Open Database Connectivity (ODBC) for 16-bit Windows 3.1. ODBC essentially replaced its forerunner, embedded SQL, as the primary database access mechanism. Embedded SQL was not very flexible, but worse, it was closely tied to the target database system. Using embedded SQL, it was basically impossible to attempt to build a single application that could access multiple database platforms. Plus, syntax differences usually prohibited the source code from being compatible as well. ODBC was the first truly successful attempt to provide database interoperability to applications. Since that time, Microsoft's data access technologies have continued to evolve, both addressing the types of environments that they need to work in and the effort required to develop database applications. Microsoft's subsequent database access technologies, DAO, RDO, and ODBCDirect, were all built with ODBC-based data access in mind. It wasn't until the advent of Component Object Model (COM) that Microsoft began to move away from ODBC to its successor OLE DB. Active Data Object (ADO), an OLE DB consumer, became the preferred database access programming model for the new OLE DB technology. Although OLE DB and ADO did a great job of addressing the data access issues involved in client/server style applications, they weren't the best fit for *n*-tiered Web applications. Plus, these technologies faced difficulties in enterprise-wide deployment. Microsoft developed the .NET Framework and ADO.NET in response to these issues. In this section, you'll get a little deeper look at each of Microsoft's database access architectures leading up to the development of ADO.NET.

Open Database Connectivity (ODBC)

ODBC is a database access standard that was defined by Microsoft. ODBC was designed to provide a standard method of desktop database access for SQL databases on different platforms. An ODBC application can be used to access data that's on a local PC database, but it is really intended to access databases on heterogeneous platforms such as SQL Server, Oracle, or DB2. Although ODBC originated as a Windows standard, it has also been implemented on several other platforms, including UNIX.

ODBC is essentially a database access Application Program Interface (API). The ODBC API is database independent and is based on the SQL/Call Level Interface (SQL/CLI) specifications developed by X/Open and ISO/IEC. The ODBC 3.0 standard was the final version of the ODBC API, and it is comprised of 76 functions, which are documented in Microsoft's three-volume *ODBC 3.0 Reference and SDK Guide*. Although, on the surface, the ODBC API consists of a set of function calls, the heart of ODBC is SQL. The primary purpose of the ODBC functions is to send SQL statements to the target database and then process the results of those SQL statements. Obviously, the server must be able to support SQL to be accessed through ODBC.

As a programming interface, ODBC required the use of the specific function calls that were part of the ODBC API. Although it was possible to use these API from languages such as VB, they were really much easier to use in C, the language the API was written in. Using the API was relatively difficult because it required an understanding of the required order of the function calls, as well as the required parameters for each API function and their data types.

Although ODBC is implemented through a set of standard function calls, one of the biggest benefits of ODBC is that it is a widely adopted desktop standard. End users typically didn't need to know or understand those functions to use ODBC— all the code required to use ODBC is built into ODBC-enabled applications such as Microsoft Access, Word, Excel, or Visio. There are literally hundreds of ODBC-enabled desktop applications.

Data Access Objects (DAO)

DAO was Microsoft's first attempt to build a COM-based database access technology. DAO has been a part of the original Visual Basic since DAO 1 was released with Visual Basic 3. DAO was Visual Basic's default data access method, and it was primarily intended to provide Visual Basic applications with data access to local Access databases via the Jet engine. However, Microsoft designed DAO to be able to accommodate a number of other databases, such as dBase, Paradox, and even ODBC databases such as Oracle and SQL Server. This flexibility was one of DAO's strong points. DAO and the Jet engine can access a number of different databases using the same code. Being a local query processor, the Microsoft Jet Database Engine gives DAO certain capabilities not found in most other client/server data access mechanisms. For instance, DAO and Jet provide the capability to perform heterogeneous joins on data from separate and dissimilar databases.

Although DAO is flexible, this flexibility carries a price. Having its own local query processor gave DAO applications a very high amount of overhead. Plus DAO was not primarily designed to work with ODBC-based data sources. It was really designed to work as a one tier–style desktop database application where the database and the program both reside on the same platform. In essence, DAO treated ODBC data sources the same as it did local data sources. This often resulted in grossly inefficient data access code that frequently performed expensive operations like frequent opens and closes that might work well for local file-based databases but killed the performance of client/server ODBC-based database applications.

Remote Data Objects (RDO)

RDO, the immediate successor to DAO, combines the ease of programming offered by DAO with the high performance offered by the ODBC API. Whereas DAO is an object layer over the Microsoft Jet engine, RDO is an object layer that encapsulates the ODBC API. RDO wasn't meant to access local Access-like databases. Instead, RDO was expressly designed for client/server-style network database access. The absence of the high-overhead Jet engine, combined with RDO's close relationship to ODBC, gave it a decided performance advantage over DAO when accessing ODBC-compliant databases such as SQL Server. RDO provided programmatic access to ODBC-compatible databases without the overhead of a local query processor like the Microsoft Jet engine. RDO provides access to virtually all the capabilities provided by the ODBC API, but being COM based makes it significantly easier to use. RDO eliminates the need to declare all the functions manually in a BAS or CLS file. Instead, RDO's COM implementation gives it seamless integration into the Visual Basic and other COM development environments by adding References to the IDE. These References allow the IDE to provide Intellisense prompting for all of the RDO object methods and properties.

Although RDO provided a good solution to the ODBC database access problems of DAO, it was a short-lived technology. RDO was ODBC based, and it was soon replaced by the OLE DB–based ADO data access technology, which provided a simpler programming model and access to heterogeneous data sources.

ODBCDirect

As is often the case, Microsoft provided more than one technology to address the ODBC database access problems encountered by DAO. Although RDO was the first of these, it was quickly followed up by ODBCDirect. ODBCDirect is a cross between DAO and RDO. ODBCDirect uses an object model similar to DAO. However, like RDO, ODBCDirect was an object layer over ODBC, and it did not use the Microsoft Jet Database Engine. In fact, exactly like RDO, ODBCDirect could be used only to connect to ODBC data sources; it couldn't be used to connect to local Access databases. ODBCDirect also supports most of the advanced ODBC capabilities provided by RDO. Like RDO, ODBCDirect supports using ODBC cursors, as well as prepared SQL statements, parameterized queries, and stored procedure return parameters. Although ODBCDirect seemed to have most of the same capabilities as RDO, it did offer one important advantage—ODBCDirect was a part of DAO 3.6 and was therefore available in the lower-cost Visual Basic Professional Edition. RDO is available only as part of the much higher-priced VB Enterprise Edition. ODBCDirect also shared RDO's short-lived fate, and it was soon replaced by the OLE DB and ADO.

OLE DB

Microsoft introduced OLE DB as the successor to ODBC. Considering the widespread success of ODBC, this left OLE DB with some big shoes to fill. The ODBC API has enjoyed near-universal acceptance. In addition to providing database support for thousands of custom database applications, most shrink-wrapped desktop applications, such as Microsoft Office, support the ODBC API. ODBC drivers exist for virtually all the major database systems. However, ODBC was primarily designed to handle relational data— it was never really intended to work with nonrelational data sources.

OLE DB was built as a universal data access technology. Like ODBC, OLE DB provides access to relational data, but OLE DB extends the functionality provided by ODBC. OLE DB has been designed as a standard interface for all types of data. In addition to relational database access, OLE DB provides access to a wide variety of data sources, including tabular data such as Excel spreadsheets, ISAM files like Access and dBase, Active Directory, and even IBM host DB2 data. OLE DB could be used to access virtually any data source that can return data in a row and column format. OLE DB was also built using the more modern COM interface—freeing the developer from ODBC's older call level interface. Each OLE DB provider delivers data access and reflects its capabilities through its exposed COM interfaces. However, the OLE DB COM interface is a low-level interface that requires support for pointers, data structures, and direct memory allocation. These low-level constructs were best suited for C++ programmers. The direct use of OLE DB was unsuitable for development environments that didn't support low-level functions like pointers, such as Visual Basic, ASP, VBA, VBScript, Java, JScript, JavaScript, and others.

ActiveX Data Objects (ADO)

This is where ADO fits in: ADO allows OLE DB providers to be accessed by interactive and scripting languages that need data access but don't support low-level memory access and manipulation. ADO is essentially an OLE DB consumer that provides application-level access to OLE DB data sources. Essentially ADO is a middleware layer on top of OLE DB that enables VB, ASP, and other scripting environments that don't have support for pointer and direct memory allocation to make use of the OLE DB data access technology. ADO introduced a new simplified object model that flattened out the hierarchical object models employed by it predecessors: DAO, RDO, and ODBCDirect. This new object model made ADO much easier to develop with, and OLE DB extended–data source support enabled ADO-based applications to access not only database resources such as SQL Server but also other system resources such as Active Directory.

As database access middleware, ADO supports all of the sophisticated database features provided by SQL Server and most other databases. ADO provides the ability to return result sets, use client- and server-side cursors, execute parameterized queries, support transactions, and support executing stored procedures. ADO is also an efficient and high-performance data access platform, making it a much better solution for developing two-tiered–style database applications than any of its forerunners. However, ADO was not really designed to support *n*-tiered Web-based applications. Although ADO does support *n*-tiered–oriented features, such as connection pooling and disconnected Recordsets, these features were really implemented on top of ADO's connection-oriented design. Although maintaining persistent database connections is fine for two-tiered desktop applications, they don't scale well for Web applications. Each connection consumes system resources whether it's active or not. In addition, although the number of desktop connections tends to be known for two-tired applications, it's not known for *n*-tiered Web applications where usage can spike unpredictably. Massive increases in the number of connections and holding those connections open tended to result in applications that didn't scale well. That's not to say that you can't use ADO to write scalable *n*-tiered applications. You certainly can. However, you had to take pains to carefully develop your applications in the right way to allow them to deal with the disconnected Web environment. In addition, ADO is COM based, which makes deployment of applications difficult—requiring registration of objects in the Windows Registry before an application can use them. Although that scenario works well for local applications, it makes it difficult to distribute a Web application to remote Web and application servers.

ADO.NET

Microsoft designed ADO.NET to address the issues of Web and distributed applications. Like its name implies, ADO.NET is based on ADO, but it's the next evolutionary step beyond COM-based ADO. ADO.NET is built using managed code from the Microsoft .NET Framework, which means it enjoys the benefits of a type-safe and memory-managed environment, making ADO.NET a more robust database access platform than ADO. As a data access framework, ADO.NET has been redesigned to allow it to handle disconnected data architecture that's required by today's *n*-tiered Web-based applications. For example, when the browser requests a page containing database data from the Web server, the Web application requests the data from the backend database server and sends it as an HTML stream back to the browser. There's no further connection with the browser until the next request is made. Therefore, there's no persistent connection between the client application and the Web server or the database server. There's also no need to hold open any database connections between the Web application and the database server. ADO.NET has been designed in a fashion that allows it to address the loosely coupled Web application environment where the different components are inherently disconnected.

At the heart of the new ADO.NET architecture is the DataSet. The DataSet is essentially a cache of records that have been retrieved from the database. You can think of the DataSet like a mini database. It contains tables, columns, constraints, rows, and relations. Applications typically need to access many different pieces of related information in order to present useful information to the end user. For instance, to place an order, an application would typically need to access a number of different database tables including product information, customer information, inventory information, and shipping information. In the disconnected model, going back to the data source to get each different piece of related information would be impractical and inefficient. All of the related information from this set of tables can be grouped together in the DataSet. A database connection is opened to fill the DataSet and then quickly closed, after which the DataSet operates independent of the backend database. The data in the DataSet is persisted as XML. In addition to handling these disconnected scenarios, the ADO.NET framework also has classes that allow it to work in a more traditional connected fashion. You can see a high-level overview of the ADO.NET application architecture in Figure 1-1.

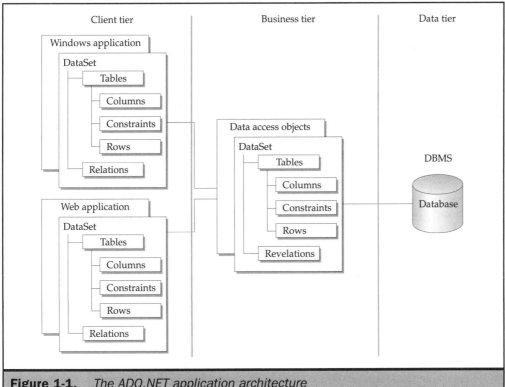

Figure 1-1.   *The ADO.NET application architecture*

ADO.NET's disconnected design enables it to be easily scalable for enterprise applications. The DataSet is maintained independent of the backend database and connections are opened only to populate the DataSet or to post changes made to the data in the DataSet back to the database. Eliminating persistent connections minimizes the system overhead and improves application throughput and scalability. Maintaining the data and the database relations in the DataSet also improves application performance by eliminating round trips to the database server. The DataSet is an in-memory data store that provides very high performance and is capable of enforcing database constraints and relations without being connected to the database. Being managed .NET applications, ADO.NET applications are also easily deployable because there's no need to remotely register objects before they can be used. Managed .NET applications contain metadata that internally identify all of the required application components, which eliminates the need to rely on an external registry. This enables ADO.NET applications to be deployed by simply copying the application to its intended destination.

You've seem how ADO.NET has been designed to address the problems faced by Microsoft's earlier data access technologies. We present more detailed information about the core ADO.NET architecture and object classes in Chapter 3, as well as in the appendixes at the back of the book. The next part of this chapter provides you with some of the essential information that you need to know about where ADO.NET fits into the Microsoft .NET Framework as an application development platform.

The .NET Framework

ADO.NET is a part of the bigger Microsoft .NET Framework. Microsoft's primary goal for the .NET Framework is to provide a platform that simplifies the application deployment and development of robust Web applications. The Microsoft .NET Framework provides several benefits over older COM-based development models, including the following:

■ **Simplified Web application development** A new programming construct known as WebForms was introduced with the .NET Framework that enables the visual development of Web applications using the same type of visual design environment that Visual Basic has long enjoyed. The new WebForms development model makes building Web applications almost as easy as building standard Windows applications. Like you might expect, there's also a new set of Windows development classes known as WinForms that facilitate the development of rich Windows-based applications.

■ **New Web Services component model** Support for Web services is one of the primary enhancements supported by the .NET Framework. Web services essentially extend the component object model to the Web. Based on the industry standard XML and SOAP protocols, Web services enable B2B applications integration by making it possible for business to create and publish Web Services that can be easily migrated into your .NET applications.

- **Consistent programming model** The .NET Framework offers a completely object-oriented programming model that eliminates the need to understand and incorporate arcane Win32 APIs or complex OLE DB GUID, IUnKnown, or AddRef calls into your applications. Instead, groups of related classes known as Namespaces are referenced by .NET application code. You can then use a consistent object-oriented methodology to create and use instances of these .NET classes to build your applications and access system resources.

- **Seamless language integration** For the first time in any development paradigm, the .NET Framework enables the seamless integration of multiple languages. Objects created using any of the .NET languages, such as Visual Basic.NET, Visual C# .NET, or Visual C++ .NET, can be freely used in any of the other .NET languages. Even more, you can also take objects created in any of the .NET languages and create new objects using any of the other .NET languages.

- **Automatic memory management** One of the most common bugs in current Windows programs is memory leakage due to failure to correctly free up or deallocate system resources that are used by a program. The .NET Framework implements its own garbage collection system that automatically manages memory and system resources. This removes the cleanup burden from the programmer and eliminates one of the most common sources of system problems.

- **Type safety** Another important feature that Microsoft introduced with the .NET Framework is type safety. In essence, type safety ensures that objects are always accessed in appropriate ways. For instance, the .NET Framework will prohibit a program from attempting to access an array element that's out of bounds or attempting to write a fifth byte to a four-byte value. Type safety eliminates another common source of programming bugs and system instability.

- **Standardized error handling** The .NET Framework also provides a standard method for error handling for all .NET languages. In previous versions, the way each language and even different API sets handled errors were different. The .NET Framework handles all errors by raising exceptions. All of the .NET languages support variations of the Try=Catch block for trapping error conditions.

- **Integrated security** The .NET Framework provides finer control over application security than just relying on the underlying OS to establish code rights. Instead, the .NET Framework implements a new evidence-based security system where privileges are based on important aspects of the code itself. For example, the .NET Framework is able to restrict the execution of any code that's not digitally signed.

- **Xcopy application deployment** Deployment was one of the biggest problems with distributed COM-based applications. These applications typically require the distribution of many files, almost all of which must be registered before they can be used. Any mistakes or failures to correctly register a component will result in application errors. .NET applications do not rely on the Windows Registry to locate application components. Instead, .NET programs are self-describing. Metadata contained in the .NET executable files themselves identify the components that are required and their versions.

- **Multiple platform support** Previous Microsoft development products have all been Windows-centric. However, Microsoft released both C# and the Common Language Infrastructure (CLI) to ECMA, the international standards committee. Because the CLI is an open standard, it is possible for other software vendors to develop their own implementations of the Common Language Runtime (CLR) that can run on other platforms. Versions of the CLR are being developed for Linux, FreeBSD, and the Mac OS X 10. In addition, the Compact .NET Framework enables the development of .NET applications for mobile devices such as the Pocket PC. You can find more information about the CLR in the next section of this chapter.

Components of the .NET Framework

The .NET Framework is essentially composed of the CLR and the class libraries that are used by the applications. In Figure 1-2, you can see a high-level overview of the .NET Framework

Microsoft .NET Framework applications are created using either the integrated development and debugging tools found in Visual Studio .NET or the free Microsoft ASP.NET Web Matrix product available at www.asp.net, or, if you are very determined and sufficiently stubborn, you can even develop them using a text editor such as Notepad in conjunction with .NET command-line compilers provided by the Microsoft .NET Framework SDK (available at http://msdn.microsoft.com/netframework/downloads/howtoget.asp). The essential difference between VS.NET and the .NET Framework is that VS.NET is an application development tool that is used to design and write .NET applications, whereas the .NET Framework provides the infrastructure required to run those applications.

The Microsoft .NET Framework provides a set of classes that you can use to develop applications and a runtime engine that interacts with the operating system. The most central part of the .NET Framework is the Common Language Runtime (CLR) shared by all of the .NET languages. The .NET Framework's CLR provides the underlying support for several new application types called WinForms, WebForms, and Web Services. Like you would expect, WinForms are used for Windows applications, WebForms are Web applications, and Web Services are a new distributed Web application building-block component. The .NET code that runs in the CLR is known as managed code because the CLR handles the resource management for the applications. You develop these new application by types using the various Namespaces (a .NET term that refers to a collection of related classes) provided by the .NET Framework. To access system, network, Web, and database resources, the .NET applications include references to

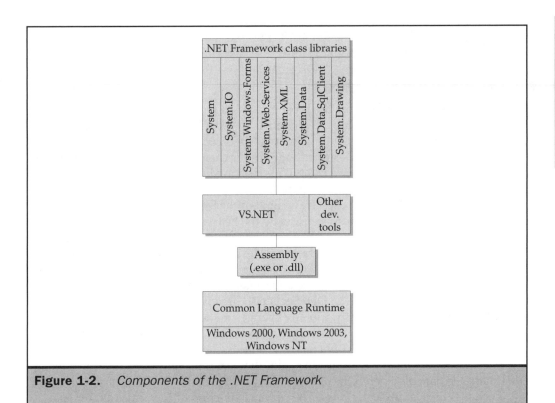

Figure 1-2.   *Components of the .NET Framework*

the appropriate Namespaces after which the application can use the classes, methods, and properties that are contained in the Namespace. For example, the System.IO Namespace contains classes that are used to read and write to the operating system; the System.Windows.Forms Namespace contains classes used to create and display Windows applications; the System.Web Namespace contains classes used to create ASP.NET Web applications; the System.Data Namespace contains classes that are used for ADO.NET database access applications.

The .NET Framework compiler then combines your source code and the .NET class references into an object called an Assembly. An Assembly is a file that ends in .exe or .dll and contains the Microsoft Intermediate Language (MSIL) code along with metadata that identifies the version of the application along and the different components used by the application. Including this metadata in the Assembly frees .NET application from any reliance on the Registry to locate DLLs and other application components. This effectively puts an end to "DLL Hell" once and for all.

When an Assembly is executed, the CLR parses the Assembly discovering the executable components. The CLR then takes the IL code contained in the Assembly and uses its Just In Time (JIT) complier to convert the IL into native code that will be executed by the operating system. It's the responsibility of the CLR to provide memory management, thread management, and application security.

The ADO.NET Namespaces

It almost goes without saying that the most important part of the new Microsoft .NET Framework to DBAs and database developers is the ADO.NET architecture. Unlike COM-based ADO, ADO.NET is built using managed code that runs on the CLR. Also unlike ADO, which was really designed for two-tier client server applications that use a persistent database connection, ADO.NET is designed for *n*-tiered applications that run primarily disconnected from the database.

The core ADO.NET Namespaces are located in the System.Data.DLL. Like its name suggests, the System.Data Namespace is really the heart of the ADO.NET architecture. Within the System.Data Namespace, the DataSet is the most important component. The DataSet is an in-memory database cache that's designed to be used in a disconnected fashion. The DataSet consists of a complete collection of tables, columns, constraints, rows and relationships and appropriately named DataTables, DataColumns, DataConstraints, DataRows, and DataRelations. The DataSet is not directly connected to the database. Instead, it operates independently and any changes made to the data in the DataSet are posted back to the database in a batch mode via the DataSets' Update method.

Another important ADO.NET Namespace is the System.Data.Common Namespace. The System.Data.Common Namespace contains the classes that are shared by the different .NET managed data providers. One of the primary classes in the System.Data.Common Namespace is the DataAdapter class. The primary function of the DataAdapter is to connect the DataSet to the data source. An overview of the ADO.NET Namespaces is illustrated in Figure 1-3.

For SQL Server developers, one of the most important Namespaces is the System.Data.SqlClient. The System.Data.SqlClient is the .NET managed data provider for SQL Server. Unlike earlier versions of ADO, which used OLE DB on top of the appropriate Net Library to access SQL Server, the System.Data.SqlClient Namespace uses SQL Server's native Tabular Data Stream (TDS) protocol to connect to the SQL Server system. Using native TDS brings ADO.NET one level closer to the wire, making it the fastest database connection possible between the application and SQL Server. This is essentially as close as an application can get to the SQL Server database.

For Oracle database developers, the System.Data.OracleClient Namespace provides access to Oracle databases. The OracleClient Namespace requires the Oracle Client software be installed on the application system. The OracleClient NamesapceNamespace provides access to the Oracle database using the Oracle Call Interface (OCI), and it's compatible with the Oracle Client versions 8.1.7 and above. The System.Data.OracleClient Namespace is not included in the version 1.0 of the .NET Framework. Developers using the .NET Framework 1.0 can download this Namespace from http://msdn.microsoft.com/downloads.

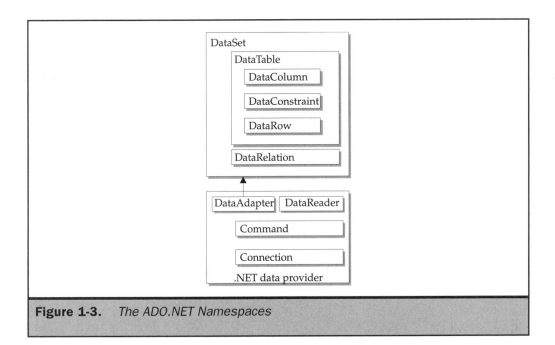

Figure 1-3.   *The ADO.NET Namespaces*

The System.Data.OleDb Namespace is essentially analogous to the System.Data .SqlClient Namespace with the primary difference being that the System.Data.OleDb is the .NET managed data provider for OLE DB data sources. Whereas the System.Data .SqlClient Namespace is used exclusively for SQL Server access, the System.Data .OleDb Namespace is used to access legacy database systems or for mixed SQL Server and heterogeneous database system access. System.Data.OleDb data provider communicates to the data source via OLE DB and can be used to connect .NET applications to Oracle, SQL Server, or Microsoft Access databases.

To enable legacy application development, the System.Data.Odbc is provided as a part of .NET Framework 1.1. The System.Data.Odbc managed provider is intended to work with all ODBC drivers, but Microsoft has only tested this driver with the Microsoft SQL Server ODBC driver, the Microsoft ODBC driver for Oracle, and the Microsoft Jet ODBC driver. This Namespace requires MDAC 2.7 to be installed as a prerequisite. The System.Data.Odbc Namespace was not included in version 1.0 of the .NET Framework. Developers using the .NET Framework 1.0 can download the Microsoft.System.Odbc Namespace from http://msdn.microsoft.com/downloads. Although Namespaces are named differently, they provide identical functionality.

Finally, the System.Data.SqlTypes Namespace contains classes that represent SQL Server's native data types.

Summary

This chapter provided you with an introduction to Microsoft's evolving database technologies. In the first section of this chapter, you saw how ADO.NET solves the application data access problems that were encountered by Microsoft's previous database access technologies. The second part of this chapter provided a brief overview of the .NET Framework and ADO.NET. You'll find much more detailed information about the ADO.NET Namespaces in Chapter 3, as well as in the appendixes at the back of the book. In the next chapter, you'll get a closer look at the .NET Framework.

The
Complete
Reference

Chapter 2

Understanding the
.NET Framework

Before launching into building ADO.NET applications, it's good to have a solid understanding of the new Microsoft .NET Framework. The .NET Framework is Microsoft's new development platform that brings with it enormous changes in the nature of the applications that are developed, as well as the development tools and methodologies that are used to develop those applications. To help you get a more complete understanding of the applications that you develop using ADO.NET and the Microsoft .NET Framework, this chapter starts out with an introduction to the new Microsoft .NET architecture, where you'll learn about the Common Language Runtime (CLR) and the Common Type System (CTS). The next part of this chapter provides a general overview of the major Namespaces in the .NET Framework. Very few applications are stand-alone database applications that just need to access database resources and nothing else. In order to access other system resources, you need to understand which of the .NET Namespaces you need to include in your applications. Next, you'll get a more in-depth look at the anatomy of programs (aka assemblies) that are created when you build .NET applications. Understanding the context of the .NET assemblies can help you understand the deployment issues that are encountered when deploying .NET applications.

.NET System Requirements

The first thing you need to know about .NET applications is where they can run. In this section, you can see the hardware and software requirements for .NET Client and .NET Server applications.

Hardware Requirements

Table 2-1 lists the .NET hardware requirements. These hardware requirements are divided into requirements for client/desktop applications, as well as server-side ASP.NET applications. This table lists the Microsoft minimum and recommended system specifications. In typical Microsoft fashion, they've low-balled their hardware recommendations. Although .NET applications may run in these low-powered systems specified in the minimum columns, in my experience, you'll be a lot happier with a faster system. We've included a "Better" column indicating a more desirable system specification. But bear in mind that, like most computer systems, "more is better" and you'll definitely get a better .NET experience running .NET applications on faster hardware.

Platform	CPU Minimum (MHz)	CPU Recommended (MHz)	CPU Better (MHz)	RAM Minimum (MB)	RAM Recommended (MB)	RAM Better (MB)
.NET Client	90	90+	350+	32	96+	128+
.NET Server	133	133+	450+	128	256+	512+

Table 2-1.   *.NET Hardware Requirements*

Operating System Requirements

In addition to the hardware requirements, .NET applications also have a minimum required operating system level to support the various .NET features. Table 2-2 shows the .NET Framework software requirements.

Platform	Operating System	Additional Software
.NET Client	Windows 98	
	Windows 98 SE	
	Windows ME	
	Windows NT 4.0 Workstation	Service Pack 6a
	Windows NT 4.0 Server	Service Pack 6a
	Windows 2000 Professional	
	Windows 2000 Server	

Table 2-2.   *.NET Operating System Requirements*

Platform	Operating System	Additional Software
	Windows 2000 Advanced Server	
	Windows 2000 Datacenter Server	
	Windows XP Home Edition	
	Windows XP Professional	
.NET Server	Windows 2000 Professional	Service Pack 2
	Windows 2000 Server	Service Pack 2
	Windows 2000 Advanced Server	Service Pack 2
	Windows 2000 Datacenter Server	Service Pack 2
	Windows XP Professional	
	Windows 2003 Server Family	

Table 2-2.   *.NET Operating System Requirements* (continued)

Database Access Requirements

In addition to the previously mentioned hardware and software prerequisites, certain database access features used by the .NET Framework have minimum MDAC (Microsoft Data Access Components) levels that are required (see Table 2-3). MDAC is included in the installation process for the .NET Framework and Visual Studio.NET, so you don't need to worry about it in a development environment. However, you do need to be concerned about this when you deploy your client and server applications.

You can download the Microsoft MDAC support from http://www.microsoft .com/data.

Platform	Middleware	Notes
.NET Client	MDAC 2.6	Needed by the SQL Server .NET Data Provider
.NET Server	MDAC 2.7	Needed by the SQL Server .NET Data Provider

Table 2-3.   *NET Database Access Requirements*

The .NET Architecture

The three primary components of the .NET architecture are the Common Language Runtime (CLR), the Common Type System (CTS), and the .NET Framework class libraries. The CLR is essentially the runtime engine that executes .NET applications; the CTS defines all of the basic data types as well as the operations that can be performed on those data types. The .NET Framework class libraries is a base set of classes grouped into Namespaces that provide access to system resources as well as standard language capabilities, such as string manipulation, I/O, and numerical functions. Figure 2-1 presents the overall architecture of the .NET Framework.

In the following sections, you'll get a more detailed look into each of these core components that comprise the .NET architecture.

The Common Language Runtime

The job of the CLR is basically to load and run .NET applications. The CLR marks a big change from Microsoft's earlier methods of software development where your application glues together many separate components in order to perform various functions. In many ways, the CLR is analogous to Java's JVM (Java Virtual Machine) or to VB 6's MSVBSM.DLL in that it's a runtime layer over the operating system. However, the CLR goes beyond the capabilities of either of these by enabling cross-language integration, self-describing components, xcopy deployment, and integrated security. The CLR's most essential task is to compile .NET code into native machine instructions and execute those instructions. The code that runs in the CLR is called *managed code*; any code that runs outside of the CLR is referred to as *unmanaged code*. Managed code basically describes the situation where the CLR—not the programmer—is responsible for performing tasks such as memory allocation and exception handling.

The CLR enables a couple of key improvements over previous Microsoft development scenarios. First, the CLR enables cross-language object inheritance and exception handling, and, in addition, it provides resource management for program objects. Code that's developed using any language that targets the .NET runtime can be used to create

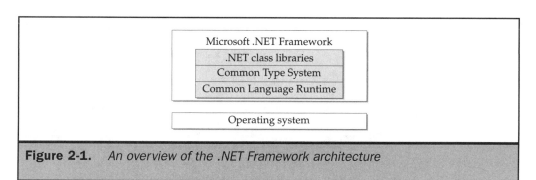

Figure 2-1.   *An overview of the .NET Framework architecture*

objects that can be inherited by other languages. For example, objects that are created using C#, J#, or Managed VC++ can be seamlessly integrated into Visual Basic.NET applications. Likewise, any exceptions raised in those objects will appear exactly like native Visual Basic.NET exceptions because they all conform to the .NET error handling standards. The CLR also automatically handles memory management tasks. The CLR is responsible for allocating the memory required by an object. Further, its automatic garbage collection takes care of releasing those resources when they're no longer used—freeing the programmer from that responsibility. Cross-language integration results in more easily reusable code, and automatic resource management results in more robust programs.

When .NET programs are created, the compiler doesn't produce code that can be natively executed. Instead, the .NET compiler outputs assemblies that contain a combination of Microsoft Intermediate Language (MSIL) and metadata information. See the "Assemblies" section, later in this chapter, for more detailed information.

 The .NET Framework SDK provides both an MSIL compiler (ILasm.exe), as well as an MSIL decompiler (ILDasm.exe).

In Figure 2-2, you can see an overview of the basic process that the CLR uses for execution and assembly.

As Figure 2-2 illustrates, .NET source code is compiled into an assembly either using one of the command-line compilers provided by the .NET Framework SDK

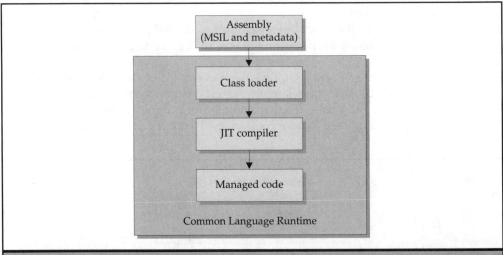

Figure 2-2. *Program execution in the CLR*

or by Visual Studio.NET. Much like standard unmanaged code, the files containing these assemblies typically end in the extension .exe or .dll. When the CLR executes an assembly, the class loader first parses the metadata contained in the assembly to pull out the MSIL code as well as discover any dependencies that the assembly has. Next, the CLR's Just-In-Time (JIT) compiler will compile the MSIL code into native code that can be executed on the system. However, don't think that the entire program is compiled all at once. Instead, the JIT compiles each function as it is called. Once the JIT has compiled a function, it stores the address of the compiled code, which will be directly executed for all future function calls. In addition, the .NET Framework also includes an install-time compile option that will convert the entire assembly to native code as part of the installation process.

As you might expect, there's no such thing as a free lunch, and the CLR is no exception to this axiom. Although the CLR enables a number of powerful new language capabilities, it does come at a price. The CLR is required to run .NET applications, and it doesn't come preinstalled with Windows XP or Windows 2000 Professional, or any Windows platform other than Windows 2003 Server. Instead, either the CLR must be deployed along with your .NET applications or it must be deployed prior to deploying your .NET applications. Moreover, the CLR's footprint weighs in at a hefty 20MB, making it a significant consideration, especially for client installations.

The Common Type System

The CTS implements the formal specifications for the type system used by the .NET Framework. All data types represented by the CTS are objects. The CTS defines how a type is defined and the operators that it can accept. One of the primary goals of the CTS is to enable deep language integration by allowing code that's written in one language to be inherited and used by another language. Sharing a common system of data types is one of the most fundamental building blocks that enable this to happen.

Classes of Types

The .NET Framework supports two basic classes of types: value types and reference types. The following section describes these types in more detail.

Value Types   Value types are very similar to the built-in data types provided by most programming languages. Typical data types that are used to store variable values include characters, integers, strings, and floating-point numbers. In the .NET Framework, they are termed *value types* because they are copied when they are passed as arguments. In other words, they are passed by value. The .NET Framework stores value types on the stack. Table 2-4 lists the value type supported by the .NET Framework along with their VB.NET and C# data type keywords.

Type	Description	VB.NET	C#
Boolean	A Boolean value (true or false)	Boolean	bool
Byte	An 8-bit unsigned integer	Byte	byte
Char	A Unicode (16-bit) character	Char	char
Decimal	A 96-bit decimal value	Decimal	decimal
Double	A double-precision (64-bit) floating-point number	Double	double
Int16	A 16-bit signed integer	Short	short
Int32	A 32-bit signed integer	Integer	int
Int64	A 64-bit signed integer	Long	long
IntPtr	A signed integer whose size depends on the underlying platform	IntPtr	IntPtr
Object	The root of the object hierarchy	Object	object
SByte	An 8-bit signed integer	SByte	sbyte
Single	A single-precision (32-bit) floating-point number	Single	float
String	An immutable, fixed-length string of Unicode characters	String	string
UInt16	A 16-bit unsigned integer	UInt16	ushort
UInt32	A 32-bit unsigned integer	UInt32	uint
UInt64	A 64-bit unsigned integer	UInt64	ulong
UIntPtr	An unsigned integer whose size depends on the underlying platform	UIntPtr	UIntPtr

Table 2-4. *CTS Value Types*

Reference Types   Reference types store a reference to the value's memory address, and are allocated on the heap. Reference types can be self-describing types, pointer types, or interface types. Unlike value types, reference types are passed between procedures using the address. In other words, a reference to the original object is passed rather than a copy of that object, as is the case with value types. Table 2-5 lists the CTS reference types.

Type	Description	VB.NET	C#
Classes	A class is a data structure that may contain data members (constants, variables, and events), function members (methods, properties, indexers, operators, and constructors), and nested types.	Class	class
Delegates	A delegate is a reference type that refers to a shared method of a type or to an instance method of an object.	Delegate	delegate
Arrays	An array is a data structure that contains a number of variables (elements of the array).	Dim MyArray(5) As Integer	int[] myArray =
Interfaces	Interfaces are implemented by other types to guarantee that they support certain operations. An interface defines a contract. A class or structure that implements an interface must adhere to that contract.	Interface	interface
Pointers	Pointers reference blocks of memory. There are three kinds of pointers supported by the runtime: managed pointers, unmanaged pointers, and unmanaged function pointers.	N/A	int*

Table 2-5.   *CTS Reference Types*

The .NET Framework Class Library

The .NET Framework class library contains a collection of programming classes that enable your applications to perform various functions. These classes are organized into related groupings referred to as Namespaces. As the name implies, all class names with a given Namespace must be unique. The .NET Framework Namespaces use a dot notation syntax scheme to describe a hierarchical organization. This naming scheme allows developers to easily group together related classes as well as to extend the functionality of a Namespace in an organized and easy-to-understand manner. Namespaces adhere to the following naming pattern: *companyname.tecnologyname.* One clear example of this is the Microsoft.Win32 Namespace, which is a Microsoft-created Namespace that contains classes that enable an application to access the Win32 API set. Another example of this naming scheme within the .NET Framework is the System.Data Namespace, which is the root level of the ADO.NET classes. Two examples of the classes that are grouped together at the next level of the System.Data class hierarchy are the System.Data.SqlClient and the System.Data.OledbClient. Each of these sets of classes are independent. No functions in the System.Data.SlqClient require the System.Data.OleDbClient, and vice versa. Further, each of these sets of classes are dependent on and subordinate to the System.Data level.

Using the different .NET Namespaces and classes in your applications is really quite easy. To use the classes contained in a given Namespace in your application, you just need to include an import directive for that Namespace. The most difficult part of using the .NET Framework class libraries is knowing which Namespace provides support for what type of functionality. By default, all .NET applications include the System Namespace, which provides basic support for variables and data types like Objects, Bytes, Int32, and Strings, as well as the Exception classes that provide structured error handling. However, to provide support for other functions, you need to include various Namespaces from the .NET Framework class libraries. Using the ADO.NET System.Data Namespace to provide database access is one of the best examples of this. In order to use ADO.NET and access databases from your .NET application, you need to include the System.Data Namespace, which enables your application to use the data access classes and methods provided by the ADO.NET technology. More detailed information about ADO.NET is presented in the next chapter of this book. Familiarizing yourself with the basic Namespaces in the .NET Framework is a vital step toward using the .NET Framework effectively and productively. The following section provides an overview of the class libraries provided with the Microsoft .NET Framework.

Microsoft Namespaces

Table 2-6 provides a brief overview of the different Microsoft Namespaces provided as a part of the .NET Framework.

Namespace	Description
Microsoft.CSharp	Contains the classes required to compile C# source code
Microsoft.JScript	Contains the classes required to support the JScript runtime

Table 2-6. *Microsoft Namespaces in the .NET Framework Class Library*

Namespace	Description
Microsoft.VisualBasic	Contains the classes required to compile Visual Basic.NET source code as well as the Visual Basic runtime
Microsoft.Vsa	Provides classes that enable you to integrate the .NET scripting interface in your applications
Microsoft.Win32	Contains the classes that enable your application to handle events that are raised by the system as well as classes that enable your application to read and write to the Registry

Table 2-6. *Microsoft Namespaces in the .NET Framework Class Library* (continued)

System Namespaces

Table 2-7 provides a brief overview of the different Namespaces provided by the System Namespace in the .NET Framework class library.

Namespace	Description
System	The most fundamental of all the .NET Framework Namespaces; it must be used by all applications, and it contains the classes that represent the basic data types that were presented earlier in the "Common Type System" section.
System.CodeDom	Contains classes that are used to represent a source code document.
System.Collections	Contains classes used to manage collections of objects.
System.ComponentModel	Provides classes that control the design-time and runtime behavior of components and controls.
System.Configuration	Contains classes that enable your application to access the .NET Framework configuration settings.

Table 2-7. *System Namespaces in the .NET Framework Class Library*

Namespace	Description
System.Data	Provides support for ADO.NET and its database access classes and data types. The basic ADO.NET data management classes contained in the System.Data Namespace are the DataSet and DataTable classes that enable disconnected data access for Windows and Web-based applications. The specific System.Data classes are discussed in more detail in the next chapter.
System.Diagnostics	Contains classes that enable your application to manage system processes as well as read the system event logs and performance monitor counters.
System.DirectoryServices	Contains classes that enable your application to access the Active Directory via the ADSI (Active Directory Services Interface).
System.Drawing	Contains classes that access the system's GDI+ functions, which provide graphics support.
System.EnterpriseServices	Contains classes that provide access to COM+ for *n*-tiered enterprise application support.
System.Globalization	Contains classes that enable National Language Support (NLS) as well as support for Calendar objects.
System.IO	Contains classes that enable your applications to read and write to data streams either synchronously or asynchronously.
System.Management	Contains classes that provide access to the WMI (Windows Management Interface) infrastructure to provide systems monitoring and management support.
System.Messaging	Contains classes that enable your application to read and write messages for the Microsoft Messaging Queuing technology.
System.Net	Contains classes that enable your application to conduct network communications using HTTP, as well as TCP and UDP sockets.
System.Reflection	Contains classes that enable the application to read the metadata of a loaded assembly.

Table 2-7. *System Namespaces in the .NET Framework Class Library* (continued)

Namespace	Description
System.Resources	Contains classes that enable your application to store and load regional-specific resources.
System.Runtime.ComplierServices	Contains classes that allow compiler developers to control aspects of the runtime behavior of the CLR.
System.Runtime.InteropServices	Contains classes that enable your .NET applications to interface with COM (Component Object Model) objects and native Win32 APIs (Application Program Interfaces).
System.Runtime.Remoting	Contains classes that enable your application to manage remote objects required for developing distributed applications.
System.Runtime.Serialization	Contains classes that allow your applications to store and load objects by converting them into a sequential stream of bytes (serialization).
System.Security	Contains classes that enable your application to control .NET Framework security features. These classes can manage security features such as permissions, policies, and cryptography.
System.ServiceProcess	Contains classes that allow your applications to create, install, and manage Windows services.
System.Text	Contains classes that represent ASCII, Unicode, UTF-7, and UTF-8 character sets.
System.Threading	Contains classes that enable you to develop multithreaded applications.
System.Timers	Contains classes that permit your application to raise an event following a specified interval of time.
System.Web	Contains a set of classes that define ASP.NET. These classes essentially provide support for Web browser to Web server interaction. For example, different classes contained in this Namespace support Web hosting, mail, security, and user interface components.
System.Windows.Forms	Contains the classes that enable the development of Windows-based applications.
System.Xml	Contains a set of classes that enable your application to work with XML documents.

Table 2-7. *System Namespaces in the .NET Framework Class Library* (continued)

Assemblies

Now that you've seen an overview of the different Namespaces that are included in the .NET Framework, it's time to look a little closer at the executable programs, or in .NET parlance, the assemblies that are created using the classes contained in those Namespaces. Assemblies are basically a new way of packaging executable code. Like the programs produced by earlier compilers, such as Visual C++, the assemblies that are created by the .NET compilers typically end with the file extension of .exe or .dll. However, unlike those programs that contain native x86 machine instructions, which can be directly executed by the Windows operating system, the assemblies output by the .NET compilers contain a combination of MSIL, metadata, and resources such as bitmaps. Assemblies cannot be executed without the presence of the .NET CLR. The metadata information that's stored in the assembly is known as the *manifest*, and it contains information about the resources within the assembly, as well as its dependencies. The Type metadata contain the CTS types that are used in the assembly. The executable code, or MSIL, is a platform-independent intermediate language that is a higher level than the native machine code produced by older compilers. Unlike standard x86 executable code, MSIL understands objects and has instructions that can instantiate and manipulate object properties. Similarly, MSIL contains facilities to raise and catch exceptions. Finally, the resources in an assembly typically contain the bitmaps, icons, and other binary resources that are used by the application. Figure 2-3 presents an overview of the internal stature of a single file assembly.

Unlike standard executable files, assemblies can be single file, or they can be contained in multiple files. For instance, an assembly could be split into three different files where one contained the metadata, another contained the MSIL, and another contained the resource and bitmaps used by the application. Multifile assemblies are typically used to support multiple-language applications. Figure 2-4 illustrates an example multifile assembly.

In Figure 2-4, you can see that the code and resources are split between three different physical files. In this case, note that the manifest contained in the base

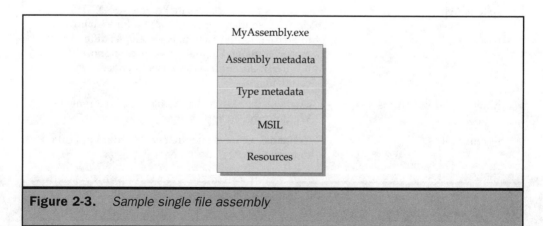

Figure 2-3.   *Sample single file assembly*

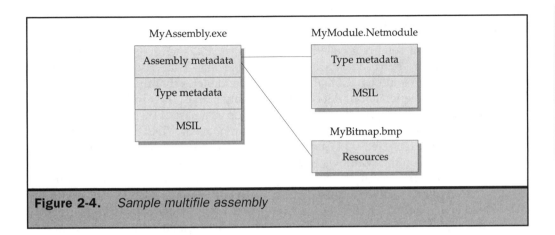

Figure 2-4.   *Sample multifile assembly*

MyAssembly.exe points to the other assemblies that are used. There are no Registry entries or other on-disk structures that are used to link together the different assembly components. The self-describing metadata is responsible for managing the assembly components. You'll find more information about the metadata contained in the assembly in the next section, "Assembly Manifest."

In addition to containing the executable program instructions, assemblies fulfill several important roles in the .NET Framework. First, assemblies define a security boundary. The assembly is the unit to which .NET permissions are granted. This security information enables a very granular level of security that was never possible with Win32 applications. .NET security can restrict and grant access at the function level of an application. Next, the assembly's manifest contains versioning information. This versioning information both identifies the current assembly and defines the version requirements for any required assemblies. Because each assembly carries with it its own version identification, as well as the version information of all dependant components, there is no possibility of an older version of a component or some otherwise incorrect but like-named component being accidentally installed and used. Next, the assembly limits the scope of the types contained in the assembly. Each type is contained within the bounds of its assembly. Identically named types in different assemblies are managed independently. Finally, an assembly forms the basic unit of deployment for a .NET application. When deploying a .NET application, you essentially just need to copy the assembly to the target system. The assembly's metadata is responsible for finding any required components.

When an assembly is created, it can be made as private or shared. Private assemblies can be used only by a single application, whereas shared assemblies can be used by multiple applications. Multiple versions of a given assembly can be simultaneously installed on the same machine. Assemblies can also be either static or dynamic. A static assembly resides in a PE (Portable Executable) file that's stored as an on-disk structure. A dynamic assembly is created and executed directly in memory, and it's not saved to disk.

Assembly Manifest

The metadata in an assembly is called an *assembly manifest,* and it contains information about the types and resources that are externally visible outside the assembly. In addition, the metadata contains information about any dependencies that the assembly has. This includes information about dependent assembly names, their locations and their version number. Including the metadata information as a part of the assembly has a couple of important advantages. First, it finally eliminates the "DLL Hell" situation that continues to plague COM-based Windows applications; second, it frees the application from dependencies on the Windows Registry. "DLL Hell" describes an all-too-common error condition experienced by Windows applications where required new software installs inadvertently replace required application components such as DLLs with like-named components of a different version—which unfortunately are not completely compatible with the component they replace. When this happens, the new application typically works, but some existing application that depended on the old component broke. This was typically exacerbated by reinstalling the old software, which restored the original component and predictably broke the new application. Maintaining this versioning information in the metadata makes it possible to have side-by-side deployment where multiple versions of an assembly can be used simultaneously. Each assembly can load the dependent assemblies it needs without fear of using an incompatible component because the metadata specifies exactly which version of the component is required and where it is located. Because assemblies are self-describing, using the Registry isn't necessary to locate any of the dependent assemblies used in an application. Registering an assembly during installation is also unnecessary. This vastly simplifies the installation process and essentially enables xcopy style of deployment where assemblies can simply be copied to their destination system and executed. Table 2-8 presents the information that's contained in an assembly's manifest.

Item	Description
Assembly name	The assembly name.
Version number	The assembly's major and minor version number, and a revision and build number.
Culture	The region- and language-specific information about an assembly.

Table 2-8. *Assembly Manifest Information*

Item	Description
Strong name	The public key from the publisher for assemblies that use strong names. You can find more information about strong names in the "Assembly Security" section, later in this chapter.
List of all files	A list of all the files contained in the assembly and their filenames.
Type references	The information used by the CLR to map a type reference to the file that contains its declaration and implementation.
Referenced assemblies	A list of assemblies that are statically referenced by the current assembly. This list includes the assembly's name, metadata, and public key, if the assembly is strong named.

Table 2-8.   *Assembly Manifest Information* (continued)

Viewing Assembly Metadata

You can view the contents of an assembly by using the Ildasm.exe tool that is supplied with the .NET Framework SDK. The Ildasm.exe tool is essentially an assembly disassembler. You run the Ildasm.exe utility by selecting Start | Programs | Microsoft Visual Studio.NET | Visual Studio .NET Tools | Visual Studio Command Prompt. From there, you can enter **ILDASM** followed by the path and name of the .NET assembly that you want to inspect. Figure 2-5 illustrates viewing an assembly's metadata using the ILDASM utility.

In Figure 2-5, you can see the assembly information for the ADONetSample application that accompanies this book. In the metadata information shown in the figure, you can see that the manifest information is listed at the top of the assembly followed by the information about the MSIL executable code in the assembly. Double-clicking the Manifest line displays the following metadata information, which lists the contents of the assembly including its name, external dependencies, and resources.

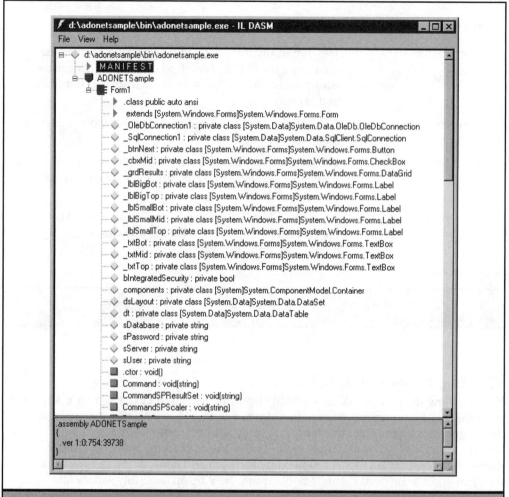

Figure 2-5. *Assembly metadata*

```
.assembly extern mscorlib
{
  .publickeytoken = (B7 7A 5C 56 19 34 E0 89 )                              //
.z\V.4..
  .ver 1:0:3300:0
}
.assembly extern Microsoft.VisualBasic
{
```

```
  .publickeytoken = (B0 3F 5F 7F 11 D5 0A 3A )                           //
.?_....:
  .ver 7:0:3300:0
}
.assembly extern System
{
  .publickeytoken = (B7 7A 5C 56 19 34 E0 89 )                           //
.z\V.4..
  .ver 1:0:3300:0
}
.assembly extern System.Data
{
  .publickeytoken = (B7 7A 5C 56 19 34 E0 89 )                           //
.z\V.4..
  .ver 1:0:3300:0
}
.assembly extern System.Drawing
{
  .publickeytoken = (B0 3F 5F 7F 11 D5 0A 3A )                           //
.?_....:
  .ver 1:0:3300:0
}
.assembly extern System.Windows.Forms
{
  .publickeytoken = (B7 7A 5C 56 19 34 E0 89 )                           //
.z\V.4..
  .ver 1:0:3300:0
}
.assembly extern System.Xml
{
  .publickeytoken = (B7 7A 5C 56 19 34 E0 89 )                           //
.z\V.4..
  .ver 1:0:3300:0
}
.assembly extern Microsoft.Data.Odbc
{
  .publickeytoken = (B7 7A 5C 56 19 34 E0 89 )                           //
.z\V.4..
  .ver 1:0:3300:0
}
.assembly ADONETSample
{
  // --- The following custom attribute is added automatically, do not
uncomment -------
  // NOTE: The following information has been truncated for presentation
purposes
  //   .custom instance void [mscorlib]System.Diagnostics.DebuggableAttribute::
```

```
  .custom instance void
 [mscorlib]System.Runtime.InteropServices.GuidAttribute::
  .custom instance void [mscorlib]System.CLSCompliantAttribute::
  .custom instance void
[mscorlib]System.Reflection.AssemblyTrademarkAttribute::
  .custom instance void
[mscorlib]System.Reflection.AssemblyCopyrightAttribute::
  .custom instance void
 [mscorlib]System.Reflection.AssemblyCompanyAttribute::
  .custom instance void
 mscorlib]System.Reflection.AssemblyDescriptionAttribute::
  .custom instance void [mscorlib]System.Reflection.AssemblyTitleAttribute::
  .hash algorithm 0x00008004
  .ver 1:0:754:39738
}
.mresource public ADONETSample.Form1.resources
{
}
.module ADONETSample.exe
// MVID: {7ECCFC40-17DF-46D6-8E60-3188CD279A0A}
.imagebase 0x11000000
.subsystem 0x00000002
.file alignment 512
.corflags 0x00000001
// Image base: 0x02d90000
```

Global Assembly Cache

The Global Assembly Cache (GAC) is a .NET mechanism that's used to explicitly share
assemblies between applications. As a rule, you should use the Global Assembly Cache
only for assemblies that are expressly intended to be shared among multiple .NET
applications. If your application's assembly is not shared, it should remain private, and
you shouldn't add it to the Global Assembly Cache.

*If you place an application in the Global Assembly Cache, you can't subsequently
deploy the application using xcopy because the GAC of the target system would
need to be updated in order to execute the assembly.*

You can view the GAC by using Windows Explorer and navigating to the
\%windows%\assembly folder. An example of the GAC is shown in Figure 2-6.
.NET applications are added to the GAC by using a .NET-aware installer, or
you can manually drag and drop files from Windows Explorer onto the Global
Assembly Cache.

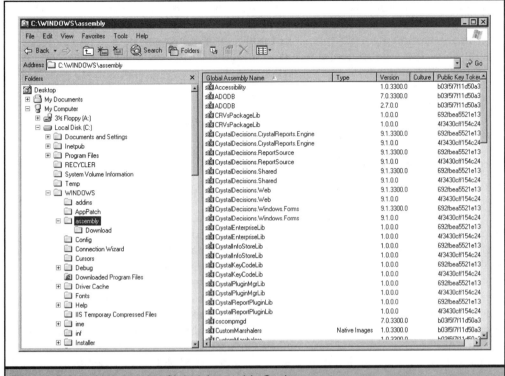

Figure 2-6. *Viewing the Global Assembly Cache*

Assembly Security

Assembly security is controlled by policies that are enforced by the CLR. When an assembly is executed, the CLR checks to ensure that the code about to be executed is allowed by the existing security polices. When the CLR first loads an assembly, it checks the available security policy to determine the assembly's permissions. In .NET parlance, the assembly security information is referred to as *evidence*. Evidence includes the assembly's publisher, its site, and its zone.

Setting Permissions

An administrator can set the security polices for a .NET application by using the .NET Framework Configuration tool, mscorcfg.msc, an MMC snap-in that's included with the .NET Framework. The permissions set by the .NET Framework Configuration tool are set after the application is deployed by an administrator, and they control the application's runtime behavior—they are not set during the development process. The .NET Framework Configuration tool can set security policies based on an enterprise-based policy, a machine-based policy, or a user-based policy. Table 2-9 lists the security configuration files that are modified using the .NET Framework Security Configuration tool.

You can start the by selecting Start | Programs | Microsoft Visual Studio.NET | Visual Studio .NET Tools | Visual Studio Command Prompt. From there, you can enter **mscorcfg.msc** at the command line. Figure 2-7 presents an example of the .NET Framework Configuration tool.

Signing an Assembly

In addition to setting an assembly's permissions, you can also sign the assembly to ensure its authenticity. There are two ways of signing an assembly. You can give an assembly a strong name and/or you can add a signcode digital signature to the assembly. Signing an assembly with a strong name adds a public key encryption to the assembly. Strong names ensure name uniqueness, and they are designed to prevent name spoofing. The strong name is stored in the file containing the assembly manifest. Signcode is a different and potentially complementary method of ensuring trust. No level of trust is associated with a strong name, whereas signcode does enable trusting code based on its publisher. Signcode is implemented using PKI and requires a publisher to prove their identity to a third-party authority and obtain a certificate. This certificate is then embedded in your assembly and can be used by the CLR to trust the code's authenticity. The signcode signature is stored in a reserved slot in the assembly. Signcode signing of an assembly is best used when you already have a trust hierarchy that's using signcode signatures.

Security Policy	Location
Enterprise	%runtime install path%\Config\Enterprisesec.config
Machine	%runtime install path%\Config\Security.config
User	%USERPROFILE%\Application data\Microsoft\CLR security config\vxx.xx\Security.config (Windows 2000 and NT)
	%WINDIR%\username\CLR security config\vxx.xx\Security.config

Table 2-9. *Security Policy Files*

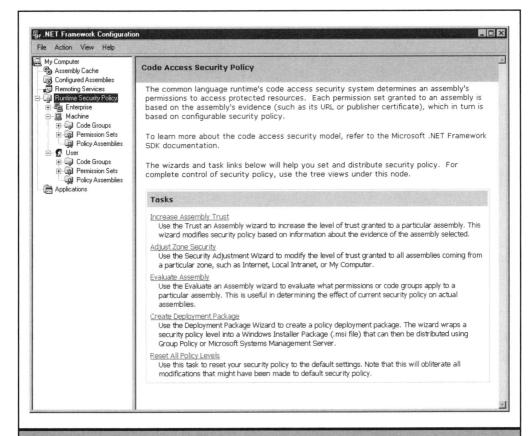

Figure 2-7.   *Using the .NET CFramework Configuration tool to set assembly security*

Summary

In this chapter, you got a high-level overview of the .NET Framework. The .NET Framework, however, involves a lot more than you can fit into one chapter. In fact, several books have been written about it. For more detailed information about the .NET Framework, you can refer to Microsoft's .NET Framework Developer's Guide.

In the next chapter, you'll get a closer look at the part of the .NET Framework that we database developer's really care about—namely, the System.Data Namespace, which provides the classes that make up ADO.NET.

The
Complete
Reference

ADO.NET

Chapter 3

The ADO.NET
Architecture

With an overall understanding of the .NET Framework under your belt, now it's time to jump into the ADO.NET data access architecture. The first part of the chapter provides you with an overview of the ADO.NET data access technology. Then the second part of this chapter introduces you to the different ADO.NET Namespaces and gives you an overall understanding of the functions of the different classes that comprise the ADO.NET architecture. Next, the last section of this chapter covers the classes that are used by the ADO.NET DataSet object. In this part of the chapter, you'll get an understanding of DataTable, DataColumn, DataRow, and other classes used by the new ADO.NET DataSets.

At its essence, ADO.NET is data access middleware that enables the development of database applications. ADO.NET builds on the platform provided by the .NET Framework. ADO.NET is built using managed code from the Microsoft .NET Framework, which means that it enjoys the benefits of the robust .NET execution time environment. Designed primarily to address the issues of Web and distributed applications, ADO.NET consists of a set of classes or Namespaces within the .NET Framework that provide data access and management capabilities to .NET applications.

As a data access framework, ADO.NET has been primarily designed to allow it to work in the disconnected data access model that is required by *n*-tiered Web-based applications. ADO, the direct predecessor of ADO.NET, was primarily designed to accommodate two-tiered client/server style of applications, which typically open a database connection when the application first starts and then hold that connection open until the application ends. This technique works fine for most intranet-style applications where the total number of client connections is a known quantity, and the state of the application is typically controlled by the application and therefore is also a known quantity. Although this approach worked well for single-tier desktop applications and two-tiered client/server style applications, it ran into serious limitations for *n*-tiered Web-style applications. Because the Web is a public environment, the total number of open connections required by Web applications isn't a known quantity. It could vary greatly and quickly: at one minute, an application may need only a handful of connections but then jump to thousands of connections just a few minutes later. Keeping open connections in this type of environment hurts scalability because each connection must go through the overhead of initializing the connection with the backend database, plus each open connection requires system resources to be held open—reducing the resources available for other database operations. As ADO evolved, Microsoft added mechanisms such as disconnected Recordsets to help deal with Web-style applications, but these were never part of ADO's original design.

Microsoft designed ADO.NET to be able to handle the disconnected computing scenario required by Web-based applications. This disconnected design enables ADO.NET to be readily scalable for enterprise applications because an open connection isn't maintained between each client system and the database. Instead, when client connection is initiated, a connection to the database is briefly opened, the requested data is retrieved from the database server, and the connection is closed. The client application then uses the data completely independently from the data store maintained by the database server. The client application can navigate through its subset of the data, as well as make changes to the data, and the data remains cached at the client until the application indicates that it needs to post any changes back to the database server. At that point, a new connection is briefly opened to the server, and all of the changes made by the client application are posted to the database in an update batch and the connection is closed.

The core ADO.NET component that enables this disconnected scenario is the DataSet. The DataSet is essentially a miniature in-memory database that is maintained independently of the backend database. Connections to the data source are opened only to populate the DataSet or to post changes made to the data in the DataSet back to the database. This disconnected computing scenario minimizes the system overhead and improves application throughput and scalability. The in-memory database provided by the ADO.NET DataSet provides many of the functions that you'll find in a fully blown database including support for data relations, the capability to create views, and support for data constraints, as well as support for foreign key constraints. However, being an in-memory structure, it doesn't provide support for many of the more advanced database features that you would find in enterprise-level database products like SQL Server. For example, the DataSet doesn't support triggers, stored procedures, or user-defined functions.

Support for disconnected Web-based applications was one of Microsoft's priorities in the design of ADO.NET; however, that isn't all that ADO.NET is capable of. The disconnected model may be appropriate for Web applications, but it really isn't the best model for client/server and desktop applications. These types of applications can be more efficient and better performing when they run in a connected fashion. To support this connected style of computing, ADO.NET also provides a DataReader object. The DataReader essentially provides fast forward-only cursor style of data access that operates in a connected fashion. While the DataSet provides the basis for disconnected Web applications, the DataReader enables the fast connected style of data access needed by desktop and client/server applications.

This section has given you a high-level overview of the ADO.NET data access middleware. You have seen that ADO.NET provides the tools to build applications that support both disconnected Web applications and connected client/server-style applications. In the next section, you'll get a close look at the different Namespaces that make up the ADO.NET architecture.

ADO.NET Namespaces

ADO.NET is implemented as a set of classes that exist within the .NET Framework. These ADO.NET classes are grouped together beneath the .NET Framework's System .Data Namespace. Several important Namespaces comprise the ADO.NET data access technology. First, the .NET Data Providers are implemented in the System.Data.SqlClient, System.Data.OracleClient, System.Data.OleDbClient, and System.Data.Odbc Namespaces. The classes in these four Namespaces provide the underlying database connectivity that's required by all of the other ADO.NET objects. The System.Data.SqlClient Namespace provides connectivity to SQL Server 7 and SQL Server 2000 databases. The System.Data.OracleClient Namespace provides connectivity to Oracle 8 and 9 databases. The System.Data.OleDbClient Namespace provides connectivity to SQL Server 6.5 and earlier databases, as well as Access and Oracle databases. And the System .Data.Odbc Namespace provides connectivity to legacy databases using ODBC drivers. These classes also provide support for executing commands, retrieving data in a fast forward-only style of access, and loading ADO.NET DataSets. Next, there are the classes contained in the System.Data Namespace itself. These classes can be considered the core of the ADO.NET technology, and they provide support for the new ADO.NET DataSet class and its supporting classes. As you learned earlier in this chapter, the DataSet is an in-memory database cache that's designed to be used in a disconnected fashion. The DataSet consists of a complete collection of tables, columns, constraints, rows, and relationships, and appropriately named DataTables, DataColumns, DataConstraints, DataRows, and DataRelations. You can see an example of the overall ADO.NET architecture shown in Figure 3-1.

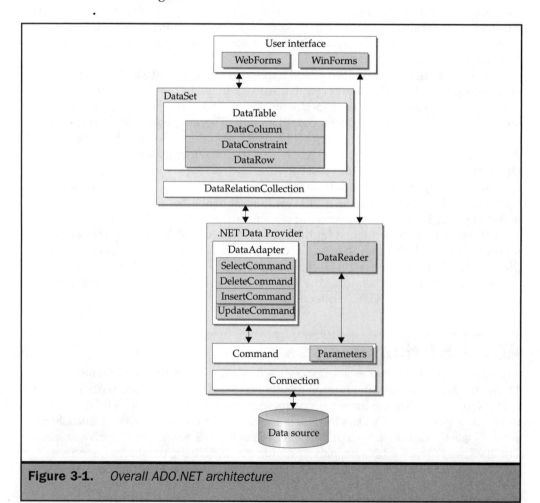

Figure 3-1.   *Overall ADO.NET architecture*

 .NET Data Providers

The.NET Data Providers are responsible for connecting your .NET application to a data source. The .NET Framework comes with four built-in .NET Data Providers. Each of the .NET Data Providers are maintained in their own Namespaces within the .NET Framework

Namespaces for the .NET Data Providers

Four .NET Data Providers are delivered with the .NET Framework: the .NET Data Provider for SQL Server, the .NET Data Provider for Oracle, the .NET Data Provider for OLE DB, and the .NET Data Provider for ODBC. The .NET Data Provider for SQL Server is contained in the System.Data.SqlClient Namespace. The .NET Data Provider for Oracle is contained in the System.Data.OracleClient Namespace. The .NET Data Provider for OLE DB is contained in the System.Data.OleDbClient. And the .NET Data Provider for ODBC is contained in the System.Data.Odbc Namespace.

System.Data.SqlClient

The System.Data.SqlClient is the .NET managed data provider for SQL Server. The System.Data.SqlClient Namespace uses SQL Server's native TDS (Tabular Data Stream) protocol to connect to the SQL Server system. Using the native TDS protocol makes the .NET Data Provider for SQL Server the fastest possible connection between a client application and SQL Server.

System.Data.OleDb

The System.Data.OleDb Namespace is the .NET managed data provider for OLE DB data sources. Whereas the System.Data.SqlClient Namespace can be used only to access SQL Server 7 or 2000 databases, the System.Data.OleDb Namespace is used to access SQL Server 6.5 databases or earlier, as well as Oracle and Access databases. Theoretically, the .NET Data Provider for OLE DB can access any database where there's an OLE DB Provider—with the exception of the Microsoft OLE DB Provider for ODBC. Microsoft purposely restricted the capability to access ODBC from the .NET Data Provider for OLE DB.

System.Data.OracleClient

The System.Data.OracleClient Namespace is the .NET managed data provider for Oracle databases. The .NET Data Provider for Oracle requires that the Oracle 8 or higher client be installed on the system. The System.Data.OracleClient Namespace uses Oracle's native OCI (Oracle Call Interface) to connect to Oracle 8 and higher databases.

System.Data.Odbc

The System.Data.Odbc Namespace is the .NET managed data provider for ODBC data sources. Microsoft designed the .NET Data Provider for ODBC to be able to access any ODBC-compliant database. However, Microsoft officially supports only connections using the Microsoft SQL Server ODBC driver, the Microsoft ODBC driver for Oracle, and the Microsoft Jet ODBC driver. However, I have successfully used this provider to connect to DB2 databases as well.

Core Classes for the .NET Data Providers

All of the.NET Data providers included in the .NET Framework are essentially architected the same. In other words, the classes contained in each Namespace have nearly identical methods, properties, and events. However, the classes use a slightly different naming convention. For instance, all of the classes in the .NET Data Provider for SQL Server, found in the System.Data.SqlClient Namespace, all begin with a prefix of "Sql"; the classes that are part of the .NET Provider for OLE DB, found in the System.Data.OleDb Namespace, all begin with the prefix of "OleDb." Both Namespaces contain classes that are used to initiate a connection to a target data source. For the System.Data.SqlClient Namespace, this class is named SqlConnection. For the System.Data.OleDb Namespace, this class is named OleDbConnection. In each case, the methods that are provided and their parameters are basically the same. Because the function and usage of these classes are basically the same, they are grouped together in the following section under their generic function names. The following section presents an overview of the primary classes contained in the .NET Data Provider Namespaces.

Connection

The Connection class is used to open a connection to a target data source. A Connection object is required in order to populate either the DataReader or the DataSet objects with data from the target data source. Likewise, an active Connection object is required in order to execute any commands or stored procedures that exist on the database from the client .NET applications. Unlike most other .NET Objects, Connection objects are not automatically destroyed when they go out of scope. This means that you must explicitly close any open ADO.NET Connection objects in your applications. If multiple Connection objects are opened that use the same connection string, they will be automatically added to the same connection pool.

  The actual functionality provided by the OleDbConnection class and the OdbcConnection class is dependent on the capabilities of the underlying OLE DB Provider and ODBC driver. Not all providers and drivers will necessarily support the same functionality.

Command

The Command class is used to execute either a stored procedure or a SQL statement on the data source that's associated with the active Connection object. Three types of commands are supported: ExecuteReader, ExecuteNonQuery, and ExecuteScalar. ExecuteReader commands return a result set. ExecuteNonQuery commands are used to execute SQL action queries like Insert, Update, and Delete statements that do not

return any rows. ExecuteScalar commands are used to execute stored procedures or
SQL queries that return a single value.

Parameter

The Parameter class is used to represent a parameter that's passed to a Command
object. Parameter objects have properties that define their attributes. For instance, the
different properties of a Parameter object specify the parameter's name, its direction,
its data type, its size and its value. Parameter names are not case-sensitive; but when
naming Parameter objects that represent stored procedure parameters, naming the
parameter the same as the stored procedure parameter is typically a good idea and is
required by some of the different .NET data providers. For instance, if the Parameter
object represents a stored procedure parameter named @CustomerID, using that same
name when instantiating the Parameter object is a good practice. A Parameter object
can also be mapped to DataColumn in the DataSet.

DataReader

The DataReader class returns a forward-only stream of data from the target data source
that's associated with the active connection object. Unlike most other ADO.NET classes that
are instantiated by calling the constructor, objects created from the DataReader class are
instantiated by calling the ExecuteReader method.

DataAdapter

The basic task of the DataAdapter class is to serve as a link between a DataSet object
and the data source represented by the active Connection object. The DataAdapter
class includes properties that allow you to specify the actual SQL statements that
will be used to interact between the DataSet and the target database. In other words,
the DataAdapter is responsible for both filling up the DataSet and sending changes
made in the DataSet back to the data source. For example, the DataAdapter class
provides the SelectCommand property, which controls the data that will be retrieved;
the InsertCommand property, which indicates how new data in the DataSet will be
added to the database; the UpdateCommand property, which controls how changed
rows in the DataSet will be posted to the database; and the DeleteCommand property,
which controls how rows deleted in the DataSet will be deleted from the database.

CommandBuilder

The CommandBuilder class provides a mechanism for automatically generating the SQL
commands that will be used to update the target database with changes in an attached
DataSet. The CommandBuilder uses the metadata returned by the SQL statement in
the DataAdapter's SelectCommand property to generate any required Insert, Update,
and Delete statements. Changes made in the DataSet are not automatically posted to
the database unless SQL commands are assigned to the DataAdapter InsertCommand,
UpdateCommand, and DeleteCommand properties, or unless a CommandBuilder object
is created and attached to the active DataAdapter object. Only one CommandBuilder
object can be associated with a given DataAdapter at one time.

Transaction

The Transaction class represents a SQL transaction. SQL transactions basically allow multiple database transactions to be treated as a unit where an entire group of database updates can either be posted to the database or they can all be undone as a unit. The Transaction object uses the BeginTransaction method to specify the start of a transaction, and then either the Commit method to post the changes to the database or the Rollback method to undo the pending transaction. A Transaction object is attached to the active Connection object.

Error

The Error class contains error information that is generated by the target data source. The active Connection object is automatically closed when an error with a severity of greater than 20 is generated by the target database. However, the connection can be subsequently reopened.

Exception

The Exception class is created whenever the .NET Data Provider encounters an error generated by one of its members. An Exception object always contains at least one instance of the Error object. You trap exceptions in your code by using the .NET Frameworks Try-Catch structure error handling.

A complete reference for the System.Data.Odbc Namespace is presented in Appendix C. The reference for the System.Data.OleDb Namespace is presented in Appendix D. The reference for the System.Data.OracleClient is in Appendix E, and the reference for the System.Data.SqlClient is in Appendix F.

Core Classes in the ADO.NET System.Data Namespace

The core classes that make up the ADO.NET technology are found in the .NET Framework's System.Data Namespace. The following section presents an overview of the functionality of the most important classes found in the System.Data Namespace.

DataSet

At the heart of the new ADO.NET architecture is the DataSet. The DataSet class is located in the .NET Framework at System.Data.DataSet. The DataSet is essentially a cache of records that have been retrieved from the database. You can think of the DataSet like a miniature database. It contains tables, columns, constraints, rows, and relations. These DataSet objects are called DataTables, DataColumns, DataRows, Constraints, and Relations. The DataSet essentially allows a disconnected application to function like it's actively connected to a database. Applications typically need to access multiple pieces of related database information in order to present useful information to the end user. For example, to work with an order, an application would typically need to access a number of different database tables including product tables, customer tables, inventory tables, and shipping tables. All of the related information from this set of tables can be grouped together in the DataSet providing the disconnected application with the capability to work with all of the related order information that it needs.

In the disconnected model, going back to the data source to get each different piece of related information would be inefficient, so the DataSet is typically populated all at once via the active Connection object and DataAdapter from the appropriate .NET Data Provider. A database connection is briefly opened to fill the DataSet and then closed. Afterward, the DataSet operates independently of the backend database. The client application then accesses the Table, DataRow, Data Column, and DataView objects that are contained within the DataSet. Any changes made to the data contained in the DataSet can be posted back to the database via the DataAdapter object. In a multi-tier environment, a clone of the DataSet containing any changed data is created using the GetChanges method. Then the cloned DataSet is used as an argument of the DataApdapter's Update method to post the changes to the target database. If any changes were made to the data in the cloned DataSet, these changes can be posted to the original DataSet using the DataSet's Merge method. Figure 3-2 provides an overview of the ADO.NET DataSet architecture.

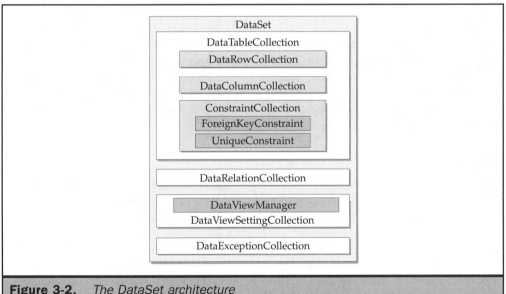

Figure 3-2.   *The DataSet architecture*

DataTable

The DataTable class is located in the .NET Framework at System.Data.DataTable. The DataTable class represents a table of in-memory data that is contained with a DataSet object. The DataTable object can be created automatically by returning result sets from the DataAdapter to the DataSet object. DataTable objects can also be created programmatically by adding DataColumns objects to the DataTable's DataColumns collection. Each DataTable object in a DataSet is bindable to data-aware user interface objects found in the .NET Framework's WinForm and WebForm classes.

When changes are made to the data contained in a DataTable object, the ColumnChanging, ColumnChanged, RowChanging, and RowChanged events are fired. When data is deleted from a DataTable object, the RowDeleting and RowDeleted events are fired. New rows are added to a DataTable by calling the DataTable's NewRow method and passing it a DataRow object. The maximum number of rows that can be stored in a DataTable is 16,777,216. The DataTable is also used as a basis to create DataView objects.

DataColumn

The DataColumn class is located in the .NET Framework at System.Data.DataColumn. The DataColumn class represents the schema of a column in a DataTable object. The DataColumn class contains several properties that are used to define the type of data contained in the DataColumn object. For example, the DataType property controls the type of data that can be stored in the DataColumn object, the DataValue property contains the DataColumn's value, the AllowDBNull property specifies whether the DataColumn can contain NULL values, the MaxLength property sets the maximum length of a Text DataType, and the Table property specifies the DataTable object that the DataColumn belongs to. DataColumns can be made to contain unique values by associating a UniqueConstraint object with the DataColumn object. In addition, you can relate a DataColumn object to another DataColumn object by creating a DataRelation object and adding it to the DataSet's DataRelationCollection.

DataRow

Found in the .NET Framework at System.Data.DataRow, the DataRow class represents a row of data in the DataTable object. The DataRow class and the DataColumn class represent the primary objects that comprise the DataTable class. The DataRow object is used to insert, update and delete rows from a DataTable. Rows can be added to a DataTable by either creating a new DataRow object using the NewRow method or by adding a DataRow object to the DataSet's DataRowCollection. DataRow objects are updated by simply changing the DataRow object's DataValue property. You delete a DataRow object by executing the DataRow object's Delete method or by calling the DataSet's DataRowCollection object's Remove method.

DataView

Found in the .NET Framework at System.Data.DataView, the DataView class offers a customized view of a subset of rows in a DataTable object. Like the DataTable object, DataView objects can be bound to both WinForm and WebForm controls. The DataView classes's RowFilter and Sort properties can allow the data presented by the DataView to be displayed in a different order than the data presented by the base DataTable object. Like the DataTable object, the data contained in a DataView object is updateable. You can add new rows by using the AddNew method, and you can delete rows by using the Delete method.

DataViewManager

The DataViewManager class is located in the .NET Framework at SystemData.Data ViewManager. The DataViewManager class is a bit different than the other classes in the System.Data Namespace. Essentially, the DataViewManager class tracks the Data-ViewSetting objects for each DataTable in the DataSet in its DataViewSettingsCollection. The DataViewSettingsCollection is a group of DataViewSetting objects where each DataViewSetting object contains properties like the RowFilter, RowStateFilter, and Sort that define each DataView object.

DataRelation

The DataRelation class is located in the .NET Framework at System.Data.DataRelation. The DataRelation class is used to represent parent-child relationships between two DataTable objects contained in a DataSet. For example, you could create a DataRelation object between an OrderID DataColumn in an Order Header table to the corresponding OrderID DataColumn in an Order Detail table. The basic function of the DataRelation object is to facilitate navigation and data retrieval from related DataTables. In order to create a relationship between two DataTable objects, the two DataTables must contain DataColumn objects that have matching attributes. When a DataRelation is first created, the .NET Framework checks to make sure that the relationship is valid and then it adds the DataRelation object to the DataRelationCollection, which tracks all of the data relations for the DataSet. The DataRelation class supports cascading changes from the parent table to the child table and this is controlled through the ForeignKeyConstraint class.

Constraint

Found in the .NET Framework at System.Data.Constraint, the Constraint class represents a set of data integrity rules that can be applied to a DataColumn object. There is no base constructor for the Constraint class. Instead, constraint objects are created using either the ForeignKeyConstraint constructor or the UniqueConstraint constructor.

ForeignKeyConstraint

The ForeignKeyConstraint class is located in the .NET Framework at SystemData .ForeignKeyConstraint. The ForeignKeyConstraint class governs how changes in a parent table affect rows in the child table when a DataRelation exists between the two tables. For example, when you delete a value that is used in one or more related tables, a ForeignKeyConstraint classes' DeleteRule property determines whether the values in the related tables are also deleted. Deleting a value from the parent table can delete the child rows, set the values in the child table's rows to null values, set the values in the child table's rows to default values, or throw an exception.

UniqueConstraint

The UniqueConstraint class is located in the .NET Framework at SystemData .UniqueConstraint. The UniqueConstraint class ensures that all values entered into a DataColumn object have a unique value.

DataException

Found in the .NET Framework at System.Data.DataException, the DataException class represents an error that is thrown by one of the System.Data classes. For example, code that violates a UniqueConstraint on a DataColumn by attempting to add a duplicate value to the DataColumn will cause a DataException object to be created and added to the DataExceptionCollection. You can use the DataException objects to report error conditions in your ADO.NET applications.

Collections in the System.Data Namespace

Table 3-1 lists the collections that are found in the ADO.NET System.Data Namespace.

Collection	Description
ConstraintCollection	A collection of Constraint objects that relate to a DataTable
DataColumnCollection	A collection of DataColumn objects that belong to a DataTable
DataRelationCollection	A collection of DataRelation objects that belong to a DataSet
DataRowCollection	A collection of DataRow objects that belong to a DataTable
DataTableCollection	A collection of DataTable objects that belong to a DataSet
DataViewSettingCollection	A collection of DataViewSetting objects that define a DataView
PropertyCollection	A collection of user-defined properties that can be added to DataSet, DataTable, or DataColumn objects

Table 3-1. *System.Data Collections*

Exceptions in the System.Data Namespace

Table 3-2 lists the Exception classes that are found in the ADO.NET System.Data Namespace.

A complete reference of the System.Data Namespace is presented in Appendix A.

Exception Class	Descriptions
ConstraintException	Thrown by the violation of a DataColumn Constraint
DBConcurrencyException	Thrown by the DataAdapter object when attempting to update zero rows
DeletedRowInaccessibleException	Thrown by the DataRow when an attempt is made to access a deleted row
DuplicateNameException	Thrown by the DataSet when an attempt is made to add an object with an existing name
EvaluateException	Thrown by the DataColumn object when the value in the Expression property cannot be evaluated
InRowChangingEventException	Thrown by the DataRow object when attempting to call the EndEdit method during the RowChanging event
InvalidConstraintException	Thrown by the DataSet object when attempting to create an invalid constraint
InvalidExpressionException	Thrown by the DataColumnCollection when attempting to add a DataColumn containing an invalid Expression property
MissingPrimaryKeyException	Thrown by the DataRowCollection when attempting to access a row that has no primary key
NoNullAllowedException	Thrown by the DataRow object when attempting to add a row with a null value in a column where the AllowDBNull property has been set to False
ReadOnlyException	Thrown by the DataRow object when an attempt is made to change the value of a read-only column
RowNotInTableException	Thrown by the DataRow object when attempting to perform an operation on a row that's not included in the DataTable
StrongTypingException	Thrown by a strongly typed DataSet object when any attempt is made to access the DBNull value
SyntaxErrorException	Thrown by the DataColumn object when the Expression property contains an invalid value

Table 3-2. *System.Data Exception Classes*

Exception Class	Descriptions
TypedDataSetGeneratorException	Thrown by a strongly typed DataSet when a name conflict occurs
VersionNotFoundException	Thrown by the DataRow object when attempting to access the version information of a row that has been deleted

Table 3-2. *System.Data Exception Classes* (continued)

Summary

In this chapter, you got an overview of the ADO.NET architecture and its primary components. In the next section of the book, you'll get a chance to dive into the ADO.NET implementation details, where you'll see how to establish a database connection using the .NET Data Providers. This section starts by showing you how to use the SQL Server .NET Data Provider, and then it takes those basic concepts and applies them to the Oracle .NET Provider, the OLE DB .NET Data Provider, and the ODBC .NET Data Provider.

The Complete Reference

Part II

The ADO.NET Connection Object

The
Complete
Reference

ADO.NET

Chapter 4

Data Provider
for SQL Server

In this chapter, you'll see how to connect to SQL Server using the .NET Framework Data Provider for SQL Server. In the first part of the chapter, you'll see how to use the visual connection objects provided by the Visual Studio.NET designer to connect to SQL Server. In the second part of this chapter, we dive in a little deeper and show you how to use the code-based ADO.NET SqlConnection objects to connect your ADO.NET applications to a SQL Server database.

Connecting with the .NET Framework Data Provider for SQL Server

The .NET Framework Data Provider for SQL Server, the .NET Framework Data Provider for OLE DB, and the .NET Framework Data Provider for ODBC can all connect to SQL Server databases. However, if your application only needs to connect to SQL Server and it doesn't need to connect to any other database systems, you'll get a significant performance advantage using the .NET Framework Data Provider for SQL Server. When accessing SQL Server databases, the .NET Framework Data Provider for SQL Server is more efficient than the .NET Framework Data Provider for OLE DB or ODBC because it communicates between the client application and the SQL Server system using SQL Server's native TDS (Tabular Data Stream) protocol. You can see an overview of the communications layers in Figure 4-1.

As you can see in Figure 4-1, the .NET Framework Data Provider for SQL Server's direct use of TDS makes it an extremely low overhead and efficient way to connect to SQL Server. Microsoft's benchmarks have shown that the .NET Framework Data

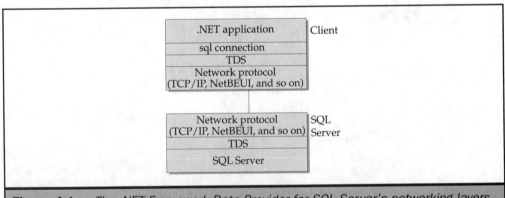

Figure 4-1.   *The .NET Framework Data Provider for SQL Server's networking layers*

Provider for SQL Server is faster than any of the other .NET Data Providers, as well as being faster than COM-based ADO for retrieving data from SQL Server. In contrast, the .NET Framework Data Provider for OLE DB and the .NET Framework Data Provider for ODBC have significantly higher overhead because the database requests must pass though either the OLE DB provider or ODBC driver as well as the appropriate network library before being converted into the TDS protocol used by SQL Server. However, don't discount these providers just because they're slower than the .NET Framework Data Provider for SQL Server. Their support for multiple OLE DB providers and ODBC drivers gives them the flexibility to connect to other databases such as Access, Oracle, and DB2, as well as SQL Server. You'll find more detailed information about the .NET Framework Data Provider for OLE DB and the .NET Framework Data Provider for ODBC .NET in Chapters 6 and 7.

Using the Visual Studio SqlConnection Object

It's easiest to get started with ADO.NET by using the visual component provided as a part of Visual Studio.NET. Using the same drag-and-drop paradigm that's used by the Visual Studio.NET interface components, you can drag and drop the different ADO.NET data components from the Visual Studio.NET Data Toolbox onto the visual designer. To create a new connection to SQL Server using the .NET Framework Data Provider for SQL Server objects in Visual Studio.NET, you must first create a Visual Studio VB.NET or C# project and then add a new form to the project. After the form has been created, you can display the form in the Visual Studio Designer window by clicking the newly created form in the Visual Studio Project Explorer window that's displayed on the right side of the Visual Studio.NET development environment. Displaying the form in the Designer window causes the Data Toolbox to be added to the collection of toolboxes displayed on the left side of the Visual Studio.Net development environment. Click the Data tab to open the Data Toolbox, and then double-click the SqlConnection object that's displayed in the Data Toolbox to add a SqlConnection object to your project. A new SqlConnection object like the one shown in Figure 4-2 will be added to your project.

Adding a SqlConnection object to your project using the Visual Studio.NET Designer is almost exactly the same as using code to add a SqlConnection object to your application. Both the visual object and the code-based object have the same capabilities and support exactly the same methods and properties. For more information on the specific methods and properties supported by the SqlConnection object, you can refer to Appendix F, the System.Data.SQLClient Namespace reference.

After adding the SqlConnection object to your project, you must set its ConnectionString property and then execute its Open method to establish a connection to the SQL Server system. You can set the ConnectionString property interactively by entering a connection string in the Properties window shown in the lower-right corner

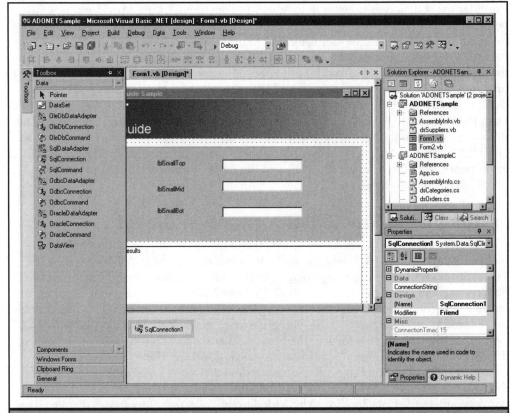

Figure 4-2. *Adding a SqlConnection object in the VS.NET Designer*

of the Visual Studio.NET design environment, or you can set the ConnectionString property using code. The following example illustrates VB.NET code that will enable you to connect to SQL Server using a SqlConnection object that was added from the Data Toolbox.

```vbnet
Private Sub SQLConnectComponent()
    SqlConnection1.ConnectionString = "SERVER=myServer;" & _
        "INTEGRATED SECURITY=True"
    Try
        SqlConnection1.Open()
    Catch ex As Exception
        MessageBox.Show("Connection error: " & ex.ToString())
```

```
      End Try
      SqlConnection1.Close()
End Sub
```

The C# version of this code is shown here:

```
private void SQLConnectComponent()
{
    sqlConnection1.ConnectionString = "SERVER=myServer;" +
        "INTEGRATED SECURITY=True";
    try
    {
        sqlConnection1.Open();
    }
    catch (Exception ex)
    {
        MessageBox.Show("Connection error: :" + ex.ToString());
    }
    sqlConnection1.Close();
}
```

In this example, the SqlConnection object uses the default name that was supplied by the VisualStudio.NET design environment. For the VB.NET example, the default name is SqlConnection1 while the C# name defaults to sqlConnection1. In both cases, the ConnectionString property of the SqlConnection object is assigned a string that uses the SERVER keyword to identify the instance of the SQL Server system that will be connected to and the INTEGRATED SECURITY keyword, which specifies that the client will be authenticated to the SQL Server system using their Windows login identification. You can find more information about the specific values used by the SqlConnection object in the next section of this chapter.

Next, a Try-Catch loop is set up in order to capture any connection errors that may occur. Within the Try-Catch loop, the SqlConnection1 object's Open method is used to establish a connection to the SQL Server system named myServer. It's always a good idea to implement structured error handling for any condition that could cause the application to terminate abnormally. For instance, if the SQL Server system named myServer is not available, then the error condition would cause an exception to be raised. If the exception isn't handled, the application would terminate abnormally and the user would see a very unfriendly message informing him or her of an application error. The Try-Catch loop enables your application to catch any exceptions that are raised and handle them in a predetermined manner. In this case, if the SqlConnection object's Open method used in the Try block fails, the code in the Catch block will be executed and the application will continue to run. Within this example, a simple instance of an Exception object named "ex" is created in the Catch block, and that object's ToString method is used to display any resulting error messages in a Message box. If the Open method succeeds, the code in the Catch block is never executed. In this case, after the Open method succeeds, the application will continue on to use the SqlConnection1 object's Close method to end the connection to SQL Server.

Adding the System.Data.SqlClient Namespace

Although the visual connection components that are provided by the Visual Studio.NET design environment make it pretty easy to create an initial connection to a SQL Server system, they also tend to clutter up the design environment. After you've used these components to make the first couple of connections, you'll probably be ready to forego the visual components in the Data Toolbox and establish your database connection exclusively using code. Using the ADO.NET objects in code requires only a couple of extra steps. In return, you get more screen real estate for the Designer window and more control over exactly when and how the SqlConnection objects get created.

Before you can use the .NET Framework Data Provider for SQL Server in your code, you must first specify an import directive for the System.Data.SqlClient Namespace in your project. This step isn't required when using the visual data components, but it is required in order to use the objects contained in the System.Data.SqlClient Namespace with code. The System.Data.SqlClient Namespace contains all of the related SQL Server connection and data access classes. To add an import directive for the System.Data.SQLClient to a VB.NET project, you would add the following code to the declaration section of your source file:

```
Imports System.Data.SqlClient
```

To add an import directive for the System.Data.SqlClient Namespace to a C# project, the code would appear as follows:

```
using System.Data.SqlClient;
```

 C# is case sensitive, so you need to be careful to choose the appropriate case for both your import directives and your code.

Connecting with a Connection String

Once you've added an import directive to your code, you're ready to begin using the different classes contained in the System.Data.SqlClient Namespace. As you saw in Chapter 3, the most essential of those classes is the Connection class. As its name implies, the System.Data.SqlClient Connection class is used to connect to a SQL Server database. You can use several different techniques to connect the System.Data.SqlClient Namespace to SQL Server. The technique that's probably most familiar to developers with previous ADO experience is to set the ConnectionString property with a valid connection string and then invoke the Open method. The following example illustrates how to make a SQL Server connection by setting the System.Data.SqlClient Namespace's ConnectionString property:

```
Private Sub SQLConnectString(ByVal sServer, ByVal sUser, _
        ByVal sPassword)
    Dim cn As New SqlConnection()
    cn.ConnectionString = "SERVER=" & sServer & ";" _
        & "UID=" & sUser & ";PWD=" & sPassword
    Try
        cn.Open()
    Catch ex As Exception
        MessageBox.Show("Connection error: :" & ex.ToString())
    End Try
    cn.Close()
End Sub
```

The C# version of this routine is as follows:

```
private void SQLConnectString(string sServer, string sUser,
        string sPassword)
{
    SqlConnection cn = new SqlConnection();
    cn.ConnectionString = "SERVER=" + sServer + ";"
        + "UID=" + sUser + ";PWD=" + sPassword;
    try
    {
        cn.Open();
    }
    catch (Exception ex)
    {
        MessageBox.Show("Connection error: :" + ex.ToString());
    }
    cn.Close();
}
```

In both cases, string variables containing the name of the SQL Server system to connect to along with the user ID and password are passed into the top of the routine. Next, a new instance of the System.Data.SqlClient Connection object, named cn, is created. Then the ConnectionString property of the System.Data.SqlClient

Connection object is assigned to the .NET Framework Data Provider for SQL Server connection string. This connection string uses the SERVER keyword to identify the SQL Server system that will be connected to. The UID and PWD keywords provide the authentication values required to log in to SQL Server if you are connecting using mixed security. A complete list of the valid .NET Framework Data Provider for SQL Server connection string keywords is presented in the section that follows. Once the ConnectionString property has been assigned the appropriate connection string, a Try-Catch block is used to execute the cn Connection object's Open method. After the Open method completes, a connection to the SQL Server system identified in the connection string is initiated. If an error occurred with the connection string or the specified SQL Server system is not available, the code in the Catch block will be executed and a message box will be displayed showing the error information. After a successful connection has been established, the Connection object is closed using the Close method.

> **Note**   *To ensure that the resources allocated by the Connection object are released when they are no longer needed, it is very important in ADO.NET to explicitly use the Close method. In .NET applications, the connection object is not necessarily destroyed when it goes out of scope. Executing either the Close or Dispose method is required to make sure that the connection resources are released. The Close method closes the current connection, but the underlying .NET-managed resources used for connection pooling will remain available. Close can be called multiple times (even when the connection is already closed) without raising an error. The Dispose method can release all managed and unmanaged resources used by a connection, and it can only be called for an active connection.*

The .NET Framework Data Provider for SQL Server Connection String Keywords

The SQL Server .Net Data Provider connection string is much like the OLE DB connection string that was used by ADO. However, unlike the OLE DB connection string, the login values contained in the connection string are not returned to the application unless you explicitly tell the provider to do so via the PERSIST SECURITY INFO connection string keyword. In addition, the SQL Server .NET Data Provider also supports a few new keywords. Table 4-1 lists all the SQL Server .NET Data Provider–specific keywords supported by the SqlConnection object's ConnectionString property.

> **Note**   *Some of the keywords in Table 4-1 contain spaces. Those spaces are required. In addition, for those items that have more than one keyword option, you can choose whichever you prefer. The .NET Framework Data Provider for SQL Server connection string keywords are not case sensitive. However, it's good programming practice to be consistent in your choice of keyword case in all of your applications.*

Keyword	Description
Application Name	Identifies the current application.
AttachDBFilename -or- Extended properties -or- Initial File Name	Identifies the full path and name of a file that will be attached as a SQL Server database. This keyword must be used in conjunction with the DATABASE keyword.
Connect Timeout -or- Connection Timeout	Specifies the length of time in seconds to wait before terminating a connection attempt. The default is 15.
Connection Lifetime	Specifies the length of time in seconds to wait before destroying a connection returned to the connection pool. This keyword is used to facilitate load balancing in cluster. The default is 0.
Connection Reset	Specifies that a connection will be reset when it is returned from the connection pool. The default is True.
Current Language	Specifies the SQL Server language name to be used for this connection.
Data Source -or-Server -or- Address -or-Addr -or- Network Address	Identifies the name or network address of a SQL Server instance to connect to.
Enlist	Determines whether the current thread will be enlisted as part of the current transaction context. The default value is True.
Encrypt	Determines whether SSL will be used to encrypt the data stream sent between the application and SQL Server. The default value is False.
Initial Catalog -or- Database	The SQL Server target database name.
Integrated Security -or- Trusted_Connection	Uses a value of True or SSPI to indicate where Windows authentication is to be used to connect to the database and a value of False to indicate that mixed or SQL Sever authentication should be used.

Table 4-1.   *SQL Server .NET Data Provider Connection String Keywords*

Keyword	Description
Max Pool Size	The default value is 100.
Min Pool Size	The default value is 0.
Network Library -or-Net	Specifies the network library DLL to be used. Supported values include dbnmpntw (Named Pipes), dbmsrpcn (Multiprotocol), dbmsadsn (Apple Talk), dbmsgnet (VIA), dbmsipcn (Shared Memory) and dbmsspxn (IPX/SPX), and dbmssocn (TCP/IP). The default value is dbmssocn. The value used by this keyword should not include the path of the .dll file extension.
Packet Size	Used to alter the network packet size. The default packet size is 8192.
Password -or-Pwd	The password associated with the login ID (used for SQL Server authentication).
Persist Security Info	Specifies whether security-sensitive information such as the login information is returned to the application after a successful connection. The default value is False.
Pooling	The default value is True.
User ID -or-UID	The login ID for the data source (used for SQL Server authentication).
Workstation ID	Identifies the client workstation.

Table 4-1. *SQL Server .NET Data Provider Connection String Keywords* (continued)

Opening a Trusted Connection

The previous example illustrated how to establish a SQL Server connection using a connection string that specified the UID and PWD keywords along with an associated SQL Server login. (This is also known as using Mixed Mode Security.) However, because this incorporates the actual user ID and password into your code this certainly isn't the most secure way to authenticate your connection to the SQL Server system.

Using Windows Authentication, also known as *Integrated Security*, provides for a more secure connection because the same values used for the client's Windows NT/

2000/NET login are also used for SQL Server authentication—there's no need to specify the user ID or the password from the application. In addition, Integrated Security makes administration easier because it eliminates the need to create a separate set of SQL Server login IDs that must be maintained independently from the Windows NT/2000/NET login information. The following example illustrates how to use VB.NET to make a trusted connection to SQL Server using the .NET Framework Data Provider for SQL Server:

```
Private Sub SQLConnectSSPI(ByVal sServer As String)
    Dim cn As New SqlConnection("SERVER=" & sServer & _
        ";INTEGRATED SECURITY=True")

    Try
        cn.Open()
    Catch ex As Exception
        MessageBox.Show("Connection error: :" & ex.ToString())
    End Try
    cn.Close()

End Sub
```

The C# version of this code follows.

```
private void SQLConnectSSPI(string sServer)
{
    SqlConnection cn  = new SqlConnection("SERVER=" + sServer
            + ";INTEGRATED SECURITY=True");
    try
    {
        cn.Open();
    }
    catch (Exception ex)
    {
        MessageBox.Show("Connection error: :" + ex.ToString());
    }
    cn.Close();
}
```

At the beginning of these subroutines, the server name is passed in as a string value. Next, an instance of the SqlConnection object is created and the ConnectionString property is assigned as one of the arguments of the constructor. As in the previous example, the connection string uses the SERVER keyword to specify the SQL Server to connect to, and the INTEGRATED SECURITY keyword is set to True, indicating that the SQL Server authentication will be performed using Windows Authentication rather than by passing in a login ID and password as part of the connection string.

After an instance of the SqlConnection object named cn has been instantiated, a Try-Catch block is used to execute the Open method. Again, if the Open method fails, then the code in the Catch block will be executed and a message box will be displayed showing the specific error message. After the connection has been established, it is immediately closed using the Connection object's Close method.

Using Connection Pooling

Connection pooling is an important scalability feature that's particularly important to *n*-tier–style Web applications, which may need to quickly support hundreds of simultaneous connections. Each open connection to SQL Server requires system overhead and management. Establishing the initial connection is the highest overhead activity associated with each connection. Connection pooling makes the overall connection process more efficient by sharing a group or pool of connections between incoming users. Rather than immediately opening individual connections for each user, with connection pooling, all connections that share exactly the same connection characteristics share the same connection, which reduces the total number of new connections that must be established and maintained by SQL Server. To further improve efficiency, open connections are not immediately closed when a given client disconnects from the server. Rather, the connection is left open for a short period of time (determined by the Connection Lifetime keyword that's used in the SqlConnection object's ConnectionString property), which means it's available immediately for any new clients that can share the same connection characteristics and you avoid the overhead associated with establishing a new connection.

Better still, the .NET Framework Data Provider for SQL Server automatically performs connection pooling without requiring any special setup. When a connection is opened, a connection pool is created based on the values used in the ConnectionString property of the SqlConnection object. Each connection pool is associated with a unique connection string. When a new connection is opened, the SqlConnection object checks to see if the value in the ConnectionString property matches the connection string used for an existing pool. If the string matches, the new connection is added to the existing pool. If not, a new pool is created. The SqlConnection object will not destroy a connection pool until the application ends. The following VB.NET example illustrates two different connections that are both added to the same connection pool:

```
Private Sub SQLConnectPool(ByVal sServer As String)
    ' Create the first connection object
    Dim cn As New SqlConnection("SERVER=" & sServer & _
        ";INTEGRATED SECURITY=True")
    Dim cn2 As New SqlConnection("SERVER=" & sServer & _
        ";INTEGRATED SECURITY=True")
```

```
     ' Create the second identical connection object
     Try
         cn.Open()
         cn2.Open()
     Catch ex As Exception
         MessageBox.Show("Connection error: :" & ex.ToString())
     End Try

     cn.Close()
     cn2.Close()
 End Sub
```

The following is the C# version of this same routine:

```
private void SQLConnectPool(string sServer)
{
    // Create the first connection object
    SqlConnection cn  = new SqlConnection("SERVER=" + sServer
         + ";INTEGRATED SECURITY=True");
    // Create the second identical connection object
    SqlConnection cn2 = new SqlConnection("SERVER=" + sServer
         + ";INTEGRATED SECURITY=True");
    try
    {
        cn.Open();
        cn2.Open();
    }
    catch (Exception ex)
    {
        MessageBox.Show("Connection error: :" + ex.ToString());
    }
    cn.Close();
    cn2.Close();
}
```

A string variable containing the server name is passed in to the beginning of this subroutine. Next, two SqlConnection objects, cn and cn2, are created and have identical connection strings. In both cases, the ConnectionString property uses the SERVER keyword to identify the SQL Server to connect to and the INTEGRATED SECURITY keyword to specify that Windows Integrated Security will be used.

After the two SqlConnection objects have been created, a Try-Catch loop is used to open the connection to SQL Server and capture any runtime errors. Because the values of these connection strings are identical, they will both be part of the same connection pool. If the connection strings were different in any way, then two separate connection pools would have been created. After the connections have been established, the Close method is used to close each connection.

Pooling Related Connection String Keywords

While the .NET Framework Data Provider for SQL Server automatically handles connection pooling for you, there are still several connection string keywords that you can use to alter the SqlConnection object's connection pooling behavior. Table 4-2 presents the ConnectionString values you can use to customize the SQL Server .NET Data Provider's connection pooling behavior.

Name	Description
Connection Lifetime	After a connection is closed, it's returned to the pool. Then its creation time is compared with the current time and the connection is destroyed if the difference exceeds the value specified by Connection Lifetime. A value of 0 specifies that pooled connections will have the maximum lifespan.
Connection Reset	When True, this specifies that the connection is reset when it's removed from the pool. For Microsoft SQL Server version 7.0, you can set this value to False to avoid an additional server roundtrip after opening a connection. However, the previous connection state and database context will not be reset.
Enlist	When True, the connection is automatically created in the current transaction context of the creation thread if a transaction context exists.
Max Pool Size	Specifies the maximum number of connections allowed in the pool.
Min Pool Size	Specifies the minimum number of connections maintained in the pool.
Pooling	When True, connection pooling is automatically enabled. False allows you to turn off connection pooling.

Table 4-2. *Pooling Related Connection String Keywords*

For those connection string keywords that contain spaces, the spaces are a required part of the keyword.

Performance Counters for Connection Pooling

You can track the SqlConnection object's use of connection pooling with System Monitor. When the .NET Framework is installed, several performance counters are added to the operating system that enable you to monitor the .NET Framework Data Provider for SQL Server's use of connection pooling. On Windows 2000 Server, you can start the System Monitor by using the Start | Programs | Administrative Tools | Performance menu option. Right-clicking the graph and selecting the Add counter option will display the Add Counter dialog box where you can select the .NET CLR Data option from the list of Performance objects. The System Monitor will display System.Data.SQLClient performance counters in a window like the one in Figure 4-3.

Table 4-3 lists the connection pooling counters that can be accessed in System Monitor using the .NET CLR Data performance object.

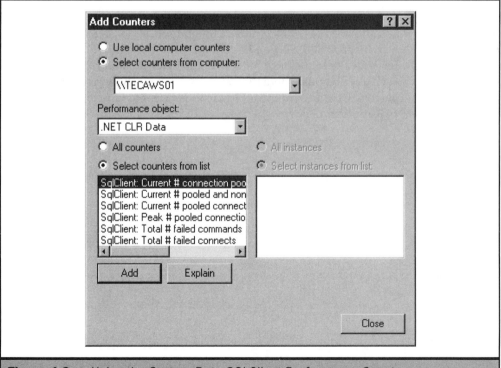

Figure 4-3. *Using the System.Data.SQLClient Performance Counters*

Counter	Description
SqlClient: Current # pooled and non-pooled connections	Current number of both pooled and nonpooled connections
SqlClient: Current # pooled connections	Current number of connections in all pools
SqlClient: Current # connection pools	Current number of connection pools
SqlClient: Peak # pooled connections	The highest number of connections in all pools
SqlClient: Total # failed connects	The total number of failed connection attempts

Table 4-3.   *Performance Counters for the SQL Server .NET Data Provider*

Summary

In this chapter, you saw several ways to connect to a target database using the .NET Framework Data Provider for SQL Server. In general, the .NET Framework Data Provider for SQL Server is the best choice for connecting to SQL Server 7.0 and higher databases. The next chapter begins where this one leaves off by showing you how to use the .NET Framework Data Provider for Oracle to connect to Oracle databases from your ADO.NET applications.

The
Complete
Reference

Chapter 5

Using the .NET Framework Data Provider for Oracle

In this chapter, you will learn how to use the .NET Framework Data Provider for Oracle to connect your ADO.NET application to an Oracle databse. In the first part of this chapter, you will learn how to install and configure the Oracle Client. The Oracle Client software is required by the ADO.NET classes to connect to an Oracle database. The next part of this chapter shows you how to use the visual OracleConnection component provided by the Visual Studio.NET IDE to establish a connection to an Oracle database. Finally, you will learn how to use the OracleClient classes provided in the System.Data.OracleClient Namespace to perform code-based connections, as well as to connect to the database using connection pooling.

Note	*This chapter covers the Microsoft .NET Framework Data Provider for Oracle, which is provided as a part of the .NET Framework 1.1. Oracle also makes a .NET Data Provider called the Oracle Provider for .NET. Oracle's .NET Data Provider is not covered in this book, but if you are interested in it, you can download it from Oracle's Web site at http:// otn.oracle.com/tech/windows/odpnet/.*

Connecting with the .NET Framework Data Provider for Oracle

The .NET Framework Data Provider is used to connect to Oracle 8i and Oracle 9i databases. The .NET Framework Data Provider for OLE DB and .NET Framework Data Provider for ODBC can also connect to Oracle databases. However, you'll get a significant performance advantage using the .NET Framework Data Provider for Oracle if your application only needs to connect to Oracle 8i and 9i databases, and it doesn't need to connect to older versions of Oracle or any other database systems. This performance advantage results because the .NET Framework Data Provider for Oracle is more efficient than the .NET Framework Data Provider for OLE DB or the .NET Framework Data Provider for ODBC. Each of these other .NET Framework Data Providers imposes additional layers of software and, therefore, overhead. This overhead provides greater flexibility, but at the cost of performance. You can see an overview of the communications layers used by the .NET Framework Data Provider for Oracle in Figure 5-1.

In Figure 5-1, you can see that on the client side, the .NET Framework Data Provider for Oracle interfaces directly with the Oracle Client software layer. The .NET Framework Data Provider for Oracle uses Oracle's native Oracle Call Interface (OCI) to communicate with the Oracle Client software. The OCI is provided by Oracle's OCI.DLL dynamic link library. The Oracle Client then converts the data access requests into Oracle's proprietary Transport Network Substrate (TNS) protocol before sending them on to the Oracle database server.

In contrast, the .NET Framework Data Provider OLE DB and .NET Framework Data Provider ODBC have significantly higher overhead because the database requests must pass through two additional layers of software before being passed on to the Oracle Client software. For example, when an ADO.NET application uses the .NET Framework Data Provider for OLE DB, the .NET Framework Data Provider for OLE DB must first pass

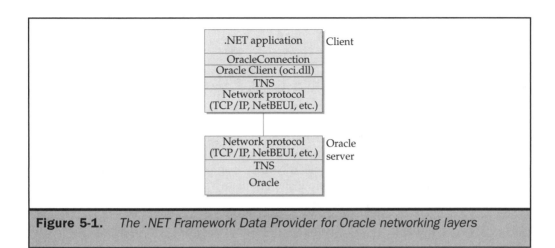

Figure 5-1.   *The .NET Framework Data Provider for Oracle networking layers*

requests to the OLE DB Service Provider, and then on to the OLE DB Provider for Oracle before these requests reach the Oracle Client software. Likewise, when using the .NET Framework Data Provider for ODBC, data access requests must first pass through the ODBC Driver Manager, and then through the Oracle ODBC driver before being passed on to the Oracle Client interface. However, remember that although the .NET Data Provider OLE DB and .NET Data Provider ODBC providers are slower than the .NET Data Provider for Oracle, they support multiple OLE DB providers and ODBC drivers, which gives them the flexibility to connect to other databases as well as older versions of the Oracle database server.

Installing the Oracle Client

Before using the .NET Framework Data Provider for Oracle, you need to install the Oracle Client software on the source system. This system might be either a networked client PC in the two-tiered design, or it might be a Web server or an application server in an *n*-tiered design. At first glance this might seem a little different than the requirements for the .NET Framework Data Provider for SQL Server, but that's really not the case. The .NET Framework Data Provider for SQL Server requires the installation of Microsoft Data Access Components (MDAC) on the client system. However, the main difference lies in the fact that MDAC is often installed as a part of Windows 2000, Windows XP, and Windows .NET Server operating systems, as well as a number of other popular software products, such as Microsoft Office, and the .NET Framework itself. So, in actuality, the .NET Framework Data Provider for Oracle's requirements for the installation of client software are really no different than SQL Server's. The only real difference is that the Oracle Client software isn't installed by default on the client system so it must always be installed separately. You can find the Oracle client software on the Oracle Client installation CD-ROM, or it can be downloaded from http://technet.oracle.com.

After beginning the Oracle Client setup program from either the CD-ROM or the download, you'll see the Oracle Universal Installer Welcome dialog box. Clicking the Next button displays the Oracle Universal Installer File Locations dialog box, shown in Figure 5-2.

 While this example uses an interactive setup procedure, the Oracle Client software also supports unattended installations using a response file.

The Oracle Universal Installer File Locations dialog box enables you to enter the location of the Oracle products.jar file and select the location on your system where you want to install the Oracle software. By default, the Oracle Universal Installer will look for the product.jar file in the \stage directory from the same drive where you ran the setup program. The Oracle software installation path for Oracle 9i is c:\oracle\ora92, but you can change this to any valid local path. In Figure 5-2, you can see that the Oracle software will be installed from the F: drive, which is the client system's CD drive while the target install directory has been changed from the default to D:\oracle\ora92. Once you have selected the appropriate file locations, click the Next button to display the Installation Types dialog box, shown in Figure 5-3.

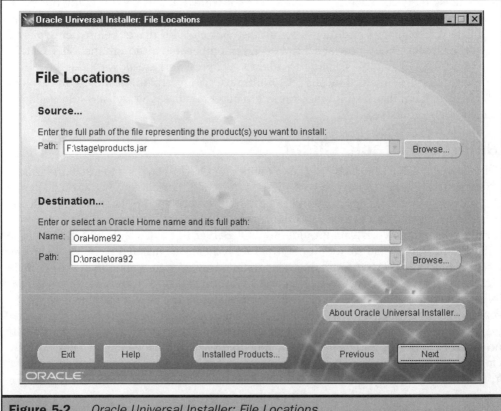

Figure 5-2. *Oracle Universal Installer: File Locations*

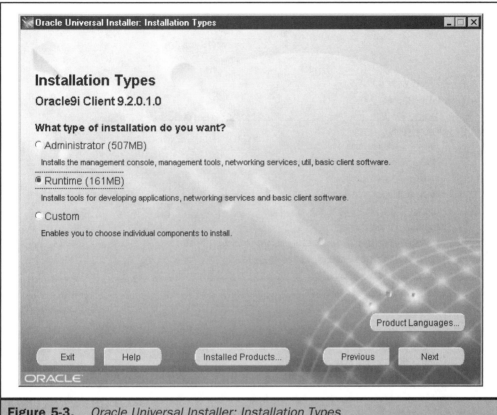

Figure 5-3. *Oracle Universal Installer: Installation Types*

The next screen displayed by the Oracle Universal Installer determines what type of installation you will be performing. You can select to install either the Oracle Administrator software or the Oracle Runtime software. The Oracle Administrator option is a superset of the Oracle Runtime option. In addition to the basic Oracle Client components, the Administrator option also installs the Oracle management console and management tools and utilities. The Runtime option installs only the basic Oracle Client files, which include the essential OCI and networking support, as well as SQL Plus, the Configuration Assistant, and the Net Manager. To install the Oracle Client software, you should select the Runtime option, as shown in Figure 5-3. The Oracle Client runtime files require a total of 161MB. Click the Next button to display the Oracle Universal Installer Summary dialog box, shown in Figure 5-4.

The Oracle Universal Installer Summary dialog box presents a list showing all of the selections that you made using the installation dialog boxes. Click the Install button to begin the process of copying the files from the installation point to the target directory. Once the installation process has copied the Oracle Client file to the target directory you'll be prompted to run the Oracle Net Configuration Assistant to configure the client connection.

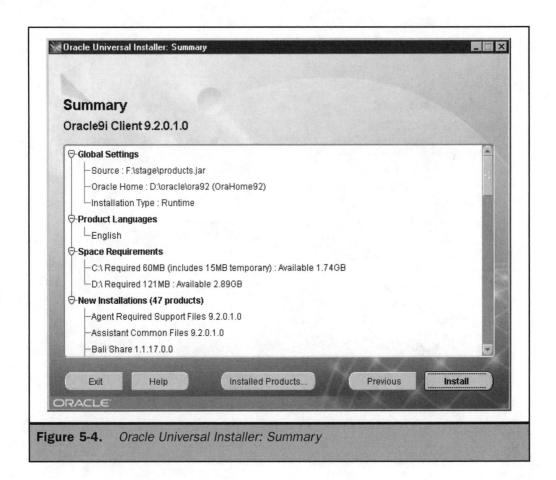

Figure 5-4.   *Oracle Universal Installer: Summary*

Configuring the Oracle Client

The Oracle Net Configuration Assistant starts automatically following the installation of the Oracle Runtime components. It can also be run at any time using the Start | Programs | Oracle – OraHome92 menu option from the Windows NT/2000/XP desktop. The first screen displayed by the Oracle Net Configuration Assistant enables you to select the type of name service that you're using to connect to the Oracle database server. You can see the Oracle Net Configuration Assistant Welcome dialog box in Figure 5-5.

The Oracle Net Configuration Assistant Welcome dialog box first asks what type of naming system the client will be using to locate the Oracle server. If you're using a directory service such as Active Directory or Sun's Network Information service (NIS), you can select the first option. In this example, I'll assume that no naming service exists and will step through the manual net service naming process. The option "No, I will

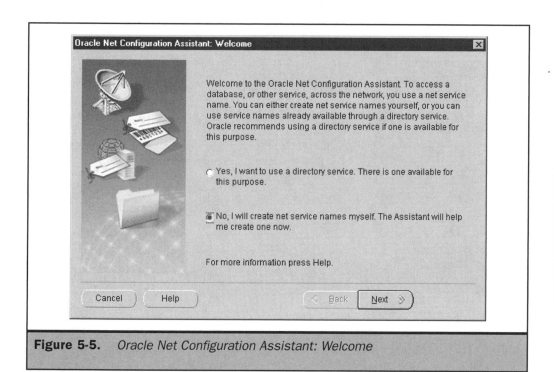

Figure 5-5.   *Oracle Net Configuration Assistant: Welcome*

create net service names myself. The Assistant will help me create one now." will begin the procedure of creating a new net service name. Select this option and click the Next button to display the Oracle Net Configuration Assistant dialog box, shown in Figure 5-6.

The next screen displayed by the Oracle Net Configuration Assistant allows you to specify the version of the Oracle database server that you want to connect to. You can choose to connect to an Oracle 8i or higher database or you can choose to connect to an Oracle 8 database. Your choice here controls the subsequent dialog boxes displayed by the Net Configuration Assistant. If you choose Oracle 8i or higher, the assistant prompts you for a service name. If you choose Oracle 8, the Net Configuration Assistant prompts you for an Oracle SID. In Figure 5-6, you can see that the database server for this connection is 8i or higher. After selecting the level of database server that you want to connect to, click the Next button to display the Net Configuration Assistant dialog box, shown in Figure 5-7.

This dialog box allows you to enter the service name for the Oracle database. The service name is comprised of the database name and domain name, and it is defined during the Oracle server installation process. It is a logical representation of a database, and it determines the way a database is presented to clients. An Oracle database can be presented as multiple services, and a service can be implemented as multiple database instances.

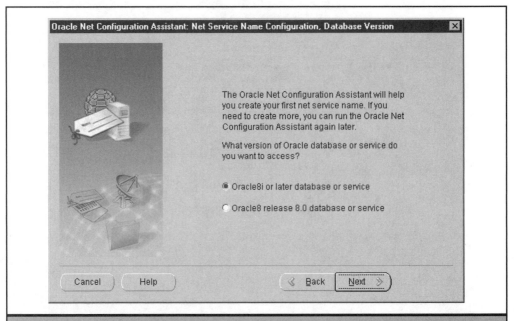

Figure 5-6. *Oracle Net Configuration Assistant: Net Service Name Configuration, Database Version*

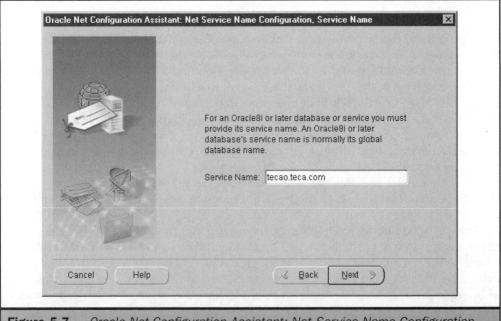

Figure 5-7. *Oracle Net Configuration Assistant: Net Service Name Configuration, Service Name*

In Figure 5-7, you can see that in this instance the service name of tecao.teca.com will be used to identify the Oracle database server. Clicking the Next button displays the Oracle Net Configuration Assistant screen, shown in Figure 5-8.

In Figure 5-8 you can see the Oracle Net Configuration Assistant, Select Protocols dialog box. This dialog box allows you to select the network protocol that you will use to connect the client to the Oracle server. In Figure 5-8, you can see that the TCP network protocol has been selected. After selecting the network protocol and clicking the Next button, the Net Configuration Assistant displays the dialog box shown in Figure 5-9.

The Net Configuration Assistant dialog box shown in Figure 5-9 allows you to enter the specific network protocol configuration information required to connect to the Oracle database. At the Host Name prompt, you need to enter either the TCP/IP host name for the Oracle server or its TCP/IP address. In Figure 5-9, you can see that the value of teca5 has been entered. This is the DNS name that's used to identify the Oracle server. Next, the TCP/IP port number is specified. This value must match the port that the Oracle Database Listener is using. In Figure 5-9, you can see that the default port of 1521 will be used. If you've selected to use a different TCP/IP port value, then you can use that value by clicking the Use Another Port Number radio button and then entering the alternative value in the text box. Once you have entered the TCP/IP connection properties of the database server that you want to connect to, click the Next button to display the Net Configuration Assistant dialog box shown in Figure 5-10.

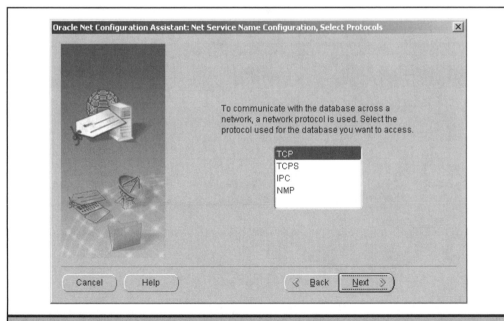

Figure 5-8. *Oracle Net Configuration Assistant: Net Service Name Configuration, Select Protocols*

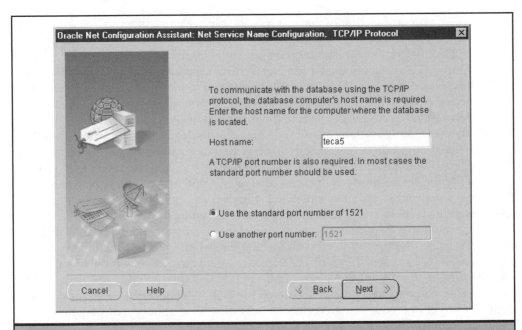

Figure 5-9.   Oracle Net Configuration Assistant: Net Service Name Configuration, TCP/IP Protocol

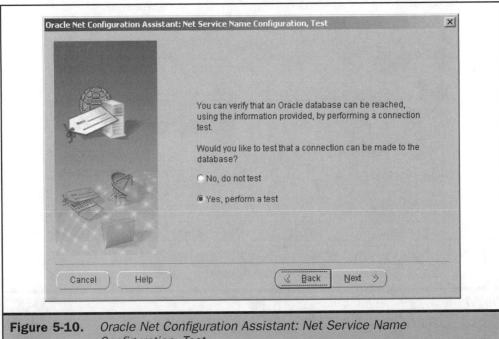

Figure 5-10.   Oracle Net Configuration Assistant: Net Service Name Configuration, Test

After all of the database server and network protocol information has been entered, you're ready to test your connection to the Oracle database server. Testing the configuration is optional. You can proceed and save the connection information without performing a test. However, testing the configuration does give you an easy method to verify the database and network configuration parameters. To test your connection, select the option Yes, Perform A Test and click the Next button. Once you have selected the test option and clicked the Next button, the Net Configuration Assistant displays the dialog box shown in Figure 5-11.

In Figure 5-11, you can see the Oracle Net Configuration Assistant, Connecting dialog box. If all of your net service configuration parameters are correct, you'll see a "Connecting… Test successful" message like the one shown in Figure 5-11. If your configuration information is correct, the test succeeds and you can save your configuration information. If the text fails, then you can click the Back button to step your way back through the Net Configuration Assistant dialog boxes, checking and changing whatever values may be incorrect. After selecting the TCP/IP protocol and clicking the Next button, the Net Configuration Assistant displays the dialog box shown in Figure 5-12.

This dialog box enables you to enter the service name for the Oracle database. The Net Service Name is the name that this configuration will be known as on the local computer. This name can be anything that you choose. In many ways, the Oracle Net Service Name is analogous to the ODBC Data Source Name in that it is a user-defined value that identifies a target data source. This name will later be used in the OracleConnection object's

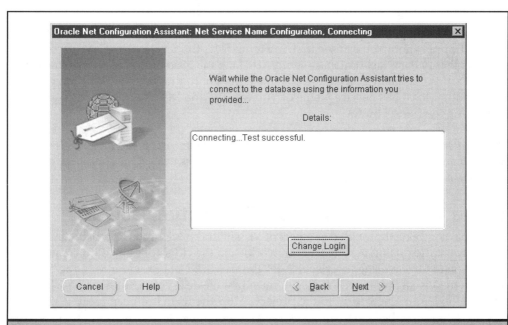

Figure 5-11. *Oracle Net Configuration Assistant: Net Service Name Configuration, Connecting*

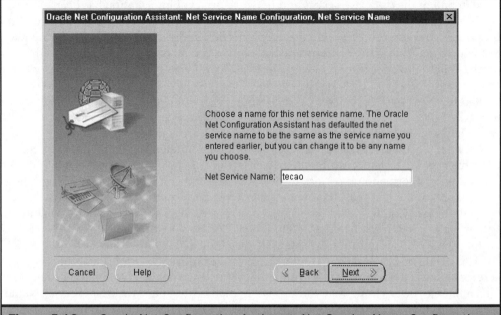

Figure 5-12. *Oracle Net Configuration Assistant: Net Service Name Configuration, Net Service Name*

ConnectionString property to establish a connection to the target Oracle database from the .NET application. You can see that, in Figure 5-12, the service name of tecao will be used to identify the Oracle database server. Clicking the Next button ends the Oracle Net Configuration Assistant's Net Service Name entry configuration. At this point, you can enter another local Net Service Name or you can end the Net Configuration Assistant by clicking the Cancel button.

After installing the Oracle client, you must reboot your system in order to register the Oracle client DLLs. Otherwise, your .NET applications will get the error message "Unable to load DLL (oci.dll)."

Using the Visual Studio OracleConnection Object

The visual component provided as a part of Visual Studio.NET offers probably the easiest way to get started using the .NET Framework Data Provider for Oracle. To create a new connection to Oracle using the visual .NET Framework Data Provider for Oracle objects found in the Visual Studio.NET IDE, you must first create a Visual Studio VB.NET or C# project. Next, add a new form to the project. After the form has been created, you can display the form in the Visual Studio Designer window by clicking the form in the Visual Studio Project Explorer window that's displayed on the right side of the Visual Studio .NET development environment. Displaying the form in the Designer window causes the Data Toolbox to be added to the collection of toolboxes that are displayed on the left side of the Visual Studio.NET development environment. Open the Data Toolbox by clicking the Data tab, and then double-click the OracleConnection object. This adds a new OracleConnection object to your project like the one shown in Figure 5-13.

Using the visual OracleConnection object in your project is very much like using the OracleConnection class using code. They both have the same capabilities and support exactly the same methods, properties, and events. For more information on the specific methods, properties, and events supported by the OracleConnection object, you can refer to Appendix E, the System.Data.OracleClient Namespace reference.

Once the OracleConnection has been added to your project, you must set its ConnectionString property and then execute its Open method to establish a connection to the Oracle server. Although you can set the ConnectionString property interactively, you don't want to do so for the OracleConnection object. Attempting to set the

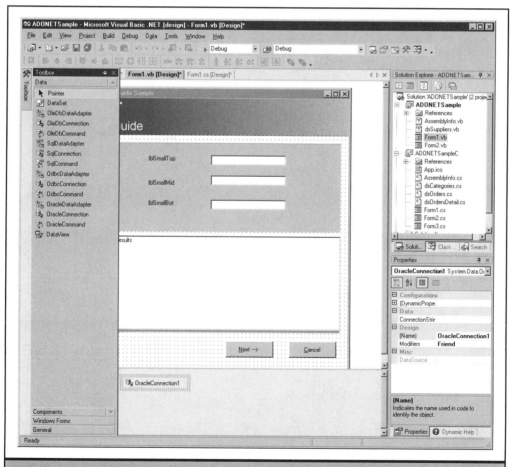

Figure 5-13.   *Adding an OracleConnecton Object in the VS.NET Designer*

ConnectionString property interactively using the Visual Studio.NET IDE will display the Data Link dialog box, which will create an OLE DB connection rather than a connection using the .NET Framework Data Provider for Oracle. To use the .NET Framework Data Provider for Oracle, you really need to set the required connection properties using code. The following examples illustrate the code required to connect to an Oracle system using the ADO.NET OracleConnection object that was added from the Data Toolbox.

```
Private Sub OracleConnectComponent()
    Cursor.Current = Cursors.WaitCursor
    OracleConnection1.ConnectionString = _
        "DATA SOURCE=tecao;UID=scott;PWD=tiger"
    Try
        OracleConnection1.Open()
    Catch ex As Exception
        Cursor.Current = Cursors.Default
        MessageBox.Show("Connection error: :" & ex.ToString())
    End Try
    OracleConnection1.Close()
    Cursor.Current = Cursors.Default
End Sub
```

The C# version of this subroutine is as follows:

```
private void OracleConnectComponent()
{
    Cursor.Current = Cursors.WaitCursor;
    odbcConnection1.ConnectionString =
        "DATA SOURCE=tecao;UID=scott;PWD=tiger";
    try
    {
        oracleConnection1.Open();
    }
    catch (Exception ex)
    {
        Cursor.Current = Cursors.Default;
        MessageBox.Show("Connection error: :" + ex.ToString());
    }
    oracleConnection1.Close();
    Cursor.Current = Cursors.Default;
}
```

In the preceding code listing, the OracleConnection object uses the default name that was supplied by the Visual Studio.NET IDE. For the VB.NET example, the default name is OracleConnection1, whereas the C# name defaults to oracleConnection1 (note the difference in case). In both examples, the ConnectionString property of the OracleConnection object is assigned a string that uses the DATA SOURCE keyword to identify the Oracle database server that will be connected. This is the Net Service Name that was defined earlier using the Oracle Net Configuration Assistant. For simplicity, these first examples illustrate passing a hard-coded Oracle login ID and password in order to connect to the Oracle server. The code shown in the preceding listing uses the Oracle example login of scott with the UID keyword and tiger with the PWD keyword. However, this is just for ease of understanding the first code example. You wouldn't want to use hard-coded authentication in your production applications. A better alternative is to use variables or to take advantage of integrated security. Oracle supports authentication to the operation system using the INTEGRATED SECURITY keyword. More information about the valid .NET Framework Data Provider for Oracle Connection String keywords is presented in the next section of this chapter.

After the ConnectionString property is set, a Try-Catch loop is used to capture any connection errors that may occur when the OracleConnection1 object's Open method is used to establish a connection to the Oracle server named tecao. You should always use this style of structured error handling for any condition that could cause the application to terminate abnormally. For instance, if the Oracle server is not available, then executing the Open method would result in an error condition that would cause the .NET Framework to raise an exception. If the exception isn't handled, the application would terminate abnormally and the user would see a very ugly message informing him or her of an application error. Using the Try-Catch Loop enables your application to catch any exceptions that are raised and handle them in a predetermined manner. Here, if the OracleConnection1 object's Open method fails, then the code in the Catch block will be executed and the application will continue to run. An instance of an Exception object named ex is created in the Catch block, and that object's ToString method is used to display any resulting error messages in a message box to the user. If the Open method succeeds, the code in the Catch block is never executed. After the OracleConnection1.Open method succeeds, the application will continue on to use the Close method to end the connection to the Oracle server.

Adding the System.Data.OracleClient Namespace

The visual connection components that are provided in the Visual Studio.NET design environment make it pretty easy to create an initial connection to an Oracle database server. However, they also tend to clutter up the design environment, and, once you've spent a little bit of time coding with ADO.NET, you'll probably be ready to bypass the visual components and establish your database connection exclusively using code. Using a completely code-based connection requires only a couple of extra steps, and in return you get more screen real estate in the IDE and more control over exactly when and how the OracleConnection objects get created.

The first step toward creating a code-based connection using the .NET Framework Data Provider for Oracle is to specify an import directive for the System.Data.OracleClient Namespace in your project. This isn't required when using the visual data components, but it is needed if you are using a code-based connection. The System.Data.OracleClient

Namespace contains all of the related Oracle connection and data access classes. To add an import directive for the System.Data.OracleClient to a VB.NET project, you would add the following code to the declarations section of your source file:

```
Imports System.Data.OracleClient
```

To add an import directive for the System.Data.OracleClient Namespace to a C# project, the code would appear as follows:

```
using System.Data.OracleClient;
```

Note   *Unlike VB.NET, C# is case sensitive, so you need to be careful about matching the appropriate case for both your import directives and your code.*

Connecting with a Connection String

After the import directive has been added to your project, you're ready to begin using the classes contained in the System.Data.OracleClient Namespace. The Connection class is the most important of those classes. As its name implies, the System.Data.OracleClient Connection class is used to connect to an Oracle database. For developers with previous ADO experience, the most straightforward method of connecting to the database is to set the ConnectionString property to a valid connection string and then invoke the Open method. The following example illustrates how to connect to an Oracle database by setting the System.Data.OracleClient Connection class ConnectionString property:

```
Private Sub OracleConnectString(ByVal sServer As String, _
        ByVal sUser As String, ByVal sPassword As String)
    Cursor.Current = Cursors.WaitCursor
    Dim cn As New OracleConnection("DATA SOURCE=" & sServer _
        & ";UID=" & sUser & ";PWD=" & sPassword)
    Try
        cn.Open()
    Catch ex As Exception
        Cursor.Current = Cursors.Default
        MessageBox.Show("Connection error: :" & ex.ToString())
    End Try
    cn.Close()
    Cursor.Current = Cursors.Default
End Sub
```

The C# version of the OracleConnectString routine is as follows:

```
private void OracleConnectString(string sServer, string sUser,
    string sPassword)
```

```
{
    Cursor.Current = Cursors.WaitCursor;
    OracleConnection cn = new OracleConnection("DATA SOURCE="
        + sServer + ";UID=" + sUser + ";PWD=" + sPassword);
    try
    {
        cn.Open();
    }
    catch (Exception ex)
    {
        Cursor.Current = Cursors.Default;
        MessageBox.Show("Connection error: :" + ex.ToString());
    }
    Cursor.Current = Cursors.Default;
    cn.Close();
}
```

In both examples, string variables containing the Oracle Net Service Name along with the user ID and password are passed into the top of the routine. Then, a new instance of the System.Data.OracleClient Connection object named cn is created. The ConnectionString property of the cn Connection object is assigned a connection string that's valid for the .NET Framework Data Provider for Oracle. This connection string uses the DATA SOURCE keyword to specify the Oracle Net Service Name representing the Oracle database that will be connected to. The UID and PWD keywords provide the authentication values required to log in to the Oracle database if you are connecting using Oracle authentication. A complete list of the valid .NET Framework Data Provider for Oracle connection string keywords is presented in the next section. After the ConnectionString property has been assigned the appropriate connection string, a Try-Catch block is used to execute the OracleConnection object's Open method. After the Open method completes, a connection to the Oracle server is initiated. If there is an error with the connection string or the specified Oracle server is not available, the code in the Catch block is executed. That code displays a message box showing the error information. After a successful connection has been established, the OracleConnection object is closed using the Close method.

Note *It is very important in ADO.NET to use the Close method to ensure that the resources allocated by the Connection object are released when they are no longer needed. In .NET applications, the Connection object is not necessarily destroyed when it goes out of scope. Executing either the Close or Dispose method is required to make sure that the connection resources are released. The Close method closes the current connection, but the underlying .NET-managed resources used for connection pooling will remain available. Close can be called multiple times (even when the connection is already closed) without raising an error. The Dispose method can release all managed and unmanaged resources used by a connection, and it can only be called once for an active connection.*

.Net Framework Data Provider for Oracle Connection String Keywords

The connection string keywords used by the .Net Framework Data Provider for Oracle are essentially a subset of the connection string keywords that are supported by the .NET Framework Data Provider for SQL Server. It's important to note that, like the .NET Framework Data Provider for SQL Server, the login values contained in the connection string are not returned to the application unless you explicitly tell the provider to do so via the Persist Security Info connection string keyword. Table 5-1 lists all the .NET Framework for Oracle Data Provider keywords supported by the OracleConnection class ConnectionString property.

For those items that have two keywords, you can use either keyword. In addition, some of the keywords displayed contain spaces. If so, those spaces are required. The .NET Framework Data Provider for Oracle connection string keywords are not case sensitive.

Keyword	Description
Data Source – or – Server	Identifies the name or network address of an instance of an Oracle database to connect to.
Integrated Security	Uses a value of True to indicate where Windows authentication is to be used to connect to the database and a value of False to indicate that Oracle authentication should be used. The default value is False.
Password – or – Pwd	The password associated with the login ID (used for Oracle authentication).
Persist Security Info	Specifies whether security-sensitive information such as login information is returned to the application after a successful connection. The default value is False.
Unicode	Specifies whether the .NET Framework Data Provider for Oracle will use the UTF16 character set for API calls. This value can only be used with Oracle 9i client software. The default value is False.
User ID – or –UID	The login ID for the data source (used for Oracle authentication).

Table 5-1. *.NET Framework Data Provider for Oracle Connection String Keywords*

Opening a Trusted Connection

The preceding example illustrated how to establish a connection to an Oracle database using a connection string that specified the UID and PWD keywords along with their associated login values. However, because this method sends the actual user ID and passwords across the network, it isn't the most secure way to authenticate your connection to the database. Integrated Security, also known as a trusted connection, provides for a more secure connection because the same values used for the client's Windows NT/2000/NET login are also used for Oracle server authentication. You don't need to specify the user ID or the password from the application, and these values are not passed over the network. The following example illustrates how to use the INTEGRATED SECURITY keywords from a VB.NET application to establish a trusted connection to an Oracle database:

```vbnet
Private Sub OracleConnectIntegrated(ByVal sServer As String)
    Cursor.Current = Cursors.WaitCursor
    Dim cn As New OracleConnection("DATA SOURCE=" & sServer _
        & ";INTEGRATED SECURITY=yes")
    Try
        cn.Open()
        MessageBox.Show("Server: " & cn.DataSource.ToString() _
            & ControlChars.Cr _
            & "ServerVersion: " & cn.ServerVersion.ToString() _
            & ControlChars.Cr _
            & "State: " & cn.State.ToString())
    Catch ex As Exception
        Cursor.Current = Cursors.Default
        MessageBox.Show("Connection error: :" & ex.ToString())
    End Try
    cn.Close()
    Cursor.Current = Cursors.Default
End Sub
```

The C# version of this subroutine is as follows:

```csharp
private void OracleConnectIntegrated(string sServer)
{
    Cursor.Current = Cursors.WaitCursor;
    OracleConnection cn = new OracleConnection("DATA SOURCE="
        + sServer + ";INTEGRATED SECURITY=yes");
    try
    {
```

```
        cn.Open();
        MessageBox.Show("Server: " + cn.DataSource.ToString()
            + "\nServerVersion: " + cn.ServerVersion.ToString()
            + "\nState: " + cn.State.ToString());
    }
    catch (Exception ex)
    {
        Cursor.Current = Cursors.Default;
        MessageBox.Show("Connection error: :" + ex.ToString());
    }
    Cursor.Current = Cursors.Default;
    cn.Close();
}
```

At the beginning of these subroutines, you can see where the server name is passed in as a string value. Then an instance of the OracleConnection object name cn is created. In this example, the ConnectionString property is assigned as one of the arguments of the OracleConnection object's constructor. The connection string uses the DATA SOURCE keyword to specify the Oracle Net Service name to connect to, and the INTEGRATED SECURITY keyword is set to yes, indicating that the current Windows authentication information will be passed to the Oracle database server, thus eliminating the need to specify the user ID and password as part of the connection string.

After the OracleConnection object has been instantiated, a Try-Catch block is used to execute the Open method. If the Open method succeeds, then a message box is displayed showing some of the important properties found in the OracleConnection object. In this example, the OracleConnection object's DataSource name, the ServerVersion, and the OracleConnection object's current State will be displayed. You can see the message box in Figure 5-14.

If the Open method fails, then the code in the Catch block is executed and a message box is displayed showing the specific error message. After the connection has been established, it is immediately closed using the OracleConnection object's Close method.

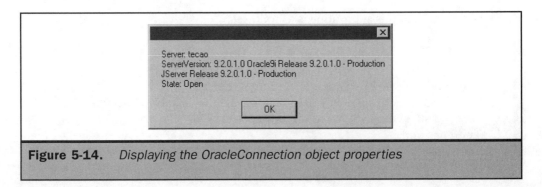

Figure 5-14.   *Displaying the OracleConnection object properties*

Enabling Connection Pooling

Connection pooling is an important scalability feature that's particularly important to *n*-tier–style Web applications. Web applications often need to support hundreds of simultaneous connections, and each open connection requires server overhead and management. The highest overhead activity of all is initially establishing the connection.

Connection pooling is a technology supported by ADO.NET that makes the overall connection process more efficient by sharing a group or pool of connections between incoming users. Rather than opening individual connections for each user, with connection pooling, all connections that share the same connection string are placed into a common connection pool, which reduces the total number of new connections that must be established and maintained by the Oracle database server. With connection pooling, open connections are not immediately closed when a given client disconnects from the server. Rather, the connection is left open for a short period of time. The period of time the connection is left open is determined by the Connection Lifetime keyword that's used in the OracleConnection object's ConnectionString property. These open connections can then be immediately available for any new database connections that can share the same connection characteristics. This avoids the overhead associated with establishing a new connection.

Like the other .NET Data Providers, the .NET Framework Data Provider for Oracle automatically performs connection pooling without requiring any special programming by the application developer. Each time a connection is opened, a connection pool is automatically created based on the values used in the ConnectionString property of the OracleConnection object. Each connection pool is associated with a unique connection string. When a new connection is opened, the OracleConnection object checks whether the value in the ConnectionString property matches the connection string used for an existing pool. If the value in the new ConnectionString property string matches an existing connection, then the new connection is added to the existing pool. If the ConnectionString doesn't match an existing connection, then a new pool is created. Connection pools are not destroyed until the application ends. The following OracleConnectPool subroutine illustrates the creation of two different connections, both of which are added to the same connection pool:

```
Private Sub OracleConnectPool(ByVal sServer As String, _
    ByVal sUser As String, ByVal sPassword As String)
  Cursor.Current = Cursors.WaitCursor
  Dim cn As New OracleConnection("DATA SOURCE=" & sServer _
    & ";UID=" & sUser & ";PWD=" & sPassword)
  Dim cn2 As New OracleConnection("DATA SOURCE=" & sServer _
    & ";UID=" & sUser & ";PWD=" & sPassword)
  Try
    cn.Open()
```

```
            cn2.Open()
      Catch ex As Exception
            Cursor.Current = Cursors.Default
            MessageBox.Show("Connection error: :" & ex.ToString())
      End Try
      cn.Close()
      cn2.Close()
      Cursor.Current = Cursors.Default
End Sub
```

The C# version of this same routine that creates two connection objects belonging to the same connection pool is shown here:

```
private void OracleConnectPool(string sServer, string sUser,
      string sPassword)
{
      Cursor.Current = Cursors.WaitCursor;
      OracleConnection cn = new OracleConnection("DATA SOURCE="
            + sServer + ";UID=" + sUser + ";pwd=" + sPassword);
      OracleConnection cn2 = new OracleConnection("DATA SOURCE="
            + sServer + ";UID=" + sUser + ";pwd=" + sPassword);
      try
      {
            cn.Open();
            cn2.Open();
      }
      catch (Exception ex)
      {
            Cursor.Current = Cursors.Default;
            MessageBox.Show("Connection error: :" + ex.ToString());
      }
      Cursor.Current = Cursors.Default;
      cn.Close();
      cn2.Close();
}
```

At the beginning of these subroutines, you can see where three string variables containing the server name, user ID, and password are passed in to the OracleConnectPool subroutine. Then two OracleConnection objects, cn and cn2, are created and have identical connection strings. In both cases, the ConnectionString property uses the DATA SOURCE keyword to identify the Oracle Net Service to connect to and the UIS and PWD keywords to provide the database authentication values. Remember that in order to be added to the same pool, the values in the ConnectionString properties of the two OracleConnection objects must match exactly. In this case, that means that the User ID and Password used in both connections must be the same.

Next, a Try-Catch loop is used to open both OracleConnection objects and capture any runtime errors. If any errors are encountered, the code in the Catch block is executed and the end user sees the error text in a message box. After the connections have been successfully opened, the OracleConnection object's Close method is used to close each connection.

Pooling Related Connection String Keywords

The .NET Framework Data Provider for Oracle automatically handles connection pooling for you. However, there are still several connection string keywords that you can use to customize the pooling behavior of the OracleConnection object. Table 5-2 presents the ConnectionString values you can use to customize the .NET Framework Data Provider for Oracle's connection pooling behavior.

Name	Description
Connection Lifetime	After a connection is closed, it's returned to the pool. Then its creation time is compared with the current time, and the connection is destroyed if the difference exceeds the value specified by Connection Lifetime. The default value of 0 specifies that pooled connections will have the maximum lifespan.
Enlist	When True, the connection is automatically created in the current transaction context of the creation thread if a transaction context exists. The default value is True.
Max Pool Size	Specifies the maximum number of connections allowed in the pool. The default value is 100.
Min Pool Size	Specifies the minimum number of connections maintained in the pool. The default value is 0.
Pooling	When True, connection pooling is automatically enabled. False allows you to turn off connection pooling.

Table 5-2. *Pooling-Related Connection String Keywords*

Summary

In this chapter, you saw several options for connecting to an Oracle database using the .NET Framework Data Provider for Oracle. The .NET Framework Data Provider for Oracle is the best choice for connecting to Oracle 8i and higher databases. If you need to connect to older versions of Oracle, you should use either the .NET Framework Data Provider for OLE DB or the .NET Framework Data Provider for ODBC. The next chapter covers using the .NET Framework Data Provider for OLE DB.

Chapter 6

Using the .NET Framework Data Provider for OLE DB

In this chapter, you learn how to use the .NET Framework Data Provider for OLE DB. The first part of this chapter covers how to use the visual OleDbConnection components that are provided with Visual Studio.NET. In the second part of this chapter, you'll see how to write the ADO.NET code required to connect to an OLE DB–compliant data source using both the ConnectionString properties and a UDL file.

Connecting with the .NET Framework Data Provider for OLE DB

While the .NET Framework Data Provider for SQL Server provides the best way to connect to SQL Server databases, ADO.NET would lack a great deal of usefulness if SQL Server were the only supported database platform. That's where the .NET Framework Data Provider for OLE DB comes in. The .NET Framework Data Provider for OLE DB theoretically enables you to use ADO.NET to connect to any other databases that provide OLE DB Providers. Although the OLE DB .NET Data Provider may work with other OLE DB Providers, Microsoft officially supports database connectivity using the three OLE DB Providers listed in Table 6-1.

> **Note** *One Microsoft OLE DB Provider that is explicitly not supported by the OLE DB .NET Data Provider is the Microsoft OLE DB Provider for ODBC (MSDASQL). Microsoft felt that the added overhead of running OLE DB on top of ODBC would result in unacceptable performance. Instead, to provide ODBC connectivity, Microsoft released the .NET Framework Data Provider for ODBC that's covered in Chapter 7.*

Although Microsoft understandably supports only its own OLE DB Providers, the company has documented the list of OLE DB interfaces that an OLE DB Provider must support in order to be compatible with the OLE DB .NET Data Provider. Table 6-2 lists the required OLE DB interfaces used by the OLE DB .Net Data Provider.

> **Note** *The .NET Framework Data Provider for OLE DB does not provide support for OLE DB 2.5 interfaces.*

Provider	Description
SQLOLEDB	Microsoft OLE DB Provider for SQL Server
MSDAORA	Microsoft OLE DB Provider for Oracle
Microsoft.Jet.OLEDB.4.0	Microsoft OLE DB Provider for the Microsoft Jet Engine

Table 6-1. *OLE DB Providers Supported by the .NET Framework Data Provider for OLE DB*

OLE DB Object	Interfaces
OLE DB Services	IDataInitialize
DataSource	IDBInitialize IDBCreateSession IDBProperties IPersist IDBInfo
Session	ISessionProperties IOpenRowset IDBSchemaRowset ITransactionLocal IDBCreateCommand
Command	ICommandText ICommandProperties ICommandWithParameters IAccessor ICommandPrepare
MultipleResults	IMultipleResults
RowSet	IRowset IAccessor IColumnsInfo IColumnsRowset IRowsetInfo
Row	IRow
Error	IErrorInfo IErrorRecords ISQLErrorInfo

Table 6-2.   *OLE DB Interfaces Used by the .NET Framework Data Provider for OLE DB*

The .NET Framework Data Provider for OLE DB essentially provides a managed .NET object wrapper over the older COM-based OLE DB providers. You can see an overview of the .NET Framework Data Provider for OLE DB communications layers illustrated in Figure 6-1.

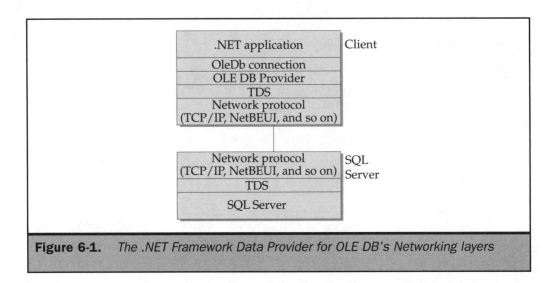

Figure 6-1.   *The .NET Framework Data Provider for OLE DB's Networking layers*

As Figure 6-1 demonstrates, the OLE DB .NET Data Provider doesn't have quite the same efficiency as the SQL Server .NET Provider. Database requests from the client application must first pass through the OLE DB Service Provider, and then the database-specific OLE DB provider as well as the appropriate network library, before being converted into the TDS protocol used by SQL Server. This added overhead reduces the performance available when compared to the SQL Server .NET Data Provider. However, in return, the support for OLE DB enables the OLE DB .NET Data Provider to connect to multiple databases.

 The OLE DB .NET Data Provider is a good choice when your application must connect to SQL Server 6.5 databases.

Using the Visual Studio OleDbConnection Objects

Much like the .NET Framework Data Provider for SQL Server, the easiest place to get started using the .NET Framework Data Provider for OLE DB is in the Visual Studio design environment. To create a new connection to SQL Server using the OLE DB .NET Data Provider, you must first create a Visual Studio VB.NET or C# project. Next, add a new form to the project. After the form has been created, you can bring the form into the Visual Studio Designer window by clicking the newly created form in the Visual Studio Project Explorer window. When you display the form in the Designer window, the Data Toolbox is added to the toolboxes that are displayed on the left side of the Visual Studio.NET development environment. Click the Data tab to open the Data Toolbox, and then double-click the OleDbConnection object that's displayed in the Data Toolbox. A new OleDbConnection object like the one shown in Figure 6-2 is added to your project.

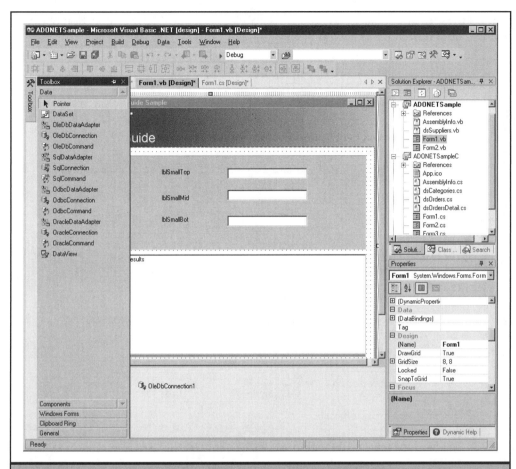

Figure 6-2. *Adding an OleDbConnection object in the VS.NET Designer*

An OleDbConnection object that is added to your project using the Visual Studio.NET Designer is exactly the same as one that is created using application code. Both objects provide the same methods and properties. For more information on the specific methods and properties supported by the OleDbConnection object, you can refer to Appendix D, the System.Data.OleDb Namespace reference.

Once the OleDbConnection object has been added to your project, you must then set its ConnectionString property and, finally, execute the Open method to establish a connection to the target database system. You can set the ConnectionString property interactively by entering a connection string in the Properties window of the Visual Studio.NET design environment. Alternatively, you can set the ConnectionString property using code. The following examples illustrate the VB.NET code that will connect to SQL Server using a SQLOLEDB provider and the OleDbConnection object that was added from the Data Toolbox:

```
Private Sub OLEDBConnectComponent()
    OleDbConnection1.ConnectionString = "PROVIDER=SQLOLEDB;" _
        & "SERVER=myServer;TRUSTED_CONNECTION=Yes"
    Try
        OleDbConnection1.Open()
    Catch ex As Exception
        MessageBox.Show("Connection error: :" & ex.ToString())
    End Try
    OleDbConnection1.Close()
End Sub
```

The C# version of this code is as follows:

```
private void OLEDBConnectComponent()
{
    oleDbConnection1.ConnectionString = "PROVIDER=SQLOLEDB;"
        + "SERVER=myServer;TRUSTED_CONNECTION=Yes";
    try
    {
        oleDbConnection1.Open();
    }
    catch (Exception ex)
    {
        MessageBox.Show("Connection error: :" + ex.ToString());
    }
    oleDbConnection1.Close();
}
```

In these examples, the OleDbConnection object uses the default name of OleDbConnection1 or oleDbConnection1 (the default object named used by C#) that was assigned by the Visual Studio.NET design environment. In both cases, the ConnectionString property of the OleDbConnection object is assigned a string that uses the PROVIDER keyword to specify the OLE DB provider that will be used. The SERVER keyword identifies the instance of the SQL Server system that will be connected to, and the TRUSTED_CONNECTION keyword specifies that the client application will be authenticated to the SQL Server system using Integrated Security. More information about the specific connection string keyword values used by the OleDbConnection object appears in the next section of this chapter.

Next, a Try-Catch loop is set up in order to capture any connection errors that may occur. Within the Try-Catch loop, the OleDbConnection1 object's Open method is used to establish a connection to the SQL Server system named myServer. If the OleDbConnection object's Open method used in the Try block fails, the code in the Catch block is executed and the resulting error message is displayed in a message box. If the Open method succeeds, the code in the Catch block is never executed and the routine continues on to use the OleDbConnection1 object's Close method to end the connection to the data source.

Adding the System.Data.OleDb Namespace

The .NET Framework Data Provider for OLE DB is supplied in the .Net Framework's System.Data.OleDb Namespace. However, before you can use any of the classes contained in the System.Data.OleDb Namespace in your application, you first need to add an import directive for the System.Data.OleDb Namespace to your project. The VB.NET code that you use to import the System.Data.OleDb Namespace into your project is shown here. This code should be placed in the declarations section of your source module:

```
Imports System.Data.OleDb
```

Similarly, you also need to add an import directive for the System.Data.OleDb Namespace to a C# project. The code appears as follows:

```
using System.Data.OleDb;
```

Connecting with a Connection String

After adding an import directive to your code, you're ready to begin using the classes contained in the System.Data.OleDb Namespace. The System.Data.OleDb OleDbConnection class is used to connect to an OLE DB–compatible database. As in the previous section, you'll see how to connect to the target database by setting the OleDbConnection object's ConnectionString property with a valid OLE DB connection string. This technique is very similar to setting the connection string for a standard ADO connection object. First, you set the ConnectionString property with a valid connection string, and then invoke the Open method. The following example illustrates how to use the OleDbConnection object to connect to a SQL Server system using Microsoft's SQLOLEDB provider:

```
Private Sub OLEDBConnectString(ByVal sServer As String, _
      ByVal sUser As String, ByVal sPassword As String)
   Dim cn As New OleDbConnection("PROVIDER=SQLOLEDB;SERVER=" & _
      sServer & ";" & "UID=" & sUser & ";PWD=" & sPassword)
   Try
      cn.Open()
```

```
Catch ex As Exception
    MessageBox.Show("Connection error: :" & ex.ToString())
End Try
cn.Close()
End Sub
```

The C# version of the OLEDBConnectString subroutine is as follows:

```csharp
private void OLEDBConnectString(string sServer, string sUser,
    string sPassword)
{
    OleDbConnection cn = new OleDbConnection("PROVIDER=SQLOLEDB;" +
        "SERVER=" + sServer + ";" + "UID=" + sUser +
        ";PWD=" + sPassword);
    try
    {
        cn.Open();
    }
    catch (Exception ex)
    {
        MessageBox.Show("Connection error: :" + ex.ToString());
    }
    cn.Close();
}
```

In both subroutines, string variables containing the name of the target SQL Server system, the user ID, and the password are passed into the top of the routine. Then, a new instance of the OleDbConnection object named cn is created. The ConnectionString property of the cn OleDbConnection object is assigned a .NET Framework Data Provider for OLE DB connection string. This connection string uses the PROVIDER keyword to indicate that the Microsoft SQL Server OLE DB Provider, SQLOLEDB, will be used. Next, the SERVER keyword is used to identify the SQL Server system that will be connected to. Then the UID and PWD keywords are used to provide the authentication values required to log in to the SQL Server system. You can find a complete list of the valid OLE DB .NET Data Provider connection string keywords in the next section

After the ConnectionString property has been assigned the appropriate connection string, a Try-Catch block is used to execute the cn Connection object's Open method. After the Open method completes, a connection to the SQL Server system will be initiated. If there is an error executing the Open method, the code in the Catch block is executed and a message box is displayed showing the error information. After a successful connection has been established, the Connection object is closed using the Close method.

Note   *Just like the .NET Framework Data Provider for SQL Server, explicitly using the Close method with the OLE DB .NET Data Provider is very important. Unlike ADO, the connection object is not necessarily destroyed when it goes out of scope. Executing either the Close or Dispose method is required to make sure that the connection resources are released. The Close method closes the current connection, but the underlying .NET managed resources used for connection pooling will remain available. Close can be called multiple times—even when the connection is already closed—without raising an error. The Dispose method can release all managed and unmanaged resources used by a connection and it can only be called for an active connection.*

The .NET Framework Data Provider for OLE DB Connection String Keywords

Because they are both based on OLE DB, the OLE DB .Net Data Provider connection string keywords are essentially identical to the OLE DB connection string keywords that are used by ADO. Table 6-3 lists all the support OLE DB .NET Data Provider connection string keywords that can be used in the OleDbConnection object's ConnectionString property.

Keyword	Description
PROVIDER	This optional keyword can be used to identify the name of the OLE DB provider that will be used.
DATASOURCE or SERVER	The name of an existing SQL Server instance.
DATABASE or INITIAL CATALOG	The SQL Server target database name.
FILE NAME	The name of a UDL file that contains connection information.
USER ID or UID	The login ID for the data source (used for SQL Server authentication).
PASSWORD or PWD	The password associated with the login ID (used for SQL Server authentication).
OLE DB Services	Used to disable specific OLE DB services. The value of –1 is the default, which indicates all services are enabled; –2 disables connection pooling; –4 disables connection pooling and auto enlistment; –5 disables client cursors; –6 disables pooling, auto enlistment, and client cursors; 0 disables all services.

Table 6-3.   *Adding an OleDbConnection object in the VS.NET Designer*

Unlike the SQL Server .NET Data Provider, which has only one set of connection string keywords, each OLE DB provider typically supports all of the common connection string keywords, as well as a set of the provider-specific keywords. Table 6-4 lists all of the provider-specific keywords that are provided by Microsoft's OLE DB Provider for SQL Server.

 For the .NET Framework Data Provider for OLE DB, the connection string format is identical to the connection string format used in ADO, with the following exceptions: the Provider keyword is required; the URL, Remote Provider, and Remote Server keywords are not supported.

Keyword	Description
TRUSTED_CONNECTION	Uses a value of YES or NO, where YES indicates that Windows NT authentication will be used and a value of NO indicates that mixed or SQL Server authentication will be used.
CURRENT LANGUAGE	Specifies the SQL Server language name that will be used for this connection.
NETWORK ADDRESS	Specifies the SQL Server network address.
NETWORK LIBRARY	Specifies the network library DLL that will be used. The value used by this keyword should not include the path of the .dll file extension.
USE PROCEDURE FOR PREPARE	Uses a value of YES or NO to indicate whether SQL Server should create temporary stored procedures for each prepared command.
AUTO TRANSLATE	Uses a value of TRUE or FALSE, where FALSE prevents automatic ANSI/multibyte character conversions. The default value of TRUE automatically converts the values transfer between SQL Server and the client.
PACKET SIZE	Used to alter the network packet size. Accepts values from 512 to 32767. If no value is specified, a default packet size of 4096 will be used.
APPLICATION NAME	Identifies the current application.
WORKSTATION ID	Identifies the client workstation.

Table 6-4. *Connection String Keywords for the OLE DB Provider for SQL Server*

Using a UDL File

The previous example illustrated how to connect the .NET Framework Data Provider for OLE DB to a target database by setting the ConnectionString property. This method is very similar to the way that you connect the .NET Framework Data Provider for SQL Server to a SQL Server database. However, for application compatibility, the OLE DB Provider also supports an ADO-style connection where the connection information is kept in a *Universal Data Link* (*UDL*) file. A UDL file is basically the OLE DB equivalent to an ODBC File DSN (Data Source Name). Like an ODBC File DSN, a UDL file stores OLE DB connection information, such as the provider, server, database, username, password, and other connection options. You can create UDL files in a couple of different ways but probably the easiest method is to simply start Notepad and then select the Save option to save an empty text file. Make sure that the saved file extension is .udl. After the file has been saved, you can double-click the file in Windows Explorer to display the Data Link Properties dialog box shown in Figure 6-3.

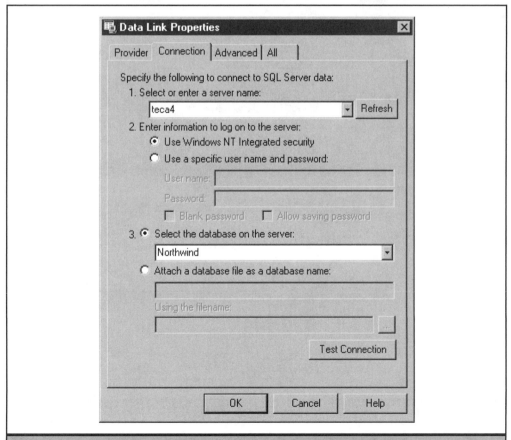

Figure 6-3. *Creating a UDL file using the Data Link Properties dialog box*

The Data Link Properties dialog box allows you to enter, test, and save your database connection information. The Data Link Properties dialog box initially displays the Provider tab that lists all the OLE DB Providers that are installed on the system. The Data Link Properties dialog box lets you both configure and connect to a target data source. To connect to SQL Server using the Data Link Properties dialog box, the user must first select the OLE DB Provider to be used from the list of the OLE DB providers displayed on the Provider tab. Clicking the Next button or selecting the Connection tab displays the OLE DB Connection information dialog box, as shown in Figure 6-4.

The Connection tab lets the user select the name of the SQL Server system that will be connected to, as well as enter authentication information and specify a default database. In Figure 6-4, you can see the Data Link Properties dialog box is being used to connect to

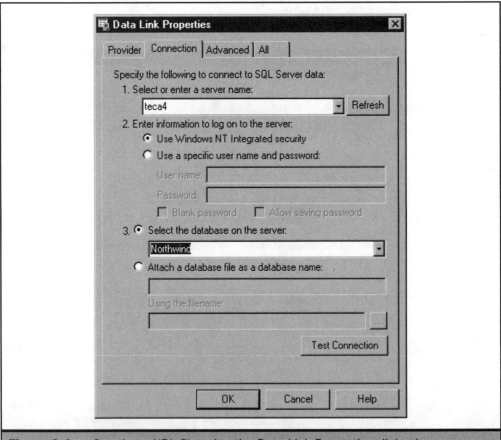

Figure 6-4. *Creating a UDL file using the Data Link Properties dialog box*

a system named teca4, that Integrated Security will be used to authenticate to the SQL Server system, and Northwind will be set as the default database. When all the connection information has been entered, clicking OK on the Connection tab will save the connection information into the UDL file and close the Data Link Properties dialog box.

One of the advantages of using a UDL file is that an administrator or developer can centrally create the UDL file, which can then be distributed to all networked clients along with the application. However, using UDL files with the .NET Framework Data Provider for OLE DB carries a performance penalty because UDL files can be modified externally outside of the current ADO.NET. To ensure that the correct connection information is retrieved, that UDL file must be read and parsed every time a new connection is opened, which can slow performance. For a Windows Form-style application, this isn't a big issue; but this could be a very serious bottleneck for a Web application, which can potentially perform hundreds or even thousands of opens. From an application developer's standpoint, using a UDL file to connect to SQL Server is similar to using the standard OLE DB connection string. The following example illustrates how you can use an existing UDL file to connect to SQL Server:

```
Private Sub OLEDBConnectUDL()
    Dim cn As New OleDbConnection("FILE NAME=myudl.udl")
    Try
        cn.Open()
    Catch ex As Exception
        MessageBox.Show("Connection error: :" & ex.ToString())
    End Try
    cn.Close()
End Sub
```

The C# version of the OLEDBConnectUDL subroutine is as follows:

```
private void OLEDBConnectUDL()
{
    OleDbConnection cn  = new OleDbConnection(
        "FILE NAME=myudl.udl");
    try
    {
        cn.Open();
    }
    catch (Exception ex)
    {
        MessageBox.Show("Connection error: :" + ex.ToString());
    }
    cn.Close();
}
```

THE ADO.NET CONNECTION OBJECT

First, an instance of the OleDbConnection object named cn is created. Then the ConnectionString property of the cn OleDbConnection object is assigned a string consisting of the FILE NAME=keyword, followed by the full path and filename of the UDL that contains the SQL Server connection information. In this example, the myudl.udl file is located in the same directory as the VB database application. If the application were located in the c:\DBApp directory, the resolved connection string would then appear as follows:

```
"FILE NAME=C:\DBApp\udlsample.udl"
```

After the OleDbConnection object's ConnectionString property has been assigned the FILE NAME keyword and the path to the existing UDL, the Open method is used within a Try-Catch block to connect to the database system specified in the UDL file. The connection is then closed using the OleDbConnection object's Close method.

Using Connection Pooling

Like the .NET Framework Data Provider for SQL Server that was presented in the previous chapter, the .NET Framework Data Provider for OLE DB automatically performs connection pooling on your behalf without requiring any special actions on your part. The essential thing that allows the provider to enable connection pooling is to use a connection string that matches a connection string that has already been used to open a previous connection. Each time a connection is opened, a connection pool is created based on the values used in the ConnectionString property of the OleDbConnection object. For each new connection, the OleDbConnection object looks to match the connection string with an existing pool. If the string matches, the new connection is added to the existing pool. Otherwise, a new pool is created. Connection pools are not destroyed until the application ends. The following VB.NET example illustrates the creation of two different connections that are both added to the same connection pool:

```
Private Sub OLEDBConnectPool(ByVal sServer As String)
    Dim cn As New OleDbConnection("PROVIDER=SQLOLEDB;SERVER=" & _
        sServer & ";TRUSTED_CONNECTION=Yes")
    Dim cn2 As New OleDbConnection("PROVIDER=SQLOLEDB;SERVER=" & _
        sServer & ";TRUSTED_CONNECTION=Yes")
    Try
        cn.Open()
        cn2.Open()
    Catch ex As Exception
        MessageBox.Show("Connection error: :" & ex.ToString())
    End Try
```

```
    cn.Close()
    cn2.Close()
End Sub
```

This subroutine written in C# is as follows:

```
private void OLEDBConnectPool(string sServer)
{
  OleDbConnection cn = new OleDbConnection("PROVIDER=SQLOLEDB;"
   + "SERVER=" + sServer + ";TRUSTED_CONNECTION=Yes");
  OleDbConnection cn2 = new OleDbConnection("PROVIDER=SQLOLEDB;"
   + "SERVER=" + sServer + ";TRUSTED_CONNECTION=Yes");
  try
    {
        cn.Open();
        cn2.Open();
    }
  catch (Exception ex)
    {
        MessageBox.Show("Connection error: :" + ex.ToString());
    }
  cn.Close();
  cn2.Close();
}
```

For both code examples, a string variable containing the name of a SQL Server system server name is passed in to the beginning of this subroutine. Then two OleDbConnection objects, cn and cn2, are created. To make sure that they both go into the same connection pool, they have identical connection strings: the ConnectionString property uses the PROVIDER keyword to specify that the SQLOLEDB provider is used; the SERVER keyword is used to identify the SQL Server system to connect to and the TRUSTED_CONNECTION keyword is used to specify that Windows Integrated Security will be used.

After the two OleDbConnection objects have been created, a Try-Catch loop is used to open the connections to SQL Server and capture any runtime errors. Because the values of these connection strings are identical, they will both be part of the same connection pool. If the connection strings were different in any way, two separate connection pools would have been created. After the connections have been established, the Close method is used to close each connection.

Summary

In this chapter, you saw how to connect to an OLE DB–compliant database using the .NET Framework Data Provider for OLE DB. The .NET Framework Data Provider for OLE DB is the best choice for connecting to SQL Server 6.5 and earlier databases. It is also a good choice for connecting to Oracle and Access databases. The next chapter continues to explore the various .NET Framework Data Providers by showing you how to use the .NET Framework Data Provider for ODBC.

The
Complete
Reference

Chapter 7

Using the .NET Framework Data Provider for ODBC

113

In this chapter, you will learn how to establish a connection to a target ODBC-compliant database using the .NET Framework Data Provider for ODBC. First, the chapter covers how to establish a basic ODBC connection using the data access components supplied in the Visual Studio.NET Toolbox. Next, the chapter covers how to connect to an ODBC-compliant database using a Data Source Name (DSN). Then you will see how to perform a code-centric DNS-less connection using the .NET Framework Data Provider for ODBC. Finally, you will see how to use connection pooling with the .NET Framework Data Provider for ODBC.

Connecting with the ODBC .NET Data Provider

The .NET Framework Data Provider for ODBC fills an important role in the ADO.NET framework: the capability to provide ODBC-compliant database access. Like the way the .NET Framework Data Provider for OLE DB uses multiple OLE DB providers, the .NET Framework Data Provider for ODBC can work with a number of different ODBC drivers. However, Microsoft understandably officially supports only its own ODBC drivers for use with the .NET Framework Data Provider for ODBC. Microsoft's supported ODBC drivers for the ODBC .NET Data Provider include the following:

- Microsoft SQL ODBC driver
- Microsoft ODBC driver for Oracle
- Microsoft Jet ODBC driver

Note *For the .NET Framework 1.0, the ODBC .NET Data Provider was released by Microsoft as an add-on to the .NET Framework, which means it must be downloaded and installed separately. If you're using the .NET Framework 1.0, you can download the ODBC .NET Data Provider from www.microsoft.com/data. After downloading and installing the add-on, the ODBC objects will be available in the Microsoft.Data.Odbc Namespace.*

The architecture of the ODBC .NET Data Provider is essentially analogous to the .NET Framework Data Provider for OLE DB, in that the .NET Framework Data Provider for ODBC is essentially an object wrapper over the underlying data access middleware. For the .NET Framework Data Provider for OLE DB, that middleware is the OLE DB Provider. For the .NET Framework Data Provider for ODBC, it's the ODBC driver. You can see an overview of the ODBC .NET Data Provider's network communication layers in Figure 7-1.

Note *The ODBC .NET Data Provider requires the installation of MDAC (Microsoft Data Access Components) 2.7 or higher. You can download MDAC from the same page as the ODBC .NET Data Provider: www.microsoft.com/data.*

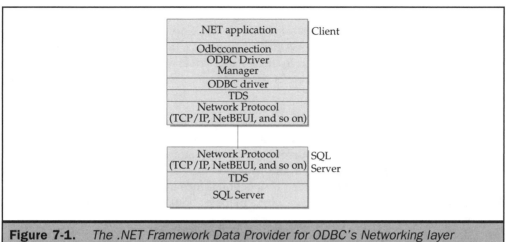

Figure 7-1. *The .NET Framework Data Provider for ODBC's Networking layer*

The ODBC Driver Manager

An ODBC-enabled application such as VB.NET makes calls to the ODBC Driver Manager, the ODBC32.DLL. For a .NET application this means that your managed application must make calls into unmanaged ODBC code. It's important to note that the application does not make calls directly to the ODBC drivers. The application calls the functions that are contained in the ODBC Driver Manager, and the ODBC Driver Manager in turn makes calls to the appropriate ODBC driver. This ensures that the ODBC functions are always called in the same way, whether you are connecting to SQL Server or another database platform such as Oracle. This layered architecture also allows multiple ODBC drivers to coexist and be active simultaneously.

The ODBC Driver Manager is responsible for loading the appropriate ODBC drivers into memory and routing subsequent requests to the correct ODBC driver. When the ODBC Driver Manager loads an ODBC driver, the ODBC Driver Manager builds a table of pointers to the functions that are in the ODBC driver. The ODBC Driver Manager uses an identifier called a *connection handle* to identify the function pointers for each loaded ODBC driver.

The ODBC Driver

The ODBC driver is responsible for sending SQL requests to the relational database management system and returning the results to the ODBC Driver Manager, which in turn passes them on to the ODBC client application. Each ODBC-compatible database has its own ODBC driver. For instance, the SQL Server ODBC driver communicates exclusively with SQL Server, and it can't be used to access an Oracle database. Likewise, the Oracle ODBC driver can't be used to access a SQL Server database.

The ODBC driver processes the ODBC function calls that are passed to it from the ODBC Driver Manager. The functions in each ODBC driver are called via function pointers that are maintained by the ODBC Driver Manager.

The Data Source

Applications that use ODBC to connect to the target database can either use a data source or a DSN-less connection. A data source is essentially a stored database configuration that contains the database connection information that will be used by the application. DSN-less connections pass the required connection information to the ODBC Driver Manager at runtime. You can find more information about using DSN-less connections later in this chapter.

A data source is created with a program called the ODBC Administrator. The data source insulates the user from the underlying mechanics of an ODBC connection by associating a target relational database and ODBC driver with a user-created name. The user then accesses the database by using the meaningful data source name and doesn't need to know the technical details about the ODBC driver or relational database.

When the ODBC application first connects to a target database, it passes the data source name to the ODBC Driver Manager. The ODBC Driver Manager then uses the data source to determine which ODBC driver to load. The ODBC driver typically requires the relational database login ID and password to connect to the target database.

Creating an ODBC Data Source

To create an ODBC data source, you need to open the ODBC Data Sources icon that's found in the Windows 9x or Windows NT Control Panel, or the Windows 2000 Administrative Tools folder. Opening the ODBC Data Sources icon displays a window like the one you can see in Figure 7-2.

The ODBC Data Source Administrator program displays all of the currently installed data sources. The different tabs enable you to work with the different types of data sources. The User DSN tab displays a list of the data sources for the currently logged on user. The System DSN tab displays a list of the system data sources that are available to all users of the system. The File DSN tab displays a list of files ending in the extension of .dsn that contain connection information. Unlike User and System DSNs, which store their configuration information in the registry, a File DSN stores its connection information in an operating system file. This makes it possible to distribute and install the DSN with your applications. The Drivers tab displays all of the different ODBC drivers that are currently installed on the system. The Tracing tab allows you to trace all of the activity for a given ODBC driver.

Although ODBC tracing is very useful in solving application performance problems you need to take care when using ODBC tracing. Tracing has a very noticeable performance impact and is capable of creating very large logging files.

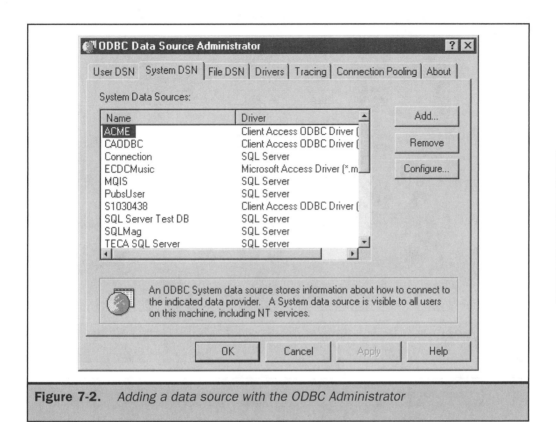

Figure 7-2.   *Adding a data source with the ODBC Administrator*

The Connection Pooling tab allows you to share a set of open connections between multiple clients. You can find more information about connection pooling later in this chapter. The About tab displays a list of the DLLs that are used by the ODBC Data Source Administrator.

To configure a new system data source, you must click the System DSN tab. If this is the first time that you've run the ODBC Administrator, the list will be blank. If you've already installed other ODBC drivers and set up data sources, they will appear in the list that's displayed. To add a new data source for SQL Server, select the Add button from the ODBC Administrator dialog box. This action displays the Create New Data Source dialog box shown in Figure 7-3.

All of the ODBC drivers that are currently installed on the system will be listed in the dialog box shown in Figure 7-3. Select the ODBC driver that you want to use with the new data source by clicking the name of ODBC driver and then clicking the Finish button. The next dialog box displayed varies depending on the ODBC driver selected. Selecting the SQL Server ODBC driver displays the Create A New Data Source To SQL Server dialog box that is shown in Figure 7-4.

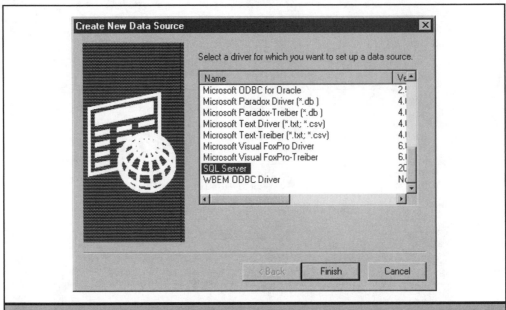

Figure 7-3. *Selecting an ODBC driver*

Figure 7-4. *Creating a new data source to SQL Server*

In the first text box of the SQL Server DSN Configuration Wizard, you enter the data source name. This name can be anything that you choose. Its primary purpose is to associate a meaningful name with the ODBC driver and target RDBMS. This data source name is used when an ODBC application first attempts to connect to the data. Either the application must specify the data source name or the ODBC Driver Manager will display a dialog box that allows the user to select a data source from a list of all configured data sources. The Description is simply an optional text field that you can use to help identify the data source. The data source description is really only used in the ODBC Administrator. Finally, you can select from the drop-down combo box the SQL Server system that you want this data source to connect to. The drop-down combo box is used to list the available SQL Server systems on your network. If you're configuring this data source on the SQL Server system itself, you can enter the name of (**local**). to connect the data source to a SQL Server that's running on the same physical system.

Click the Next button to display the next wizard screen, shown in Figure 7-5.

The second screen of the SQL Server DSN Configuration Wizard enables you to specify the SQL Server security authentication that will be performed. The radio buttons at the top of the window enable you to select between using the Windows NT's login or a SQL Server login. Logging in to SQL Server using the Windows NT login ID requires a trusted connection and an implementation of Windows NT Authentication Mode or Mixed Security. Using SQL Server's authentication does not require a trusted connection, but it does require that a login ID and password are entered by the user and that these logins are defined in each SQL Server database. If you selected SQL Server authentication, then you need to enter the login ID and password that you will use to connect to SQL Server. Clicking the Next button initiates a connection with SQL Server and displays the next wizard screen shown in Figure 7-6.

The check box at the top of the SQL Server DSN Configuration Wizard shown in Figure 7-6 enables you to override the default database that's specified in the SQL Server login. Leaving this check box blank specifies that the default database that's entered in SQL Server's Login ID will be used.

The "Attach database filename" check box enables you to specify the name of a primary file for the attachable database that will be used as the default database for the connection.

The "Create temporary stored procedures for prepared SQL statements" check box is only enabled for SQL Server 6.5 connections. Selecting the "Create temporary stored procedures for prepared SQL statements" check box causes a temporary stored procedure to be created when the ODBC driver calls the SQLPrepare function. Generally, checking this option for SQL Server 6.5 databases improves the performance of ODBC applications that use prepared statements. SQL Server 7.0 and SQL Server 2000 databases automatically create a shared execution plan in SQL Server's Procedure Cache for prepared SQL statements. Two radio buttons follow that control when these temporary stored procedures will be dropped. Selecting the first of these radio buttons causes the temporary stored

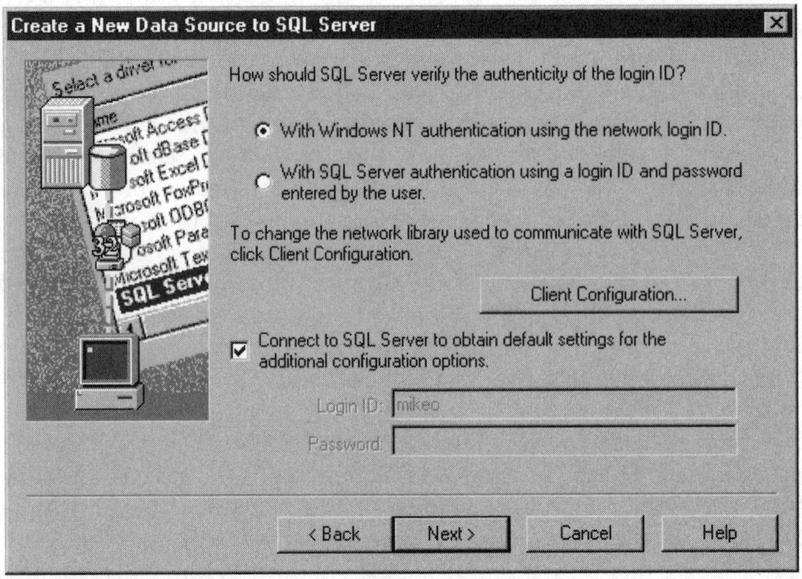

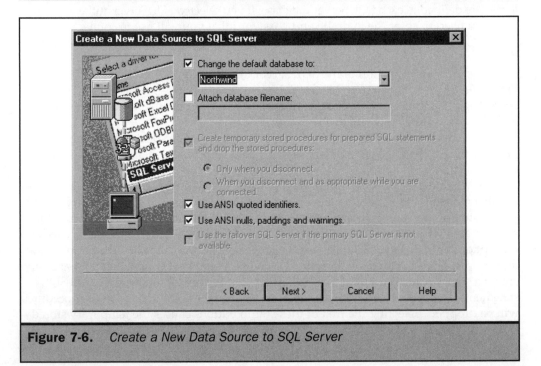

Figure 7-5. *Configuration options in the Create A New Data Source tTo SQL Server dialog box*

Figure 7-6. *Create a New Data Source to SQL Server*

procedures to be deleted when you disconnect. Selecting the second radio button causes the temporary stored procedures to be dropped when a subsequent SQLPrepare is issued for the same statement handle, when the SQLFreeStmt function is issued, or when the ODBC application disconnects.

Selecting the "Use ANSI quoted identifiers" check box causes the SQL Server ODBC driver to enforce ANSI rules for quotation marks in SQL statements. Selecting the "Use ANSI nulls, paddings, and warning" check box causes the SQL Server ODBC driver to enforce ANSI rules for handling null columns, padding trailing blanks on varchar fields, and issuing warnings on ANSI rule violations.

Finally, the "Use the failover SQL Server" check box enables you to indicate a backup SQL Server system in case of the failure of a primary SQL Server system. If a failover server has been defined for the primary SQL Server system and the "Use the failover SQL Server" option has been enabled, when the ODBC driver connects to the primary server, it also retrieves the information needed to connect to the failover server. In the event that the connection to the primary SQL Server is lost, the ODBC driver ends the current transaction and then attempts to reestablish a connection to the failover server. Clicking the Next button displays the wizard dialog box shown in Figure 7-7.

The SQL Server DSN Configuration Wizard shown in Figure 7-7 specifies the language, character set, regional settings, and log files that will be used by the SQL Server ODBC driver. The first check box specifies which language will be used to display ODBC

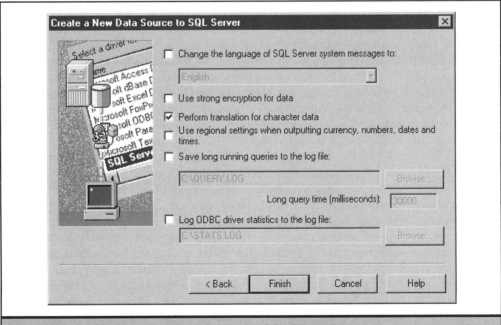

Figure 7-7.   *Create a New Data Source to SQL Server*

messages. This check box and its associated drop-down combo box will not be available if there is only one language installed on the connected SQL Server.

Selecting the "Use strong encryption" check box causes the ODBC driver to encrypt the data stream that's being sent between the ODBC client and the SQL Server system.

The next check box controls how the ODBC driver performs character set translation. Selecting the option "Perform translation for character data" specifies that the ODBC driver will use Unicode to convert ANSI strings sent between the ODBC client and the SQL Server system. If this option is not selected, ANSI data is sent directly to SQL Server, which requires that the client and the SQL Server system use the same code page.

The "Use regional settings when outputting currency, numbers, dates and times" check box enables you to override the default settings that are specified in the SQL Server login information.

The next two check boxes enable you to set a maximum time in milliseconds for long running queries, as well as control whether the SQL Server ODBC driver will record driver statistics. If these options are enabled, they will record their activity in the files that are specified in the text boxes. The default settings disable both of these options.

Clicking the Finish button completes the SQL Server data source configuration and displays the confirmation dialog box.

Using the Visual Studio OdbcConnection Object

The easiest place to get started using ODBC in your ADO.NET applications is through the visual components that are provided in the Visual Studio.NET IDE. Following the same drag-and-drop paradigm that's used by the Visual Studio.NET interface components, you can drag and drop the different ADO.NET data components from the Visual Studio .NET Data Toolbox onto the visual designer. To create a new connection to a SQL Server database using the .NET Framework Data Provider for ODBC objects in Visual Studio.NET, you first create a Visual Studio VB.NET or C# project and then add a new form to the project. You can display the form in the Visual Studio Designer window by clicking the newly created form in the Visual Studio Project Explorer window. Displaying the form in the Designer window causes the Data Toolbox to be added to the collection of toolboxes that is displayed on the left side of the Visual Studio.NET development environment. Clicking the Data tab opens up the Data Toolbox. From there, double-click the OdbcConnection object to add an OdbcConnection object to your project. A new OdbcConnection object like the one shown in Figure 7-8 will be added to your project.

The visual OdbcConnection object and the code-based OdbcConnection object are essentially the same. They have the same functionality and support the same methods and properties. For more information on the methods and properties supported by the OdbcConnection object, refer to Appendix C, the System.Data.Odbc Namespace reference.

After adding the OdbcConnection object to the VS.NET visual designer, you must set its ConnectionString property and then execute its Open method to establish a connection to the target data source. You can set the ConnectionString property interactively by entering a connection string in the Properties window shown in the

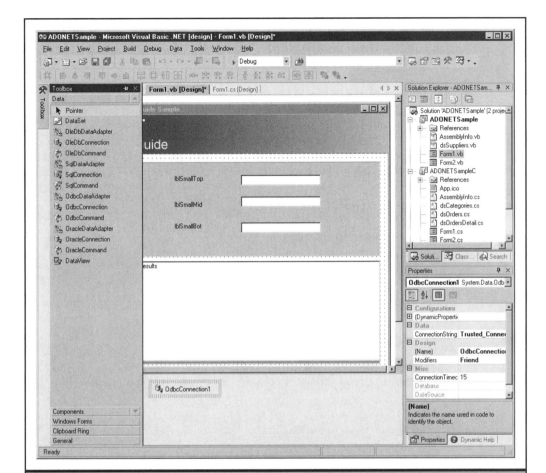

Figure 7-8.   *Adding an OdbcConnection object in the VS.NET Designer*

lower-right corner of the Visual Studio.NET design environment of Figure 7-8, or you can set the ConnectionString property using code, as is illustrated in the following listing:

```
Private Sub ODBCConnectComponent()
    Cursor.Current = Cursors.WaitCursor
    OdbcConnection1.ConnectionString = "DSN=MyDSN"
    Try
        OdbcConnection1.Open()
```

```
    Catch ex As Exception
        Cursor.Current = Cursors.Default
        MessageBox.Show("Connection error: :" & ex.ToString())
    End Try
    OdbcConnection1.Close()
    Cursor.Current = Cursors.Default
End Sub
```

The C# version of this code is shown here:

```
private void ODBCConnectComponent()
{
    Cursor.Current = Cursors.WaitCursor;
    odbcConnection1.ConnectionString = "DSN=MyDSN";
    try
    {
        odbcConnection1.Open();
    }
    catch (Exception ex)
    {
        Cursor.Current = Cursors.Default;
        MessageBox.Show("Connection error: :" + ex.ToString());
    }
    odbcConnection1.Close();
    Cursor.Current = Cursors.Default;
}
```

Here, the OdbcConnection object uses the default name of OdbcConnect1 (or
odbcConnect1 for C#) that was assigned by the Visual Studio.NET design environment.
In both cases, the ConnectionString property of the OdbcConnection1 object is set to
a string that uses the DSN keyword to identify the data source that will be used by the
OdbcConnection object to connect to the target data source. Next, a Try-Catch loop is
used to capture any errors that may occur during the connection process. Within the
Try-Catch loop, the OdbcConnection1 object's Open method is executed to establish a
connection to the database specified in the myDSN data source. If the target data source
is not available, an exception is raised. If the exception isn't handled, the application
would terminate abnormally. Using a Try-Catch Loop to catch any exceptions allows
your application to gracefully handle error conditions. In the preceding example, if the
OdbcConnection.Open method fails, the code in the Catch block is executed and the
application will continues to run. An instance of an Exception object named ex is created

in the Catch block, and that Exception object's ToString method is used to display any resulting error messages to the user. If the Open method succeeds, the code in the Catch block is never executed and the application continues on using the OdbcConnection1 object's Close method to terminate the connection.

Adding the System.Data.Odbc Namespace

In order to begin using the System.Data.Odbc classes in your ADO.NET code-based applications, you need to add an import directive for the System.Data.Odbc Namespace to your project. The following examples illustrate how you can add the System.Data .Odbc Namespace into your VB or C# projects. For VB, this directive should be placed in the declarations section of the source module:

```
Imports System.Data.Odbc
```

For a C# project, you would add a reference to the System.Data.Odbc Namespace as follows:

```
using System.Data.Odbc;
```

Connecting with a Connection String

Once you've added an import directive to your code, you're ready to begin using the .NET Framework Data Provider for ODBC to connect to your ODBC databases. Like the other .NET data providers that were presented earlier in this section, to connect to a target data source with the .NET Framework Data Provider for ODBC, you need to create a connection object, set the ConnectionString properties of the connection object, and then invoke the Open method to establish a connection. The following VB.NET example illustrates how to connect to a SQL Server database by setting the OdbcConnection object's ConnectionString property:

```
Private Sub ODBCConnectString()
    Dim cn As New OdbcConnection("DSN=myDSN")
    Try
        cn.Open()
    Catch ex As Exception
        MessageBox.Show("Connection error: :" & ex.ToString())
    End Try
    cn.Close()
End Sub
```

The C# version of this subroutine is as follows:

```
private void ODBCConnectString()
{
    OdbcConnection cn = new OdbcConnection("DSN=myDSN");
    try
    {
        cn.Open();
    }
    catch (Exception ex)
    {
        MessageBox.Show("Connection error: :" + ex.ToString());
    }
    cn.Close();
}
```

In both cases, a new instance of the OdbcConnection object is created. Then the ConnectionString property of the OdbcConnection object is assigned an ODBC connection string. In these examples, the connection string uses the DSN keyword to indicate that the required connection information will come from a Data Source Name (DSN) that has been created using the Data Sources (ODBC) option found in the Win2K Administrative Tools folder. You can find a complete list of the valid .NET Framework Data Provider for ODBC connection string keywords in the next section of this chapter.

After the ConnectionString property has been set up, a Try-Catch block is used to execute the cn.Open method. After the Open method completes, a connection to the SQL Server system identified in the connection string is initiated. If an error occurs with the connection, the code in the Catch block is executed and a message box showing the error information appears. After a successful connection has been established, the Connection object is closed using the Close method.

The Close method is required to ensure that the resources allocated by the OdbcConnection object are released when they are no longer needed.

.NET Framework Data Provider for ODBC Connection String Keywords

Table 7-1 lists the connection string keywords supported by the ODBC .NET Data Provider. The most common keywords are presented at the top of the list and the lesser-used keywords follow in alphabetical order.

Keyword	Description
DSN	The name of an existing data source created using the ODBC Administrator.
FILEDSN	The name of an existing file data source created using the ODBC Administrator.
DRIVER	The name of an existing ODBC driver.
SERVER	The name of an existing SQL Server system.
SAVEFILE	The name of a file data source that contains the saved connection information.
ADDRESS	The network address of the SQL Server system.
ANSINPW	Uses a value of YES or NO, where YES specifies that ANSI-defined behaviors are to be used for handling NULLs.
APP	Specifies the name of the client application.
ATTACHDBFILENAME	Specifies the name of an attachable database. The path to the data file must be included (for example, c:\\mssql\Mydatabase.mdf). If the database was detached, it automatically becomes attached after the connection completes. The database then becomes the default database for the connection.
AUTOTRANSLATE	Uses a value of TRUE or FALSE, where FALSE prevents automatic ANSI/multibyte character conversions. The default value of TRUE automatically converts the values transfer between SQL Server and the client.
FALLBACK	Uses a value of YES or NO, where YES specifies the ODBC driver should attempt to connect to the fallback server specified by an earlier SQLSetConnectAttr ODBC function call. (SQL Server 6.5 only.)
LANGUAGE	Specifies the SQL Server language name to be used for this connection.
NETWORK	Specifies the network library DLL to be used. The value used by this keyword should not include the path of the .dll file extension.
QUERYLOGFILE	Specifies the full path of the file used to store query logs.

Table 7-1.   *NET Framework Data Provider for ODBC Connection String Keywords*

THE ADO.NET
CONNECTION OBJECT

Keyword	Description
QUERYLOG_ON	Uses a value of YES or NO, where YES specifies that long-running queries are to be logged to the query log file specified by the QUERYLOGFILE keyword.
QUOTEDID	Uses a value of YES or NO, where YES specifies that Quoted Identifiers will be turned on for the connection.
REGIONAL	Uses a value of YES or NO, where YES specifies that SQL Server uses client setting when converting date, time, currency, and data.
STATSLOGFILE	Specifies the full path of the file used to store ODBC driver performance statistics.
STATSLOG_ON	Uses a value of YES or NO, where YES specifies ODBC driver statistics are to be logged to the stats log file specified by the STATSLOGFILE keyword.
TRUSTED_CONNECTION	Uses a value of YES or NO, where a value of YES indicates Windows NT authentication is to be used and a value of NO indicates mixed or SQL Server authentication is to be used.
USEPROCFORPREPARE	Uses a value of YES or NO to indicate whether SQL Server should create temporary stored procedures for each prepared command. (SQL Server 6.5 only.)

Table 7-1.   *NET Framework Data Provider for ODBC Connection String Keywords (continued)*

Connecting with a DNS-less Connection String

The previous example illustrated how to establish a database connection using the OdbcConnection object and an existing DSN. Instances occur in which your application may need to make an ODBC-based connection, however, and it can't rely on a DSN being preconfigured. Luckily, the .NET Framework Data Provider for ODBC also supports using DSN-less connections, which removes the need for an existing data source. The following VB.NET code illustrates how to use the OdbcConnection object and the SQL Server ODBC driver to make a DSN-less connection to SQL Server:

```
Private Sub ODBCConnectDSNless(ByVal sServer As String, _
        ByVal sUser As String, ByVal sPassword As String)
    Dim cn As New OdbcConnection("driver={SQL Server};server=" _
```

```
            & sServer & ";" & "uid=" & sUser & ";pwd=" & sPassword)
    Try
        cn.Open()
    Catch ex As Exception
        MessageBox.Show("Connection error: :" & ex.ToString())
    End Try
    cn.Close()
End Sub
```

In C#, this subroutine would appear as follows:

```
private void ODBCConnectDSNless(string sServer, string sUser,
        string sPassword)
{
    OdbcConnection cn = new OdbcConnection("driver={SQL Server};" +
        "server=" + sServer + ";" + "uid=" + sUser +
        ";pwd=" + sPassword);
    try
    {
        cn.Open();
    }
    catch (Exception ex)
    {
        MessageBox.Show("Connection error: :" + ex.ToString());
    }
    cn.Close();
}
```

First, these examples create a new OdbcConnection object named cn where the ConnectionString property is assigned as part of the constructor. Because this connection string is intended to establish a DSN-less connection, it's quite a bit different than the connection string presented in the previous example. As you might guess, the DSN keyword isn't needed to establish a DSN-less connection. Instead, the DRIVER keyword has the value of "SQL Server" to indicate the SQL Server ODBC driver should be used.

Note *This example encloses the value used by the DRIVER keyword c in {}, as in {SQL Server}, but this isn't a requirement.*

In addition to specifying the ODBC driver to be used, a DSN-less ODBC connection string must also indicate the server and database to be used. These values are supplied by the SERVER and DATABASE keywords. Finally, the UID and PWD keywords supply the required SQL Server login information.

After setting the ConnectionString property with a DSN-less ODBC connection string, the OdbcConnection object's Open method is used with a Try=Catch block to start a connection to the SQL Server system. Then the OdbcConnection object's Close method is used to end the connection.

Enabling Connection Pooling

The .NET Framework Data Provider for ODBC automatically performs connection pooling without requiring any special actions on your part. The essential ingredient is to be sure that the connection string matches an existing connection string that has already been used and remains open. For every new connection, the OdbcConnection object tries to match the connection string with an existing pool. If the string matches, the new connection is added to the existing pool. Otherwise, a new pool is created. The following VB.NET example shows how to create two different connections that are both added to the same connection pool through their matching connection strings:

```
Private Sub ODBCConnectPool(ByVal sServer As String)
    Dim cn As New OdbcConnection("driver={SQL Server};server=" & _
        sServer & ";" & "trusted_connection=yes")
    Dim cn2 As New OdbcConnection("driver={SQL Server};server=" & _
        sServer & ";" & "trusted_connection=yes")
    Try
        cn.Open()
        cn2.Open()
    Catch ex As Exception
        MessageBox.Show("Connection error: :" & ex.ToString())
    End Try
    cn.Close()
    cn2.Close()
End Sub
```

The C# version of the ODBCConnectionPool subroutine is as follows:

```
private void ODBCConnectPool(string sServer)
{
    OdbcConnection cn = new OdbcConnection("driver={SQL Server};" +
        "server=" + sServer + ";" + "trusted_connection=yes");
    OdbcConnection cn2 = new OdbcConnection("driver={SQL Server};" +
        "server=" + sServer + ";" + "trusted_connection=yes");
```

```
    try
    {
        cn.Open();
        cn2.Open();
    }
    catch (Exception ex)
    {
        MessageBox.Show("Connection error: :" + ex.ToString());
    }
    cn.Close();
    cn2.Close();
}
```

Here, a string variable containing the name of a SQL Server system server name is passed in to the beginning of this subroutine. Then two OdbcConnection objects are created that have identical connection strings. After the two OdbcConnection objects have been created, a Try-Catch loop is used to open the connections to SQL Server and capture any runtime errors. Because the values of these connection strings are identical, they will both be part of the same connection pool. If the connection strings were different in any way, then two separate connection pools would have been created. After the connections have been established, the Close method is used to close each connection.

Summary

In this chapter, you saw several options for connecting to a target database using .NET Framework Data Provider for ODBC. The .NET Framework Data Provider for ODBC is a good choice when you need to connect to legacy databases or when your application may need to connect to several different database platforms.

The
Complete
Reference

Part III

The ADO.NET Command Object

Chapter 8

Using the SqlCommand Object

I n this chapter, you see how to use the .NET Framework Data Provider for SQL Server's SqlCommand object to execute commands on a target SQL Server system. In the first part of this chapter, you learn how to execute simple SQL action queries that don't return any values. Next, you see how to execute scalar queries using both SQL statements and stored procedures that return single values. The chapter closes with a discussion of how to use the SqlCommand object to commit and roll back transactions.

Executing SQL Statements and Stored Procedures Using the SqlCommand Object

Executing dynamic SQL statements and stored procedures are two of the most common database actions that are required by an application. Dynamic SQL statements are SQL statements that are read by the database server and executed when they are sent to the database server from the client application. When the database receives these SQL statements, they are first parsed to ensure that their syntax is correct, and then the database engine creates an access plan—essentially determining the best way to process the SQL statement—and then executes the statements. Unlike dynamic SQL statements, which are often used for executing SQL DML operations like creating tables or for data access operations like performing ad hoc queries, stored procedures are typically used to perform predefined queries and database update operations. Stored procedures form the backbone of most database applications. The primary difference between dynamic SQL statements and stored procedures is that stored procedures are typically created before the application is executed and they reside in the database itself. This gives stored procedures a significant performance advantage over dynamic SQL statements because the jobs of parsing the SQL statement and creating the data access plan have already been completed. It's worth noting that changes made to data contained in an ADO.NET DataSet either can be posted back to the database using dynamic SQL statements created by the SqlCommandBuilder class, or can be written back to the database using stored procedures. However, you don't need to use the DataSet and DataAdapter in order to update the database. In cases where you don't need the data binding and navigation functions provided by the DataSet, the Command objects can provide a much lighter-weight and more-efficient method of updating the database. In the next sections, you'll see how to use the SqlCommand object to execute an ad hoc query, and then to execute a SQL DDL statement to build a table on the target database, followed by two examples using the stored procedure. The first stored procedure example illustrates passing parameters to a stored procedure, and the second example illustrates executing a stored procedure that supplies a return value.

Using the Visual Studio SqlCommand Object

The easiest place to get started with the SqlCommand object is probably using the visual component provided as a part of Visual Studio.NET. Using the same drag-and-drop paradigm that's implemented for interface components, you can drag and drop an instance of the SqlCommand from the Visual Studio.NET Data Toolbox onto the visual designer. After you've done this, you'll see a new SqlCommand object in the components pane, as shown in Figure 8-1.

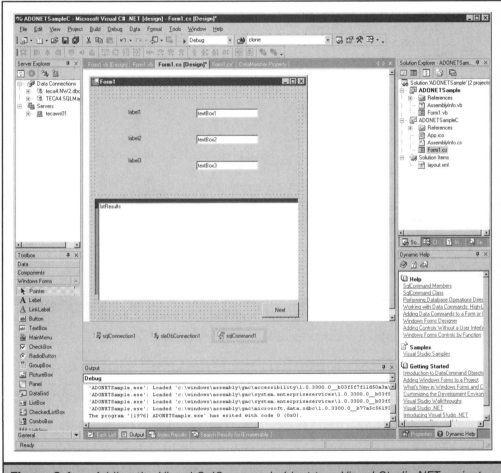

Figure 8-1. *Adding the Visual SqlCommand object to a Visual Studio.NET project*

Dragging and dropping the SqlCommand component from the Data tab to the Design window results in the creation of the SqlCommand1 object that is displayed in the component window at the bottom of the screen. After that, the SqCommand1 component is ready to use. The follow example illustrates executing a simple ad hoc query with the visual SqlCommand component:

```
Private Sub SQLCommandComponent(ByVal sServer As String, _
    ByVal sDB As String)
    SqlConnection1.ConnectionString = "SERVER=" & sServer _
        & ";" & "INTEGRATED SECURITY=True;DATABASE=" & sDB
    'Set up a simple query
    SqlCommand1.CommandText = "SELECT * FROM customers"
    ' Set the active connection
    SqlCommand1.Connection = SqlConnection1
    Try
        ' Open a connection
        SqlConnection1.Open()
        ' Execute the query
        Dim dr As System.Data.SqlClient.SqlDataReader = _
            SqlCommand1.ExecuteReader()
        ' The reader can now be processed
    Catch ex As Exception
        MessageBox.Show("Connection error: :" & ex.ToString())
    End Try
    SqlConnection1.Close()
End Sub
```

An example of the SQLCommandComponent subroutine written in C# is shown here:

```
private void SQLCommandComponent(string sServer, string sDB)
{
    sqlConnection1.ConnectionString = "SERVER=" + sServer + ";"
        + "INTEGRATED SECURITY=True;DATABASE=" + sDB;
    sqlCommand1.CommandText = "SELECT * FROM customers";
    // Set the active connection
    sqlCommand1.Connection = sqlConnection1;
    try
    {
        // Open a connection
        sqlConnection1.Open();
```

```
        // Execute the query
        System.Data.SqlClient.SqlDataReader dr =
            sqlCommand1.ExecuteReader();
        // The reader can now be processed
    }
    catch (Exception ex)
    {
        MessageBox.Show(ex.Message);
    }
    sqlConnection1.Close();
}
```

At the top of the SQLCommandComponent routine, you can see where two variables are passed in as parameters. The sServer variable contains the name of the SQL Server system that will be the database server; the sDB variable contains the name of the database that will be accessed. These examples all use the Northwind database that's supplied as a sample database with SQL Server.

The first action within the routine sets the SqlConnection1 object's connection string using the server and database values that were passed into the routine. The Integrated Security keyword indicates that Windows authentication will be used for the connection. You should note that even though this example is using the visual SqlCommand component, it still requires a SqlConnection object to actually connect to the target database. Although this example uses the visual SqlConnection1 object, this could also use a code-based SqlConnection object as well.

Next the CommandText property of the SqlCommand1 object is assigned a simple SQL SELECT statement that will query all of the rows and columns from the Customers table found in the Northwind database. The next statement sets the Sql1Command1 object's Connection property to the SqlConnect1 object. Then a Try-Catch block is set up to open the connection and execute the command. The SqlConnection1.Open method is used to initiate a connection to the target SQL Server system; then the SqlCommand1 object's ExecuteReader command is used to create a SqlDataReader object named dr. The ExecuteReader method is used to return a fast forward-only data stream from the target data source. Table 8-1 lists all of the different SQL command execution methods supported by both the SqlCommand object and the OleDbCommand object.

After the ExecuteReader method has completed, the results of the query can then be accessed using the dr SqlDataReader object. The detailed usage of the SqlDataReader will be presented in the next chapter. If an error occurs during the execution of either the Open method or the ExecuteReader, a message box will be displayed to the user showing the exception text.

THE ADO.NET
COMMAND OBJECT

Method	Description
ExecuteNonQuery	The ExecuteNonQuery method is used to execute a SQL statement on the connected data source. It is used for DDL statements and action queries like Insert, Update, and Delete operations, as well as ad hoc queries. The number of rows affected is returned, but no output parameters or resultsets are returned.
ExecuteReader	The ExecuteReader method is used to execute a SQL Select statement on the data source. A fast forward-only result is returned. More examples of the ExecuteReader method are shown in Chapter 6.
ExecuteScalar	The ExecuteScalar method is used to execute a stored procedure or a SQL statement that returns a single scalar value. The first row of the first column of the resultset is returned to the calling application. Any other returned values are ignored.
ExecuteXMLReader	The ExecuteXMLReader method is used to execute a FOR XML SELECT statement that returns an XML data stream from the data source. More examples of the ExecuteXMLReader method are shown in Chapter 30. The ExecuteXMLReader command is compatible only with SQL Server 2000 and later.

Table 8-1.   *SqlCommand SQL Statement Execution Methods*

Adding the System.Data.SqlClient Namespace

Although using the visual connection components provided by the Visual Studio.NET design environment is pretty easy, in the long run, you'll probably find it simpler to use the ADO.NET objects by just writing code. To use the SqlCommand class in your project, you first need to add an import directive for the System.Data.SqlClient Namespace in your project. The following example illustrates how to do this for a VB.NET project:

```
Imports System.Data.SqlClient
```

For a C# project, you need to add an import directive for the System.Data.SqlClient Namespace as follows:

```
using System.Data.SqlClient;
```

After the import directive has been added, you're ready to use code-based SqlCommand objects in your projects.

Executing Dynamic SQL Statements Using SqlCommand

Dynamic SQL provides an extremely flexible mechanism for working with the database. Dynamic SQL allows you to execute ad hoc queries and return the results from action queries, as well as execute SQL DDL statements to create database objects. The following SQLCommandNonQuery subroutine provides an example illustrating how you can use dynamic SQL with the ADO.NET SqlCommand object to check for the existence of a table and conditionally create it if it doesn't exist:

```
Private Sub SQLCommandNonQuery(ByVal sServer As String, _
    ByVal sDB As String)
  Dim cn As New SqlConnection("SERVER=" & sServer _
    & ";INTEGRATED SECURITY=True;DATABASE=" & sDB)
  Dim sSQL As String
  Dim cmd As New SqlCommand(sSQL, cn)
  Try
    ' Open the connection
    cn.Open()
    ' First drop the table
    sSQL = "IF EXISTS " _
      & "(SELECT * FROM dbo.sysobjects WHERE id = " _
      & "object_id(N'[Department]') " _
      & "AND OBJECTPROPERTY(id, N'IsUserTable') = 1) " _
      & "DROP TABLE [department]"
    cmd.CommandText = sSQL
    cmd.ExecuteNonQuery()
    ' Then create the table
    sSQL = "CREATE TABLE Department " _
      & "(DepartmentID Int NOT NULL, " _
      & "DepartmentName Char(25), PRIMARY KEY(DepartmentID))"
    cmd.CommandText = sSQL
    cmd.ExecuteNonQuery()
  Catch e As Exception
    MsgBox(e.Message)
  End Try
  ' Close the connection
  cn.Close()
End Sub
```

The C# version of the SQLCommandNonQuery subroutine is shown here:

```csharp
private void SQLCommandNonQuery(string sServer, string sDB)
{
    SqlConnection cn = new SqlConnection("SERVER=" + sServer
        + ";INTEGRATED SECURITY=True;DATABASE=" + sDB);
    string sSQL;
    SqlCommand cmd = new SqlCommand("", cn);
    try
    {
        // Open the connection
        cn.Open();
        // First drop the table
        sSQL = "IF EXISTS "
            + "(SELECT * FROM dbo.sysobjects "
            + "WHERE id = object_id(N'[Department]') "
            + "AND OBJECTPROPERTY(id, N'IsUserTable') = 1) "
            + "DROP TABLE [department]";
        cmd.CommandText = sSQL;
        cmd.ExecuteNonQuery();
        // Then create the table
        sSQL = "CREATE TABLE Department "
            + "(DepartmentID Int NOT NULL, "
            + "DepartmentName Char(25), "
            + "PRIMARY KEY(DepartmentID))";
        cmd.CommandText = sSQL;
        cmd.ExecuteNonQuery();
    }
    catch(Exception ex)
    {
        MessageBox.Show(ex.Message);
    }
    // Close the connection
    cn.Close();
}
```

In the first part of the SQLCommandNonQuery subroutine, you can see where the sServer and sDB variables are passed as parameters. The values of these two variables are used to specify the SQL Server database server and database that will be used. Next, a new SqlConnection object named cn is created. In this example, the connection string is passed in as the first parameter of the SqlConnection object's constructor. The connection string uses Integrated Security to connect to the server and database specified using the server and database keywords. For more information about the Sql Connection object's connection string keywords, you can refer to Chapter 4.

After the Connection object has been created, the sSQL variable that will be used to contain the dynamic SQL statements and an instance of the SqlCommand object named cmd are instantiated. In this example, the constructor of the cmd SqlCommand object uses two parameters—the first being a string containing the SQL statement that will be executed, and the second being the SqlConnection object that will provide the connection to the target database server. Here the sSQL string is initially empty. Next, a Try-Catch structure is set up to execute the SQL commands. The first action that you can see within the Try-Catch block uses the cn SqlConnection object's Open method to open a connection to the SQL Server database that was specified earlier in the connection string used in the SqlConnection object's constructor. Then, the sSQL variable is assigned a SQL statement that checks for the existence of the department table. In this SQL statement, you can see that a Select statement queries the SQL Server sysobjects table to determine if a User Table named Department exists. If the Department table is found, a DROP TABLE statement will be executed to remove the table from the target database. Otherwise, if the Department table isn't found, no further action will be taken. In order to actually execute the SQL statement, that value in the sSQL variable is then assigned to the CommandText property of the cmd object, and then the ExcuteNonQuery method of the cmd SqlCommand object is used to send the command to the SQL Server system. The ExecuteNonQuery method is used to execute a SQL statement that doesn't return a resultset or a specific return value.

After the first DROP TABLE SQL command has been issued, the same sequence is followed to execute a Create Table command. First, the sSQL variable is assigned a SQL CREATE TABLE statement that creates a table named Department that consists of two columns. The first column is an integer data type named DepartmentID, which is also the primary key, and the second column is a 25-character data type named DepartmentName. Then the value in the sSQL variable is copied to the cmd object's CommandText property, and the ExecuteNonQuery method is called to execute the CREATE TABLE SQL statement. Following the successful completion of the ExecuteNonQuery method, the Department Table will exist in the database that was earlier identified in the sDB variable.

If an error occurs during any of these operations, the SqlConnection object's Open method or either instance of the SqlCommand object's ExecuteNonQuery method, then the code in the Catch block will be executed, and a message box will be displayed showing the text of the exception condition.

At the end of the CommandNonQuery subroutine, the SqlConnection object's Close method is executed to end the connection to the SQL Server database.

Executing Parameterized SQL Statements

In addition to executing dynamic SQL statements, the SqlCommand object can also be used to execute stored procedures and parameterized SQL statements. The primary difference between dynamic SQL and prepared SQL is that dynamic SQL statements must be parsed and an access plan must be created before each run. (Technically, some database systems like SQL Server are very smart about the way this is handled, and they will actually store dynamic statements for a period of time. Then when the statement is subsequently executed, the existing access plan will be used. Even so, this depends on the database activity; and with dynamic SQL, there's no guarantee that the plan will be immediately available.) You can think of prepared SQL statements as sort of a cross between stored procedures and dynamic SQL. Like stored procedures, they can accept different parameter values at runtime. Like dynamic SQL, they are not persistent in the database. The SQL statement is parsed and the access plan is created when the application executes the SQL statements. However, unlike dynamic SQL, the prepared SQL is parsed and the access plan is only created once when the statement is first prepared. Subsequent statement execution takes advantage of the existing access plan. The access plan will typically remain in the procedure cache until the connection is terminated. The following example shows how to create and execute a prepared SQL statement using the ADO.NET SqlCommand object:

```
Private Sub SQLCommandPreparedSQL(ByVal sServer As String, _
    ByVal sDB As String)
  Dim cn As New SqlConnection("SERVER=" & sServer _
    & ";INTEGRATED SECURITY=True;DATABASE=" & sDB)
  'Set up the Command object's parameter types
  Dim cmd As New SqlCommand("INSERT INTO department VALUES" _
    & "(@DepartmentID, @DepartmentName)", cn)
  Dim parmDepartmentID = _
    New SqlParameter("@DepartmentID", SqlDbType.Int)
  parmDepartmentID.Direction = ParameterDirection.Input
  Dim parmDepartmentName = _
    New SqlParameter("@DepartmentName", SqlDbType.Char, 25)
  parmDepartmentName.Direction = ParameterDirection.Input
  ' Add the parameter objects to the cmd Parameter's collection
  cmd.Parameters.Add(parmDepartmentID)
  cmd.Parameters.Add(parmDepartmentName)
  Try
    ' Open the connection & prepare the command
    cn.Open()
    cmd.Prepare()
    ' Execute the prepared SQL statement to insert 10 rows
    Dim i As Integer
    For i = 0 To 10
      parmDepartmentID.Value = i
      parmDepartmentName.Value = "New Department " & CStr(i)
      cmd.ExecuteNonQuery()
    Next
```

```
      Catch e As Exception
          MsgBox(e.Message)
      End Try
      cn.Close()
End Sub
```

The C# version of the SQLCommandPrepareSQL subroutine is shown in the following listing:

```csharp
private void SQLCommandPreparedSQL(string sServer, string sDB)
{
    SqlConnection cn = new SqlConnection("SERVER=" + sServer
        + ";INTEGRATED SECURITY=True;DATABASE=" + sDB);
    //Set up the Command object's parameter types
    SqlCommand cmd = new SqlCommand("INSERT INTO department VALUES"
        + "(@DepartmentID, @DepartmentName)", cn);
    SqlParameter parmDepartmentID =
        new SqlParameter("@DepartmentID", SqlDbType.Int);
    parmDepartmentID.Direction = ParameterDirection.Input;
    SqlParameter parmDepartmentName =
        new SqlParameter("@DepartmentName", SqlDbType.Char, 25);
    parmDepartmentName.Direction = ParameterDirection.Input;
    // Add the parameter objects to the cmd Parameter's collection
    cmd.Parameters.Add(parmDepartmentID);
    cmd.Parameters.Add(parmDepartmentName);
    try
    {
        // Open the connection & prepare the command
        cn.Open();
        cmd.Prepare();
        // Execute the prepared SQL statement to insert 10 rows
        for (int i = 1; i <= 10; i++)
        {
            parmDepartmentID.Value = i;
            parmDepartmentName.Value = "New Department " + i;
            cmd.ExecuteNonQuery();
        }
    }
    catch (Exception ex)
    {
        MessageBox.Show(ex.Message);
    }
```

```
            // Close the connection
            cn.Close();
    }
```

At the top of the CommandPrepareSQL subroutine, you can see where the target database server name and the database name are passed into the subroutine using the sServer and sDB variables. Next, a new SqlConnection object named cn is created, followed by a new SqlCommand object named cmd. In this example, the constructor takes two arguments. The first argument is used to assign a SQL statement to the cmd object. This can be either SQL statement or it can be the name of a stored procedure. Here, the SQL statement is an INSERT statement that adds that values of two columns to the Department table.

Note *The Department table was created in the earlier section of this chapter.*

The important point to note in this example is the format of the parameter markers that are used in the SQL statement. Parameter markers are used to indicate the replaceable characters in a prepared SQL statement. At runtime, these parameters will be replaced with the actual values that are supplied by the SqlCommand object's Parameters collection. Unlike ADO or the OleDbCommand object, which uses the question mark character (?) to indicate replaceable parameters, the SqlCommand object requires that all parameter markers begin with the @ symbol. This example shows two parameter markers: @DepartmentID and @DepartmentName. The second argument of the SqlCommand constructor associates the cmd SqlCommand object with the cn SqlConnection object that was created earlier.

Next, you can see where two SqlParameter objects are created. The first parameter object named parmDepartmentID will be used to supply values to the first parameter marker (@DepartmentID). Likewise, the second parameter object named parmDepartmentName will supply the values used by the second replaceable parameter (@DepartmentName). The code example used in this subroutine shows three parameters being passed to the SqlParameter's constructor. The first parameter supplies the parameter name. Here you need to make sure that the name supplied to the SqlParameter object's constructor matches the name that was used in the parameter marker of the prepared SQL statement. The second parameter that's passed to this overloaded version of the SqlParameter constructor specifies the parameter's data type. Table 8-2 lists all of the valid DbType enumerations that can be used to specify the SqlParameter's data type.

Here the Direction property is set to input using the ParameterDirection.Input enumeration. Table 8-3 lists the valid enumerations for the SqlParameter Direction property.

DbType Enumeration	.NET Data Type
BigInt	Int64
Binary	Array of type Byte
Bit	Boolean
Char	String
DateTime	DateTime
Decimal	Decimal
Float	Double
Image	Array of type Byte
Int	Int32
Money	Decimal
nChar	String
nText	String
nVarChar	String
Real	Single
SmallDateTime	DateTime
SmallInt	Int16
SmallMoney	Decimal
Text	String
Timestamp	DateTime
TinyInt	Byte
UniqueIdentifier	Guid
VarBinary	Array of type Byte
VarChar	String
Variant	Object

Table 8-2. *DbType Enumerations*

Enumeration	Description
ParameterDirection.Input	The parameter is an input parameter.
ParameterDirection.InputOutput	The parameter is capable of both input and output.
ParameterDirection.Output	The parameter is an output parameter.
ParameterDirection.ReturnValue	The parameter represents a return value.

Table 8-3. *SqlParameterDirection Enumeration*

After the SqlParameter objects have been created, the next step is to add them to the SqlCommand object's Parameters collection. In the previous listings, you can see that you use the Add method of the SqlCommand object's Parameters collection to add both the parmDepartmentID and parmDepartmentName SqlParameter objects to the cmd SqlCommand object. The order in which you add the SqlParameter objects isn't important. Next, within the Try-Catch block, the cn SqlConnection object's Open method is used to open a connection to SQL Server and then the Prepare statement is used to prepare the statement. Note that the Prepare method is executed after all of the parameter attributes have been described.

Note *Using the Prepare operation provides an important performance benefit for parameterized queries because it instructs SQL Server to issue an sp_prepare statement, thereby ensuring that the statement will be in the Procedure cache until the statement handle is closed.*

Next, a For-Next loop is used to add 10 rows to the newly created Department table. Within the For-Next loop, the Value property of each parameter object is assigned a new data value. For simplicity, the parmDepartmentID parameter is assigned the value of the loop counter contained in the variable i while the parmDepartmentName parameter is assigned a string containing the literal "New Department" along with the current value of the loop counter. Last, the SqlCommand object's ExecuteNonQuery method is used to execute the SQL statement. In this case, ExecuteNonQuery was used because this example is using a SQL action query that doesn't return any values. From the SQL Server perspective, running the ExecuteNonQuery method results in the server issuing an sp_execute command to actually perform the insert.

Note *If you need to pass a null value as a parameter, you need to set the parameter to the value DBNull.Value.*

If an error occurs during any of these operations, the code in the Catch block will be executed and a message box will be displayed showing the text of the exception condition.

At the end of the subroutine, the SqlConnection object's Close method is executed to end the connection to the SQL Server database.

Executing Stored Procedures with Return Values

Stored procedures are the core of most database applications—and for good reason. In addition to their performance benefits, stored procedures can also be a mechanism for restricting data access to the predefined interfaces that are exposed by the stored procedures. Similar to prepared SQL statements, stored procedures get significant performance benefits from the fact that they are compiled before they are used. This allows the database to forego the typical parsing steps that are required, skipping the need to create an access plan. Stored procedures are the true workhorse of most database applications, and they are almost always used for database insert, update, and delete operations, as well as for retrieving single values and result sets. In the following examples, you see how to execute SQL Server stored procedures using the SqlCommand object. In the first example that follows, you'll see how to execute a stored procedure that accepts a single input parameter and returns a scalar value.

The following listing presents the T-SQL source code required to create the StockValue stored procedure that will be added to the sample Northwind database. You can create this stored procedure by executing this code using Query Analyzer.

```
CREATE PROCEDURE StockValue
    @ProductID int
AS

DECLARE @StockValue money

SELECT StockValue = (UnitsInStock * UnitPrice)
FROM Products WHERE ProductID = @ProductID

RETURN @StockValue
```

In the preceding listing, you can see that the StockValue stored procedure accepts a single input parameter. That parameter is an Integer value that's used to identify the ProductID. The StockValue stored procedure returns the stock value of that ProductID from the Products table in the Northwind database. The stock value is calculated by retrieving the UnitsInStock number and multiplying it by the value in the UnitPrice column. The results are then assigned to the @StockValue variable, which is returned as a scalar value by the stored procedure. After the sample stored procedure has been created in the Northwind database, it can be called by your ADO.NET applications. The following example shows how to use the SqlCommand class form VB.NET to execute the StockValue stored procedure and retrieve the scalar value that it returns:

```
Private Sub SQLCommandSPScalar(ByVal sServer As String, _
```

```
        ByVal sDB As String)
    Dim cn As New SqlConnection("SERVER=" & sServer _
        & ";INTEGRATED SECURITY=True;DATABASE=" & sDB)
    ' Create the command object and set the SQL statement
    Dim cmd As New SqlCommand("StockValue", cn)
    cmd.CommandType = CommandType.StoredProcedure
    'Create the parameter
    cmd.Parameters.Add("@ProductID", SqlDbType.Int)
    cmd.Parameters("@ProductID").Direction = _
        ParameterDirection.Input
    cmd.Parameters("@ProductID").Value = 1
    Try
        Dim nStockValue As Decimal
        ' Open the connection and execute the command
        cn.Open()
        nStockValue = cmd.ExecuteScalar()
        txtMid.Text = nStockValue
    Catch e As Exception
        MsgBox(e.Message)
    End Try
    ' Close the connection
    cn.Close()
End Sub
```

Following is the C# version of the SQLCommandSPScalar subroutine that calls a SQL stored procedure and returns a scalar value:

```
private void SQLCommandPSScalar(string sServer, string sDB)
{
    SqlConnection cn = new SqlConnection("SERVER=" + sServer
        + ";INTEGRATED SECURITY=True;DATABASE=" + sDB);
    // Create the command object and set the SQL statement
    SqlCommand cmd = new SqlCommand("StockValue", cn);
    cmd.CommandType = CommandType.StoredProcedure;
    // Create the parameter
    cmd.Parameters.Add("@ProductID", SqlDbType.Int);
    cmd.Parameters["@ProductID"].Direction =
        ParameterDirection.Input;
    cmd.Parameters["@ProductID"].Value = 1;
    try
    {
        decimal nStockValue;
        // Open the connection and execute the command
```

```
        cn.Open();
        nStockValue = (decimal)cmd.ExecuteScalar();
        txtMid.Text = nStockValue.ToString();
    }
    catch (Exception ex)
    {
        MessageBox.Show(ex.Message);
    }
    // Close the connection
    cn.Close();
}
```

In the beginning of this routine you can see where the cn SqlConnection object is created, followed by the creation of the SqlCommand object named cmd. In this example, the constructor for the SqlCommand object uses two parameters. The first parameter is a string that accepts the command that will be executed. This can be either a SQL statement or the name of the stored procedure. In this example, you can see that the name of the StockValue stored procedure is used. The second parameter is used for the name of the SqlConnection object that will be used to connect to the target database. After the cmd SqlCommand object has been created, its CommandType property is set to CommandType.StoredProcedure indicating that a stored procedure will be executed. The CommandType property can accept any of the values shown in the following table:

CommandType Values	Description
CommandType.StoredProcedure	The command is a stored procedure.
CommandType.TableDirect	The command is the name of a database table.
CommandType.Text	The command is a SQL statement.

After the SqlCommand object's CommandType property is set to CommandType .StoredProcedure, the SqlParameter object used to supply the input value to the StockValue stored procedure is created. SqlParameter objects can be created either by using the SqlParameter class constructor or by executing the SqlCommand object's Parameters collection Add method. In this example, the parameter is created using the Add method of the SqlCommand object's Parameters collection. The first parameter supplied to the Add method is a string containing the name of the parameter. In this case "@ProductID". Again, note that replaceable parameters used by the SQLParameter object must begin with the at symbol (@). The second parameter uses the SqlDbType.Int enumeration to indicate that the parameter will contain an Integer value. The next line sets the Direction property to the value ParameterDirection.Input to indicate that this is an input parameter. Last, the SqlParameter object's Value property is set to 1—storing a value of 1 to pass to the StockValue stored procedure.

The next section of code sets up a Try-Catch block to open the connection to the SQL Server system and then executes the StockValue stored procedure. The important point to note in the Try-Catch block is that the cmd SqlCommand object's ExecuteScalar method is used to execute the StockValue stored procedure and the return value is assigned to the nStockValue variable. The contents of the nStockValue variable are then assigned to a text box. Like the earlier examples, if the connection or the stored procedure fails, a message box showing the error text will be displayed to the end user. Then the connection will be closed.

Executing Transactions

Transactions enable you to group together multiple operations that can be performed as a single unit of work, which helps to ensure database integrity. For instance, transferring funds from your savings account to your checking account involves multiple database operations, and the transfer cannot be considered complete unless all of the operations are successfully completed. A typical transfer from your savings account to your checking account requires two separate but related operations: a withdrawal from your savings account and a deposit to your checking account. If either operation fails, the transfer is not completed. Therefore, both of these functions would be considered part of the same logical transaction. From the database standpoint, to ensure database integrity, both the withdrawal and the deposit would be grouped together as a single transaction. If the withdrawal operation succeeded but the deposit failed, the entire transaction could be rolled back, which would restore the database to the condition it had before the withdrawal operation was attempted. Using transactions is an essential part of most production-level database applications.

ADO.NET supports transactions using the Transaction classes. In order to incorporate transactions into your ADO.NET application you first need to create an instance of the SqlTransaction object and then execute the BeginTransaction method to mark the beginning of a transaction. Under the covers this will cause the database server to begin a transaction. For instance, using the SqlTransaction object to issue a BeginTransaction statement will send a T-SQL BEGIN TRANSACTION command to SQL Server. After the transaction has started, the database update operations are performed and then the Commit method is used to actually write the updates to the target database. If an error occurs during the process, then the RollBack operation is used to undo the changes. The following SQLCommandTransaction subroutine shows how to start a transaction and then either commit the results of the transaction to the database or roll back the transaction in the event of an error:

```
Private Sub SQLCommandTransaction(ByVal sServer As String, _
    ByVal sDB As String)
  Dim cn As New SqlConnection("SERVER=" & sServer _
    & ";INTEGRATED SECURITY=True;DATABASE=" & sDB)
  Dim cmd As New SqlCommand()
```

```
        Dim trans As SqlTransaction
        ' Start a local transaction
        cn.Open()
        trans = cn.BeginTransaction()
        cmd.Connection = cn
        cmd.Transaction = trans
        Try
            ' Insert a row  transaction
            cmd.CommandText = _
                "INSERT INTO Department VALUES(100, 'Transaction 100')"
            cmd.ExecuteNonQuery()
            ' This will result in an error
            cmd.CommandText = _
                "INSERT INTO Department VALUES(100, 'Transaction 101')"
            cmd.ExecuteNonQuery()
            trans.Commit()
        Catch e As Exception
            MsgBox(e.Message)
            trans.Rollback()
        Finally
            cn.Close()
        End Try
End Sub
```

You can see the C# version of the SQLCommandTransaction subroutine in the following listing:

```
private void SQLCommandTransaction(string sServer, string sDB)
{
    SqlConnection cn = new SqlConnection("SERVER=" + sServer
        + ";INTEGRATED SECURITY=True;DATABASE=" + sDB);
    SqlCommand cmd = new SqlCommand();
    SqlTransaction trans;
    // Start a local transaction
    cn.Open();
    trans = cn.BeginTransaction();
    cmd.Connection = cn;
    cmd.Transaction = trans;
    try
    {
        // Insert a row transaction
```

```
        cmd.CommandText =
            "INSERT INTO Department VALUES(100, 'Transaction 100')";
        cmd.ExecuteNonQuery();
        // This will result in an error
        cmd.CommandText =
            "INSERT INTO Department VALUES(100, 'Transaction 101')";
        cmd.ExecuteNonQuery();
        trans.Commit();
    }
    catch (Exception ex)
    {
        MessageBox.Show(ex.Message);
        trans.Rollback();
    }
    finally
    {
        cn.Close();
    }
}
```

In the beginning of this subroutine, you can see where new instances of the SqlConnection and SqlCommand objects are created, followed by the definition of a SqlTransaction object named trans. Next, a local transaction is started by first opening the connection and then using the cn SqlConnection object's BeginTransaction method to create a new instance of a SqlTransaction object. Note that the connection must be open before you execute the BeginTransaction method. Next, the cmd SqlCommand Connection property is assigned with the cn SqlConnection and the Transaction property is assigned with the trans SqlTransaction object.

Within the Try-Catch block, two commands are issued that are within the local transaction scope. The first command is an INSERT statement that inserts two columns into the Department table that was created previously in this chapter. The first insert statement adds the DepartmentID of 100 along with a DepartmentName value of 'Transaction 100'. The SqlCommand ExecuteNonQuery method is then used to execute the SQL statement. Next, the cmd object's CommandText property is set to another SQL INSERT statement. However, this statement will cause an error because it is attempting to insert a duplicate primary key value. In this second case, the DepartmentID of 100 is attempted to be inserted along with the DepartmentName value of 'Transaction 101'. This causes an error because the DepartmentID of 100 was just inserted by the previous INSERT statement. When the ExecuteNonQuery method is executed, the duplicate primary key error will be issued and the code in the Catch portion of the Try-Catch block will be executed.

Displaying the exception message in a message box is the first action that happens within the Catch block. You can see an example of this message in Figure 8-2.

Figure 8-2. *A duplicate primary key error prevents the Commit operation.*

After the message box is displayed, the trans SqlTransaction object's RollBack method is used to roll back the attempted transaction. Note that because both insert statements were within the same transaction scope both insert operations will be rolled back. The resulting department table will not contain either DepartmentID 100 or DepartmentID 101.

In this example, a Finally block is used to close the cn SqlConnection object. If the Finally block is attached to the Try-Catch structure, the code in the Finally block will always be executed.

Summary

In this chapter, you saw several examples illustrating how to execute commands using the .NET Framework Data Provider for SQL Server's SqlCommand object. The examples in the first part of the chapter illustrated how to use the SqlCommand object to execute SQL statements and stored procedures. In the second part of the chapter, you learned how to use transactions. The next chapter begins where this chapter leaves off: you'll see how to execute commands using the OracleCommand object.

THE ADO.NET
COMMAND OBJECT

The Complete Reference

ADO.NET

Chapter 9

Using the OracleCommand Object

In the previous chapter, you saw how to use the SqlCommand object to execute SQL statements and stored procedures on a SQL Server database. This chapter picks up where Chapter 8 leaves off, and here you see how to use the OracleCommand object to execute SQL statements and stored procedures on an Oracle 9i database. In the first part of this chapter, you learn how to use the visual OracleCommand object to execute simple SQL DDL action queries on the target database. Next, the chapter provides an example that illustrates how to execute an Oracle stored procedure with named parameters. In the final example, you see how to use the OracleCommand object to execute transactions.

Executing SQL Statements and Stored Procedures Using the OracleCommand Object

The OracleCommand object is used to execute SQL action queries, stored procedures, and packages on an Oracle 8i or later database. Two of the most essential database application actions, executing dynamic SQL statements and stored procedures, are the basis for most production ADO.NET applications. Dynamic SQL statements are parsed by the database server and executed when they are sent to the database server from the client application. In contrast, stored procedures are typically created in advance by the DBA and then called by the database applications. Stored procedures offer both a performance and security advantage over dynamic SQL. Packages and stored procedures enjoy a performance advantage because the jobs of parsing the SQL statements and creating the data access plan are enacted when the procedure is first created—not at runtime. They gain a security advantage because they allow the developer to funnel database access through a predefined interface supplied by the procedure rather than permitting access to the base tables. This helps to prevent hackers from using techniques such as SQL injection to gain knowledge about the underlying database structure and contents. The first example in this chapter illustrates how to use the OracleCommand object to execute a SQL DDL statement that creates a stored procedure. The next example illustrates how to call that stored procedure.

Using the Visual Studio OracleCommand Object

The simplest place to start using the OracleCommand object is the visual component provided as a part of Visual Studio.NET IDE. You can drag and drop an instance of the OracleCommand from Visual Studio.NET's Data Toolbox onto the visual designer, which adds a new OracleCommand object to your project's components pane, as shown in Figure 9-1.

Once the visual OracleCommand component has been added, it is ready to use. The following example illustrates how to execute a dynamic SQL DDL statement that creates a stored procedure with the visual OracleCommand component. Dynamic SQL provides an extremely flexible mechanism for working with the database. You can use

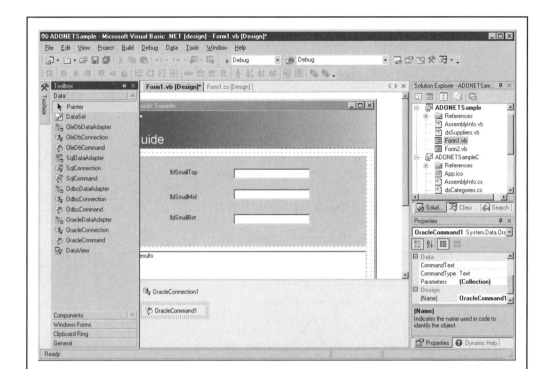

Figure 9-1. *Adding the visual OracleCommand object to a Visual Studio.NET project*

it to execute ad hoc queries and return the results from action queries, as well as to execute SQL DDL statements to create database objects as shown here:

```
Private Sub OracleCommandComponent(ByVal sServer As String, _
     ByVal sUser As String, ByVal sPassword As String)
  Cursor.Current = Cursors.WaitCursor
  OracleConnection1.ConnectionString = "DATA SOURCE=" & sServer _
     & ";UID=" & sUser & ";PWD=" & sPassword
  'Set up a query
  OracleCommand1.CommandText = _
     "CREATE OR REPLACE PROCEDURE GETEMPDETAILS" _
     & " ( I_EMPNO IN number," _
     & "O_ENAME OUT varchar," _
     & "O_JOB OUT varchar," _
     & "O_SAL OUT number " _
```

```
            & " ) IS " _
            & "BEGIN" _
            & " SELECT ENAME, JOB, SAL " _
            & " INTO O_ENAME, O_JOB, O_SAL" _
            & " FROM EMP WHERE EMPNO=I_EMPNO;" _
            & " END; "
        ' Set the active connection
        OracleCommand1.Connection = OracleConnection1
        Try
            ' Open a connection and execute the command
            OracleConnection1.Open()
            OracleCommand1.ExecuteNonQuery()
        Catch ex As Exception
            Cursor.Current = Cursors.Default
            MessageBox.Show("Connection error: :" & ex.ToString())
        End Try
        OracleConnection1.Close()
        Cursor.Current = Cursors.Default
    End Sub
```

The following is an example of the OracleCommandComponent subroutine
written in C#:

```
private void OracleCommandComponent(string sServer, string sUser,
        string sPassword)
{
    Cursor.Current = Cursors.WaitCursor;
    oracleConnection1.ConnectionString = "DATA SOURCE=" + sServer
        + ";UID=" + sUser + ";PWD=" + sPassword;
    // Set up a query
    oracleCommand1.CommandText =
        "CREATE OR REPLACE PROCEDURE GETEMPDETAILS"
        + " ( I_EMPNO IN number,"
        + "O_ENAME OUT varchar,"
        + "O_JOB OUT varchar,"
        + "O_SAL OUT number "
        + " ) IS "
        + "BEGIN"
        + " SELECT ENAME, JOB, SAL "
        + " INTO O_ENAME, O_JOB, O_SAL"
        + " FROM EMP where EMPNO=I_EMPNO;"
```

```
        + " END; ";
    // Set the active connection
    oracleCommand1.Connection = oracleConnection1;
    try
    {
        // Open a connection and execute the command
        oracleConnection1.Open();
        oracleCommand1.ExecuteNonQuery();
    }
    catch(Exception ex)
    {
        Cursor.Current = Cursors.Default;
        MessageBox.Show("Connection error: :" + ex.ToString());
    }
    oracleConnection1.Close();
    Cursor.Current = Cursors.Default;
}
```

In the beginning of the OracleCommandComponent routine, you can see where three variables are passed in as parameters. The sServer variable contains the name of the Oracle database system, the sUser variable contains the name of the database user, and the sPassword variable contains the password for the Oracle database login. This example login has been set up to use the Oracle sample SCOTT database. Next, the routine sets the OracleConnection1 object's ConnectionString property using the DATA SOURCE, UID, and PWD keywords in conjunction with the variables passed in at the top of the subroutine. Then the OracleCommand1 object's CommandText property is assigned a SQL statement that will create an Oracle stored procedure named GETEMPDETAILS. This stored procedure takes one input parameter, which consists of the employee number. It returns three parameters containing the employee name, job description, and salary that are retrieved from the EMP table.

The next statement sets the OracleCommand1 object's Connection property to the OracleConnect1 object. Then a Try-Catch block is set up to open the connection to the Oracle database and execute the SQL statement. First the OracleConnection1.Open method is used to start a connection to the Oracle database and then the OracleCommand1 object's ExecuteNonQuery method is used to execute the SQL statement. The OracleCommand object supports several different command execution methods, which are listed in Table 9-1.

After the ExecuteNonQuery method has finished, the OracleConnection object is closed and the subroutine ends. If an error occurs during the execution of either the Open method or the ExecuteNonQuery method, a message box appears showing the exception text.

Method	Description
ExecuteNonQuery	The ExecuteNonQuery method is used to execute a SQL statement on the connected data source. It is used for DDL statements and action queries such as Insert, Update, and Delete operations, as well as ad hoc queries. The number of rows affected is returned, but no output parameters or resultsets are returned.
ExecuteOracleNonQuery	Like the ExecuteNonQuery method, the ExecuteOracleNonQuery is used to execute a SQL statement on the connected data source. Unlike the ExecuteNonQuery method, the ExecuteOracleNonQuery method is able to accept a parameter containing the row ID of the server. The number of rows affected is returned, but no output parameters or resultsets are returned.
ExecuteOracleScalar	The ExecuteOracleScalar method is used to execute a stored procedure or a SQL statement that returns a single scalar value. This function returns the value as an Oracle data type. The first row of the first column of the resultset is returned to the calling application. Any other returned values are ignored.
ExecuteReader	The ExecuteReader method is used to execute a SQL Select statement on the data source. A fast forward-only result is returned.
ExecuteScalar	The ExecuteScalar method is used to execute a stored procedure or a SQL statement that returns a single scalar value. The first row of the first column of the resultset is returned to the calling application. Any other returned values are ignored.

Table 9-1.   *OracleCommand SQL Statement Execution Methods*

Executing Stored Procedures with Output Parameters

Stored procedures are the core of most database applications. Stored procedures have significant performance benefits because they are compiled before they are used. This allows the database to forego the typical parsing steps that are required to process dynamic SQL, as well as skip the creation of an access plan. The OracleCommand object is the primary ADO.NET mechanism for executing stored procedures against an Oracle database. To use the OracleCommand class in your project, you first need to add an import directive for the System.Data.OracleClient Namespace in your project. You can find an example showing how to create an import directive for the System.Data.OracleClient in Chapter 5.

The following listing presents the code required to use the GETEMPDETAILS stored procedure that was created in the preceding example in this chapter. If you look back at the preceding code listing, you can see that the GETEMPDETAILS stored procedure accepts a single numeric input parameter. That's used to identify the employee whose information will be retrieved. The GETEMPDETAILS stored procedure returns the employee name, job description, and salary from the EMP table in the Oracle sample SCOTT database. After the GETEMPDETAILS stored procedure has been created in the SCOTT database, it can then be called from your ADO.NET applications using the OracleCommand object. The following shows how to use the OracleCommand object to execute the GETEMPDETAILS stored procedure and retrieve the value that it returns:

```
Private Sub OracleCommandSPParms(ByVal sServer As String, _
        ByVal sUser As String, ByVal sPassword As String)
    Cursor.Current = Cursors.WaitCursor
    Dim cn As New OracleConnection("DATA SOURCE=" & sServer _
        & ";UID=" & sUser & ";PWD=" & sPassword)
    'Setup the Command object's Connection, SQL and parameter types
    Dim cmd As New OracleCommand("GETEMPDETAILS", cn)
    cmd.CommandType = CommandType.StoredProcedure
    Dim parmEMPNO = New OracleParameter("I_EMPNO", _
        OracleType.Number)
    parmEMPNO.Direction = ParameterDirection.Input
    Dim parmENAME = New OracleParameter("O_ENAME", _
        OracleType.VarChar, 10)
    parmENAME.Direction = ParameterDirection.Output
    Dim parmJOB = New OracleParameter("O_JOB", _
        OracleType.VarChar, 9)
    parmJOB.Direction = ParameterDirection.Output
    Dim parmSAL = New OracleParameter("O_SAL", OracleType.Number)
    parmSAL.Direction = ParameterDirection.Output
    ' Add the parameter objects to the Command Parameters collection
```

THE ADO.NET
COMMAND OBJECT

```
    cmd.Parameters.Add(parmEMPNO)
    cmd.Parameters.Add(parmENAME)
    cmd.Parameters.Add(parmJOB)
    cmd.Parameters.Add(parmSAL)
    Try
        ' Open the connection & prepare the command
        cn.Open()
        ' Execute the prepared SQL statement to retrieve EMPNO 7788
        parmEMPNO.Value = 7788
        cmd.ExecuteNonQuery()
        Debug.WriteLine(parmENAME.Value)
        Debug.WriteLine(parmJOB.Value)
        Debug.WriteLine(parmSAL.Value)
    Catch e As Exception
        Cursor.Current = Cursors.Default
        MsgBox(e.Message)
    End Try
    cn.Close()
    Cursor.Current = Cursors.Default
End Sub
```

Following is the C# version of the OracleCommandSPParms subroutine:

```
private void OracleCommandSPParms(string sServer, string sUser,
        string sPassword)
{
    Cursor.Current = Cursors.WaitCursor;
    OracleConnection cn = new OracleConnection("DATA SOURCE=" +
        sServer + ";UID=" + sUser + ";PWD=" + sPassword);
    //Setup the Command object's Connection, SQL and parameter types
    OracleCommand cmd = new OracleCommand("GETEMPDETAILS", cn);
    cmd.CommandType = CommandType.StoredProcedure;
    OracleParameter parmEMPNO = new OracleParameter("I_EMPNO",
        OracleType.Number);
    parmEMPNO.Direction = ParameterDirection.Input;
    OracleParameter parmENAME = new OracleParameter("O_ENAME",
        OracleType.VarChar, 10);
    parmENAME.Direction = ParameterDirection.Output;
    OracleParameter parmJOB = new OracleParameter("O_JOB",
        OracleType.VarChar, 9);
```

```
        parmJOB.Direction = ParameterDirection.Output;
        OracleParameter parmSAL = new OracleParameter("O_SAL",
            OracleType.Number);
        parmSAL.Direction = ParameterDirection.Output;
        // Add the parameter objs to the Command Parameters collection
        cmd.Parameters.Add(parmEMPNO);
        cmd.Parameters.Add(parmENAME);
        cmd.Parameters.Add(parmJOB);
        cmd.Parameters.Add(parmSAL);
        try
        {
            // Open the connection & prepare the command
            cn.Open();
            // Execute the prepared SQL statement to retrieve EMPNO 7788
            parmEMPNO.Value = 7788;
            cmd.ExecuteNonQuery();
            Debug.WriteLine(parmENAME.Value);
            Debug.WriteLine(parmJOB.Value);
            Debug.WriteLine(parmSAL.Value);
        }
        catch (Exception ex)
        {
            Cursor.Current = Cursors.Default;
            MessageBox.Show("Connection error: :" + ex.ToString());
        }
        cn.Close();
        Cursor.Current = Cursors.Default;
    }
```

Three string variables are passed as parameters into the beginning of this subroutine. The sServer variable contains the .NET Service name of the Oracle database. The sUser variable contains the Oracle user's login, and the sPassword variable contains the user's password. Next, the cn OracleConnection object is created, followed by an OracleCommand object named cmd. The OracleCommand object's constructor uses two parameters. The first parameter of the OracleCommand object's constructor is a string that contains the name of the stored procedure that will be executed: GETEMPDETAILS. For stored procedures, this parameter contains the name of the stored procedure but it can also contain SQL statements that will be executed. The second parameter contains the name of the active OracleConnection object. After the OracleCommand object has been created, its CommandType property is set to CommandType.StoredProcedure, which indicates that a stored procedure will be executed. The OracleCommand object's CommandType property can accept any of the values shown in the table that follows.

CommandType Values	Description
CommandType.StoredProcedure	The command is a stored procedure.
CommandType.TableDirect	The command is the name of a database table.
CommandType.Text	The command is a SQL statement.

After the OracleCommand object has been created and its CommandType property is set to CommandType.StoredProcedure, four OracleParameter objects are created. These OracleParameter objects are used to supply the input value to the GETEMPDETAILS stored procedure, as well as return the values in the output parameters to the ADO.NET application. In this example, the OracleParameter objects are instantiated using the OracleParameter object's constructor. Two parameters are passed to the OracleParameter class constructor. The first parameter is a string containing the name of the parameter. The second parameter specifies the data type of the parameter. Because the OracleCommand object uses named parameters, this string must exactly match the name of the parameter as it is defined in the Oracle stored procedure. However, because named parameters are used, the order that the OracleParameters objects are created in or added to the OracleCommand object doesn't matter. The names are used to identify each parameter, not their position. Here the first OracleParameter object uses the parameter name of the "I_EMPNO"—matching the name of the first parameter in the GETEPDETAILS stored procedure.

Oracle named parameters use the colon character to designate a named parameter. You can optionally use or omit the colon in your OracleParameter objects. In this case, the first parameter could have been named either I_EMPNO or :I_EMPNO.

The second parameter used in the OracleParameter object's constructor specifies the data type that is used in the parameter. This is stored in the OracleType property. Table 9-2 shows the valid values for the OracleType property.

Unfortunately ADO.NET doesn't provide a convenient way to set up the Direction property along with the other parameter attributes. The next line following the parameter object's constructor sets the Direction property of the OracleParameter object. Table 9-3 lists the valid enumerations for the OracleParameter Direction property.

Once the OracleParameter objects have been created, they are added to the cmd OracleCommand object's Parameters collection.

Next, a Try-Catch block is used to open the connection to the Oracle server and then set the value of the parmEMPNO inout parameter to 7788. Then the OracleCommand object's ExecuteNonQuery method is used to execute the GETEMPDETAILS stored procedure. The ExecuteNonQuery method doesn't return a resultset, but after the stored procedure has executed, the returned values will be available in the output parameter objects. Here, the contents of the parmENAME, parmJob, and parmSAL Value properties are written to the Debug console. If the connection or the stored procedure fails, a message box showing the error text appears. Closing the connection is the last action in the subroutine.

OracleType	Description
BFile	Contains a reference to binary data with a maximum size of 4GB that is stored in an external file. Passed as an OracleBFileType data type.
Blob	Contains binary data with a maximum size of 4GB. Passed as an OracleLOB data type.
Byte	Not a native Oracle data type. The Byte type contains an integral type representing unsigned 8-bit integers with values between 0 and 255. Passed as a .NET Byte data type.
Char	Contains a string of up to 2000 bytes. Passed as either a .NET String or an OracleString data type.
Clob	Contains character data with a maximum size of 4GB. Passed as an OracleLob data type.
Cursor	Contains an Oracle REF Cursor, which can be read using the OracleDataReader.
DateTime	Represents dates ranging from January 1, 4712 B.C., to A.D December, 31, 4712. The default format is *dd-mmm-yy*. Passed as a .NET DataTime or an OracleDataTime data type.
Double	Not a native Oracle data type, the Double contains a double precision floating point value. Passed as a .NET Double or an OracleNumber data type.
Float	Not a native Oracle data type, the Float contains a single precision floating point value. Passed as a .NET Single or an OracleNumber data type.

Table 9-2. *OracleType Enumerations*

OracleType	Description
Int16	Not a native Oracle data type, the Int16 integral type represents signed 16-bit integers with values between –32768 and 32767. Passed as a .NET Int16 or an OracleNumber data type.
Int32	Not a native Oracle data type, the Int32 integral type represents signed 32-bit integers with values between –2147483648 and 2147483647. Passed as a .NET Int32 or an OracleNumber data type.
IntervalDayToSecond	Contains an interval of time in days, hours, minutes, and seconds, and has a fixed size of 11 bytes. Passed as a .NET TimeSpan or OracleTimeSpan data type. (Only on Oracle 9i and later.)
IntervalYearToMonth	Contains an interval of time in years and months, and has a fixed size of 5 bytes. Passed as a .NET Int32 or an OracleMonthSpan data type. (Only on Oracle 9i and later.)
LongRaw	Contains variable-length binary data with a maximum size of 2 gigabytes. Passed as a .NET Byte array or an OracleBinary data type.
LongVarChar	Contains a variable-length character string with a maximum size of 2 gigabytes. Passed as a .NET String or an OracleString data type.
NChar	Contains a fixed-length Unicode character string with a maximum size of 2000 bytes. Passed as a .NET String or an OracleString data type.
NClob	Contains Unicode character data with a maximum size of 4GB. Passed as an OracleLob data type.
Number	Contains variable-length numeric data with a maximum precision and scale of 38. Passed as a .NET Decimal or OracleNumber data type.
NVarChar (nVarChar2)	Contains a variable-length Unicode string with a maximum size of 4000 bytes. Passed as a .NET String or an OracleString data type.

Table 9-2. *OracleType Enumerations* (continued)

OracleType	Description
Raw	Contains variable-length binary data with a maximum size of 2000 bytes. Passed as a .NET Byte array or an OracleBinary data type.
RowID	Contains a base64 string representing an Oracle RowID data type. Passed as a.NET String or an OracleString data type.
SByte	Not a native Oracle data type, the sByte data type is an integral type representing signed 8-bit integers with values between –128 and 127. Passed as a .NET SByte data type.
Timestamp	Contains the date and time and ranges in size from 7 to 11 bytes. Passed as a .NET DateTime or an OracleDateTime data type. (Only on Oracle 9i and later.)
TimestampLocal	Contains the date, time, and a reference to the original time zone, and ranges in size from 7 to 11 bytes. Passed as a .NET DateTime or an OracleDateTime data type. (Only on Oracle 9i and later.)
TimestampwithTZ	Contains the date, time, and a specified time zone, and has a fixed size of 13 bytes. Passed as a .NET DateTime or an OracleDateTime data type. (Only on Oracle 9i and later.)
UInt16	Not a native Oracle data type, the UInt16 contains an integral type representing unsigned 16-bit integers with values between 0 and 65535. Passed as a .NET UInt16 or an OracleNumber data type.
UInt32	Not a native Oracle data type, the UInt16 contains an integral type representing unsigned 32-bit integers with values between 0 and 4294967295. Passed as a .NET UInt32 or an OracleNumber data type.
VarChar (VarChar2)	Contains a variable-length character string with a maximum size of 4000 bytes. Passed as a.NET String or an OracleString data type.

Table 9-2. *OracleType Enumerations* (continued)

Enumeration	Description
ParameterDirection.Input	The parameter is an input parameter.
ParameterDirection.InputOutput	The parameter is capable of both input and output.
ParameterDirection.Output	The parameter is an output parameter.
ParameterDirection.ReturnValue	The parameter represents a return value.

Table 9-3.   *OracleParameterDirection Enumeration*

Executing Transactions with Parameterized SQL Statements

Transactions are an essential part of most production-level database applications. Transactions ensure database integrity by enabling you to group together multiple operations as a single unit of work. For instance, when a product is shipped, an update would be required to the shipping table to indicate an in-transit status and a corresponding update would be required to the inventory table to reflect the new inventory levels. To ensure database integrity, both the shipment and the inventory update are combined into a single transaction. If either operation fails, the transaction is not completed and both operations need to be rolled back, restoring the database to its original condition.

To incorporate Oracle database transactions into your ADO.NET applications, you first need to create an instance of the OracleTransaction object and then execute the BeginTransaction method to mark the beginning of a transaction. After the transaction has started, the database update operations are performed and then the Commit method is used to write the updates to the target database. If an error occurs during the process, the RollBack operation is used to undo the changes. In the following OracleCommandTransaction subroutine, you'll see how to commit and roll back database transactions using the OracleCommand object.

```
Private Sub OracleCommandTransaction(ByVal sServer As String, _
        ByVal sUser As String, ByVal sPassword As String)
    Cursor.Current = Cursors.WaitCursor
    Dim cn As New OracleConnection("DATA SOURCE=" & sServer _
        & ";UID=" & sUser & ";PWD=" & sPassword)
```

```
    Dim cmd As New OracleCommand
    cmd.CommandType = CommandType.Text
    Dim trans As OracleTransaction
    ' Start a local transaction
    cn.Open()
    cmd.Connection = cn
    trans = cn.BeginTransaction()
    cmd.Transaction = trans
    cmd.CommandText = _
        "INSERT INTO DEPT(DEPTNO, DNAME, LOC) " & _
        "VALUES(:I_DEPTNO, :I_DNAME, :I_LOC)"
    'Create the input parameters
    Dim parmDEPTNO = _
        New OracleParameter("I_DEPTNO", OracleType.Number)
    parmDEPTNO.Direction = ParameterDirection.Input
    parmDEPTNO.Value = 50
    Dim parmDNAME = _
        New OracleParameter("I_DNAME", OracleType.VarChar, 14)
    parmDNAME.Direction = ParameterDirection.Input
    parmDNAME.Value = "IT"
    Dim parmLOC = _
        New OracleParameter("I_LOC", OracleType.VarChar, 13)
    parmLOC.Direction = ParameterDirection.Input
    parmLOC.Value = "SAN JOSE"
    ' Add the parameter objects to the Parameter's collection
    cmd.Parameters.Add(parmDEPTNO)
    cmd.Parameters.Add(parmDNAME)
    cmd.Parameters.Add(parmLOC)
    Try
        ' Insert a row transaction
        cmd.Prepare()
        cmd.ExecuteNonQuery()
        trans.Commit()
    Catch e As Exception
        trans.Rollback()
        Cursor.Current = Cursors.Default
        MsgBox(e.Message)
    Finally
        cn.Close()
    End Try
    Cursor.Current = Cursors.Default
End Sub
```

You can see the C# version of the OracleCommandTransaction subroutine in the following listing:

```
private void OracleCommandTransaction(string sServer,
        string sUser, string sPassword)
{
    Cursor.Current = Cursors.WaitCursor;
    OracleConnection cn = new OracleConnection("DATA SOURCE=" +
        sServer + ";UID=" + sUser + ";PWD=" + sPassword);
    OracleCommand cmd = new OracleCommand();
    cmd.CommandType = CommandType.Text;
    OracleTransaction trans;
    // Start a local transaction
    cn.Open();
    cmd.Connection = cn;
    cmd.CommandText = "DELETE DEPT WHERE DEPTNO = 50";
    cmd.ExecuteNonQuery();
    trans = cn.BeginTransaction();
    cmd.Transaction = trans;
    cmd.CommandText =
        "INSERT INTO DEPT(DEPTNO, DNAME, LOC) " +
        "VALUES(:I_DEPTNO, :I_DNAME, :I_LOC)";
    // Create the input parameters
    OracleParameter parmDEPTNO =
        new OracleParameter("I_DEPTNO", OracleType.Number);
    parmDEPTNO.Direction = ParameterDirection.Input;
    parmDEPTNO.Value = 50;
    OracleParameter parmDNAME =
        new OracleParameter("I_DNAME", OracleType.VarChar, 14);
    parmDNAME.Direction = ParameterDirection.Input;
    parmDNAME.Value = "IT";
    OracleParameter parmLOC =
        new OracleParameter("I_LOC", OracleType.VarChar, 13);
    parmLOC.Direction = ParameterDirection.Input;
    parmLOC.Value = "SAN JOSE";
    // Add the parameter objects to the Parameter's collection
    cmd.Parameters.Add(parmDEPTNO);
    cmd.Parameters.Add(parmDNAME);
    cmd.Parameters.Add(parmLOC);
    try
    {
        // Insert a row  transaction
```

```
        cmd.Prepare();
        cmd.ExecuteNonQuery();
        trans.Commit();
    }
    catch(Exception ex)
    {
        trans.Rollback();
        Cursor.Current = Cursors.Default;
        MessageBox.Show("Connection error: :" + ex.ToString());
    }
    finally
    {
        cn.Close();
    }
    Cursor.Current = Cursors.Default;
}
```

At the top of the OracleCommandTransaction subroutine, you can see where new instances of the OracleConnection and OracleCommand objects are created. Next, an instance of an OracleTransaction object named trans is instantiated. The database transaction is started by first opening the connection and then using the OracleConnection object's BeginTransaction method. Next, the cmd OracleComm and Transaction is assigned with the new OracleTransaction object named trans.

The next section of code sets up the parameterized SQL statement and its associated parameter objects. First, the OracleCommand object's CommandText property is assigned a SQL Insert statement. The important thing to note about this line is the use of the named parameters. Following the Oracle conventions, all of the parameter names begin with a colon. The next section of code creates three OracleParameter objects: parmDEPTNO, parmDNAME, and parmLOC. These OracleParameter objects are used to supply the input values to the parameterized Insert statement. In this example, the first parameter associated with the parmDEPTNO object is set to a value of 50. The second parameter represented by the parmDname object is set to a value of "IT". And the third parameter represented by the parmLOC OracleParameter object is assigned the value of "SAN JOSE". Then all of the OracleParameter objects are added to the Parameters collection of the OracleCommand object named cmd.

In the next section of code, a Try-Catch-Finally block is used to prepare the SQL statement and then execute the statement and commit the transactions to the database. The Prepare method parses the SQL statement and causes the database to create an execution plan. The ExecuteNonQuery method is then used to execute the Insert statement. At this point, the transaction can still be rolled back. The transaction is committed to the database using the OracleTransaction object's Commit method. If an error occurs, the code in the Catch block is executed. Within the Catch block, the transaction is first rolled back using the OracleTransaction object's Rollback method. Then a message box displays the error message to the end user. A Finally block is used to close the cn OracleConnection object. The Finally block is always executed, which in this case means that the Oracle connection is always closed at the end of the Try-Catch-Finally block.

Summary

The examples in this chapter illustrated how to use the OracleCommand object to execute SQL statements and stored procedures. The next chapter continues the discussion of the ADO.NET Command objects by illustrating how to use the OleDbCommand object.

Chapter 10

Using the
OleDbCommand Object

In this chapter, you'll learn how to use the OleDbCommand object to execute SQL commands on a target database. The first part of this chapter covers how to execute a simple SELECT statement using the visual OleDBCommand object that's supplied with Visual Studio.NET. Next, the chapter covers how to execute a stored procedure that returns output parameters. The chapter closes with a discussion of how to use the OleDbCommand object to commit and roll back transactions.

Executing SQL Statements and Stored Procedures Using the OleDbCommand Object

In the previous chapters, you saw numerous examples of issuing SQL commands and executing stored procedures using the SqlCommand object and the OracleCommand object. This chapter will focus on showing how to do these same types of database actions using the OleDbCommand object. Unlike the SqlCommand classes, which can only be used with SQL Server 7 and 2000 databases, the OleDbCommand classes can be used with Oracle and Access databases, in addition to all version of SQL Server. Both the SqlCommand and OleDbCommand objects are conceptually very similar, so the exact same code will not be presented in this section. Instead, this chapter will focus on presenting those aspects of using the OleDbCommand object that are different from the SqlCommand object, as well as bringing out areas of the various ADO.NET command functions that weren't presented in the previous section. First, the section will begin by presenting the basics of using the visual OleDbCommand component followed by the Namespace requirements that you need in order to use the OleDbCommand classes in your projects. Next, it will present examples of using stored procedures with output parameters, as well as transactions that take advantage of the new save point features.

Using the Visual Studio OleDbCommand Object

You can create a visual instance of the OleDbCommand object by dragging and dropping the OleDbCommand object from the Visual Studio.NET Data Design toolbar to the visual designer. A new OleDbCommand object like the one shown in Figure 10-1 will be added to your project.

Dragging and dropping the OleDbCommand component from the Data Design toolbox results in the creation of the OleDbCommand1 object that you can see near the bottom of Figure 10-1. The following VB.NET example shows how to use the OleDbCommand component to execute an ExecuteNonQuery command that creates a new table based on the columns from an existing table.

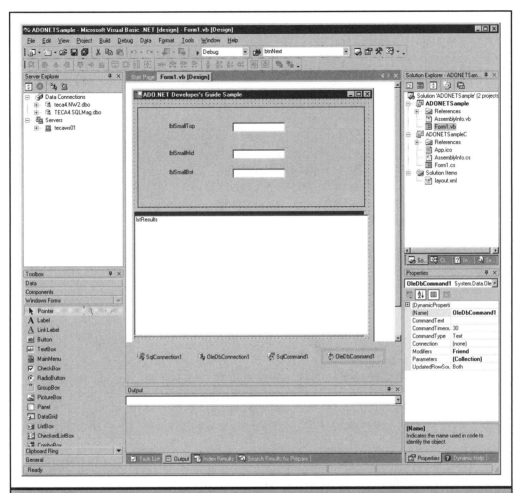

Figure 10-1. *Adding an OleDbCommand object in the VS.NET Designer*

```vb
Private Sub OLEDBCommandComponent(ByVal sServer As String, _
    ByVal sDB As String)
    OleDbConnection1.ConnectionString = _
        "PROVIDER=SQLOLEDB;SERVER=" & sServer & _
```

```
            ";TRUSTED_CONNECTION=Yes;DATABASE=" & sDB
        'Set up a query
        OleDbCommand1.CommandText = "SELECT LastName, FirstName " & _
            "INTO #EmployeeNames FROM Employees"
        ' Set the active connection
        OleDbCommand1.Connection = OleDbConnection1
        Try
            ' Open a connection and execute the command
            OleDbConnection1.Open()
            OleDbCommand1.ExecuteNonQuery()
            ' The reader can now be processed
        Catch ex As Exception
            MessageBox.Show("Connection error: :" & ex.ToString())
        End Try
        OleDbConnection1.Close()
    End Sub
```

Here is the C# version of the OLEDBCommandComponent subroutine:

```
private void OLEDBCommandComponent(string sServer, string sDB)
{
    oleDbConnection1.ConnectionString =
        "PROVIDER=SQLOLEDB;SERVER=" + sServer
        + ";TRUSTED_CONNECTION=Yes;DATABASE=" + sDB;
    // Set up a query
    oleDbCommand1.CommandText = "SELECT LastName, FirstName " +
        "INTO #EmployeeNames FROM Employees";
    // Set the active connection
    oleDbCommand1.Connection = oleDbConnection1;
    try
    {
        // Open a connection and execute the command
        oleDbConnection1.Open();
        oleDbCommand1.ExecuteNonQuery();
    }
    catch (Exception ex)
    {
        MessageBox.Show(ex.Message);
    }
    oleDbConnection1.Close();
}
```

Once the visual OleDBCommand component has been added to the Visual Studio .NET Design Window, using it is very much like using the standard OleDBCommand classes. In the preceding OLEDBCommandComponent routines, you can see where an OLE DB connection string is assigned to the ConnectionString property of the visual oleDbConnection1 object. Just like the class-based OleDbCommand objects, the visual OleDbCommand component requires an OleDbConnection object in order to connect to the data source. This can either be the visual OleDbConnection component, as is shown in this example, or it can be a code-based OleDbConnection object. Next, the OleDbCommand1 object's CommandText property is set to a valid SQL statement or to the name of a stored procedure. The preceding example illustrates using the Select Into statement that will create a temporary table named #EmployeeNames, which contains the FirstName and LastName column from the Employees table in the Northwind database. Then the oleDbCommand1 object's Connection property is set to the OleDbConnection object, and a Try-Catch block is used to actually open the database connection and execute the command. Because this command doesn't return a resultset, the ExecuteNonQuery method is used to send the command to the data source. Like the earlier examples, if an error occurs within the Try block, the code in the Catch block will display a message showing the exception message. The OleDbConneciton1 object is then closed at the end of the routine.

Adding the System.Data.OleDb Namespace

Using the ADO.NET OleDbCommand objects in code is only slightly harder than using the visual object in the Visual Studio.NET Designer. To use the classes in code requires only that you add an import directive for the OleDBClient Namespace and then manually instantiate the OleDbCommand objects. The payoff is better control over your development environment and more screen real estate. You can see how to add the System.Data.OleDb Namespace to your project in Chapter 6.

Executing Stored Procedures with Output Parameters

One of the most significant differences between the OleDbCommand object and the SqlCommand object is the way that they deal with parameters. The OleDbCommand object treats replaceable parameters in much the same way as ADO, where parameters are not named and each parameter marker is represented using the question mark character (?). This is quite different from either the SqlCommand command object or the OracleCommand object, which both require the use of named parameters. This makes creating the parameterized statement a bit easier using the OleDbCommand object. It uses the same coding techniques that you probably already know, and the actual statement creation is a bit more concise. However, there is a tradeoff. Being identified by name, SqlCommand parameters are not sensitive to the order in which they are added to the SqlCommand object. This makes it more robust because there is less chance of inadvertently attempting to pass incorrect data to a given parameter.

In the following example, you'll see how to use the OleDbCommand object to execute a stored procedure that provides returned data using output parameters:

```
Private Sub OLEDBCommandParms(ByVal sServer As String, _
        ByVal sDB As String)
    Dim cn As New OleDbConnection("PROVIDER=SQLOLEDB;SERVER=" _
        & sServer & ";DATABASE=" & sDB & ";TRUSTED_CONNECTION=Yes")
    ' Create the command object and set the SQL statement
    Dim cmd As New OleDbCommand _
        ("SELECT COUNT(*) FROM Orders WHERE EmployeeID = ?", cn)
    cmd.CommandType = CommandType.Text
    'Add the input parameter
    cmd.Parameters.Add("", OleDbType.Integer)
    cmd.Parameters(0).Direction = ParameterDirection.Input
    cmd.Parameters(0).Value = 2
    Try
        'Open the connection and execute the SQL
        cn.Open()
        txtMid.Text = cmd.ExecuteScalar()
    Catch ex As Exception
        MessageBox.Show("Connection error: :" & ex.ToString())
    End Try
    cn.Close()
End Sub
```

The C# version of the OLEDBCommandParms subroutine follows:

```
private void OLEDBCommandParms(string sServer, string sDB)
{
    OleDbConnection cn = new OleDbConnection
        ("PROVIDER=SQLOLEDB;SERVER=" + sServer + ";DATABASE="
        + sDB + ";TRUSTED_CONNECTION=Yes");
    // Create the command object and set the SQL statement
    OleDbCommand cmd = new OleDbCommand
        ("SELECT COUNT(*) FROM Orders WHERE EmployeeID = ?", cn);
    cmd.CommandType = CommandType.Text;
    // Add the input parameter
    cmd.Parameters.Add("", OleDbType.Integer);
    cmd.Parameters[0].Direction = ParameterDirection.Input;
    cmd.Parameters[0].Value = 2;
    try
    {
```

```
        cn.Open();
        txtMid.Text = cmd.ExecuteScalar().ToString();
    }
    catch (Exception ex)
    {
        MessageBox.Show(ex.Message);
    }
    cn.Close();
}
```

At the top of the OLEDBCommandParms subroutine, you can see where instances of the OleDbConnection and OleDbCommand objects are created. Two parameters are passed to the OleDbCommand constructor. The first parameter is a string that contains the SQL statement that will be executed, and the second parameter is used for the name of the OleDbConnection object that will be used to connect to the target data source.

 Using this overloaded version of the OleDbCommand constructor automatically assigns the value of the first parameter to the OleDbCommand object's CommandText property, and the value of the second parameter is assigned to the OleDbCommand object's Connection property.

You should pay particular attention to the formation of the parameterized SQL statement that's used in the first parameter. Unlike the parameterized SQL statements that were used in the earlier SqlCommand examples, replaceable parameters are represented to the OleDbCommand object using the question mark character (?). This particular SQL statement returns a single value that contains the number of orders from the Northwind database where the value in the EmployeeID column is equal to the value supplied to the OleDbCommand object at runtime. After the OleDbCommand object has been instantiated, the next line sets its CommandType property to CommandType .Text, indicating that a SQL statement is being used in the CommandText property.

The Parameter object is created in the next section of code. In this example, the Parameter object is created using the Add method of the OleDbCommand object's Parameters collection. Unlike SqlCommand objects, OleDbCommand objects do not need to be named. Here, the first parameter that's passed to the Add method is an empty string. Because this parameter object is not named, subsequent references to the parameter must be performed using the index value of the parameter. Like all other .NET arrays and collections, the OleDbCommand object's Parameters collection uses a zero-based index. Therefore, the index of the first element of the collection is 0. The second parameter of the Add method specifies the data type that will be used. In this case, the parameter is created as an Integer data type. Next the Parameter object's Direction property is set to

ParameterDirection.Input, specifying that this is an input parameter. The next line sets the value of the parameter to 2. The SQL statement will be evaluated using the value of 2 for EmployeeID 2.

The OleDbCommand object is executed within the following Try-Catch block. The ExecuteScalar method is used because the SQL statement is known to return a single value—the row count of the number of orders for EmployeeID 2. If either the Open method or the ExecuteScalar method throws an exception, the code in the Catch block will be executed and a message box will be displayed.

Executing Transactions

Executing database transactions using the OleDbCommand object is a lot like using the SqlCommand object that was shown earlier in the chapter. In the following example, you'll see how to use the OleDbCommand object to execute a transaction that consists of a parameterized INSERT statement that inserts rows into the Department table. (The SQL definition for the Department table was shown earlier in Chapter 8.) After the insert transaction has been completed, the Transaction object's Commit operation is used to commit the transaction to the database.

```
Private Sub OLEDBCommandTransaction(ByVal sServer As String, _
      ByVal sDB As String)
  Dim cn As New OleDbConnection("PROVIDER=SQLOLEDB;SERVER=" _
      & sServer & ";DATABASE=" & sDB & ";TRUSTED_CONNECTION=Yes")
  ' Create the command and transaction objects
  Dim cmd As New OleDbCommand()
  Dim trans As OleDbTransaction
  cmd.CommandText = "INSERT INTO Department VALUES(?,?)"
  'Create the input parameters
  Dim parmDepartmentID = _
      New OleDbParameter("@DepartmentID", OleDbType.Integer)
  parmDepartmentID.Direction = ParameterDirection.Input
  Dim parmDepartmentName = _
      New OleDbParameter("@DepartmentName", OleDbType.Char, 25)
  parmDepartmentName.Direction = ParameterDirection.Input
  ' Add the parameter objects to the Parameter's collection
  cmd.Parameters.Add(parmDepartmentID)
  cmd.Parameters.Add(parmDepartmentName)
  ' Start a local transaction
  cn.Open()
  trans = cn.BeginTransaction()
  cmd.Connection = cn
  cmd.Transaction = trans
```

```
    Try
        ' Insert a row  transaction
        parmDepartmentID.Value = 100
        parmDepartmentName.Value = "Transaction 100"
        cmd.ExecuteNonQuery()
        ' Commit the transaction
        trans.Commit()
    Catch e As Exception
        MsgBox(e.Message)
        trans.Rollback()
    Finally
        cn.Close()
    End Try
End Sub
```

Using C#, the OLEDBCommandTransaction subroutine is coded as you can see in the following listing:

```
private void OLEDBCommandTransaction(string sServer, string sDB)
{
    OleDbConnection cn = new OleDbConnection
        ("PROVIDER=SQLOLEDB;SERVER=" + sServer + ";DATABASE=" + sDB
        + ";TRUSTED_CONNECTION=Yes");
    // Create the command and transaction objects
    OleDbCommand cmd = new OleDbCommand();
    OleDbTransaction trans;
    cmd.CommandText = "INSERT INTO Department VALUES(?,?)";
    // Create the input parameters
    OleDbParameter parmDepartmentID =
        new OleDbParameter("@DepartmentID", OleDbType.Integer);
    parmDepartmentID.Direction = ParameterDirection.Input;
    OleDbParameter parmDepartmentName =
        new OleDbParameter("@DepartmentName", OleDbType.Char, 25);
    parmDepartmentName.Direction = ParameterDirection.Input;
    // Add the parameter objects Parameter's collection
    cmd.Parameters.Add(parmDepartmentID);
    cmd.Parameters.Add(parmDepartmentName);
    // Start a local transaction
    cn.Open();
    trans = cn.BeginTransaction();
    cmd.Connection = cn;
    cmd.Transaction = trans;
```

```
    try
    {
        // Insert a row  transaction
        parmDepartmentID.Value = 100;
        parmDepartmentName.Value = "Transaction 100";
        cmd.ExecuteNonQuery();
        // Commit the transaction
        trans.Commit();
    }
    catch (Exception ex)
    {
        MessageBox.Show(ex.Message);
        trans.Rollback();
    }
    finally
    {
        cn.Close();
    }
}
```

Like the earlier example, these subroutines begin by creating an instance of the OleDbConnection object and an OleDbCommand object. Next, to support transactions, an instance of the OleDbTransaction object named trans is created. Then the cmd OleDbCommand object's CommandText property is assigned a parameterized SQL INSERT statement. You should note that in this case the INSERT statement uses two parameters—one for each column in the Department table

The next section of code creates two OleDbParameter objects. The first object is named parmDepartmentID and the second object is named parmDepartmentName. The parmDepartmentID object is used to input an integer value that will be written to the DepartmentID column. The parmDepartmentName object is used to input a character value that will be written to the DepartmentName column.

Note   *Unlike the previous example, which created unnamed parameters using the Parameters collection's Add method, this example explicitly creates the OleDbParameter objects using the OleDbParameter classes' constructor. Using explicitly named parameter objects makes it easier to reference the objects in code and obviates the need to use an index in order to reference each object. Any time you have multiple parameters, using explicitly named objects is a good idea.*

After the two OleDbParameter objects are created, they need to be added to the OleDbCommand object's Parameters collection. Be sure that you add the OleDbParameter objects in the same order as they occur in the SQL statement. Next, the database connection is opened and then the cn OleDbConnection object's BeginTransaction method is used to start a new transaction. After the transaction has been started, a Try-Catch block is used to execute the parameterized INSERT statement. Within the Try block, the value of each replaceable parameter is set by assigning a value to the OleDbParameter object's Value property, and then the ExecuteNonQuery method is used to execute the SQL statement. If no exception is raised during the insert operation, the OleDbTransaction object's Commit method is used to commit the insert to the database. If an exception is thrown, the code in the Catch block will be executed, the error message will be displayed, and the RollBack method is used to undo the insert. Then a Finally block is used to close the connection. Note that the code in the Finally block is always executed no matter whether the Try operation generates an exception or completes successfully.

Summary

In this chapter, you saw several examples that illustrated how to execute commands using the OleDbCommand object. The examples in the first part of the chapter demonstrated how to use the visual OleDblCommand object to execute SQL statements and stored procedures. The next section showed you how to use positional parameters with the OleDbCommand object, and, finally, you saw how to execute transactions. The next chapter covers how to use the OdbcCommand object to execute SQL commands and stored procedures on ODBC-compliant databases.

Chapter 11

Using the
OdbcCommand Object

In this chapter, you'll see how to use the OdbcCommand object to execute SQL commands and stored procedures on an ODBC-compliant data source. In the first part of this chapter, you will learn how to execute a stored procedure using the visual OdbcCommand object that's provided with Visual Studio.NET. Next, you see how to execute a stored procedure that returns output parameters. The chapter closes with a discussion of how to use the OdbcCommand object to execute transactions.

Executing SQL Statements and Stored Procedures Using the OdbcCommand Object

The OdbcCommand object can be used to execute SQL statements and stored procedures on ODBC-compliant databases. Using the OdbcCommand object is conceptually similar to using the SqlCommand, OracleCommand, and OleDbCommand objects, but there are differences—especially regarding how you use the OdbcCommand object to execute stored procedures. The following section covers how to execute a simple stored procedure using the OdbcCommand object. Then, you'll see an example showing how to call a parameterized stored procedure using the OdbcCommand object. Finally, the chapter provides an example that shows how to execute transactions.

Using the Visual Studio OdbcCommand Object

You can create a visual instance of the OdbcCommand object by dragging and dropping the OdbcCommand object from the Visual Studio.NET Data Design toolbar to the visual designer. A new OdbcCommand object like the one shown in Figure 11-1 will be added to your project.

After the OdbcCommand object has been added to the Visual Studio.NET IDE, you can then use that object in your ADO.NET project. The following VB.NET example shows how to use the OdbcCommand component to execute a stored procedure and then how to use the OdbcDataReader to read through the result set returned by that stored procedure.

```
Private Sub ODBCCommandComponent()
    Cursor.Current = Cursors.WaitCursor
    OdbcConnection1.ConnectionString = "DSN=MyDSN"
    'Set up a query
    OdbcCommand1.CommandText = "{CALL[Ten Most Expensive Products]}"
    ' Set the active connection
    OdbcCommand1.Connection = OdbcConnection1
    OdbcCommand1.CommandType = CommandType.StoredProcedure
    Dim rdr As OdbcDataReader
    Try
```

```
      ' Open a connection and execute the command
      OdbcConnection1.Open()
      rdr = OdbcCommand1.ExecuteReader()
      Do While rdr.Read()
          Debug.WriteLine(rdr.GetString(0) & " " & _
              rdr.GetString(1))
      Loop
      rdr.Close()
      ' The reader can now be processed
    Catch ex As Exception
      Cursor.Current = Cursors.Default
      MessageBox.Show("Connection error: :" & ex.ToString())
    End Try
    OdbcConnection1.Close()
    Cursor.Current = Cursors.Default
End Sub
```

Here is the C# version of the ODBCCommandComponent subroutine:

```
private void ODBCCommandComponent()
{
    Cursor.Current = Cursors.WaitCursor;
    odbcConnection1.ConnectionString = "DSN=MyDSN";
    // Set up a query
    odbcCommand1.CommandText =
        "{CALL[Ten Most Expensive Products]}";
    // Set the active connection
    odbcCommand1.Connection = odbcConnection1;
    odbcCommand1.CommandType = CommandType.StoredProcedure;
    OdbcDataReader rdr;
    try
    {
        // Open a connection and execute the command
        odbcConnection1.Open();
        rdr = odbcCommand1.ExecuteReader();
        while (rdr.Read())
        {
            Debug.WriteLine(rdr.GetString(0) + " " +
                rdr.GetString(1));
        }
        rdr.Close();
```

```
    }
    catch (Exception ex)
    {
        Cursor.Current = Cursors.Default;
        MessageBox.Show(ex.Message);
    }
    Cursor.Current = Cursors.Default;
    odbcConnection1.Close();
}
```

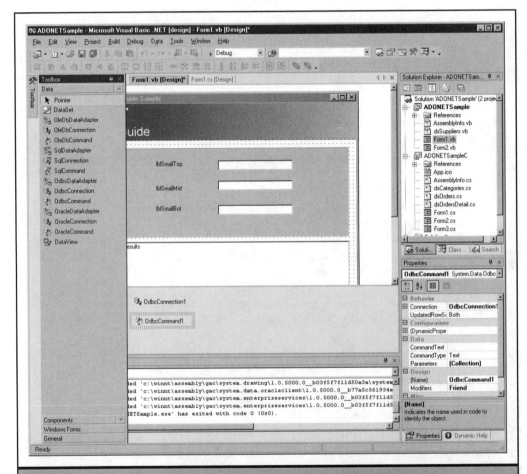

Figure 11-1. *Adding the OdbcCommand object in the VS.NET Designer*

After the visual OdbcCommand component has been added to the Visual Studio .NET Design Window, you use it almost exactly like you use the standard OdbcCommand classes. In the preceding subroutines, you can see where an ODBC connection string is assigned to the ConnectionString property of the visual OdbcConnection1 object. In this example, the ConnectionString uses a DSN named MyDSN to get the connection information for a SQL Server system. You can find the details of how this DSN was created in Chapter 7. Next, the OdbcCommand1 object's CommandText property is set to an ODBC string that will execute a stored procedure named Ten Most Expensive Products. Then the OdbcCommand1 object's Connection property is set to the visual OdbcConnection object that was also created previously in Chapter 7. Next, a Try-Catch block is used to open the database connection and execute the stored procedure. This command returns a resultset, so the ExecuteReader method is used to send the command to the ODBC-compliant database. Then a While loop is used to read through all of the results returned by the Ten Most Expensive Products stored procedure. If an error occurs within the Try block, the code in the Catch block will display the exception message. The OdbcConnection1 object is then closed at the end of the routine.

Adding the System.Data.ODBC Namespace

Before beginning to write code using the System.Data.Odbc classes, you should add an import directive for the System.Data.Odbc Namespace to your project. You can see the code required to add the System.Data.ODBC in Chapter 7.

Executing Dynamic SQL Statements

Like its name implies, you can use the OdbcCommand object to execute commands against ODBC-based data sources. In the following example, you'll see how to execute a dynamic SQL statement that creates a stored procedure using the OdbcCommand objects:

```
Private Sub ODBCCommand(ByVal sServer As String, _
        ByVal sDB As String)
    Dim cn As New OdbcConnection("DRIVER={SQL Server};SERVER=" _
        & sServer & ";DATABASE=" & sDB & ";TRUSTED_CONNECTION=yes")
    Dim cmd As New OdbcCommand()
    cmd.CommandType = CommandType.Text
    cmd.Connection = cn
    Try
        ' Open a connection
        cn.Open()
        'Set up a query
        cmd.CommandText = _
            "IF EXISTS (SELECT * FROM dbo.sysobjects " _
```

```
                        & "WHERE id = object_id(N'ProductStatus') " _
                        & "AND OBJECTPROPERTY(id, N'IsProcedure') = 1)" _
                        & "DROP PROCEDURE ProductStatus"
            ' Execute the command
            cmd.ExecuteNonQuery()
            cmd.CommandText = "CREATE PROCEDURE ProductStatus " _
                        & "(@ProductID int," _
                        & "@UnitsInStock int OUTPUT," _
                        & "@UnitsonOrder int OUTPUT) " _
                        & "AS " _
                        & "SELECT @UnitsInStock = UnitsInStock, " _
                        & "@UnitsOnOrder = UnitsOnOrder " _
                        & "FROM Products " _
                        & "WHERE ProductID = @ProductID " _
                        & "RETURN"
            ' Execute the command
            cmd.ExecuteNonQuery()
        Catch ex As Exception
            MessageBox.Show("Connection error: :" & ex.ToString())
        End Try
        cn.Close()
    End Sub
```

You can see the C# version of the ODBCCommand subroutine in the following listing:

```
private void ODBCCommand(string sServer, string sDB)
{
    OdbcConnection cn = new OdbcConnection
        ("DRIVER={SQL Server};SERVER=" + sServer
        + ";DATABASE=" + sDB + ";TRUSTED_CONNECTION=yes");
    OdbcCommand cmd = new OdbcCommand();
    cmd.CommandType = CommandType.Text;
    cmd.Connection = cn;
    try
    {
        // Open a connection
        cn.Open();
        // Set up a query
        cmd.CommandText =
            "IF EXISTS (SELECT * FROM dbo.sysobjects "
```

```
                + "WHERE id = object_id(N'ProductStatus') "
                + "AND OBJECTPROPERTY(id, N'IsProcedure') = 1)"
                + "DROP PROCEDURE ProductStatus";
        // Execute the command
        cmd.ExecuteNonQuery();
        cmd.CommandText =  "CREATE PROCEDURE ProductStatus "
                + "(@ProductID int,"
                + "@UnitsInStock int OUTPUT,"
                + "@UnitsonOrder int OUTPUT) "
                + "AS "
                + "SELECT @UnitsInStock = UnitsInStock, "
                + "@UnitsOnOrder = UnitsOnOrder "
                + "FROM Products "
                + "WHERE ProductID = @ProductID "
                + "RETURN";
        // Execute the command
        cmd.ExecuteNonQuery();
    }
    catch (Exception ex)
    {
        MessageBox.Show(ex.Message);
    }
    cn.Close();
}
```

In the beginning of the OdbcCommand subroutine, a new OdbcConnection object is created. This OdbcConnection object uses a DSN-less connection to attach to the target database. In this example, the DRIVER keyword is used to load the SQL Server ODBC driver, and the connection will use Windows security to authenticate to the database. Next, a new OdbcCommand object named cmd is created, and the CommandType is set to CommandText to indicate that a SQL command will be executed.

Next, a Try-Catch block is used to execute two SQL commands using the OdbcCommand object. The first SQL statement checks for the existence of a stored procedure named ProductStatus and drops that stored procedure if it is found. The OdbcCommand object's ExecuteNonQuery method is used to execute the command because there is no return data that needs to be brought back into the subroutine. Next, the CommandText property of the cmd OdbcCommand object is assigned a string that contains a SQL statement that will create the ProductStatus stored procedure. By examining the string, you can see that the ProductStatus stored procedure will accept three parameters—one input parameter and two output parameters. The input parameter is used to supply a ProductID code that will be used to query the Northwind products table. The two output parameters will return the total units in stock and units on order value for the specified product ID.

Again, the ExecuteNonQuery method is used to execute the command because there are no results that need to be returned by the statement. If an error occurs, a message box will be displayed by the Catch block.

Executing Stored Procedures with Output Parameters

The previous example created the ProductStatus stored procedure that used one input parameter and two output parameters. In this section, you'll see how to code an OdbcCommand object that will execute that stored procedure and retrieve the values that are returned in the two output parameters. The following ODBCSPParms subroutine presents the VB.NET code that uses the OdbcCommand object to execute the stored procedure and retrieve returned values:

```
Private Sub ODBCSPParms(ByVal sServer As String, _
    ByVal sDB As String)
  Dim cn As New OdbcConnection("DRIVER={SQL Server};SERVER=" _
    & sServer & ";DATABASE=" & sDB & ";TRUSTED_CONNECTION=yes")
  ' Create the command object and set the SQL statement
  Dim cmd As New OdbcCommand( _
      "{ CALL ProductStatus(?, ?, ?) }", cn)
  cmd.CommandType = CommandType.StoredProcedure
  'Add the input parameter
  Dim parmProductID = _
      New OdbcParameter("@ProductID", OdbcType.Int)
  parmProductID.Direction = ParameterDirection.Input
  parmProductID.Value = 1
  'Add the output parameters
  Dim parmUnitsInStock = _
      New OdbcParameter("@UnitsInStock", OdbcType.Int)
  parmUnitsInStock.Direction = ParameterDirection.Output
  Dim parmUnitsOnOrder = _
      New OdbcParameter("@UnitsOnOrder", OdbcType.Int)
  parmUnitsOnOrder.Direction = ParameterDirection.Output
  ' Add the parameter objects to the Parameters collection
  cmd.Parameters.Add(parmProductID)
  cmd.Parameters.Add(parmUnitsInStock)
  cmd.Parameters.Add(parmUnitsOnOrder)
  Try
      ' Open the connection and execute the command
      cn.Open()
      cmd.ExecuteNonQuery()
      ' Put the return values into text boxes
```

```
        txtMid.Text = parmUnitsInStock.Value
        txtBot.Text = parmUnitsOnOrder.Value
    Catch ex As Exception
        MessageBox.Show("Connection error: :" & ex.ToString())
    End Try
    cn.Close()
End Sub
```

The C# version of the ODBCSPParms subroutine is shown here:

```
private void ODBCSPParms(string sServer, string sDB)
{
    OdbcConnection cn = new OdbcConnection(
        "DRIVER={SQL Server};server=" + sServer
        + ";DATABASE=" + sDB + ";TRUSTED_CONNECTION=yes");
    OdbcCommand cmd = new OdbcCommand(
        "{ CALL ProductStatus(?, ?, ?) }", cn);
    cmd.CommandType = CommandType.StoredProcedure;
    // Add the input parameter
    OdbcParameter parmProductID =
        new OdbcParameter("@ProductID", OdbcType.Int);
    parmProductID.Direction = ParameterDirection.Input;
    parmProductID.Value = 1;
    // Add the output parameters
    OdbcParameter parmUnitsInStock =
        new OdbcParameter("@UnitsInStock", OdbcType.Int);
    parmUnitsInStock.Direction = ParameterDirection.Output;
    OdbcParameter parmUnitsOnOrder =
        new OdbcParameter("@UnitsOnOrder", OdbcType.Int);
    parmUnitsOnOrder.Direction = ParameterDirection.Output;
    // Add the parameter objects to the Parameters collection
    cmd.Parameters.Add(parmProductID);
    cmd.Parameters.Add(parmUnitsInStock);
    cmd.Parameters.Add(parmUnitsOnOrder);
    try
    {
        // Open the connection and execute the command
        cn.Open();
        cmd.ExecuteNonQuery();
        // Put the return values into text boxes
        txtMid.Text = parmUnitsInStock.Value.ToString();
```

```
            txtBot.Text = parmUnitsOnOrder.Value.ToString();
        }
        catch (Exception ex)
        {
            MessageBox.Show(ex.Message);
        }
        cn.Close();
    }
```

At the beginning of the ODBCSPParms subroutine, you can see where an instance of a new DSN-less OdbcConnection object is created, followed by an OdbcCommand object. In this example, the constructor for the OdbcCommand object uses two parameters. The first parameter is a string that contains the ODBC command that will be executed, and the second parameter contains the name of the OdbcCommand object that will be used to connect to the target data source.

Note *The OdbcCommand object executes stored procedures much differently than the SqlCommand and OleDbCommand objects. Whereas the SqlCommand and OleDbCommand objects allow you to just use the stored procedure name in the CommandText property, the OdbcCommand object requires that you use the older call style syntax where the ODBC CALL keyword is used prior to the name of the stored procedure. Any parameters are then passed within parentheses.*

After the OdbcCommand object is created, three OdbcParameter objects are created. The parmProductID object is an input parameter that's used to pass an integer value to the ProductStatus stored procedure. The parmUnitsInStock and parmUnitsOnOrder OdbcParameter objects are output parameters that are used to return the output values from the stored procedure to the ODBCSPParms subroutine. Once all of the OdbcParameter objects have been created, they are then all added to the cmd OdbcCommand object. Note that the parameter objects must be added in the same order as the parameter markers that they represent in the SQL statement.

Next, a Try-Catch structure is used to open the database connection and execute the SQL command. The ExecuteNonQuery method is used to execute the ProductStatus stored procedure because no resultset or return value is generated by the stored procedure. After the ExecuteNonQuery method successfully completes, the parmUnitsInStock and parmUnitsOnOrder OdbcParameter objects will contain the values returned by the stored procedure's output parameters. Those values are then assigned to two text boxes. If an error occurs, a message box will be displayed by the Catch block.

Executing Transactions

The OdbcCommand object also provides support for database transactions much like the SqlCommand and OleDbCommand objects. The following example shows how to use the OdbcCommand object to issue a database transaction that deletes a row from a table:

```
Private Sub ODBCCommandTransaction(ByVal sServer As String, _
    ByVal sDB As String)
    Dim cn As New OdbcConnection("DRIVER={SQL Server};SERVER=" _
        & sServer & ";DATABASE=" & sDB & ";TRUSTED_CONNECTION=yes")
    Dim cmd As New OdbcCommand()
    Dim trans As OdbcTransaction
    cmd.CommandText = _
        "DELETE FROM Department WHERE DepartmentID = ?"
    ' Create the parameter object and add it to the collection
    Dim parmDepartmentID = _
        New OdbcParameter("@DepartmentId", OdbcType.Int)
    parmDepartmentID.Direction = ParameterDirection.Input
    cmd.Parameters.Add(parmDepartmentID)
    ' Start a local transaction
    cn.Open()
    trans = cn.BeginTransaction()
    cmd.Connection = cn
    cmd.Transaction = trans
    Try
        ' Delete a row
        parmDepartmentID.Value = 100
        cmd.ExecuteNonQuery()
        ' Commit the transaction
        trans.Commit()
    Catch e As Exception
        MsgBox(e.Message)
        trans.Rollback()
    Finally
        cn.Close()
    End Try
End Sub
```

Written in C#, the ODBCCommandTransaction subroutine appears as follows:

```
private void ODBCCommandTransaction(string sServer, string sDB)
{
    OdbcConnection cn = new OdbcConnection
        ("DRIVER={SQL Server};SERVER=" + sServer
        + ";DATABASE=" + sDB + ";TRUSTED_CONNECTION=yes");
    OdbcCommand cmd = new OdbcCommand();
    OdbcTransaction trans;
    cmd.CommandText =
        "DELETE FROM Department WHERE DepartmentID =?";
    // Create the parameter object and add it to the collection
```

```
OdbcParameter parmDepartmentID =
    new OdbcParameter("@DepartmentId", OdbcType.Int);
parmDepartmentID.Direction = ParameterDirection.Input;
cmd.Parameters.Add(parmDepartmentID);
// Start a local transaction
cn.Open();
trans = cn.BeginTransaction();
cmd.Connection = cn;
cmd.Transaction = trans;
try
{
    // Delete a row
    parmDepartmentID.Value = 100;
    cmd.ExecuteNonQuery();
    // Commit the transaction
    trans.Commit();
}
catch (Exception ex)
{
    MessageBox.Show(ex.Message);
    trans.Rollback();
}
finally
{
    cn.Close();
}
```

The ODBCCommandTransaction subroutine shown in the preceding examples starts by creating OdbcConnection, OdbcCommand, and OdbcTransaction objects. When the OdbcCommand object is created, it is assigned a parameterized SQL DELETE statement that will delete a specific row from the Department table. In this example, the DELETE statement will delete the row where the value of the DepartmentId column is the same as the value that is supplied to the replaceable parameter of the SQL statement. Next, the OdbcParameter object representing the replaceable value is created and the OdbcParameter object is added to the OdbcCommand Parameters collection. Then the connection is opened and a database transaction is started. After the transaction is started, the Try-Catch block is set up to execute the transaction. Within the Try block, a value is assigned to the OdbcParameter object representing the input parameter. Then the SQL DELETE statement is executed and the transaction is committed. If an error occurred during the Delete operation, the code in the Catch block will display the error in a message box, and the transaction will be rolled back.

Summary

In this chapter, you saw several examples illustrating how to execute SQL commands and stored procedures using the OdbcCommand object. The examples in the first part of the chapter illustrated how to use the visual OdbcCommand object from the Visual Studio.NET IDE. The next examples illustrated how to create and call a parameterized stored procedure, as well as how to execute transactions. The next section of this book will go on to cover how to retrieve data using the ADO.NET Data Reader objects.

The
Complete
Reference

ADO.NET

Part IV

The ADO.NET DataReader Object

The Complete Reference

Chapter 12

Using the SqlDataReader

In this chapter, you'll see how to use the SqlDataReader to retrieve a stream of results from a target database. The first part of this chapter focuses on how to retrieve and manipulate a simple forward-only results stream. Here you learn how to access the different elements of the data stream returned from the SQL Server database. Next, you learn how you can use the SqlDataReader to retrieve multiple results. The chapter provides an example to demonstrate how you can retrieve the schema of the returned resultset. The chapter also provides an example to illustrate how to populate a DataSet using the results returned by SqlDataReader. Finally, this chapter illustrates how you can use the SqlDataReader to retrieve BLOB data.

Using the SqlDataReader

The DataReader is a unique entity in the ADO.NET Framework. While the rest of the ADO .NET Framework was explicitly designed to work in a disconnected model, the DataReader has been designed to work in a more traditional connected fashion. The DataReader essentially provides a fast forward-only stream of data that's sent from the database server to the application. Thanks to these qualities, this type of fast forward-only resultset is also known as a fire hose cursor. Unlike the much more feature-laden DataSet, the DataReader is a very lightweight, high-performance object. Also unlike the DataSet, the DataReader is one-way. In other words, it doesn't allow you to directly update the data that's retrieved. That doesn't mean that the data retrieved by the DataReader can't be changed: it can, but the DataReader doesn't have any built-in mechanisms that allow updating. To update the data retrieved by the DataReader, you would either need to execute SQL statements or stored procedures, or move the data into a DataSet. The DataReader is also created a bit differently than the other ADO.NET objects. While most of the other ADO.NET objects such as the Connection and Command objects can be instantiated using a constructor (for instance, when you use the New keyword), to create a DataReader, you must call the ExecuteReader method of the Command object. It's important to remember that while the DataReader is in use, it will monopolize the associated Connection object. No other operations can be performed using the Connection object (other than closing it) until the Close method of the DataReader is executed.

Adding the System.Data.SqlClient Namespace

Before using the SqlDataReader classes in your code, you should first add an import directive for the System.Data.SqlClient Namespace. This enables you to use the classes in the System.Data.SqlClient Namespace without having to prefix all of the class names with System.Data.SqlClient. Your code will be easier to write, and more readable to boot. You can see how to add an import directive for the System.Data.SqlClient Namespace in Chapter 4.

Retrieving a Fast Forward-Only Resultset
with the SqlDataReader

Retrieving a fast read-only stream of results from a SQL Server database is the SqlDataReader's primary purpose. Retrieving quick read-only subsets of data is one of the most common operations for a SQL Server database application, and the SqlDataReader is the best ADO.NET object for this task because it provides the best data read performance of any ADO.NET object and has minimal overhead. The SqlDataReader maintains a stately connection to the database from the time the query is started until the database has returned the result stream, which means that the SqlConnection object can't be used for anything else while the SqlDataReader is active. The following example illustrates the basic usage of the SqlDataReader. In this example, you'll see how to retrieve a basic read-only resultset from the SQL Server Northwind database and then process the individual data elements that comprise the result stream.

```vb
Private Sub SQLReaderForward(ByVal sServer As String, _
        ByVal sDB As String)
    Cursor.Current = Cursors.WaitCursor
    ' Setup the  connection and command
    Dim cn As New SqlConnection("SERVER=" & sServer _
        & ";INTEGRATED SECURITY=True;DATABASE=" & sDB)
    Dim cmd As New SqlCommand _
        ("SELECT CustomerID, CompanyName FROM Customers " _
        & "WHERE Country = 'USA'", cn)
    cmd.CommandType = CommandType.Text
    Dim rdr As SqlDataReader
    Try
        ' Open the connection and create the reader
        cn.Open()
        rdr = cmd.ExecuteReader(CommandBehavior.CloseConnection)
        ' Read the results and add them to a list box
        lstResults.Items.Clear()
        Do While rdr.Read()
            lstResults.Items.Add(rdr("CustomerID") & vbTab _
            & rdr.Item("CompanyName"))
        Loop
        rdr.Close()
    Catch e As Exception
        Cursor.Current = Cursors.Default
        MsgBox(e.Message)
    End Try
    cn.Close()
    Cursor.Current = Cursors.Default
End Sub
```

THE ADO.NET DATAREADER OBJECT

The C# version of the SQLReaderForward subroutine is as follows:

```csharp
private void SQLReaderForward(string sServer, string sDB)
{
    Cursor.Current = Cursors.WaitCursor;
    // Setup the connection and command
    SqlConnection cn = new SqlConnection("SERVER=" + sServer
        + ";INTEGRATED SECURITY=True;DATABASE=" + sDB);
    SqlCommand cmd = new SqlCommand
        ("Select CustomerID, CompanyName from Customers "
        + "where Country = 'USA'", cn);
    cmd.CommandType = CommandType.Text;
    SqlDataReader rdr;
    try
    {
        // Open the connection and create the reader
        cn.Open();
        rdr = cmd.ExecuteReader(CommandBehavior.CloseConnection);
        // Read the results and add them to a list box
        lstResults.Items.Clear();
        while (rdr.Read())
        {
            lstResults.Items.Add(rdr["CustomerID"].ToString() + '\t'
                + rdr["CompanyName"].ToString());
        }
        rdr.Close();
    }
    catch (Exception ex)
    {
        Cursor.Current = Cursors.Default;
        MessageBox.Show(ex.Message);
    }
    cn.Close();
    Cursor.Current = Cursors.Default;
}
```

In the beginning of the SQLReaderForward subroutine, a new SqlConnection object named cn is created that uses integrated security to attach to the target database. Next, a new SqlCommand object named cmd is created and the constructor sets the Command Property to a SQL Select statement that retrieves the value of the CustomerID and

CompanyName columns from the Customer Table in the Northwind database for all rows where the Country column is equal to USA. Because this is a SQL command, the CommandType is set to CommandText and then a new SqlDataReader named rdr is declared.

Note *At this point you can't use the SqlDataReader, because although the SqlDataReader object is declared, it has not been instantiated. The SqlDataReader is only instantiated after the SqlCommand object's ExecuteReader method has been called.*

Inside the Try block, the SqlConnection object's Open method is used to open a connection to the target database, and then the cmd SqlCommand object's ExecuteReader is used to instantiate the SqlDataReader. The SqlDataReader is then opened and ready to be used. You might notice that the ExecuteReader method uses CommandBehavior .CloseConnection enumeration, which automatically closes the connection when the SqlDataReader is closed. The CommandBehavior member provides the Command object a description of the results of the query and also influences the effects of the query on the database. Table 12-1 describes the available CommandBehavior options.

Next, a While loop is used to read the forward-only data stream returned by the SqlDataReader. Within the While loop, the two different data elements in the data stream are added to a list box named lstResults. In this example, each column in the resultset is accessed using a string that identifies the column name. In other words, rdr("CustomerID") is used to access the CustomerID column and rdr("CustomerName") is used to access the CompanyName column. Alternatively you could also access the column returned by the DataReader in a couple of other fashions. First, you could use each column's ordinal position rather than the column name. In this case, you could use rdr(0) and rdr(1). Using ordinals may execute a tiny bit faster, but the price you pay in code readability isn't worth the minuscule performance difference. Next, each of the columns in the resultset returned by the SqlDataReader could also have been accessed using the rdr.GetInt32(0) and rdr .GetString(1) methods. The main difference between these options is that when you reference the DataReader columns directly using the named columns, you get back the native .NET Data Provider data type types. Using GetInt32, GetString, or other similar data access methods returns the .NET Framework data type. An error is thrown if the data doesn't match the data type expected by the method. In addition, GetString, GetInt32, and the other data access methods only accept ordinal values, and they can't be used with string identifiers. You should note that in all of these cases, each column must be accessed in the order it appears in the resultset. You cannot access the columns out of order because the DataReader provides one-way streams of results to the client application. After all of the results have been retrieved, the rdr.Read method returns the value of False and the While loop is terminated. Then the rdr.Close method is used to close the SqlDataReader. Because the CommandBehavior.CloseConnection flag was used earlier by the ExecuteReader method, the connection to the SQL Server database is also closed.

THE ADO.NET
DATAREADER OBJECT

CommandBehavior	Description
CloseConnection	The associated Connection object is closed when the DataReader object is closed.
Default	No options are set. This is equivalent to calling ExecuteReader().
KeyInfo	The query returns column and primary key information. This flag causes the SQL Server .NET Data Provider to append a FOR BROWSE clause to the statement being executed.
SchemaOnly	The query only returns column metadata and does not return a resultset.
SequentialAccess	This flag is used to handle access to BLOB (Binary Large Objects). When this option is used, the DataReader loads data as a stream rather than loading the entire row. The GetBytes or GetChars methods can then be used to read the data buffer that's returned.
SingleResult	The query is restricted to returning a single resultset.
SingleRow	The query is expected to return a single row. Using the SingleRow flag with the ExecuteReader method of the OleDbCommand object causes the object to perform single row binding using the OLE DB IRow interface. Otherwise, the OLE DB .NET Provider will perform binding using the IRowset interface.

Table 12-1. *ExecuteReader CommandBehavior Enumeration*

Note

Explicitly closing all of the ADO.NET objects is especially important because unlike ADO, the objects aren't destroyed when they go out of scope. Instead, they are destroyed when the .NET Garbage collector decides to remove them. However, closing the DataReader is particularly important because the connection can't be used for anything else until the DataReader is closed.

The code in the Catch block is executed if an error occurs while either opening the connection or using the SqlDataReader. In this case, the exception message will be

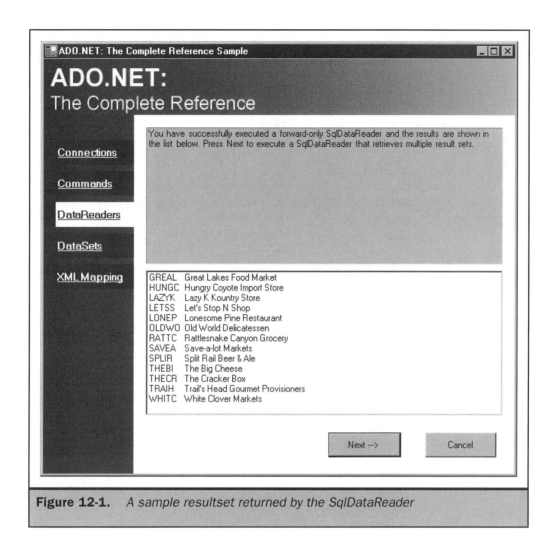

Figure 12-1.   *A sample resultset returned by the SqlDataReader*

captured and displayed in a message box. You can see the results of the SQLReaderForward subroutine in Figure 12-1.

Returning Multiple Resultsets

While the DataReader is limited in that it provides only a forward-only, read-only resultset, it is most certainly not limited to returning a single resultset. The DataReader can easily handle multiple resultsets returned either by a stored procedure or by executing multiple SQL statements as part of a batch. In the next example, you'll see how to

execute multiple SQL Select statements using the SqlDataReader and how to process
the different resultsets that are returned.

```vb
Private Sub SQLReaderMultipleRS(ByVal sServer As String, _
        ByVal sDB As String)
    Cursor.Current = Cursors.WaitCursor
    Dim cn As New SqlConnection("SERVER=" & sServer _
        & ";INTEGRATED SECURITY=True;DATABASE=" & sDB)
    Dim cmd As New SqlCommand _
        ("SELECT CategoryID, CategoryName FROM Categories;" _
        & "SELECT ProductID, ProductName FROM Products", cn)
    Try
        ' Open the connection and create the reader
        cn.Open()
        Dim rdr As SqlDataReader = cmd.ExecuteReader()
        ' Loop through all the result sets
        lstResults.Items.Clear()
        Dim bMoreResults As Boolean = True
        Do Until Not bMoreResults
            lstResults.Items.Add(rdr.GetName(0) & vbTab & _
                    rdr.GetName(1))
                Do While rdr.Read()
                    lstResults.Items.Add(rdr.GetInt32(0) & _
                        vbTab & rdr.GetString(1))
                Loop
            bMoreResults = rdr.NextResult()
        Loop
        rdr.Close()
    Catch e As Exception
        Cursor.Current = Cursors.Default
        MsgBox(e.Message)
    End Try
    cn.Close()
    Cursor.Current = Cursors.Default
End Sub
```

The SQLReaderMultipleRS subroutine written in C# is as follows:

```csharp
private void SQLReaderMultipleRS(string sServer, string sDB)
{
    Cursor.Current = Cursors.WaitCursor;
    // Create the connection and command
```

```
SqlConnection cn = new SqlConnection("SERVER=" + sServer
    + ";INTEGRATED SECURITY=True;DATABASE=" + sDB);
SqlCommand cmd = new SqlCommand(
    "SELECT CategoryID, CategoryName FROM Categories;"
    + "SELECT ProductID, ProductName FROM Products", cn);
cmd.CommandType = CommandType.Text;
SqlDataReader rdr;
try
{
    // Open the connection and create the reader
    cn.Open();
    rdr = cmd.ExecuteReader(CommandBehavior.CloseConnection);
    // Loop through all the result sets
    lstResults.Items.Clear();
    bool bMoreResults = true;
    while (bMoreResults)
    {
        lstResults.Items.Add(rdr.GetName(0) + '\t' +
            rdr.GetName(1));
        while (rdr.Read())
        {
            lstResults.Items.Add(rdr.GetInt32(0) + '\t' +
                rdr.GetString(1));
        }
        bMoreResults = rdr.NextResult();
    }
    rdr.Close();
}
catch (Exception ex)
{
    Cursor.Current = Cursors.Default;
    MessageBox.Show(ex.Message);
}
cn.Close();
Cursor.Current = Cursors.Default;
}
```

THE ADO.NET
DATAREADER OBJECT

As in the previous example, the SQLReaderMultipleRS subroutine begins by creating a new SqlConnection object named cn and a new SqlCommand object named cmd. The primary thing to note about the SqlCommand object in this example is that the SqlCommand constructor sets the Command Property to multiple SQL SELECT statements where each statement is separated by a semicolon. The first SELECT statement retrieves the CategoryID and CategoryName columns from the Categories table. The second SQL SELECT statement retrieves the ProductID and ProductName from the Products table. Both of these tables are from the SQL Server Northwind database. Because this SqlCommand object will be executing SQL statements, the CommandType is set to CommandText. Then a new SqlDataReader named rdr is declared.

The resultsets returned by the SqlDataReader are processed in the Try block. If an error occurs within the Try block, the code in the Catch block is executed and a message box appears. Inside the Try block, the SqlConnection object is opened and then the SqlCommand object's ExecuteReader method is used to create the rdr SqlDataReader object. Next, a While loop is set up to process each of the different resultsets. Before the While loop is entered, a Boolean variable named bMoreResults is declared and assigned a value of True, ensuring that the While loop will be executed at least one time. This variable is used to track the availability of additional resultsets.

The first action that occurs within the While loop is writing the column names to the lstResults list box. Notice that the SqlDataReader's GetName function is used with the ordinal position of each column to retrieve the column names. A tab character is added between the names to allow the entries to be lined up neatly in the list box. The data stream that's returned by the rdr SqlDataReader is processed using another nested While loop. In this case, the nested While loop continues to be executed until all of the data has been read in the current resultset and the Read method returns a value of False. Within the inner While loop, the data values returned by the SqlDataReader are added to the lstResults list box with a tab character between each value. In this example, the rdr.GetInt32 method is used to retrieve the value of the first column, which is an integer value, while the rdr.GetString method is used to retrieve the character data contained in the second column.

| Note | *In the preceding code, the use of ordinals allowed more generic code to be employed because the same code could be used to process the different columns returned in each of the different resultsets. It's important to note that the data types returned are the same, which allows this routine to work.* |

After all of the data has been retrieved from the first resultset, the second While loop is exited and the SqlDataReader's NextResult method is used to assign a value to the bMoreResults variable. If another resultset is available, the NextResult method returns a value of True and the outer While loop is processed again. Otherwise, if no more resultsets are available, the NextResults method returns a value of False and the While loop is exited. You can see the results of the SQLReaderMultipleRS subroutine in Figure 12-2.

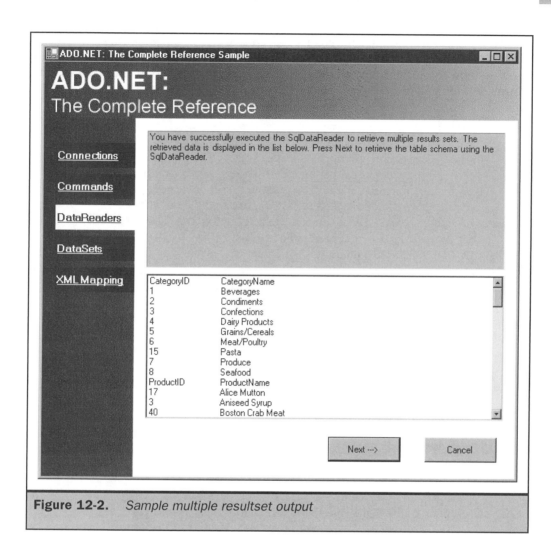

Figure 12-2.   *Sample multiple resultset output*

Reading Schema-Only Information

The previous examples illustrated how to retrieve the data and basic column headings using the SqlDataReader. However, the SqlDataReader can also retrieve more-detailed table schema information. The metadata returned can help you determine how to process the columns that are returned by the DataReader. The column schema information returned includes the column name and its data type, as well as other information such as whether the column can accept null values. The following SQLReaderSchema subroutine illustrates how to use the SqlDataReader's GetTableSchema method to return the schema information for a given query.

```vb
Private Sub SQLReaderSchema(ByVal sServer As String, _
        ByVal sDB As String)
    Cursor.Current = Cursors.WaitCursor
    ' Setup the  connection and command
    Dim cn As New SqlConnection("SERVER=" & sServer _
        & ";INTEGRATED SECURITY=True;DATABASE=" & sDB)
    Dim cmd As New SqlCommand("SELECT * FROM Customers", cn)
    cmd.CommandType = CommandType.Text
    Dim rdr As SqlDataReader
    Try
        ' Open the connection and create the reader
        cn.Open()
        rdr = cmd.ExecuteReader(CommandBehavior.SchemaOnly)
        ' bind the returned DataTable to the grid & close
        grdResults.SetDataBinding(rdr.GetSchemaTable(), "")
        rdr.Close()
    Catch e As Exception
        Cursor.Current = Cursors.Default
        MsgBox(e.Message)
    End Try
    cn.Close()
    Cursor.Current = Cursors.Default
End Sub
```

The C# version of the SQLReaderSchema subroutine is as follows:

```csharp
private void SQLReaderSchema(string sServer, string sDB)
{
    Cursor.Current = Cursors.WaitCursor;
    // Setup the connection and command
    SqlConnection cn = new SqlConnection("SERVER=" + sServer
        + ";INTEGRATED SECURITY=True;DATABASE=" + sDB);
    SqlCommand cmd = new SqlCommand("SELECT * FROM Customers "
        + "WHERE Country = 'USA'", cn);
    cmd.CommandType = CommandType.Text;
    SqlDataReader rdr;
```

```
try
{
    // Open the connection and create the reader
    cn.Open();
    rdr = cmd.ExecuteReader(CommandBehavior.SchemaOnly);
    // bind the returned DataTable to the grid & close
    grdResults.SetDataBinding(rdr.GetSchemaTable(), "");
    rdr.Close();
}
catch (Exception ex)
{
    Cursor.Current = Cursors.Default;
    MessageBox.Show(ex.Message);
}
Cursor.Current = Cursors.Default;
cn.Close();
}
```

As in the previous examples, the SQLReaderSchema subroutine begins by creating a new SqlConnection object named cn and a new SqlCommand object named cmd. In this case, the SqlCommand object contains a SQL SELECT statement that retrieves all of the columns from the Customers table. You might note that because this example doesn't actually retrieve any data, it's okay to use an unqualified query such as this. However, if this were a production query you would make sure to specify the exact columns and rows that your application needed. Next, the CommandText property is set to CommandType .Text and a SqlDataReader object named rdr is declared.

Next, a Try block is used to open the connection and execute the SqlDataReader. If an error occurs inside the Try block, the code in the Catch block is executed and a message box appears. It's important to note that the cmd SqlCommand object's ExecuteReader method uses the CommandBehavior.SchemaOnly enumeration to specify that only schema metadata should be returned by the SqlDataReader and that no data will be returned to the calling application. You should also note the use of the rdr SqlDataReader's GetSchemaTable method to actually retrieve the metadata for the query. The GetTableSchema method returns a DataTable object, which is then bound to the DataGrid named grdResults using the grid's SetDataBinding method. For more information on creating and using the DataTable object, refer to Chapter 16. You can see the returned results in Figure 12-3.

Note *While this example illustrates retrieving the column metadata information from a single table, the DataReader's GetTableSchema method works just as well with the results of multiple table joins.*

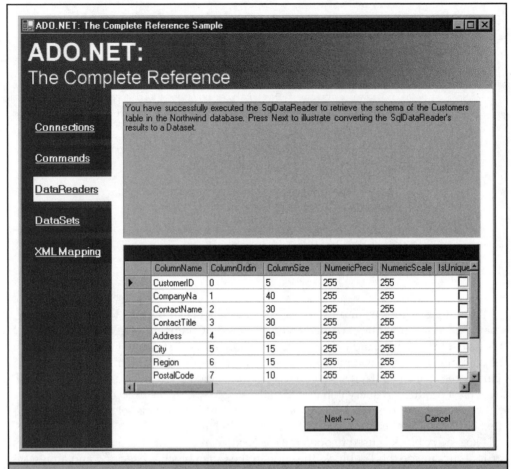

Figure 12-3. *Table schema information returned by the SqlDataReader's GetTableSchema method*

Populating a DataSet from the SqlDataReader

The previous examples illustrate how to process multiple results returned by a DataReader, as well as how to use the DataReader to retrieve column metadata information. The next example combines and extends both of those techniques by illustrating how you can convert the results returned by a DataReader into a DataSet. Certainly, the most straightforward method of doing this is to populate the DataSet using the DataAdapter, as described in Chapters 17–20. However, there are scenarios for which you want the application to run as efficiently as possible by utilizing the fast forward-only result stream supplied by the DataReader, and you don't want to incur the additional overhead of the DataSet. Even so, either you still may need to conditionally update the data returned, or you may need to conditionally display the data in different order or perform some other action on the results that can be supported by the DataSet but not the DataReader. To accommodate these types of scenarios, you'll need to be able to convert the results returned by the DataReader into a DataSet. The following SqlReaderDataSet subroutine shows how to do exactly that by combining several of the techniques presented earlier in this chapter. You can see the code for the SqlReaderDataSet subroutine in the listings that follow.

```
Private Sub SQLReaderDataSet(ByVal sServer As String, _
        ByVal sDB As String)
    Cursor.Current = Cursors.WaitCursor
    Dim cn As New SqlConnection("SERVER=" & sServer _
        & ";INTEGRATED SECURITY=True;DATABASE=" & sDB)
    Dim cmd As New SqlCommand( _
        "SELECT * FROM Customers WHERE Country = 'USA';" _
        & "SELECT * FROM Orders WHERE ShipCountry = 'USA';" _
        & "SELECT * FROM Suppliers WHERE Country = 'USA'", cn)
    Dim rdr As SqlDataReader
    Dim ds As New DataSet()
    Try
        cn.Open()
        rdr = cmd.ExecuteReader()
        Dim bMoreResults As Boolean = True
        Do Until Not bMoreResults
            ' Create new data table
            Dim dtSchemaTable As DataTable = rdr.GetSchemaTable()
            Dim dtData As New DataTable()
            Dim i As Integer
            For i = 0 To dtSchemaTable.Rows.Count - 1
                Dim dr = dtSchemaTable.Rows(i)
                ' Create a unique column name in the data table
                Dim columnName As String = dr("ColumnName")
                ' Add the column definition to the data table
                Dim dc As New DataColumn(columnName, dr.GetType)
                dtData.Columns.Add(dc)
            Next i
            ds.Tables.Add(dtData)
            ' Fill the data table
            While rdr.Read()
                Dim dr = dtData.NewRow()
                For i = 0 To rdr.FieldCount - 1
                    dr(i) = rdr.GetValue(i)
                Next i
                dtData.Rows.Add(dr)
            End While
```

```
                ' Get the next result set
                bMoreResults = rdr.NextResult()
            Loop
            grdResults.DataSource = ds
        Catch e As Exception
            Cursor.Current = Cursors.Default
            MsgBox(e.Message)
        End Try
        rdr.Close()
        cn.Close()
        Cursor.Current = Cursors.Default
    End Sub
```

You can see the C# version of the SQLReaderDataSet subroutine in the listing that follows:

```csharp
private void SQLReaderDataSet(string sServer, string sDB)
{
    Cursor.Current = Cursors.WaitCursor;
    // Create the connection and command
    SqlConnection cn = new SqlConnection("SERVER=" + sServer
        + ";INTEGRATED SECURITY=True;DATABASE=" + sDB);
    SqlCommand cmd = new SqlCommand(
        "SELECT * FROM Customers WHERE Country = 'USA';"
        + "SELECT * FROM Orders WHERE ShipCountry = 'USA';"
        + "SELECT * FROM Suppliers WHERE Country = 'USA'", cn);
    cmd.CommandType = CommandType.Text;
    SqlDataReader rdr;
    DataSet ds = new DataSet();
    try
    {
        // Open the connection and create the reader
        cn.Open();
        rdr = cmd.ExecuteReader(CommandBehavior.CloseConnection);
        // Loop through all the result sets
        bool bMoreResults = true;
        while (bMoreResults)
        {
            //' Create new data table
            DataTable dtSchemaTable = rdr.GetSchemaTable();
            DataTable dtData = new DataTable();
            int i;
            for (i = 0; i < dtSchemaTable.Rows.Count; i++)
            {
```

```
            DataRow dr = dtSchemaTable.Rows[i];
            // Create a unique column name in the data table
            string columnName = dr["ColumnName"].ToString();
            // Add the column definition to the data table
            DataColumn dc = new DataColumn(columnName,
                dr.GetType());
            dtData.Columns.Add(dc);
        }
        ds.Tables.Add(dtData);
        // Fill the data table
        while (rdr.Read())
        {
            DataRow dr = dtData.NewRow();
            for( i = 0; i < rdr.FieldCount; i++)
            {
                dr[i] = rdr.GetValue(i);
            }
            dtData.Rows.Add(dr);
        }
        // Get the next result set
        bMoreResults = rdr.NextResult();
    }
    rdr.Close();
    grdResults.DataSource = ds;
}
catch (Exception ex)
{
    Cursor.Current = Cursors.Default;
    MessageBox.Show(ex.Message);
}
cn.Close();
Cursor.Current = Cursors.Default;
}
```

THE ADO.NET
DATAREADER OBJECT

In the preceding code, you can see that the SQLReaderDataSet subroutine begins by creating a new SqlConnection object named cn and a new SqlCommand object named cmd. The most important thing to note about the SqlCommand object in this example is that the SqlCommand constructor sets the Command property to three different SQL SELECT statements. As you saw in the earlier example showing multiple resultsets, each SQL statement is separated by a semicolon. In this example, the first SELECT statement retrieves all of the columns from the Customers table where the Country column is equal to the value of USA. The second SQL SELECT statement retrieves all of the columns from the Orders table where the ShipCountry column is equal to the value of USA. Last, the third SQL SELECT statement retrieves all of the columns from the Suppliers table where the Country column is equal to the value of USA. All of these tables are from the SQL Server Northwind example database. Next, the SqlCommand object's CommandType property is set to CommandType.Text. Then a new SqlDataReader named rdr is declared and the new DataSet named ds is instantiated.

Next, a Try block is used to open the connection and execute the SqlDataReader. If an error occurs inside the Try block, the code contained in the Catch block is executed and a message box showing the exception message appears. Inside the Try block, the SqlConnection object is opened and the SqlCommand object's ExecuteReader method is used to instantiate the SqlDataReader object. Next, a Boolean variable named bMoreResults is declared and assigned a value of True. This variable is used to control the processing of the following While loop, which is used to process each of the different resultsets. The first action that occurs within the inner While loop is the use of the rdr SqlDataReader's GetSchemaTable method to retrieve the metadata for the query. The GetTableSchema method returns a DataTable object that is named dtSchemaTable. As its name suggests, this DataTable object is used to capture the metadata of the columns returned by the SqlDataReader. Next, a second DataTable named dtData is created. The dtData DataTable object will be built with DataColumns based on the names and types of the column metadata recorded in the dtSchemaTable. Then the dtData DataTable will be populated using the data returned by the SqlDataReader.

After the DataTable containing the column schema has been created and a new DataTable that will contain the data itself has been created, a For-Next loop is used to parse the dtSchemaTable. The For-Next loop processes each of the rows in the dtSchemaTable DataTable. Each row of the dtSchemaDataTable contains the definition of a column that was returned by the DataReader. Within the For-Next loop, as each row is read from the dtSchemaTable DataTable, a DataColumn object named dc is added to the dtDataTable. The name of the column returned by the DataReader is retrieved using the dr("ColumnName") property while the data type of the new DataColumn is retrieved using the dr.GetType method. After the attributes of the new DataColumn have been defined, the Add method of the dtDataTable's Columns collection adds the new DataRow to the dtData DataTable. When the For-Next loop has completed, all of the schema will have been set up for the dtDataTable, at which point it is added to the ds DataSet's Tables collection using the Add method.

Once the dtData DataTable's schema has been set up, the table can then be populated, and that's exactly what the following While loop does. The While loop will be executed until all of the data has been returned from the rdr SqlDataReader object and the rdr object's Read method returns a value of False. Inside the While loop, a new DataRow object named dr is created for every row read in by the SqlDataReader. Then a For-Next loop is used to parse the column data that's in the row returned by the rdr SqlDataReader object. The For-Next loop executes once for every column in the returned resultset, which is determined by checking the rdr.FieldCount property. Within the For-Next loop, the value of each column is retrieved using the SqlDataReader's GetValue method. The GetValue method uses the integer value of i to identify the index of each column in the resultset. The data value retrieved by the GetValue method is then assigned to the column in the dr DataRow object that is likewise identified by the integer i. After all of the data values have been copied from the column in the rdr SqlDataReader to the dr DataRow object, the DataRow object is then added to the dtData DataTables object's Rows collection using the Add method.

When all of the results have been retrieved from the resultset, the rdr SqlDataReader's NextResult property is assigned to the bMoreResults variable, which is then checked to determine if multiple resultsets are being returned. In the preceding example, if you look back to where the cmd SqlCommand object is instantiated at the top of this routine, you can see that this process is repeated three times, once for each of the resultsets returned by the three SELECT statements. After all of the resultsets have been processed, the rdr SqlDataReader object's Close method is used to close the SqlDataReader and the DataSet is bound to a DataGrid named grdResults, which will be displayed to the end user. You can see the output of the SQLReaderDataSet subroutine shown in Figure 12-4.

More information about creating and using DataSets is presented in Chapter 16.

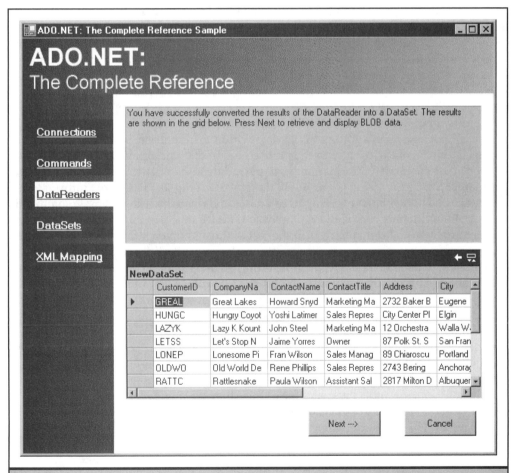

Figure 12-4.   *Sample DataSet created from the DataReader*

Retrieving BLOB Data Using the SqlDataReader

The previous examples illustrated how to retrieve resultsets that are comprised of standard character and numeric data. However, it's common for modern databases to also contain large binary objects, more commonly referred to as BLOBs (Binary Large Objects). BLOBs are typically graphical images such as product and employee photos contained in .bmp, .jpg or .tif files. They can also be small sound bytes like .wav files or MP3s. Although these are some of the common types of data files that are stored as BLOBs in the database, the BLOB storage provided by most modern databases such as SQL Server, Oracle, and UDB can accommodate all kinds of objects including Microsoft Word documents, PowerPoint presentations, standard executable files (.EXEs) and even XML documents. Although the database is fully capable of storing BLOB data, the potential size of these objects means that they must be accessed and managed differently than standard text and numeric data types. SQL Server uses three different data types for BLOB storage: Text, nText, and Image. The Text and nText data types can be used to store variable-length text data. The Text data type can accommodate up to 2GB of non-Unicode text data while the nText data can accommodate up to 1GB of Unicode text data. The Image data type is undoubtedly the most versatile of the SQL Server BLOB storage types. The Image data type can store up to 2GB of binary data, which also enables it to store standard text data. In this section, you'll see how to retrieve BLOB data from a SQL Server database using the SqlDataReader.

Before jumping directly into the code, it's worth briefly exploring the advantages and disadvantages of integrating BLOB data within the database. Storing these types of objects in the database along with the more common text and numeric data enables you to keep all of the related information for a given database entity together. This enables easy searching and retrieval of the BLOB data by querying its related text information. For instance, you can retrieve an employee's name and photo by using a simple command such as SELECT name, photo FROM Employee WHERE Id = 1. In this scenario, the photo information is stored right along with the rest of the employee information and can be retrieved in much the same way. The common alternative to this is storing the binary files outside of the database and then including a file path or URL to the object within the database. This separate storage method has a couple of advantages. It is somewhat easier to program for and it does allow your databases to be smaller because they don't include the binary objects, which can be quite large. However, you must manually create and maintain some type of link between the database and external system files, which can easily become out of sync. Next, some type of unique naming scheme for the OS files is usually required to keep the potentially hundreds or even thousands of files separate. Storing the BLOB data within the database eliminates these problems.

The following example illustrates how to use the SqlDataReader to retrieve the photo images stored in the Northwind Categories table. As you'll see, using the SqlDataReader to retrieve BLOB data is similar to retrieving character and number data but there are some important differences. The main difference is the use of the CommandBehavior .SequentialAccess access flag on the Command object ExecuteReader method. As you saw in an earlier example, the DataReader is always instantiated by calling the

ExecuteReader method, and the CommandBehavior flag influences how the database will send information to the DataReader. When you specify SequentialAccess, it changes the default behavior of the DataReader in a couple of ways. First, you are not required to read from the columns in the order they are returned. In other words, you can jump ahead to an offset in the data stream. However, once your application has read past a location in the returned stream of data, it can no longer read anything prior to its current location. Next the CommandBehavior.SequentialAccess flag turns off the DataReader's normal buffering mode where the DataReader always returns one row at a time and, instead, results are streamed back to the application. Because this subroutine writes data to the file system, you need to import the .NET System.IO Namespace into your application to enable access to the file system. To import the System.IO Namespace, you need to add the following code to your projects:

```
Imports System.IO
```

For a C# project, you need to add an import directive for the System.IO Namespace as follows:

```
using System.IO;
```

Note *While the native 16-color bitmap images that are stored in the Picture column of the Categories table in the Northwind database can be retrieved by the SqlDataReader, unfortunately they cannot be displayed by the .NET controls. In order to display these images in the .NET Label control, the image first needed to be edited using Access, and then saved as a 256-color bitmap and reimported to the database.*

The following SQLReaderBLOB subroutine illustrates how to retrieve BLOB data from the SQL Server database. You can find more information on inserting BLOB data in Chapter 29.

```
Private Sub SQLReaderBLOB(ByVal sServer As String, _
        ByVal sDB As String)
    Dim cn As New SqlConnection("SERVER=" & sServer _
        & ";INTEGRATED SECURITY=True;DATABASE=" & sDB)
    Dim cmd As SqlCommand = New SqlCommand( _
        "SELECT Picture FROM Categories WHERE CategoryId = 1", cn)
    ' Declare object to write to a file
    Dim fs As FileStream
    Dim bw As BinaryWriter
    ' Set up byte array
    Dim iBufferSize As Integer = 1000
```

```
Dim bBLOBStorage(iBufferSize - 1) As Byte
Dim lRetval As Long
Dim lStartIndex As Long = 0
Dim sOutputFileName As String
sOutputFileName = "tempExportBLOBFile"
Cursor.Current = System.Windows.Forms.Cursors.WaitCursor
' Open the file for writing
fs = New FileStream( _
    sOutputFileName, FileMode.OpenOrCreate, FileAccess.Write)
bw = New BinaryWriter(fs)
Dim rdr As SqlDataReader
Try
    ' Open the connection and read data into the DataReader.
    cn.Open()
    rdr = cmd.ExecuteReader(CommandBehavior.SequentialAccess)
    ' Write BLOB chunks to file
    Do While rdr.Read()
        ' Reset the starting byte
        lStartIndex = 0
        ' Read bytes into bBLOBStorage
        lRetval = rdr.GetBytes(0, lStartIndex, bBLOBStorage, _
            0, iBufferSize)
        ' Continue reading and writing while there are
        ' bytes beyond the size of the buffer.
        Do While lRetval = iBufferSize
            bw.Write(bBLOBStorage)
            bw.Flush()
            ' Reposition the start index to the end of the
            ' last buffer and fill the buffer.
            lStartIndex = lStartIndex + iBufferSize
            lRetval = rdr.GetBytes( _
                0, lStartIndex, bBLOBStorage, 0, iBufferSize)
        Loop
        ' Write the remaining buffer.
        bw.Write(bBLOBStorage)
        bw.Flush()
        ' Close the output file.
        bw.Close()
        fs.Close()
    Loop
    rdr.Close()
    ' Set image to Label
    lblBigBot.Image = Image.FromFile("tempExportBLOBFile")
Catch e As Exception
```

```
        MsgBox(e.Message)
    Finally
        ' Close  the connection.
        cn.Close()
        Cursor.Current = Cursors.Default
    End Try
End Sub
```

The C# version of the SQLReaderBLOB subroutine is shown here:

```
private void SQLReaderBLOB(string sServer, string sDB)
{
    Cursor.Current = Cursors.WaitCursor;
    // Create the  connection and command
    SqlConnection cn = new SqlConnection("SERVER=" + sServer
        + ";INTEGRATED SECURITY=True;DATABASE=" + sDB);
    SqlCommand cmd = new SqlCommand(
        "SELECT Picture FROM Categories WHERE CategoryId = 1", cn);
    // Declare object to write to a file
    FileStream fs;
    BinaryWriter bw;
    // Setup byte array
    int iBufferSize = 1000;
    byte[] bBLOBStorage;
    bBLOBStorage = new byte[iBufferSize];
    long lRetval;
    long lStartIndex = 0;
    string sOutputFileName;
    sOutputFileName = "tempExportBLOBFile";
    Cursor.Current = System.Windows.Forms.Cursors.WaitCursor;
    // Open the file for writing
    fs = new FileStream(
        sOutputFileName, FileMode.OpenOrCreate, FileAccess.Write);
    bw = new BinaryWriter(fs);
    SqlDataReader rdr;
    try
    {
        // Open the connection and read data into the DataReader.
        cn.Open();
        rdr = cmd.ExecuteReader(CommandBehavior.SequentialAccess);
        // Write BLOB chunks to file
        while(rdr.Read())
        {
```

```
            // Reset the starting byte
            lStartIndex = 0;
            // Read bytes into bBLOBStorage
            lRetval = rdr.GetBytes(
                0, lStartIndex, bBLOBStorage, 0, iBufferSize);
            // Continue reading and writing while there are
            //  bytes beyond the size of the buffer.
            while(lRetval == iBufferSize)
            {
                bw.Write(bBLOBStorage);
                bw.Flush();
                // Reposition the start index to the end of the
                //  last buffer and fill the buffer.
                lStartIndex = lStartIndex + iBufferSize;
                lRetval = rdr.GetBytes(
                    0, lStartIndex, bBLOBStorage, 0, iBufferSize);
            }
            // Write the remaining buffer.
            bw.Write(bBLOBStorage);
            bw.Flush();
            // Close the output file.
            bw.Close();
            fs.Close();
        }
        rdr.Close();
        lblBigBot.Image = Image.FromFile("tempExportBLOBFile");
    }
    catch (Exception ex)
    {
        MessageBox.Show(ex.Message);
    }
    finally
    {
        cn.Close();
        Cursor.Current = Cursors.Default;
    }
}
```

The SQLReaderBLOB subroutine begins by creating a new SqlConnection object named cn and a new SqlCommand object named cmd. Here, the SqlCommand object contains a SQL SELECT statement that retrieves the Picture column from the Categories table in the Northwind database where the value of CategoryID is equal to 1.

Because the purpose of this subroutine is to export the contents of a BLOB column to the file system, this subroutine needs a mechanism capable of writing binary files and that is precisely what the fs FileStream and bw BinaryWriter objects do. The fs FileStream object is created by passing three parameters to the FileStream's constructor. The first parameter specifies the filename. The second parameter uses the FileMode enumerator of FileMode.OpenOrCreate to specify that if the file already exists it will be opened; otherwise a new file will be created. The third parameter uses the FileAccess.Write enumerator to indicate that the file will be opened for writing, thereby allowing the subroutine to write binary data to the file. Next, a BinaryWriter object named bw is created and attached to the fs FileStream object.

Next, a new SqlDataReader named rdr is declared and then a Try block is used to open the connection and execute the SqlDataReader. If an error occurs inside the Try block, the code in the Catch block is executed and a message box appears. In this example, the most important point to notice is that the ExecuteReader's CommandBehavior .SequentialAccess option is used to enable streaming access to BLOB data. Then a While loop is used to read the data that's returned by the query associated with the SQLCommand object, which in this case will be the contents of the Picture column. While this example retrieved only a single Image column, for the sake of simplicity there's no restriction on mixing Image columns and character and numeric data in the same resultset. Inside the While loop, the code basically reads a chunk of binary data from the Image column and writes them a chunk at a time to the bw BinaryWriter object. The lStartIndex variable tracks the offset of data that marks that spot where the binary data will be read. Then the rdr SqlDataReader's GetBytes method is used to actually read the data from the DataReader. The first parameter of the GetBytes method specifies the index value of the column in the resultset. In this example, there's only a single column, so the value of this parameter is set at 0. The second parameter specifies the offset from the beginning of the data stream where the GetBytes method will begin retrieving data. The third parameter is a byte array named bBLOBStorage that will store the binary data returned by the GetByte method. The fourth parameter indicates the offset in the column to begin reading the data. Last, the fifth parameter of the GetByte method specifies the number of bytes that will be retrieved by the GetBytes method. If the number of bytes specified in the fifth parameter exceeds the available size of the buffer identified in the third parameter, then an exception is thrown. The While loop continues writing the binary data from the rdr SqlDataReader to the bBLOBStorage array until the lRetval variable is equal to the iBuffersize, which indicates that all of the data from the SqlDataReader has been read. Next, the BinaryWriter's Write method is called to write the last chunk of binary data to the file system. The Flush method is called to ensure that all of the data will be cleared from the bw BinaryWriter's internal buffer and written out to disk. Then the bw BinaryWriter and the associated fs FileStream objects are closed.

After all of the data has been returned from the SqlDataReader, the outer While loop is ended and the SqlDataReader is closed using the Close method. The tempExportBLOBFile that was created is then read in from disk using the Image class's FromFile method and assigned to the Image property of a Label control. You can see the results of the SQLReaderBLOB subroutine in Figure 12-5.

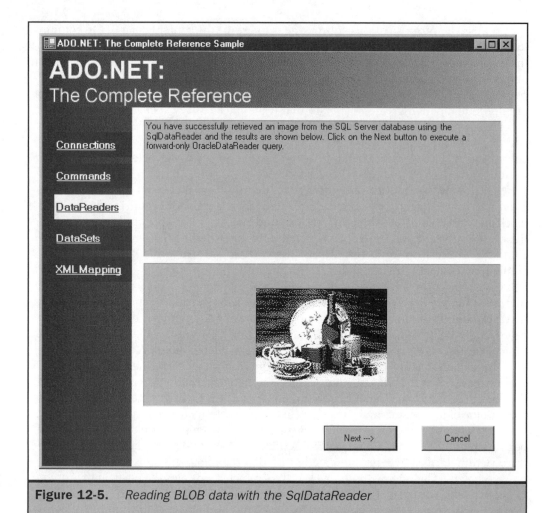

Figure 12-5. *Reading BLOB data with the SqlDataReader*

Summary

In this chapter you saw several examples that illustrated how to retrieve resultsets from a SQL Server database using the SqlDataReader object. The next chapter tackles the OracleDataReader object and demonstrates how you can use ADO.NET to retrieve data from an Oracle database.

Chapter 13

Using the OracleDataReader

In this chapter, you will see how to use the ADO.NET OracleDataReader to retrieve a stream of results from an Oracle database. The first part of this chapter covers how to retrieve a simple fast forward-only results stream. Next, the chapter covers how to use the OracleDataReader to retrieve a resultset from an Oracle package that uses Ref Cursor as an output parameter. Then the chapter goes on to illustrate how to use the OracleDataReader to process the results from multiple Oracle Ref Cursors.

Using the OracleDataReader

The OracleDataReader provides a fast forward-only stream of data that's sent from the Oracle server to the application. Unlike the heavier-weight DataSet, the OracleDataReader works in a connected fashion, keeping a connection open to the target database until all of the results returned have been read. The OracleDataReader itself provides a read-only mechanism. In order to update the data retrieved by the OracleDataReader you either need to execute SQL statements using the OracleCommand object, or move the data into a DataSet. Unlike the other ADO.NET objects such as OracleConnection and OracleCommand, the OracleDataReader is not instantiated using the New keyword. Instead, the OracleDataReader is created by calling the ExecuteReader method of the OracleCommand object. One important difference between the OracleDataReader and the SqlDataReader is that the OracleDataReader allows multiple OracleDataReader objects to be opened simultaneously.

Adding the System.Data.OracleClient Namespace

Before using the OracleDataReader classes in your code, you should first add an Import directive for the System.Data.OracleClient Namespace. This allows you to use the classes in the System.Data.OracleClient Namespace without needing to prefix all of the class names with System.Data.OracleClient. Your code will be both easier to write and more readable to boot. You can see the specific code to import the System.Data .OracleClient Namespace in Chapter 5.

Retrieving a Fast Forward-Only Resultset with the OracleDataReader

Retrieving read-only subsets of data is one of the most common operations for a database application and the OracleDataReader provides the best data read performance of any ADO.NET object. The OracleDataReader maintains an open connection to the database from the time the OracleDataReader is first opened until the database has returned the result stream. The following example illustrates the basic usage of the OracleDataReader. Here you'll see how to retrieve a forward-only, read-only resultset that's based on a simple join between the EMP and DEPT tables in the Oracle sample Scott database.

```vb
Private Sub OracleReaderForward(ByVal sServer As String, _
      ByVal sUser As String, ByVal sPassword As String)
    Cursor.Current = Cursors.WaitCursor
    ' Setup the  connection and command
    Dim cn As New OracleConnection("DATA SOURCE=" & sServer _
        & ";UID=" & sUser & ";PWD=" & sPassword)
    Dim cmd As New OracleCommand(
        "SELECT EMPNO, ENAME, LOC FROM EMP " _
        & "INNER JOIN DEPT ON EMP.DEPTNO = DEPT.DEPTNO", cn)
    cmd.CommandType = CommandType.Text
    Dim rdr As OracleDataReader
    Try
        ' Open the connection and create the reader
        cn.Open()
        rdr = cmd.ExecuteReader()
        lstResults.Items.Clear()
        lstResults.Items.Add(rdr.GetName(0) & vbTab _
            & rdr.GetName(1) & vbTab & rdr.GetName(2))
        Do While rdr.Read()
            lstResults.Items.Add(rdr("EMPNO") & vbTab _
            & rdr("ENAME") & vbTab & rdr("LOC"))
        Loop
        rdr.Close()
    Catch e As Exception
        Cursor.Current = Cursors.Default
        MsgBox(e.Message)
    End Try
    cn.Close()
    Cursor.Current = Cursors.Default
End Sub
```

The C# version of the OracleReaderForward subroutine is as follows:

```csharp
private void OracleReaderForward(string sServer, string sUser,
    string sPassword)
{
    Cursor.Current = Cursors.WaitCursor;
    // Setup the connection and command
    OracleConnection cn = new OracleConnection("DATA SOURCE="
        + sServer + ";UID=" + sUser + ";PWD=" + sPassword);
    OracleCommand cmd = new OracleCommand(
        "SELECT EMPNO, ENAME, LOC FROM EMP "
```

THE ADO.NET
DATAREADER OBJECT

```
            + "INNER JOIN DEPT ON EMP.DEPTNO = DEPT.DEPTNO", cn);
    cmd.CommandType = CommandType.Text;
    OracleDataReader rdr;
    try
    {
        // Open the connection and create the reader
        cn.Open();
        rdr = cmd.ExecuteReader();
        lstResults.Items.Clear();
        lstResults.Items.Add(rdr.GetName(0) + '\t'
            + rdr.GetName(1) + '\t' + rdr.GetName(2));
        while (rdr.Read())
        {
            lstResults.Items.Add(rdr.GetValue(0).ToString() + '\t'
            + rdr.GetValue(1).ToString() + '\t'
            + rdr.GetValue(2).ToString());
        }
        rdr.Close();
    }
    catch (Exception ex)
    {
        Cursor.Current = Cursors.Default;
        MessageBox.Show(ex.Message);
    }
    cn.Close();
    Cursor.Current = Cursors.Default;
}
```

At the top of the OracleReaderForward subroutine, a new OracleConnection object named cn is instantiated. Then a new OracleCommand object named cmd is created. The OracleCommand object's constructor sets the Command property to a SQL Select statement that retrieves the EMPNO, ENAME, and LOC columns from the EMP and DEPT tables in the Scott database. Next, the CommandType is set to CommandText to indicate that the OracleCommand object will be used to execute a SQL statement. Then a new OracleDataReader named rdr is declared.

Next, a Try-Catch block is used to open a connection to the target Oracle server, and then the OracleCommand object's ExecuteReader is used to instantiate the OracleDataReader named rdr. At this point, the OracleDataReader is opened but the Read method must be called before there is any data available to the application. A list box named lstResults is cleared, and then the column names of each of the columns returned in the results are added to the first line in the list box by calling the OracleDataReader object's GetName method. In this example, the GetName method uses ordinals to identify each of the columns in the resultset. Next, a While loop is used to read the data stream returned by the OracleDataReader. Within the While loop, each column in the resultset is accessed using the GetValue method in conjunction with the ordinal value that identifies the column. In other words, the rdr.GetValue(0) method retrieves the value in the EMPNO column, the rdrGetValue(1) method is used to access the ENAME column, and the GetValue(2) method is used to retrieve the value in the LOC column. You should note that in all of these cases, each column must be accessed in the order it appears in the resultset. You cannot access the columns out of order because the OracleDataReader provides a one-way stream of results to the client application. After all of the results have been retrieved, the rdr.Read method returns the value of False, the While loop is terminated, and then the rdr.Close method is used to close the OracleDataReader.

Note   *While this example accessed the column data using ordinals, you could also access the data returned by the OracleDataReader in a couple of other ways. For example, you could use the column names [for example, rdr.Item(("EMPNO")] or you could access the data using OracleDataReader's typed data access methods [for example, rdr.GetOracleNumber(0)]. The main difference between these options is that when you reference the OracleDataReader columns directly using the named columns, you get back the native .NET Data Provider data type types.*

The code in the Catch block is executed if an error occurs while opening the connection or reading results using the OracleDataReader. Here, if an error is encountered, the exception message will be captured and displayed in a message box. Finally, at the end of the routine, the cn OracleConnection object is closed. You can see the results of the OracleReaderForward subroutine in Figure 13-1.

Retrieving Data Using an Oracle Ref Cursor

A Ref Cursor is a database feature that's unique to the Oracle database system. It is a special type of output parameter and, as its name implies, it is a reference to a cursor on the Oracle database. From the ADO.NET application developer's standpoint, you use Ref Cursors very much like a standard resultset. In this section, you'll see how to use Oracle's Ref Cursor feature with the OracleDataReader.

Ref Cursors are defined in an Oracle stored procedure or package. Oracle packages are essentially database objects that allow you to group together logically related procedures. The following example PL/SQL code illustrates how to create an Oracle package that contains two procedures that both use Ref Cursors as parameters. The first procedure, GetEmpAboveSal, returns a list of employees from the Scott schema who have salaries above a specified amount. The second procedure, GetDeptAndEmp, returns two parameters that are both Ref Cursors. This section shows you the basics of working with Ref Cursors by illustrating how to retrieve data from the GetEmpAboveSal procedure. You'll see how to use multiple Ref Cursors in the next section.

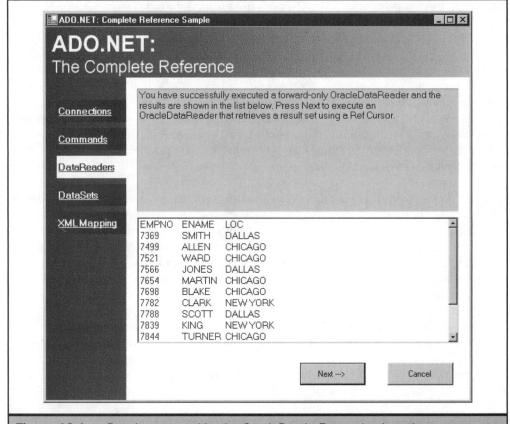

Figure 13-1. *Results returned by the OracleReaderForward subroutine*

```
CREATE OR REPLACE PACKAGE EMP_PKG AS
    TYPE cur is REF CURSOR;
    PROCEDURE GetEmpAboveSal(i_sal IN NUMBER, o_emplist OUT cur);
    PROCEDURE GetDeptAndEmp(o_dept OUT cur, o_emp OUT cur);
END EMP_PKG;
CREATE OR REPLACE PACKAGE BODY EMP_PKG AS
    PROCEDURE GetEmpAboveSal(i_sal IN NUMBER, o_emplist OUT cur)
    IS
    BEGIN
        OPEN o_emplist FOR
            SELECT EMPNO, ENAME, MGR FROM EMP
            WHERE SAL > i_sal
            ORDER BY ENAME;
    END GetEmpAboveSal;
```

```
        PROCEDURE GetDeptAndEmp(o_dept OUT cur, o_emp OUT cur)
        IS
        BEGIN
          OPEN o_dept FOR SELECT * FROM DEPT;
          OPEN o_emp FOR SELECT * FROM EMP;
        END GetDeptAndEmp;
     END EMP_PKG;
```

In the preceding EMP_PKG Oracle package, three declarations are made in the package header. First, a Ref Cursor named cur is declared, and then the GetEmpAboveSal and the GetDeptAndEmp procedures are declared. The GetEmpAboveSal procedure uses one input parameter, an Oracle Number type that specifies a given salary level, and one output parameter, an Oracle Ref Cursor that returns a list of employee data. The GetDeptAndEmp procedure contains only two output parameters—both Ref Cursor types that return a list of department and employee information, respectively. You can see the logic for each of these procedures in the package body. In the GetEmpAboveSal procedure, a Select statement returns only those rows in which the contents of the SAL column is greater than the i_sal input parameter. The GetDeptAndEmp procedure returns all of the rows and columns from both the Dept and Emp tables in the Oracle Scott schema.

Now that you've seen how the Oracle Ref Cursor is declared, in the following code listing you'll see how to call the GetEmpAboveSal procedure in the Oracle package and access the data returned in the Ref Cursor parameter.

```
Private Sub OracleReaderRefCursor(ByVal sServer As String, _
        ByVal sUser As String, ByVal sPassword As String)
    Cursor.Current = Cursors.WaitCursor
    ' Create the command and connection
    Dim cn As New OracleConnection("DATA SOURCE=" & sServer _
        & ";UID=" & sUser & ";PWD=" & sPassword)
    Dim cmd As New OracleCommand("EMP_PKG.GetEmpAboveSal", cn)
    cmd.CommandType = CommandType.StoredProcedure
    Dim parmSAL = New OracleParameter("i_sal", OracleType.Number)
    parmSAL.Direction = ParameterDirection.Input
    parmSAL.Value = 1000
    Dim parmCURSOR = New OracleParameter("o_emplist", _
        OracleType.Cursor)
    parmCURSOR.Direction = ParameterDirection.Output
    cmd.Parameters.Add(parmSAL)
    cmd.Parameters.Add(parmCURSOR)
    Dim rdr As OracleDataReader
    Try
        ' Open the connection and create the reader
        cn.Open()
```

```
            rdr = cmd.ExecuteReader()
            lstResults.Items.Clear()
            lstResults.Items.Add(rdr.GetName(0) & vbTab _
                & rdr.GetName(1) & vbTab & rdr.GetName(2))
            Do While rdr.Read()
                lstResults.Items.Add(rdr.Item(0) & vbTab _
                & rdr.Item(1) & vbTab & rdr.Item(2))
            Loop
            rdr.Close()
        Catch e As Exception
            Cursor.Current = Cursors.Default
            MsgBox(e.Message)
        End Try
        cn.Close()
        Cursor.Current = Cursors.Default
    End Sub
```

The C# version of the OracleReaderRefCursor subroutine is as follows:

```
private void OracleReaderRefCursor(string sServer, string sUser,
        string sPassword)
{
    Cursor.Current = Cursors.WaitCursor;
    // Create the command and connection
    OracleConnection cn = new OracleConnection("DATA SOURCE="
        + sServer + ";UID=" + sUser + ";PWD=" + sPassword);
    OracleCommand cmd = new OracleCommand(
        "EMP_PKG.GetEmpAboveSal", cn);
    cmd.CommandType = CommandType.StoredProcedure;
    OracleParameter parmSAL = new OracleParameter("i_sal",
        OracleType.Number);
    parmSAL.Direction = ParameterDirection.Input;
    parmSAL.Value = 1000;
    OracleParameter parmCURSOR = new OracleParameter("o_emplist",
        OracleType.Cursor);
    parmCURSOR.Direction = ParameterDirection.Output;
    cmd.Parameters.Add(parmSAL);
    cmd.Parameters.Add(parmCURSOR);
    OracleDataReader rdr;
    try
    {
        // Open the connection and create the reader
        cn.Open();
```

```
            rdr = cmd.ExecuteReader();
            lstResults.Items.Clear();
            lstResults.Items.Add(rdr.GetName(0) + '\t'
                + rdr.GetName(1) + '\t' + rdr.GetName(2));
            while (rdr.Read())
                lstResults.Items.Add(rdr.GetValue(0).ToString() + '\t'
                    + rdr.GetValue(1).ToString() + '\t'
                    + rdr.GetValue(2).ToString());
            rdr.Close();
        }
        catch (Exception ex)
        {
            Cursor.Current = Cursors.Default;
            MessageBox.Show(ex.Message);
        }
        cn.Close();
        Cursor.Current = Cursors.Default;
    }
```

The OracleReaderRefCursor subroutine begins by creating a new OracleConnection object named cn followed by an OracleCommand object named cmd. The OracleCommand object contains the qualified name of the package and stored procedure that will be executed. Here, you can see that the GetEmpAboveSal procedure in the EMP_PKG will be called. Then the cmd OracleCommand object's CommandType property is set to the CommandType.StoredProcedure. Next, two OracleParameter objects are created. The first OracleParameter object, parmSQL, is an input parameter of the OracleNumber data type. The value of this parameter is then set to 1000. The second OracleParameter object, parmCURSOR, is an output parameter and its type is set to OracleTypeCursor—indicating that it will be used for a Ref Cursor. After both the OracleParameter objects have been created, they are then added to the Parameter's collection of the OracleCommand object named cmd.

Next, an OracleDataReader named rdr is declared, and then a Try-Catch block is used to open the connection to the Oracle database server. If an error occurs inside the Try block, the code in the Catch block is executed and a message box appears. Within the Try block, the OracleCommand object's ExecuteReader method is used to execute the GetEmpAboveSal procedure. Next, the lstResult list box is cleared and the column names in the resultset are added to the first row in the list box. Each name is separated using the tab character. Then a While loop is used to read the data that's returned in the Ref Cursor parameter. Here the contents of the first three columns—identified by the ordinal numbers 0, 1, and 2—are written to the lstResults list box. After all of the data has been returned, the OracleDataReader is closed using the Close method. Finally, the cn OracleConnection object is closed. You can see the results of the OracleReaderRefCursor subroutine in Figure 13-2.

THE ADO.NET
DATAREADER OBJECT

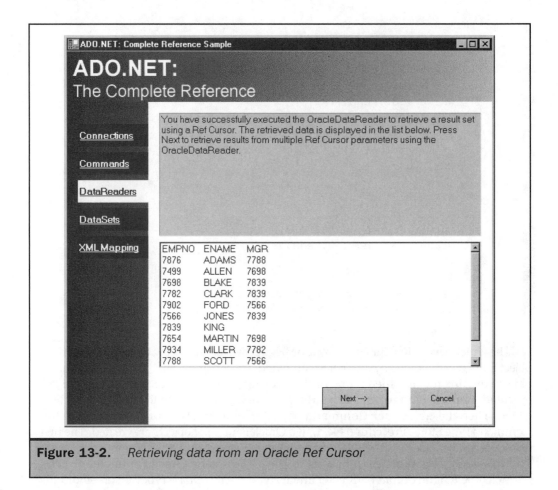

Figure 13-2. *Retrieving data from an Oracle Ref Cursor*

Retrieving Data from Multiple Ref Cursors

In the previous example, you saw the basics of dealing with an Oracle Ref Cursor using the OracleDataReader. This example picks up where that one leaves off by illustrating how you can use the OracleDataReader to retrieve data from multiple Ref Cursor parameters. In the following example, you'll see how to execute the GetDeptAndEmp Oracle package, which was defined in the previous section. This package returns two Oracle Ref Cursor parameters. The following OracleReaderMultiRefCursor subroutine executes that Oracle package and processes the two different resultsets that are returned in each Ref Cursor parameter.

```
Private Sub OracleReaderMultiRefCursor(ByVal sServer As String, _
        ByVal sUser As String, ByVal sPassword As String)
    Cursor.Current = Cursors.WaitCursor
    ' Create the command and connection
    Dim cn As New OracleConnection("DATA SOURCE=" & sServer _
        & ";UID=" & sUser & ";PWD=" & sPassword)
    Dim cmd As New OracleCommand("EMP_PKG.GetDeptAndEmp", cn)
    cmd.CommandType = CommandType.StoredProcedure
    Dim parmDEPT = New OracleParameter("o_dept", OracleType.Cursor)
    parmDEPT.Direction = ParameterDirection.Output
    Dim parmEMP = New OracleParameter("o_emp", OracleType.Cursor)
    parmEMP.Direction = ParameterDirection.Output
    cmd.Parameters.Add(parmDEPT)
    cmd.Parameters.Add(parmEMP)
    Dim rdr As OracleDataReader
    Try
        ' Open the connection and create the reader
        cn.Open()
        rdr = cmd.ExecuteReader()
        lstResults.Items.Clear()
        lstResults.Items.Add(rdr.GetName(0) & vbTab _
            & rdr.GetName(1))
        Do While rdr.Read()
            lstResults.Items.Add(rdr.Item(0) & vbTab _
                & rdr.Item(1))
        Loop
        rdr.NextResult()
        lstResults.Items.Add(rdr.GetName(0) & vbTab _
            & rdr.GetName(1) & vbTab & rdr.GetName(2))
        Do While rdr.Read()
            lstResults.Items.Add(rdr.Item(0) & vbTab _
                & rdr.Item(1) & vbTab & rdr.Item(2))
        Loop
        rdr.Close()
    Catch e As Exception
        Cursor.Current = Cursors.Default
        MsgBox(e.Message)
    End Try
    cn.Close()
    Cursor.Current = Cursors.Default
End Sub
```

The C# version of the OracleReaderMultiRefCursor subroutine is as follows:

```csharp
private void OracleReaderMultiRefCursor(string sServer,
    string sUser, string sPassword)
{
    Cursor.Current = Cursors.WaitCursor;
    // Create the command and connection
    OracleConnection cn = new OracleConnection("DATA SOURCE="
        + sServer + ";UID=" + sUser + ";PWD=" + sPassword);
    OracleCommand cmd = new OracleCommand(
        "EMP_PKG.GetDeptAndEmp", cn);
    cmd.CommandType = CommandType.StoredProcedure;
    OracleParameter parmDEPT = new OracleParameter("o_dept",
        OracleType.Cursor);
    parmDEPT.Direction = ParameterDirection.Output;
    OracleParameter parmEMP = new OracleParameter("o_emp",
        OracleType.Cursor);
    parmEMP.Direction = ParameterDirection.Output;
    cmd.Parameters.Add(parmDEPT);
    cmd.Parameters.Add(parmEMP);
    OracleDataReader rdr;
    try
    {
        // Open the connection and create the reader
        cn.Open();
        rdr = cmd.ExecuteReader();
        lstResults.Items.Clear();
        lstResults.Items.Add(rdr.GetName(0) + '\t'
            + rdr.GetName(1));
        while (rdr.Read())
        {
            lstResults.Items.Add(rdr.GetValue(0).ToString() + '\t'
                + rdr.GetValue(1).ToString());
        }
        rdr.NextResult();
        lstResults.Items.Add(rdr.GetName(0) + '\t'
            + rdr.GetName(1) + '\t' + rdr.GetName(2));
        while (rdr.Read())
        {
            lstResults.Items.Add(rdr.GetValue(0).ToString() + '\t'
                + rdr.GetValue(1).ToString() + '\t'
                + rdr.GetValue(2).ToString());
        }
        rdr.Close();
```

```
        }
    catch (Exception ex)
    {
        Cursor.Current = Cursors.Default;
        MessageBox.Show(ex.Message);
    }
    cn.Close();
    Cursor.Current = Cursors.Default;
}
```

The OracleReaderMultRefCursor subroutine begins by creating an OracleConnection object named cn followed by an OracleCommand object named cmd. In this example, the OracleCommand constructor sets the Command property to the value of EMP_PKG.GetDeptAndEmp, the qualified name of the PL/SQL procedure that will be executed. Next, because this OracleCommand object will be executing a procedure, the CommandText is set to CommandText. Then two OracleParameter objects are declared. The first OracleParameter object, parmDept, corresponds to the o_dept output parameter used by the GetDeptAndEmp procedure. The second OracleParameter object, parmEMP, corresponds to the o_emp output parameter. In both cases, the Direction property is set to Parameter.Direction.Output and the data type is set to OracleType.Cursor, which indicates that a Ref Cursor will be used. Next, an OracleDataReader named rdr is declared and a Try-Catch loop is used to execute the procedure.

If an error occurs within the Try block, the code in the Catch block is executed and a message box appears. Within the Try block, the cn OracleConnection object is opened, and then the OracleCommand object's ExecuteReader method is used to execute the GetDeptAndEmp procedure and instantiate the rdr OracleDataReader object. Next, the lstResults list box is cleared and the column headings returned with the first Ref Cursor resultset written to the list box. The OracleDataReader's GetName function is used with the ordinal position of each column to retrieve the column names. A tab character is added between the names to allow the entries to be lined up neatly in the list box. Then a While loop is used to process the first resultset. Inside the While loop, the values of the first three columns returned by the first Ref Cursor are written to the lstResults list box. The data values returned by the OracleDataReader are added to the lstResults list box with a tab character between each value. In this example, the rdr.GetValue method is used with the ordinal for the first three columns to retrieve the data values. After all of the contents of the first Ref Cursor are retrieved, the rdr OracleDataReader's NextResult method is executed to enable the subroutine to process the resultset returned by the second Ref Cursor. The same logic is essentially repeated to first read the column headings and write them to the list box, and then a second While loop is used to retrieve the contents of the second Ref Cursor. After all of the data has been retrieved from the second Ref Cursor, the OracleDataReader and the OracleConnection objects are closed. You can see the results of the OracleReaderMultiRefCursor subroutine in Figure 13-3.

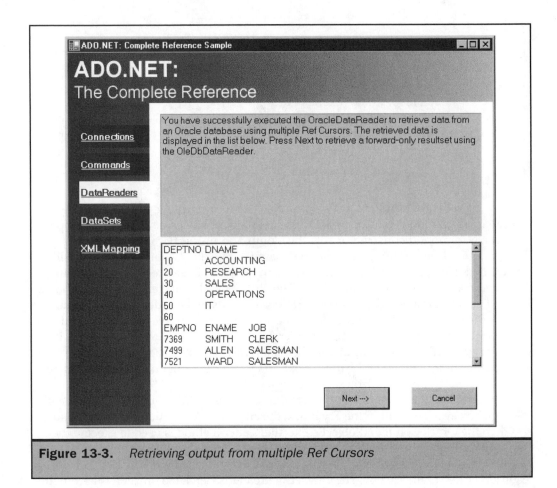

Figure 13-3. *Retrieving output from multiple Ref Cursors*

Summary

In this chapter, you saw several examples illustrating how to use the OracleDataReader to retrieve simple fast forward-only resultsets from an Oracle database. You saw how to execute Oracle packages and retrieve resultsets returned by an Oracle Ref Cursor. The next chapter will go on to cover how to use the OleDbDataReader.

The
Complete
Reference

Chapter 14

Using the OleDbDataReader

In this chapter, you learn how to use the ADO.NET OleDbDataReader to retrieve a stream of results from a target database. You'll see how the OleDbDataReader is conceptually similar to the SqlDataReader and the OracleDataReader, but you'll also see some important differences. The first example in the chapter illustrates the basic use of the OleDbDataReader by retrieving a simple forward-only resultset. The next example utilizes some of the unique features of the .NET Framework Data Provider for OLE DB to show you how to submit and process a hierarchical query using the OleDbDataReader.

Using the OleDbDataReader

Exactly like the SqlDataReader and the OracleDataReader objects that were covered earlier in this book, the OleDbDataReader works in a connected fashion, providing a fast forward-only, read-only resultset from the target database. Also like the SqlDataReader and the OracleDataReader, the OleDbDataReader requires that you retrieve all column data in the order that they appear in the resultset. The primary difference between the OleDbDataReader and the SqlDataReader or the OracleDataReader lies in the type of databases that they can connect to and the different data type conversions that are supported by each object. While the SqlDataReader can only connect to SQL Server 7 and higher databases, and the OracleDataReader can connect to Oracle 8i and later databases, the OleDbDataReader can be used to read data from all versions of SQL Server as well as Oracle, DB2, and even Access.

Using the OleDbDataReader is conceptually very similar to using the SqlDataReader. However, the OleDbDataReader offers some unique possibilities thanks to its capability to support hierarchical resultsets via the OLE DB Provider. In this section, you'll see the declarations required for using the OleDbDataReader in your projects. This section offers an example subroutine showing how to retrieve a simple forward-only resultset, as well as an example showing how to retrieve a hierarchical resultset.

Adding the System.Data.OleDb Namespace

To use the OleDbDataReader classes in your code you should first add an import directive for the System.Data.OleDb Namespace. This allows you to use the classes in the System .Data.OleDb Namespace without always needing to prefix all of the class names with System.Data.OleDb. Chapter 6 provides an example of how to add an import directive for the System.Data.OleDb Namespace.

Retrieving a Fast Forward-Only Resultset with the OleDbDataReader

The primary function of the OleDbDataReader is to retrieve a fast read-only stream of results from the target database. Quickly retrieving subsets of data is one of the most common database actions, and the OleDBDataReader is well suited to this task.

It provides the best read-only performance of any of the ADO.NET objects with the exception of the SqlDataReader. It also shares the SqlDataReader's small footprint. Like the SqlDataReader, the OleDbDataReader functions in a connected fashion, essentially opening a connection and retrieving the entire resultset in a single operation, and then closing the connection. The associated OleDbConnection object can't be used for any other operations while the OleDbDataReader is open. The following example shows the basic use of the OleDbDataReader. Here you'll see how to retrieve a forward-only, read-only resultset from the target database. In this example, you'll also see how to set custom tab stops in the list box, which allows the returned data to be displayed in columns that line up nicely.

```
Private Sub OLEDBReaderForward(ByVal sServer As String, _
      ByVal sDB As String)
   Cursor.Current = Cursors.WaitCursor
   ' Create the connection and command
   Dim cn As New OleDbConnection("PROVIDER=SQLOLEDB;SERVER=" _
      & sServer & ";DATABASE=" & sDB & ";TRUSTED_CONNECTION=Yes")
   Dim cmd As New OleDbCommand("CustOrderHist", cn)
   cmd.CommandType = CommandType.StoredProcedure
   Dim parm = New OleDbParameter("@CustomerID", OleDbType.Char, 5)
   parm.Value = "ALFKI"
   cmd.Parameters.Add(parm)
   'Setup custom tabs stops for the ListBox
   Dim ListBoxTabs() As Integer = {160, 240}
   Dim result As Integer
   'Send LB_SETTABSTOPS message to ListBox
   result = SendMessage(Me.lstResults.Handle, LB_SETTABSTOPS, _
      ListBoxTabs.Length, ListBoxTabs(0))
   Me.lstResults.Refresh()
   Try
        cn.Open()
        Dim rdr As OleDbDataReader
        rdr = cmd.ExecuteReader()
        lstResults.Items.Clear()
        ' Setup the list headings and populate the list
        lstResults.Items.Add("Product Name" & vbTab & _
            "Total Orders")
        Do While rdr.Read()
            lstResults.Items.Add(rdr.GetValue(0) _
                & vbTab & rdr.GetValue(1))
        Loop
        rdr.Close()
```

```
    Catch e As Exception
        Cursor.Current = Cursors.Default
        MsgBox(e.Message)
    End Try
    cn.Close()
    Cursor.Current = Cursors.Default
End Sub
```

That was the VB.NET version of the OLEDBReaderForward subroutine. The C#
version of this same subroutine is as follows:

```
private void OLEDBReaderForward(string sServer, string sDB)
{
    Cursor.Current = Cursors.WaitCursor;
    // Create the Connection and Command
    OleDbConnection cn = new OleDbConnection(
        "PROVIDER=SQLOLEDB;SERVER=" + sServer +
        ";DATABASE=" + sDB + ";TRUSTED_CONNECTION=Yes");
    OleDbCommand cmd = new OleDbCommand("CustOrderHist", cn);
    cmd.CommandType = CommandType.StoredProcedure;
    OleDbParameter parm = new OleDbParameter(
        "@CustomerID", OleDbType.Char, 5);
    parm.Value = "ALFKI";
    cmd.Parameters.Add(parm);
    // Setup tab stops
    int[] ListBoxTabs = {160, 240};
    int iResult;
    // Send LB_SETTABSTOPS message to ListBox
    iResult = SendMessage(this.lstResults.Handle.ToInt32(),
        LB_SETTABSTOPS, ListBoxTabs.Length, ref ListBoxTabs[0]);
    this.lstResults.Refresh();
    try
    {
        cn.Open();
        OleDbDataReader rdr;
        rdr = cmd.ExecuteReader();
        lstResults.Items.Clear();
        // Setup list headings and populate the list
        lstResults.Items.Add("Product Name" + '\t' +
            "Total Orders");
        while( rdr.Read())
```

```
        {
            lstResults.Items.Add(rdr.GetValue(0).ToString() + '\t'
                + rdr.GetValue(1).ToString());
        }
        rdr.Close(0);
    }
    catch (Exception ex)
    {
        Cursor.Current = Cursors.Default;
        MessageBox.Show(ex.Message);
    }
    cn.Close(0);
    Cursor.Current = Cursors.Default;
}
```

At the beginning of this subroutine, the OleDbConnection and OleDbCommand objects are created. In this example, the OleDbCommand object will be executing the CustOrderHist stored procedure that's found in the SQL Server Northwind database. The CustOrderHist stored procedure returns a resultset showing the orders placed for a given customer and it takes as input one parameter that specifies the CustomerID of the orders that will be retrieved. This example supplies a customer ID of ALFKI.

Next, an array called ListBoxTabs is created to supply a set of custom tab stops to the List Box control. The values in this array are in pixels and they essentially correspond to tab stops at columns 40 and 60. Next the SendMessage function is used to communicate with the ListBox. If you've looked at your .NET Framework declarations you might have noticed that the SendMessage function is neither part of any of the .NET languages nor is it declared in the .NET Class library. Instead, it's a part of the underlying Win32 API set. To call the Win32 SendMessage function, you must first include the System.Runtime .InteropServices Namespace in the declarations section of your application using the VB.NET's Import directive or C#'s user directive. Then you need to add the following declaration for the function to your application:

```
<DllImport("user32.dll")> _
Private Shared Function SendMessage( _
    ByVal hWnd As IntPtr, _
    ByVal wMsg As Int32, _
    ByVal wParam As Int32, _
    ByRef lParam As Int32) _
    As Int32
End Function
Private Const LB_SETTABSTOPS As Int32 = &H192
```

The C# version of the SendMessage function declaration is shown in the following code listing:

```
[DllImport("user32.dll")]
private static extern int SendMessage (int hWnd, int wMsg,
    int wParam, ref int lParam);
private const int LB_SETTABSTOPS = 0x192;
```

The DLLImport statement identifies the DLL that contains the function that will be imported into the application. Next, the function name is defined along with its parameters. In this case, the SendMessage function accepts four parameters. The first parameter is an Integer value that identifies the list box's windows handle. The value for this parameter is supplied with the this.lstResults.Handle.ToInt32() method. The second parameter is an enumerator of the message that will be sent to the windows component. In this case, the LB_SETTABSTOP constant tells the given list box to reset its tab stops. The third parameter contains the length data for the message that will be sent. Here, the length of the ListBoxTabs array is used. The fourth parameter contains the message data itself. In this example, this data is supplied by passing the address of the ListBoxTabs array. After the SendMessage function has completed, the Refresh method of the lstResults list box is called to make sure that the change is activated in the list box.

After the new tab stops have been set into the lstResults list box, a Try-Catch block is used to open the connection, execute the OleDbDataReader, and populate the list box with the resultset retrieved by the OleDbDataReader. Notice that in the Try block, where the column heading are added to the top of the list, literals are used to set the column headings and one tab is used to separate each column. Next, a While loop is used to read the data from the OleDbDataReader. Inside the While loop, the Add method of the lstResults Items collection is used to add entries to the list box that contain the data from the OleDbDataReader. The rdr OleDbDataReader object's GetValue method is used to get the value of each column returned, and the ToString method is used to convert that value to a string. Again, the string value returned for each column is separated by one tab stop. After all of the data has been read from the OleDbDataReader and added to the list box, the OleDbDataReader and the OleDbConnection objects are closed. You can see the results of the OLEDBReaderForward subroutine in Figure 14-1.

Retrieving Hierarchical Resultsets

As you saw in the preceding example, the basic usage of the OleDbDataReader is pretty much the same as the SqlDataReader. However, there are differences. One of the biggest differences comes from the underlying capabilities of the connection mechanisms themselves. While the SqlConnection object is a bit faster than the OleDbConnection object thanks its use of the TDS data stream, the OleDbConnection object has some functionality that's not present in the SqlConnection object. Probably the best example of this is the support for hierarchical resultsets that is built into the Microsoft OLE DB

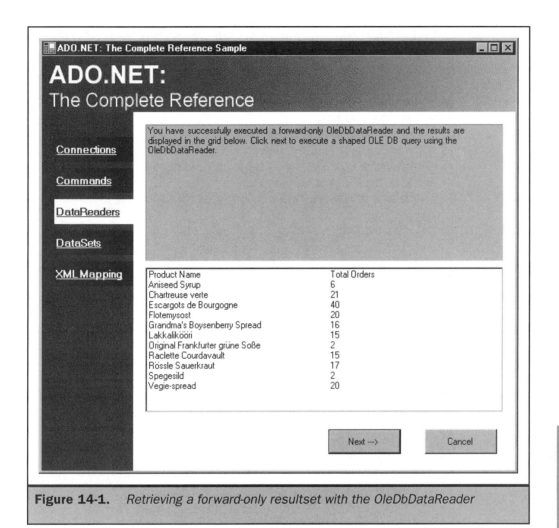

Figure 14-1.   *Retrieving a forward-only resultset with the OleDbDataReader*

Provider. Also known as Shaped resultsets, hierarchical resultsets basically consist of two or more recordsets that are related in a parent/child relationship. Hierarchical recordsets can be nested to any depth. For example, order header data and the corresponding order detail data is one example of a parent and child recordset. Another example might be customers and their related orders. Hierarchical recordsets are essentially a recordset within a recordset. When the related column from the parent recordset is read, the OLE DB Provider automatically retrieves the related results for the child recordset. In OLE DB terminology, the child recordset is referred to as a *chapter*. For SqlConnections, retrieving these types of results requires the use of a DataSet and DataRelations objects. However, using the MSDataShape provider, the OleDbDataReader can return hierarchical resultsets through just the OleDbDataReader. The following example shows how to retrieve a hierarchical resultset using the Microsoft MSDataShape provider and the OleDbDataReader.

```vb
Private Sub OLEDBReaderShaped(ByVal sServer As String, _
        ByVal sDB As String)
    ' Use the OleDB Shape Provider
    Dim cn As OleDbConnection = New OleDbConnection( _
        "PROVIDER=MSDataShape;DATA PROVIDER=SQLOLEDB;" _
        & "DATA SOURCE=" & sServer _
        & ";INTEGRATED SECURITY=SSPI;INITIAL CATALOG=" & sDB)
    ' Setup the Shape command
    Dim cmd As OleDbCommand = New OleDbCommand( _
        "SHAPE {SELECT CustomerID, CompanyName FROM Customers} " & _
        " APPEND ({SELECT CustomerID, OrderID FROM Orders} " & _
        " AS CustomerOrders " & _
        " RELATE CustomerID TO CustomerID)", cn)
    Try
        cn.Open()
        ' create two readers
        Dim rdrCust As OleDbDataReader = cmd.ExecuteReader()
        Dim rdrOrder As OleDbDataReader
        lstResults.Items.Clear()
        ' Setup the list headings and populate the list
        lstResults.Items.Add("Orders per Customer")
        ' Read the Customers
        Do While rdrCust.Read()
            lstResults.Items.Add(rdrCust("CompanyName"))
            ' Set the chapter for the Orders Reader
            rdrOrder = rdrCust.GetValue(2)
            Do While rdrOrder.Read()
                lstResults.Items.Add(rdrOrder("OrderID"))
            Loop
            rdrOrder.Close()
        Loop
        rdrCust.Close()
    Catch e As Exception
        MsgBox(e.Message)
    Finally
        cn.Close()
        Cursor.Current = Cursors.Default
    End Try
End Sub
```

The C# version of the OLEDBReaderShaped subroutine is as follows:

```
private void OLEDBReaderShaped(string sServer, string sDB)
{
    Cursor.Current = Cursors.WaitCursor;
    // Use the OleDB Shape Provider
    OleDbConnection cn = new OleDbConnection(
        "PROVIDER=MSDataShape;DATA PROVIDER=SQLOLEDB;"
        + "DATA SOURCE=" + sServer
        + ";INTEGRATED SECURITY=SSPI;INITIAL CATALOG=" + sDB);
    // Setup the Shape command
    OleDbCommand cmd = new OleDbCommand(
        "SHAPE {SELECT CustomerID, CompanyName FROM Customers} "
        + " APPEND ({SELECT CustomerID, OrderID FROM Orders} "
        + " AS CustomerOrders "
        + " RELATE CustomerID TO CustomerID)", cn);
    try
    {
        cn.Open();
        // create two readers
        OleDbDataReader rdrCust = cmd.ExecuteReader();
        OleDbDataReader rdrOrder;
        lstResults.Items.Clear();
        // Setup the list headings and populate the list
        lstResults.Items.Add("Orders per Customer");
        // Read the Customers
        while( rdrCust.Read())
        {
            lstResults.Items.Add(rdrCust["CompanyName"]);
            // Set the chapter for the Orders Reader
            //rdrOrder = rdrCust["OrderID"];
            rdrOrder = (OleDbDataReader)rdrCust.GetValue(2);
            while(rdrOrder.Read())
            {
                lstResults.Items.Add(rdrOrder["OrderID"]);
            }
            rdrOrder.Close();
        }
        rdrCust.Close();
    }
    catch (Exception ex)
    {
        MessageBox.Show(ex.Message);
```

```
    }
    finally
    {
        cn.Close();
        Cursor.Current = Cursors.Default;
    }
}
```

The most important thing to note at the beginning of the OLEDBReaderShaped subroutine is the OLE DB connection string that's used to instantiate the cn OleDbConnection object. In this connection string you can see that the PROVIDER keyword is used to specify the use of the OLE DB Shaping Service, MSDataShape. The DATA PROVIDER keyword is used to specify the OLE DB Provider that will be used. In this case, the value of SQLOLEDB indicates that the Microsoft OLE DB Provider for SQL Server is being used. As their names imply, the MSDataShape Provider supplies the data shaping capability while the SQLOLEDB Data Provider provides the database connectivity. The remaining keywords are used the same as in the other OLE DB connection examples: the DATA SOURCE keyword is used to identify the database server, the INTEGRATED SECURITY keyword is used to indicate that Windows authentication will be used to log in to the database, and the INITIAL CATALOG keyword sets the default database.

You should also note the use of the Shape command that's supplied as a parameter for the cmd OleDbCommand object's constructor. The Shape command that you can see in this example utilizes three different keywords specific to the Microsoft MSDataShape shaping service. The first is the Shape command itself. The Shape command is followed by any command that can be issued by the underlying OLE DB Provider. Typically, however, this is a SELECT statement because the purpose of the Shaping service is to relate returned resultsets. In this case, you can see that the Shape command is followed by a SELECT statement that retrieves the Customer ID and CompanyName columns from the Customers table in the SQL Server Northwind database. The next Shape-specific keyword is APPEND, which is used to add a chapter to the parent resultset. In this example, the chapter that's added consists of the CustomerID, and OrderID columns from the Orders table. The AS keyword is used to name this chapter CustomerOrders. RELATE is the third important Shape keyword that's used in this example. The RELATE keyword tells the shaping service how the parent and the child resultsets are related. In this case, the RELATE keyword is used to join the two resultsets based on the CustomerID column.

In the Try-Catch block, you can see the code used to process the results of the Shape command. First, the connection to the data source is opened, and then two OleDbDataReader objects are created. The first OleDbDataReader, named rdrCust, is used to read the parent resultset returned by the Shape command, and the second OleDbDataReader, named rdrOrder, is used to read the CustomerOrder chapter. The next section of code initializes the list box that will be used to display the results, and then a While loop is used to begin reading from the parent results using the rdrCust object's Read method. Inside that While loop, the value of the CompanyName column is first added to the list box. Then the rdrCust object's GetValue method is used to assign the first rdrOrder object with a reference to an OLE DB–shaped chapter. Next, an inner While loop is used to read the data from that chapter using the rdrOrder OleDbDataReader object's Read method and write the contents of the OrderID column to the list box. After all of the results have been read, the OleDbDataReader objects are closed. You can see the results of the OLEDBReaderShaped subroutine in Figure 14-2.

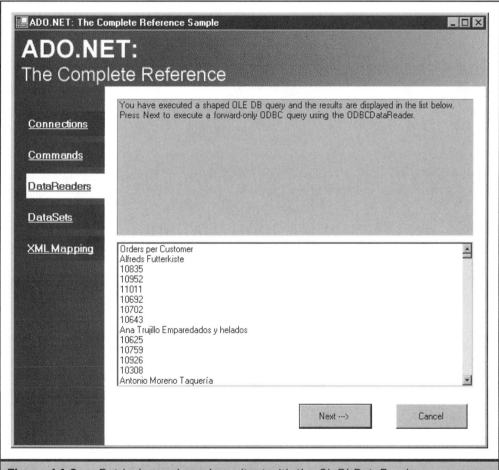

Figure 14-2.   *Retrieving a shaped resultset with the OleDbDataReader*

Summary

In this chapter, you saw a couple of core examples illustrating how to retrieve resultsets using the OleDbDataReader object. The next chapter provides examples of how to use the OdbcDataReader that is part of the .NET Framework Data Provider for ODBC.

ADO.NET

Chapter 15

Using the
OdbcDataReader

This chapter provides examples that use the OdbcDataReader that's provided with the .NET Framework Data Provider for ODBC. The first example illustrates how the OdbcDataReader retrieves a simple, forward-only resultset. This example also shows how you can take advantage of the SQL alias capability to provide custom column headings for the resultset returned by the OdbcDataReader. The second example illustrates how you can retrieve BLOB data using the OdbcDataReader. Unlike the previous BLOB retrieval example, which used the SqlDataReader and wrote the BLOB data to a temporary file before loading the binary data to the Image property of a .NET Label control, this example forgoes the use of the file system, and retrieves the BLOB data from the database and then loads it into a memory stream. The memory stream will then be used to load the .NET Label control's Image property.

Using the OdbcDataReader

The OdbcDataReader is very much like the SqlDataReader, the OracleDataReader, and the OleDbDataReader. The OdbcDataReader works in a connected manner, and it returns a fast forward-only, read-only resultset from the target database. Like the other DataReaders, the OdbcDataReader requires that you access all of the column data in the exact order that they appear in the resultset. The primary difference between the OdbcDataReader and DataReader objects provided by the other .NET Framework Data Providers is in the different databases that they support and the different data type conversions supplied by each method. The OdbcDataReader can connect to all versions of SQL Server, as well as to most other ODBC-compliant databases.

Adding the System.Data.ODBC Namespace

After starting your project, you should add an import directive for the System.Data.Odbc Namespace to your project. Importing the Namespace enables you to directly refer to the classes in the Namespace without having to prefix them with System.Data.Odbc, which means that your code is easier to write and much more readable. You can see an example of importing the System.Data.Odbc Namespace in Chapter 7.

Retrieving a Fast Forward-Only Resultset with the OdbcDataReader

The primary purpose of the OdbcDataReader is to retrieve a fast read-only stream of results from an ODBC-compliant database. The OdbcDataReader works in a connected fashion. You use the OdbcDataReader by opening a connection to the target database, retrieving the entire resultset, and closing the connection. The associated OdbcConnection object can't be used for any other operations while the OdbcDataReader is open. The following example

shows how to use the OdbcCommand object and the OdbcDataReader to issue a SQL
SELECT statement to the target database that returns all of the orders for a given customer.
This example also shows how the SQL AS keyword can be used to provide custom alias
column headings for the columns in the resultset.

```vb
Private Sub ODBCReaderForward(ByVal sServer As String, _
        ByVal sDB As String)
    Cursor.Current = Cursors.WaitCursor
    Dim cn As New OdbcConnection("DRIVER={SQL Server};SERVER=" _
        & sServer & ";DATABASE=" & sDB _
        & ";TRUSTED_CONNECTION=yes")
    ' Set the SQL join statement using Aliases
    Dim sSQL As String = _
        "SELECT Customers.CompanyName AS Company," _
        & "Orders.OrderID AS [Order]," _
        & "[Order Details].ProductID AS Product " _
        & "FROM Customers " _
        & "INNER JOIN Orders " _
        & "ON Customers.CustomerID = " _
        & "Orders.CustomerID " _
        & "INNER JOIN [Order Details] " _
        & "ON Orders.OrderID = " _
        & "[Order Details].OrderID"
    Dim cmd As New OdbcCommand(sSQL, cn)
    Try
        cn.Open()
        Dim rdr As OdbcDataReader
        rdr = cmd.ExecuteReader()
        lstResults.Items.Clear()
        ' Set up the list headings and populate the list
        lstResults.Items.Add(rdr.GetName(0) & vbTab _
            & rdr.GetName(1) & vbTab & rdr.GetName(2))
        Do While rdr.Read()
            lstResults.Items.Add(rdr("Company") & vbTab _
            & rdr("Order") & vbTab & rdr("Product"))
        Loop
        rdr.Close()
    Catch e As Exception
        Cursor.Current = Cursors.Default
        MsgBox(e.Message)
```

```
        End Try
        cn.Close()
        Cursor.Current = Cursors.Default
    End Sub
```

The following code listing shows the C# version of the ODBCReaderForward subroutine.

```
private void ODBCReaderForward(string sServer, string sDB)
{
    Cursor.Current = Cursors.WaitCursor;
    OdbcConnection cn = new OdbcConnection(
        "DRIVER={SQL Server};SERVER=" + sServer +
        ";DATABASE=" + sDB + ";TRUSTED_CONNECTION=yes");
    // Set up the SQL JOIN using Aliases
    string sSQL =
        "SELECT Customers.CompanyName AS Company, "
        + "Orders.OrderID AS [Order], "
        + "[Order Details].ProductID AS Product "
        + "FROM Customers "
        + "INNER JOIN Orders "
        + "ON Customers.CustomerID = "
        + "Orders.CustomerID "
        + "INNER JOIN [Order Details] "
        + "ON Orders.OrderID = "
        + "[Order Details].OrderID";
    OdbcCommand cmd = new OdbcCommand(sSQL, cn);
    try
    {
        cn.Open();
        OdbcDataReader rdr;
        rdr = cmd.ExecuteReader();
        lstResults.Items.Clear();
        // Set up the list headings and populate the list
        lstResults.Items.Add(rdr.GetName(0) + '\t'
            + rdr.GetName(1).ToString() + '\t'
            + rdr.GetName(2).ToString());
        while( rdr.Read())
        {
            lstResults.Items.Add(rdr["Company"].ToString() + '\t'
```

```
                    + rdr["Order"].ToString() + '\t'
                    + rdr["Product"].ToString());
        }
        rdr.Close();
    }
    catch (Exception ex)
    {
        MessageBox.Show(ex.Message);
    }
    finally
    {
        cn.Close();
        Cursor.Current = Cursors.Default;
    }
}
```

In the beginning of the ODBCReaderForward subroutine, a new OdbcConnection object is created that uses a DSN-less connection to attach to the target database. In this example, the DRIVER keyword is used to load the SQL Server ODBC driver, and the TRUSTED_CONNECTION keyword indicates that the connection will use Windows security to authenticate to the database. The SERVER and DATABASE keyword specify the data source and default database.

Next, a new string variable named sSQL is created that contains a SELECT statement that joins the Customers table with the Orders table in the CustomerID column. The AS keyword is used to supply an alias for the columns returned by the SELECT statement. The CompanyName column will be returned with the column name of Company, while the OrderID and ProductID columns will be returned as Order and Product, respectively. Next, an OdbcCommand object named cmd is created and the sSQL string variable and the cn OdbcConnection object are passed as arguments for the OdbcCommand object's constructor.

Within the Try-Catch block, the connection to the database is opened, and an OdbcDataReader object named rdr is declared and then instantiated using the cmd object's ExecuteReader method. The next lines initialize the list box that will be used to display the results. First, the contents of the lstResults list box are cleared, and then the names of each of the columns in the resultset are written to the first line of the list box. Tab stops are added between each of the names to allow the data to line up in neat columns in the list box. Then a While loop is used to read the data returned by the OdbcDataReader, and the content of each column is written to the list separated by tab stops. After all of the data has been read, the OdbcDataReader will return a value of False to end the While loop. Then the OdbcDataReader is closed. You can see the output of the ODBCReaderForward subroutine in Figure 15-1.

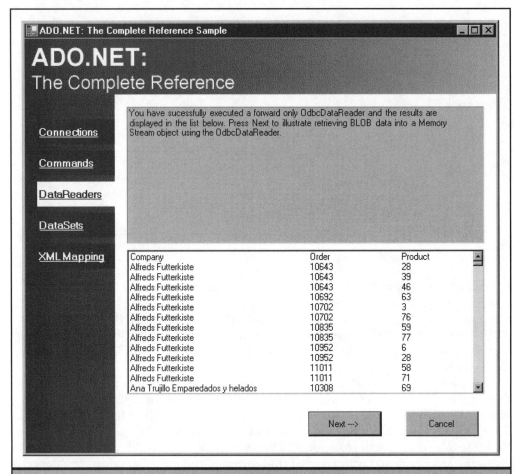

Figure 15-1. *Retrieving data with the OdbcDataReader*

Retrieving BLOB Data Using the OdbcDataReader

As you saw in the preceding example, the OdbcDataReader has essentially the same characteristics as the SqlDataReader, the OracleDataReader, and the OdbcDataReader, including the capability to work with BLOB objects as well as standard character and numeric data. In the next example, you'll see how the OdbcDataReader can be used to retrieve BLOB data from the database and display the binary image in a Label control. This example illustrates a couple of more advanced BLOB retrieval techniques. Here, you'll see how you can retrieve the entire contents of the BLOB column in a single operation. While this isn't the best for large BLOB objects, it can be very effective for smaller objects such as photos. In addition, you'll see how to write the BLOB to a memory stream and assign that Memory Stream object to a Label control's Image property, rather than writing the binary image to disk. Again, this is a technique that's best suited for smaller BLOB objects, but it can result in performance gains by avoiding the extra I/O that's required to first write and then subsequently read the binary data to disk. Because this subroutine uses a memory stream to store the binary data, you need to import the .NET System.IO Namespace into your application to enable access to the file system. To import the System.IO Namespace, add the following code to your projects.

```
Imports System.IO
```

For a C# project, add an import directive for the System.IO Namespace as follows:

```
using System.IO;
```

The following is the code for the ODBCReaderBLOB subroutine:

```
Private Sub ODBCReaderBLOB(ByVal sServer As String, _
      ByVal sDB As String)
    Dim cn As New OdbcConnection("DRIVER={SQL Server};SERVER=" _
        & sServer & ";DATABASE=" & sDB _
        & ";TRUSTED_CONNECTION=yes")
    Dim cmd As OdbcCommand = New OdbcCommand( _
        "SELECT Picture FROM Categories WHERE CategoryId = 2", cn)
    Dim iBufferSize As Integer
    Dim lRetval As Long
    Cursor.Current = System.Windows.Forms.Cursors.WaitCursor
    Dim rdr As OdbcDataReader
    Try
        ' Open the connection and read data
        cn.Open()
        rdr = cmd.ExecuteReader(CommandBehavior.SequentialAccess)
        Do While rdr.Read()
            ' Size the byte array
            iBufferSize = rdr.GetBytes(0, 0, Nothing, 0, 0)
            Dim bBLOBStorage(iBufferSize - 1) As Byte
            ' Read bytes into bBLOBStorage
            lRetval = rdr.GetBytes(0, 0, bBLOBStorage, 0, _
                iBufferSize)
            Dim ms As New MemoryStream(bBLOBStorage)
```

```
                lblBigBot.Image = Image.FromStream(ms)
            Loop
            rdr.Close()
        Catch e As Exception
            MsgBox(e.Message)
        Finally
            ' Close the reader and the connection
            cn.Close()
            Cursor.Current = Cursors.Default
        End Try
End Sub
```

The C# version of the OdbcReaderBLOB subroutine is as follows:

```csharp
private void ODBCReaderBLOB(string sServer, string sDB)
{
    Cursor.Current = Cursors.WaitCursor;
    OdbcConnection cn = new OdbcConnection(
        "DRIVER={SQL Server};SERVER=" + sServer +
        ";DATABASE=" + sDB + ";TRUSTED_CONNECTION=yes");
    OdbcCommand cmd = new OdbcCommand(
        "SELECT Picture FROM Categories WHERE CategoryId = 2", cn);
    int iBufferSize;
    long lRetval;
    OdbcDataReader rdr;
    try
    {
        // Open the connection and read the data stream
        cn.Open();
        rdr = cmd.ExecuteReader(CommandBehavior.SequentialAccess);
        while(rdr.Read())
        {
            // Set the buffer size
            iBufferSize = (int)rdr.GetBytes(0, 0, null, 0, 0);
            byte[] bBLOBStorage;
            bBLOBStorage = new byte[iBufferSize];
            // Read bytes into bBLOBStorage()
            lRetval = rdr.GetBytes(0, 0, bBLOBStorage, 0,
                iBufferSize);
            MemoryStream ms = new MemoryStream(bBLOBStorage);
```

```
        lblBigBot.Image = Image.FromStream(ms);
    }
    rdr.Close();
}
catch (Exception ex)
{
    MessageBox.Show(ex.Message);
}
finally
{
    cn.Close();
    Cursor.Current = Cursors.Default;
}
}
```

The ODBCReaderBLOB subroutine begins by creating a new OdbcConnection object named cn and a new OdbcCommand object named cmd. Here the SqlCommand object contains a SQL SELECT statement that retrieves the Picture column from the Categories table in the Northwind database, where the value of CategoryID is equal to 2.

Note *The native 16-color bitmap images that are stored in the Picture column of the Categories table were converted to 256-bit color images in order to be displayed in the .NET Label control.*

Next, a new OdbcDataReader named rdr is declared, and then a Try block is used to open the connection and execute the OdbcDataReader. The ExecuteReader's CommandBehavior.SequentialAccess option is used to enable streaming access to BLOB data. Next, a While loop is used to retrieve the binary data from the Picture column. Inside the While loop, the rdr OdbcDataReader object's GetBytes method is used twice. The first instance is used to retrieve the number of bytes in the BLOB column by passing a null value in to GetBytes method's third parameter (which would normally be used from the returned data buffer). The returned value is then used to dynamically size the bBLOBStorage byte array. The rdr OdbcDataReader's GetBytes method is called a second time to read the data from the BLOB column. In this case, the first parameter of the GetBytes method specifies the index value of the column in the resultset, which is 0 for the first column. The second parameter specifies the offset (0) from the beginning of the data stream. This value controls where the GetBytes method will begin retrieving data. The third parameter is the bBLOBStorage byte array, which has been sized large enough to contain the BLOB data. The fourth parameter indicates the offset in the column to begin reading the data.

The fifth and last parameter specifies the number of bytes that will be retrieved by the GetBytes method. In this case, the data contained in the iBufferSize variable is equal to the total number of bytes, and all of the BLOB data will be read into the bBLOBStorage array in a single operation.

After the GetBytes method has completed, a new Memory Stream object named ms is created and assigned the contents of the bBLOBStorage byte array. Then the Image class's FromStream method is used to assign the binary image data in the ms Memory Stream object to the Image property of a Label control. You can see the results of the OdbcReaderBLOB subroutine in Figure 15-2.

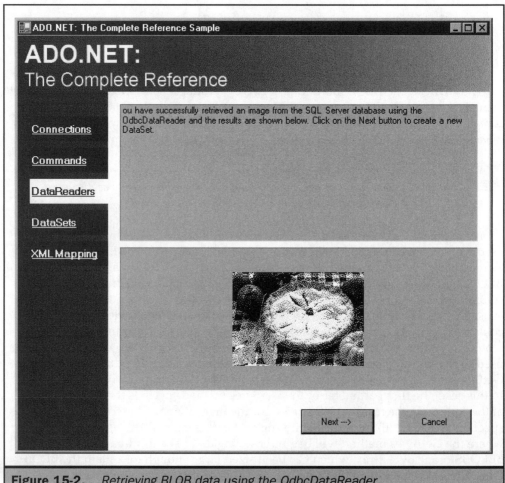

Figure 15-2. *Retrieving BLOB data using the OdbcDataReader*

 ## Summary

In this chapter, you saw how to use the OdbcDataReader to retrieve binary and text data from an ODBC-compliant data source. The next chapter tackles a completely different aspect of the ADO.NET Framework. You'll see how to create an ADO.NET DataSet and the supporting objects that it contains.

THE ADO.NET
DATAREADER OBJECT

The
Complete
Reference

ADO.NET

Part V

The ADO.NET DataSet Object

The
Complete
Reference

Chapter 16

Building a DataSet

The DataSet is at the heart of the ADO.NET development environment. A DataSet is an in-memory database that represents a relational set of data consisting of data tables, constraint rules, and table relation information. DataSets are completely separated from a data source, so any changes you make to the data in your DataSet does not affect your data source until you are ready to propagate the changes back to the data source. You can see an overview of a DataSet and its essential objects in Figure 16-1.

As you can see in Figure 16-1, the DataSet contains two collections, a Tables collection and a Relations collection. As their names suggest, the Tables collection contains the

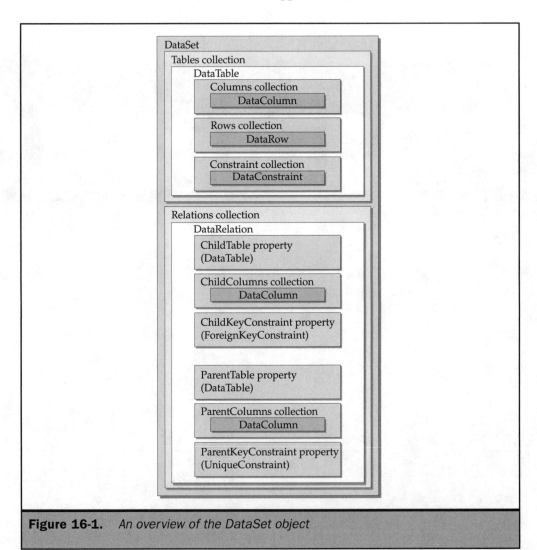

Figure 16-1. *An overview of the DataSet object*

DataTable objects for the DataSet and the Relations collection contains the DataRelation objects for the DataSet. In the first part of this chapter, you will see how to create an ADO.NET DataSet. You will then learn how to create data tables that contain columns and rows of data and add the DataTable objects to the Tables collection of the DataSet. Next, you will see how to create data relations and add the DataRelation objects to the Relations collection of the DataSet. In the second part of the chapter, you will learn how to create a strongly typed DataSet and add it to your .NET applications. A strongly typed DataSet is inherited from the base DataSet class. It has a schema file (an XML XSD file) that describes the structures of the objects contained in the DataSet.

Creating a DataSet

You can create a new DataSet in several different ways, and the creation method that you use depends on the type of DataSet you want. You can create a DataSet by calling the DataSet constructor, which will create an empty DataSet object. When you create a DataSet using this method, you may specify a name for the DataSet. If you do not specify a name for the DataSet, a default name of NewDataSet is given to your DataSet. You may also create a DataSet by using the DataSet.Copy method to make an exact copy of an existing DataSet. The DataSet.Copy method copies the original DataSet's schema, or relational structure, plus all data rows, row versions, and row states into your new DataSet. You create a DataSet that contains only the original DataSet's schema information by using the DataSet.Clone method. You may then add data to your new cloned DataSet by using the DataTable .ImportRows method. Finally, you can create a subsetted copy of an existing DataSet that contains the original DataSet's schema and filtered rows of data that represent added, modified, or deleted rows. This is accomplished by using the DataSet.GetChanges method and passing in a DataRowState value as a parameter. The following example illustrates how to use VB.NET to create an empty DataSet using the DataSet constructor:

```
Private Sub CreateDataSet(ByVal sDSName As String)

    Dim ds = New DataSet(sDSName)

End Sub
```

The C# version of this code follows:

```
private void CreateDataSet(string sDSName)
{
    DataSet ds = new DataSet(sDSName);
}
```

In both cases, a string variable containing the name of the new DataSet is passed into the top of the routine. Next, a new instance of an empty DataSet object named ds is created using the DataSet constructor.

Using the DataTable Class

Once you've created the DataSet, you will want to create and add DataTables to it. A DataTable consists of DataColumns, which define the schema of the table by specifying the data type of each column; DataRows, which represent the actual data contained in the table; and Constraints, which define the rules and actions that are performed against the tables when the data in the rows changes. After you create a DataTable and its associated columns, rows, and data rules, you add the DataTable to the DataSet by adding the DataTable to the Tables collection of the DataSet. You may create a DataTable by calling the DataTable constructor and specifying a name for the DataTable. If you do not specify a name, an incremental default name (Table1, Table2, and so on) will be given to your DataTable when it is added to the DataSet.Tables collection. Also, several properties are set to their default values. The following table describes these default property settings.

Property	Default Property Value
CaseSensitive	False. Unless the DataTable has been added to a DataSet, this property is set to the DataSet.CaseSensitive value.
DisplayExpression	Empty string. Set this string to display a description of this table in the user interface.
Locale	Current system CultureInfo. Unless the DataTable has been added to a DataSet, this property is set to the DataSet.Locale value.
MinimumCapacity	25 rows.

The documentation states that the MinimumCapacity property default is 25 rows; however, the sample used in this chapter actually uses a default value of 50 rows.

You may also create a DataTable by calling the DataTableCollection.Add method, which creates a DataTable and adds it to the DataSet.Tables collection. The following example illustrates how to create a DataTable object and add it to a DataSet:

```
Private Sub CreateDataTable(ByVal sDTName As String)
    Dim ds = New DataSet()

    ds.Tables.Add(sDTName)
End Sub
```

The C# version of this code follows:

```
private void CreateDataTable(string sDTName)
{
     DataSet ds = new DataSet();

     ds.Tables.Add(sDTName);
}
```

In both cases, a string variable containing the name of the new DataTable is passed into the top of the routine. Next, a new instance of an empty DataSet object named ds is created using the DataSet constructor. The next statement shows the use of the DataTableCollection.Add method to create a new DataTable and add it to the DataSet's table collection.

DataColumn

After creating a new DataTable object, you will want to define the DataTable's structure. DataColumn objects, along with Constraint objects, make up the schema of a DataTable by defining the type of data that is allowed in each column and any rules imposed on the data. After you create a DataColumn, you add it to the DataTable by adding the DataColumn to the Columns collection of the DataTable. You create a DataColumn by calling the DataColumn constructor and optionally specifying a ColumnName, DataType, Expression, and MappingType for the DataColumn. If you do not specify a name, an incremental default name (Column1, Column2, and so on) will be given to your DataColumn when it is added to the DataTable.Columns collection. You may also create a DataColumn by calling the DataColumnCollection.Add method and optionally specifying a ColumnName, DataType, and Expression for the DataColumn, which creates a DataColumn and adds it to the DataTable.Columns collection. Alternatively, you can call the DataColumnCollection.Add method and specify an existing DataColumn to add to the DataTables.Columns collection. Two of the most important properties that you can set for the DataColumn are the DataType and Expression properties.

DataType Property   Setting the DataType property to the correct value is crucial to ensure the correct storing and updating of data. Trying to store the wrong type of data in a column or changing the DataType of a column after data has been stored in it will result in an exception error being thrown. The DataType property supports the following .NET Framework types: Boolean, Byte, Char, DateTime, Decimal, Double, Int16, Int32, Int64, SByte, Single, String, TimeSpan, UInt16, UInt32, and UInt64. These data types are explained in more detail in Appendix A of this book.

Expression Property   The Expression argument for the DataColumn constructor allows you to calculate or filter the value of a column, or create a summative column.

For example, to calculate the discount on a sale item, you use the price of the item multiplied by a discount amount as shown:

```
DataSet1.Tables("Sales").Columns("Discount").Expression =
    "ItemPrice * 0.15"
```

You use the column name to refer to the DataColumn in your expressions; so in this example, the value in the column named ItemPrice is multiplied by 15 percent, and the column named Discount contains the result. You may also add columns to a DataTable that reflect a True/False value after checking a filter expression. A filter expression evaluates the specified column value against the specified literal and returns the result. For example, to check a column for a certain value, you designate the column to check and the literal to check for as shown here:

```
DataTable.Columns.Add("OregonSales",
    System.Type.GetType("System.String"), "Region = 'OR'");
```

In this example, when the value of the column Region contains the literal 'OR', the column OregonSales is set with the value of True. Otherwise, the column OregonSales will contain the value of False. This capability to filter and calculate column data is very useful and supports many operators and functions, such as string operators, wildcard characters, regular operators, aggregates, and functions. A brief description of these features is listed here:

String operators	You may concatenate string values with the + symbol. Case sensitivity of string values is determined by the CaseSensitive property of the DataTable. When you want to filter a string type column, you need to enclose the string in single quotes, for example, "FirstName = 'Michael'"
Wildcard characters	The two wildcard characters that you can use with the LIKE comparison keyword in a string expression are the * (asterisk) symbol and the % (percent) symbol. You can use a wildcard character at the beginning and end of the string value, at the beginning of the string value, or at the end of a string value, but not in the middle of a string value, for example, "SalesRegion LIKE 'North*'" valid expression "SalesRegion LIKE '*west'" valid expression "SalesRegion LIKE '*North*'" valid expression "SalesRegion LIKE 'North*west'" not a valid expression

Operators   Operators are supported in expressions to calculate column values and concatenate clauses of your expression. You may use parentheses to group clauses together and press clause priority. The following are the supported operators:

> Concatenation
> Comparison
> Arithmetic
> + (addition)
> – (subtraction)
> * (multiplication)
> / (division)
> < (less than)
> > (greater than)
> <= (less than or equal to)
> >= (greater than or equal to)
> <> (not equal to)
> = (equal to)
> % (modulus)
> AND
> OR
> NOT
> IN
> LIKE

Aggregates   An aggregate will perform an action on the entire set of rows in a DataTable. An aggregate column used in a single table will display the same value in the DataColumn for all rows. However, when an aggregate column is created in a parent/child DataRelation, group-by functionality is employed. Parent/child DataRelations are discussed later in this chapter, in the section "Using the DataRelation Class." The aggregate types that are supported are

> Sum (sum)
> Ave (average)
> Min (minimum)
> Max (maximum)
> Count (count)
> StDev (statistical standard deviation)
> Var (statistical variance)

Functions   The following functions are supported in an expression.

CONVERT
Converts the specified column to the specified .NET Framework type:

```
Convert(ItemPrice, System.Int64)
```

LEN
Returns the length of the specified column:

```
Len(FirstName)
```

ISNULL
If the column is not null, returns the value; else returns the specified default value:

```
IsNull(Sales, 0)
```

IIF
Evaluates expression and returns either the true or false specified values:

```
IIF(Sales>100, 'true', 'false')
```

TRIM
Trims leading and trailing blank characters from the column:

```
Trim(LastName)
```

SUBSTRING
Returns a substring of the specified length from the specified column, starting at the specified point:

```
Substring(Zip4, 1, 5)
```

DataRow

When you have finished creating a DataTable and defining its structure through DataColumn objects, you are ready to add new rows of data to the DataTable. A DataRow object represents a row of data in a DataTable. The DataTable.NewRow method is used to create a DataRow object based on the schema of the table. Once the new row has been created in the DataTable, you then add data to the row using the column name or integer index of the column. After adding the data to the new row, you call the DataRowCollection.Add method with the DataRow object as an argument to add the DataRow to the DataTable.Rows collection. Alternatively, you may call the DataRowCollection.Add method with an array of Object types as an argument, to create a new row in the DataTable and set the data to the values of the Object array values. The following example illustrates how to create a DataTable, add table schema using DataColumn objects, and then add a row of data to the table:

```
Private Sub CreateDataColumnRow(ByVal sDCName As String)
    Dim dt = New DataTable()
```

```
      Dim dc = New DataColumn(sDCName, _
          System.Type.GetType("System.String"))
      dc.AllowDBNull = False
      dc.MaxLength = 50
      dt.Columns.Add(dc)
      dt.Columns.Add("RowCount", _
          System.Type.GetType("System.Int32"), _
          "Count(" & dc.ColumnName & ")")
      Dim dr = dt.NewRow()
      dr(sDCName) = "Michael"
      dt.Rows.Add(dr)
  End Sub
```

The C# version of this code follows:

```
private void CreateDataColumn(string sDCName)
{
    DataTable dt = new DataTable();
    DataColumn dc = new DataColumn(sDCName,
        System.Type.GetType("System.String"));
    dc.AllowDBNull = false;
    dc.MaxLength = 50;
    dt.Columns.Add(dc);
    dt.Columns.Add("RowCount",
        System.Type.GetType("System.Int32"),
        "Count(" + dc.ColumnName + ")");
    DataRow dr = dt.NewRow();
    dr[sDCName] = "Michael";
    dt.Rows.Add(dr);
}
```

In both cases, a string variable containing the name of the new DataColumn is passed into the top of the routine. Next, a new instance of an empty DataTable object named dt is created using the DataTable constructor. The next statements create a string type DataColumn with the column name set to the passed-in string variable, and then set the AllowDBNull property to False and the maximum length of the column data to 50 characters. The next statement then adds the DataColumn, dc, to the table's Columns collection. Next, a new DataColumn named RowCount is created and added to the DataTable using the DataColumnCollection.Add method. The RowCount DataColumn is an integer type column, and the Count aggregate expression is used to count the number of rows added to the DataTable. The next statement creates a new DataRow object, dr, using the DataTable's NewRow method. Next, data is placed into the DataRow at the named column. Last, the DataRow, dr, is added to the DataTable's Rows collection. Note here that when the row is added to the table, the aggregate Count expression is executed and the RowCount column data is automatically updated to "1" to reflect that one row was added to the DataTable.

UniqueConstraint

Rules and restrictions may be forced on the data in a DataTable by means of a constraint. A constraint helps to maintain the integrity of the data and determines the action that results when data in the row changes. When the EnforceConstraints property of the DataSet is set to True, constraint rules on the data are enforced. ADO.NET contains two types of constraints: ForeignKeyConstraints and UniqueConstraints. ForeignKeyConstraints are used with related objects and will be discussed in the next section, "Using the DataRelation Class." A UniqueConstraint is a simple constraint that ensures that the data in the specified column or columns of a DataTable is unique. You may create a UniqueConstraint by calling the UniqueConstraint constructor and specifying a DataColumn or array of DataColumns to place the constraint on. You may optionally specify a constraint name and whether this DataColumn or array of DataColumns is a primary key. After creating the UniqueConstraint, you add it to the DataTable.Constraints collection. Alternatively, if you set the DataTable's PrimaryKey property, a UniqueConstraint is automatically created and added to the table's Constraints collection. The following example illustrates how to create a UniqueConstraint for a DataColumn and also how to set a primary key for the DataTable:

```
Private Sub CreateDataConstraint(ByVal sUCName As String, _
        ByVal sPKName As String)
    Dim dt = New DataTable()
    Dim dc As DataColumn = dt.Columns.Add(sUCName)
    dt.Columns.Add(sPKName)
    Dim uc As UniqueConstraint = New UniqueConstraint(dc)
    dt.Constraints.Add(uc)
    Dim dtKey(1) As DataColumn
    dtKey(0) = dt.Columns(sPKName)
    dt.PrimaryKey = dtKey
End Sub
```

The C# version of this code follows:

```
private void CreateDataConstraint(string sUCName, string sPKName)
{
    DataTable dt = new DataTable();
    DataColumn dc = dt.Columns.Add(sUCName);
    dt.Columns.Add(sPKName);
    UniqueConstraint uc = new UniqueConstraint(dc);
```

```
    dt.Constraints.Add(uc);
    DataColumn[] dtKey = new DataColumn[1];
    dtKey[0] = dt.Columns[sPKName];
    dt.PrimaryKey = dtKey;
}
```

In both cases, two string variables containing the names of the new DataColumns are passed into the top of the routine. Next, a new instance of an empty DataTable object named dt is created using the DataTable constructor. The next two statements create and add two DataColumns to the DataTable using the DataColumnCollection.Add method and the two passed-in string variables as parameters. Next, a new UniqueConstraint object is created using the UniqueConstraint constructor and the DataColumn, dc, as an argument. Then the UniqueConstraint is added to the DataTable using the ConstraintCollection.Add method. The next statement creates an array of DataColumn objects. Next, the DataColumn array, dtKey, is set with the DataColumn named sPKName. Last, the dtKey DataColumn array is set as the primary key for the DataTable.

 Note here that when the primary key is set in the table, a UniqueConstraint for this column or columns is automatically created and added to the DataTable's Constraints collection.

Using the DataRelation Class

Along with DataTables, a DataSet may contain another important object, a DataRelation. A DataRelation is used to associate two DataTable objects together through their DataColumn objects. Relationships may be made between DataColumns of the tables that have the same DataType property. The primary function of the DataRelation in the DataSet is to allow you to navigate from one DataTable object to another. For example, you could create a parent/child DataRelation on an OrderHeader table and an OrderDetail table to help associate order information. When a DataRelation object is created, it checks for the existence of the DataTable objects in the DataSet and verifies that the DataColumns have matching types. You create a DataRelation by calling the DataRelation constructor and specifying a name for the DataRelation, and a parent column and child column from the DataTables you wish to build a relationship between. If you do not specify a name, an incremental default name (Relation1, Relation2, and so on) will be given to your DataRelation when it is added to the DataSet.Relations collection. You may create a DataRelation that is based on more than one parent/child column combination by calling the DataRelation constructor and specifying a DataRelation name, and an array of parent column objects and an array of child column objects. Again, the parent column type must match the corresponding child column type or an exception will be thrown. Once the DataRelation has been created, you need to add it to the DataSet.Relations collection. When a DataRelation is added to the DataSet, both a UniqueConstraint and a ForeignKeyConstraint are automatically created, unless you specify *createConstraints=false* when creating the DataRelation or set the DataSet property EnforceConstraints to False. The following example illustrates how to create a DataSet, add two DataTable objects, create a DataRelation object to associate the two tables through a DataColumn, and then add the DataRelation to the DataSet:

```
Private Sub CreateDataRelation(ByVal sDRelName As String)
    Dim dsSales = New DataSet("Sales")
    Dim dtStaff = dsSales.Tables.Add("Products")
    Dim dtInvoices = dsSales.Tables.Add("Invoices")
    Dim dcParent As DataColumn = dtStaff.Columns.Add("ProductID")
    Dim dcChild As DataColumn = dtInvoices.Columns.Add("ProductID")
    Dim drelSales = New DataRelation(sDRelName, dcParent, _
        dcChild, True)
    dsSales.Relations.Add(drelSales)
End Sub
```

The C# version of this code follows:

```
private void CreateDataRelation(string sDRelName)
{
    DataSet dsSales = new DataSet("Sales");
    DataTable dtStaff = dsSales.Tables.Add("Products");
    DataTable dtInvoices = dsSales.Tables.Add("Invoices");
    DataColumn dcParent = dtStaff.Columns.Add("ProductID");
    DataColumn dcChild = dtInvoices.Columns.Add("ProductID");
    DataRelation drelSales = new DataRelation(sDRelName, dcParent,
        dcChild, true);
    dsSales.Relations.Add(drelSales);
}
```

In both cases, a string variable containing the name of the new DataRelation is passed into the top of the routine. Next, a new instance of an empty DataSet object is created using the DataSet constructor. The next statements add two DataTable objects to the DataSet: one for a table named Products and another for a table named Invoices. Next, a DataColumn named ProductID is created and added to each of the DataTable's Columns collections. The next statement shows the DataRelation object being created using the string variable that was passed in as the DataRelation name, and the DataColumn from each of the DataTables that will create the association between the tables. Finally, the DataRelation is added to the DataSet.

ForeignKeyConstraint

A ForeignKeyConstraint dictates what happens to data in related DataTables when the values in the rows of the tables are updated or deleted. The UpdateRule property and the DeleteRule property define the action that is taken on the data in the child-related DataTable. For example, if a row in the parent table is deleted and a ForeignKeyConstraint's DeleteRule property is set to Cascade, the related row in the child table will also be deleted. You may also restrict changes to data in the parent DataTable. For example, if the ForeignKeyConstraint's DeleteRule property is set to None, trying to delete a row from the parent table when there is a related row in the child table will fail, and an exception will be thrown. You may create a ForeignKeyConstraint by calling the ForeignKeyConstraint constructor and specifying a parent DataColumn and child DataColumn, or an array of parent DataColumns and an array of child DataColumns. You may optionally specify a constraint name and AcceptRejectRule, UpdateRule, and DeleteRule properties. After creating the ForeignKeyConstraint, you add it to the DataTable.Constraints collection. The following example illustrates how to create two DataTable objects and add a DataColumn to each table, how to create a ForeignKeyConstraint object to associate the two tables through a DataColumn, and then how to add the constraint to the DataTable's Constraints collection.

```
Private Sub CreateForeignKeyConstraint(ByVal sFKName As String)
    Dim dtStaff = New DataTable("Staff")
    Dim dtInvoices = New DataTable("Invoices")
    Dim dcParent As DataColumn = dtStaff.Columns.Add("StaffID")
    Dim dcChild As DataColumn = dtInvoices.Columns.Add("StaffID")
    Dim fk = New ForeignKeyConstraint(sFKName, dcParent, dcChild)
    dtInvoices.Constraints.Add(fk)
End Sub
```

The C# version of this code follows:

```
private void CreateForeignKeyConstraint(string sFKName)
{
    DataTable dtStaff = new DataTable("Staff");
    DataTable dtInvoices = new DataTable("Invoices");
    DataColumn dcParent = dtStaff.Columns.Add("StaffID");
    DataColumn dcChild = dtInvoices.Columns.Add("StaffID");
    ForeignKeyConstraint fk = new ForeignKeyConstraint(sFKName,
        dcParent, dcChild);
    dtInvoices.Constraints.Add(fk);
}
```

In both cases, a string variable containing the name of the new ForeignKeyConstraint is passed into the top of the routine. The next statements create two new DataTable objects: one for a table named Sales and another for a table named Invoices. Next, a DataColumn named StaffID is created and added to each of the DataTable's Columns collections. The next statement shows the ForeignKeyConstraint object being created using the string variable that was passed in as the constraint name, and the DataColumn from the Sales table that will be the parent column and the DataColumn from the Invoices table that will be the child column. Finally, the ForeignKeyConstraint, fk, is added to the Invoices table's Constraints collection.

Here you add the ForeignKeyConstraint to the child column's table and a UniqueConstraint is automatically created and added to the parent table's Constraints collection.

Using the DataView Class

A DataView is another object that may be added to your DataSet and is often used in data-binding applications. DataViews allow you to dynamically view, search, and navigate through the data in DataTables with a different sort order, or filter the data through filter expressions. A DataView is not a DataTable, but rather a different view of an existing DataTable; therefore, you may not exclude columns that exist in the source table or append columns that do not exist in the source table. You may create a DataView by calling the DataView constructor and optionally specifying a DataTable name, filter, sort, and rowstate criteria, or you may create a reference to a DataTables's DefaultView property. If you do not specify a DataTable when creating a DataView, you will not be able to use the DataView until you set the table property to an existing DataTable. The following example illustrates how to create a DataView for an existing DataTable:

```
Private Sub CreateDataView()
    Dim dt = New DataTable("Counter")
    Dim dr As DataRow
    dt.Columns.Add("Count", System.Type.GetType("System.Int32"))
    Dim i As Integer
    For i = 1 To 10
        dr = dt.NewRow()
        dr("Count") = i
        dt.Rows.Add(dr)
    Next i
    Dim dv = New DataView(dt, "Count > 5", "", _
        DataViewRowState.CurrentRows)
End Sub
```

The C# version of this code follows:

```
private void CreateDataView()
{
    DataTable dt = new DataTable("Counter");
    DataRow dr;
    dt.Columns.Add("Count", System.Type.GetType("System.Int32"));
    for (int i = 1; i <= 10; i++)
    {
        dr = dt.NewRow();
        dr["Count"] = i;
        dt.Rows.Add(dr);
    }
    DataView dv = new DataView(dt, "Count > 5", "",
        DataViewRowState.CurrentRows);
}
```

In both cases, the routine starts by creating a DataTable object named dt. The next statement creates an instance of a DataRow object, and the next adds a DataColumn to the table with a column name of Count and a data type of integer. Next, a For loop adds 10 rows to the table, each containing an incremented number starting at 1 and going through 10 in the Count column of the table. Finally, the DataView is created using the dt table object and a filter expression of Count > 5, no sorting, and a row state of all the current rows. This results in a DataView object that contains only 5 rows instead of 10, because the filter expression specified to include only rows where the data in column Count was greater than the value of 5.

Creating a Strong Typed DataSet

A strong typed DataSet is a DataSet that is inherited from the base DataSet class. It has a schema file (an XML XSD file) that describes the structures of the objects contained in the DataSet. The information provided by this schema contains the DataTable and DataColumn names, the DataColumn's data types, and information about the DataConstraints that are in place. In contrast, an untyped DataSet has no corresponding schema. You can use either type of DataSet in your applications. However, typed DataSets make programming with the DataSet less error-prone because data type mismatch errors are caught at compile time rather than at runtime. When you use a typed DataSet, it generates an object model that allows the DataTable objects and DataColumn objects to become first-class objects—thereby allowing you direct access to them. You may create a strongly typed DataSet using the xsd.exe tool, which is included with the .NET Framework SDK (Software Development Kit). This utility tool generates a schema or class file from a specified source file, such as an XML file, which you may then compile and use in an ADO.NET application. An overview of the steps to create a strongly typed DataSet is shown in Figure 16-2.

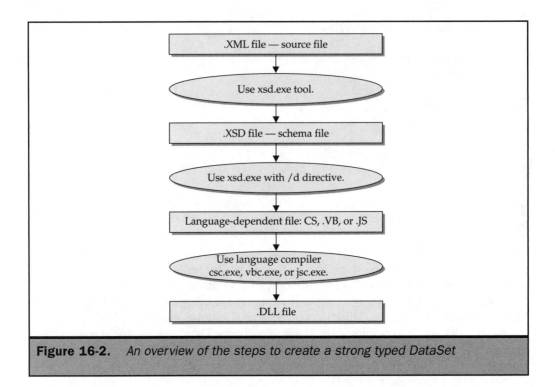

Figure 16-2. *An overview of the steps to create a strong typed DataSet*

As you can see in the figure, an XML file is used as a source for the schema file that is generated. Then a language-dependent file is generated from the schema file. Finally, the language-dependent file is compiled into a library for use in your project. The following example shows how to use the xsd.exe tool to generate a schema file inferred from the data in an XML file:

```
xsd.exe C:\ADONETSample\layout.xml /o:C:\ADONETSample
```

In this example, the xsd command is executed on an XML file named layout.xml, which will generate a schema file named layout.xsd. The /o directive indicates the output directory for the layout.xsd schema file. Once the schema file has been generated, you create the typed DataSet by using the xsd.exe tool and pass in the schema file as an argument. The following example shows how to create a DataSet using the layout.xsd schema file for use in a VB application:

```
xsd.exe C:\ADONETSample\layout.xsd /d /l:VB
    /n:layoutSchemaVB.Namespace
```

This creates a DataSet using the layout.xsd schema file for use in a C# application:

```
xsd.exe C:\ADONETSample\layout.xsd /d /l:CS
    /n:layoutSchemaCS.Namespace
```

The examples show executing the xsd command on the layout.xsd schema file, which generated a file named layout.vb in the VB example and layout.cs in the C# example. The /d directive creates a DataSet from the specified schema file and the /l directive informs the tool which language to use. The /n directive instructs the xsd utility to generate a Namespace for the DataSet using the specified name. The output files from the previous command may now be manually compiled into a library or a module and used in your ADO application, or you may add the file to your Solution Explorer window and Visual Studio will compile it automatically. To manually compile the layout.vb file, you use the Visual Basic .NET compiler tool vbc.exe; to compile the layout.cs file, you use the Visual C# .NET compiler tool csc.exe. The following example shows how to use the vbc.exe utility to compile the layout.vb file into a library DLL file:

```
vbc.exe C:\ADONETSample\layout.vb /t:library /r:System.dll
    /r:System.Data.dll /r:System.Xml.dll
```

This compiles the layout.cs file into a library DLL file using the csc.exe compiler:

```
csc.exe /t:library C:\ADONETSample\layout.cs /r:System.dll
    /r:System.Data.dll /r:System.Xml.dll
```

The examples show the creation of a library file called layout.dll using the appropriate language compiler. The /t directive instructs the compiler to create a library file and the /r directive designates the resource files to include in the compile. After the library file has been created, you add the references of your .NET project, and include and import statements for the Namespace at the top of your project code. You add a reference to your project by selecting Project | References to display the Add References dialog box. Click Browse, go to the directory where you compiled the DLL file, and select it as shown in Figure 16-3.

After selecting the file, click OK in the Add References dialog box to exit the dialog box and add a reference to the DLL file to your project. Next, you will add an import directive for the Namespace to your project. The following example shows how to add the layout Namespace to a VB project. Place this directive in the declarations section of your source code:

```
Imports layoutSchemaVB.Namespace;
```

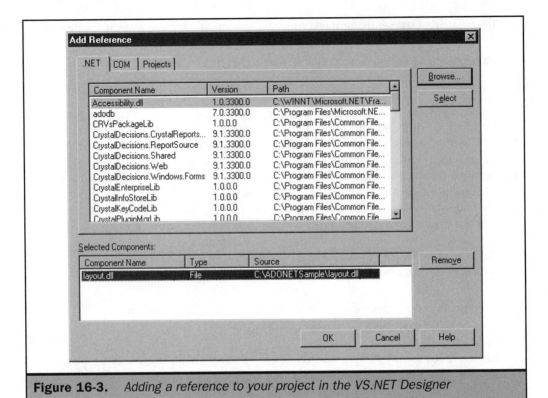

Figure 16-3. *Adding a reference to your project in the VS.NET Designer*

For a C# project, add a Namespace reference as follows:

```
using layoutSchemaCS.Namespace;
```

You are now ready to use your strong typed DataSet. You create your DataSet just like a standard DataSet by calling its constructor. For example, the following shows how to create an instance of the typed DataSet from the previous examples:

```
Dim dsl = New dslayout()
```

The C# version of this code is as follows:

```
dslayout dsl = new dslayout();
```

Strong typed DataSets improve development by catching any data type discrepancies at compile time rather than runtime, and they are integrated into your VS.NET environment, which enables automatic completion of lines as you type your code. Here you've seen how to create a strong typed DataSet using information inferred from an XML file. For more information on XML files and data mapping using XML, refer to Chapter 30 of this book.

Summary

In this chapter, you saw how to create a DataSet, and create and add the DataTables, DataColumns, DataRows, DataRelations, and constraints for the DataSet. The DataSet is at the heart of ADO.NET data access and contains all the elements needed to work with data in an environment that is detached from the data source. In the next chapter, you learn how to populate the DataSet by using the DataAdapter. You will also work with Command objects, which execute SQL statements against a data source, and table mappings, which describe the table relationships while populating a DataSet.

Chapter 17

Populating the DataSet Using the SqlDataAdapter

In the preceding chapter, you saw how to create a DataSet, an in-memory subset of a database that is separate from the data source, and add to it DataTables, Constraints, and DataRelations. You also saw how to set up the table schema by creating DataColumns, and you added data to the DataSet through the DataRows. In this chapter, you will see how to populate the DataSet with information through a DataAdapter. A DataAdapter is the tunnel between the DataSet and the data source, where data is read from a data source and populates the tables and constraints of a DataSet and also resolves the information from the DataSet back to the data source. The DataAdapter contains a database connection and a set of data commands— SelectCommand, InsertCommand, UpdateCommand, and DeleteCommand—to fill a DataSet and update a data source. The SelectCommand is used to fill the DataSet from the database, and the InsertCommand, UpdateCommand, and DeleteCommand are used to update the information back to the data source. These last commands are discussed in Chapters 25 though 29 of this book.

Each .NET Framework Data Provider includes its own DataAdapter object. The.NET Framework Data Provider for SQL Server contains the SqlDataAdapter object for interacting with a Microsoft SQL Server database. Figure 17-1 shows an overview of the SqlDataAdapter object.

As you can see in Figure 17-1, the .NET Framework Data Provider for SQL Server supplies the SqlConnection, SqlCommand, and SqlDataAdapter classes and objects that allow information to be retrieved and updated between the SQL Server database and the DataSet. In the first part of this chapter, you will see how to use the DataAdapter Configuration Wizard to create a visual SqlDataAdapter component object to populate a DataSet by selecting data using a SQL query statement. You will use the Query Builder tool to generate the SQL SELECT statement that is used in the SqlCommand object of the SqlDataAdapter. The next part of this chapter covers how to use the SqlDataAdapter class to select data and fill the DataSet using a SQL query statement.

Using the SqlDataAdapter

The SqlDataAdapter is used in combination with the SqlConnection object and the SqlCommand object to fill a DataSet with table schema and data from a Microsoft SQL Server database. These objects are included in the .NET Framework Data Provider for SQL Server and they provide enhanced performance of your application when you only need to connect to a SQL Server database.

Using the Visual Studio SqlDataAdapter Object

One way to populate a DataSet is to use the visual SqlDataAdapter component provided as a part of Visual Studio .NET. You use the same drag-and-drop method that's used by the Visual Studio .NET interface components to add the ADO.NET data components from the Visual Studio .NET Data Toolbox onto the visual designer. To create and use a new SqlDataAdapter component you must first create a Visual Studio VB.NET project, a C# project, or a J# project, and then add a new form to

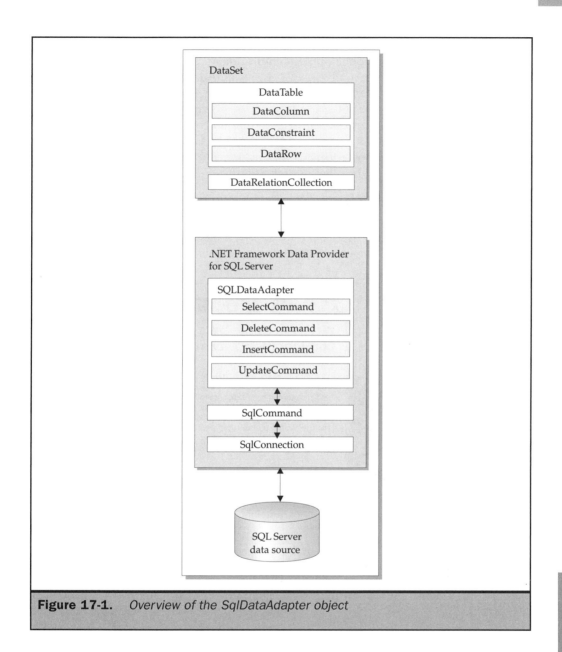

Figure 17-1.   *Overview of the SqlDataAdapter object*

the project. After the form has been created, you can display the form in the Visual Studio Designer window by clicking on the newly created form in the Visual Studio Project Explorer window that's displayed on the right side of the Visual Studio.NET development environment. Displaying the form in the Designer window causes the

Data Toolbox to be added to the collection of toolboxes that is displayed on the left side of the Visual Studio.Net development environment. Click the Data tab to open up the Data Toolbox, and then double-click the SqlDataAdapter object that's displayed in the Data Toolbox to add a SqlDataAdapter to the component pane of your project and start the DataAdapter Configuration Wizard, as shown in Figure 17-2.

The DataAdapter Configuration Wizard steps you through the process of setting up a SqlConnection object and commands that the DataAdapter will use against the database. Click the Next button on the Configuration Wizard to display the Choose Your Data Connection dialog box, as shown in Figure 17-3, and select a SQL Server database to connect to.

You may select a data connection from the drop-down list or create a new SQL Server connection to use with the DataAdapter. The drop-down list shows the data connections that have already been created using Server Explorer. If the connection you want to use is not listed in the drop-down list, you can click the New Connection button to display the

Figure 17-2. *DataAdapter Configuration Wizard Welcome dialog box*

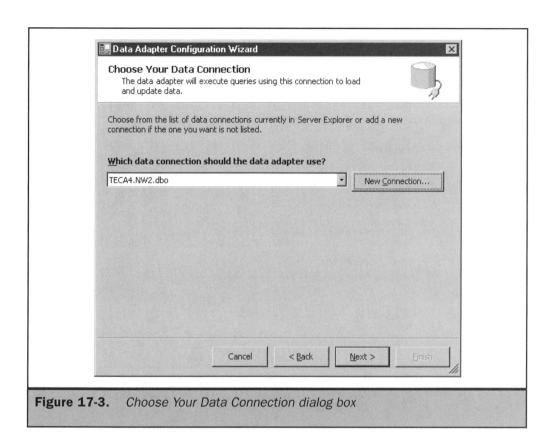

Figure 17-3.   *Choose Your Data Connection dialog box*

Data Link Properties dialog box and configure a new SQL Server connection. You can see in Figure 17-3 that the TECA4.NW2.dbo database has been selected. After selecting your data connection, click the Next button to display the Choose A Query Type dialog box shown in Figure 17-4.

Retrieving Data Using SQL Statements

The DataAdapter can use either SQL statements or stored procedures to access the SQL Server database. In Figure 17-4, you can see that the Use SQL Statements option has been selected. When this option is selected, you specify the SQL Select statement used to retrieve data from the database, and the wizard generates the corresponding Insert, Update, and Delete statements to be used when the data is resolved back to the data source. The Create New Stored Procedure option enables you to specify a SQL statement, and then the wizard generates stored procedures for each of the commands: Select, Insert, Update, and Delete. The Use Existing Stored Procedures option enables you to select a stored procedure from a drop-down list for each of the commands. These stored procedures must already exist in

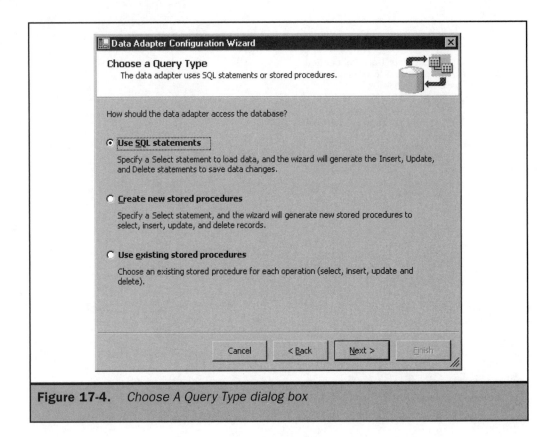

Figure 17-4. *Choose A Query Type dialog box*

the database. After selecting your query type option, click the Next button to display the Generate the SQL Statements dialog box shown in Figure 17-5.

In the Generate the SQL Statements dialog box, you can manually enter a SQL statement into the displayed text box or click the Query Builder button to display the Query Builder dialog box, shown in Figure 17-6, and graphically design your SQL statement.

The Query Builder allows you to graphically select tables, views, or functions to include in your SQL statement. You may select the columns, sort type, sort order, and criteria to be met for your query. As you select each element of your query, the SQL statement is built and displayed in the SQL pane of the Query Builder dialog box. Figure 17-6 shows the selection of the Orders table of the NW2 database in the top pane of the Query Builder dialog box. The second pane of the dialog box shows the selection of four columns to include in the query: OrderID, CustomerID, EmployeeID, and OrderDate. A Sort Type of Descending has also been added to the CustomerID

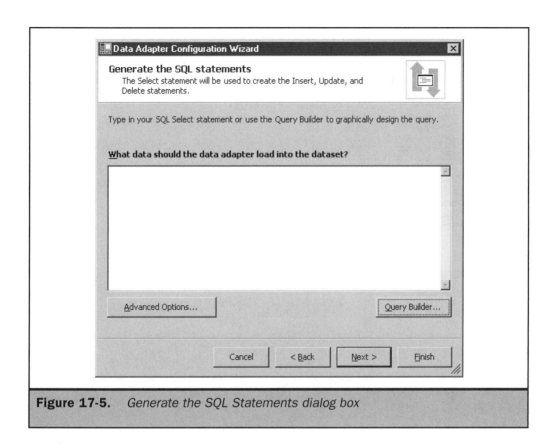

Figure 17-5.   *Generate the SQL Statements dialog box*

column. The third pane of the Query Builder shows the completed SQL statement that the SqlDataAdapter will use to retrieve data from the database. Once you are satisfied with your query selections, click OK to return to the Generate the SQL Statements dialog box. The SQL statement you built with the Query Builder will be shown in the text box of the dialog box.

The other button on the Generate the SQL Statements dialog box is the Advanced Options button. Click this button to display the Advanced SQL Generation Options dialog box shown in Figure 17-7.

The Advanced SQL Generation Options enable you to specify whether the wizard will generate the Insert, Update, and Delete command from the SELECT statement. It also enables you to set up optimistic concurrency to prevent concurrency conflicts and automatic refresh of the DataSet after an Insert or Update command executes. These advanced SQL generation options are discussed in Chapter 25. Click OK to return to the Generate the SQL Statements dialog box. Click the Next button to display the

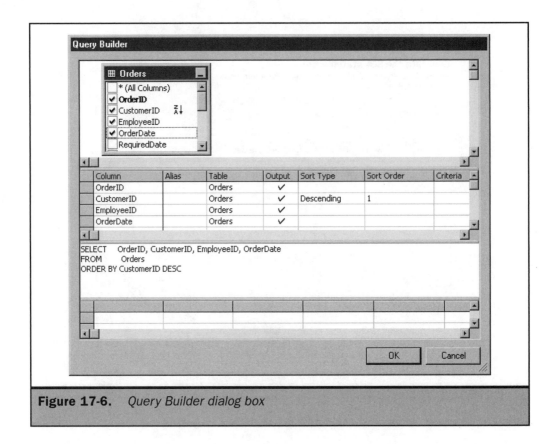

Figure 17-6. *Query Builder dialog box*

View Wizard Results dialog box, as shown in Figure 17-8, and verify the results of the DataAdapter Configuration Wizard.

Once you have selected the Finish button on the DataAdapter Configuration Wizard, a SqlDataAdapter component named sqlDataAdapter1 and a SqlConnection component named sqlConnection1 are added to your project. You then need to generate a DataSet from the SqlDataAdapter schema information that you just configured. Right-click the SqlDataAdapter component to display a pop-up menu and select the Generate DataSet option, as shown in Figure 17-9.

The Generate DataSet dialog box shown in Figure 17-10 appears and enables you to create a DataSet and add the tables specified in the SqlDataAdapter. You may choose an existing DataSet to add tables from the SqlDataAdapter to, or create a new DataSet and add the tables to it. In this example, the New DataSet option is chosen and a DataSet name of dsOrders is input. Note here that the Add This dataset To The Designer option is selected. When you select this option, a DataSet component is added to your project that is used as a data source for displaying data information in bound controls such as text boxes and data grids.

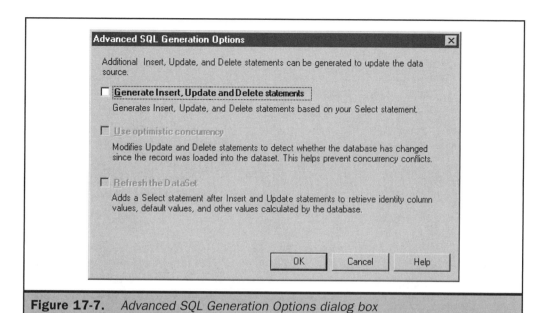

Figure 17-7. *Advanced SQL Generation Options dialog box*

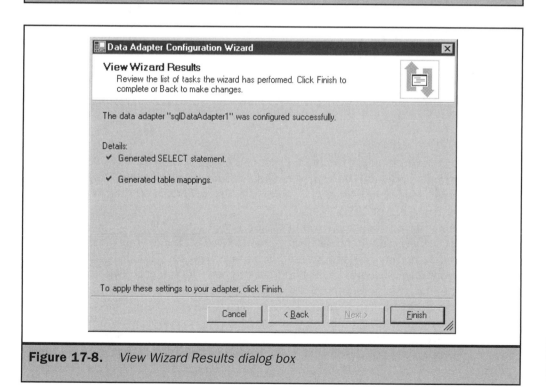

Figure 17-8. *View Wizard Results dialog box*

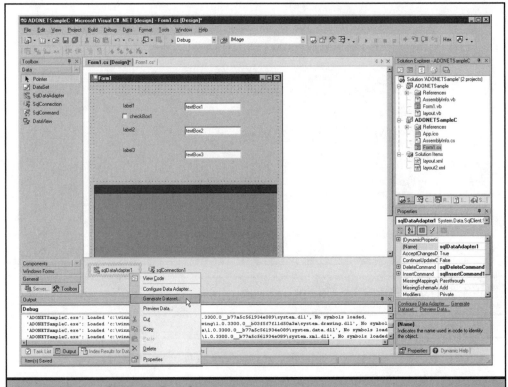

Figure 17-9. *Generate DataSet pop-up menu*

Click the OK button on the Generate DataSet dialog box, and a DataSet component named dsOrders1 is added to your project. Visual Studio also uses the information in the DataAdapter to generate an XML schema file, dsOrders.xsd, and adds it to your project, as shown in Figure 17-11.

This schema file may be used in other projects or components you create.

After the DataSet component has been generated and added to your project, you are ready to bind the DataSet to a Windows interface component such as a data grid. To add a data grid to your form, display the form in the Designer window and select the Windows Forms tab from the collection of toolboxes that is displayed on the left side of the Visual Studio.NET development environment. Then double-click the DataGrid object. Right-click the DataGrid to display a pop-up menu and select the Properties option. Scroll down the list of properties to DataSource and click its drop-down arrow to display the available data sources. Then select the DataSet/DataTable, dsOrders1.Orders, and the DataGrid will

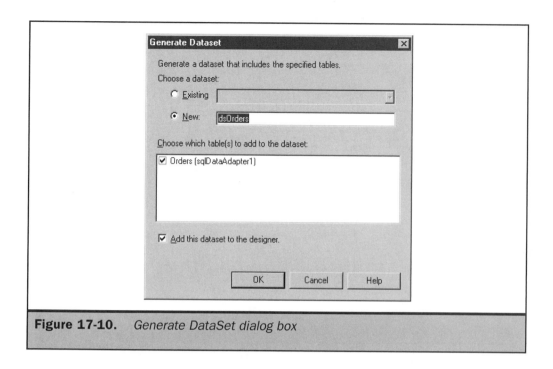

Figure 17-10.   *Generate DataSet dialog box*

display the columns from the table that were selected through the SqlDataAdapter object, as shown in Figure 17-12.

Finally, to populate the DataSet object from the data source, you call the SqlDataAdapter's Fill method using the DataSet as the first argument. In this example, call the SqlDataAdapter's Fill method from the form's Load method so that the data will be displayed as soon as the application starts. Double-click the Form object to display the code for the Form1_Load method, and add the Fill method to this subroutine as illustrated here:

```
Private Sub Form1_Load(ByVal sender As System.Object, _
        ByVal e As System.EventArgs) Handles MyBase.Load
    SqlDataAdapter1.Fill(dsOrders1)
End Sub
```

The C# version of this code is as follows:

```
private void Form1_Load(object sender, System.EventArgs e)
{
    sqlDataAdapter1.Fill(dsOrders1);
}
```

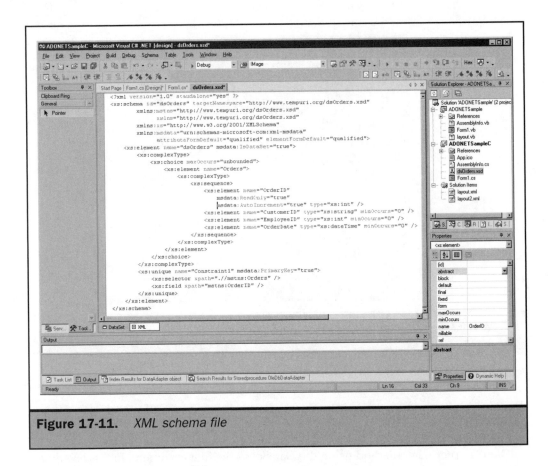

Figure 17-11. *XML schema file*

In this example, the dsOrders1 object that was generated earlier is passed to the Fill method of the sqlDataAdapter1 object. The sqlDataAdapter1's SelectCommand property was configured earlier in this chapter to select four columns from the Orders table in the SQL Server database, and the DataGrid's DataSource property was set to the DataSet object. When this program is run, the SelectCommand of the SqlDataAdapter will populate the DataSet and display the results in the DataGrid, as shown in Figure 17-13.

Using the SqlDataAdapter Class

The visual SqlDataAdapter component that is provided by the Visual Studio.NET design environment makes it pretty easy to create, populate, and display results to a bound control; but in many cases, you will want more control over exactly when and how the DataSet is created and populated by the SqlDataAdapter.

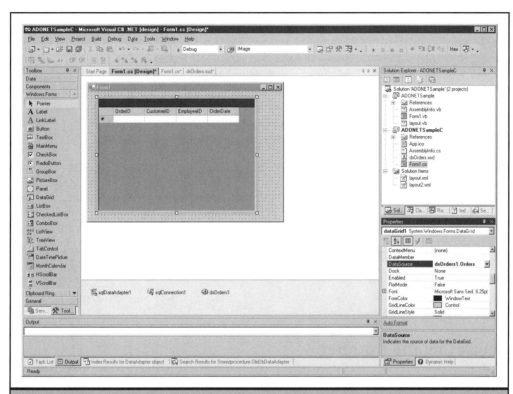

Figure 17-12. *DataGrid in design mode*

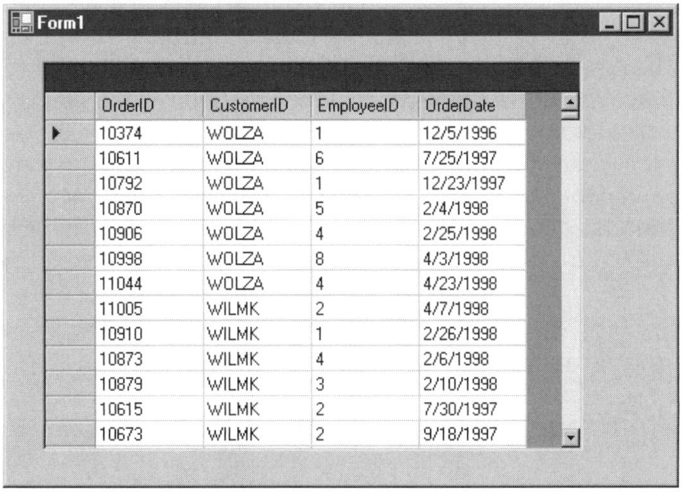

Figure 17-13. *DataGrid results form*

Adding the System.Data.SqlClient Namespace

Before you can use the .NET Framework Data Provider for SQL Server in your code, you must first specify an import directive for the System.Data.SqlClient Namespace in your project. This step isn't required when using the visual data components, but it is required in order to use the ADO.NET SQL Server objects in code. The System.Data.SqlClient Namespace contains all of the related SQL Server connection and data access classes. To add an import directive for the System.Data.SQLClient to a VB.NET project, you would add the following code to the declarations section of your source file:

```
Imports System.Data.SqlClient
```

To add an import directive for the System.Data.SqlClient Namespace to a C# project the code would appear as follows:

```
using System.Data.SqlClient;
```

 C# is case sensitive, so you need to be careful about matching the appropriate case for both your import directives and your code.

Populating the DataSet

After adding an import directive to your code, you're ready to begin using the different classes contained in the System.Data.SqlClient Namespace. The SqlDataAdapter uses the SqlConnection object of the .NET Framework Data Provider for SQL Server to connect to a SQL Server data source, and a SqlCommand object that specifies the SQL statements to execute to retrieve and resolve changes from the DataSet back to the SQL Server database. The SqlConnection object is explained in more detail in Chapter 4, and the SqlCommand object is explained in more detail in Chapter 8. Once a SqlConnection object to the SQL Server database has been created, a SqlCommand object is created and set with a SELECT statement to retrieve records from the data source. The SqlDataAdapter is then created, and its SelectCommand property is set to the SqlCommand object. Next, you create a new DataSet and use the Fill method of the SqlDataAdapter to retrieve the records from the SQL Server database and populate the DataSet. The following example illustrates how to make a SQL Server connection, create a SqlCommand object, and populate a new DataSet with the SqlDataAdapter. The contents of the DataSet will then be displayed to the user in a grid.

```
Private Sub FillDataSetSql(ByVal sServer As String, _
    ByVal sDB As String, ByVal sTable As String)
  Dim sqlCn = New SqlConnection("SERVER=" & sServer & _
    ";INTEGRATED SECURITY=True;DATABASE=" & sDB)
  Dim cmdSelect = New SqlCommand("SELECT * FROM " & sTable, _
    sqlCn)
```

```vb
    Dim sqlDA = New SqlDataAdapter()
    sqlDA.SelectCommand = cmdSelect
    Dim ds = New DataSet()
    Try
        sqlDA.Fill(ds, sTable)
    Catch e As Exception
        MsgBox(e.Message)
    End Try
    grdResults.DataSource = ds
    grdResults.DataMember = sTable
End Sub
```

The C# version of this code follows:

```csharp
private void FillDataSetSql(string sServer,string sDB,string sTable)
{
    SqlConnection sqlCn = new SqlConnection("SERVER=" + sServer +
        ";INTEGRATED SECURITY=True;DATABASE=" + sDB);
    SqlCommand cmdSelect = new SqlCommand("SELECT * FROM " + sTable,
        sqlCn);
    SqlDataAdapter sqlDA = new SqlDataAdapter();
    sqlDA.SelectCommand = cmdSelect;
    DataSet ds = new DataSet();
    try
    {
        sqlDA.Fill(ds, sTable);
    }
    catch (Exception ex)
    {
        MessageBox.Show("Fill SqlDataAdapter error: :" +
            ex.ToString());
    }
    grdResults.DataSource = ds;
    grdResults.DataMember = sTable;
}
```

String variables containing the name of a SQL Server system, a database, and a table in the database are passed into the top of the routine. Next, an instance of a SqlConnection object is created and its ConnectionString property is set as the argument of the constructor. The next statement creates a SqlCommand object and sets its CommandText property to a SQL SELECT statement and Connection property to the previously created SqlConnection object. Next, an instance of a SqlDataAdapter is created and its SelectCommand property is set to the SqlCommand object. An empty DataSet is then created, which will be populated with the results of the SELECT query command. The DataSet is then filled using the SqlDataAdapter's Fill method, which is executed inside a Try-Catch block. If the Fill method fails, the code in the Catch block is executed and a message box appears showing the error message. Last, a DataGrid's DataSource property is set to the DataSet, and the DataGrid's DataMember property is set to the table and displayed to the user. Notice here that the SqlConnection object was not explicitly opened or closed. When the Fill method of the SqlDataAdapter is executed, it opens the connection it is associated with, provided the connection is not already open. Then, if the Fill method opened the connection, it also closes the connection after the DataSet has been populated. This helps to keep connections to the data source open for the shortest amount of time possible, which frees resources for other user applications.

Summary

In this chapter, you saw how to populate a DataSet using the visual SqlDataAdapter component object provided with the .NET Framework Data Provider for SQL Server. You learned how to create a SqlConnection object to connect to the SQL database and then create a SqlCommand object to execute a SQL SELECT query command. The SqlDataAdapter's Fill method then uses the SqlConnection and SqlCommand query objects to retrieve the data and populate the DataSet. The next chapter covers how to populate a DataSet using the OracleDataAdapter that is included in the .NET Framework Data Provider for Oracle.

Chapter 18

Populating the DataSet Using the OracleDataAdapter

In the preceding chapter, you saw how to create a SqlDataAdapter and fill a DataSet using a SQL statement. In this chapter, you will see how to populate the DataSet with information through the OracleDataAdapter that is included with the .NET Framework Data Provider for Oracle. Figure 18-1 shows an overview of the OracleDataAdapter object.

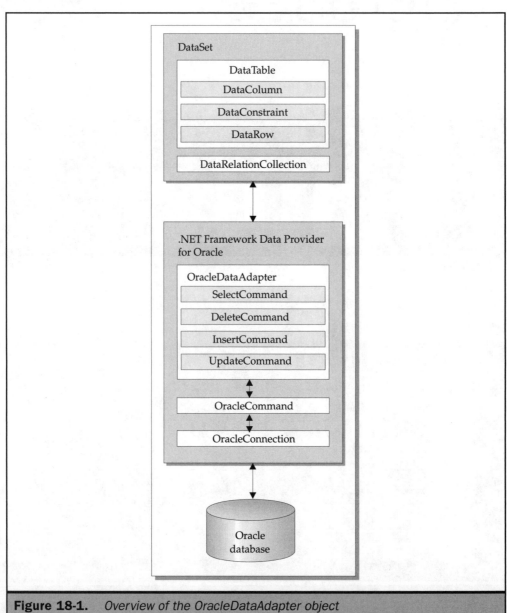

Figure 18-1. *Overview of the OracleDataAdapter object*

As you can see in Figure 18-1, the .NET Framework Data Provider for Oracle supplies the OracleConnection, OracleCommand, and OracleDataAdapter classes and objects that allow information to be retrieved and updated between the Oracle database and the DataSet. In the first part of this chapter, you will see how to use the visual OracleDataAdapter object in the Visual Studio development environment. In the second part of this chapter, table mappings and column mappings will be added to the OracleDataAdapter's TableMappings collection in your program code.

Using the OracleDataAdapter

The OracleDataAdapter is used in combination with the OracleConnection object and the OracleCommand object to fill a DataSet with table schema and data from an Oracle database. These objects are included in the .NET Framework Data Provider for Oracle. This Data Provider enhances the performance of your application when you need to connect to an Oracle database.

Using the Visual Studio OracleDataAdapter Object

Like the visual SqlDataAdapter component, the OracleDataAdapter component is provided as a part of Visual Studio.NET development environment. To create and use an OracleDataAdapter component, you create a Visual Studio project and then add a new form to the project. After the form has been created, you display the form in the Visual Studio Designer window, which causes the Data Toolbox to be added to the collection of toolboxes that are displayed on the left side of the Visual Studio.Net development environment. Click the Data tab to open up the Data Toolbox, and then double-click the OracleDataAdapter object that's displayed in the Data Toolbox to add an OracleDataAdapter to the component pane of your project and start the DataAdapter Configuration Wizard. Using the DataAdapter Configuration Wizard, step through the process of setting up an OracleConnection object that the OracleDataAdapter will use to connect to the database. After selecting an Oracle connection, click the Next button to display the Choose A Query Type dialog box shown in Figure 18-2.

Because the .NET Framework Data Provider for Oracle does not handle stored procedures in the same way as a SQL Server database, the Configuration Wizard does not allow automatic generation of stored procedure usage in the OracleDataAdapter. You can see in Figure 18-2 that the Create New Stored Procedures and Use Existing Stored Procedure options have been disabled and the Use SQL Statements option is selected. Click the Next button to display the Generate SQL Statements dialog box, and click the Query Builder button to graphically design your query command or type your SQL statement into the list box.

Click the Next button to display the View Wizard Results dialog box. Once you've viewed the results of the DataAdapter Configuration Wizard, click the Finish button and an OracleDataAdapter component named oracleDataAdapter1 and an OracleConnection

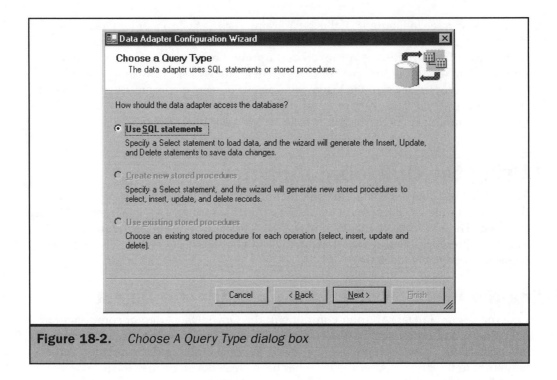

Figure 18-2. *Choose A Query Type dialog box*

component named oracleConnection1 will be added to your project. You then generate a DataSet from the OracleDataAdapter schema information that you just configured by right-clicking the OracleDataAdapter component to display a pop-up menu and select the Generate DataSet option. The Generate Dataset dialog box appears and enables you to create a DataSet and add the tables specified in the OracleDataAdapter, as shown in Figure 18-3.

In this example, an existing DataSet is chosen from the drop-down list and the EMP table is selected from the list box to be included in the DataSet and DataSet schema. The Add This Dataset To The Designer option is also selected. Click the OK button on the Generate DataSet dialog box to generate a DataSet component and add it to your project. The schema for your DataSet is also generated in the form of an XMD schema file and added to your project.

Preview or Edit the DataSet XML Schema

The visual DataAdapter components enable you to preview and edit the data schema of the DataSet. To view the schema, right-click the DataSet object. A pop-up menu like the one shown in Figure 18-4 appears.

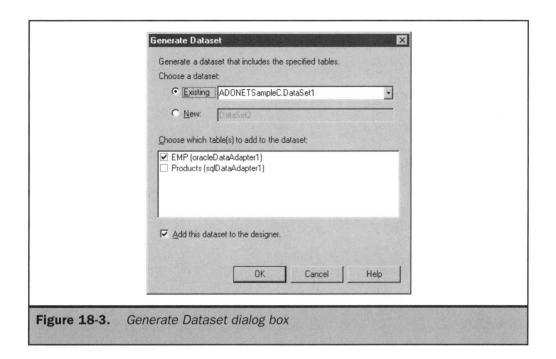

Figure 18-3.   *Generate Dataset dialog box*

Select the View Schema option to display the DataSet1.xsd file in the Visual Studio design environment window, as shown in Figure 18-5.

You can see in Figure 18-5 that the columns of the EMP table of the DataSet are defined and the key element is flagged. Notice that an XML Schema Toolbox is added to the toolbox collection on the left side of the development environment, in which you may interactively add or edit your DataSet XML schema as you would edit a Windows form. This is a handy tool that allows you to graphically build XML files that you can use in other applications.

After the DataSet component has been generated and added to your project, you are ready to bind the DataSet to a Windows or Web interface component such as a data grid. To add a data grid to your form, display the form in the Designer window, select the Windows Forms tab from the collection of toolboxes, and double-click the DataGrid object. Right-click the DataGrid object to display a pop-up menu and select the Properties option. Scroll down the list of properties to DataSource, and click its drop-down arrow to display the available data sources. Then select the DataSet/DataTable, dataSet1.EMP. To populate the DataSet object from the data source, you call the OracleDataAdapter's Fill method using the DataSet as the first argument. The OracleDataAdapter's Fill method will be called from the form's Load method, so that the data will be displayed as soon

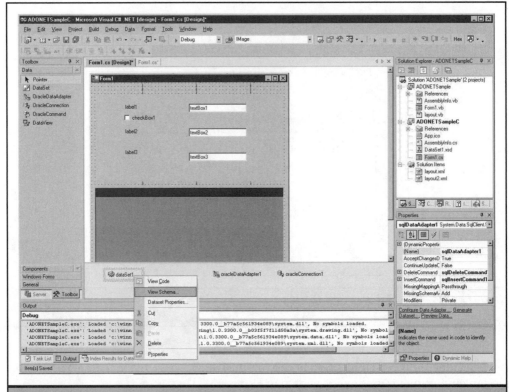

Figure 18-4. *View Schema pop-up menu*

as the application starts. Double-click the form object to display the code for the Form1_
Load method, and add the Fill method to this subroutine as illustrated here:

```
Private Sub Form1_Load(ByVal sender As System.Object, _
        ByVal e As System.EventArgs) Handles MyBase.Load
    OracleDataAdapter1.Fill(dataSet1)
End Sub
```

The C# version of this code is as follows:

```
private void Form1_Load(object sender, System.EventArgs e)
{
    oracleDataAdapter1.Fill(dataSet1);
}
```

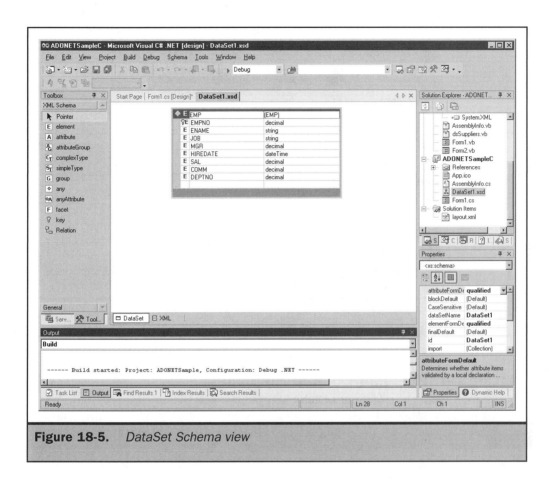

Figure 18-5.   *DataSet Schema view*

In this example, the dataSet1 object that was generated earlier is passed to the Fill method of the oracleDataAdapter1 object. The oracleDataAdapter1's SelectCommand property was configured to select the records from the EMP table in the database, and the data grid's DataSource property was set to the DataSet object. When this program is run, the SelectCommand of the OracleDataAdapter will populate the DataSet and display the results in the data grid, as shown in Figure 18-6.

Using the OracleDataAdapter Class

The visual OracleDataAdapter component offers an easy and fast way to populate a DataSet and display the results in a bound control—but for more advanced applications, you will want to use the OracleDataAdapter class to populate a DataSet. This next section demonstrates how to use the OracleDataAdapter class to fill your DataSet in program code.

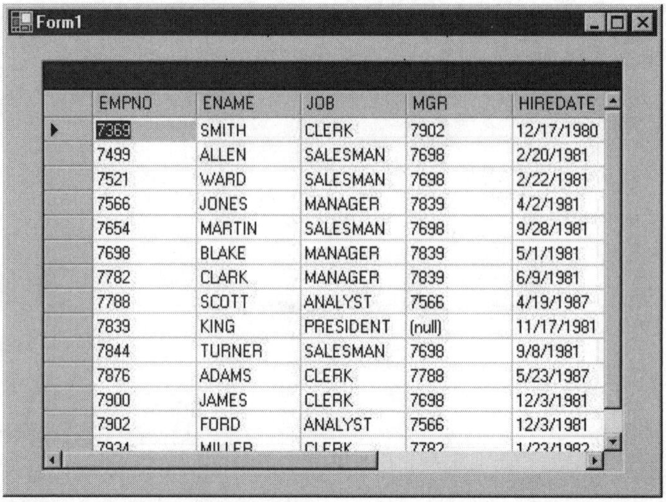

	EMPNO	ENAME	JOB	MGR	HIREDATE
▸	7369	SMITH	CLERK	7902	12/17/1980
	7499	ALLEN	SALESMAN	7698	2/20/1981
	7521	WARD	SALESMAN	7698	2/22/1981
	7566	JONES	MANAGER	7839	4/2/1981
	7654	MARTIN	SALESMAN	7698	9/28/1981
	7698	BLAKE	MANAGER	7839	5/1/1981
	7782	CLARK	MANAGER	7839	6/9/1981
	7788	SCOTT	ANALYST	7566	4/19/1987
	7839	KING	PRESIDENT	(null)	11/17/1981
	7844	TURNER	SALESMAN	7698	9/8/1981
	7876	ADAMS	CLERK	7788	5/23/1987
	7900	JAMES	CLERK	7698	12/3/1981
	7902	FORD	ANALYST	7566	12/3/1981
	7934	MILLER	CLERK	7782	1/23/1982

Figure 18-6. *Data grid results*

Setting Up Table and Column Mappings

DataAdapters contain collections of TableMapping objects that are used for defining table names in a DataSet, and that are different or more user friendly than the table names used in a database. For example, if you have a Customers table in your database and you want to fill a DataSet table with data from that Customers table that only includes customers from the West Coast area, you would use a select SQL statement that limits the retrieval of data to just the West Coast customers. To better identify this West Coast Customers table in the DataSet, you could add a TableMapping to name the DataTable "WestCoastCustomers." This does not change the name of the original Customers table in the database, but rather helps the DataTable in the DataSet be more recognizable. DataColumns in the DataTable may also be mapped to more useful names. The example that follows shows the mapping of tables and columns in the database to DataTables and DataColumns in the DataSet.

Populating the DataSet in Program Code

Before you use the .NET Framework Data Provider for Oracle in your code, you need to specify an import directive for the System.Data.OracleClient Namespace in your project. The technique for including the import directive for the OracleClient Namespace is described in Chapter 5, "Using the .NET Framework Data Provider for Oracle."

After adding an import directive to your code, you may use the different classes contained in the System.Data.OracleClient Namespace. The OracleDataAdapter uses an OracleConnection object and an OracleCommand object to retrieve data from the database and resolve changes from the DataSet back to the data source. You first create an OracleConnection object to the database using a valid connection string and then create an OracleCommand object using a select SQL statement that will retrieve the records. You then create the OracleDataAdapter using the OracleCommand object as an argument. This sets the selectCommand property of the OracleDataAdapter to use the OracleCommand's SQL statement to query the database and retrieve the specified records. Next, you add table mappings and column mappings to specify the names you would like to use in the DataTable. Then you create a new DataSet and use the Fill method of the OracleDataAdapter to retrieve the records from the database and populate the DataSet. The following example illustrates how to make a connection, create an OracleCommand object, and populate a new DataSet with the OracleDataAdapter and table and column mappings:

```vb
Private Sub FillDataSetOracle(ByVal sServer As String)
    Cursor.Current = Cursors.WaitCursor
    ' Create the connection, command, dataadapter objects
    Dim oracleCn = New OracleConnection("DATA SOURCE=" & sServer _
        & ";INTEGRATED SECURITY=yes")
    Dim cmdSelect = New OracleCommand("SELECT * FROM EMP", oracleCn)
    Dim oracleDA = New OracleDataAdapter(cmdSelect)
    ' Create the table mappings
    Dim dtMap As System.Data.Common.DataTableMapping = _
        oracleDA.TableMappings.Add("Table", "Employees")
    dtMap.ColumnMappings.Add("EMPNO", "EmployeeNumber")
    dtMap.ColumnMappings.Add("ENAME", "EmployeeName")
    dtMap.ColumnMappings.Add("MGR", "Manager")
    Dim ds = New DataSet
    Try
        ' Populate the dataset
        oracleDA.Fill(ds)
    Catch e As Exception
        Cursor.Current = Cursors.Default
        MsgBox(e.Message)
    End Try
    ' Display the results
    grdResults.DataSource = ds
    Cursor.Current = Cursors.Default
End Sub
```

The C# version of this code is as follows:

```csharp
private void FillDataSetOracle(string sServer)
{
    Cursor.Current = Cursors.WaitCursor;
    // Create the connection, command, and dataadapter objects
```

```
OracleConnection oracleCn = new OracleConnection(
    "DATA SOURCE=" + sServer + ";INTEGRATED SECURITY=yes");
OracleCommand cmdSelect = new OracleCommand(
    "SELECT * FROM EMP", oracleCn);
OracleDataAdapter oracleDA = new OracleDataAdapter(cmdSelect);
// Create the table mappings
System.Data.Common.DataTableMapping dtMap =
    oracleDA.TableMappings.Add("Table", "Employees");
dtMap.ColumnMappings.Add("EMPNO", "EmployeeNumber");
dtMap.ColumnMappings.Add("ENAME", "EmployeeName");
dtMap.ColumnMappings.Add("MGR", "Manager");
DataSet ds = new DataSet();
try
{
    // Populate the dataset
    oracleDA.Fill(ds);
}
catch (Exception ex)
{
    Cursor.Current = Cursors.Default;
    MessageBox.Show("Fill OracleDataAdapter error: :" +
        ex.ToString());
}
// Display the results
grdResults.DataSource = ds;
Cursor.Current = Cursors.Default;
}
```

In this example, a string variable containing the name of an Oracle system is passed into the top of the subroutine. Next, an instance of an OracleConnection object is created using a ConnectionString as the argument of the constructor. The next statement shows the creation of an OracleCommand object with its first argument set to a query statement and its second argument set to the previously created connection object. This example is using a table named EMP that is located in the sample Oracle database. Next, a DataTableMapping object named dtMap is created and added to the TableMappings collection of the OracleDataAdapter object. The DataTableMapping object is part of the System.Data.Common Namespace instead of the .NET Framework Data Provider Namespace, so the object creation has been qualified with the System.Data.Common Namespace. Notice here that the first argument of the Add method (the source table) is "Table" and not "EMP" as you might expect. When the DataAdapter's Fill or Update methods are called without specifying a table name, the DataAdapter will look for a default DataTableMapping of "Table". By setting the source table argument to "Table", you are overriding the default table mapping in the DataAdapter to your DataTableMapping. Next, several ColumnMappings are added to the DataTableMapping object. You can see that the first argument of the ColumnMappings.Add method is the source column name and the second argument is the name that will be used in the DataSet. A new DataSet is then created and filled using the OracleDataAdapter's Fill method, which is executed inside a Try-Catch block. If the Fill method fails, then the code in the Catch block will be executed and a message box will be displayed showing the error message. Last, a data grid's DataSource property is set to the DataSet and displayed to the user, as shown in Figure 18-7.

Notice that the OracleConnection object was not explicitly opened or closed. The Fill method will open the connection if it is not already open and will also close the connection after the DataSet has been populated.

Summary

In this chapter, you saw how to populate a DataSet using the OracleDataAdapter object included with the .NET Framework Data Provider for Oracle. You saw how to create an OracleConnection to the data source and then use the OracleDataAdapter's Fill method to retrieve the data and populate the DataSet from an Oracle database. You also saw how to graphically edit an XML schema file and map tables and columns in the DataSet to more user-friendly names. In the next chapter, you will see how to populate a DataSet using the OleDbDataAdapter that is included in the .NET Framework Data Provider for OLE DB and stored procedures.

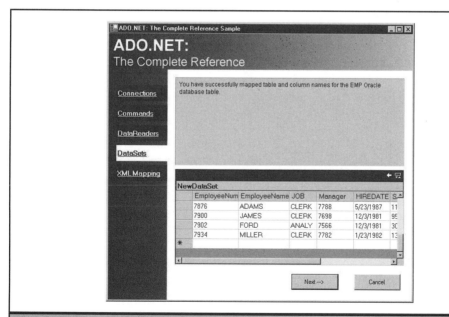

Figure 18-7.   *Results of table and column mapping*

Chapter 19

Populating the DataSet Using the OleDbDataAdapter

In Chapter 16, you saw how to create a DataSet and add to it DataTables, Constraints, and DataRelations. A DataSet is an in-memory subset of a database that is separate from the data source. You also saw how to set up the table schema by creating DataColumns and add data to the DataSet through the DataRows. In this chapter, you will learn how to populate the DataSet with information through the OleDbDataAdapter that is included with the .NET Framework Data Provider for OLE DB. The OleDbDataAdapter is the tunnel between a DataSet and an OLE DB–compliant database, where data is read from a database and fills the tables and constraints of a DataSet. The OleDbDataAdapter also resolves the information from the DataSet back to the database. Figure 19-1 shows an overview of the OleDbDataAdapter object.

As you can see in Figure 19-1, the .NET Framework Data Provider for OLE DB supplies the OleDbConnection, OleDbCommand, and OleDbDataAdapter classes and objects that allow information to be retrieved and updated between the data source and the DataSet. The first part of this chapter covers how to create an OleDbDataAdapter component using the DataAdapter Configuration Wizard. The DataAdapter Configuration Wizard steps you through the creation of a new stored procedure to use with the OleDbDataAdapter to populate a DataSet. The next part of this chapter shows you how to use the OleDbDataAdapter class in code to call your newly created stored procedure to fill the DataSet.

Using the OleDbDataAdapter

The OleDbDataAdapter is used in combination with the OleDbConnection object and the OleDbCommand object to fill a DataSet with table schema and data from a database such as Access. These objects are included in the.NET Framework Data Provider for OLE DB to enhance the performance of your application when you need to connect to an OLE DB–compliant database.

Using the Visual Studio OleDbDataAdapter Object

Like the visual SqlDataAdapter component, the OleDbDataAdapter component is provided as a part of the Visual Studio .NET development environment. To create and use a new OleDbDataAdapter component, you must first create a Visual Studio project, and then add a new form to the project. After the form has been created, you can display the form in the Visual Studio Designer window by clicking on the newly created form in the Visual Studio Project Explorer window. Displaying the form in the Designer window causes the Data Toolbox to be added to the collection of toolboxes that is displayed on the left side of the Visual Studio.Net development environment. Click the Data tab to open up the Data Toolbox, and then double-click the OleDbDataAdapter object that's displayed in the Data Toolbox to add an OleDbDataAdapter to the component pane of your project and start the DataAdapter Configuration Wizard. The DataAdapter Configuration Wizard steps you through the process of setting up an OleDbConnection object and an OleDbCommand object that the OleDbDataAdapter will use against

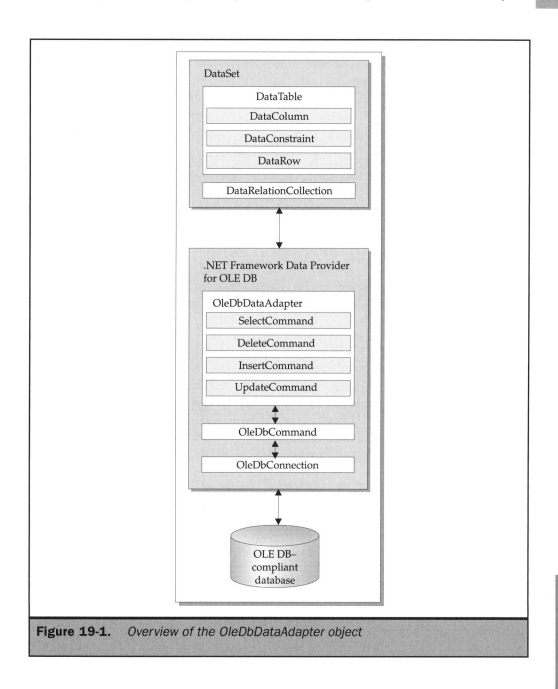

Figure 19-1.   *Overview of the OleDbDataAdapter object*

the database. Click the Next button on the DataAdapter Configuration Wizard to select an OLE DB–compliant database to connect to, and then click the Next button to display the Choose A Query Type dialog box, shown in Figure 19-2.

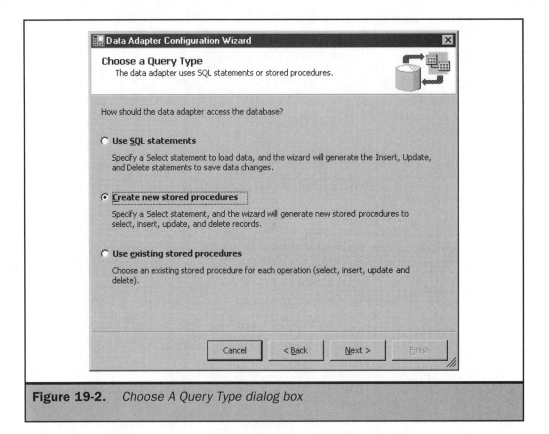

Figure 19-2. *Choose A Query Type dialog box*

Retrieving Data Using a Stored Procedure

The DataAdapter can use either SQL statements or stored procedures to access the database. As you can see in Figure 19-2, the Create New Stored Procedures option has been selected, which specifies to the wizard to generate the stored procedures for each of the commands used in the DataAdapter. Click the Next button to display the Generate the SQL Statements dialog box, and then enter a SQL statement into the displayed textbox or click the Query Builder button to graphically design your query command, as you saw in Chapter 17. After you've designed your query command, click the Next button to display the Create the Stored Procedures dialog box shown in Figure 19-3 and name your new stored procedures.

As you can see in Figure 19-3, names for each of the stored procedures to be created have been input and the option for the wizard to automatically create and store the procedures in the database has been selected. You may preview the SQL script that is

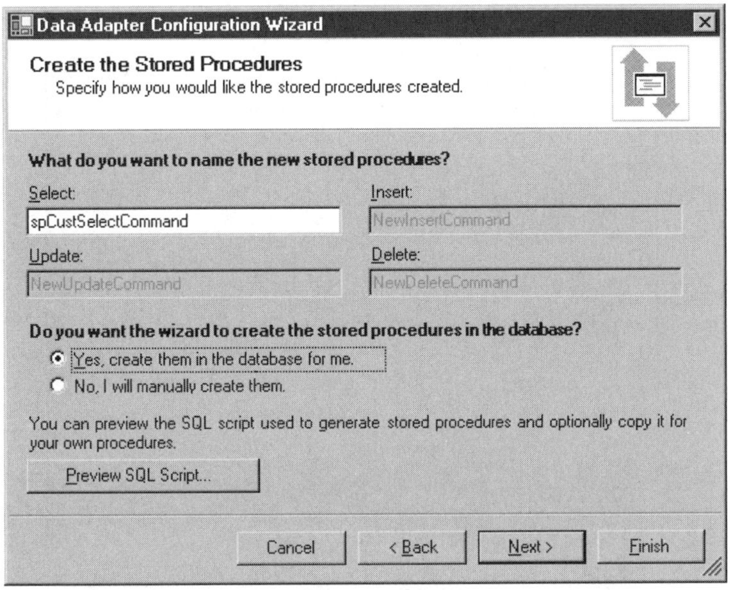

Figure 19-3.   *Create The Stored Procedures dialog box*

used to create your stored procedures by clicking the Preview SQL script button to display the Preview SQL Script dialog box shown in Figure 19-4.

The Preview SQL Script dialog box allows you to review the SQL script for each of the stored procedures and optionally copy them or save them to a file. After you've previewed your SQL script, click the Close button to return to the Create the Stored Procedures dialog box, and click the Next button to display the View Wizard Results dialog box. Once you've viewed the results of the DataAdapter Configuration Wizard, click the Finish button, and an OleDbDataAdapter component named oleDbDataAdapter1 and an OleDbConnection component named oleDbConnection1 will be added to your project. You then need to generate a DataSet from the OleDbDataAdapter schema information that you just configured. Right-click the OleDbDataAdapter component to display a pop-up menu and select the Generate DataSet option. The Generate DataSet dialog box appears and allows you to create a DataSet and add the tables specified in the OleDbDataAdapter. In this example, the New DataSet option is chosen and a DataSet name of dsCustList is input. Note here that the Add This Dataset To The Designer option is selected. When you select this option, a DataSet component is added to your project that is used as a data source for

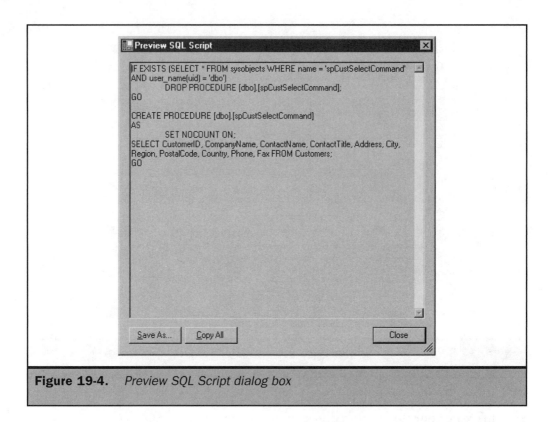

Figure 19-4.   *Preview SQL Script dialog box*

displaying data information in bound controls such as textboxes and data grids. After selecting the OK button on the Generate DataSet dialog box, a DataSet component named dsCustList1 is added to your project and an XML schema file named dsCustList.xsd is generated and also added to your project.

Another feature of the visual DataAdapter components is the capability to preview the data that will be retrieved by the DataAdapter. To preview the data, right-click the OleDbDataAdapter component to display a pop-up menu and select the Preview Data option. The DataAdapter Preview dialog box appears, and you can click the Fill DataSet button to display the resulting data that is retrieved from the database. The DataAdapter Preview dialog box is shown in Figure 19-5.

After the DataSet component has been generated and added to your project, you are ready to bind the DataSet to a Windows interface component such as a data grid. To add a data grid to your form, display the form in the Designer window, and select the Windows Forms tab from the collection of toolboxes and double-click the DataGrid object. Right-click the DataGrid to display a pop-up menu and select the Properties option. Scroll down the list of properties to DataSource, and click its drop-down arrow to display the available data sources. Then select the DataSet/

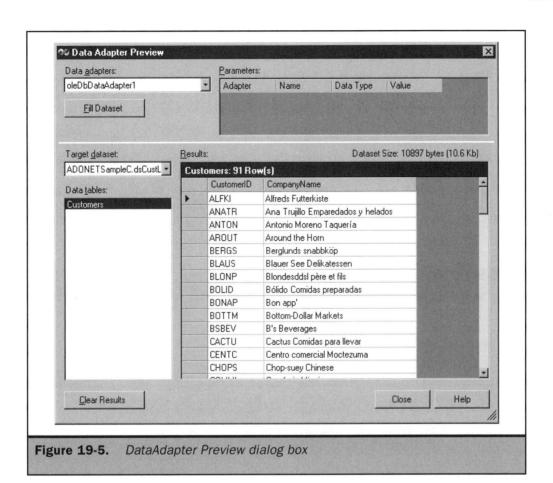

Figure 19-5.   *DataAdapter Preview dialog box*

DataTable, dsCustList1.Customers, and the DataGrid will display the columns from the table that was selected through the OleDbDataAdapter object. Finally, to populate the DataSet object from the data source, you call the OleDbDataAdapter's Fill method using the DataSet as the first argument. Again, the OleDbDataAdapter's Fill method will be called from the form's Load method, so the data will be displayed as soon as the application starts. Double-click the form object to display the code for the Form1_Load method, and add the Fill method to this subroutine as illustrated in the code that follows.

```
Private Sub Form1_Load(ByVal sender As System.Object, _
        ByVal e As System.EventArgs) Handles MyBase.Load
    OleDbDataAdapter1.Fill(dsCustList1)
End Sub
```

The C# version of this code is as follows:

```
private void Form1_Load(object sender, System.EventArgs e)
{
    oleDbDataAdapter1.Fill(dsCustList1);
}
```

In this example, the dsCustList1 object that was generated earlier is passed to the Fill method of the oleDbDataAdapter1 object. The oleDbDataAdapter1's SelectCommand property was configured earlier in this chapter to select all the records from the Customers table in the database, and the DataGrid's DataSource property was set to the DataSet object. When this program is run, the SelectCommand of the OleDbDataAdapter populates the DataSet and displays the results in the DataGrid, as shown in Figure 19-6.

Using the OleDbDataAdapter Class

Using the visual OleDbDataAdapter component makes it easy to populate a DataSet and display the results in a bound control. However, for more flexibility in your applications you will want to use the OleDbDataAdapter class to populate a DataSet. This next section demonstrates using the OleDbDataAdapter class.

Figure 19-6. *DataGrid results form*

Adding the System.Data.OleDb Namespace

You can use the OLE DB .NET Data Provider in your code by first specifying an import directive for the System.Data.OleDb Namespace in your project. The System.Data.OleDb Namespace contains all of the related OLE DB connection and data access classes. The VB.NET code you use to add an import directive for the System.Data.OleDb Namespace to your project is shown here. You add the following code to the declarations section of your source file:

```
Imports System.Data.OleDb
```

To add an import directive for the System.Data.OleDb Namespace to a C# project, the code is as follows:

```
using System.Data.OleDb;
```

Populating the DataSet

After adding an import directive to your code, you're ready to begin using the different classes contained in the System.Data.OleDb Namespace. The OleDbDataAdapter uses an OleDbConnection object and an OleDbCommand object to retrieve data from the database and resolve changes from the DataSet back to the data source. The OleDbConnection object is explained in more detail in Chapter 6, and the OleDbCommand object is explained in more detail in Chapter 10. Once an OleDbConnection object to the database has been created, an OleDbCommand object is created and set with a stored procedure to retrieve records from the data source. The OleDbDataAdapter is then created and its SelectCommand property is set to the OleDbCommand object. Next, you create a new DataSet and use the Fill method of the OleDbDataAdapter to retrieve the records from the database and populate the DataSet. The following example illustrates how to make a connection, create an OleDbCommand object, and populate a new DataSet with the OleDbDataAdapter:

```
Private Sub FillDataSetOleDb(ByVal sServer As String, _
    ByVal sDB as String)
    Dim oleDbCn = New OleDbConnection( _
        "PROVIDER=SQLOLEDB;SERVER=" & sServer & _
        ";TRUSTED_CONNECTION=Yes;DATABASE=" & sDB)
    Dim cmdSelect = New OleDbCommand("spCustSelectCommand",oleDbCn)
    cmdSelect.CommandType = CommandType.StoredProcedure
    Dim oleDbDA = New OleDbDataAdapter(cmdSelect)
    Dim ds = New DataSet()
    Try
        oleDbDA.Fill(ds)
```

```
    Catch e As Exception
        MsgBox(e.Message)
    End Try
    grdResults.DataSource = ds
End Sub
```

The C# version of this code is as follows:

```csharp
private void FillDataSetOleDb(string sServer, string sDB)
{
    OleDbConnection oleDbCn = new OleDbConnection(
        "PROVIDER=SQLOLEDB;SERVER=" + sServer +
        ";TRUSTED_CONNECTION=Yes;DATABASE=" + sDB);
    OleDbCommand cmdSelect = new OleDbCommand("spCustSelectCommand",
        oleDbCn);
    cmdSelect.CommandType = CommandType.StoredProcedure;
    OleDbDataAdapter oleDbDA = new OleDbDataAdapter(cmdSelect);
    DataSet ds = new DataSet();
    try
    {
        oleDbDA.Fill(ds);
    }
    catch (Exception ex)
    {
        MessageBox.Show("Fill OleDbDataAdapter error: :" +
            ex.ToString());
    }
    grdResults.DataSource = ds;
}
```

A String variable containing the name of a SQL Server system is passed into the top of the routine. Next, an instance of an OleDbConnection object is created and its ConnectionString property is set as the argument of the constructor. The next statement creates an OleDbCommand object with its first argument set to a stored procedure name and its second argument set to the previously created OleDbConnection object. This example uses the spCustSelectCommand stored procedure, which was created earlier in this chapter. Next, an instance of an OleDbDataAdapter is created with the argument of the constructor set to the OleDbCommand object. An empty DataSet is then created, which will be populated with the results of the stored procedure. The DataSet is then filled using the OleDbDataAdapter's Fill method, which is executed inside a Try-Catch block. If the Fill method fails, the code in the Catch block is executed and a message box appears showing the error message. Last, a DataGrid's

DataSource property is set to the DataSet and displayed to the user. Again, notice here that the OleDbConnection object was not explicitly opened or closed. When the Fill method of the OleDbDataAdapter is executed, it opens the connection it is associated with, provided that the connection is not already open. If the Fill method opened the connection, it will also close the connection after the DataSet has been populated.

Summary

In this chapter, you learned how to populate a DataSet using the visual SqlDataAdapter component and the SqlDataAdapter class, the visual OleDbDataAdapter object included with the .NET Framework Data Provider for OLE DB. You saw how to create an OleDbConnection to the data source and then create a OleDbCommand object to execute a stored procedure. The OleDbDataAdapter's Fill method then uses the connection and stored procedure to retrieve the data and populate the DataSet. In the next chapter, you will see how to populate a DataSet using the OdbcDataAdapter that is included in the .NET Framework Data Provider for ODBC.

Chapter 20

Populating the DataSet Using the OdbcDataAdapter

In Chapter 16, "Building a DataSet," you saw how to create a DataSet, an in-memory subset of a database that is separate from the data source, and add DataTables, constraints, and DataRelations to it. You also saw how to set up the table schema with DataColumns and add data with DataRows. In this chapter, you will see how o populate the DataSet with information through the OdbcDataAdapter, which is included with the .NET Framework Data Provider for ODBC. The OdbcDataAdapter is the tunnel between a DataSet and an ODBC-compliant database, where data is read from a database and fills a DataSet. The OdbcDataAdapter also resolves the information from the DataSet back to the database. Figure 20-1 shows an overview of the OdbcDataAdapter object.

As you can see in Figure 20-1, the .NET Framework Data Provider for ODBC supplies the OdbcConnection, OdbcCommand, and OdbcDataAdapter classes and objects that allow information to be retrieved and updated between the ODBC database and the DataSet. In the first part of this chapter, you will use the DataAdapter Configuration Wizard to create an OdbcDataAdapter object to populate a DataSet using stored procedures that already exist in your database. The next section will show how to use the OdbcDataAdapter class to fill a DataSet in the code section of your projects.

Using the OdbcDataAdapter

The OdbcDataAdapter is used in combination with the OdbcConnection object and the OdbcCommand object to populate DataSets from ODBC-compliant databases. These objects are included in the .NET Framework Data Provider for ODBC.

Using the Visual Studio OdbcDataAdapter Object

The OdbcDataAdapter component is provided as a part of Visual Studio .NET development environment. You create a new OdbcDataAdapter component by first creating a Visual Studio project and then adding a form to the project. After the form has been created, you can click the newly created form in the Visual Studio Project Explorer window to display it in the Visual Studio Designer window. The Data Toolbox will be added to the collection of toolboxes that is displayed on the left side of the Visual Studio.Net development environment. Double-click the OdbcDataAdapter object to add an OdbcDataAdapter to the component pane of your project. The DataAdapter Configuration Wizard will start and step you through the process of setting up an OdbcConnection object and OdbcDataAdapter to interact with the database.

Use Existing Stored Procedures to Retrieve Data

Click the Next button on the DataAdapter Configuration Wizard to select an ODBC data connection, and then click the Next button to display the Choose A Query Type dialog box shown in Figure 20-2.

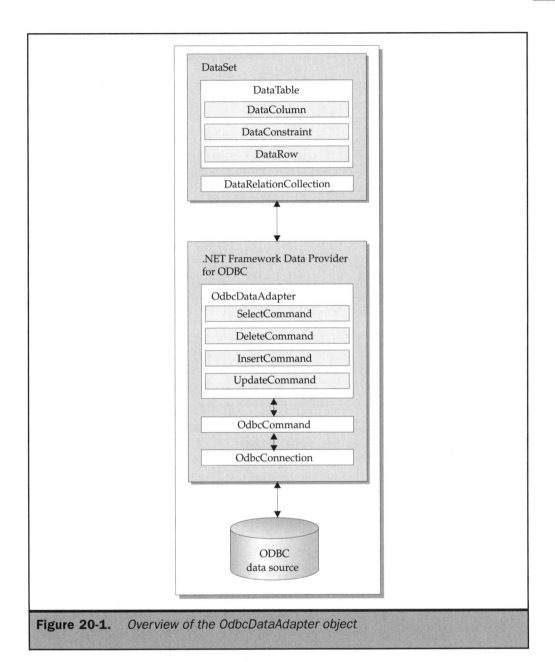

Figure 20-1. *Overview of the OdbcDataAdapter object*

The OdbcDataAdapter can use either SQL statements or stored procedures to access the database. You can see in Figure 20-2 that the Use Existing Stored Procedures option has been selected. This option specifies to the wizard to use stored procedures for each of the commands that already exist in the database. Click the Next button to display the Bind Commands To Existing Stored Procedures dialog box shown in Figure 20-3.

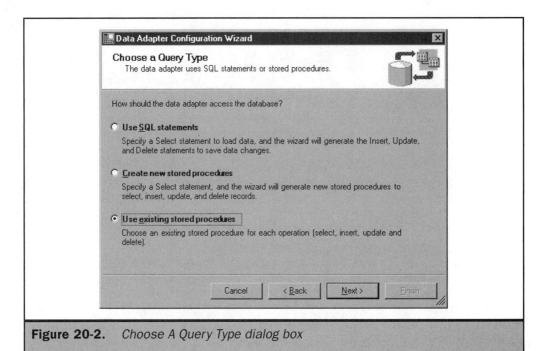

Figure 20-2. *Choose A Query Type dialog box*

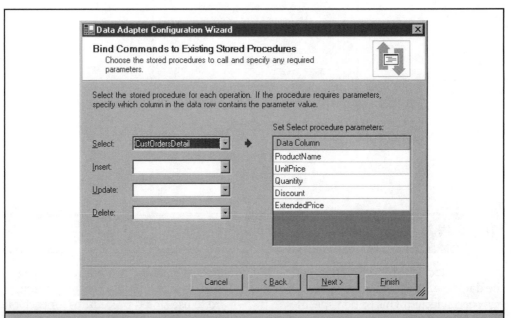

Figure 20-3. *Bind Commands To Existing Stored Procedures dialog box*

As you can see in Figure 20-3, a stored procedure named CustOrdersDetail has been selected from the Select drop-down box, and the data columns in the stored procedure have been added to the list on the right portion of the dialog box. You may also select the data column to use as a parameter value if your stored procedure uses parameters. Click the Next button to display the View Wizard Results dialog box shown in Figure 20-4.

After viewing the results of the DataAdapter Configuration Wizard, click the Finish button to add the odbcDataAdapter1 and odbcConnection1 components to your project. You then generate a DataSet by right-clicking the odbcDataAdapter1 component to display a pop-up menu and selecting the Generate Dataset option. The Generate Dataset dialog box, shown in Figure 20-5, will be displayed, allowing you to create a DataSet and add the tables specified in the OdbcDataAdapter.

In Figure 20-5, you can see that the New DataSet option is chosen, a DataSet name of dsCustOrdDet is input, and the Add This Dataset To The Designer option is selected. Click OK on the Generate Dataset dialog box to add the dsCustOrdDet1 DataSet and the dsCustOrdDet.xsd file to your project.

After the DataSet component has been generated from the DataAdapter and added to your project, you bind the DataSet to a Windows interface component such as a data grid. Add a data grid to your form by displaying the form in the Designer window, selecting the Windows Forms tab from the collection of toolboxes, and double-clicking the DataGrid object. Right-click the DataGrid and select the Properties option from the pop-up menu. Scroll down the list of properties to DataSource and select the DataSet/ DataTable, dsCustOrdDet1.CustOrdersDetail.

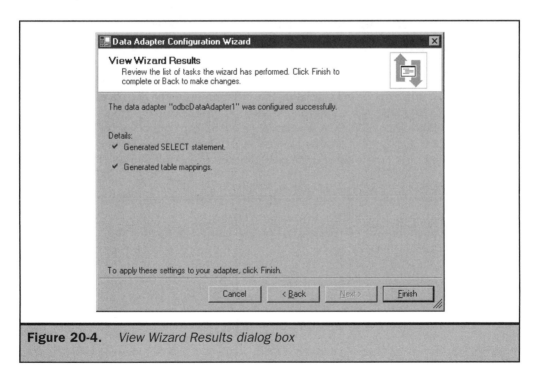

Figure 20-4.   *View Wizard Results dialog box*

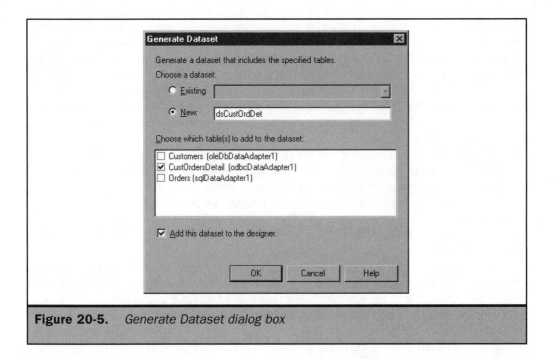

Figure 20-5. *Generate Dataset dialog box*

Using Parameter Values for Stored Procedures to Retrieve Data

The stored procedure in this example uses an input parameter of OrderID and is an integer type. You set the parameter value and then populate the DataSet object from the data source by calling the OdbcDataAdapter's Fill method using the DataSet as the first argument. The parameter value and the Fill method will be called from the form's Load method, so that the data will be displayed as soon as the application starts. Double-click the form object to display the code for the Form1_Load method and add the parameter value and Fill method to this subroutine as illustrated in the following:

```
Private Sub Form1_Load(ByVal sender As System.Object, _
      ByVal e As System.EventArgs) Handles MyBase.Load
   OdbcDataAdapter1.SelectCommand.Parameters("@OrderID").Value = _
      10259
   OdbcDataAdapter1.Fill(dsCustOrdDet1)
End Sub
```

The C# version of this code follows:

```
private void Form1_Load(object sender, System.EventArgs e)
{
    odbcDataAdapter1.SelectCommand.Parameters["@OrderID"].Value =
        10259;
    odbcDataAdapter1.Fill(dsCustOrdDet1);
}
```

A value of 10259 is set for the input parameter; and the DataSet, dsCustOrdDet1, that was generated earlier is passed to the Fill method of the odbcDataAdapter1 object. When this program is run, the stored procedure that was put into the SelectCommand property of the OdbcDataAdapter will populate the DataSet and the results will be displayed in the DataGrid, as shown in Figure 20-6.

Using the OdbcDataAdapter Class

Using the visual OdbcDataAdapter is a fast and easy way to populate a DataSet and bind your Windows form controls to data in the DataSet, but for more in-depth programming you will need to use the OdbcDataAdapter class. In the next section, you will see how to use stored procedures and fill a DataSet with the OdbcDataAdapter class.

Before you can use the .NET Framework Data Provider for ODBC in your code, you must first specify an import directive for the System.Data.Odbc Namespace in your project, as described in Chapter 7, "Using the .NET Framework Data Provider for ODBC."

Populating the DataSet in Program Code

After adding an import directive to your code, you're ready to use the classes contained in the System.Data.Odbc Namespace. Like the other Data Providers, the OdbcDataAdapter uses an OdbcConnection object to connect to a data source, and an OdbcCommand object to execute statements to retrieve and resolve changes from the DataSet back

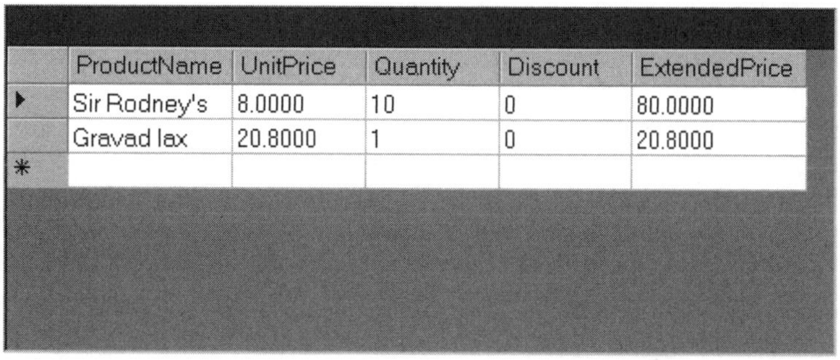

	ProductName	UnitPrice	Quantity	Discount	ExtendedPrice
▶	Sir Rodney's	8.0000	10	0	80.0000
	Gravad lax	20.8000	1	0	20.8000
✳					

Figure 20-6.   *Results of the CustOrdersDetail stored procedure*

to the database. You first create an OdbcConnection object, and then you create an OdbcCommand object using the name of a stored procedure. You then create an OdbcDataAdapter and set its SelectCommand property to the OdbcCommand object. Here, you will also set the parameter value of the OdbcDataAdapter's @OrderID parameter to the order number that will be retrieved. Next, you create a new DataSet and use the Fill method of the OdbcDataAdapter to retrieve the records from the database that match the specified parameter value and populate the DataSet. The following example illustrates how to make a connection, create an OdbcCommand object, and populate a new DataSet with the OdbcDataAdapter:

```
Private Sub FillDataSetOdbc(ByVal sServer As String, _
    ByVal sUser As String, ByVal sPassword As String, _
    ByVal sDB As String, ByVal sTable As String)
    Dim odbcCn = New OdbcConnection("DRIVER={SQL Server};SERVER=" _
        & sServer & ";UID=" & sUser & ";pwd=" & sPassword & _
        ";DATABASE=" & sDB)
    Dim cmdSelect = New OdbcCommand("spCustOrdDet", odbcCn)
    cmdSelect.CommandType = CommandType.StoredProcedure
    Dim odbcDA = New OdbcDataAdapter()
    odbcDA.SelectCommand = cmdSelect
    OdbcDataAdapter1.SelectCommand.Parameters("@OrderID").Value = _
        10259
    Dim ds = New DataSet()
    Try
        odbcDA.Fill(ds, sTable)
    Catch e As Exception
        MsgBox(e.Message)
    End Try
    grdResults.DataSource = ds
    grdResults.DataMember = sTable
End Sub
```

The C# version of this code follows:

```
private void FillDataSetOdbc(string sServer, string sUser,
    string sPassword, string sDB, string sTable)
{
    OdbcConnection odbcCn = new OdbcConnection(
        "DRIVER={SQL Server};SERVER=" + sServer + ";UID=" +
        sUser + ";PWD=" + sPassword + ";DATABASE=" + sDB);
    OdbcCommand cmdSelect = new OdbcCommand("spCustOrdDet", odbcCn);
```

```
        cmdSelect.CommandType = CommandType.StoredProcedure;
        OdbcDataAdapter odbcDA = new OdbcDataAdapter();
        odbcDA.SelectCommand = cmdSelect;
        odbcDataAdapter1.SelectCommand.Parameters["@OrderID"].Value =
            10259;
        DataSet ds = new DataSet();
        try
        {
            odbcDA.Fill(ds, sTable);
        }
        catch (Exception ex)
        {
            MessageBox.Show("Fill OdbcDataAdapter error: :" +
                ex.ToString());
        }
        grdResults.DataSource = ds;
        grdResults.DataMember = sTable;
    }
```

String variables containing the name of a server system, user, password, database, and a table in the database are passed into the top of the routine. Next, an OdbcConnection object is created and its ConnectionString property is set as the argument of the constructor. The next statements create an OdbcCommand object, set its CommandType property to Stored Procedure, and create an instance of an OdbcDataAdapter. The OdbcDataAdapter's SelectCommand property is set to the OdbcCommand object that was created, and its @OrderID parameter from the Parameters Collection is set to a value of 10259. The DataSet is then filled using the OdbcDataAdapter's Fill method inside a Try-Catch block, and a DataGrid's properties are set to the DataSet and table to display the information to the user.

Summary

In this chapter, you saw how to populate a DataSet using the OdbcDataAdapter object included with the .NET Framework Data Provider for ODBC. You saw how to create a connection to the data source, create a command object to execute an existing stored procedure, and set a parameter value in the OdbcDataAdapter's Parameters Collection. The DataAdapter's Fill method was then used to populate the DataSet with the specified information by executing the stored procedure. In the next chapter, you will see how to use multiple DataAdapters to retrieve data from different data sources.

Chapter 21

Populating the DataSet Using Multiple Tables and DataAdapters

In the last few chapters, you saw several techniques for populating a DataSet using the DataAdapter objects that are included in each of the .NET Framework Data Providers. The DataAdapter makes mapping and filling data from a data source to a DataTable in the DataSet quite simple and straightforward. Many times you will find that the information you need in your DataSet requires that the data come from multiple data sources. In the first part of this chapter, you will use visual DataAdapter components to retrieve information from multiple tables in a database into a DataTable in the DataSet. The second part of this chapter will show you how to use the DataAdapter classes in your program code to populate your DataSet with data that comes from a number of different sources.

Filling a DataSet from Multiple Tables

In some cases, you will need information from different tables in a database populated to a DataTable in the DataSet. For example, you may want a simple report on your customers and their corresponding "Ship to" addresses, but this data is found in different tables in the data source. You can bring all the relevant information together in a single DataTable in the DataSet. The data may be retrieved by using a SQL statement or stored procedure with a join tables clause and setting the SelectCommand of a DataAdapter. Figure 21-1 shows an overview of multiple tables filling the DataSet.

In Figure 21-1 you can see that two tables are selected from a single data source and passed to the .NET Data Provider's DataAdapter object to fill a single DataTable. In this section, you will see how to load data from more than one table in a database to a DataTable.

Using the Visual Studio DataAdapter Objects

As in the previous chapters, you create a new DataAdapter component by first creating a Visual Studio project and then adding a form to the project. After the form has been created, you select the form, and then double-click one of the DataAdapter objects found on the Data Toolbox to add a DataAdapter to the component pane of your project. The DataAdapter Configuration Wizard will start and step you through the process of setting up a Connection object and DataAdapter to retrieve data from the database.

Select Multiple Tables from the Data Source

After the DataAdapter Configuration Wizard's Welcome dialog box is displayed, click Next to select a data connection, and then click Next to display the Choose A Query Type dialog box. Select the Use SQL Statements radio button, and then click Next to display the Generate SQL Statements dialog box. Click the Query Builder button to graphically build a SQL statement that includes multiple tables from the database.

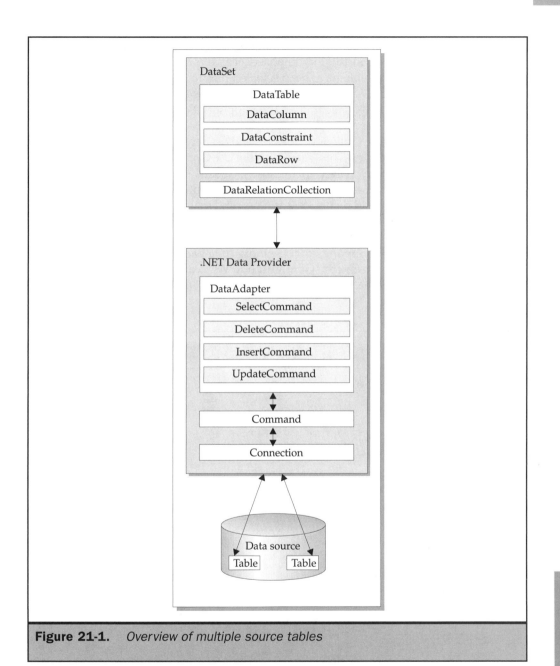

Figure 21-1.   *Overview of multiple source tables*

Figure 21-2 shows the Query Builder dialog box with the tables Products and Suppliers selected from the Northwind database located on a SQL Server. All of the columns from the Products table have been selected for inclusion in the query, and the columns SupplierID and CompanyName have been selected from the Suppliers table. There is an INNER JOIN specified on the SupplierID column for the tables. Click OK to close the Query Builder dialog box. Click the Advanced Options button to display the Advanced SQL Generation Options dialog box, and deselect the Generate Insert, Update, And Delete Statements check box. This will disable the Use Optimistic Concurrency and Refresh The Dataset check boxes. If the Generate Insert, Update, And Delete Statements check box is selected and you continue through the steps of the Configuration Wizard, the View Wizard Results dialog box will display warning errors, as you can see in Figure 21-3.

In this situation, where tables are joined in the SQL statement, the query will execute and populate a *single* DataTable from multiple tables in the database. However, in this case, DataAdapter commands for resolving data back to the data source cannot be automatically generated using the Configuration Wizard because the table and column mappings between the DataTable in the DataSet and the database table do not correspond to one another.

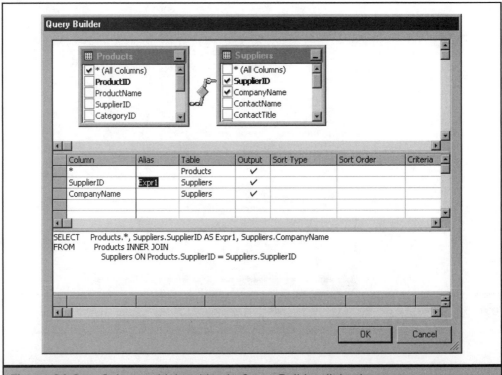

Figure 21-2. *Select multiple tables in Query Builder dialog box*

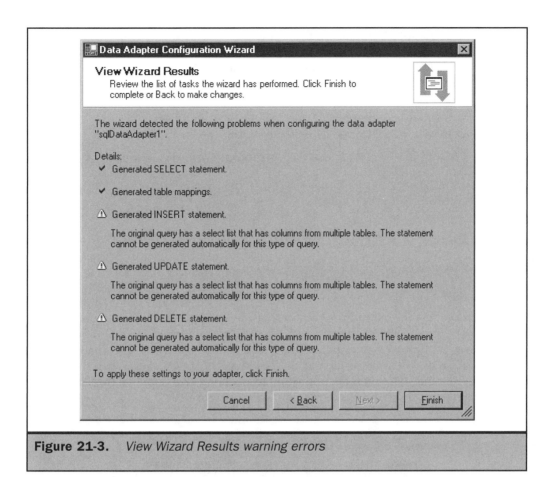

Figure 21-3.   *View Wizard Results warning errors*

Click the Finish button to add the sqlDataAdapter1 and sqlConnection1 components to your project. Then generate a DataSet by right-clicking the sqlDataAdapter1 component to display a pop-up menu and selecting the Generate Dataset option. The Generate Dataset dialog box appears, allowing you to create a DataSet and add it to your project. In this example, the New Dataset radio button is selected and a DataSet name of dsProducts is typed into the text box.

After the DataSet component has been generated from the DataAdapter and added to your project, you bind the DataSet to a Windows interface component such as a data grid. Add a data grid to your form by selecting the Windows Forms tab from the collection of toolboxes, and double-click the DataGrid object. Right-click the DataGrid and select the Properties option from the pop-up menu. Scroll down the list of properties to DataSource, and select the DataSet/DataTable, dsProducts1.Products.

Finally, to populate the DataSet object from the data source, you call the SqlDataAdapter's Fill method using the generated DataSet as the first argument.

Call the SqlDataAdapter's Fill method from the form's Load method, so that the data will be displayed as soon as the application starts. Double-click the form object to display the code for the Form1_Load method, and add the Fill method to this subroutine as illustrated here:

```
Private Sub Form1_Load(ByVal sender As System.Object, _
        ByVal e As System.EventArgs) Handles MyBase.Load
    SqlDataAdapter1.Fill(dsProducts1)
End Sub
```

The C# version of this code follows:

```
private void Form1_Load(object sender, System.EventArgs e)
{
    sqlDataAdapter1.Fill(dsProducts1);
}
```

You can see that the dsProducts1 object that was generated earlier is passed to the Fill method of the sqlDataAdapter1 object. The sqlDataAdapter1's SelectCommand property was configured to join the Products table and Suppliers table from the SQL Server database and fill a single table named Products in the DataSet. When this program is run, the SQL statement of the SqlDataAdapter will populate the DataSet and display the results in the DataGrid, as shown in Figure 21-4.

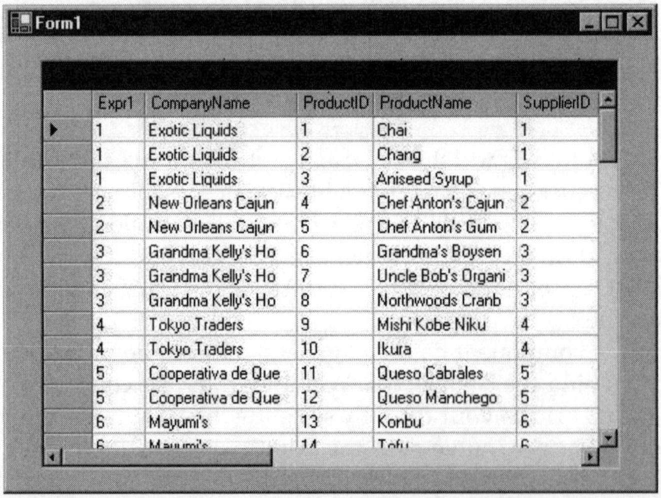

Figure 21-4.   *DataGrid results form*

Filling a DataSet from Multiple DataAdapters

In this section, you will see that each DataAdapter is responsible for exchanging data between a single table in a data source and a corresponding DataTable in a DataSet. This allows your ADO.NET application to seamlessly integrate data from heterogeneous data sources. If a DataSet contains multiple DataTables, then you need multiple DataAdapters populating the DataSet and resolving the changes back to the data source. Figure 21-5 shows an overview of the relationship of multiple DataAdapters to the DataSet.

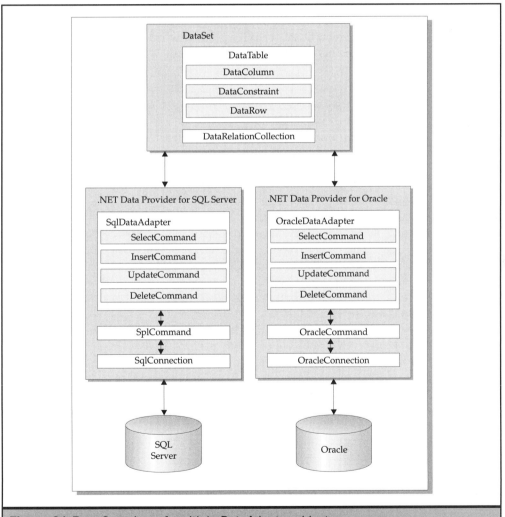

Figure 21-5.   *Overview of multiple DataAdapter objects*

This flexibility allows the DataSet to contain data from various data sources. For example, a DataSet may contain data from a SQL Server database, an Access database, and a data source that streams XML data.

Using the DataAdapter Classes

Each DataAdapter is included in its associated .NET Framework Data Provider. Before you can use the .NET Framework Data Provider objects in your code, you must first specify an import directive for the Namespace in your project. The import directives are described in Chapters 4–7.

After specifying the import directive you need, you will create a Connection and DataAdapter object for each DataTable you wish to fill in the DataSet. The following example illustrates populating a DataSet from the Northwind database on a SQL Server 2000 system, from the NWIND Access database, and also from the sample Scott Oracle database.

```
Private Sub FillDataSetMultiple(ByVal sServer1 As String, _
        ByVal sServer2 As String)
    Dim sqlCn As SqlConnection = New SqlConnection( _
        "SERVER=" & sServer1 & ";INTEGRATED SECURITY=True;" & _
        "DATABASE=Northwind")
    Dim sqlDA As SqlDataAdapter = New SqlDataAdapter( _
        "SELECT * FROM Products", sqlCn)
    Dim oleDbCn As OleDbConnection = New OleDbConnection( _
        "PROVIDER=Microsoft.Jet.OLEDB.4.0;DATA SOURCE=" & _
        "C:\\Program Files\\Microsoft Visual Studio\\NWIND.MDB;")
    Dim oleDbDA As OleDbDataAdapter = New OleDbDataAdapter( _
        "SELECT * FROM Suppliers", oleDbCn)
    Dim oracleCn As New OracleConnection("DATA SOURCE=" & _
        sServer2 & ";INTEGRATED SECURITY=yes")
    Dim oracleDA As OracleDataAdapter = New OracleDataAdapter( _
        "SELECT * FROM EMP", oracleCn)
    Dim dsMult = New DataSet()
    Try
        sqlDA.Fill(dsMult, "Products")
        oleDbDA.Fill(dsMult, "Suppliers")
        oracleDA.Fill(dsMult, "Employees")
    Catch e As Exception
        MsgBox(e.Message)
    End Try
    grdResults.DataSource = dsMult
End Sub
```

The C# version of this code follows:

```
private void FillDataSetMultiple(string sServer1, string sServer2)
{
    SqlConnection sqlCn = new SqlConnection("SERVER=" + sServer1
        + ";INTEGRATED SECURITY=True;DATABASE=Northwind");
    SqlDataAdapter sqlDA = new SqlDataAdapter(
        "SELECT * FROM Products", sqlCn);
    OleDbConnection oleDbCn = new OleDbConnection(
        "PROVIDER=Microsoft.Jet.OLEDB.4.0;DATA SOURCE=" +
        "C:\\Program Files\\Microsoft Visual Studio\\NWIND.MDB;");
    OleDbDataAdapter oleDbDA = new OleDbDataAdapter(
        "SELECT * FROM Suppliers", oleDbCn);
    OracleConnection oracleCn = new OracleConnection(
        "DATA SOURCE=" + sServer2 + ";INTEGRATED SECURITY=yes");
    OracleDataAdapter oracleDA = new OracleDataAdapter(
        "SELECT * FROM EMP", oracleCn);
    DataSet dsMult = new DataSet();
    try
    {
        sqlDA.Fill(dsMult, "Products");
        oleDbDA.Fill(dsMult, "Suppliers");
        oracleDA.Fill(dsMult, "Employees");
    }
    catch (Exception ex)
    {
        MessageBox.Show("Fill MultipleDataAdapters error: :" +
            ex.ToString());
    }
    grdResults.DataSource = dsMult;
}
```

Two server names are passed to the subroutine: one for the SQL Server and one for the Oracle database. A SqlConnection object is then created with a connection string passed as an argument to the constructor. The connection string designates the SQL Server system that was passed into the routine, with integrated security set to True and the initial database set to Northwind. The next statement creates a SqlDataAdapter passing to the constructor a SQL Select statement and the sqlCn SqlConnection object. Notice here that you may pass a SQL Select statement into the SqlDataAdapter's constructor, which will automatically set the SqlDataAdapter's selectCommand property to the statement. This allows you to bypass the need to create a SqlCommand object with the Select statement and then manually set the SqlDataAdapter's selectCommand to the SqlCommand object. Next, an OleDbConnection is created to the NWIND.mdb Access database located on the local hard drive. An OleDbDataAdapter is then created using the same method of passing in the SQL Select statement during its construction. A third Connection object and DataAdapter are created to an Oracle database source, and a statement to select all the records of the EMP table is specified. Creating the Oracle data source is discussed in Chapter 5, "Using the .NET Framework Data Provider for Oracle." A DataSet named dsMult is then created, and each of the DataAdapter's Fill methods are called to populate the DataSet from their respective data sources. The sqlDA SqlDataAdapter will build and fill a DataTable in the DataSet named Products, the oleDbDA OleDbDataAdapter will build and fill a DataTable in the DataSet named Suppliers, and the oracleDA OracleDataAdapter will build and fill a DataTable in the DataSet named Employees. The Fill methods are called within a Try-Catch loop to display to the user any errors that may occur during the population of the DataSet. Again, each respective Fill method will handle the opening and closing of the data source it is working with, so no explicit call is needed to open or close the SqlConnection, the OleDbConnection, or the OracleConnection. Last, a DataGrid's DataSource property is set to the DataSet and the DataTables are displayed to the user, as you can see in Figure 21-6.

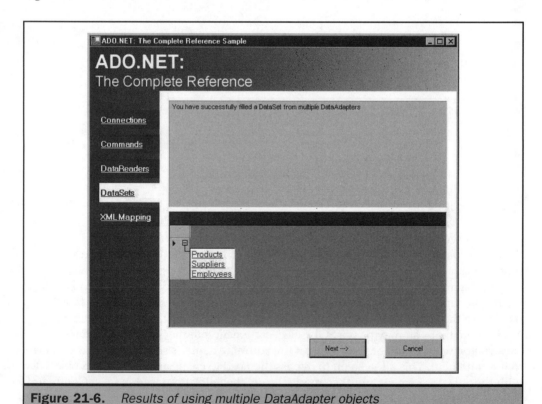

Figure 21-6. *Results of using multiple DataAdapter objects*

By looking at Figure 21-6, you can see that the DataTables included in the DataSet are listed in the DataGrid area, and the user may now click on each DataTable to expand it into the full grid area.

Summary

In this chapter, you saw how to populate a single DataTable in a DataSet using multiple tables of a data source. You also saw how to use multiple DataAdapters from multiple data sources to create a one-on-one correspondence between DataTables and database tables. In the next chapters, you will explore navigating through the DataSet by using Windows data-bound controls, selecting DataRows using a DataView, and setting up DataRelations.

The Complete Reference

ADO.NET

Chapter 22

Navigating the DataSet Using Windows Data-Bound Forms Controls

In the previous chapters, you saw how to populate a DataSet using the DataAdapter. You saw that each .NET Framework Data Provider includes its own DataAdapter object, Connection object, and Command object for filling the DataSet with information from the data source. In this chapter, you will see how to navigate through the DataSet and find and retrieve DataRows. In the first part of this chapter, you will see how to navigate through a DataTable in the DataSet and display the results in data-bound text boxes on a Windows form. You will navigate through DataSet rows using the data-bound management objects, BindingContext and CurrencyManager, for Windows Forms controls. In the second part of this chapter, you will navigate through the DataSet using the DataTable's Rows collection and manually manage the row position of the records in the DataSet.

Navigating Data with Windows Data-Bound Controls

In Windows applications, when a data source is bound to Windows Forms controls, the Windows application will also have a related CurrencyManager object. The CurrencyManager object manages a list of bindings to that data source. For example, if several TextBox controls are bound to the same DataTable, they will share the same CurrencyManager. However, if the TextBoxes are bound to multiple data sources, the form will have multiple CurrencyManager objects, each keeping track of the record position and data associated with their own data source. Windows Forms also contain a BindingContext object that keeps track of one or more CurrencyManagers. An overview of the Windows Forms controls, BindingContext, CurrencyManager, and data source interaction is shown in Figure 22-1.

As you can see in Figure 22-1, the data source is associated with a CurrencyManager object, the BindingContext then manages the CurrencyManager objects, and the Windows Forms controls communicate through the BindingContext to bind the controls to the data source. One of the important properties of the CurrencyManager is the Position property. The term "Currency" refers to the current position within the data. In earlier data access technologies, a cursor was maintained to keep track of record position and to help navigate to other records. Now, without cursors, the data is unaware of its current record, and you may have several positions set within the same data. The CurrencyManager's Position property is used to track the record position within the data, making it simple to move from record to record.

Using the Windows Forms Controls

To create and use Windows Forms controls, you must first create a Visual Studio VB.NET or C# project and then add a new form to the project. After you create the form, you can add several TextBox controls and Button controls to the form by double-clicking these controls from the Windows Forms tab of the toolbox that is displayed on the left side of the Visual Studio.NET development environment.

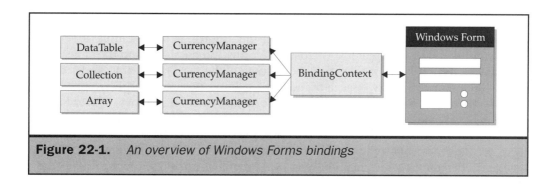

Figure 22-1. *An overview of Windows Forms bindings*

You may then add a DataAdapter to the form using the technique explained in Chapter 17. Figure 22-2 shows a Windows form with several TextBox controls, Button controls, and a DataAdapter and DataSet created.

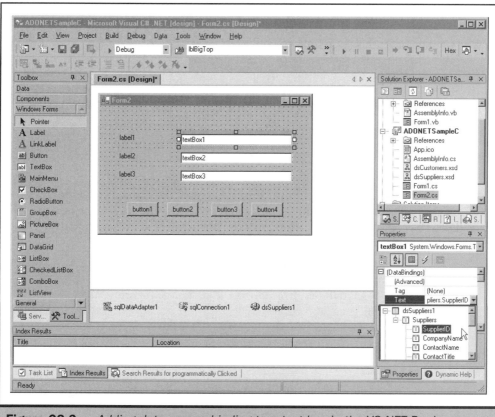

Figure 22-2. *Adding data source binding to a text box in the VS.NET Designer*

As you can see in Figure 22-2, textBox1 has been selected and the Text property of the DataBindings properties has been set to the data source. In this example, the data source for the sqlDataAdapter1 is Microsoft's Northwind database; and the table in the DataSet, dsSuppliers1, is Suppliers. Select each of the TextBox controls and set the DataBindings.Text property of each of them to a column from the Suppliers table. Next, select each of the Button objects on the form and set their Text property to First, Previous, Next, and Last. These will be the navigation buttons for moving through the DataSet. Double-click the First button to display the code for the button1_Click method. Here, the Position property of the CurrencyManager is set through the BindingContext object so when the First button is clicked, the data will be positioned to the first record in the table:

```
Private Sub button1_Click(ByVal sender As System.Object, _
        ByVal e As System.EventArgs) Handles button1.Click
    ' move to the First record
    Me.BindingContext(DsSuppliers1, "Suppliers").Position = 0
End Sub
```

The C# version of this code follows:

```
private void button1_Click(object sender, System.EventArgs e)
{
    // move to the First record
    this.BindingContext[dsSuppliers1, "Suppliers"].Position = 0;
}
```

You see here that the BindingContext object is supplied with the DataSet and table name and the Position property is set to zero. Set each of the other navigation buttons to the appropriate action of incrementing, decrementing, or moving to the last record in the data. The code for the navigation buttons is listed here, along with warning messages for beginning-of-file and en-of-file conditions:

```
Private Sub button2_Click(ByVal sender As System.Object, _
        ByVal e As System.EventArgs) Handles button2.Click
    ' move to the Previous record
    If Me.BindingContext(DsSuppliers1,"Suppliers").Position = 0 _
        Then
        MsgBox("You are already at the beginning of the data")
    Else
        Me.BindingContext(DsSuppliers1,"Suppliers").Position -= 1
    End If
```

```
End Sub

Private Sub button3_Click(ByVal sender As System.Object, _
        ByVal e As System.EventArgs) Handles button3.Click
    ' move to the Next record
    If Me.BindingContext(DsSuppliers1, "Suppliers").Position = _
      Me.BindingContext(DsSuppliers1, "Suppliers").Count - 1 Then
        MsgBox("You are already at the end of the data")
    Else
        Me.BindingContext(DsSuppliers1,"Suppliers").Position += 1
    End If
End Sub

Private Sub button4_Click(ByVal sender As System.Object, _
        ByVal e As System.EventArgs) Handles button4.Click
    ' move to Last record
    Me.BindingContext(DsSuppliers1, "Suppliers").Position = _
        Me.BindingContext(DsSuppliers1, "Suppliers").Count - 1
End Sub
```

The C# version of this code follows:

```
private void button2_Click(object sender, System.EventArgs e)
{
    // move to the Previous record
    if (this.BindingContext[dsSuppliers1,"Suppliers"].Position == 0)
    {
        MessageBox.Show("You are at the beginning of the data");
    }
    else
    {
        this.BindingContext[dsSuppliers1,"Suppliers"].Position -= 1;
    }
}

private void button3_Click(object sender, System.EventArgs e)
{
    // move to the Next record
    if (this.BindingContext[dsSuppliers1, "Suppliers"].Position ==
        this.BindingContext[dsSuppliers1, "Suppliers"].Count - 1)
    {
```

```
            MessageBox.Show("You are already at the end of the data");
        }
        else
        {
            this.BindingContext[dsSuppliers1,"Suppliers"].Position += 1;
        }
    }


private void button4_Click(object sender, System.EventArgs e)
{
    // move to the Last record
    this.BindingContext[dsSuppliers1, "Suppliers"].Position =
        this.BindingContext[dsSuppliers1, "Suppliers"].Count - 1;
}
```

The button2_Click routine checks the current position of the data, and if already zero, issues a message to the user that they are currently at the beginning of the data. If the current position is not zero, the Position property is decremented by one and the previous record is automatically displayed in the text boxes. Likewise, the button3_Click routine checks the current position of the data against the total records in the data, and if they are equal, issues a message to the user that they are currently at the end of the data. If the current position is not equal to the total number of records in the data, the Position property is incremented by one, and the next record is automatically displayed in the text boxes. The button4_Click routine simply sets the Position property equal to the last record in the data.

Finally, call the SqlDataAdapter's Fill method from the form's Load method, so that the data will be displayed as soon as the application starts. Double-click the form object to display the code for the Form2_Load method, and add the Fill method to this subroutine as illustrated here:

```
Private Sub Form2_Load(ByVal sender As System.Object, _
        ByVal e As System.EventArgs) Handles MyBase.Load
    SqlDataAdapter1.Fill(DsSuppliers1, "Suppliers")
End Sub
```

The C# version of this code follows:

```
private void Form2_Load(object sender, System.EventArgs e)
{
    sqlDataAdapter1.Fill(dsSuppliers1, "Suppliers");
}
```

Here, the dsSuppliers1 object that was generated earlier is passed to the Fill method of the sqlDataAdapter1 object. The sqlDataAdapter1 was configured to select the columns from the Suppliers table in the SQL Server. When this program is run, the DataSet will be populated with the data from the Suppliers table and displayed in the text boxes on the form, as shown in Figure 22-3. You may then move through the data by clicking each of the navigation buttons, and the data in the text boxes will change to reflect the current record.

Using the Collection Classes

Using the visual Windows Forms components provided by the Visual Studio.NET design environment makes it easy to bind data and display and move through the data on the form, but it is also fairly simple to navigate through the data using the DataTable's Rows collection. Instead of using the exposed BindingContext method to automatically display the data in the Forms controls, you can manually set the text of the controls in your code. You need to create a DataSet with a DataTable and a DataAdapter to retrieve the data from the data source and populate the DataSet.

Adding the Namespace

Before you can use the .NET Framework Data Provider in your code, you must first specify an import directive. To use the .NET Framework Data Provider for SQL Server, you import the System.Data.SqlClient Namespace into your project. To use the .NET Framework Data Provider for Oracle, you import the System.Data.OracleClient Namespace into your project. To use the .NET Framework Data Provider for OLE DB, you import the System.Data.OleDb Namespace into your project. To use the .NET

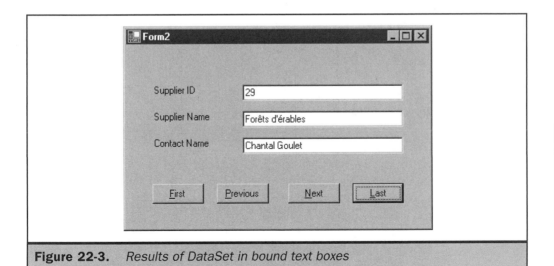

Figure 22-3.   *Results of DataSet in bound text boxes*

Framework Data Provider for ODBC, you import the System.Data.Odbc Namespace into your project. This step isn't required when using the visual data components, but it is required in order to use the ADO.NET Framework DataProvider objects in code. The Namespaces contain all of the related connection and data access classes. To add an import directive for the System.Data.SqlClient to a VB.NET project, you would add the following code to the declarations section of your source file:

```
Imports System.Data.SqlClient
```

To add an import directive for the System.Data.SqlClient Namespace to a C# project, the code would appear as follows:

```
using System.Data.SqlClient;
```

To add an import directive for the System.Data.OracleClient to a VB.NET project, you would add the following code to the declarations section of your source file:

```
Imports System.Data.OracleClient
```

To add an import directive for the System.Data.OracleClient namespace to a C# project, the code would appear as follows:

```
using System.Data.OracleClient;
```

To add an import directive for the System.Data.OleDb to a VB.NET project, you would add the following code to the declarations section of your source file:

```
Imports System.Data.OleDb
```

To add an import directive for the System.Data.OleDb Namespace to a C# project, the code would appear as follows:

```
using System.Data.OleDb;
```

To add an import directive for the System.Data.Odbc to a VB.NET project, you would add the following code to the declarations section of your source file:

```
Imports System.Data.Odbc
```

To add an import directive for the System.Data.Odbc Namespace to a C# project, the code would appear as follows:

```
using System.Data.Odbc;
```

In the following example, the data source will be the same Northwind database and Suppliers table used earlier. The same form with text boxes and navigation buttons will also be used. Here, instead of using the visual DataAdapter component from the .NET design environment, a Connection object and DataAdapter object will be constructed in the form's Load method. A global DataSet will also be constructed and filled with the data from the data source, and a global integer instantiated to keep track of the current data position. These two objects are declared global and placed in the declarations section of the Form2 class to allow the button subroutines shown later to access their values. The following example shows the creation of the global objects in the declarations section of the form:

```
Public Class Form2
    Inherits System.Windows.Forms.Form

    Dim dsSuppliers = New DataSet()
    Dim iPos As Integer
```

The C# code for these declarations is as follows:

```
public class Form2 : System.Windows.Forms.Form
{
    DataSet dsSuppliers = new DataSet();
    int iPos;
```

Next, the creation of the connection object and the DataAdapter object and the filling of the DataSet is done in the form's Load method. In the previous example using the visual components, the connection string was configured when the Connection object was placed on the project. Here the connection string needs to be stated in code. You can employ several different methods to retrieve server and database variables, including adding a login screen or passing the variables from another form. For simplicity's sake in this example, the server and database names have been hard-coded into the connection string argument of the Connection object:

```
Private Sub Form2_Load(ByVal sender As System.Object, _
        ByVal e As System.EventArgs) Handles MyBase.Load
    Dim oleDbCn As OleDbConnection = New OleDbConnection( _
```

```
          "PROVIDER=SQLOLEDB;SERVER=TECA4;" & _
          "INITIAL CATALOG=Northwind;TRUSTED_CONNECTION=Yes")
    Dim oleDbDA As OleDbDataAdapter = New OleDbDataAdapter( _
        "SELECT * FROM Suppliers", oleDbCn)
    Try
        ' fill the global dsSuppliers DataSet
        oleDbDA.Fill(dsSuppliers, "Suppliers")
        ' set the global position tracker
        iPos = 0
        textBox1.Text = _
            dsSuppliers.Tables("Suppliers").Rows(iPos) _
            ("SupplierID").ToString()
        textBox2.Text = _
            dsSuppliers.Tables("Suppliers").Rows(iPos) _
            ("CompanyName").ToString()
        textBox3.Text = _
            dsSuppliers.Tables("Suppliers").Rows(iPos) _
            ("ContactName").ToString()
    Catch ex As Exception
        MsgBox(ex.Message)
    End Try
End Sub
```

The C# version of this code follows:

```
private void Form2_Load(object sender, System.EventArgs e)
{
    OleDbConnection oleDbCn = new OleDbConnection(
        "PROVIDER=SQLOLEDB;SERVER=TECA4;" +
        "INITIAL CATALOG=Northwind;TRUSTED_CONNECTION=Yes");
    OleDbDataAdapter oleDbDA = new OleDbDataAdapter(
        "SELECT * FROM Suppliers", oleDbCn);
    try
    {
        // fill the global dsSuppliers DataSet
        oleDbDA.Fill(dsSuppliers, "Suppliers");
        // set the global position tracker
        iPos = 0;
        textBox1.Text =
            dsSuppliers.Tables["Suppliers"].Rows[iPos]
            ["SupplierID"].ToString();
        textBox2.Text =
```

```
                    dsSuppliers.Tables["Suppliers"].Rows[iPos]
                    ["CompanyName"].ToString();
            textBox3.Text =
                    dsSuppliers.Tables["Suppliers"].Rows[iPos]
                    ["ContactName"].ToString();
        }

        catch (Exception ex)
        {

        MessageBox.Show("Suppliers table error: " + ex.ToString());

        }

    }
```

At the top of the routine, an OleDbConnection object is created using the server named TECA4 and the Northwind database. The next statement creates an OleDbDataAdapter passing to the constructor a SQL Select statement and the OleDbCn OleDbConnection object. Notice here that you may pass a SQL Select statement into the OleDbDataAdapter's constructor, which will automatically set the OleDbDataAdapter's selectCommand property to the statement. This allows you to bypass creating an OleDbCommand object with the Select statement and then manually setting the OleDbDataAdapter's selectCommand to the OleDbCommand object. A DataSet named dsSuppliers is then created, and the DataAdapter's Fill method is called to populate the DataSet from the data source. The Fill method is called within a Try-Catch block to display to the user any errors that may occur during the population of the DataSet. The integer iPos is set to zero and used to manually set the current position of the data to the first record. The Text properties of the three text boxes on the form are then manually set with the data in the DataTable's Rows collection from the indicated position.

Note *The OleDbConnection object was not explicitly opened or closed. When the Fill method of the OleDbDataAdapter is executed, it will open the connection it is associated with, provided that the connection is not already open. Then, if the Fill method opened the connection, it will also close the connection after the DataSet has been populated.*

The form's First, Previous, Next, and Last navigation buttons will be used to move through the data; however, instead of using the BindingContext object, you can set the data into the text boxes from the Rows collection manually. This does mean that you will need to manually keep track of the current position of the data also. The following example shows the code navigation buttons:

```
Private Sub button1_Click(ByVal sender As System.Object, _
        ByVal e As System.EventArgs) Handles button1.Click
```

```
    ' move to the First record
    iPos = 0
    SetTextBoxes()
End Sub

Private Sub button2_Click(ByVal sender As System.Object, _
        ByVal e As System.EventArgs) Handles button2.Click
    ' move to the Previous record
    If iPos = 0 Then
        MsgBox("You are already at the beginning of the data")
    Else
        iPos -= 1
        SetTextBoxes()
    End If
End Sub

Private Sub button3_Click(ByVal sender As System.Object, _
        ByVal e As System.EventArgs) Handles button3.Click
    ' move to the Next record
    If iPos = dsSuppliers.Tables("Suppliers").Rows.Count - 1 Then
        MsgBox("You are already at the end of the data")
    Else
        iPos += 1
        SetTextBoxes()
    End If
End Sub

Private Sub button4_Click(ByVal sender As System.Object, _
        ByVal e As System.EventArgs) Handles button4.Click
    ' move to Last record
    iPos = dsSuppliers.Tables("Suppliers").Rows.Count - 1
    SetTextBoxes()
End Sub

Private Sub SetTextBoxes()
    textBox1.Text = _
        dsSuppliers.Tables("Suppliers").Rows(iPos) _
        ("SupplierID").ToString()
    textBox2.Text = _
        dsSuppliers.Tables("Suppliers").Rows(iPos) _
        ("CompanyName").ToString()
    textBox3.Text = _
```

```
            dsSuppliers.Tables("Suppliers").Rows(iPos) _
            ("ContactName").ToString()
End Sub
```

The C# version of this code follows:

```csharp
private void button1_Click(object sender, System.EventArgs e)
{
    // move to the First record
    iPos = 0;
    SetTextBoxes();
}

private void button2_Click(object sender, System.EventArgs e)
{
    // move to the Previous record
    if (iPos == 0)
    {
        MessageBox.Show("You are at the beginning of the data");
    }
    else
    {
        iPos -= 1;
        SetTextBoxes();
    }
}

private void button3_Click(object sender, System.EventArgs e)
{
    // move to the Next record
    if (iPos == dsSuppliers.Tables["Suppliers"].Rows.Count-1)
    {
        MessageBox.Show("You are already at the end of the data");
    }
    else
    {
        iPos += 1;
        SetTextBoxes();
    }
}
```

```
private void button4_Click(object sender, System.EventArgs e)
{
    // move to the Last record
    iPos = dsSuppliers.Tables["Suppliers"].Rows.Count-1;
    SetTextBoxes();
}

private void SetTextBoxes()
{
    textBox1.Text =
        dsSuppliers.Tables["Suppliers"].Rows[iPos]
        ["SupplierID"].ToString();
    textBox2.Text =
        dsSuppliers.Tables["Suppliers"].Rows[iPos]
        ["CompanyName"].ToString();
    textBox3.Text =
        dsSuppliers.Tables["Suppliers"].Rows[iPos]
        ["ContactName"].ToString();
}
```

The button1_Click routine sets the iPos variable to zero to indicate a move to the beginning of the data. The SetTextBoxes routine is then called to manually set the Text property of the three text boxes on the form, with the data in the DataTable's Rows collection from the indicated position. The button2_Click routine checks the value of the iPos variable and, if already zero, issues a message to the user that he or she is currently at the beginning of the data. If the variable is not zero, the iPos variable is decremented by one and the text boxes are set with the previous record's data. Likewise, the button3_Click routine checks the iPos variable against the total records in the data and, if they are equal, issues a message to the user that he or she is currently at the end of the data. If the variable is not equal to the total number of records in the data the iPos variable is incremented by one, and the text boxes are set with the next record's data. The button4_Click routine simply sets the iPos variable equal to the last record in the data.

Summary

In this chapter, you saw how to navigate through a DataSet using the visual Windows Forms controls and the data-bound management objects. You also saw how to move through the DataSet one record at a time using the DataTable's Rows collection object and manually set the record position. In the next chapter, you will see how to find a row or group of rows in a DataSet using the DataView object.

The
Complete
Reference

Chapter 23

Navigating Through the DataSet Using DataViews

In this chapter, you will see how to navigate through the DataSet and find and retrieve DataRows using the powerful sorting and filtering methods of DataViews. A DataView is a customized view of a DataTable that can be data-bound. The first part of this chapter shows how to find a single row in a DataTable by searching on single or multiple columns of a DataRow in the table. The second part of this chapter shows how to find multiple rows in a DataTable by searching on single or multiple columns, and return a DataRowView object. A DataRowView is a customized view of a DataRow rather than a DataTable.

Navigating Data with the DataView Class

Navigating through a DataTable one record at a time and displaying the data on a form is fairly simple and straightforward; however, you may want to go to a particular record or group of records without having to move through the entire table. The DataView class contains the methods Find and FindRows to accommodate this task. A DataView allows you to navigate through the data in a DataTable with a different sort order, or filter the data through filter expressions. One important property of the DataView object is its Sort property. You must set a sort order in order to use the Find or FindRows method on a DataView or an exception will be thrown.

Finding a Record in the DataTable

To find a specific record in a DataTable, you use the Find method of a DataView over that table and search according to the sort key value. The Find method returns an integer value containing the index of the first row that matches the search criteria. You may search on a single column or multiple columns of the DataView; however, the Sort property must correspond to the number of columns and the order the columns are being searched in. The following example illustrates searching data for a specific record using a single column:

```
Private Sub DataViewFind(ByVal sServer As String, _
        ByVal sDB As String)
    Dim sqlCn As SqlConnection = New SqlConnection("SERVER=" & _
        sServer & ";INTEGRATED SECURITY=True;DATABASE=" & sDB)
    Dim sqlDA As SqlDataAdapter = New SqlDataAdapter( _
        "SELECT * FROM Categories", sqlCn)
    Dim ds = New DataSet()
    Try
        sqlDA.Fill(ds, "Categories")
        Dim dv = New DataView(ds.Tables("Categories"), "", _
            "CategoryName", DataViewRowState.CurrentRows)
        Dim iRow As Integer
        iRow = dv.Find("Confections")
```

```
            lstResults.Items.Add(dv(iRow)("CategoryID").ToString() & _
                        dv(iRow)("CategoryName").ToString() & _
                        dv(iRow)("Description").ToString())
    Catch e As Exception
        MsgBox(e.Message)
    End Try
End Sub
```

The C# version of this code follows:

```
private void DataViewFind(string sServer, string sDB)
{
    SqlConnection sqlCn = new SqlConnection("SERVER=" + sServer +
        ";INTEGRATED SECURITY=True;DATABASE=" + sDB);
    SqlDataAdapter sqlDA = new SqlDataAdapter(
        "SELECT * FROM Categories", sqlCn);
    DataSet ds = new DataSet();
    try
    {
        sqlDA.Fill(ds, "Categories");
        DataView dv = new DataView(ds.Tables["Categories"], "",
            "CategoryName", DataViewRowState.CurrentRows);
        int iRow = dv.Find("Confections");
        lstResults.Items.Add(dv[iRow]["CategoryID"].ToString() +
                    '\t' + dv[iRow]["CategoryName"].ToString() +
                    '\t' + dv[iRow]["Description"].ToString());
    }
    catch (Exception ex)
    {
        MessageBox.Show("DataViewFind: :" + ex.ToString());
    }
}
```

In both cases, string variables containing the name of the server and database are passed into the top of the routine. Next, an instance of a SqlConnection object is created and its ConnectionString property is set as the argument of the constructor. The next statement creates a SqlDataAdapter passing to the constructor a SQL Select statement and the sqlCn SqlConnection object. An empty DataSet is then created, which will be populated with the results of the SELECT query command. The DataSet is then filled using the SqlDataAdapter's Fill method, which is executed inside a Try-Catch block. If the Fill method fails, the code in the Catch block will be executed and a message box appears showing the error message. Next, a DataView object is created against all the current rows of the Categories table and sets the Sort argument to CategoryName.

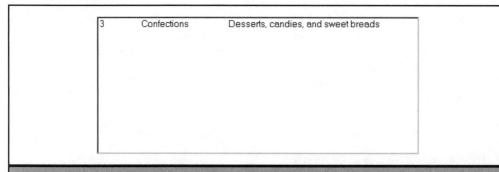

Figure 23-1.   *A sample result row from a single column search using the DataView Find method*

The DataView Find method is then executed to find the row where CategoryName is equal to "Confections," and an integer, iRow, is set with the resulting row index. Last, the retrieved row is added to the lstResults list box and displayed to the user, as shown in Figure 23-1.

The following example shows how to search data using a multiple-column sort order:

```
Private Sub DataViewFindCols(ByVal sServer As String, _
        ByVal sDB As String)
    Dim sqlCn As SqlConnection = New SqlConnection("SERVER=" & _
        sServer & ";INTEGRATED SECURITY=True;DATABASE=" & sDB)
    Dim sqlDA As SqlDataAdapter = New SqlDataAdapter( _
        "SELECT * FROM Products", sqlCn)
    Dim ds = New DataSet()
    Try
        sqlDA.Fill(ds, "Products")
        Dim dv = New DataView(ds.Tables("Products"), "", _
          "SupplierID, CategoryID", DataViewRowState.CurrentRows)
        Dim iRow As Integer iRow = dv.Find(New Object() {3, 2})
        lstResults.Items.Add(dv(iRow)("SupplierID").ToString() & _
                        dv(iRow)("CategoryID").ToString() & _
                        dv(iRow)("ProductName").ToString())
    Catch e As Exception
        MsgBox(e.Message)
    End Try
End Sub
```

The C# version of this code follows:

```
private void DataViewFindCols(string sServer, string sDB)
{
```

```
SqlConnection sqlCn = new SqlConnection("SERVER=" + sServer +
    ";INTEGRATED SECURITY=True;DATABASE=" + sDB);
SqlDataAdapter sqlDA = new SqlDataAdapter(
    "SELECT * FROM Products", sqlCn);
DataSet ds = new DataSet();
try
{
    sqlDA.Fill(ds, "Products");
    DataView dv = new DataView(ds.Tables["Products"], "",
        "SupplierID, CategoryID", DataViewRowState.CurrentRows);
    int iRow = dv.Find(new object[]{3, 2});
    lstResults.Items.Add(dv[iRow]["SupplierID"].ToString() +
                '\t' + dv[iRow]["CategoryID"].ToString() +
                '\t' + dv[iRow]["ProductName"].ToString());
}
catch (Exception ex)
{
    MessageBox.Show("DataViewFindCols: :" + ex.ToString());
}
}
```

In both cases, string variables containing the name of the server and database are passed into the top of the routine. Again, an instance of a SqlConnection, a SqlDataAdapter, and an empty DataSet are created. The DataSet is then filled using the SqlDataAdapter's Fill method, which is executed inside a Try-Catch block. Next, a DataView object is created against all the current rows of the Products table and the Sort argument is set to SupplierID and CategoryID. The DataView Find method is then executed to find the row where SupplierID is equal to 3 and CategoryID is equal to 2. An integer, iRow, is set with the index of the first match for the search criteria. Last, the row is added to the lstResults list box and displayed to the user, as shown in Figure 23-2.

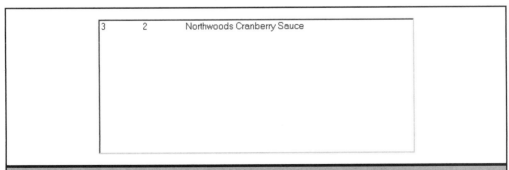

| 3 | 2 | Northwoods Cranberry Sauce |

Figure 23-2. *A sample result row from a multiple-column search using the DataView Find method*

Finding Multiple Rows in the DataTable

You may also search for a group of rows in a DataTable that match a given search criteria. To find and return multiple rows in a DataTable, you use the FindRows method of a DataView. The FindRows method returns a DataRowView array containing a reference to the rows that match the search criteria. Again, you may search on a single column or multiple columns of the DataView. The Sort property must correspond to the number of columns and the order that the columns are being searched in. The following example illustrates searching data for a group of rows using a single column:

```
Private Sub DataViewFindRows(ByVal sServer As String, _
     ByVal sDB As String)
   Dim sqlCn As SqlConnection = New SqlConnection("SERVER=" & _
       sServer & ";INTEGRATED SECURITY=True;DATABASE=" & sDB)
   Dim sqlDA As SqlDataAdapter = New SqlDataAdapter( _
       "SELECT * FROM Products", sqlCn)
   Dim ds = New DataSet()
   Try
       sqlDA.Fill(ds, "Products")
       Dim dv = New DataView(ds.Tables("Products"), "", _
           "SupplierID", DataViewRowState.CurrentRows)
       Dim drView() As DataRowView = dv.FindRows(12)
       Dim drv As DataRowView
       For Each drv In drView
           lstResults.Items.Add(drv("SupplierID").ToString() & _
               vbTab & drv("ProductID").ToString() & vbTab & _
               drv("ProductName").ToString())
       Next
   Catch e As Exception
       MsgBox(e.Message)
   End Try
End Sub
```

The C# version of this code follows:

```
private void DataViewFindRows(string sServer, string sDB)
{
   SqlConnection sqlCn = new SqlConnection("SERVER=" + sServer +
       ";INTEGRATED SECURITY=True;DATABASE=" + sDB);
   SqlDataAdapter sqlDA = new SqlDataAdapter(
       "SELECT * FROM Products", sqlCn);
   DataSet ds = new DataSet();
   try
```

```
    {
          sqlDA.Fill(ds, "Products");
          DataView dv = new DataView(ds.Tables["Products"], "",
               "SupplierID", DataViewRowState.CurrentRows);
          DataRowView[] drView = dv.FindRows(12);
          foreach (DataRowView drv in drView)
          {
                lstResults.Items.Add(drv["SupplierID"].ToString() +
                            '\t' + drv["ProductID"].ToString() +
                            '\t' + drv["ProductName"].ToString());
          }
    }
    catch (Exception ex)
    {
          MessageBox.Show("DataViewFindRows: :" + ex.ToString());
    }
}
```

In this example, string variables containing the name of the server and database are passed into the top of the routine. Next, an instance of a SqlConnection object is created and its ConnectionString property is set. The next statement creates a SqlDataAdapter using a SQL Select statement and the sqlCn object. The DataSet is then created and filled using the SqlDataAdapter's Fill method, which is executed inside a Try-Catch block. Next, a DataView object is created against all the current rows of the Products table and the Sort argument is set to SupplierID. The DataView FindRows method is then executed to find all the rows where SupplierID is equal to 12, and a DataRowView array is set with the resulting rows. A foreach loop is then used to read through the DataRowView array and add each row to the lstResults list box. The lstResults list box is shown in Figure 23-3.

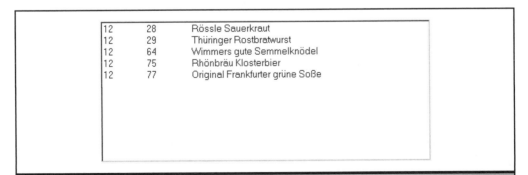

Figure 23-3.   *Sample result rows from a single-column search using the DataView FindRows method*

The next example shows searching data using a multiple-column sort order:

```
Private Sub DataViewFindRowsCols(ByVal sServer As String, _
        ByVal sDB As String)
    Dim sqlCn As SqlConnection = New SqlConnection("SERVER=" & _
        sServer & ";INTEGRATED SECURITY=True;DATABASE=" & sDB)
    Dim sqlDA As SqlDataAdapter = New SqlDataAdapter( _
        "SELECT * FROM Orders", sqlCn)
    Dim ds = New DataSet()
    Try
        sqlDA.Fill(ds, "Orders")
        Dim dv = New DataView(ds.Tables("Orders"), "", _
            "CustomerID, EmployeeID", DataViewRowState.CurrentRows)
        Dim drView() As DataRowView = _
            dv.FindRows(New Object() {"ANTON", 3})
        Dim drv As DataRowView
        For Each drv In drView
            lstResults.Items.Add(drv("OrderID").ToString() & _
                vbTab & drv("CustomerID").ToString() & vbTab & _
                drv("EmployeeID").ToString())
        Next
    Catch e As Exception
        MsgBox(e.Message)
    End Try
End Sub
```

The C# version of this code follows:

```
private void DataViewFindRowsCols(string sServer, string sDB)
{
    SqlConnection sqlCn = new SqlConnection("SERVER=" + sServer +
        ";INTEGRATED SECURITY=True;DATABASE=" + sDB);
    SqlDataAdapter sqlDA = new SqlDataAdapter(
        "SELECT * FROM Orders", sqlCn);
    DataSet ds = new DataSet();
    try
    {
        sqlDA.Fill(ds, "Orders");
        DataView dv = new DataView(ds.Tables["Orders"], "",
            "CustomerID, EmployeeID", DataViewRowState.CurrentRows);
```

```
            DataRowView[] drView = dv.FindRows(new object[]{"ANTON", 3});
            foreach (DataRowView drv in drView)
            {
                lstResults.Items.Add(drv["OrderID"].ToString() + '\t' +
                                drv["CustomerID"].ToString() + '\t' +
                                drv["EmployeeID"].ToString());
            }
        }
        catch (Exception ex)
        {
            MessageBox.Show("DataViewFindRowsCols: :" + ex.ToString());
        }
    }
```

In this example, string variables containing the name of the server and database are passed into the top of the routine. Next, an instance of a SqlConnection object, a SqlDataAdapter, and a DataSet are created. The DataSet is then filled using the SqlDataAdapter's Fill method, which is executed inside a Try-Catch block. Next, a DataView object is created against all the current rows of the Orders table, and the Sort argument is set to CustomerID and EmployeeID. The DataView FindRows method is then executed to find all the rows where CustomerID is equal to ANTON and EmployeeID is equal to 3. A DataRowView array is set with the resulting rows, and a foreach loop is then used to read through the DataRowView array and add each row to the lstResults list box. The lstResults list box is shown in Figure 23-4.

Figure 23-4.   *Sample result rows from a multiple-column search using the DataView FindRows method*

Summary

In this chapter, you saw how to navigate through a DataSet using the Find and FindRows methods of the DataView object. DataViews help you sort, search, and filter data into views that match certain criteria without your having to move through a DataTable one record at a time. In the next chapter, you will see how to navigate through related rows of multiple DataTables using a DataRelation.

The
Complete
Reference

Chapter 24

Navigating Through
the DataSet Using
DataRelations

In the preceding chapters, you saw how to navigate through DataSets using Windows data-bound controls, and how to search and sort functions found in the DataView class. In this chapter, you see how to retrieve related rows of data from multiple DataTables using a DataRelation. DataRelations enable you to associate DataTables through like fields of information.

Navigating Data with the DataRelation Class

One of the main functions of the DataRelation class is to enable you to retrieve the related DataRow objects in a DataTable when you specify a DataRow from another DataTable. DataRelations set up a parent/child relationship between tables in a DataSet using the tables' DataColumns. For example, you may retrieve all the OrderDetail rows for a particular OrderHeader row. The following example creates a DataRelation between Northwind's Orders table, OrderDetails table, and Products table to display a description of products for each order:

```
Private Sub DataRelationRelatedRows(ByVal sServer As String, _
    ByVal sDB As String)
  Cursor.Current = Cursors.WaitCursor
  Dim oleDbCn As OleDbConnection = New OleDbConnection( _
      "PROVIDER=SQLOLEDB;SERVER=" & sServer & _
      ";TRUSTED_CONNECTION=Yes;DATABASE=" & sDB)
  Dim oleDbDAOrders = New OleDbDataAdapter( _
      "SELECT * FROM Orders", oleDbCn)
  Dim oleDbDAODetails = New OleDbDataAdapter( _
      "SELECT * FROM [Order Details]", oleDbCn)
  Dim oleDbDAProducts = New OleDbDataAdapter( _
      "SELECT * FROM Products", oleDbCn)
  Dim dsOrders = New DataSet()
  Try
      oleDbDAOrders.Fill(dsOrders, "Orders")
      oleDbDAODetails.Fill(dsOrders, "OrderDetails")
      oleDbDAProducts.Fill(dsOrders, "Products")
      Dim drelOrders = dsOrders.Relations.Add( _
          "RelOrderDetail", _
          dsOrders.Tables("Orders").Columns("OrderID"), _
          dsOrders.Tables("OrderDetails").Columns("OrderID"), _
          False)
      Dim drelProducts = dsOrders.Relations.Add( _
          "RelOrderProducts", _
          dsOrders.Tables("Products").Columns("ProductID"), _
          dsOrders.Tables("OrderDetails").Columns("ProductID"), _
```

```
                False)
        Dim drOrder As DataRow
        Dim drODetail As DataRow
        Dim drProduct As DataRow
        For Each drOrder In dsOrders.Tables("Orders").Rows
            lstResults.Items.Add("Order ID:  " & _
                drOrder("OrderID").ToString())
            For Each drODetail In drOrder.GetChildRows(drelOrders)
                For Each drProduct In drODetail.GetParentRows( _
                        drelProducts)
                    lstResults.Items.Add(vbTab & "    Product:  " _
                        & drProduct("ProductName"))
                Next
            Next
        Next
        Cursor.Current = Cursors.Default
    Catch e As Exception
        Cursor.Current = Cursors.Default
        MsgBox(e.Message)
    End Try
End Sub
```

The C# version of this code follows:

```
private void DataRelationRelatedRows(string sServer, string sDB)
{
    OleDbConnection oleDbCn = new OleDbConnection(
        "PROVIDER=SQLOLEDB;SERVER=" + sServer +
        ";TRUSTED_CONNECTION=Yes;DATABASE=" + sDB);
    OleDbDataAdapter oleDbDAOrders = new OleDbDataAdapter(
        "SELECT * FROM Orders", oleDbCn);
    OleDbDataAdapter oleDbDAODetails = new OleDbDataAdapter(
        "SELECT * FROM [Order Details]", oleDbCn);
    OleDbDataAdapter oleDbDAProducts = new OleDbDataAdapter(
        "SELECT * FROM Products", oleDbCn);
    DataSet dsOrders = new DataSet();
    try
    {
        oleDbDAOrders.Fill(dsOrders, "Orders");
        oleDbDAODetails.Fill(dsOrders, "OrderDetails");
        oleDbDAProducts.Fill(dsOrders, "Products");
```

```
DataRelation drelOrders = dsOrders.Relations.Add(
    "RelOrderDetail",
    dsOrders.Tables["Orders"].Columns["OrderID"],
    dsOrders.Tables["OrderDetails"].Columns["OrderID"],
    false);
DataRelation drelProducts = dsOrders.Relations.Add(
    "RelOrderProducts",
    dsOrders.Tables["Products"].Columns["ProductID"],
    dsOrders.Tables["OrderDetails"].Columns["ProductID"],
    false);
foreach (DataRow drOrder in dsOrders.Tables["Orders"].Rows)
{
    lstResults.Items.Add("Order ID:   " +
        drOrder["OrderID"].ToString());
    foreach (DataRow drODetail in
        drOrder.GetChildRows(drelOrders))
    {
        foreach(DataRow drProduct in
            drODetail.GetParentRows(drelProducts))
        {
            lstResults.Items.Add("\t   Product:   " +
                drProduct["ProductName"]);
        }
    }
}
}
catch (Exception ex)
{
    MessageBox.Show("DataRelationRelatedRows:" + ex.ToString());
}
}
```

In this example, string variables containing the name of the server and database are passed into the top of the routine and an instance of an OleDbConnection object is created. Next, three DataAdapters are created, one for each of the tables that will be added to the DataSet. A DataSet is then created and each DataAdapter's Fill method is called to populate the DataSet with their corresponding tables. Next, a DataRelation object named drelOrders is created to relate the Orders DataTable and the OrderDetails DataTable in the DataSet. The DataColumn that relates the tables is OrderID. The next

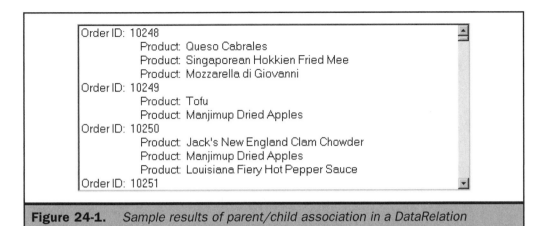

Figure 24-1.   *Sample results of parent/child association in a DataRelation*

statement creates a DataRelation, drelProducts, and relates the OrderDetails DataTable with the Products DataTable using the ProductID DataColumn. Next, a foreach loop is used to read each order out of the Orders table and add the OrderID to the lstResults list box. The next foreach loop then retrieves the OrderDetail records that relate to the OrderID of the Orders table, and the next foreach loop retrieves the corresponding Products rows for each of the OrderDetail records. The ProductName for each of the Products rows is then added to the lstResults list box and displayed to the user. In this example, the lstResults list box will display each Order in the Orders table and the ProductNames of each order, as shown in Figure 24-1.

Summary

In this chapter, you saw how to navigate through a DataSet by selecting DataTable relations and setting up parent/child associations in a DataRelation. In the next few chapters, you will see how to edit and update the DataSet information back to the data source using the different .NET Framework Data Providers.

Chapter 25

Updating the Database using the SqlDataAdapter

In the previous three chapters, you saw how to navigate through a DataSet and display the contents of a DataTable on a Windows Form. You also saw how to use the Rows collection of the DataTable to move through the data and how to find rows and retrieve related data from multiple tables with a DataView and a DataRelation. In the next four chapters you will see how to update the database with the changed information in the DataSet. The DataAdapter's Update method is used to resolve changes in the DataSet and post them back to the database. The DataAdapter contains three built-in methods that allow it to update a data source: the InsertCommand, the UpdateCommand, and the DeleteCommand. The DataSet's Update method calls the appropriate InsertCommand, UpdateCommand, or DeleteCommand after the DataAdapter analyzes the changed information in the DataSet.

This chapter focuses on updating a SQL Server database using the SqlDataAdapter that's provided as a part of the .NET Framework Data Provider for SQL Server. You will see how to use the visual SqlDataAdapter object to automatically generate the update commands. You'll also see examples of how to use the SqlDataAdapter class and the CommandBuilder object to generate the update commands and update the database.

Updating a Database Using the SqlDataAdapter

The SqlDataAdapter is used in combination with the SqlConnection object and the SqlCommand object to fill a DataSet with data and then resolve the information back to a Microsoft SQL Server database.

Using the Visual Studio SqlDataAdapter Object

The visual SqlDataAdapter component included as part of Visual Studio .NET, provides a fast and effective way to generate update commands for resolving changes to the DataSet back to the data source. To use the SqlDataAdapter component you must first create a Visual Studio VB.NET or C# project and then add a new form to the project. After the form has been created, you can add several TextBoxes and Buttons to the form by double-clicking these controls from the Windows Forms tab of the toolbox that is displayed on the left side of the Visual Studio.NET development environment. You then add a SqlDataAdapter to the form using the technique explained in Chapter 17. The DataAdapter Configuration Wizard will step you through the configuration of the SqlDataAdapter object. The following example will use the familiar Northwind database.

Using the Advanced SQL Generation Options

As you step through the DataAdapter Configuration Wizard, the Generate the SQL Statements dialog box offers an Advanced Options button. Click the Advanced Options button to display the Advanced SQL Generation Options dialog box of the Configuration Wizard. This dialog box enables you to specify whether Insert, Update, and Delete commands are automatically generated from the DataAdapter's Select statement. The Advanced SQL Generation Options dialog box is shown in Figure 25-1.

You can see from Figure 25-1 that the option to generate Insert, Update, and Delete statements has been selected. In this case, the Configuration Wizard will create SQL statements for the DataAdapter's InsertCommand, UpdateCommand, and DeleteCommand properties. The Use optimistic concurrency and Refresh the DataSet options have also been selected. The Use optimistic concurrency option checks whether the database has been changed since the record was loaded into the DataSet. Concurrency issues are discussed in the next chapter. The Refresh the DataSet option will add a SELECT statement to the corresponding command object. This SELECT statement will be executed right after the Update or Insert command and will return just the record that was updated or inserted. This is not always the most efficient way to keep the DataSet synchronized. If you have many updates to do, it is better to refill the entire DataSet after all the updates are finished.

Complete the steps to configure the SqlDataAdapter, and then right-click the sqlDataAdapter1 object that was added to your Visual Studio project to display a pop-up menu and select the Properties option to review the object's properties, as shown in Figure 25-2.

Figure 25-2 shows that the InsertCommand, UpdateCommand, and DeleteCommand properties of the sqlDataAdapter1 object have been set with the automatically generated objects sqlInsertCommand1, sqlUpdateCommand1, and sqlDeleteCommand1 respectively.

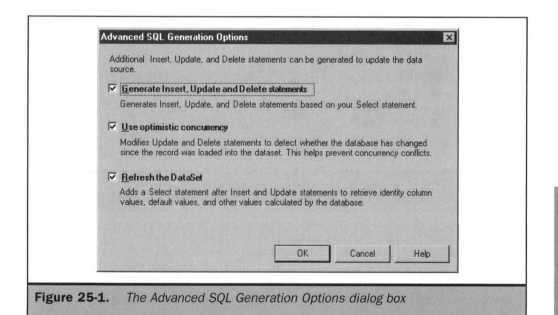

Figure 25-1.   *The Advanced SQL Generation Options dialog box*

THE ADO.NET
DATASET OBJECT

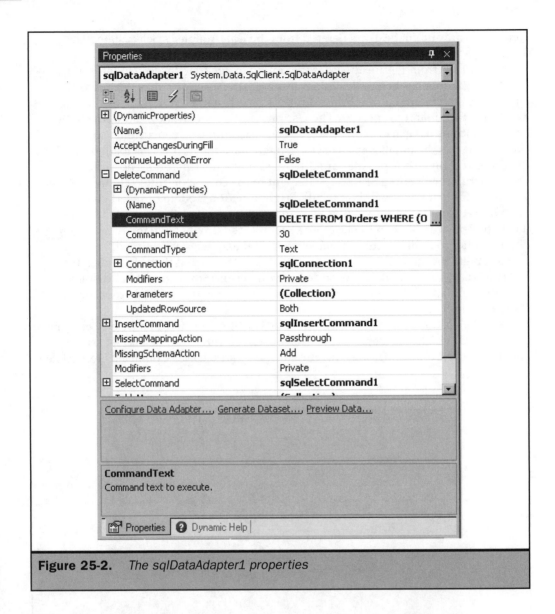

Figure 25-2. *The sqlDataAdapter1 properties*

To see the SQL statements that are generated and to show the sqlDeleteCommand1 statement attributes, open the DeleteCommand property by clicking the plus sign next to the property. You can see that the CommandText property of the sqlDeleteCommand1 object has been set with the actual DELETE statement that will be executed against the database. Click on the ellipsis of the CommandText property to display the entire DELETE statement, as shown in Figure 25-3.

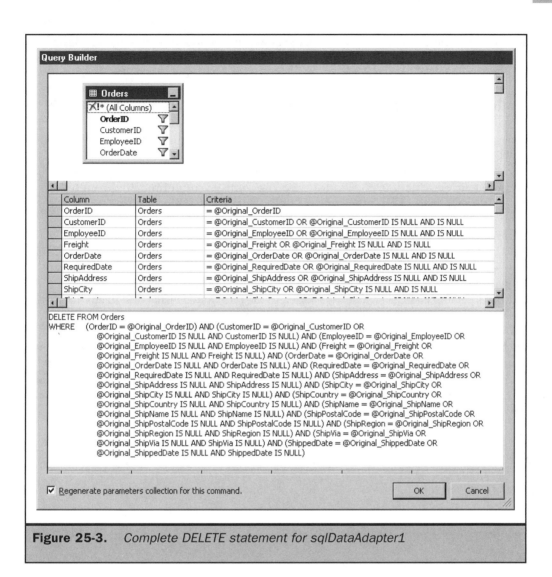

Figure 25-3.   *Complete DELETE statement for sqlDataAdapter1*

You can see in Figure 25-3 that the SqlDataAdapter object uses named parameters in the command statements, as in @CustomerID. In contrast, the OracleDataAdapter uses the colon (:) character as a placeholder and the OleDbDataAdapter and OdbcDataAdapter use the question mark (?) symbol as a placeholder for the command statement parameters.

Next, right-click the sqlDataAdapter1 object in your Visual Studio project design window to display a pop-up menu and select the Generate DataSet option. The Generate DataSet dialog box appears, enabling you to create a DataSet and add the tables specified in the SqlDataAdapter. Choose an existing DataSet to add tables to, or create a new DataSet and add the tables to it. In this example, the new DataSet option is chosen and a DataSet name of dsOrders is input. A DataSet component is added to your project that is used as a data source for displaying data information in bound controls.

Updating using BindingContext and Windows Form controls

In Windows applications, when you bind data from a data source to Windows Forms controls, the Windows application has a related CurrencyManager object. The CurrencyManager object manages a list of bindings to that data source. Windows Forms also contain a BindingContext object that keeps track of one or more CurrencyManagers. Windows Forms controls communicate through the BindingContext to bind the controls to the data source. BindingContext and CurrencyManager objects are discussed in Chapter 22, "Navigating Through the DataSet Using Windows Data-Bound Form Controls."

The next illustration will describe how you update data from the DataSet to the data source using bound Windows Form controls and the BindingContext object. Figure 25-4 shows a Visual Studio project Windows form with several Textboxes, Buttons, and a DataAdapter and DataSet created and added to the form in the visual design environment.

In this example, the data source for the sqlDataAdapter1 is Microsoft's Northwind database and the table in the DataSet, dsOrders1, is Orders. You need to populate the DataSet object from the data source. Call the SqlDataAdapter's Fill method using the DataSet as the first argument. In this example, call the SqlDataAdapter's Fill method from the form's Load method, so that the data will be displayed as soon as the application starts. Double-click the form object to display the code for the Form1_Load method and add the Fill method to this subroutine as illustrated here:

```
Private Sub Form1_Load(ByVal sender As System.Object, _
        ByVal e As System.EventArgs) Handles MyBase.Load
    SqlDataAdapter1.Fill(DsOrders1)
End Sub
```

The C# version of this code is as follows:

```
private void Form1_Load(object sender, System.EventArgs e)
{
    sqlDataAdapter1.Fill(dsOrders1);
}
```

The dsOrders1 object that was generated earlier is passed to the Fill method of the sqlDataAdapter1 object. The sqlDataAdapter1's SelectCommand property was configured to select the columns from the Orders table in the SQL Server database and the form's text boxes will be bound to several of the columns. When the DataAdapter's Fill method is executed, the SelectCommand of the SqlDataAdapter will populate the DataSet and display the results on the form. You then add, update, or delete records in the database using the appropriate action button.

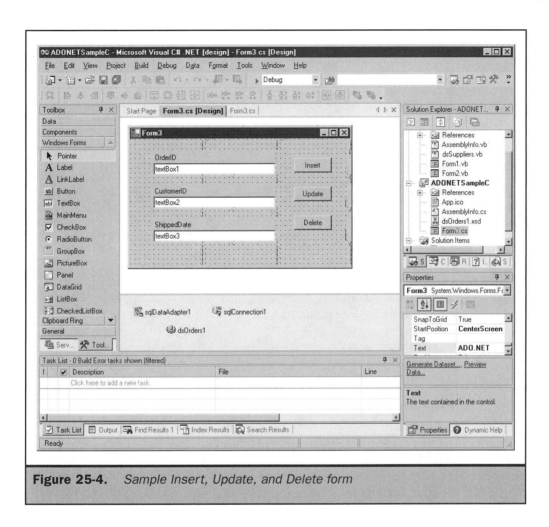

Figure 25-4. *Sample Insert, Update, and Delete form*

To bind the Textbox objects shown in Figure 25-4 to the DataSet, select each of the TextBoxes and set the DataBindings.Text property of each of them to a column from the Orders table. Next, select each of the Button objects on the form and set their Text property to Insert, Update, and Delete respectively. Double-click the Insert button to display the code for the button1_Click method as shown in the code that follows.

Set the Insert Button Using BindingContext

```
Private Sub button1_Click(ByVal sender As System.Object, _
        ByVal e As System.EventArgs) Handles button1.Click
    ' insert button
```

```
     Try
          Me.BindingContext(DsOrders1, "Orders").EndCurrentEdit()
          Me.BindingContext(DsOrders1, "Orders").AddNew()
     Catch ex As Exception
          MsgBox(ex.Message)
     End Try
End Sub
```

The C# version of this code is as follows:

```
// Insert button
private void button1_Click(object sender, System.EventArgs e)
{
     try
     {
          this.BindingContext[dsOrders1, "Orders"].EndCurrentEdit();
          this.BindingContext[dsOrders1, "Orders"].AddNew();
     }
     catch (Exception ex)
     {
          MessageBox.Show("InsertError: :" + ex.ToString());
     }
}
```

You see here that the BindingContext object is supplied with the DataSet and table name, and the EndCurrentEdit method is called. The EndCurrentEdit method tells the BindingContext manager that all current edits are complete. This transfers the information contained in the bound control from the control properties to the DataSet. The AddNew method is then called to clear the text boxes and ready the DataSet for a new record.

Set the Update button and Delete button to the appropriate action of updating or deleting the data. The code for the Update button and Delete button is listed here.

Set the Update and Delete Buttons Using BindingContext

```
Private Sub button2_Click(ByVal sender As System.Object, _
     ByVal e As System.EventArgs) Handles button2.Click
  ' update button
  Try
       Me.BindingContext(DsOrders1, "Orders").EndCurrentEdit()
       SqlDataAdapter1.Update(DsOrders1, "Orders")
  Catch ex As Exception
       MsgBox(ex.Message)
```

```vb
        End Try
    End Sub
    Private Sub button3_Click(ByVal sender As System.Object, _
            ByVal e As System.EventArgs) Handles button3.Click
        ' delete button
        Try
            Me.BindingContext(DsOrders1, "Orders").RemoveAt( _
                Me.BindingContext(DsOrders1, "Orders").Position)
            SqlDataAdapter1.Update(DsOrders1, "Orders")
        Catch ex As Exception
            MsgBox(ex.Message)
        End Try
    End Sub
```

The C# version of this code is as follows:

```csharp
// Update button
private void button2_Click(object sender, System.EventArgs e)
{
    try
    {
        this.BindingContext[dsOrders1, "Orders"].EndCurrentEdit();
        sqlDataAdapter1.Update(dsOrders1, "Orders");
    }
    catch (Exception ex)
    {
        MessageBox.Show("UpdateError: :" + ex.ToString());
    }
}
// Delete button
private void button3_Click(object sender, System.EventArgs e)
{
    try
    {
        this.BindingContext[dsOrders1, "Orders"].RemoveAt(
            this.BindingContext[dsOrders1, "Orders"].Position);
        sqlDataAdapter1.Update(dsOrders1, "Orders");
    }
    catch (Exception ex)
    {
        MessageBox.Show("DeleteError: :" + ex.ToString());
    }
}
```

Here the Update button's click event calls the EndCurrentEdit method, which transfers the information in the text boxes to the DataSet. Then the sqlDataAdapter1's Update method is called passing the DataSet and table name as arguments. The sqlDataAdapter's Update method will resolve the changed DataSet information to the SQL Server database table.

The Delete button's click event calls the RemoveAt method to remove the DataRow from the current position in the DataTable. The sqlDataAdapter's Update method is then called to resolve the DataSet information back to the data source. Figure 25-5 shows the application with data in the bound text boxes.

Using the SqlDataAdapter Class

Using the visual SqlDataAdapter component that is provided by the Visual Studio.NET design environment enables you to easily create update commands for updating the database, but you may also use the CommandBuilder class in code to automatically create update commands. The CommandBuilder is useful when a Select command is specified at runtime instead of at design time. For example, a user may dynamically create a textual Select command in an application. You may then create a CommandBuilder object to automatically create the appropriate Insert, Update, and Delete commands for the specified Select command. To do this, you create a DataAdapter object and set its SelectCommand property with a SQL select statement. Then you create a CommandBuilder object specifying as an argument the DataAdapter for which you want to create the update commands. The CommandBuilder is used when the DataTable in the DataSet is mapped to a single table in the data source.

Before you can use the .NET Framework Data Provider for SQL Server in your code, you must first specify an import directive for the System.Data.SqlClient Namespace in your project, as described in Chapter 4, "Using the .NET Framework Data Provider for SQL Server."

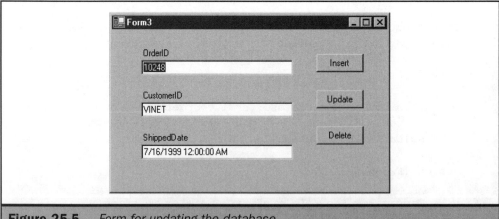

Figure 25-5. *Form for updating the database*

Using the CommandBuilder Object

After adding an import directive to your code, you're ready to begin using the different classes contained in the System.Data.SqlClient Namespace. The following example uses a SqlDataAdapter and CommandBuilder objects to automatically generate Insert, Update, and Delete commands to change the data in the Categories table of the Northwind database.

The first bit of code shows inserting a new record into the Categories table.

Insert Using the CommandBuilder

```
Private Sub DataSetInsertSql(ByVal sServer As String, _
    ByVal sDB As String)
    Cursor.Current = Cursors.WaitCursor
    ' Create the connection, dataadapter, and commandbuilder
    Dim sqlCn As SqlConnection = New SqlConnection("SERVER=" & _
        sServer & ";INTEGRATED SECURITY=True;DATABASE=" & sDB)
    Dim sqlDA As SqlDataAdapter = New SqlDataAdapter( _
        "SELECT * FROM Categories", sqlCn)
    Dim ds = New DataSet()
    Dim sqlCB = New SqlCommandBuilder(sqlDA)
    Try
        ' Populate the dataset
        sqlDA.Fill(ds, "Categories")
        ' Add a new record to the datatable
        Dim sqlDR = ds.Tables("Categories").NewRow()
        sqlDR("CategoryName") = "Pasta"
        sqlDR("Description") = "Dried or fresh noodles"
        ds.Tables("Categories").Rows.Add(sqlDR)
        ' Insert the record into the database table
        sqlDA.Update(ds, "Categories")
        Cursor.Current = Cursors.Default
    Catch e As Exception
        Cursor.Current = Cursors.Default
        MsgBox(e.Message)
    End Try
End Sub
```

The C# version of this code follows:

```
private void DataSetInsertSql(string sServer, string sDB)
{
    Cursor.Current = Cursors.WaitCursor;
```

```
// Create the connection, dataadapter, and commandbuilder
SqlConnection sqlCn = new SqlConnection("SERVER=" + sServer +
    ";INTEGRATED SECURITY=True;DATABASE=" + sDB);
SqlDataAdapter sqlDA = new SqlDataAdapter(
    "SELECT * FROM Categories", sqlCn);
DataSet ds = new DataSet();
SqlCommandBuilder sqlCB = new SqlCommandBuilder(sqlDA);
try
{
    // Populate the dataset
    sqlDA.Fill(ds, "Categories");
    // Add a new record to the datatable
    DataRow sqlDR = ds.Tables["Categories"].NewRow();
    sqlDR["CategoryName"] = "Pasta";
    sqlDR["Description"] = "Dried or fresh noodles";
    ds.Tables["Categories"].Rows.Add(sqlDR);
    // Insert the record into the database table
    sqlDA.Update(ds, "Categories");
    Cursor.Current = Cursors.Default;
}
catch (Exception ex)
{
    Cursor.Current = Cursors.Default;
    MessageBox.Show("DataSetInsertSql: :" + ex.ToString());
}
}
```

String variables containing the name of a SQL Server system and database are passed into the top of the routine. Next, an instance of a SqlConnection object is created and its ConnectionString property is set as the argument of the constructor. The next statement creates a SqlDataAdapter passing to the constructor a SQL Select statement and the sqlCn SqlConnection object. This automatically sets the SqlDataAdapter's selectCommand property to the SQL SELECT statement. An empty DataSet is then created, which will be populated with the results of the SELECT query command. The next statement creates a CommandBuilder object and takes as an argument the SqlDataAdapter. At this point the CommandBuilder executes the Select SQL statement contained in the selectCommand property of the SqlDataAdapter and automatically creates the InsertCommand, UpdateCommand, and DeleteCommand based on the contents of the SQL SELECT statement. The automatically created commands are set to the SqlDataAdapter's insertCommand, updateCommand, and deleteCommand properties respectively. If a command already exists for one of these properties, then the existing property will be used. The DataSet is then filled using the SqlDataAdapter's Fill method, which is executed inside a Try-Catch block. Next, the table's NewRow method is called to create an empty record in the Categories DataTable in the DataSet and a DataRow object is returned. The CategoryName column and Description column of the DataRow are set with text. Now that the DataRow object contains the data that you want to insert, you need to add the DataRow to the DataTable's Rows collection, as shown in the next statement. Lastly, the SqlDataAdapter's Update method is called. The Update method will evaluate the changes that have been made to the DataTable in the DataSet and determine which of the commands to execute. In this case, the Table.Rows.RowState property shows Added for the new row so the InsertCommand is executed and the new record is added to the Categories table in the database.

The next example shows how to change existing data in a DataSet and then send those changes to the database.

Update Using the CommandBuilder

```
Private Sub DataSetUpdateSql(ByVal sServer As String, _
        ByVal sDB As String)
    Cursor.Current = Cursors.WaitCursor
    ' Create the connection, dataadapter, and commandbuilder
    Dim sqlCn As SqlConnection = New SqlConnection("SERVER=" & _
        sServer & ";INTEGRATED SECURITY=True;DATABASE=" & sDB)
    Dim sqlDA As SqlDataAdapter = New SqlDataAdapter( _
        "SELECT * FROM Categories", sqlCn)
    Dim ds = New DataSet()
    Dim sqlCB = New SqlCommandBuilder(sqlDA)
    Try
        ' Populate the dataset
        sqlDA.Fill(ds, "Categories")
        ' Update a record in the datatable
        Dim sqlDR = ds.Tables("Categories").Rows( _
            ds.Tables("Categories").Rows.Count - 1)
        sqlDR("Description") = "oodles of noodles"
        ' Update the record in the database table
        sqlDA.Update(ds, "Categories")
        Cursor.Current = Cursors.Default
    Catch e As Exception
        Cursor.Current = Cursors.Default
        MsgBox(e.Message)
    End Try
End Sub
```

THE ADO.NET
DATASET OBJECT

The C# version of this code follows:

```csharp
private void DataSetUpdateSql(string sServer, string sDB)
{
    Cursor.Current = Cursors.WaitCursor;
    // Create the connection, dataadapter, and commandbuilder
    SqlConnection sqlCn = new SqlConnection("SERVER=" + sServer +
        ";INTEGRATED SECURITY=True;DATABASE=" + sDB);
    SqlDataAdapter sqlDA = new SqlDataAdapter(
        "SELECT * FROM Categories", sqlCn);
    DataSet ds = new DataSet();
    SqlCommandBuilder sqlCB = new SqlCommandBuilder(sqlDA);
    try
    {
        // Populate the dataset
        sqlDA.Fill(ds, "Categories");
        // Update a record in the datatable
        DataRow sqlDR = ds.Tables["Categories"].Rows
            [ds.Tables["Categories"].Rows.Count-1];
        sqlDR["Description"] = "oodles of noodles";
        // Update the record in the database table
        sqlDA.Update(ds, "Categories");
        Cursor.Current = Cursors.Default;
    }
    catch (Exception ex)
    {
        Cursor.Current = Cursors.Default;
        MessageBox.Show("DataSetUpdateSql: :" + ex.ToString());
    }
}
```

Here you can see again the server and database name have been passed in at the top of the routine. A connection object, DataAdapter, DataSet, and CommandBuilder object are then created. The DataSet is then filled inside the Try-Catch loop. The next statement shows retrieving the last row in the Categories table into a DataRow object. The Description field of the DataRow is then set with a new value, which changes the Table.Rows.RowState property for this row to reflect Modified. The next statement calls the DataAdapter's Update method. The Update method determines the appropriate command to execute based on the value of the RowState property and, in this case, will call the UpdateCommand of the DataAdapter to resolve the changed row back to the data source.

The next example shows how to delete a record from the database.

Delete Using the CommandBuilder

```
Private Sub DataSetDeleteSql(ByVal sServer As String, _
    ByVal sDB As String)
    Cursor.Current = Cursors.WaitCursor
    ' Create the connection, dataadapter, and commandbuilder
    Dim sqlCn As SqlConnection = New SqlConnection("SERVER=" & _
        sServer & ";INTEGRATED SECURITY=True;DATABASE=" & sDB)
    Dim sqlDA As SqlDataAdapter = New SqlDataAdapter( _
        "SELECT * FROM Categories", sqlCn)
    Dim ds = New DataSet()
    Dim sqlCB = New SqlCommandBuilder(sqlDA)
    Try
        ' Populate the dataset
        sqlDA.Fill(ds, "Categories")
        ' Mark the record in the datatable for deletion
        Dim sqlDR = ds.Tables("Categories").Rows( _
            ds.Tables("Categories").Rows.Count - 1)
        sqlDR.Delete()
        ' Delete the record from the database table
        sqlDA.Update(ds, "Categories")
        Cursor.Current = Cursors.Default
    Catch e As Exception
        Cursor.Current = Cursors.Default
        MsgBox(e.Message)
    End Try
End Sub
```

The C# version of this code follows:

```
private void DataSetDeleteSql(string sServer, string sDB)
{
    Cursor.Current = Cursors.WaitCursor;
    // Create the connection, dataadapter, and commandbuilder
    SqlConnection sqlCn = new SqlConnection("SERVER=" + sServer +
        ";INTEGRATED SECURITY=True;DATABASE=" + sDB);
    SqlDataAdapter sqlDA = new SqlDataAdapter(
        "SELECT * FROM Categories", sqlCn);
    DataSet ds = new DataSet();
    SqlCommandBuilder sqlCB = new SqlCommandBuilder(sqlDA);
    try
    {
```

THE ADO.NET
DATASET OBJECT

```
        // Populate the dataset
        sqlDA.Fill(ds, "Categories");
        // Mark the record in the datatable for deletion
        DataRow sqlDR = ds.Tables["Categories"].Rows
                [ds.Tables["Categories"].Rows.Count-1];
        sqlDR.Delete();
        // Delete the record from the database table
        sqlDA.Update(ds, "Categories");
        Cursor.Current = Cursors.Default;
    }
    catch (Exception ex)
    {
        Cursor.Current = Cursors.Default;
        MessageBox.Show("DataSetDeleteSql: :" + ex.ToString());
    }
}
```

Again you can see the server and database name passed into the routine, and the connection, DataAdapter, DataSet, and CommandBuilder objects being created. Then the DataSet is filled in the Try-Catch loop. The next statement retrieves the last row from the Categories DataTable into a DataRow object. Then the DataRow's Delete method is called to delete the row from the DataTable Categories. In reality, this does not physically delete the row from the DataTable, but instead sets the Table.Rows.RowState property to Deleted. Next, when the DataAdapter's Update method is called, the DeleteCommand of the DataAdapter will execute and delete the record from the database. In contrast, if you call the DataTable's Remove or RemoveAt methods, the row will be physically removed from the DataTable in the DataSet. If you use the Remove or RemoveAt methods and then call the Update method, the row in the data source will not be deleted because the DataAdapter's Update method determines what action to take based on the Table.Rows.RowState property and all of the remaining rows in the DataTable have a RowState of Unmodified; therefore no action will take place at the data source.

Summary

In this chapter, you saw how to update the database from the DataSet by using the SqlDataAdapter's Update method. You saw how the Update method calls the appropriate InsertCommand, UpdateCommand, or DeleteCommand after the DataAdapter analyzes the changed information in the DataSet. The visual SqlDataAdapter object that is provided by the .NET Framework Data Provider for SQL Server was used to automatically generate the update commands. The CommandBuilder object that is included in the SqlDataAdapter class was also used to generate the update commands and update the database. In the next chapter, you will use the OracleDataAdapter to update an Oracle database.

The Complete Reference

Chapter 26

Updating the Database Using the OracleDataAdapter

In this chapter, you'll see how to use the OracleDataAdapter and optimistic locking to update a record in the Oracle database only if the record has not been changed by another user. You will also see how to use the Parameter Collection Editor dialog box to interactively add, update, or delete parameters from the parameters collection of the DataAdapter. Last, you will see how to build custom update commands that use parameters and SQL statements to update a data source in program code.

Updating a Database Using the OracleDataAdapter

The OracleDataAdapter, OracleConnection object, and OracleCommand object are included in the .NET Framework Data Provider for Oracle. This Data Provider enhances the performance of your application when you need to connect to an Oracle database.

Using the Visual Studio SqlDataAdapter Object

The visual OracleDataAdapter component is included as part of Visual Studio.NET and offers an effective way to generate update commands for resolving changes from the DataSet back to the Oracle database. You can use the OracleDataAdapter component by first creating a Visual Studio.NET project and then adding a new form to the project. After the form has been created, you add an OracleDataAdapter to the form by double-clicking the OracleDataAdapter object that's displayed in the Data Toolbox in the design environment. The DataAdapter Configuration Wizard steps you through the configuration of the OracleDataAdapter object. Step through the Configuration Wizard to the Generate The SQL Statements dialog box, and click the Advanced Options button. The Advanced SQL Generation Options dialog box appears, as shown in Figure 26-1.

You can see from Figure 26-1 that the option to generate Insert, Update, and Delete statements has been selected, along with the Use Optimistic Concurrency radio button.

Using Optimistic Concurrency

When you select the optimistic concurrency option, the DataAdapter Configuration Wizard automatically generates SQL command statements that contain a WHERE clause for each column in the record. Figure 26-2 shows an example of the generated UPDATE SQL statement for the EMP table of the sample SCOTT Oracle database, with the Optimistic Concurrency option selected.

You see from Figure 26-2 that the WHERE clause of the SQL statement contains each of the columns in the EMP table. In contrast, Figure 26-3 shows the same UPDATE SQL statement, but without the Optimistic Concurrency option.

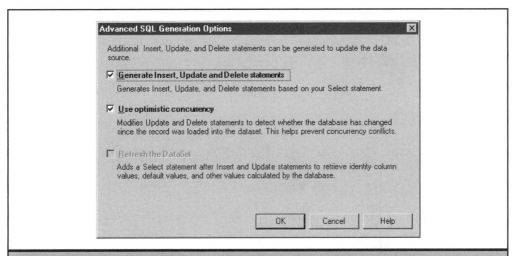

Figure 26-1. *The Advanced SQL Generation Options dialog box*

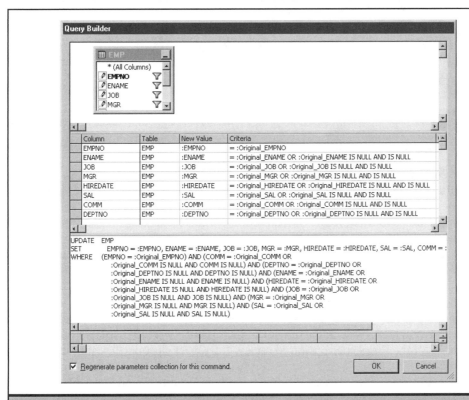

Figure 26-2. *Command statement with Optimistic Concurrency selected*

THE ADO.NET
DATASET OBJECT

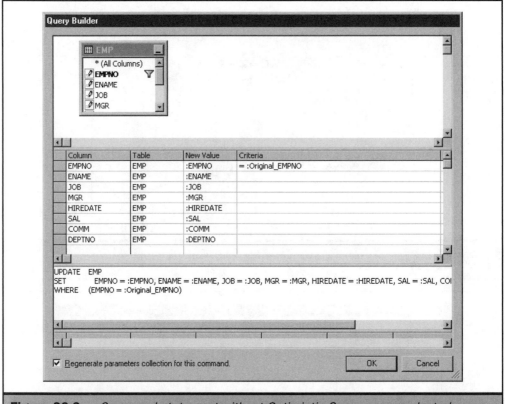

Figure 26-3. *Command statement without Optimistic Concurrency selected*

Figure 26-3 shows that the WHERE clause of the SQL statement contains only the key column, EMPNO, in the EMP table. When you elect to use the Optimistic Concurrency option, the result is that each of the column values will be checked as the command is executed. If any of the column values has changed since you read the record into your DataSet (in other words, another user has changed the data in the database), then your SQL command will fail. If you choose not to use optimistic concurrency, then changes by other users to the record in the database can potentially be overridden without warning by your SQL command.

Complete the steps to configure the OracleDataAdapter, and you will see an oracleDataAdapter1 object and an oracleConnection1 object added to the components pane of your project. Right-click the oracleDataAdapter1 object to display a pop-up menu, and select the Properties option to review the object's properties, shown in Figure 26-4.

Figure 26-4 shows that the InsertCommand, UpdateCommand, and DeleteCommand properties of the oracleDataAdapter1 object have been set with the automatically generated objects oracleInsertCommand1, oracleUpdateCommand1, and oracleDeleteCommand1, respectively.

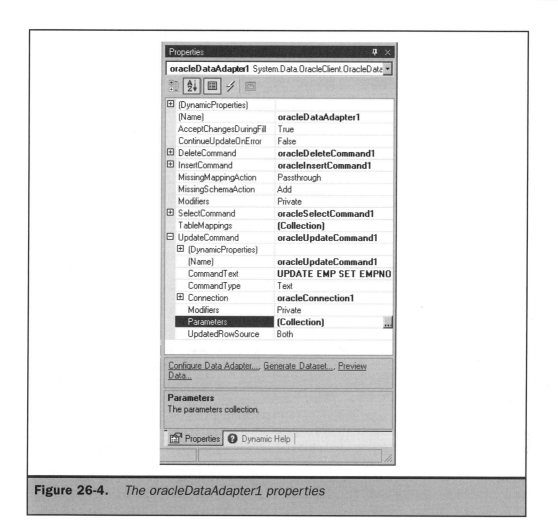

Figure 26-4.   *The oracleDataAdapter1 properties*

The Visual Parameter Collection Editor Dialog Box

To see the parameter collection for the commands that are generated, open the UpdateCommand property by clicking the plus sign next to the property to show the oracleUpdateCommand1 statement attributes. You can see that the Parameters property of the oracleUpdateCommand1 object contains a collection of column objects. Click the ellipsis of the Parameters property to display the Collection Editor dialog box, as shown in Figure 26-5.

Figure 26-5 shows the OracleParameter collection that was generated for the UPDATE command statement of the OracleDataAdapter. The parameter Collection Editor is a handy tool that allows you to add, delete, or change the parameters of the command statements for your DataAdapter. The Parameter Collection Editor displays each of the parameters in the collection along with the parameter direction and attributes of the associated column. Parameters in the collection are matched to the

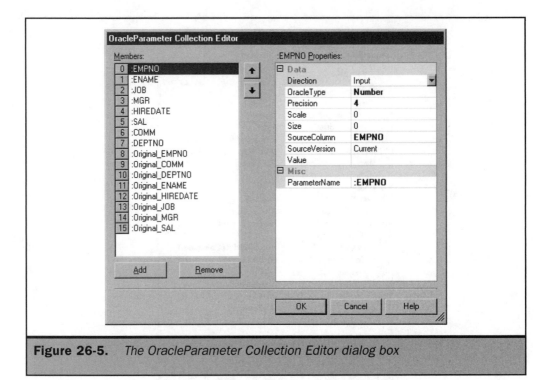

Figure 26-5. The OracleParameter Collection Editor dialog box

parameter placeholders in the command statement by position, so it is important that the parameters in the collection are placed in the correct order.

Close the OracleParameter Collection Editor dialog box and right-click the oracleDataAdapter1 object in your Visual Studio project design window to display a pop-up menu. Select the Generate DataSet option to display the Generate DataSet dialog box that allows you to create a DataSet and add the tables specified in the OracleDataAdapter. Choose an existing DataSet, or create a new DataSet and add the tables to it.

Binding Data to Windows Form Controls

After the DataSet is created, you need to populate it from the data source. Call the OracleDataAdapter's Fill method from the form's Load method, so that the data will be displayed as soon as the application starts. Use the DataSet as the first argument and the name of the DataTable to be created as the second argument. Double-click the form object to display the code for the Form1_Load method, and add the Fill method to this subroutine as illustrated here:

```
Private Sub Form1_Load(ByVal sender As System.Object, _
        ByVal e As System.EventArgs) Handles MyBase.Load
    OracleDataAdapter1.Fill(DsEMP1)
End Sub
```

The C# version of this code follows:

```
private void Form1_Load(object sender, System.EventArgs e)
{
    oracleDataAdapter1.Fill(dsEMP1);
}
```

The dsEMP1 object that was generated earlier is passed to the Fill method of the oracleDataAdapter1. For this example, you add several TextBoxes and Buttons to the form by double-clicking these controls from the Windows Forms tab of the toolbox that is displayed on the left side of the Visual Studio.Net development environment. To bind the TextBox objects to the DataSet, select each of the TextBoxes and set the DataBindings.Text property of each of them to a column from the table. Next, select each of the Button objects on the form and set their Text property to Insert, Update, and Delete, respectively. Then double-click each of the Button objects to display the code for the button_Click event, and write the code to use the BindingContext as described in the preceding chapter, "Updating the Database Using the SqlDataAdapter."

When the application is run, the OracleDataAdapter's Fill method will populate the DataSet from the Oracle database with the information from the EMP table, and the first record will be displayed in the text boxes as shown in Figure 26-6. You may change the data in the text boxes and click one of the buttons to either add, update, or delete this record from the DataSet and update the changes to the Oracle database.

Using the OracleDataAdapter Class

Using the visual OracleDataAdapter component that is provided by the Visual Studio.NET design environment is an easy way to create update commands for updating the database. The next section focuses on using custom update commands and parameters to insert, update, and delete records from your Oracle database.

Before you use the .NET Framework Data Provider for Oracle in your code, you need to specify an import directive for the System.Data.OracleClient Namespace in your

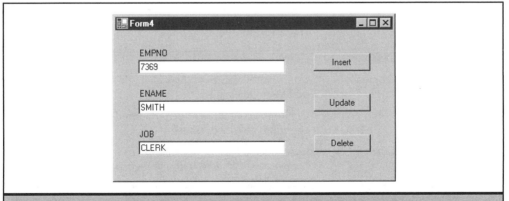

Figure 26-6.   *Form for updating the database*

project. The technique for including the import directive for the OracleClient Namespace is described in Chapter 5, "Using the .NET Framework Data Provider for Oracle."

Using Custom Update Commands

After adding an import directive to your code, you may use the different classes contained in the System.Data.OracleClient Namespace. In the next section, you'll see an example that illustrates how to use the OracleDataAdapter class to manually set the InsertCommand, UpdateCommand, and DeleteCommand with custom SQL statements that use parameter markers to change the value of the rows in the data source. Parameter markers for OracleDataAdapter use the colon symbol (:), such as :DEPTNO, whereas the parameter markers for the SqlDataAdapter use named parameter markers such as @CustomerID, and the OleDbDataAdapter uses the question mark symbol (?). For each of the DataAdapter's commands, you build a corresponding SQL command. For example, to delete a row at the data source, you build a Command object that contains a DELETE statement and set the DataAdapter's DeleteCommand property with the Command object. For more information about Command objects and parameterized query statements, refer to Chapter 9, "Using the OracleCommand Object."

In the following examples, you will see how to create OracleParameter objects and add them to the Parameters collection of the OracleDataAdapter. The OracleParameter objects relate the parameter markers in the SQL statement to the columns in the DataTable. The SourceColumn property of the OracleParameter object is used to make this relationship. Another important property of the OracleParameter object is the SourceVersion. The SourceVersion specifies the value of the column that is to be used during an update of the information from the DataSet to the database. For example, when a row in a DataTable is first filled, the value of the columns reflects the original values of the database. In other words, values are set in DataRowVersion.Original. Then when changes are made to the rows in the DataTable, the DataRowVersion.Proposed reflects the changes that have been made but not yet committed to the database. As soon as the changes are sent to the database, the DataRowVersion reflects the DataRowVersion.Current values of the columns. Table 26-1 lists the valid enumerations for the DataRowVersion property.

Enumeration	Description
DataRowVersion.Default	Contains default values for a row that was added
DataRowVersion.Original	Contains the values of the DataTable when it is first added to the DataSet
DataRowVersion.Proposed	Contains data that has been modified but not committed to the database
DataRowVersion.Current	Contains the current information in the DataTable after the row is committed to the database

Table 26-1. *DataRowVersion Enumeration*

Using the DataAdapter and Insert Custom Command

The example that follows shows how to insert a record into the DEPT table of the sample SCOTT Oracle database using the OracleDataAdapter and a parameterized query.

```vb
Private Sub DataSetInsertOracleParm(ByVal sServer As String)
    Cursor.Current = Cursors.WaitCursor
    ' Create the connection and dataadapter
    Dim oracleCn = New OracleConnection("DATA SOURCE=" & sServer _
        & ";INTEGRATED SECURITY=yes")
    Dim oracleDA As OracleDataAdapter = New OracleDataAdapter( _
        "SELECT * FROM DEPT", oracleCn)
    Dim ds = New DataSet()
    Try
        oracleDA.Fill(ds)
        ' Create an insert command and set to dataadapter
        Dim oracleInsertCmd = New OracleCommand( & _
            "INSERT INTO DEPT " & _
            "(DEPTNO) VALUES (:DEPTNO)", oracleCn)
        oracleDA.InsertCommand = oracleInsertCmd
        ' Set parameter to dataadapter parameter collection
        Dim oracleParm As New OracleParameter()
        oracleParm = oracleDA.InsertCommand.Parameters.Add( _
            New OracleParameter(":DEPTNO", OracleType.Number))
        oracleParm.SourceColumn = "DEPTNO"
        oracleParm.SourceVersion = DataRowVersion.Current
        ' add a row to the datatable
        Dim oracleDR = ds.Tables(0).NewRow()
        oracleDR("DEPTNO") = 60
        ds.Tables(0).Rows.Add(oracleDR)
        ' send new row to the data source
        oracleDA.Update(ds)
        Cursor.Current = Cursors.Default
    Catch e As Exception
        Cursor.Current = Cursors.Default
        MsgBox(e.Message)
    End Try
End Sub
```

The C# version of this code follows:

```csharp
private void DataSetInsertOracleParm(string sServer)
{
    Cursor.Current = Cursors.WaitCursor;
    // Create the connection and dataadapter
```

```
OracleConnection oracleCn = new OracleConnection(
    "DATA SOURCE=" + sServer + ";INTEGRATED SECURITY=yes");
OracleDataAdapter oracleDA = new OracleDataAdapter(
    "SELECT * FROM DEPT", oracleCn);
DataSet ds = new DataSet();
try
{
    oracleDA.Fill(ds);
    // Create an insert command and set to dataadapter
    OracleCommand oracleInsertCmd = new OracleCommand(
        "INSERT INTO DEPT (DEPTNO) VALUES (:DEPTNO)", oracleCn);
    oracleDA.InsertCommand = oracleInsertCmd;
    // Set parameter to dataadapter parameter collection
    OracleParameter oracleParm = new OracleParameter();
    oracleParm = oracleDA.InsertCommand.Parameters.Add(
        new OracleParameter(":DEPTNO", OracleType.Number));
    oracleParm.SourceColumn = "DEPTNO";
    oracleParm.SourceVersion = DataRowVersion.Current;
    // add a row to the datatable
    DataRow oracleDR = ds.Tables[0].NewRow();
    oracleDR["DEPTNO"] = 60;
    ds.Tables[0].Rows.Add(oracleDR);
    // send new row to the data source
    oracleDA.Update(ds);
    Cursor.Current = Cursors.Default;
}
catch (Exception ex)
{
    Cursor.Current = Cursors.Default;
    MessageBox.Show("DataSetInsertOracleParm: :" +
        ex.ToString());
}
}
```

The server name is passed into the top of the routine, and the OracleConnection object, OracleDataAdapter, and the DataSet are created. Then the DataSet is filled in the Try-Catch loop. Next, an OracleCommand object named oracleInsertCmd is created with an INSERT statement as the first argument and the Connection object as the second argument of the constructor. The next statement sets the OracleDataAdapter's InsertCommand property with the command object. Next, an OracleParameter object named oracleParm is created and the parameter's name is set to :DEPTNO. This parameter is defined as an OracleType.Number. The SourceColumn for the OracleParameter is then set to the DEPTNO column of the DataTable, and the

SourceVersion is set to DataRowVersion.Current. A new row is then created in the DataSet's DataTable and a DataRow object named oracleDR is returned. Next, the column DEPTNO is assigned the value of 60. The DataRow object is then added to the DataTable's Rows collection. Last, the OracleDataAdapter's Update method is called to send the new row from the DataSet to the database.

Using the DataAdapter and Update Custom Command

The next example updates the DEPT record that was added to the database table. It illustrates how to use a custom UPDATE command to update a record in the DEPT table of the Oracle database.

```
Private Sub DataSetUpdateOracleParm(ByVal sServer As String)
    Cursor.Current = Cursors.WaitCursor
    ' Create the connection and dataadapter
    Dim oracleCn = New OracleConnection("DATA SOURCE=" & sServer _
        & ";INTEGRATED SECURITY=yes")
    Dim oracleDA As OracleDataAdapter = New OracleDataAdapter( _
        "SELECT * FROM DEPT", oracleCn)
    Dim ds = New DataSet()
    Try
        oracleDA.Fill(ds)
        ' Create an update command and set to dataadapter
        Dim oracleUpdateCmd = New OracleCommand("UPDATE DEPT " & _
            "SET DNAME = :DNAME WHERE DEPTNO = :DEPTNO", oracleCn)
        oracleDA.UpdateCommand = oracleUpdateCmd
        ' Set parameters to dataadapter parameter collection
        Dim oracleParm As New OracleParameter()
        oracleParm = oracleDA.UpdateCommand.Parameters.Add( _
            New OracleParameter(":DEPTNO", OracleType.Number))
        oracleParm.SourceColumn = "DEPTNO"
        oracleParm.SourceVersion = DataRowVersion.Original
        oracleParm = oracleDA.UpdateCommand.Parameters.Add( _
            New OracleParameter(":DNAME", OracleType.VarChar))
        oracleParm.SourceColumn = "DNAME"
        oracleParm.SourceVersion = DataRowVersion.Current
        ' change a row in the datatable
        Dim oracleDR = ds.Tables(0).Rows _
            (ds.Tables(0).Rows.Count - 1)
        oracleDR("DNAME") = "DOCUMENTATION"
        ' update the row in the data source
        oracleDA.Update(ds)
        Cursor.Current = Cursors.Default
    Catch e As Exception
```

```
            Cursor.Current = Cursors.Default
            MsgBox(e.Message)
        End Try
    End Sub
```

The C# version of this code follows:

```csharp
private void DataSetUpdateOracleParm(string sServer)
{
    Cursor.Current = Cursors.WaitCursor;
    // Create the connection and dataadapter
    OracleConnection oracleCn = new OracleConnection(
        "DATA SOURCE=" + sServer + ";INTEGRATED SECURITY=yes");
    OracleDataAdapter oracleDA = new OracleDataAdapter(
        "SELECT * FROM DEPT", oracleCn);
    DataSet ds = new DataSet();
    try
    {
        oracleDA.Fill(ds);
        // Create an update command and set to dataadapter
        OracleCommand oracleUpdateCmd = new OracleCommand(
            "UPDATE DEPT SET DNAME = :DNAME WHERE DEPTNO = :DEPTNO",
            oracleCn);
        oracleDA.UpdateCommand = oracleUpdateCmd;
        // Set parameters to dataadapter parameter collection
        OracleParameter oracleParm = new OracleParameter();
        oracleParm = oracleDA.UpdateCommand.Parameters.Add(
            new OracleParameter(":DEPTNO", OracleType.Number));
        oracleParm.SourceColumn = "DEPTNO";
        oracleParm.SourceVersion = DataRowVersion.Original;
        oracleParm = oracleDA.UpdateCommand.Parameters.Add(
            new OracleParameter(":DNAME", OracleType.VarChar));
        oracleParm.SourceColumn = "DNAME";
        oracleParm.SourceVersion = DataRowVersion.Current;
        // change a row in the datatable
        DataRow oracleDR = ds.Tables[0].Rows
                [ds.Tables[0].Rows.Count-1];
        oracleDR["DNAME"] = "DOCUMENTATION";
        // update the row in the data source
        oracleDA.Update(ds);
        Cursor.Current = Cursors.Default;
    }
```

```
    catch (Exception ex)
    {
        Cursor.Current = Cursors.Default;
        MessageBox.Show("DataSetUpdateOracleParm: :" +
            ex.ToString());
    }
}
```

The server name is passed into the top of the routine, and the OracleConnection object, OracleDataAdapter, and DataSet are created. Then the DataSet is filled in the Try-Catch loop. Next, an OracleCommand object is created with an UPDATE statement as the first argument and the Connection object as the second argument of the constructor. The next statement sets the OracleDataAdapter's UpdateCommand property with the command object. An OracleParameter object is then created. The parameter marker :DEPTNO is defined as an OracleType.Number and added to the oracleUpdateCommand object's Parameters collection in the OracleDataAdapter. The OracleParameter's SourceColumn property is then set to the DEPTNO column of the DataTable and its SourceVersion property is set to DataRowVersion.Original. Next, the parameter marker :DNAME is defined as an OracleType.VarChar and added to the OracleDataAdapter's Parameters collection. The SourceColumn for the OracleParameter is then set to the DNAME column of the DataTable, and the SourceVersion is set to DataRowVersion.Current. Next, you can see that the last row of the DataTable is selected and a new DataRow named oracleDR is returned. The next statement sets the retrieved DataRow's DNAME column with the new value of DOCUMENTATION. The OracleDataAdapter's Update method is then called, which executes the UPDATE statement and updates the database with the new company name.

Using the DataAdapter and Delete Custom Command

The next example shows how to use a custom DELETE command. You will see how to flag a DataSet record for deletion and then call the OracleDataAdapter Update method to remove the record from the data source.

```
Private Sub DataSetDeleteOracleParm(ByVal sServer As String)
    Cursor.Current = Cursors.WaitCursor
    ' Create the connection and dataadapter
    Dim oracleCn = New OracleConnection("DATA SOURCE=" & sServer _
        & ";INTEGRATED SECURITY=yes")
    Dim oracleDA As OracleDataAdapter = New OracleDataAdapter( _
        "SELECT * FROM DEPT", oracleCn)
    Dim ds = New DataSet()
    Try
        oracleDA.Fill(ds)
```

```
      ' Create a delete command and set to dataadapter
      Dim oracleDeleteCmd = New OracleCommand( _
          "DELETE FROM DEPT WHERE DEPTNO = :DEPTNO ", oracleCn)
      oracleDA.DeleteCommand = oracleDeleteCmd
      ' Set parameter to dataadapter parameter collection
      Dim oracleParm As New OracleParameter()
      oracleParm = oracleDA.UpdateCommand.Parameters.Add( _
          New OracleParameter(":DEPTNO", OracleType.Number))
      oracleParm.SourceColumn = "DEPTNO"
      oracleParm.SourceVersion = DataRowVersion.Original
      ' mark a row for deletion in the datatable
      Dim oracleDR = ds.Tables(0).Rows _
          (ds.Tables(0).Rows.Count - 1)
      oracleDR.Delete()
      ' delete the row from the data source
      oracleDA.Update(ds)
      Cursor.Current = Cursors.Default
    Catch e As Exception
      Cursor.Current = Cursors.Default
      MsgBox(e.Message)
    End Try
End Sub
```

The C# version of this code follows:

```
private void DataSetDeleteOracleParm(string sServer)
{
    Cursor.Current = Cursors.WaitCursor;
    // Create the connection and dataadapter
    OracleConnection oracleCn = new OracleConnection(
        "DATA SOURCE=" + sServer + ";INTEGRATED SECURITY=yes");
    OracleDataAdapter oracleDA = new OracleDataAdapter(
        "SELECT * FROM DEPT", oracleCn);
    DataSet ds = new DataSet();
    try
    {
        oracleDA.Fill(ds);
        // Create a delete command and set to dataadapter
        OracleCommand oracleDeleteCmd = new OracleCommand(
            "DELETE FROM DEPT WHERE DEPTNO = :DEPTNO ", oracleCn);
        oracleDA.DeleteCommand = oracleDeleteCmd;
        // Set parameter to dataadapter parameter collection
```

```
            OracleParameter oracleParm =
                oracleDA.DeleteCommand.Parameters.Add(
                new OracleParameter(":DEPTNO", OracleType.Number));
            oracleParm.SourceColumn = "DEPTNO";
            oracleParm.SourceVersion = DataRowVersion.Original;
            // mark a row for deletion in the datatable
            DataRow oracleDR = ds.Tables[0].Rows
                [ds.Tables[0].Rows.Count-1];
            oracleDR.Delete();
            // delete the row from the data source
            oracleDA.Update(ds);
            Cursor.Current = Cursors.Default;
        }
        catch (Exception ex)
        {
            Cursor.Current = Cursors.Default;
            MessageBox.Show("DataSetDeleteOracleParm: :" +
                ex.ToString());
        }
    }
}
```

Here again, the server name is passed into the top of the routine, and the OracleConnection object, OracleDataAdapter, and the DataSet are created. Then the DataSet is filled in the Try-Catch loop. Next, an OracleCommand object is created with a DELETE statement as the first argument and the Connection object as the second argument of the constructor. The next statement sets the OracleDataAdapter's DeleteCommand property with the command object. The parameter marker :DEPTNO is defined as an OracleType.Number and added to the command object's Parameters collection in the OracleDataAdapter. This statement also returns an OracleParameter object, oracleParm. The oracleParm's SourceColumn property is then set to the DEPTNO field in the DataTable, and its SourceVersion property is set to DataRowVersion.Original. The last row of the DataTable is then selected, and a new DataRow is returned. Next, the DataRow's Delete method is called to flag the row in the DataTable as Deleted. The OracleDataAdapter's Update method is then called to execute the DELETE command and remove the record from the database table.

Summary

In this chapter, you saw how to update the database from the DataSet by using the OracleDataAdapter's Update method. You saw how to use custom commands for the appropriate InsertCommand, UpdateCommand, and DeleteCommand to change the information in the DataSet. In the next chapter, you will see how to use the DataForm Wizard to quickly generate data forms for updating a data source.

Chapter 27

Updating the Database Using the OleDbDataAdapter

In the preceding chapter, you saw how to update an Oracle database using the
OracleDataAdapter. In this chapter, you will use the OleDbDataAdapter that is
provided as a part of the .NET Framework Data Provider for OLE DB to update
a data source. You will see how to use the visual OleDbDataAdapter object and the
Visual Studio DataForm Wizard to easily create bound data update forms. Then you
will use the OleDataAdapter class in code to update the database using a stored
procedure and parameters.

Using the OleDbDataAdapter

The OleDbDataAdapter is used in combination with the OleDbConnection object,
OleDbCommand object, and OleDbDataAdapter object to fill a DataSet with data
and resolve changes back to an OLE DB–compliant database.

Using the Visual Studio OleDbDataAdapter Object

Like the visual SqlDataAdapter component, the OleDbDataAdapter component is
provided as a part of the Visual Studio.NET development environment. To create and
use a new OleDbDataAdapter component, you must first create a Visual Studio project.
In the first example, you will create a DataForm using the DataForm Wizard to display
and update information in the Products table and Suppliers table of the Northwind
database. To start the DataForm Wizard, select Project | Add Windows Form from the
VS.NET environment menu bar. The Add New Item dialog box appears, as shown in
Figure 27-1.

Select the DataForm Wizard from the templates area of the dialog box, and click the
Open button. A DataForm will be added to your project and the DataForm Wizard will
begin to step you through configuring a connection and selecting a table or tables to
display and update. The first dialog box enables you to create a new DataSet object
or to select a DataSet that already exists in your project. As you can see in Figure 27-2,
a new DataSet named dsProducts will be created and used in this example.

Click the Next button to display the Choose A Data Connection dialog box and
select an existing connection from the drop-down box, or click the New Connection
button to create a new data connection. Click the Next button to display the Choose
Tables Or Views dialog box shown in Figure 27-3.

The Choose Tables Or Views dialog box enables you to select the tables or views
to use in your DataSet and DataForm. In this example, the Products table and the
Suppliers table have been selected. Click the Next button to create a relationship between

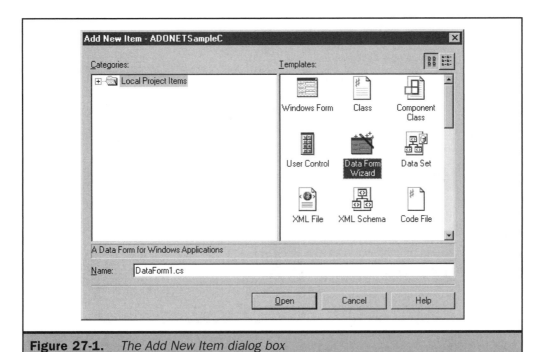

Figure 27-1.   *The Add New Item dialog box*

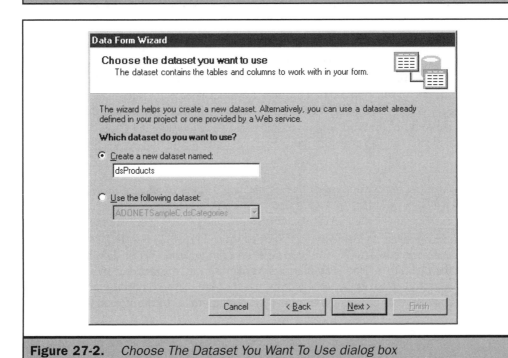

Figure 27-2.   *Choose The Dataset You Want To Use dialog box*

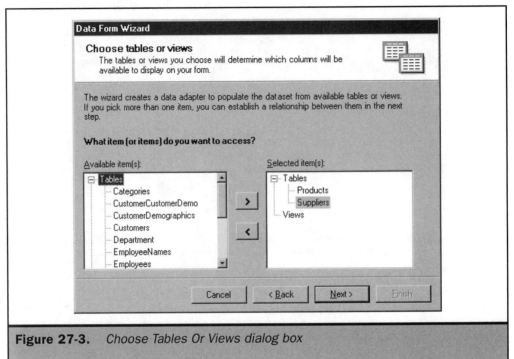

Figure 27-3. *Choose Tables Or Views dialog box*

the selected tables or views. Figure 27-4 shows the Create A Relationship Between Tables dialog box, in which the relationship has been given the name relProducts, the selected tables have been given their respective parent/child relations, and a column in each table has been selected as the common keys between the tables.

After selecting the relationship between the tables, click Next to select the columns you would like to build on the DataForm. When you've finished selecting the columns, click Next to select a display style for your DataForm from the dialog box shown in Figure 27-5.

Note *If your database table contains an Image field, you will not be allowed to select the Image field to be included on your DataForm.*

The Choose The Display Style dialog box shown in Figure 27-5 indicates that the record will be displayed in individual controls, and navigation and update buttons will be added to the DataForm. You may also opt to display the information in a data grid instead of individual controls. After selecting the display style, click the Finish button to build a DataForm that contains the requested data controls and buttons, as shown in Figure 27-6.

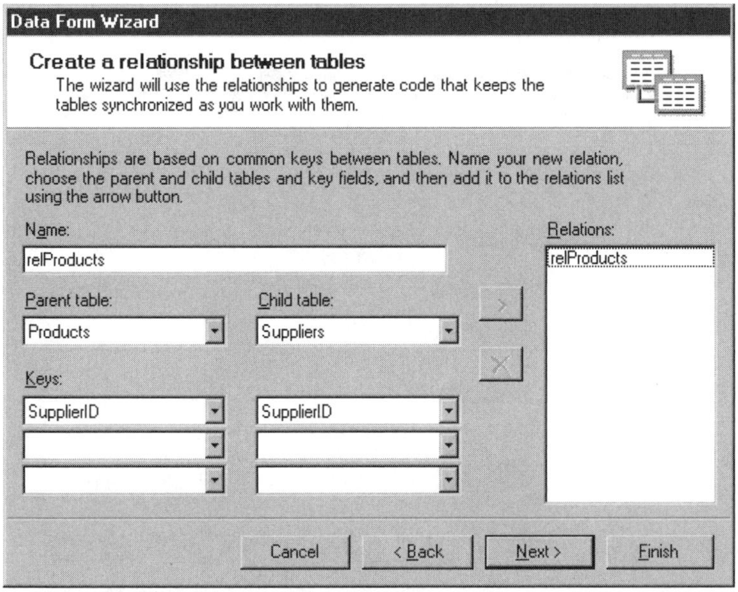

Figure 27-4.   *Create A Relationship Between Tables dialog box*

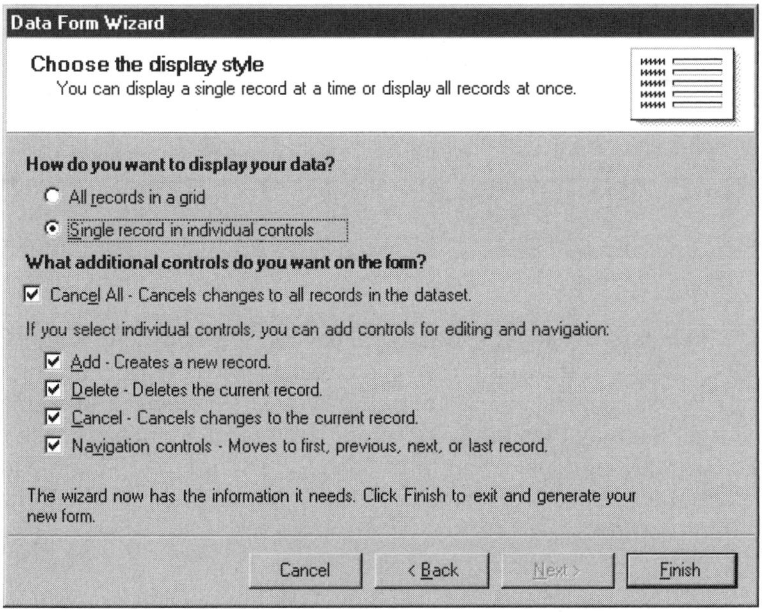

Figure 27-5.   *Choose The Display Style dialog box*

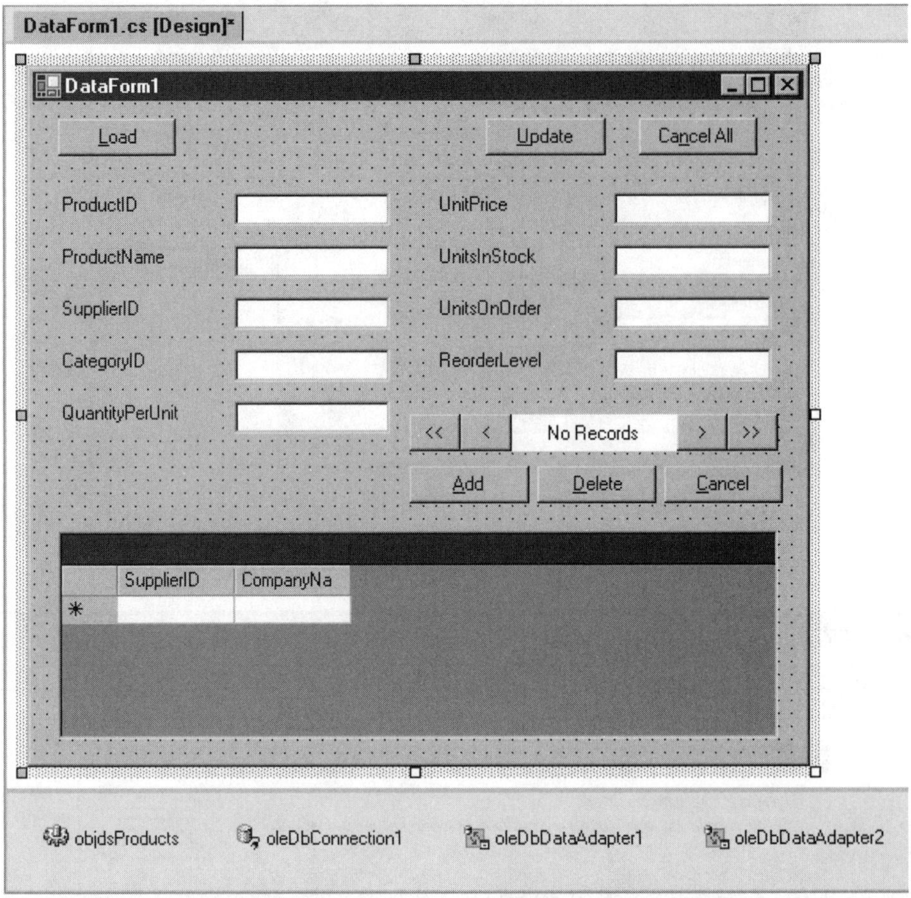

Figure 27-6. *DataForm1*

You can see in Figure 27-6 that the DataForm has been created along with a Connection object, DataSet, and two DataAdapters—one for each table you are working with. When this program is run, click the Load button to fill the DataSet and display the data on the DataForm. You may then navigate through the records or change the records using the Add, Update, and Delete buttons. Each DataAdapter will handle loading and updating data to their respective database tables. Figure 27-7 shows the DataForm with data in the bound controls.

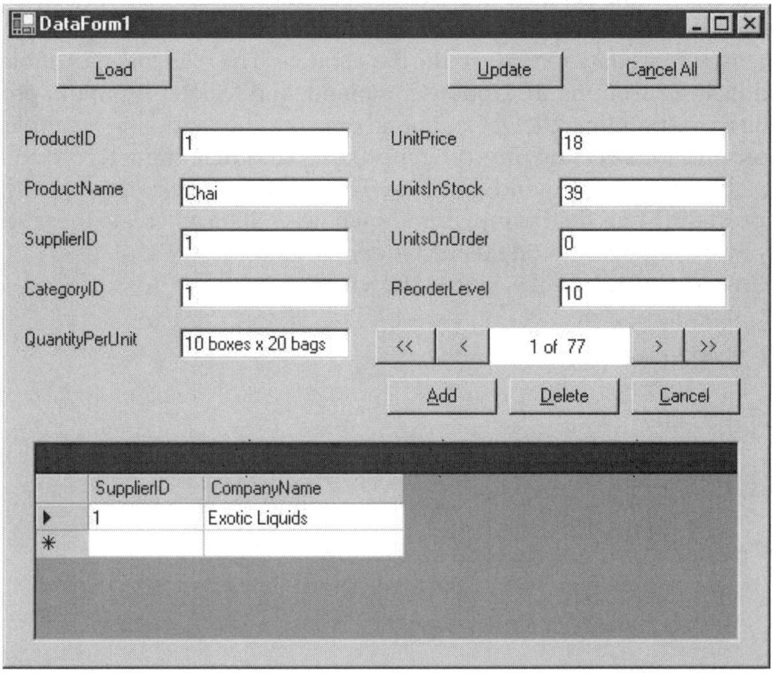

Figure 27-7. *DataForm1 with data*

Using the OleDbDataAdapter Class

As you can see in the preceding example, using the visual OleDbDataAdapter component and the DataForm Wizard makes it easy to automatically build update commands for changing database information from a DataSet. In this next section, the example uses the OleDbDataAdapter class and parameterized queries with stored procedures.

Before you can use the .NET Framework Data Provider for OLE DB in your code, you must first specify an import directive for the System.Data.OleDb Namespace in your project, as described in Chapter 6, "Using the .NET Framework Data Provider for OLE DB."

Using Parameters and Stored Procedures

After adding an import directive to your code, you're ready to begin using the different classes contained in the System.Data.OleDb Namespace. Like the SqlDataAdapter, the OleDbDataAdapter uses an OleDbConnection object and OleDbCommand objects to resolve changes from the DataSet to the database. Once an OleDbConnection object to the database has been created, OleDbCommand objects are created and set with a stored procedure to update records to the data source. The OleDbDataAdapter is then created and its InsertCommand, UpdateCommand, and DeleteCommand properties are set to the corresponding OleDbCommand objects. The following examples use stored procedures for selecting, inserting, updating, and deleting a record from the Customers table of the Northwind database. The T-SQL source code required to create the stored procedures for the examples is shown here. You can create these stored procedures by executing this code using Query Analyzer.

The spCustSelectCmd source code is shown here:

```
CREATE PROCEDURE spCustSelectCmd
AS
    SET NOCOUNT ON;
SELECT * FROM Customers
GO
```

The spCustInsertCmd source code is as follows:

```
CREATE PROCEDURE spCustInsertCmd
(
    @CustomerID nchar(5),
    @CompanyName nvarchar(40),
    @ContactName nvarchar(30),
    @ContactTitle nvarchar(30),
    @Address nvarchar(60),
    @City nvarchar(15),
    @Region nvarchar(15),
    @PostalCode nvarchar(10),
    @Country nvarchar(15),
    @Phone nvarchar(24),
    @Fax nvarchar(24),
)
AS
    SET NOCOUNT OFF;
INSERT INTO Customers(CustomerID, CompanyName, ContactName,
ContactTitle, Address, City, Region, PostalCode, Country,
Phone, Fax) VALUES (@CustomerID, @CompanyName, @ContactName,
@ContactTitle, @Address, @City, @Region, @PostalCode, @Country,
@Phone, @Fax);
GO
```

The spCustUpdateCmd source code is shown here:

```
CREATE PROCEDURE dbo.spCustUpdateCmd
(
    @CustomerID nchar(5),
    @ContactName nvarchar(30),
    @ContactTitle nvarchar(30),
    @Original_CustomerID nchar(5),
    @Original_ContactName nvarchar(30),
    @Original_ContactTitle nvarchar(30)
)
AS
    SET NOCOUNT OFF;
UPDATE Customers SET CustomerID = @CustomerID,
ContactName = @ContactName, ContactTitle = @ContactTitle
WHERE (CustomerID = @Original_CustomerID) AND
(ContactName = @Original_ContactName OR @Original_ContactName
IS NULL AND ContactName IS NULL) AND
(ContactTitle = @Original_ContactTitle OR @Original_ContactTitle
IS NULL AND ContactTitle IS NULL);
GO
```

The spCustDeleteCmd source code is as follows:

```
CREATE PROCEDURE spCustDeleteCmd
(
    @Original_CustomerID nchar(5)
)
AS
    SET NOCOUNT OFF;
DELETE FROM Customers WHERE (CustomerID = @Original_CustomerID)
GO
```

Use the DataAdapter and Insert Stored Procedure

The following example illustrates how to make a connection, create an OleDbCommand object that contains an INSERT statement, and add a new record to the Customers table in the Northwind database with the OleDbDataAdapter. The stored procedures used in this example are spCustSelectCmd and spCustInsertCmd.

```
Private Sub DataSetInsertOleDb(ByVal sServer As String, _
        ByVal sDB As String)
```

```vb
Cursor.Current = Cursors.WaitCursor
' Create the connection, command, and dataadapter
Dim oleDbCn = New OleDbConnection( _
    "PROVIDER=SQLOLEDB;SERVER=" & sServer & _
    ";TRUSTED_CONNECTION=Yes;DATABASE=" & sDB)
Dim oleDbSelectCmd = New OleDbCommand("spCustSelectCmd", _
    oleDbCn)
oleDbSelectCmd.CommandType = CommandType.StoredProcedure
Dim oleDbDA = New OleDbDataAdapter(oleDbSelectCmd)
Dim ds = New DataSet()
Try
    ' Populate the dataset
    oleDbDA.Fill(ds, "Customers")
    ' Put insert command to dataadapter property
    Dim oleDbInsertCmd = New OleDbCommand("spCustInsertCmd", _
        oleDbCn)
    oleDbInsertCmd.CommandType = CommandType.StoredProcedure
    oleDbDA.InsertCommand = oleDbInsertCmd
    ' Set parameters to the dataadapter parameters collection
    Dim oleDbParm = New OleDbParameter()
    oleDbParm = oleDbDA.InsertCommand.Parameters.Add( _
        New OleDbParameter("@CustomerID", OleDbType.Char, 5))
    oleDbParm.SourceColumn = "CustomerID"
    oleDbParm.SourceVersion = DataRowVersion.Current
    oleDbParm = oleDbDA.InsertCommand.Parameters.Add( _
        New OleDbParameter("@CompanyName", OleDbType.VarChar))
    oleDbParm.SourceColumn = "CompanyName"
    oleDbParm.SourceVersion = DataRowVersion.Current
    oleDbParm = oleDbDA.InsertCommand.Parameters.Add( _
        New OleDbParameter("@ContactName", OleDbType.VarChar))
    oleDbParm.SourceColumn = "ContactName"
    oleDbParm.SourceVersion = DataRowVersion.Current
    oleDbParm = oleDbDA.InsertCommand.Parameters.Add( _
        New OleDbParameter("@ContactTitle", OleDbType.VarChar))
    oleDbParm.SourceColumn = "ContactTitle"
    oleDbParm.SourceVersion = DataRowVersion.Current
    oleDbParm = oleDbDA.InsertCommand.Parameters.Add( _
        New OleDbParameter("@Address", OleDbType.VarChar))
    oleDbParm.SourceColumn = "Address"
    oleDbParm.SourceVersion = DataRowVersion.Current
    oleDbParm = oleDbDA.InsertCommand.Parameters.Add( _
        New OleDbParameter("@City", OleDbType.VarChar))
```

```
        oleDbParm.SourceColumn = "City"
        oleDbParm.SourceVersion = DataRowVersion.Current
        oleDbParm = oleDbDA.InsertCommand.Parameters.Add( _
            New OleDbParameter("@Region", OleDbType.VarChar))
        oleDbParm.SourceColumn = "Region"
        oleDbParm.SourceVersion = DataRowVersion.Current
        oleDbParm = oleDbDA.InsertCommand.Parameters.Add( _
            New OleDbParameter("@PostalCode", OleDbType.VarChar))
        oleDbParm.SourceColumn = "PostalCode"
        oleDbParm.SourceVersion = DataRowVersion.Current
        oleDbParm = oleDbDA.InsertCommand.Parameters.Add( _
            New OleDbParameter("@Country", OleDbType.VarChar))
        oleDbParm.SourceColumn = "Country"
        oleDbParm.SourceVersion = DataRowVersion.Current
        oleDbParm = oleDbDA.InsertCommand.Parameters.Add( _
            New OleDbParameter("@Phone", OleDbType.VarChar))
        oleDbParm.SourceColumn = "Phone"
        oleDbParm.SourceVersion = DataRowVersion.Current
        oleDbParm = oleDbDA.InsertCommand.Parameters.Add( _
            New OleDbParameter("@Fax", OleDbType.VarChar))
        oleDbParm.SourceColumn = "Fax"
        oleDbParm.SourceVersion = DataRowVersion.Current
        ' Add a new record to the datatable
        Dim oleDbDR = ds.Tables("Customers").NewRow()
        oleDbDR("CustomerID") = "BUYRT"
        oleDbDR("CompanyName") = "Buy Right Foods"
        oleDbDR("ContactName") = "Rene Wilson"
        oleDbDR("ContactTitle") = "Chef"
        oleDbDR("Address") = "12 One St"
        oleDbDR("City") = "Mealville"
        oleDbDR("Region") = "NW"
        oleDbDR("PostalCode") = "12345"
        oleDbDR("Country") = "USA"
        oleDbDR("Phone") = "555-123-1234"
        oleDbDR("Fax") = "555-123-4321"
        ds.Tables("Customers").Rows.Add(oleDbDR)
        ' Insert the record into the database table
        oleDbDA.Update(ds, "Customers")
        Cursor.Current = Cursors.Default
    Catch e As Exception
        Cursor.Current = Cursors.Default
        MsgBox(e.Message)
```

```
    End Try
End Sub
```

The C# version of this code is as follows:

```csharp
private void DataSetInsertOleDb(string sServer, string sDB)
{
    Cursor.Current = Cursors.WaitCursor;
    // Create the connection, command, and dataadapter
    OleDbConnection oleDbCn = new OleDbConnection(
        "PROVIDER=SQLOLEDB;SERVER=" + sServer +
        ";TRUSTED_CONNECTION=Yes;DATABASE=" + sDB);
    OleDbCommand oleDbSelectCmd = new OleDbCommand(
        "spCustSelectCmd", oleDbCn);
    oleDbSelectCmd.CommandType = CommandType.StoredProcedure;
    OleDbDataAdapter oleDbDA = new OleDbDataAdapter(oleDbSelectCmd);
    DataSet ds = new DataSet();
    try
    {
        // Populate the dataset
        oleDbDA.Fill(ds, "Customers");
        // Put insert command to dataadapter property
        OleDbCommand oleDbInsertCmd = new OleDbCommand(
            "spCustInsertCmd", oleDbCn);
        oleDbInsertCmd.CommandType = CommandType.StoredProcedure;
        oleDbDA.InsertCommand = oleDbInsertCmd;
        // Set parameters to the dataadapter parameters collection
        OleDbParameter oleDbParm = new OleDbParameter();
        oleDbParm = oleDbDA.InsertCommand.Parameters.Add(
            new OleDbParameter("@CustomerID", OleDbType.Char, 5));
        oleDbParm.SourceColumn = "CustomerID";
        oleDbParm.SourceVersion = DataRowVersion.Current;
        oleDbParm = oleDbDA.InsertCommand.Parameters.Add(
            new OleDbParameter("@CompanyName", OleDbType.VarChar));
        oleDbParm.SourceColumn = "CompanyName";
        oleDbParm.SourceVersion = DataRowVersion.Current;
        oleDbParm = oleDbDA.InsertCommand.Parameters.Add(
            new OleDbParameter("@ContactName", OleDbType.VarChar));
        oleDbParm.SourceColumn = "ContactName";
        oleDbParm.SourceVersion = DataRowVersion.Current;
        oleDbParm = oleDbDA.InsertCommand.Parameters.Add(
            new OleDbParameter("@ContactTitle", OleDbType.VarChar));
```

```
oleDbParm.SourceColumn = "ContactTitle";
oleDbParm.SourceVersion = DataRowVersion.Current;
oleDbParm = oleDbDA.InsertCommand.Parameters.Add(
    new OleDbParameter("@Address", OleDbType.VarChar));
oleDbParm.SourceColumn = "Address";
oleDbParm.SourceVersion = DataRowVersion.Current;
oleDbParm = oleDbDA.InsertCommand.Parameters.Add(
    new OleDbParameter("@City", OleDbType.VarChar));
oleDbParm.SourceColumn = "City";
oleDbParm.SourceVersion = DataRowVersion.Current;
oleDbParm = oleDbDA.InsertCommand.Parameters.Add(
    new OleDbParameter("@Region", OleDbType.VarChar));
oleDbParm.SourceColumn = "Region";
oleDbParm.SourceVersion = DataRowVersion.Current;
oleDbParm = oleDbDA.InsertCommand.Parameters.Add(
    new OleDbParameter("@PostalCode", OleDbType.VarChar));
oleDbParm.SourceColumn = "PostalCode";
oleDbParm.SourceVersion = DataRowVersion.Current;
oleDbParm = oleDbDA.InsertCommand.Parameters.Add(
    new OleDbParameter("@Country", OleDbType.VarChar));
oleDbParm.SourceColumn = "Country";
oleDbParm.SourceVersion = DataRowVersion.Current;
oleDbParm = oleDbDA.InsertCommand.Parameters.Add(
    new OleDbParameter("@Phone", OleDbType.VarChar));
oleDbParm.SourceColumn = "Phone";
oleDbParm.SourceVersion = DataRowVersion.Current;
oleDbParm = oleDbDA.InsertCommand.Parameters.Add(
    new OleDbParameter("@Fax", OleDbType.VarChar));
oleDbParm.SourceColumn = "Fax";
oleDbParm.SourceVersion = DataRowVersion.Current;
// Add a new record to the datatable
DataRow oleDbDR = ds.Tables["Customers"].NewRow();
oleDbDR["CustomerID"] = "BUYRT";
oleDbDR["CompanyName"] = "Buy Right Foods";
oleDbDR["ContactName"] = "Rene Wilson";
oleDbDR["ContactTitle"] = "Chef";
oleDbDR["Address"] = "12 One St";
oleDbDR["City"] = "Mealville";
oleDbDR["Region"] = "NW";
oleDbDR["PostalCode"] = "12345";
oleDbDR["Country"] = "USA";
oleDbDR["Phone"] = "555-123-1234";
oleDbDR["Fax"] = "555-123-4321";
```

```csharp
        ds.Tables["Customers"].Rows.Add(oleDbDR);
        // Insert the record into the database table
        oleDbDA.Update(ds, "Customers");
        Cursor.Current = Cursors.Default;
    }
    catch (Exception ex)
    {
        Cursor.Current = Cursors.Default;
        MessageBox.Show("DataSetInsertOleDb: :" + ex.ToString());
    }
}
```

The server and database name are passed into the top of the routine, and the Connection object, the OleDbCommand object, the OleDbDataAdapter object, and the DataSet are created. Notice here that the OleDbCommand object is created with the first argument as the stored procedure, spCustSelectCmd, and the CommandType property of the Command object is set to CommandType.StoredProcedure. Then the DataSet is populated using the OleDbDataAdapter's Fill method inside the Try-Catch loop. Next, an OleDbCommand object is created using an Insert stored procedure as the first argument and the Connection object as the second argument of the constructor, and the CommandType property of the Command object is set to CommandType .StoredProcedure. The next statement sets the OleDbDataAdapter's InsertCommand property with the oleDbParm command object. An OleDbParameter object is then created for each of the columns in the table and added to the DataAdapter's Parameters collection. The SourceColumn property of each of the OleDbParameters is set to the corresponding column names in the DataTable. A new DataRow object is then created, assigned new column values, and added to the DataTable's Rows collection. Last, the OleDbDataAdapter's Update method is called to send the new row from the DataSet to the database.

Using the DataAdapter and Update Stored Procedure

The next example updates the Shipper record that was added to the database table:

```vb
Private Sub DataSetUpdateOleDb(ByVal sServer As String, _
    ByVal sDB As String)
    Cursor.Current = Cursors.WaitCursor
    ' Create the connection, command, and dataadapter
    Dim oleDbCn = New OleDbConnection( _
        "PROVIDER=SQLOLEDB;SERVER=" & sServer & _
        ";TRUSTED_CONNECTION=Yes;DATABASE=" + sDB)
    Dim oleDbSelectCmd = New OleDbCommand("spCustSelectCmd", _
        oleDbCn)
```

```vb
oleDbSelectCmd.CommandType = CommandType.StoredProcedure
Dim oleDbDA = New OleDbDataAdapter(oleDbSelectCmd)
Dim ds = New DataSet()
Try
    ' Populate the dataset
    oleDbDA.Fill(ds, "Customers")
    ' Put update command to dataadapter property
    Dim oleDbUpdateCmd = New OleDbCommand("spCustUpdateCmd", _
        oleDbCn)
    oleDbUpdateCmd.CommandType = CommandType.StoredProcedure
    oleDbDA.UpdateCommand = oleDbUpdateCmd
    ' Set parameters to the dataadapter parameters collection
    Dim oleDbParm = New OleDbParameter()
    oleDbParm = oleDbDA.UpdateCommand.Parameters.Add( _
        New OleDbParameter("@CustomerID", OleDbType.Char, 5))
    oleDbParm.SourceColumn = "CustomerID"
    oleDbParm.SourceVersion = DataRowVersion.Original
    oleDbParm = oleDbDA.UpdateCommand.Parameters.Add( _
        New OleDbParameter("@ContactName", OleDbType.VarChar))
    oleDbParm.SourceColumn = "ContactName"
    oleDbParm.SourceVersion = DataRowVersion.Current
    oleDbParm = oleDbDA.UpdateCommand.Parameters.Add( _
        New OleDbParameter("@ContactTitle", OleDbType.VarChar))
    oleDbParm.SourceColumn = "ContactTitle"
    oleDbParm.SourceVersion = DataRowVersion.Current
    oleDbParm = oleDbDA.UpdateCommand.Parameters.Add( _
        New OleDbParameter("@Original_CustomerID", _
        OleDbType.Char, 5))
    oleDbParm.SourceColumn = "CustomerID"
    oleDbParm.SourceVersion = DataRowVersion.Original
    oleDbParm = oleDbDA.UpdateCommand.Parameters.Add( _
        New OleDbParameter("@Original_ContactName", _
        OleDbType.VarChar))
    oleDbParm.SourceColumn = "ContactName"
    oleDbParm.SourceVersion = DataRowVersion.Original
    oleDbParm = oleDbDA.UpdateCommand.Parameters.Add( _
        New OleDbParameter("@Original_ContactTitle", _
        OleDbType.VarChar))
    oleDbParm.SourceColumn = "ContactTitle"
    oleDbParm.SourceVersion = DataRowVersion.Original
    ' Change a record in the datatable
    Dim dv = New DataView(ds.Tables("Customers"), "", _
        "CustomerID", DataViewRowState.CurrentRows)
```

```
        Dim iRow As Integer
        iRow = dv.Find("BUYRT")
        ds.Tables("Customers").Rows(iRow)("ContactName") = _
            "George Martin"
        ds.Tables("Customers").Rows(iRow)("ContactTitle") = "Owner"
        ' Update the record in the database table
        oleDbDA.Update(ds, "Customers")
        Cursor.Current = Cursors.Default
    Catch e As Exception
        Cursor.Current = Cursors.Default
        MsgBox(e.Message)
    End Try
End Sub
```

The C# version of this code follows:

```
private void DataSetUpdateOleDb(string sServer, string sDB)
{
    Cursor.Current = Cursors.WaitCursor;
    // Create the connection, command, and dataadapter
    OleDbConnection oleDbCn = new OleDbConnection(
        "PROVIDER=SQLOLEDB;SERVER=" + sServer +
        ";TRUSTED_CONNECTION=Yes;DATABASE=" + sDB);
    OleDbCommand oleDbSelectCmd = new OleDbCommand(
        "spCustSelectCmd", oleDbCn);
    oleDbSelectCmd.CommandType = CommandType.StoredProcedure;
    OleDbDataAdapter oleDbDA = new OleDbDataAdapter(oleDbSelectCmd);
    DataSet ds = new DataSet();
    try
    {
        // Populate the dataset
        oleDbDA.Fill(ds, "Customers");
        // Put update command to dataadapter property
        OleDbCommand oleDbUpdateCmd = new OleDbCommand(
            "spCustUpdateCmd", oleDbCn);
        oleDbUpdateCmd.CommandType = CommandType.StoredProcedure;
        oleDbDA.UpdateCommand = oleDbUpdateCmd;
        // Set parameters to the dataadapter parameters collection
        OleDbParameter oleDbParm = new OleDbParameter();
        oleDbParm = oleDbDA.UpdateCommand.Parameters.Add(
            new OleDbParameter("@CustomerID", OleDbType.Char, 5));
        oleDbParm.SourceColumn = "CustomerID";
```

```
        oleDbParm.SourceVersion = DataRowVersion.Original;
        oleDbParm = oleDbDA.UpdateCommand.Parameters.Add(
            new OleDbParameter("@ContactName", OleDbType.VarChar));
        oleDbParm.SourceColumn = "ContactName";
        oleDbParm.SourceVersion = DataRowVersion.Current;
        oleDbParm = oleDbDA.UpdateCommand.Parameters.Add(
            new OleDbParameter("@ContactTitle", OleDbType.VarChar));
        oleDbParm.SourceColumn = "ContactTitle";
        oleDbParm.SourceVersion = DataRowVersion.Current;
        oleDbParm = oleDbDA.UpdateCommand.Parameters.Add(
            new OleDbParameter("@Original_CustomerID",
            OleDbType.Char, 5));
        oleDbParm.SourceColumn = "CustomerID";
        oleDbParm.SourceVersion = DataRowVersion.Original;
        oleDbParm = oleDbDA.UpdateCommand.Parameters.Add(
            new OleDbParameter("@Original_ContactName",
            OleDbType.VarChar));
        oleDbParm.SourceColumn = "ContactName";
        oleDbParm.SourceVersion = DataRowVersion.Original;
        oleDbParm = oleDbDA.UpdateCommand.Parameters.Add(
            new OleDbParameter("@Original_ContactTitle",
            OleDbType.VarChar));
        oleDbParm.SourceColumn = "ContactTitle";
        oleDbParm.SourceVersion = DataRowVersion.Original;
        // Change a record in the datatable
        DataView dv = new DataView(ds.Tables["Customers"], "",
                "CustomerID", DataViewRowState.CurrentRows);
        int iRow = dv.Find("BUYRT");
        ds.Tables["Customers"].Rows[iRow]["ContactName"] =
                "George Martin";
        ds.Tables["Customers"].Rows[iRow]["ContactTitle"] = "Owner";
        // Update the record in the database table
        oleDbDA.Update(ds, "Customers");
        Cursor.Current = Cursors.Default;
    }
    catch (Exception ex)
    {
        Cursor.Current = Cursors.Default;
        MessageBox.Show("DataSetUpdateOleDb: :" + ex.ToString());
    }
}
```

The server and database name are passed into the top of the routine, and the Connection object, OleDbDataAdapter, and DataSet are created. Then the DataSet is filled inside the Try-Catch loop. The OleDbCommand object is created with the first argument as the stored procedure, spCustUpdateCmd, and the CommandType property of the Command object is set to CommandType.StoredProcedure. The next statement sets the OleDbDataAdapter's UpdateCommand property with the command object. An OleDbParameter object is then created. The parameters are then created and added to the OleDbParameter's Parameters collection. The SourceColumn and SourceVersion of the parameters are then set. The next statement creates a DataView over the DataTable setting the sort order of the DataView to the CustomerID field. Next, you use the DataView's Find method to select a row of the DataTable that matches the CustomerID literal of BUYRT. The next statements change the values of the ContactName and ContactTitle columns. The OleDbDataAdapter's Update method is then called, which executes the UPDATE statement and updates the database with the new contact name and contact title values.

Using the DataAdapter and Delete Stored Procedure

The next example shows the DELETE statement:

```
Private Sub DataSetDeleteOleDb(ByVal sServer As String, _
    ByVal sDB As String)
    Cursor.Current = Cursors.WaitCursor
    ' Create the connection, command, and dataadapter
    Dim oleDbCn = New OleDbConnection( _
        "PROVIDER=SQLOLEDB;SERVER=" & sServer & _
        ";TRUSTED_CONNECTION=Yes;DATABASE=" & sDB)
    Dim oleDbSelectCmd = New OleDbCommand("spCustSelectCmd", _
        oleDbCn)
    oleDbSelectCmd.CommandType = CommandType.StoredProcedure
    Dim oleDbDA = New OleDbDataAdapter(oleDbSelectCmd)
    Dim ds = New DataSet()
    Try
        ' Populate the dataset
        oleDbDA.Fill(ds, "Customers")
        ' Put delete command to dataadapter property
        Dim oleDbDeleteCmd = New OleDbCommand("spCustDeleteCmd", _
            oleDbCn)
        oleDbDeleteCmd.CommandType = CommandType.StoredProcedure
        oleDbDA.DeleteCommand = oleDbDeleteCmd
        ' Set parameters to the dataadapter parameters collection
        Dim oleDbParm = New OleDbParameter()
        oleDbParm = oleDbDA.DeleteCommand.Parameters.Add( _
```

```
          New OleDbParameter("@CustomerID", OleDbType.Char, 5))
      oleDbParm.SourceColumn = "CustomerID"
      oleDbParm.SourceVersion = DataRowVersion.Original
      ' Mark a record for deletion from the datatable
      Dim oleDbDR = ds.Tables("Customers").Select( _
          "CustomerID = 'BUYRT'")(0)
      oleDbDR.Delete()
      ' Delete the record from the database table
      oleDbDA.Update(ds, "Customers")
      Cursor.Current = Cursors.Default
    Catch e As Exception
      Cursor.Current = Cursors.Default
      MsgBox(e.Message)
    End Try
End Sub
```

The C# version of this code is as follows:

```
private void DataSetDeleteOleDb(string sServer, string sDB)
{
    Cursor.Current = Cursors.WaitCursor;
    // Create the connection, command, and dataadapter
    OleDbConnection oleDbCn = new OleDbConnection(
        "PROVIDER=SQLOLEDB;SERVER=" + sServer +
        ";TRUSTED_CONNECTION=Yes;DATABASE=" + sDB);
    OleDbCommand oleDbSelectCmd = new OleDbCommand(
        "spCustSelectCmd", oleDbCn);
    oleDbSelectCmd.CommandType = CommandType.StoredProcedure;
    OleDbDataAdapter oleDbDA = new OleDbDataAdapter(oleDbSelectCmd);
    DataSet ds = new DataSet();
    try
    {
        // Populate the dataset
        oleDbDA.Fill(ds, "Customers");
        // Put delete command to dataadapter property
        OleDbCommand oleDbDeleteCmd = new OleDbCommand(
            "spCustDeleteCmd", oleDbCn);
        oleDbDeleteCmd.CommandType = CommandType.StoredProcedure;
        oleDbDA.DeleteCommand = oleDbDeleteCmd;
        // Set parameters to the dataadapter parameters collection
        OleDbParameter oleDbParm = new OleDbParameter();
        oleDbParm = oleDbDA.DeleteCommand.Parameters.Add(
```

THE ADO.NET
DATASET OBJECT

```
            new OleDbParameter("@CustomerID", OleDbType.Char, 5));
        oleDbParm.SourceColumn = "CustomerID";
        oleDbParm.SourceVersion = DataRowVersion.Original;
        // Mark a record for deletion from the datatable
        DataRow oleDbDR = ds.Tables["Customers"].Select(
            "CustomerID = 'BUYRT'")[0];
        oleDbDR.Delete();
        // Delete the record from the database table
        oleDbDA.Update(ds, "Customers");
        Cursor.Current = Cursors.Default;
    }
    catch (Exception ex)
    {
        Cursor.Current = Cursors.Default;
        MessageBox.Show("DataSetDeleteOleDb: :" + ex.ToString());
    }
}
```

Here again, the server and database name are passed into the top of the routine, and the Connection object, OleDbDataAdapter, and DataSet are created. Then the DataSet is filled inside the Try-Catch loop. The OleDbCommand object is created with the first argument as the stored procedure, spCustDeleteCmd, and the CommandType property of the Command object is set to CommandType.StoredProcedure. The next statement sets the OleDbDataAdapter's DeleteCommand property with the command object. An OleDbParameter object is then created. The parameter is then added to the OleDbParameter's Parameters collection. The SourceColumn and SourceVersion of the parameters are then set. Next, you can see that a row of the DataTable is selected that matches the literal BUYRT. The next statement calls the DataRow object's Delete method to flag the row for deletion. The OleDbDataAdapter's Update method is then called to execute the DELETE command and remove the record from the database table.

Summary

In this chapter, you saw how to create a Windows DataForm to update the database from the DataSet using the OleDbDataAdapter. You saw how the DataAdapter's Update method calls the appropriate InsertCommand, UpdateCommand, or DeleteCommand after the DataAdapter analyzes the changed information in the DataSet. You also saw how to use stored procedures and how to add parameters in program code. The next chapter will use the OdbcDataAdapter that is provided with the .NET Framework Data Provider for ODBC.

Chapter 28

Updating the Database Using the OdbcDataAdapter

In the preceding chapter, you saw how to use the DataForm Wizard to quickly create forms that allow updating of database information. You also used parameters and stored procedures in program code to change database tables through the OleDbDataAdapter. This chapter focuses on using the OdbcDataAdapter that's included in the .NET Framework Data Provider for ODBC. You will use the DataAdapter Configuration Wizard to create and configure an OdbcDataAdapter to use existing stored procedures from your ODBC-compliant database to populate a DataSet and then return the updated information back to the data source. You will also see how to select specific records in the DataSet to resolve to the database based on the DataRow's RowState value. This enables you to update the database in a particular order. For example, you may want to resolve the deleted records from the DataSet to the data source before you resolve the inserted records.

Using the OdbcDataAdapter

The OdbcDataAdapter is used in combination with the OdbcConnection object and the OdbcCommand object to populate DataSets from ODBC-compliant databases and resolve changes back to those databases. These objects are included in the .NET Framework Data Provider for ODBC.

Using the Visual Studio OdbcDataAdapter Object

Like other DataAdapters, the OdbcDataAdapter component is provided as a part of the Visual Studio.NET development environment. You create a new OdbcDataAdapter component by creating a Visual Studio project, adding a form to the project, and clicking the newly created form in the Visual Studio Project Explorer window to display it in the Visual Studio Designer window. After the form has been created, add a DataGrid and Button to the form by double-clicking these controls from the Windows Forms tab of the toolbox that is displayed on the left side of the Visual Studio.Net development environment. Double-click the OdbcDataAdapter object from the Data Toolbox that is displayed on the left side of the Visual Studio.Net development environment to add an OdbcDataAdapter to the component pane of your project. The DataAdapter Configuration Wizard will start and step you through the process of setting up an OdbcConnection object and an OdbcDataAdapter object to use against the database.

Updating Using Existing Stored Procedures and Windows Form Controls

Step through the DataAdapter Configuration Wizard by selecting a connection in the Choose a DataConnection dialog box and clicking the Next button to display the Choose A Query Type dialog box, as shown in Figure 28-1.

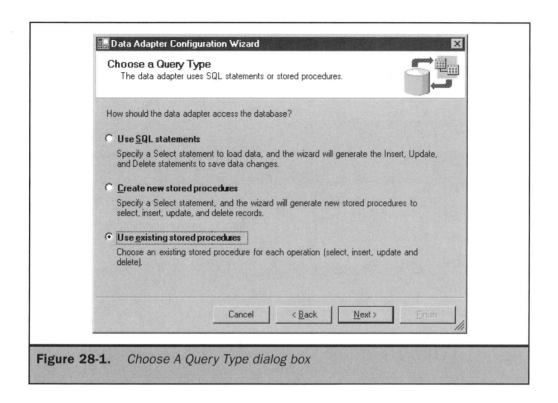

Figure 28-1. *Choose A Query Type dialog box*

In this example, you will use existing stored procedures to update the database. You can see in Figure 28-1 that the Use Existing Stored Procedures radio button is selected. Click the Next button to take you to the next dialog box, Bind Commands To Existing Stored Procedures, as shown in Figure 28-2.

Each drop-down list in this dialog box will contain the stored procedures that already exist in the database. Select each drop-down list, and choose a corresponding stored procedure for each of the command actions you wish to use. For example, in Figure 28-2, you can see that the stored procedure spCustSelectCommand has been chosen for the DataAdapter's SelectCommand property and the spCustUpdateCommand has been chosen for the UpdateCommand property.

After selecting the stored procedures for each command, click the Next button to display the View Wizard Results dialog box, ahown in Figure 28-3.

You can see in Figure 28-3 that statements for each of the command properties have been generated and that the OdbcDataAdapter has been successfully configured. Click the Finish button to return to the Visual Studio design environment.

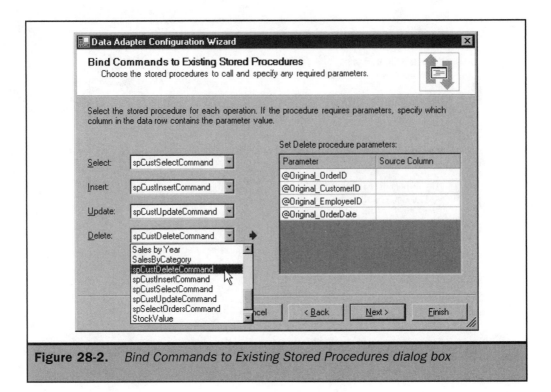

Figure 28-2. *Bind Commands to Existing Stored Procedures dialog box*

Next, right-click the odbcDataAdapter1 object in your Visual Studio project design window to display a pop-up menu and select the Generate DataSet option. The Generate Dataset dialog box will be displayed, enabling you to create a DataSet and add the tables specified in the OdbcDataAdapter. Choose an existing DataSet to add tables to, or create a new DataSet, and add the tables to it.

In Figure 28-4, the new DataSet option is chosen and a DataSet name of dsCustomer has been entered. Notice here that the table that will be added to the DataSet is based on the results of the stored procedure that has been placed in the SelectCommand property of the OdbcDataAdapter. Click OK, and a DataSet component is added to your project to be used as a data source for displaying data information in bound controls.

The DataSet is created, so now you need to populate the DataSet object from the data source. Call the OdbcDataAdapter's Fill method using the DataSet as the first argument and the name of the DataTable to be created as the second argument. In this example, call the OdbcDataAdapter's Fill method from the form's Load method, so that the data will be displayed as soon as the application starts. The DataGrid that was added to the form earlier will have its DataSource property set to the DataSet. Double-click the form object to display the code for the Form1_Load method, and add the Fill method to this subroutine as illustrated in the code that follows.

```
Private Sub Form1_Load(ByVal sender As System.Object, _
        ByVal e As System.EventArgs) Handles MyBase.Load
    OdbcDataAdapter1.Fill(DsCustomer1, "Customers")
    DataGrid1.DataSource = DsCustomer1
    DataGrid1.DataMember = "Customers"
End Sub
```

The C# version of this code is as follows:

```
private void Form1_Load(object sender, System.EventArgs e)
{
    odbcDataAdapter1.Fill(dsCustomer1, "Customers");
    DataGrid1.DataSource = dsCustomer1;
    DataGrid1.DataMember = "Customers";
}
```

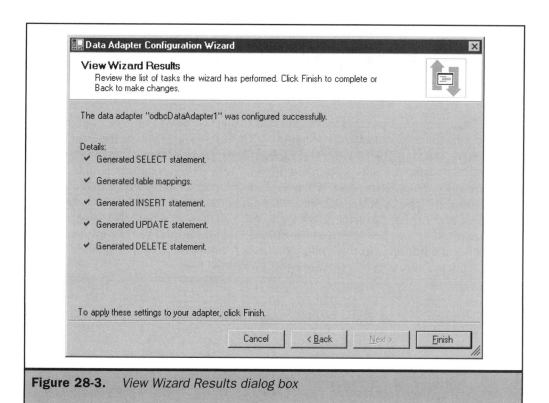

Figure 28-3.   *View Wizard Results dialog box*

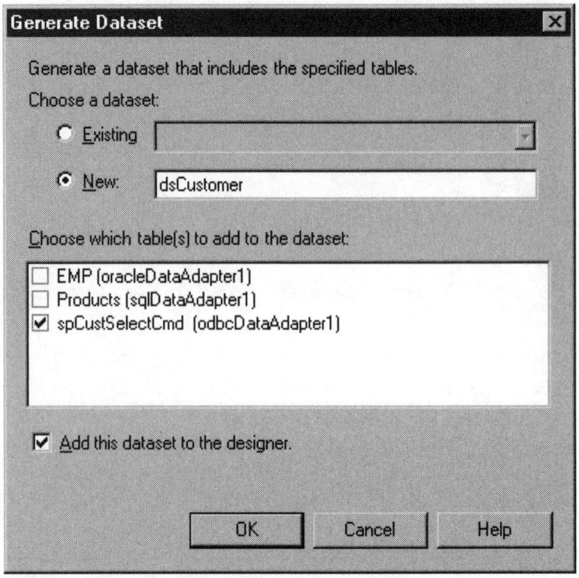

Figure 28-4. Generate DataSet dialog box

The dsCustomer1 object that was generated earlier is passed to the Fill method of the odbcDataAdapter1 object and the name of "Customers" is given to the DataTable created in the DataSet. The DataGrid's DataSource property is then set to the DataSet. The odbcDataAdapter1's SelectCommand property was configured to contain the stored procedure spCustSelectCommand. When the DataAdapter's Fill method is executed, the SelectCommand of the OdbcDataAdapter will execute the stored procedure and populate the DataSet, and display the results in the DataGrid. You then add the OdbcDataAdapter's Update method to the click action of the button that was added to the form earlier. Double-click the Button object to display the code for the button1_Click method and add the Update method to this subroutine as illustrated here:

```
Private Sub button1_Click(ByVal sender As System.Object, _
        ByVal e As System.EventArgs) Handles button1.Click
    Try
        OdbcDataAdapter1.Update(DsCustomer1, "Customers")
    Catch ex As Exception
        MsgBox(ex.Message)
    End Try
End Sub
```

The C# version of this code is as follows:

```csharp
private void button1_Click(object sender, System.EventArgs e)
{
    try
    {
        odbcDataAdapter1.Update(dsCustomer1,"Customers");
    }
    catch (Exception ex)
    {
        MessageBox.Show("Update OdbcDataAdapter error: :" +
            ex.ToString());
    }
}
```

Here, the button's click event calls the odbcDataAdapter's Update method, passing the DataSet and table name as arguments. The odbcDataAdapter's Update method will resolve the changed DataSet information to the database table. The Update method analyzes the rows in the DataTable and determines the action to take based on the DataRow's RowState property value. The actions that take place when the Update method is called are the stored procedures that were configured earlier and placed in the appropriate command property of the DataAdapter. When changes are made to the rows in the DataTable, the DataRow.RowState property reflects the changes that have been made. Table 28-1 lists the valid enumerations for the DataRow.RowState property.

Here, you run the application. The OdbcDataAdapter's Fill method will execute the stored procedure spCustSelectCommand from the DataAdapter's SelectCommand property. A DataSet will be created along with a DataTable named Customers, which

Enumeration	Description
Added	The row has been added to the DataRowCollection.
Deleted	The row was deleted.
Detached	The row has been created. The row has not been added to the DataRowCollection.
Modified	The row has been changed.
Unchanged	The row has not changed.

Table 28-1. *DataRow.RowState Enumeration*

will be filled with the data from the database and displayed in the DataGrid object. You then change, add, or delete records using the DataGrid, and your changes will reflect in the RowState property of the DataRows in the DataTable. Click the Button object on the form to call the Update method of the DataAdapter to analyze the RowState property value and execute the corresponding stored procedure contained in the DataAdapter's command property. Figure 28-5 shows the application with data in the DataGrid object. The first record's CompanyName field has been changed, so this row's RowState property in the DataTable shows a value of Modified. The button on the form is then clicked to call the odbcDataAdapter's Update method, which will call the stored procedure spCustUpdateCommand contained in the DataAdapter's UpdateCommand property, and the row will be updated in the database.

Using the OdbcDataAdapter Class

The visual OdbcDataAdapter component allows you to quickly configure a connection, and create a DataAdapter and DataSet object for retrieving and updating database information with minimal program code. But, of course, often you will want greater control over how the information in the database is updated. In the upcoming section, you will see how to resolve selected rows to the database using the DataRowView's DataViewRowState property in program code. When you sort or filter a view of a DataTable, you use a DataView. A DataRowView represents a view of a DataRow in much the same way. So, to select a subset of DataRows from a DataTable based on the RowState of the rows, you use the DataRowView's DataRowViewState property, as shown in the next section.

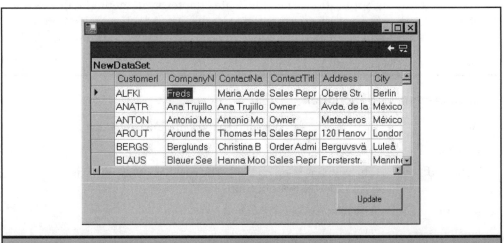

Figure 28-5. *Form for updating the database*

Updating the Database in an Ordered Manner

Sometimes the order in which changes are made through the DataSet and sent to the database is important. For example, if a key value for an existing row is changed, and then a new row is added with the original key value, you need to process the update to the changed row before you process the inserted row. This kind of ordered update may be needed when, for example, one of your customers' business situation changes. For example, you have a customer, Bart's Auto Parts, who sells new and used automobile parts. The key value for this customer is "BAP". Bart wants to scale down his business and move to a new location, so Wilbur purchases the automobile parts business from Bart. The key value of "BAP" now changes to "WAP"for Wilbur's Auto Parts. Bart moves to a new location and starts a business selling automobile accessory parts, so you add a new customer record with a key value of "BAP". In this case, the change to "WAP" needs to take place before the new "BAP" record may be added to the database. You use the Select method of the DataTable to return an array of DataRows that have a specific DataViewRowState, like ModifiedCurrent, that indicates the version of the DataRow. You then pass the DataRow array information to the Update method of the DataAdapter to process just the modified rows. This enables you to control the order in which rows are updated in the database. Table 28-2 lists the valid enumerations for the DataViewRowState.

Enumeration	Description
Added	Identifies a new row
CurrentRows	Identifies current rows, including unchanged, new, and modified rows
Deleted	Identifies deleted row
ModifiedCurrent	Identifies a current version of a row that has been modified from the original version
ModifiedOriginal	Identifies an original version of a row that has been modified and is available as ModifiedCurrent
None	None
OriginalRows	Identifies the original rows, including unchanged and deleted rows
Unchanged	Identifies a row that has not changed

Table 28-2.   *DataViewRowState Enumeration*

THE ADO.NET
DATASET OBJECT

Following is an example of ordered updates to the Suppliers table:

```
Private Sub DataSetOrdered(ByVal sServer As String, _
        ByVal sUser As String, ByVal sPassword As String, _
        ByVal sDB As String)
    Cursor.Current = Cursors.WaitCursor
    ' Create connection, command, and dataadapter
    Dim odbcCn = New OdbcConnection("DRIVER={SQL Server};SERVER=" _
        & sServer & ";UID=" & sUser & ";PWD=" & sPassword _
        & ";DATABASE=" & sDB)
    Dim cmdSelect = New OdbcCommand("SELECT * FROM Suppliers", _
        odbcCn)
    Dim odbcDA = New OdbcDataAdapter()
    odbcDA.SelectCommand = cmdSelect
    Dim ds = New DataSet()
    Try
        ' Populate the dataset
        odbcDA.Fill(ds, "Suppliers")
        Dim dtSuppliers As DataTable = ds.Tables("Suppliers")
        ' Here you make changes to the table ...
        ' Deletes.
        odbcDA.Update(dtSuppliers.Select(Nothing, Nothing, _
            DataViewRowState.Deleted))
        ' Updates.
        odbcDA.Update(dtSuppliers.Select(Nothing, Nothing, _
            DataViewRowState.ModifiedCurrent))
        ' Inserts.
        odbcDA.Update(dtSuppliers.Select(Nothing, Nothing, _
            DataViewRowState.Added))
    Catch e As Exception
        Cursor.Current = Cursors.Default
        MsgBox(e.Message)
    End Try
    Cursor.Current = Cursors.Default
End Sub
```

The C# version of this code is as follows:

```
private void DataSetOrdered(string sServer, string sUser,
        string sPassword, string sDB)
{
    Cursor.Current = Cursors.WaitCursor;
```

```
// Create connection, command, and dataadapter
OdbcConnection odbcCn = new OdbcConnection(
    "DRIVER={SQL Server};SERVER=" + sServer +";UID=" +
    sUser + ";PWD=" + sPassword + ";DATABASE=" + sDB);
OdbcCommand cmdSelect = new OdbcCommand(
    "SELECT * FROM Suppliers", odbcCn);
OdbcDataAdapter odbcDA = new OdbcDataAdapter();
odbcDA.SelectCommand = cmdSelect;
DataSet ds = new DataSet();
try
{
    // Populate the dataset
    odbcDA.Fill(ds, "Suppliers");
    DataTable dtSuppliers = ds.Tables["Suppliers"];
    // Here you make changes to the table ...
    // Deletes.
    odbcDA.Update(dtSuppliers.Select(null, null,
        DataViewRowState.Deleted));
    // Updates.
    odbcDA.Update(dtSuppliers.Select(null, null,
        DataViewRowState.ModifiedCurrent));
    // Inserts.
    odbcDA.Update(dtSuppliers.Select(null, null,
        DataViewRowState.Added));
}
catch (Exception ex)
{
    Cursor.Current = Cursors.Default;
    MessageBox.Show("DataSetOrdered error: :" + ex.ToString());
}
Cursor.Current = Cursors.Default;
}
```

As you can see at the top of the routine, the server name, database, user ID, and password are passed into the routine. These variables are then used in the connect statement of the OdbcConnection object. An OdbcCommand object is then created with a SELECT statement as its first argument and the connection object as its second argument. An OdbcDataAdapter object is then created, and its SelectCommand property is set to the previously created OdbcCommand object. Next, a DataSet is created, and then the DataAdapter's Fill method is called to fill the DataSet with information from the Suppliers table. The next statement shows a DataTable object being created. You then make changes to the rows in the DataTable. Because the code to make the change is essentially identical to the examples previously presented, the code for making changes to the DataTable is not shown here. The next statement shows the DataAdapter's Update method being called to process first only the deleted rows in the DataTable. Next, the Modified rows are processed with the DataAdapter's Update method. And, finally, any rows that were added to the DataTable are sent to the database with the DataAdapter's Update method.

Summary

In this chapter, you saw how to use existing stored procedures from your database and the visual OdbcDataAdapter object to update a data source. You also saw how to update the database from the DataSet by using the DataAdapter's Update method and DataRowViews to resolve changes to the database in a particular order. The next chapter will explore some aspects of updating the database, including updates to image fields, accepting and rejecting changes to the database, and error handling.

Chapter 29

Advanced
Database Updating

In the preceding four chapters, you saw how to update the changes made to the DataSet back to the data source using each of the DataAdapters provided by each of the .NET Framework Data Providers. You saw how to use the DataForm Wizard to quickly create data-bound Windows forms, and you explored manually binding your data to Windows Forms controls with the BindingContext and CurrencyManager objects. You used the CommandBuilder to automatically generate update commands, and you also created custom commands using parameters, SQL statements, and stored procedures.

Advanced Database Updating

This chapter covers some advanced issues you may need when updating your data source. First, you will see how to validate information in your DataSet using the Accept or Reject methods before the DataSet is sent to the database. Next, you will update your database with Binary Large Objects (BLOBs). BLOBs are usually graphical image or media files and are handled differently than most other data types. Then you will see how to work with auto-increment fields. You will see how these fields may be retrieved using an output parameter in a stored procedure or by using the RowUpdated event of the DataAdapter. Last, you will see how to handle merging the contents of a DataSet, DataTable, or DataRow into an existing DataSet.

Accepting or Rejecting Changes

The DataRows in DataTables are managed by the row's state and version. The RowState property of the DataRow contains the status of the row, such as whether the row has been added or modified. The row version maintains the value of the data stored in the row as it is being manipulated. For example, when you change a column in a DataRow, the row's RowState will be *Modified* and two row versions will then exist: one with a version of Current, which contains the row's current values, including the recent change, and one with a version of *Original*, which contains the row's original values before the change to the column. Table 29-1 lists the valid enumerations for the DataRow.RowState property.

Table 29-2 lists the valid enumerations for the DataRowVersion property value.

In many situations, you will want to check the information in the DataSet for data errors before sending the information back to the data source. To do this, you validate the row values in your program code, and, if no error exists, you can use the AcceptChanges method of the DataRow, DataTable, or DataSet to overwrite the row values in the Original row version with the values of the Current row version. Rows with a row state of Deleted are removed and the remaining rows are given a row state of Unchanged. This sets into the DataSet the changes that have been made since the DataSet was first filled from the data source.

Enumeration	Description
Added	The row has been added to the DataRowCollection.
Deleted	The row was deleted.
Detached	The row has been created. The row has not been added to the DataRowCollection.
Modified	The row has been changed.
Unchanged	The row has not changed.

Table 29-1.   *DataRow.RowState Enumeration Options*

Likewise, the RejectChanges method rolls back any changes that have been made to the DataSet since it was filled from the data source. The rows with a row state of Added are removed, the remaining rows are given a state of Unchanged, and the Original row version values overwrite the Current version values. Accepting or rejecting changes clears out the RowError information and sets the HasErrors property of the DataSet

Enumeration	Description
Current	The current values for the row. This row version does not exist for rows with a state of Deleted.
Default	Indicates the default version for a row. If row state is Added, Modified, or Unchanged, the default version is Current. If row state is Deleted, the default version is Original. If row state is Detached, the default version is Proposed.
Original	The original values for the row. This row version does not exist for rows with a state of Added.
Proposed	The proposed values for a row. This row version exists when an edit operation is being performed on a row or when the row has not yet been added to the DataRowCollection.

Table 29-2.   *DataRowVersion Enumeration Options*

THE ADO.NET
DATASET OBJECT

to False. The following example illustrates how to reject certain errors found in the
Orders table of the Northwind database:

```
Private Sub DataSetAcceptReject(ByVal sServer As String, _
    ByVal sDB As String)
    Cursor.Current = Cursors.WaitCursor
    Dim sqlCn As SqlConnection = New SqlConnection("SERVER=" & _
        sServer & ";INTEGRATED SECURITY=True;DATABASE=" & sDB)
    Dim sqlDA As SqlDataAdapter = New SqlDataAdapter( _
        "SELECT * FROM Orders", sqlCn)
    Dim ds = New DataSet()
    Try
        sqlDA.Fill(ds, "Orders")
        Dim dtOrders As DataTable = ds.Tables("Orders")
        ' The Orders table is update by users here. . . .
        If dtOrders.HasErrors Then
            Dim drError As DataRow
            For Each drError In dtOrders.GetErrors()
                If drError.RowError = "Freight cannot equal 0." Then
                    drError("Freight") = 10.0
                    drError.RowError = ""
                Else
                    drError.RejectChanges()
                End If
            Next
        dtOrders.AcceptChanges()
        End If
    Catch e As Exception
        Cursor.Current = Cursors.Default
        MsgBox(e.Message)
    End Try
    Cursor.Current = Cursors.Default
End Sub
```

The C# version of this code is as follows:

```
private void DataSetAcceptReject(string sServer, string sDB)
{
    Cursor.Current = Cursors.WaitCursor;
    SqlConnection sqlCn = new SqlConnection("SERVER=" + sServer +
        ";INTEGRATED SECURITY=True;DATABASE=" + sDB);
    SqlDataAdapter sqlDA = new SqlDataAdapter(
        "SELECT * FROM Orders", sqlCn);
    DataSet ds = new DataSet();
    try
```

```
    {
        sqlDA.Fill(ds, "Orders");
        DataTable dtOrders = ds.Tables["Orders"];
        // The Orders table is updated by users here. . . .
        if (dtOrders.HasErrors)
        {
            foreach (DataRow drError in dtOrders.GetErrors())
            {
                if (drError.RowError == "Freight cannot equal 0.")
                {
                    drError["Freight"] = 10.00;
                    drError.RowError = "";
                }
                else
                    drError.RejectChanges();
            }
        }
        dtOrders.AcceptChanges();
    }
    catch (Exception ex)
    {
        Cursor.Current = Cursors.Default;
        MessageBox.Show("DataSetAcceptReject error: :" +
            ex.ToString());
    }
    Cursor.Current = Cursors.Default;
}
```

The server and database names are passed into the top of the routine, and the SqlConnection object, SqlDataAdapter, and DataSet are created. Then the DataSet is filled in the Try-Catch loop using the DataAdapter's Fill method. The DataTable object, dtOrders, is then created, and an If statement is used to check for errors in the DataTable. Errors in the rows of a DataTable can occur for many reasons as users change the data. Or you may simply want to disallow certain values for some of the columns in your DataTable. If an error is encountered in the DataTable, the DataTable's GetErrors method is used to retrieve into a DataRow the row that contains the error. For illustration purposes in this example, a rule was established that the Freight column cannot have a value of 0 and code was added for this rule elsewhere in the project. A foreach loop is used here to iterate through each of the rows that contain errors. Inside the foreach loop, you can see that an error of "Freight cannot equal 0." is trapped and corrected, but all other errors that are encountered are rejected. The DataTable's AcceptChanges method is then called to accept the changes that were made to the DataSet.

Working with Binary Objects

The preceding example also shows the technique for inserting BLOBs (Binary Large Objects) into a database table. BLOBs are typically graphical images such as product and employee photos contained in .BMP, .JPG or .TIF files. They can also be small sound bytes such as .WAV files or MP3s. You can find more information about exporting BLOB types in the section "Retrieving BLOB Data Using the SqlDataReader" in Chapter 12. This subroutine imports a JPG file into the Picture column of the Categories table in the Northwind database; therefore you need to import the .NET System.IO Namespace into your application to enable access to the file system. To import the System.IO Namespace, you need to add the following code to your project.

```
Imports System.IO
```

For a C# project, you need to add an import directive for the System.IO Namespace as follows:

```
using System.IO;
```

Once you've imported the System.IO Namespace, your application will be able to read binary files. The DataSetInsertSql subroutine shown here illustrates how you can import binary objects into a SQL Server database using the ADO.NET DataSet.object:

```
Private Sub DataSetInsertSql(ByVal sServer As String, _
    ByVal sDB As String)
    Cursor.Current = Cursors.WaitCursor
    Dim sqlCn As SqlConnection = New SqlConnection("SERVER=" & _
        sServer & ";INTEGRATED SECURITY=True;DATABASE=" & sDB)
    Dim sqlDA As SqlDataAdapter = New SqlDataAdapter( _
        "SELECT * FROM Categories", sqlCn)
    Dim ds = New DataSet()
    Dim sqlCB = New SqlCommandBuilder(sqlDA)
    Dim fs = New FileStream("C:\pasta.jpg", _
        FileMode.OpenOrCreate, FileAccess.Read)
    Try
        sqlDA.Fill(ds, "Categories")
        Dim bBLOB(fs.Length) As Byte
        fs.Read(bBLOB, 0, fs.Length)
        fs.Close()
        Dim sqlDR = ds.Tables("Categories").NewRow()
        sqlDR("CategoryName") = "Pasta"
        sqlDR("Description") = "Dried or fresh noodles"
```

```
        sqlDR("Picture") = bBLOB
        ds.Tables("Categories").Rows.Add(sqlDR)
        sqlDA.Update(ds, "Categories")
        Cursor.Current = Cursors.Default
    Catch e As Exception
        Cursor.Current = Cursors.Default
        MsgBox(e.Message)
    End Try
End Sub
```

The C# version of this code is as follows:

```
private void DataSetInsertSql(string sServer, string sDB)
{
    Cursor.Current = Cursors.WaitCursor;
    SqlConnection sqlCn = new SqlConnection("SERVER=" + sServer +
        ";INTEGRATED SECURITY=True;DATABASE=" + sDB);
    SqlDataAdapter sqlDA = new SqlDataAdapter(
        "SELECT * FROM Categories", sqlCn);
    DataSet ds = new DataSet();
    SqlCommandBuilder sqlCB = new SqlCommandBuilder(sqlDA);
    FileStream fs = new FileStream("C:\\pasta.jpg",
        FileMode.OpenOrCreate, FileAccess.Read);
    try
    {
        sqlDA.Fill(ds, "Categories");
        Byte[] bBLOB = new Byte[fs.Length];
        fs.Read(bBLOB, 0, (int)fs.Length);
        fs.Close();
        DataRow sqlDR = ds.Tables["Categories"].NewRow();
        //"CategoryID" is an auto increment field
        sqlDR["CategoryName"] = "Pasta";
        sqlDR["Description"] = "Dried or fresh noodles";
        sqlDR["Picture"] = bBLOB;
        ds.Tables["Categories"].Rows.Add(sqlDR);
        sqlDA.Update(ds, "Categories");
        Cursor.Current = Cursors.Default;
    }
    catch (Exception ex)
    {
        Cursor.Current = Cursors.Default;
        MessageBox.Show("DataSetInsertSql error: " + ex.ToString());
    }
}
```

String variables containing the name of a SQL Server system and database are passed into the top of the routine. Next, an instance of a SqlConnection object is created and its ConnectionString property is set as the argument of the constructor. The next statement creates a SqlDataAdapter passing to the constructor a SQL SELECT statement and the sqlCn SqlConnection object. This automatically sets the SqlDataAdapter's selectCommand property to the SQL SELECT statement. An empty DataSet is then created, which will be populated with the results of the SELECT query command. The next statement creates a SqlCommandBuilder object and takes as an argument the SqlDataAdapter object. The SqlCommandBuilder object is used here to automatically create the appropriate Insert, Update, and Delete commands for the specified SELECT command. Use of the SqlCommandBuilder is described in more detail in Chapter 25, "Updating the Database Using the SqlDataAdapter." At this point, the SqlCommandBuilder executes the SELECT SQL statement contained in the selectCommand property of the SqlDataAdapter and automatically creates the InsertCommand, UpdateCommand, and DeleteCommand based on the contents of the SQL SELECT statement. The automatically created commands are assigned to the SqlDataAdapter's insertCommand, updateCommand, and deleteCommand properties, respectively. Next, a FileStream object is created and set with the filename, open method, and access method for opening and working with the pasta.jpg file located on the local hard drive. The FileMode.OpenOrCreate indicates that if the file exists it will be opened. Otherwise, it will be created. The FileAccess.Read flag indicates that the file will be opened for reading. The DataSet is then filled using the SqlDataAdapter's Fill method, which is executed inside a Try-Catch block. The next statement creates a byte array that is set to the length of the FileStream object. The FileStream is then read, the data is placed into the byte array starting at the beginning of the data, and then the FileStream is closed.

> **Note**   *This example illustrates reading the entire BLOB object in a single operation. This is a good technique when you know that the BLOB objects are only a few megabytes or less, but it would not be the best technique for very large BLOB objects.*

Next, the table's NewRow method is called to create an empty record in the Categories table and a DataRow object is returned. The CategoryName and Description fields are set with text, and the Picture field is set with the byte array that contains the JPG information that was read in from the pasta.jpg file. Now that the DataRow object contains the data that you want to insert, you need to add the DataRow to the table's Rows collection, as shown in the next statement. Finally, the SqlDataAdapter's Update method is called. The Update method will evaluate the changes that have been made to the DataTable in the DataSet and determine which of the commands to execute. In this case, the Table.Rows.RowState property shows Added for the new row, so the InsertCommand is executed and the new record is added to the Categories table in the database.

Working with AutoIncrement Fields

You will notice in the previous example that the first field in the row, CategoryID, is an auto-increment field, so its value is not set here. A column in a DataTable may be set as an auto-incrementing key in order to ensure unique values for each row. However, if several users are each working with a separate instance of the DataTable, duplicate values may be sent to the database when an Update is called. To avoid this conflict, you may let the data source set the value of the auto-increment field by defining the field as an Identity field in SQL Server or an Autonumber field in Access. In this situation, the field is incremented when the record is added to the database and not when the row is added to the DataTable. However, in some cases, the application or the user needs to know the assigned auto-increment number as soon as it is added to the database. For example, say you work in a sales office and take orders over the telephone along with several other people. You may want to input your order, and then update the database and give the confirming order number to the client immediately. To do this, you would need to have the order number incremented at the data source and returned to you to give to your client. This can be accomplished in a couple of ways. You may use an output parameter in a stored procedure, or you may use the RowUpdated method of the DataAdapter. An example of each of these techniques is illustrated next.

Returning Auto-Increment Values Using a Stored Procedure

When you are using a data source that can create stored procedures with output parameters (such as SQL Server) you can specify the automatically generated values as an output parameter and use the SqlDataAdapter to map that value back to the column in the DataSet. Following is a stored procedure that inserts an employee record into the Employees table of the Northwind database and returns the auto-increment field of EmployeeID as an output parameter.

```
CREATE PROCEDURE spEmployeesInsertCmd
(
    @LastName nvarchar(20),
    @FirstName nvarchar(10),
    @Title nvarchar(30),
    @Address nvarchar(60),
    @City nvarchar(15),
    @Region nvarchar(15),
    @PostalCode nvarchar(10),
    @Identity int OUT
)
AS
INSERT INTO Employees(LastName, FirstName,
Title, Address, City, Region, PostalCode) VALUES (@LastName,
@FirstName, @Title, @Address, @City, @Region, @PostalCode)
SET @Identity = SCOPE_IDENTITY()
```

This stored procedure can be used in the InsertCommand property of a SqlDataAdapter to return the auto-incremented EmployeeID field to the current row in the DataTable, as illustrated in the following code.

```
Private Sub AutoIncrInsertSql(ByVal sServer As String, _
    ByVal sDB As String)
    Cursor.Current = Cursors.WaitCursor
    Dim sqlCn As SqlConnection = New SqlConnection("SERVER=" & _
        sServer & ";INTEGRATED SECURITY=True;DATABASE=" & sDB)
    Dim sqlDA As SqlDataAdapter = New SqlDataAdapter( _
        "SELECT * FROM Employees", sqlCn)
    sqlDA.InsertCommand = New SqlCommand("spEmployeesInsertCmd", _
        sqlCn)
    sqlDA.InsertCommand.CommandType = CommandType.StoredProcedure
    Dim ds = New DataSet()
    Try
        sqlDA.Fill(ds, "Employess")
        Dim sqlParm = New SqlParameter()
        sqlParm = sqlDA.InsertCommand.Parameters.Add( _
            New SqlParameter("@LastName", SqlDbType.NChar, 20, _
            "LastName"))
        sqlParm = sqlDA.InsertCommand.Parameters.Add( _
            New SqlParameter("@FirstName", SqlDbType.NChar, 10, _
            "FirstName"))
        sqlParm = sqlDA.InsertCommand.Parameters.Add( _
            New SqlParameter("@Title", SqlDbType.NChar, 30, _
            "Title"))
        sqlParm = sqlDA.InsertCommand.Parameters.Add( _
            New SqlParameter("@Address", SqlDbType.NChar, 60, _
            "Address"))
        sqlParm = sqlDA.InsertCommand.Parameters.Add( _
            New SqlParameter("@City", SqlDbType.NChar, 15, _
            "City"))
        sqlParm = sqlDA.InsertCommand.Parameters.Add( _
            New SqlParameter("@Region", SqlDbType.NChar, 15, _
            "Region"))
        sqlParm = sqlDA.InsertCommand.Parameters.Add( _
            New SqlParameter("@PostalCode", SqlDbType.NChar, 10, _
            "PostalCode"))
        sqlParm = sqlDA.InsertCommand.Parameters.Add( _
            New SqlParameter("@Identity", SqlDbType.Int, 0, _
            "EmployeeID"))
        sqlParm.Direction = ParameterDirection.Output
        Dim sqlDR = ds.Tables("Employees").NewRow()
```

```
        sqlDR("LastName") = "Smith"
        sqlDR("FirstName") = "James"
        sqlDR("Title") = "Sales Temp"
        sqlDR("Address") = "1222 First St"
        sqlDR("City") = "Portland"
        sqlDR("Region") = "OR"
        sqlDR("PostalCode") = "97345"
        ds.Tables("Employees").Rows.Add(sqlDR)
        sqlDA.Update(ds, "Employees")
        Cursor.Current = Cursors.Default
    Catch e As Exception
        Cursor.Current = Cursors.Default
        MsgBox(e.Message)
    End Try
End Sub
```

The C# version of this code is as follows:

```
private void AutoIncrInsertSql(string sServer, string sDB)
{
    Cursor.Current = Cursors.WaitCursor;
    SqlConnection sqlCn = new SqlConnection("SERVER=" + sServer +
        ";INTEGRATED SECURITY=True;DATABASE=" + sDB);
    SqlDataAdapter sqlDA = new SqlDataAdapter(
        "SELECT * FROM Employees", sqlCn);
    sqlDA.InsertCommand= new SqlCommand("spEmployeesInsertCmd",
        sqlCn);
    sqlDA.InsertCommand.CommandType = CommandType.StoredProcedure;
    DataSet ds = new DataSet();
    try
    {
        sqlDA.Fill(ds, "Employees");
        SqlParameter sqlParm = new SqlParameter();
        sqlParm = sqlDA.InsertCommand.Parameters.Add(
            new SqlParameter("@LastName", SqlDbType.NChar, 20,
            "LastName"));
        sqlParm = sqlDA.InsertCommand.Parameters.Add(
            new SqlParameter("@FirstName", SqlDbType.NChar, 10,
            "FirstName"));
        sqlParm = sqlDA.InsertCommand.Parameters.Add(
            new SqlParameter("@Title", SqlDbType.NChar, 30,
            "Title"));
        sqlParm = sqlDA.InsertCommand.Parameters.Add(
```

```
            new SqlParameter("@Address", SqlDbType.NChar, 60,
                "Address"));
        sqlParm = sqlDA.InsertCommand.Parameters.Add(
            new SqlParameter("@City", SqlDbType.NChar, 15,
                "City"));
        sqlParm = sqlDA.InsertCommand.Parameters.Add(
            new SqlParameter("@Region", SqlDbType.NChar, 15,
                "Region"));
        sqlParm = sqlDA.InsertCommand.Parameters.Add(
            new SqlParameter("@PostalCode", SqlDbType.NChar, 10,
                "PostalCode"));
        sqlParm = sqlDA.InsertCommand.Parameters.Add(
            new SqlParameter("@Identity", SqlDbType.Int, 0,
                "EmployeeID"));
        sqlParm.Direction = ParameterDirection.Output;
        DataRow sqlDR = ds.Tables["Employees"].NewRow();
        sqlDR["LastName"] = "Smith";
        sqlDR["FirstName"] = "James";
        sqlDR["Title"] = "Sales Temp";
        sqlDR["Address"] = "1222 First St";
        sqlDR["City"] = "Portland";
        sqlDR["Region"] = "OR";
        sqlDR["PostalCode"] = "97345";
        ds.Tables["Employees"].Rows.Add(sqlDR);
        sqlDA.Update(ds, "Employees");
        Cursor.Current = Cursors.Default;
    }
    catch (Exception ex)
    {
        Cursor.Current = Cursors.Default;
        MessageBox.Show("AutoIncrInsertSql error: " +
            ex.ToString());
    }
}
```

The server and database name are passed into the top of the routine, and the SqlConnection object is created. Next, a SqlDataAdapter object is created using a SELECT SQL statement as the first argument in the constructor and the Connection object as the second argument. A SqlCommand object is then created and set to the InsertCommand property of the DataAdapter. Notice here that the SqlCommand object is created with the first argument as the stored procedure, spEmployeesInsertCmd, and the CommandType property of the Command object is set to CommandType.StoredProcedure. Next, a DataSet is created and populated using the SqlDataAdapter's Fill method inside the

Try-Catch loop. The next statements show how to create SqlParameter objects for each of the fields that will be used, and how to add each SqlParameter object to the parameters collection of the SqlDataAdapter's InsertCommand. Each parameter is defined with a parameter marker, data type, length, and source column that corresponds to the database column this field is associated with. The last parameter added to the parameters collection is an output parameter that contains the auto-increment field that is to be retrieved from the data source. You can see that the parameter object's Direction property is set to ParameterDirection.Output. Next, a new row is initialized in the Employees DataTable and a DataRow object is returned. Data is then entered into each of the input columns of the new DataRow and the new row is added to the Rows collection of the Employees DataTable. Finally, the SqlDataAdapter's Update method is called. The Update method will analyze the DataSet and see that a new row has been added to the Employees DataTable. The DataAdapter's InsertCommand will then execute the stored procedure and insert the new row into the database table. The auto-increment field will be advanced and the stored procedure will return the new number to the current row in the Employees DataTable.

Returning Auto-Increment Values Using the OnRowUpdated Event

In some situations, you may not want to use a stored procedure or the database may not support a stored procedure for returning the identity value using output parameters. In such cases, you can use the RowUpdated event of the DataAdapter to retrieve the newly generated auto-increment number to the DataSet row. Following is an example of how to use the RowUpdated event to return the auto-increment field of EmployeeID after an insert into the Employees table of the Northwind database.

```
Dim sqlConnect As SqlConnection = New SqlConnection
Private Sub AutoIncrInsertEventSql(ByVal sServer As String, _
    ByVal sDB As String)
    Cursor.Current = Cursors.WaitCursor
    sqlConnect.ConnectionString = "SERVER=" & _
        sServer & ";INTEGRATED SECURITY=True;DATABASE=" & sDB
    Dim sqlDA As SqlDataAdapter = New SqlDataAdapter( _
        "SELECT * FROM Employees ORDER BY EmployeeID", sqlConnect)
    sqlDA.InsertCommand = New SqlCommand("INSERT INTO Employees" & _
        "(LastName, FirstName, Title, Address, City, Region, " & _
        "PostalCode) VALUES (@LastName, @FirstName, @Title, " & _
        "@Address, @City, @Region, @PostalCode)", sqlConnect)
    sqlDA.InsertCommand.CommandType = CommandType.Text
    Dim ds = New DataSet
    Try
        sqlConnect.Open()
        sqlDA.Fill(ds, "Employees")
        Dim sqlParm = New SqlParameter
        sqlParm = sqlDA.InsertCommand.Parameters.Add( _
            New SqlParameter("@LastName", SqlDbType.NChar, 20, _
```

```
                    "LastName"))
         sqlParm = sqlDA.InsertCommand.Parameters.Add( _
             New SqlParameter("@FirstName", SqlDbType.NChar, 10, _
             "FirstName"))
         sqlParm = sqlDA.InsertCommand.Parameters.Add( _
             New SqlParameter("@Title", SqlDbType.NChar, 30, _
             "Title"))
         sqlParm = sqlDA.InsertCommand.Parameters.Add( _
             New SqlParameter("@Address", SqlDbType.NChar, 60, _
             "Address"))
         sqlParm = sqlDA.InsertCommand.Parameters.Add( _
             New SqlParameter("@City", SqlDbType.NChar, 15, _
             "City"))
         sqlParm = sqlDA.InsertCommand.Parameters.Add( _
             New SqlParameter("@Region", SqlDbType.NChar, 15, _
             "Region"))
         sqlParm = sqlDA.InsertCommand.Parameters.Add( _
             New SqlParameter("@PostalCode", SqlDbType.NChar, 10, _
             "PostalCode"))
         Dim sqlDR = ds.Tables("Employees").NewRow()
         sqlDR("LastName") = "Jones"
         sqlDR("FirstName") = "James"
         sqlDR("Title") = "Sales Temp"
         sqlDR("Address") = "2111 First St"
         sqlDR("City") = "Portland"
         sqlDR("Region") = "OR"
         sqlDR("PostalCode") = "97234"
         ds.Tables("Employees").Rows.Add(sqlDR)
         AddHandler sqlDA.RowUpdated, New _
             SqlRowUpdatedEventHandler(AddressOf OnRowUpdated)
         sqlDA.Update(ds, "Employees")
         sqlConnect.Close()
         Cursor.Current = Cursors.Default
     Catch e As Exception
         Cursor.Current = Cursors.Default
         MsgBox(e.Message)
     End Try
 End Sub
 Private Sub OnRowUpdated(ByVal sender As Object, _
           ByVal args As SqlRowUpdatedEventArgs)
     Dim iEmpId As Integer = 0
     Dim sqlCmd As SqlCommand = New SqlCommand( _
         "SELECT @@IDENTITY", sqlConnect)
     If args.StatementType = StatementType.Insert Then
         iEmpId = CInt(sqlCmd.ExecuteScalar())
         args.Row("EmployeeID") = iEmpId
     End If
 End Sub
```

The C# version of this code is as follows:

```
SqlConnection sqlConnect = new SqlConnection();
private void AutoIncrInsertEventSql(string sServer, string sDB)
{
    Cursor.Current = Cursors.WaitCursor;
    sqlConnect.ConnectionString = "SERVER=" + sServer +
        ";INTEGRATED SECURITY=True;DATABASE=" + sDB;
    SqlDataAdapter sqlDA = new SqlDataAdapter(
        "SELECT * FROM Employees ORDER BY EmployeeID", sqlConnect);
    sqlDA.InsertCommand= new SqlCommand("INSERT INTO Employees" +
        "(LastName, FirstName, Title, Address, City, Region, " +
        "PostalCode) VALUES (@LastName, @FirstName, @Title, " +
        "@Address, @City, @Region, @PostalCode)", sqlConnect);
    sqlDA.InsertCommand.CommandType = CommandType.Text;
    DataSet ds = new DataSet();
    try
    {
        sqlConnect.Open();
        sqlDA.Fill(ds, "Employees");
        SqlParameter sqlParm = new SqlParameter();
        sqlParm = sqlDA.InsertCommand.Parameters.Add(
            new SqlParameter("@LastName", SqlDbType.NChar, 20,
            "LastName"));
        sqlParm = sqlDA.InsertCommand.Parameters.Add(
            new SqlParameter("@FirstName", SqlDbType.NChar, 10,
            "FirstName"));
        sqlParm = sqlDA.InsertCommand.Parameters.Add(
            new SqlParameter("@Title", SqlDbType.NChar, 30,
            "Title"));
        sqlParm = sqlDA.InsertCommand.Parameters.Add(
            new SqlParameter("@Address", SqlDbType.NChar, 60,
            "Address"));
        sqlParm = sqlDA.InsertCommand.Parameters.Add(
            new SqlParameter("@City", SqlDbType.NChar, 15,
            "City"));
        sqlParm = sqlDA.InsertCommand.Parameters.Add(
            new SqlParameter("@Region", SqlDbType.NChar, 15,
            "Region"));
        sqlParm = sqlDA.InsertCommand.Parameters.Add(
            new SqlParameter("@PostalCode", SqlDbType.NChar, 10,
            "PostalCode"));
        DataRow sqlDR = ds.Tables["Employees"].NewRow();
        sqlDR["LastName"] = "Jones";
```

```
            sqlDR["FirstName"] = "James";
            sqlDR["Title"] = "Sales Temp";
            sqlDR["Address"] = "2111 First St";
            sqlDR["City"] = "Portland";
            sqlDR["Region"] = "OR";
            sqlDR["PostalCode"] = "97234";
            ds.Tables["Employees"].Rows.Add(sqlDR);
            sqlDA.RowUpdated += new SqlRowUpdatedEventHandler(
                OnRowUpdated);
            sqlDA.Update(ds, "Employees");
            sqlConnect.Close();
            Cursor.Current = Cursors.Default;
        }
        catch (Exception ex)
        {
            Cursor.Current = Cursors.Default;
            MessageBox.Show("AutoIncrInsertEventSql error: " +
                ex.ToString());
        }
    }
    protected void OnRowUpdated(object sender,
        SqlRowUpdatedEventArgs args)
    {
        System.Decimal iEmpId = 0;
        SqlCommand sqlCmd = new SqlCommand("SELECT @@IDENTITY",
            sqlConnect);
        if (args.StatementType == StatementType.Insert)
        {
            iEmpId = (System.Decimal)sqlCmd.ExecuteScalar();
            args.Row["EmployeeID"] = iEmpId;
        }
    }
```

This example starts with a SqlConnection object created outside the scope of the subroutine. This will allow the same Connection object to be used in both of the subroutines in this example. The server and database names are passed into the top of the routine and the SqlConnection object's ConnectionString property is set. A SqlDataAdapter object is created using a SELECT SQL statement as the first argument in the constructor and the Connection object as the second argument. A SqlCommand object is then created and set to the InsertCommand property of the SqlDataAdapter. Here, the SqlCommand object is created with the first argument as an INSERT SQL statement and the CommandType property of the Command object is set to CommandType.Text.

Next, a DataSet is created and populated using the SqlDataAdapter's Fill method inside the Try-Catch loop. In this case, instead of letting the Fill method open and close the connection to the database, the SqlConnection Open method is called to open the connection. This allows the RowUpdated event handler that will be used later in the subroutine to use the open connection. The next statements show the creation of the SqlParameter objects and how to add them to the parameters collection of the DataAdapter's InsertCommand. Each parameter is defined with a parameter marker, data type, length, and source column that corresponds to the database column this field is associated with. A new row is then initialized in the Employees DataTable and a DataRow object is returned. Data is then entered into each of the input columns of the new DataRow and the new row is added to the Rows collection of the Employees DataTable. The next statement adds an event handler for the RowUpdated event of the DataAdapter.

The OnRowUpdated will fire after a row in the database has been changed. Next, the SqlDataAdapter's Update method is called. The Update method will analyze the DataSet and see that a new row has been added to the Employees DataTable. The DataAdapter's InsertCommand will then execute the SQL statement and insert the new row into the database table. The auto-increment field will be advanced and the OnRowUpdated event handler will execute the code inside its subroutine. Inside the OnRowUpdate subroutine, you can see that an iEmpId variable is initialized to 0. Next, a SqlCommand object is created that uses a SELECT statement to return an identity column as the first argument and the open connection in the second argument. The StatementType is then checked. If the statement that fired the event is an Insert statement, the SqlCommand will execute the ExecuteScalar method. The ExecuteScalar method returns just the first column of the first row in the result of the query. The result of the SqlCommand query will return the new auto-increment number, which is placed into the EmployeeID column of the current row in the Employees DataTable. Finally, the open connection to the data source is closed.

Merging DataSets

In some situations, you will want to merge the contents of a DataSet, DataTable, or DataRow array into an existing DataSet. To do this, you use the Merge method of the DataSet. There are some important factors to consider when merging information into an existing DataSet, such as adding primary keys, preserving changes that have been made to the DataSet, dealing with incoming data that is not already part of the DataSet schema, and handling data constraints.

Merging Primary Keys

If a DataTable has a primary key, the incoming merge data is matched to existing rows using the original primary key column, and the existing rows are modified. New rows that are being merged that do not have a matching existing row are appended to the DataTable. If a merging table and a DataTable contain a column with the same name but the data types are different, or if they have primary keys that are defined on different columns, then an exception error will be thrown. If a DataTable does not have a primary key, then incoming data cannot be matched to existing rows, so the data is appended to the DataTable.

Using the preserveChanges Flag

The preserveChanges flag is an optional parameter that you may specify when calling the Merge method. The preserveChanges flag is a Boolean True or False flag. When preserveChanges is set to true, the data in the DataRow's Current row version remains the same and the data in the DataRow's Original row version is overwritten with the incoming data's Original row version. When the preserveChanges flag is set to False, both the Current and Original row versions of the DataRow are overwritten with the incoming data's Current and Original row versions. The default setting for preserveChanges is False.

Using the MissingSchemaAction Flag

Another optional parameter that you may specify when calling the Merge method is the MissingSchemaAction. The MissingSchemaAction specifies how the Merge method will handle incoming schema information that is not part of the existing DataSet. Table 29-3 shows the MissingSchemaAction enumeration options.

Using Constraints

When you use the Merge method, constraints are not checked until all the incoming data has been added to the existing DataSet. You need to make sure you have proper error handling routines in place to handle any constraint violations that may occur once the incoming data has been added to the DataSet and the constraints are enforced.

Enumeration	Description
Add	Default setting. The incoming schema is added to the DataSet, and the new columns are populated with the incoming data.
AddWithKey	The incoming schema and primary key data are added to the DataSet, and the new columns are populated with the incoming data.
Error	Throws an exception error if incoming schema does not match existing DataSet schema.
Ignore	The incoming schema is ignored.

Table 29-3. *MissingSchemaAction Enumeration Options*

Updating Only Changed Rows to the Database

The following is an example of updating the database only with rows that have been modified. A new DataSet is created that contains only modified rows. The newly created DataSet is updated to the data source, and then merged back into the original DataSet. This enables you to have greater control over which rows are sent to the database and more easily catch any errors that may occur during the update action. You will notice several error trapping points including the use of the OnRowUpdated event, which checks for errors in each DataRow, and the useful Try-Catch loop.

```vb
Private Sub MergeDataSet(ByVal sServer As String, _
        ByVal sDB As String)
    Cursor.Current = Cursors.WaitCursor
    Dim sqlCn As SqlConnection = New SqlConnection("SERVER=" & _
        sServer & ";INTEGRATED SECURITY=True;DATABASE=" & sDB)
    Dim sqlDA As SqlDataAdapter = New SqlDataAdapter( _
        "SELECT * FROM Categories", sqlCn)
    Dim sqlCmdB As SqlCommandBuilder = New SqlCommandBuilder(sqlDA)
    Dim ds = New DataSet
    Try
        sqlDA.Fill(ds, "Categories")
        ds.Tables("Categories").Rows(0)("CategoryName") = "Pizza"
        Dim dsUpd As DataSet = ds.GetChanges()
        AddHandler sqlDA.RowUpdated, New _
            SqlRowUpdatedEventHandler(AddressOf OnRowUpdated)
        sqlDA.Update(dsUpd, "Categories")
        ds.Merge(dsUpd, True, MissingSchemaAction.Add)
        Dim drErr As DataRow
        Dim drErrs() As DataRow = _
            ds.Tables("Categories").GetErrors()
        For Each drErr In drErrs
            drErr.RejectChanges()
            drErr.RowError = Nothing
        Next
        ds.AcceptChanges()
        Cursor.Current = Cursors.Default
    Catch e As Exception
        Cursor.Current = Cursors.Default
        MsgBox(e.Message)
    End Try
End Sub
Private Sub OnRowUpdated(ByVal sender As Object, _
        ByVal args As SqlRowUpdatedEventArgs)
```

```
      If args.Status = UpdateStatus.ErrorsOccurred Then
          args.Row.RowError = args.Errors.Message
          args.Status = UpdateStatus.SkipCurrentRow
      End If
End Sub
```

The C# version of this code is as follows:

```csharp
private void MergeDataSet(string sServer, string sDB)
{
    Cursor.Current = Cursors.WaitCursor;
    SqlConnection sqlCn = new SqlConnection("SERVER=" + sServer +
        ";INTEGRATED SECURITY=True;DATABASE=" + sDB);
    SqlDataAdapter sqlDA = new SqlDataAdapter(
        "SELECT * FROM Categories", sqlCn);
    SqlCommandBuilder sqlCmdB = new SqlCommandBuilder(sqlDA);
    DataSet ds = new DataSet();
    try
    {
        sqlDA.Fill(ds, "Categories");
        ds.Tables["Categories"].Rows[0]["CategoryName"] = "Pizza";
        DataSet dsUpd = ds.GetChanges();
        sqlDA.RowUpdated += new SqlRowUpdatedEventHandler(
            OnRowUpdated);
        sqlDA.Update(dsUpd, "Categories");
        ds.Merge(dsUpd, true, MissingSchemaAction.Add);
        DataRow[] drErrs = ds.Tables["Categories"].GetErrors();
        foreach (DataRow drErr in drErrs)
        {
            drErr.RejectChanges();
            drErr.RowError = null;
        }
        ds.AcceptChanges();
        Cursor.Current = Cursors.Default;
    }
    catch (Exception ex)
    {
        Cursor.Current = Cursors.Default;
        MessageBox.Show("MergeDataSet error: " + ex.ToString());
    }
}
```

```
protected void OnRowUpdated(object sender,
    SqlRowUpdatedEventArgs args)
{
    if (args.Status == UpdateStatus.ErrorsOccurred)
    {
        args.Row.RowError = args.Errors.Message;
        args.Status = UpdateStatus.SkipCurrentRow;
    }
}
```

The server and database names are passed into the top of the routine, and the Connection object is created. A SqlDataAdapter object is created using a SELECT SQL statement as the first argument in the constructor and the Connection object as the second argument. Next, a CommandBuilder object is created suing the DataAdapter as an argument in the constructor. This is a handy object in that the Update, Insert, and Delete commands will automatically be generated from the SqlDataAdapter's SELECT command and placed into the appropriate Command properties in the DataAdapter. A DataSet is then created and populated using the SqlDataAdapter's Fill method inside the Try-Catch loop. The next statement in this example selects the first row of the Categories DataTable and changes the CategoryName column. A new DataSet named dsUpd is then created that includes only the rows from the original DataSet that have been changed. The DataSet's GetChanges method is used to retrieve the changed row. The next statement adds an event handler for the RowUpdated event of the DataAdapter. The OnRowUpdated will fire after a row in the data source has been changed, added, or deleted. Next, the SqlDataAdapter's Update method is called using the new dsUpd DataSet. The Update method will see that the row in the dsUpd DataSet has been changed and will execute the UpdateCommand that was generated by the CommandBuilder. The record in the data source will be changed and the OnRowUpdated event handler will execute the code inside its subroutine.

Inside the OnRowUpdate subroutine, you can see that if the status of the SqlRowUpdatedEventArgs is equal to UpdateStatus.ErrorsOccurred, then an error occurred while the record was being updated at the data source. The SqlRowUpdatedEventArgs error message is then placed in the DataRow's RowError property, and the SqlRowUpdatedEventArgs status is changed to skip the current row. The OnRowUpdated routine will end, and the program code will continue at the statement after the SqlDataAdapter's Update method.

The next statement in the MergeDataSet subroutine shows merging the dsUpd DataSet back into the original ds DataSet with the preserveChanges flag set to True and the MissingSchemaAction parameter set to Add. The preserveChanges flag will ensure that any changes made to the DataSet will be saved when the incoming data is merged with the DataSet, and the MissingSchemaAction parameter of Add will ensure that the columns in the target DataSet data will be added to match the merged DataSet. Next, a DataRow array is created and filled with any rows that have errors. The DataTable's GetErrors method is used to check the DataRow's HasErrors property for a value of True and returns that row to the DataRow array. A foreach loop is then used to iterate through the DataRow array. Each DataRow in the array calls its RejectChanges method to overwrite the Current row version values with the Original row version values—in other words, rolling back the changes that were made to the DataRow. The RowError property is then cleared. After the errors in the DataRows have been rejected, the DataSet's AcceptChanges method is called to overwrite the row values in the Original row version with the values of the Current row version.

Summary

This chapter covered some advanced issues, showing you how to validate information in your DataSet before it is sent to the database using the Accept or Reject method. You updated your database with BLOBs and learned how to work with auto-increment fields. You also saw how to merge DataSets and set up several error trapping features.

The Complete Reference

Part VI

ADO.NET Data Integration

Chapter 30

Mapping Data to XML

If the .NET Framework is the infrastructure for building .NET applications, then XML could rightly be considered the plumbing for those applications. Nowhere is this more true than in ADO.NET. Beneath its object-oriented surface, all of the persistent structures in ADO.NET are actually represented using XML. This is a big change from the earlier versions of ADO, in which where Microsoft used a proprietary binary format to store persistent data. Microsoft chose XML as the underlying support mechanism for ADO.NET for a number of reasons. First, XML has quickly become an industry standard. The vast majority of platforms now provide support for XML, making it the *de facto* standard for cross-platform data exchange. Second, XML is a text-based protocol. Being text based enables XML documents to be freely sent over any protocol, including the HTTP Web protocol. This also allows XML data to be passed freely over firewalls, which often block ports other than port 80 and also often block the transmission of binary data. Third, XML is a flexible language. Being a self-describing, tag-based language gives XML the power to represent both simple objects such as single documents and complex data structures such as databases with their schema. This capability is particularly important for ADO.NET because it is the primary mechanism that enables the DataSet to function as a disconnected data store. Using XML as the native ADO.NET storage format isn't without its disadvantages. Because it is a text-based format, XML takes significantly more storage to represent data than older ADO, which uses a proprietary binary format. ADO's binary format allows it to be a much more efficient transport. However, the advantages inherent in XML far outweigh the performance penalty for using XML as ADO.NET's internal data representation method.

It's important to note that you don't really need to know all about XML in order to take advantage of it. While there are certainly places where understanding XML grammar and structure is important (for instance if your application is programmatically creating XML documents, then you'll need to know how to create a well-formed XML document), for the vast majority of situations, the ADO.NET Framework takes care of the heavy XML lifting for you. You can easily write database applications that fully take advantage of such XML-enabled features as disconnected data storage without once ever needing to see an XML document or manually parse any XML data.

In this chapter, you'll first get a brief primer on the XML technology itself. If you're unfamiliar with XML, this will help you understand some of the example XML documents presented in this chapter. Next, you'll see an overview of how XML relates to the ADO.NET data access framework. Then you'll see several examples illustrating the deep XML integration that's built into ADO.NET. These examples will begin by showing how the XMLDataReader can be used to read XML documents. Then you'll see several examples illustrating the interaction between XML documents and the core ADO.NET DataSet object. In addition to this, you'll see how you can issue XML XPath queries over ADO.NET data.

XML Primer

Like its close cousin HTML (Hypertext Markup Language), XML is a tag-based language. Both HTML and XML were developed by World Wide Web Consortium (www.w3.org) and they are both derived from the SGML (Standard Generalized Markup Language). SGML is a standard document-formatting language that enables a publisher to create, view, display, and print documents. Markup languages originated to enable publishers to indicate to printers how the content of a newspaper, magazine, or book should be produced. Markup languages for electronic data perform the same function for documents that can be displayed on different types of devices. However, SGML is a general purpose formatting language and is poorly suited to use over the Web. HTML and XML are subsets of SGML and are expressly designed for use over the Web. HTML was designed to describe the contents of a set of data and how the data should be output to a device or displayed in a Web page, whereas XML was primarily designed to transfer information. In HTML you can only use tags that come from a fixed subset of allowable HTML tags. In contrast, an XML document defines its own tags. This flexibility means that XML documents must be read by a parser that understands the rules behind creating XML documents.

XML Terminology

Before looking more closely at what constitutes an XML document, you'll need to know some important XML terminology. The following list presents some of the most common XML terms and their meanings:

- **XML document** A document that is formatted following the XML rules and contains XML elements and attributes.

- **Elements/Attributes** An element is one of the basic components of an XML document. An XML document contains one or more elements, where each element is enclosed in tags <Element> </Element>. Each element has one or more attributes that provides added information about the element.

- **Document Type Definition (DTD)** Defines the elements and attributes that can be used in an XML document.

- **Namespace** An XML Namespace enables you to differentiate between similarly named XML data types. Namespaces make element names uniquely recognizable to avoid name collisions for elements that have the same name. For instance, an XML Namespace for titles is used to distinguish between titles of books and titles of employees.

- **Extensible Stylesheet Language (XSL)** An XSL document is a special purpose XML document that describes how XML data is to be formatted. For instance, an XSL document might describe how the contents of an XML document might be converted into HTML.

- **XML Schema Definition (XSD)** The XML Schema definition language is a standard developed by the W3C organization that enables you to define the structure and data types for XML documents.

- **XML Data Reduced (XDR) Schema** A special-purpose XML standard that was developed by Microsoft to provide an XML view of the relational database. XDR documents map rows from a database table/view to XML while column values are mapped to attributes or elements. The XDR standard has been replaced by the more modern XSD standard.

- **Template** A special purpose XML document that contains one or more database queries or commands. Template files are used to send SQL and XPath queries to a database server such as SQL Server. Templates provide a more flexible and secure alternative to specifying queries in the URL string.

- **XPath Query** XPath is a graph navigation language that's defined by w3.org and it is used to select a set of nodes from an XML document. XPath queries specify tables/views as elements, and columns as attributes.

XML Documents, Elements, and Attributes

An XML document is considered well-formed if it contains exactly one unique root element and all the child elements are nested within the root, as well as nested properly within each other. Start and end tags must match. Elements cannot overlap. Both the beginning and ending tags of a given child element should exist within the body of the same parent element. Element names must begin with a letter, an underscore (_), or a colon (:). Afterward, the name can include letters, digits, periods (.), hyphens (-), underscores (_), or colons (:). Any attributes that are used should be quoted. Unlike HTML, XML is case-sensitive. XML also cares about blanks and white space. In addition, you must deal carefully with special characters that could potentially confuse the document structure such as <, >, / and the term "XML". As you can see, XML is a simple language. However, its flexibility allows it to be used in very sophisticated implementations.

Let's look at an example XML document. The following is an example of a well-formed XML document based on a subset of the data from the Customers table in the SQL Server example Northwind database.

```
<?xml version="1.0" encoding="utf-8" ?>
<shippers>
  <shipper ShipperID="1" CompanyName="Speedy Express" Phone="(503)555-9831" />
  <shipper ShipperID="2" CompanyName="United Package" Phone="(503)555-3199" />
  <shipper ShipperID="3" CompanyName="Federal Shipping" Phone="(503)555-9931"
/>
</shippers>
```

In this example, the shippers tag is the root of the XML document, and as the root tag it begins with the <shippers> tag and ends with the </shippers> tag. Rows in the shippers table are represented by shippers elements. For each element, the start and end tags must be contained within the confines of the parent tags, which in this case is the shippers root tag. Columns of the shippers table are represented by attributes of each element. For instance, each Element tag has the ShipperID, CompanyName, and Phone Attribute pairs that provide additional information about that particular element. In this case, that information is the data values for each column in the shippers table.

In this section, you learned the basics of XML. As you can imagine, there's much more to know about XML than can be covered in a few paragraphs. If you want to find out more, one of the first places to start is www.w3c.org. In addition, the Summary section of this chapter provides several references to help you learn more about the XML standard.

XML and ADO.NET

Now that you have a basic understanding of what XML is, this next section will look at how XML is used by the ADO.NET Framework. Unlike ADO, for which the use of XML was an afterthought added on primarily to provide an XML-compatible import and export mechanism, the XML integration with ADO.NET is deep-rooted and pervasive. The essential ADO.NET objects are built-in on top of an XML foundation, and ADO.NET itself allows you to work with XML documents exactly as if they were standard relational data. ADO.NET's double-sided programming model enables you to freely mix relational row-by-row data access with hierarchical XML document-based data access. Figure 30-1 presents an overview of the relationship between XML and ADO.NET.

In the center of Figure 30-1, you can see that the DataSet object and the XmlDataDocument object are at essentially the same level. In each case, schema and data can be freely exchanged between the .NET DataSet object and the XmlDataDocument.

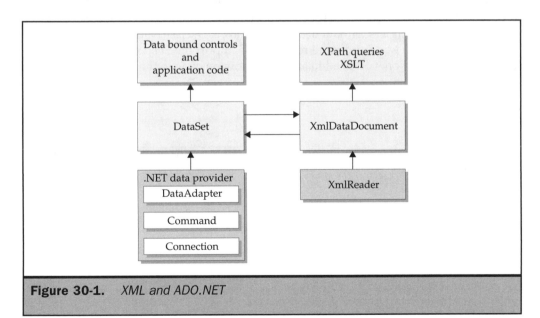

Figure 30-1. *XML and ADO.NET*

As you saw in Chapter 3, the database connection for the DataSet object is built on the SqlConnection object or the OleDbConnection object in conjunction with the SqlDataAdapter or the OleDbDataAdapter. From the application side, the contents of the DataSet are then typically surfaced to the end user either through the use of data bound controls or application code. In a similar fashion, the XmlDataDocument is populated using the XmlReader, and the contents of the XmlDataDocument can then be queried using the native XML XPath query method or can be formatted and displayed using XSLT stylesheets. From the developer's standpoint, the most important thing to remember is the close relationship between the DataSet and XML document. ADO.NET makes it very easy to read XML documents, as well as convert the contents of DataSets to XML and vice versa. In the next section of this chapter, you'll see several examples showing exactly how that can be accomplished.

Using the XmlReader

In the next section of this chapter, you get to roll up your sleeves and dig into the actual ADO.NET code that reads and writes to XML documents. Here you'll see how to use the XmlReader to read data from an XML document in a manner that's very much like using the standard ADO.NET DataReader to read data from a relational database. Then the second example in this section illustrates how to parse both the element and attribute information from an XML document using the XmlReader.

Adding the System.Xml Namespace

Before using the various XML classes in your application, you should add an import directive for the System.Xml Namespace. Importing the System.Xml Namespace enables you to work with its classes without needing to prefix each class name with System.Xml. Your code is easier to write and more readable. To import the System.Xml Namespace to a VB.NET application, you need to add the following code to the Declarations section of your project:

```
Imports System.Xml
```

For a C# project you need to add an import directive for the System.Xml Namespace as follows:

```
using System.Xml;
```

Reading XML Documents Using the DataReader

The first example in this section illustrates the basic use of the XmlReader. Very much like the SqlDataReader and OleDbDataReader, the XmlReader returns a forward-only, read-only data stream from the contents of an XML document. When the XmlReader is used, it first checks to ensure that the XML document is well-formed. If there's a problem with the XML document, the XmlReader throws an XmlException.

If you're familiar with XML it may sound like the XmlReader is the same as the SAX (simple API for XML). Both programming interfaces enable reading XML documents in a forward-only direction. Both provide fast, non-buffered stream access to the XML data. However, they're not the same. The XmlReader uses a pull model to retrieve information from the XML document, whereas the SAX model is a push model in which the parser pushes events to the application. Using the pull model allows the XmlReader to skip records of no interest to the application. In other words, the XmlReader puts the application in control of how the XML is processed rather than the parser. The XmlReader can also read streams, as well as documents.

The XmlReader is the base class that contains the code for reading XML documents and it is the focus of this section of the chapter. However, you should also be aware that there are three other closely related classes in the System.XML Namespace that are derived from the base XmlReader class. These related classes are listing in Table 30-1.

The following XmlReader subroutine shows how the XmlReader can be used to read selected data from an XML data stream returned from SQL Server. In this example, you'll

Class	Description
XmlTextReader	The fastest of the XmlReader classes. It checks for well-formed XML, but does not support data validation. It doesn't expand general entities and doesn't support default attributes.
XmlValidatingReader	Able to validate data using DTDs, XDR schema, or XSD schema. This class supports expanding general entities and default attributes.
XmlNodeReader	Able to read XML data from a node (aka subtree) in an XML document. This class does not support DTD or schema validation.

Table 30-1.   *XML Classes Derived from the XmlReader Class*

see how to retrieve a basic read-only resultset from the SQL Server Northwind database and then process the individual data elements that comprise the result stream. In this example, the data retrieved is displayed in a list box, but it could be used for other purposes, including building other XML documents or updategrams.

```vb
Private Sub XMLReader(ByVal sServer As String, ByVal sDB As String)
    Dim cn As New SqlConnection("SERVER=" & sServer _
        & ";INTEGRATED SECURITY=True;DATABASE=" & sDB)
    Dim cmd As New SqlCommand( _
        "SELECT ProductName, " & _
        "CategoryID FROM Products FOR XML AUTO", cn)
    Try
        ' Open a connection and read the XML into a list
        cn.Open()
        Dim xmlRdr As XmlReader = cmd.ExecuteXmlReader()
        lstResults.Items.Clear()
        lstResults.Items.Add("ProductName" & vbTab _
            & "CategoryID")
        Do While xmlRdr.Read()
            lstResults.Items.Add(xmlRdr("ProductName") & vbTab _
                & xmlRdr.Item("CategoryID"))
        Loop
        ' Always close the XmlReader when finished.
        xmlRdr.Close()
    Catch e As Exception
        MsgBox(e.Message)
    Finally
        Cursor.Current = Cursors.Default
        cn.Close()
    End Try
End Sub
```

The C# version of the XMLReader subroutine is shown in the listing that follows:

```csharp
private void XMLReader(string sServer, string sDB)
{
    Cursor.Current = Cursors.WaitCursor;
    // Setup the connection and command
    SqlConnection cn = new SqlConnection("SERVER=" + sServer +
        ";INTEGRATED SECURITY=True;DATABASE=" + sDB);
    SqlCommand cmd = new SqlCommand(
        "SELECT ProductName, CategoryID FROM Products FOR XML AUTO",
```

```
        cn);
    cmd.CommandType = CommandType.Text;
    try
    {
        // Open a connection and read the XML into a list
        cn.Open();
        XmlReader xmlRdr = cmd.ExecuteXmlReader();
        lstResults.Items.Clear();
        lstResults.Items.Add("ProductName" + '\t'
            + "CategoryID");
        while(xmlRdr.Read())
        {
            lstResults.Items.Add(xmlRdr["ProductName"] + '\t'
                + xmlRdr["CategoryID"]);
        }
        // Always close the XmlReader when finished.
        xmlRdr.Close();
    }
    catch (Exception ex)
    {
        MessageBox.Show(ex.Message);
    }
    finally
    {
        cn.Close();
        Cursor.Current = Cursors.Default;
    }
}
```

At the top of the XMLReader subroutine, a new SqlConnection object named cn is created that uses integrated security to attach to the target database. Next, a new SqlCommand object named cmd is created. The SqlCommand object's constructor sets the Command Property to a SQL Select statement that retrieves the ProductName and CategoryID columns from the Products table in SQL Server's example Northwind database. You should note that the SQL SELECT statement using the FOR XML AUTO keywords indicating the resultset should be returned as an XML document.

Note   *The FOR XML AUTO keywords in the SQL SELECT statement are only supported by SQL Server 2000 and higher.*

Next, a Try block is used to first execute the SqlConnection object's Open method to open a connection to the target database. Then the SqlCommand object's ExecuteXmlReader is used to instantiate a new XmlReader object named xmlRdr. At this point, the xmlRdr XmlReader is ready to be used. Next the list box that will contain the results is cleared, and new headings are set up in the List for the product and category information that will be returned by the SELECT statement. Then, a While loop is used to read the forward-only data stream returned by the XmlReader. The xmlRdr XmlReader object's Read method is used to advance the cursor through the resultset. Inside the While loop, the two different data elements are added to the list box named lstResults. Each column in the resultset is accessed using a string that identifies the column name. The CustomerID column is accessed using the rdr("CustomerID") code, and the CompanyName column is accessed using the rdr("CustomerName") identifier. Alternatively, you could also access the columns returned by the XmlReader using each column's ordinal position rather than the column name. In that case, you would use rdr(0) and rdr(1) identifiers. Using ordinals allows your code to execute faster, but you pay a price in code readability and maintainability. The XmlReader requires that each column must be accessed in the order it appears in the resultset. You can't access the columns out of order because the XmlReader provides a one-way result stream to the client application, and it doesn't for backward movement through the results stream. After all of the results have been retrieved, the xmlRdr.Read method will return the value of False, and the While loop will be terminated. Then the xmlRdr.Close method is used to close the XmlReader.

Note *When the application is connected to a database such as SQL Server, explicitly closing all of the SqlConnection and the XmlReader objects is important because the objects aren't immediately destroyed when they go out of scope. Instead, they are destroyed when the .NET Garbage collector decides to remove them, which could take a long time—even days or until the next reboot.*

The code in the Catch block will be executed if an error occurs while either opening the SqlConnection object connection or using the XmlReader. An error could occur if either a connection failure occurred or if the XML result stream was not well-formed. In that case and exception message will be captured and displayed in a message box. You can see the results of the XmlReader subroutine in Figure 30-2.

Reading XML Documents Using the DataReader

You'll notice that the XmlReader allows your application to process XML documents very much like the DataReader allows your application to process resultsets returned from a relational data source. However, there are differences. While the DataReader can read only a result stream that returned from a database, the XmlReader, can read both streams returned from a database, such as a SQL SELECT statement issued with the FOR XML keywords, as well as stand-alone XML documents. The previous example illustrated the use of the XmlReader to process an XML result stream. In this example, you'll see how to use the XmlReader to parse the node and attribute information for an XML data source. In the following listing, you can see the XMLReaderNodes subroutine,

ADO.NET DATA
INTEGRATION

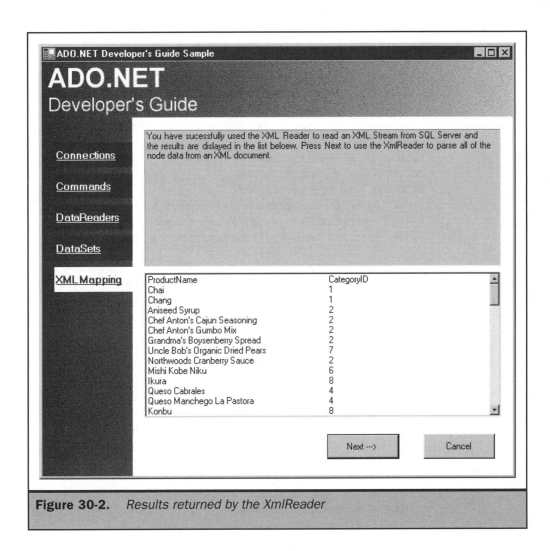

Figure 30-2. *Results returned by the XmlReader*

which reads an XML data stream and displays all of the node, element, and attribute information contained in the data stream in a list box.

```
Private Sub XMLReaderNodes(ByVal sServer As String, _
        ByVal sDB As String)
    Dim cn As New SqlConnection("SERVER=" & sServer _
        & ";INTEGRATED SECURITY=True;DATABASE=" & sDB)
    Dim cmd As New SqlCommand( _
```

```vb
              "SELECT * FROM orders WHERE ShipRegion = 'OR' " & _
              "FOR XML AUTO", cn)
    Try
        ' Open a connection and read the XML node data
        cn.Open()
        Dim xmlRdr As XmlReader = cmd.ExecuteXmlReader()
        lstResults.Items.Clear()
        Do While xmlRdr.Read()
            Select Case xmlRdr.NodeType
                Case XmlNodeType.Element
                    lstResults.Items.Add("Element:" & xmlRdr.Name)
                    While xmlRdr.MoveToNextAttribute()
                        lstResults.Items.Add("Attribute: " _
                            & xmlRdr.Name & "='" _
                            & xmlRdr.Value & "'")
                    End While
                    If xmlRdr.IsEmptyElement = True Then
                        lstResults.Items.Add("Element Empty")
                    End If
                Case XmlNodeType.Text
                    lstResults.Items.Add("Text=" & xmlRdr.Value)
                Case XmlNodeType.CDATA
                    lstResults.Items.Add("CDATA=" & xmlRdr.Value)
                Case XmlNodeType.ProcessingInstruction
                    lstResults.Items.Add("ProcessingInstruction=" _
                        & xmlRdr.Name & " " & xmlRdr.Value)
                Case XmlNodeType.Comment
                    lstResults.Items.Add("Comment=" _
                        & xmlRdr.Value)
                Case XmlNodeType.Document
                    lstResults.Items.Add("Document=" _
                        & "xml version='1.0'")
                Case XmlNodeType.Whitespace
                    lstResults.Items.Add("Whitespace=" _
                        & xmlRdr.Value)
                Case XmlNodeType.SignificantWhitespace
                    lstResults.Items.Add("SignificantWhitespace=" _
                        & xmlRdr.Value)
                Case XmlNodeType.EndElement
                    lstResults.Items.Add("Element End:" _
                        & xmlRdr.Name)
            End Select
```

```
        Loop
        ' Always close the XmlReader when finished.
        xmlRdr.Close()
    Catch e As Exception
        MsgBox(e.Message)
    Finally
        Cursor.Current = Cursors.Default
        cn.Close()
    End Try
End Sub
```

You can see the C# version of the XMLReaderNodes subroutine in the following listing:

```
private void XMLReaderNodes(string sServer, string sDB)
{
    Cursor.Current = Cursors.WaitCursor;
    // Setup the connection and command
    SqlConnection cn = new SqlConnection("SERVER=" + sServer
        + ";INTEGRATED SECURITY=True;DATABASE=" + sDB);
    SqlCommand cmd = new SqlCommand(
        "SELECT * FROM orders WHERE ShipRegion = 'OR' FOR XML AUTO",
        cn);
    cmd.CommandType = CommandType.Text;
    try
    {
        // Open a connection and read the XML node data
        cn.Open();
        XmlReader xmlRdr = cmd.ExecuteXmlReader();
        lstResults.Items.Clear();
        while(xmlRdr.Read())
        {
            switch (xmlRdr.NodeType)
            {
                case XmlNodeType.Element:
                    lstResults.Items.Add("Element: "
                        + xmlRdr.Name);
                    while (xmlRdr.MoveToNextAttribute())
                    {
                        lstResults.Items.Add("Attribute: "
                            + xmlRdr.Name
```

```
                           + "='" + xmlRdr.Value + "'");
                }
                if (xmlRdr.IsEmptyElement == true)
                    lstResults.Items.Add("Element Empty");
                break;
            case XmlNodeType.Text:
                lstResults.Items.Add("Text=" + xmlRdr.Value);
                break;
            case XmlNodeType.CDATA:
                lstResults.Items.Add("CDATA=" + xmlRdr.Value);
                break;
            case XmlNodeType.ProcessingInstruction:
                lstResults.Items.Add("ProcessingInstruction="
                    + xmlRdr.Name
                    + " " + xmlRdr.Value);
                break;
            case XmlNodeType.Comment:
                lstResults.Items.Add("Comment="
                    + xmlRdr.Value);
                break;
            case XmlNodeType.Document:
                lstResults.Items.Add("Document="
                    + "xml version='1.0'");
                break;
            case XmlNodeType.Whitespace:
                lstResults.Items.Add("Whitespace="
                    + xmlRdr.Value);
                break;
            case XmlNodeType.SignificantWhitespace:
                lstResults.Items.Add("SignificantWhitespace="
                    + xmlRdr.Value);
                break;
            case XmlNodeType.EndElement:
                lstResults.Items.Add("Element End:"
                    + xmlRdr.Name);
                break;
        }
    }
    xmlRdr.Close();
}
catch (Exception ex)
{
    MessageBox.Show(ex.Message);
```

```
        }
        finally
        {
            cn.Close();
            Cursor.Current = Cursors.Default;
        }
    }
```

In the beginning of the XMLReaderNodes subroutine you can see where new instances of the SqlConnection and SqlCommand objects are created. The constructor for the cmd SqlCommand object supplies a SQL SELECT statement that will retrieve all of the columns form the Orders table where the ShipRegion column contains the value of 'OR'. Here again, you should notice that the SELECT statement uses the FOR XML AUTO keywords to instruct SQL Server to return the result stream as XML.

The database connection and data retrieval tasks are executed within a Try-Catch block. The first action that happens inside the Try block is opening the connection to the database. Next the XmlReader xmlRdr object is instantiated using the SqlCommand object's ExecuteXmlReader method. After the XmlReader object is created it is ready to use. The list box, lstResults, which will display the data returned by the xmlRdr XmlReader object, is cleared, and then a While loop is used in conjunction with the XmlReader's Read method to retrieve the XML data stream. A Select Case statement (switch in C#) is used to parse the results returned by the XmlReader. The Select Case statement examines the contents of the XmlReader.NodeType property and writes the property type, name, and value to the lstResults list box. While the code only looks at the most common values for the XmlReader's NodeType property, Table 30-2 lists all the possible values:

NodeType	Description	Example
Attribute	An Attribute node can have the Text and EntityReference child node types. The Attribute node can't be the child node of any other node type.	attribute='data'
CDATA	CDATA sections are used to escape blocks of text that would otherwise be recognized as markup. A CDATA node can't have child nodes. It can be the child of the DocumentFragment, EntityReference, and Element nodes.	<![CDATA[text]]>

Table 30-2.   *XmlReader NodeTypes*

NodeType	Description	Example
Comment	A Comment node can't have child nodes. It can be the child of the Document, DocumentFragment, Element, and EntityReference nodes.	<!-- comment -->
Document	The root of the XML document tree. It can't appear as the child of any node types. The Document node can have the XmlDeclaration, Element, ProcessingInstruction, Comment, and DocumentType child node types.	
DocumentFragment	The DocumentFragment node associates a node with a document without being contained within that document. It cannot appear as the child of any node types. A DocumentFragment node can have the Element, ProcessingInstruction, Comment, Text, CDATA, and EntityReference child node types.	
DocumentType	A DocumentType node can have the Notation and Entity child node types. It can appear as the child of the Document node.	<!DOCTYPE ...>
Element	An Element node can have the Element, Text, Comment, ProcessingInstruction, CDATA, and EntityReference child node types. It can be the child of the Document, DocumentFragment, EntityReference, and Element nodes.	<element>
EndElement	Returned when XmlReader gets to the end of an element.	</element>
EndEntity	Returned when XmlReader gets to the end of the entity replacement as a result of a call to ResolveEntity.	
Entity	An Entity node can have child nodes that represent the expanded entity. It can be the child of the DocumentType node.	<!ENTITY ...>

Table 30-2.   *XmlReader NodeTypes* (continued)

NodeType	Description	Example
EntityReference	An EntityReference node can have the Element, ProcessingInstruction, Comment, Text, CDATA, and EntityReference child node types. It can appear as the child of the Attribute, DocumentFragment, Element, and EntityReference nodes.	&num
None	Returned by the XmlReader if a Read method has not been called.	
Notation	A Notation node can't have any child nodes. It can be the child of the DocumentType node.	<!NOTATION ...>
ProcessingInstruction	A ProcessingInstruction node can't have child nodes. It can be the child of the Document, DocumentFragment, Element, and EntityReference nodes.	<?pi code?>
SignificantWhitespace	White space between markup tags or white space within the xml:space="preserve" scope.	
Text	A Text node can't have any child nodes. It can be the child node of the Attribute, DocumentFragment, Element, and EntityReference nodes.	
Whitespace	White space between markup tags.	
XmlDeclaration	Appearing as the first node in the document. It can't have child nodes. It is a child of the Document node. It can have attributes that provide version and encoding information.	<?xml version='1.0'?>

Table 30-2. *XmlReader NodeTypes* (continued)

The structure of the basic Select Case statement is fairly straightforward: each different node type encountered is written to the lstResults list box using a literal that represents the node type along with a value associated with that particular node type. However, if you're familiar with XML documents you know that multiple attributes are often grouped together under a single element node. To handle this situation, an additional While loop is executed each time an XMLNode.Element node type is read. Within that While loop, the xmlRdr XmlReader object's MoveToNextAttribute method is used to read all of the attribute information for that element. The attribute name is retrieved using the xmlRdr.Name property, and the data value of each attribute is retrieved using the xmlRdr.Value property. When all of the attributes for the element have been read the MoveToNextAttribute method returns the value of False, the While loop is ended, and the program control drops to the bottom of the Case statement. Then the next NodeType can be processed. Likewise, when all of the data has been read by the XmlReader, the Read method returns a value of False, the outer While loop is ended, and the xmlRdr XmlReader object is closed. You can see the output of the XMLReaderNodes subroutine in Figure 30-3.

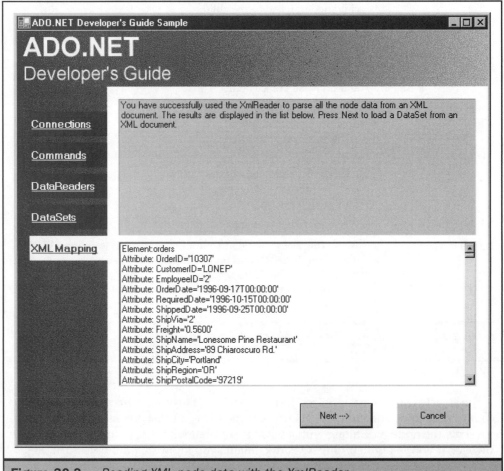

Figure 30-3. *Reading XML node data with the XmlReader*

Using DataSets and XML

In the previous section, you saw how to quickly read XML documents using the XmlReader. The XmlReader can be used to read XML data and even output new XML documents; however, because it's read-only, the XmlReader can't be used to update XML documents. The XML support found in the ADO.NET DataSet picks up where the XmlReader leaves off. The ADO.NET DataSet object provides tight XML integration. It can be used to import, update, and export XML data and schema. You can even use the DataSet to integrate data for XML data sources with data that originates from relational data sources. In the next section of this chapter, you get to roll up your sleeves and dig into the ADO.NET DataSet/XML integration features. The first example illustrates how to import, update, and export XML data using the DataSet. The next example illustrates how to map XML schema to relational schema. Finally, you'll see how to use XPath queries with ADO.NET DataSets.

Loading XML into the DataSet

In this section, you'll see the key features of the ADO.NET DataSet object's XML integration capabilities. The example that's presented in this section will illustrate how to import a standalone XML document into a DataSet. Then you'll see how to programmatically update the contents of that DataSet and the export the updated contents of the DataSet back to disk as a new XML document.

The following listing shows the example XML document that will be processed by the XmlReader. The XML document contains a subset of the Customers table from the Northwind database. You can see that the root is named customers and that the column data is represented using element attributes. For instance, the CustomerID attribute contains the different customer ID values, and the CompanyName attribute contains the company name data.

```xml
<?xml version="1.0" encoding="utf-8" ?>
<customers>
<customers CustomerID="AROUT" CompanyName="Around the Horn"
 ContactName="Thomas Hardy" ContactTitle="Sales Representative"
 Address="120 Hanover Sq." City="London" PostalCode="WA1 1DP"
 Country="UK" Phone="(171) 555-7788" Fax="(171) 555-6750" />
<customers CustomerID="BSBEV" CompanyName="B's Beverages"
 ContactName="Victoria Ashworth" ContactTitle="Sales Representative"
 Address="Fauntleroy Circus" City="London" PostalCode="EC2 5NT"
 Country="UK" Phone="(171) 555-1212" />
<customers CustomerID="CONSH" CompanyName="Consolidated Holdings"
 ContactName="Elizabeth Brown" ContactTitle="Sales Representative"
 Address="Berkeley Gardens 12 Brewery" City="London" PostalCode="WX1 6LT"
 Country="UK" Phone="(171) 555-2282" Fax="(171) 555-9199" />
```

```
<customers CustomerID="EASTC" CompanyName="Eastern Connection"
 ContactName="Ann Devon" ContactTitle="Sales Agent"
 Address="35 King George" City="London" PostalCode="WX3 6FW"
 Country="UK" Phone="(171) 555-0297" Fax="(171) 555-3373" />
<customers CustomerID="NORTS" CompanyName="North/South"
 ContactName="Simon Crowther" ContactTitle="Sales Associate"
 Address="South House 300 Queensbridge" City="London" PostalCode="SW7 1RZ"
 Country="UK" Phone="(171) 555-7733" Fax="(171) 555-2530" />
<customers CustomerID="SEVES" CompanyName="Seven Seas Imports"
 ContactName="Hari Kumar" ContactTitle="Sales Manager"
 Address="90 Wadhurst Rd." City="London" PostalCode="OX15 4NB"
 Country="UK" Phone="(171) 555-1717" Fax="(171) 555-5646" />
</customers>
```

Now that you've seen the input document, it's time to have a look at the code. In the following listing you can see the XMLDataSet subroutine, which reads through the XML customers document, loads it into a DataSet, modifies the contents of the DataSet, and finally writes the new contents back to another XML document. The method that's used to read the XML document is the DataSet's ReadXml method. Data is updated using the standard DataSet update techniques that were presented in Chapters 25–29. In this case, the example shows how to add rows so a new DataRow object is created and then added to the DataTable. Finally, the WriteXML method is used to export the content of the DataSet to a new XML document. You can see the code for this in the following subroutine.

```
Private Sub XMLDataSet()
    ' Create a DataSet
    Dim ds As New DataSet()
    Try
        ' Load DataSet with XML
        ds.ReadXml("customers.xml", XmlReadMode.Auto)
        ' Add a DataTable
        Dim dt As DataTable = ds.Tables("customers")
        ' Add a DataRow
        Dim dr As DataRow = dt.NewRow()
        dr("CustomerID") = "TESTC"
        dr("CompanyName") = "New XML Labs"
        dr("ContactName") = "Xavier M. Last"
        dr("ContactTitle") = "Engineer"
        dr("Address") = "1234 W. Data St."
        dr("City") = "London"
        dr("PostalCode") = "WA1 1DP"
        dr("Country") = "UK"
```

```
        dr("Phone") = "(171) 555-0230"
        dr("Fax") = "(171) 555-0231"
        ds.Tables("customers").Rows.Add(dr)
        ' Write out XML
        ds.WriteXml("updatedcustomers.xml")
        grdResults.DataSource = dt
    Catch ex As Exception
        MessageBox.Show(ex.ToString())
    End Try
End Sub
```

The C# version of this XMLDataSet subroutine is shown in the following listing:

```
private void XMLDataSet()
{
    // Create a DataSet
    DataSet ds = new DataSet();
    try
    {
        // Load DataSet with XML
        ds.ReadXml("customers.xml", XmlReadMode.Auto);
        // Add a DataTable
        DataTable dt = ds.Tables["customers"];
        // Add a DataRow
        DataRow dr = dt.NewRow();
        dr["CustomerID"]="TESTC";
        dr["CompanyName"]="New XML Labs";
        dr["ContactName"]="Xavier M. Last";
        dr["ContactTitle"]="Engineer";
        dr["Address"]="1234 W. Data St.";
        dr["City"]="London";
        dr["PostalCode"]="WA1 1DP";
        dr["Country"]="UK";
        dr["Phone"]="(171) 555-0230";
        dr["Fax"]="(171) 555-0231";
        ds.Tables["customers"].Rows.Add(dr);
        // Write out XML
        ds.WriteXml("updatedcustomers.xml");
        grdResults.DataSource = dt;
    }
    catch (Exception ex)
    {
```

```
        MessageBox.Show(ex.ToString());
    }
}
```

In the first part of the XMLDataSet subroutine, you can see where a new DataSet named ds is created. Then a Try-Catch block is used to import the XML document and manipulate it. If an exception is thrown by any of the objects within the Try block, the code in the Catch block will be executed and a message box will appear showing the error condition. The first action within the Try-Catch block is loading the DataSet with the content of the customers.xml document. The DataSet object's ReadXml method is used to load the DataSet. The ReadXml method works with a stream object, a file object, or an XmlReader object. The ReadXml method takes two parameters. The first argument is the stream, file or XmlReader object that contains the XML data. The second parameter is the XmlReadMode enumerator that specifies how the input stream should be processed. The code example shown in the XMLDataSet subroutine uses the XmlReadMode.Auto, which will cause the ReadXml method to create a default schema for the incoming data. The valid values for the second parameter of the ReadXml method are listed in the following table.

XmlReadMode	Description
Auto	This is the default setting. If the data is a DiffGram the XmlReadMode is set to DiffGram. If the DataSet already has a schema the XMLReadMode is set to ReadSchema. If the DataSet does not already have a schema, the XmlReadMode is set to InferSchema.
DiffGram	Reads a DiffGram and applies changes in the DiffGram to the DataSet. The target DataSet must have the same schema as the XML data, or the DiffGram merge operation will fail and an exception will be thrown.
Fragment	Reads XML documents, which may not have a root. The most common use for this is for reading XML data stream generated by SQL Server 2000's SELECT statement using the FOR XML keywords. The default Namespace is read as the inline schema.
IgnoreSchema	Ignores any inline schema and reads the XML data into the existing DataSet schema. If any data does not match the existing schema, it is discarded.
InferSchema	Ignores any inline schema, infers schema from the XML data, and loads the data to the DataSet. An exception is thrown if the inferred schema for the XML document already exists in the DataSet.
ReadSchema	Reads any inline schema and loads the XML data to the DataSet. An exception is thrown if any tables in the inline schema already exist in the DataSet.

After the ReadXml method completes, the ds DataSet will contain a new DataTable object named customers. The customers DataTable will contain DataColumn objects for each of the attribute pairs in the original XML document. In other words, the following DataColumns will be created: CustomerID, CompanyName, ContactName, ContactTitle, Address,City, PostalCode, Country, Phone, and Fax. When the schema for the DataSet is inferred, as it is in this case, there are some general guidelines that you can use to predict how the ReadXml method will create the new schema. Elements become tables if the element is repeated or contains multiple attributes. Otherwise it will become a column. Attributes become columns. Relations are created for nested table mapped elements.

The next section of code in the XMLDataSet subroutine illustrates updating the data in the DataSet. In this example, a new row is added to the customers DataTable object. To add a new row to the DataTable, first a new DataRow object named dr is created using the dt DataTable object's NewRow method. Next, the column values are assigned to each of the columns in the dr DataRow. In this example, each column is identified using a string with the column name, which makes the code more readable. For instance, dr("CompanyName") refers to the CompanyName column. Alternatively, this could also have used a zero-based ordinal to reference each column. Using ordinals offers a very slight performance advantage but a significant loss of readability. Once all of the dr DataRow column objects have been assigned new values, the dr DataRow is added to the customers DataTable object using the DataTable's Rows collection's Add method. At this point the DataSet contains the updated data, but the original XML document is unchanged.

Next, the updated contents of the ds DataSet are written out to a new XML document using the WriteXml method. In this example, the WriteXml method uses a single parameter that identifies the name of the new XML file to be created. The WriteXml method also accepts an optional second argument that controls the WriteMode. The valid values for the WriteXml XmlWriteMode parameter are listed in the following table.

XmlWriteMode	Description
DiffGram	Writes the entire DataSet as a DiffGram. The resulting Diffgram will include original and current values. To generate a DiffGram containing only changed values, you must call the GetChanges method and then call WriteXml using the value DiffGram with the XmlWrite method of the new DataSet.
IgnoreSchema	Writes the current contents of the DataSet as XML data without an XSD schema.
WriteSchema	This is the default setting. Writes the current contents of the DataSet as XML data with the relational structure as inline XSD schema.

After the new XML document has been created, the dt DataTable object is bound to a DataGrid named grdResults. You can see the output of the XMLDataSet subroutine in Figure 30-4.

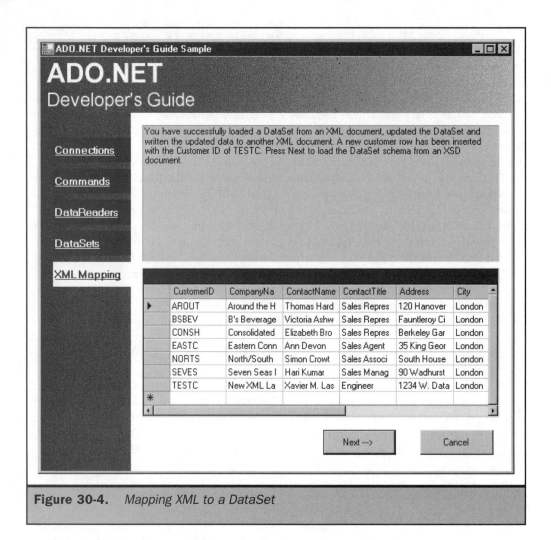

Figure 30-4.   *Mapping XML to a DataSet*

Loading XSD Schema to a DataSet

The previous example illustrated how to load an XML document into a DataSet, modifying it and then writing out a new XML document. In that example, there was no schema definition attached to the document so the schema used to create the DataTable and DataColumn objects contained in the DataSet needed to be inferred. In other words, the DataSet object's ReadXml method automatically generated a schema that matched the data that was being loaded into the DataSet. Automatically generating the schema is useful for simple documents but it isn't always reliable enough for complex documents or in cases where strict adherence to given data types is required. To address these types of scenarios, the DataSet is capable of creating schema based on an XML XSD document. XML XSD documents are a lot like SQL DDL—only applied to an XML document rather than a database. An XSD can define elements such as an order document, as well as the individual data elements and their data types that comprise that order. In addition, XSD documents can define complex elements and data relationships. For instance, an XSD is also capable of defining the relationship between a group or order elements and related order detail elements. As you can see, XSDs can perform many of the same functions that SQL DDL can perform.

To illustrate how you can import the schema contained in an XML XSD document to a DataSet, you'll need to start with an XSD document. The following listing presents a sample XML XSD definition that is representative of the Order table and Order Detail table that are found in the SQL Server example Northwind database.

```xml
<?xml version="1.0" encoding="utf-8"?>
<xs:schema id="NewDataSet" xmlns=""
xmlns:xs="http://www.w3.org/2001/XMLSchema"
xmlns:msdata="urn:schemas-microsoft-com:xml-msdata">
  <xs:element name="NewDataSet" msdata:IsDataSet="true">
    <xs:complexType>
      <xs:choice maxOccurs="unbounded">
        <xs:element name="Order_Details">
          <xs:complexType>
            <xs:attribute name="OrderID" type="xs:int" />
            <xs:attribute name="ProductID" type="xs:int" />
            <xs:attribute name="UnitPrice" type="xs:double" />
            <xs:attribute name="Quantity" type="xs:int" />
            <xs:attribute name="Discount" type="xs:double" />
          </xs:complexType>
        </xs:element>
        <xs:element name="Orders">
          <xs:complexType>
            <xs:attribute name="OrderID" type="xs:int" />
            <xs:attribute name="CustomerID" type="xs:string" />
            <xs:attribute name="EmployeeID" type="xs:int" />
            <xs:attribute name="OrderDate" type="xs:date" />
            <xs:attribute name="RequiredDate" type="xs:date" />
            <xs:attribute name="ShippedDate" type="xs:date" />
            <xs:attribute name="ShipVia" type="xs:int" />
            <xs:attribute name="Freight" type="xs:double" />
            <xs:attribute name="ShipName" type="xs:string" />
            <xs:attribute name="ShipAddress" type="xs:string" />
            <xs:attribute name="ShipCity" type="xs:string" />
            <xs:attribute name="ShipRegion" type="xs:string" />
```

```
                    <xs:attribute name="ShipPostalCode" type="xs:string" />
                    <xs:attribute name="ShipCountry" type="xs:string" />
                </xs:complexType>
            </xs:element>
            <xs:element name="Products">
                <xs:complexType>
                    <xs:attribute name="ProductID" type="xs:int" />
                    <xs:attribute name="ProductName" type="xs:string" />
                    <xs:attribute name="SupplierID" type="xs:int" />
                    <xs:attribute name="CategoryID" type="xs:int" />
                    <xs:attribute name="QuantityPerUnit" type="xs:string" />
                    <xs:attribute name="UnitPrice" type="xs:double" />
                    <xs:attribute name="UnitsInStock" type="xs:int" />
                    <xs:attribute name="UnitsOnOrder" type="xs:int" />
                    <xs:attribute name="ReorderLevel" type="xs:int" />
                    <xs:attribute name="Discontinued" type="xs:boolean" />
                </xs:complexType>
            </xs:element>
        </xs:choice>
    </xs:complexType>
</xs:element>
</xs:schema>
```

At the top of this document, you can see the XML version flag that tells whatever parsing engine reads the document the XML specification that was used to encode the data. Next, you can see that this schema consists of one element and a number of subelements. The primary element is named NewDataSet, and the subelements include three complexTypes: Order, Order_Details, and Products. Each of the complexTypes includes multiple attribute pairs that define the data names along with their corresponding data types. For example, in the Orders subelement, you can see that the OrderID, ProductID, and Quantity attributes contain integer data, whereas the data contained in the UnitPrice and Discount attribute must contain values that are double data types. Likewise, the other complexType, the Order_Detail subelement, includes definitions for attributes such as the OrderID, which is an integer data type; the CustomerID, which is a string data type; the EmployeeID attribute, an integer data type; along with definitions for the other attributes that comprise the Order_Detail subelement. You might note that these data types don't exactly match the data types used by the .NET Framework. When the XSD schema is loaded into a DataSet, the XML data types must be converted into their corresponding .NET data types. The following table shows the relationship between the XML XSD data type definitions and the data types used by the .NET Framework.

XML Schema (XSD) Type	.NET Framework Type
anyURI	System.Uri
base64Binary	System.Byte[]
Boolean	System.Boolean
Byte	System.SByte
Date	System.DateTime
dateTime	System.DateTime
decimal	System.Decimal
Double	System.Double
Duration	System.TimeSpan
ENTITIES	System.String[]
ENTITY	System.String
Float	System.Single
gDay	System.DateTime
gMonthDay	System.DateTime
gYear	System.DateTime
gYearMonth	System.DateTime
hexBinary	System.Byte[]
ID	System.String
IDREF	System.String
IDREFS	System.String[]
int	System.Int32
integer	System.Decimal
language	System.String
long	System.Int64
month	System.DateTime
Name	System.String
NCName	System.String
negativeInteger	System.Decimal
NMTOKEN	System.String
NMTOKENS	System.String[]
nonNegativeInteger	System.Decimal

XML Schema (XSD) Type	.NET Framework Type
nonPositiveInteger	System.Decimal
normalizedString	System.String
NOTATION	System.String
positiveInteger	System.Decimal
QName	System.Xml.XmlQualifiedName
short	System.Int16
string	System.String
time	System.DateTime
timePeriod	System.DateTime
token	System.String
unsignedByte	System.Byte
unsignedInt	System.UInt32
unsignedLong	System.UInt64
unsignedShort	System.UInt16

Now that you've seen the XSD schema that will be imported, it's time to take a look at the ADO.NET code that's needed to read this XSD schema and convert it into a DataSet schema. The following VB.NET XMLLoadSchemaXSD subroutine does exactly that.

```
Private Sub XMLLoadSchemaXSD()
    ' Create a DataSets
    Dim ds As New DataSet()
    Dim dt As New DataTable()
    Dim dc As New DataColumn()
    Try
        ' Load the DataSet Schema
        ds.ReadXml("ProductOrdersDetails.xsd", _
            XmlReadMode.ReadSchema)
        lstResults.Items.Clear()
        lstResults.Items.Add("DataSet Schema")
        'Parse the Dataset and show the generated schema
        For Each dt In ds.Tables
            ' Add the Table
            lstResults.Items.Add(dt.TableName)
            'List its Columns
            For Each dc In dt.Columns
```

```
                lstResults.Items.Add("  |- " & dc.ColumnName _
                    & "   " & dc.DataType.ToString)
            Next
        Next
    Catch ex As Exception
        MessageBox.Show("XML Load Error: " + ex.ToString())
    End Try
End Sub
```

You can see the C# version of the XMLSchemaXSD subroutine in the following listing.

```
private void XMLLoadSchemaXSD()
{
    // Create a DataSets
    DataSet ds = new DataSet();
    try
    {
        // Load the DataSet Schema
        ds.ReadXml("ProductOrdersDetails.xsd",
            XmlReadMode.ReadSchema);
        lstResults.Items.Clear();
        lstResults.Items.Add("DataSet Schema");
        //Parse the Dataset and show the generated schema
        foreach (DataTable dt in ds.Tables)
        {
            // Add the Table
            lstResults.Items.Add(dt.TableName);
            // List its Columns
            foreach (DataColumn dc in dt.Columns)
            {
                lstResults.Items.Add("  |- " + dc.ColumnName
                    + "   " + dc.DataType.ToString());
            }
        }
    }
    catch (Exception ex)
    {
        MessageBox.Show("XML Load Error: " + ex.ToString());
    }
}
```

New instances of a DataSet, DataTable, and DataColumn objects named ds, dt, and dc respectively are created in the beginning of this subroutine. Of these, only the DataSet object is needed in order to actually load the XSD schema. The other objects are created to parse the DataSet and display the schema information. It's most important to notice the code at the beginning of the Try-Catch structure that loads the XSD schema to the DataSet using the DataSet object's ReadXml method. Unlike the previous example, here the ReadXml method takes two arguments. The first argument supplies the name of the XSD document to read. This instance shows reading an XSD document named ProductOrdersDetails.xsd, but the XSD information could also have been supplied by a stream object or an XmlReader object. The second argument of the ReadXml method uses the XMLReadMode.ReadSchema enumerator to tell the ReadXml method to only read the schema information from the XML document.

Once the ReadXml method completes, the DataSet will contain three DataTables: Orders, Order_Details, and Products. Each of these DataTables will contain a collection of DataColumn objects that match the attributes for each of the complexTypes defined in the XSD document. At this point, the DataSet schema is defined, but none of the objects in the DataSet will contain any data.

A For Each loop is used to read and display the ds DataSet object's new schema information. The For Each loop reads each table in the DataSet object's Tables collection. For every DataTable read, the name of the DataTable will be written to a list box named lstResults. Next, a second For Each loop is used to read and display the DataColumn information associated with each DataTable object. Inside this For Each loop, the name of the DataColumn and its DataType type are written to the list box. You can see the results of the XMLLoadSchemaSXD subroutine in Figure 30-5.

Although this example shows how to import XML XSD schema to a DataSet, you can also export XSD schema from a DataSet by using the WriteXML method in conjunction with the WriteXML XMLWriteMode argument.

Using XML DiffGrams

DiffGrams are a subset of the UpdateGram document supported by SQL Server 2000. While the UpdateGram is typically used to update SQL Server databases with XML information, the DiffGram is used to update a DataSet. DiffGram's are the internal storage mechanism that ADO.NET uses to capture the changes made to a DataSet. Like the other XML documents, DiffGrams are text based and are capable of passing over firewalls, which often block binary traffic. The next example in this section shows you how to generate a DiffGram that contains just the changes made to a DataSet. Then you'll see how to take that DiffGram and update a second DataSet. It's important to remember that when sending updates between DataSets using DiffGrams, the target DataSet must have the same schema as the DataSet that produced the DiffGram. This makes sense because the DiffGram is essentially a set of changes applied to a document, and the DiffGram needs to be able to exactly match the target schema in order to apply those changes. If the

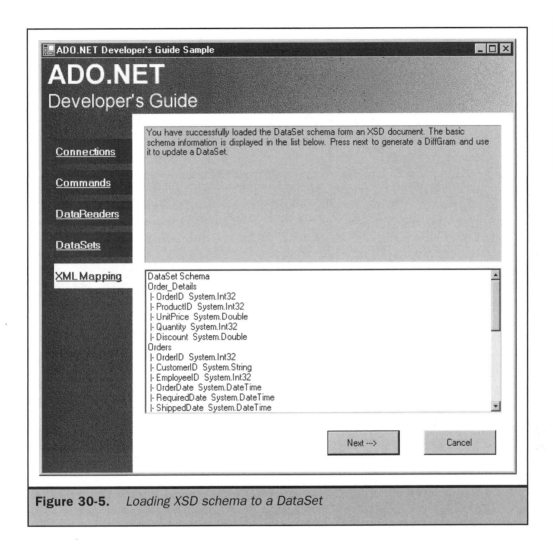

Figure 30-5. *Loading XSD schema to a DataSet*

DataSets have different schema, an exception will be thrown. You can see the sample code to produce a Diffgram and use it to update a DataSet in the following XMLDiffGram subroutine.

```
Private Sub XMLDiffGram()
    ' Create two DataSets
    Dim dsOld As New DataSet()
    Dim dsNew As New DataSet()
    Try
```

```
            ' Load the DataSet
            dsOld.ReadXml("customers.xml", XmlReadMode.Auto)
            ' Accept the new XML data
            dsOld.AcceptChanges()
            ' Clone the DataSet Structure
            dsNew = dsOld.Clone()
          ' Create a DataTable
            Dim dt As DataTable = dsOld.Tables("customers")
            ' Retrieve the first row and change it
            Dim sFilter As String = "CustomerID = 'AROUT'"
            ' Use the Select method to find all rows matching filter.
            Dim dr As DataRow = dt.Select(sFilter)(0)
            dr("CompanyName") = "Around the Cape"
            ' Create a DiffGram of the changes
            If dsOld.HasChanges(DataRowState.Modified) Then
                ' Create temporary DataSet
                Dim dsDiff As New DataSet()
                ' Get changes for modified rows
                dsDiff = dsOld.GetChanges(DataRowState.Modified)
                ' Write out the DiffGram
                dsDiff.WriteXml("TempDiffGram.xml", _
                    XmlWriteMode.DiffGram)
            End If
            ' Merge the DiffGram to the new DataSet
            dsNew.ReadXml("TempDiffGram.xml", XmlReadMode.DiffGram)
            ' Show the updated DataSet in a grid
            grdResults.DataSource = dsNew.Tables("customers")
        Catch ex As Exception
            MessageBox.Show(ex.ToString())
        End Try
End Sub
```

The C# version of the XMLDiffGram subroutine is shown here:

```
private void XMLDiffGram()
{
    // Create two DataSets
    DataSet dsOld = new DataSet();
    DataSet dsNew = new DataSet();
    try
    {
```

```
    // Load the DataSet
    dsOld.ReadXml("customers.xml", XmlReadMode.Auto);
    // Accept the new XML data
    dsOld.AcceptChanges();
    // Clone the DataSet Structure
    dsNew = dsOld.Clone();
    // Create a DataTable
    DataTable dt = dsOld.Tables["customers"];
    // Retrieve the first row and change it
    string sFilter = "CustomerID = 'AROUT'";
    // Use the Select method to find all rows matching filter
    DataRow dr = dt.Select(sFilter)[0];
    dr["CompanyName"] = "Around the Cape";
    // Create a DiffGram of the changes
    if (dsOld.HasChanges(DataRowState.Modified))
    {
        // Create temporary DataSet
        DataSet dsDiff = new DataSet();
        // Get changes for modified rows
        dsDiff = dsOld.GetChanges(DataRowState.Modified);
        // Write out the DiffGram
        dsDiff.WriteXml("TempDiffGram.xml",
            XmlWriteMode.DiffGram);
    }
    // Merge the DiffGram to the new DataSet
    dsNew.ReadXml("TempDiffGram.xml", XmlReadMode.DiffGram);
    // Show the updated DataSet in a grid
    grdResults.DataSource = dsNew.Tables["customers"];
}
catch (Exception ex)
{
    MessageBox.Show(ex.ToString());
}
}
```

At the top of the XMLDiffGram subroutine, two DataSet objects are created. The first
DataSet is named dsOld, and it will be used to hold the original information and generate
the DiffGram. The second DataSet, named dsNew, will be the target of the changes
contained in the DiffGram. Within the Try block, the dsOld DataSet is loaded with the
contents of the customer.xml document that was presented earlier in this chapter. The
XMLReadMode.Auto is used to automatically generate a schema for the XML data loaded
into the DataSet by the ReadXml method. When the data is initially loaded into the dsOld

DataSet object, the RowState for all of the rows will indicate that the row has been added. Generating a DiffGram from a DataSet in which all of the rows have an Added status will result in all of the rows in the DataSet being exported to the DiffGram. In order to reset the RowState for the newly added data, the dsOld DataSet's AcceptChanges method is called. Then the dsOld DataSet's Clone method is used to copy the schema of the dsOld DataSet to the dsNew DataSet. This is required because the schema for the target DataSet must be identical to the DataSet that's used to generate the DiffGram.

The next section of code sets up a search criterion to retrieve one row out of the dsOld DataSet. The string variable sFilter contains the value of CustomerID = 'AROUT' indicating that the row in the DataSet where the value of the CustomerID DataColumn equals AROUT will be retrieved. Then the dt DataTable's Select method is executed using the sFilter string variable to return an instance of a DataRow that contains the desired row. After the row has been retrieved and the dr DataRow object has been assigned an instance of the DataRow, the CompanyName item in the DataRow is assigned the new value of Around the Cape. Making this change will cause the DataRow's RowState property to be set to Modified.

The DiffGram is actually generated in the next section of the XMLDiffGram subroutine. An If statement is used to test the DataRowState property of the dsOld DataSet object to see if any rows have been modified. In this case, one row has been changed so the code within the If block will be executed. First, a temporary DataSet object named dsDiff is created to hold just the changed rows from the original dsOld DataSet. The GetChanges method pulls all of the updated rows out of the dsOld DataSet. Once the temporary dsDiff DataSet has been assigned all of the changed rows, the WriteXml method is used along with the XmlWriteMode.DiffGram argument to write a DiffGram to the TempDiffGram.xml file.

After the DiffGram has been created, it can then be used to update the target dsNew DataSet object. To perform the update, the dsNew DataSet object's ReadXml method is used along with the XMLReadMode.DiffGram argument to read the TempDiffGram .xml XML document and merge the changes into the dsNew DataSet. In this case, because the dsNew Data is empty, one row will be added to the dsNew DataSet object. Then the dsNew DataSet is bound to a DataGrid named grdResults and displayed. You can see the results of the XMLDiffGram subroutine in Figure 30-6.

In case you were wondering what the format of the TempDiffGram.xml document looks like, you can see it in the following listing.

```xml
<?xml version="1.0" standalone="yes"?>
<diffgr:diffgram xmlns:msdata="urn:schemas-microsoft-com:xml-msdata"
xmlns:diffgr="urn:schemas-microsoft-com:xml-diffgram-v1">
  <customers>
    <customers diffgr:id="customers1" msdata:rowOrder="0"
     diffgr:hasChanges="modified" CustomerID="AROUT"
     CompanyName="Around the Cape" ContactName="Thomas Hardy"
     ContactTitle="Sales Representative" Address="120 Hanover Sq."
     City="London" PostalCode="WA1 1DP" Country="UK"
```

```
      Phone="(171) 555-7788" Fax="(171) 555-6750" />
  </customers>
  <diffgr:before>
    <customers diffgr:id="customers1" msdata:rowOrder="0"
    CustomerID="AROUT" CompanyName="Around the Horn"
    ContactName="Thomas Hardy" ContactTitle="Sales Representative"
    Address="120 Hanover Sq." City="London" PostalCode="WA1 1DP"
    Country="UK" Phone="(171) 555-7788" Fax="(171) 555-6750" />
  </diffgr:before>
</diffgr:diffgram>
```

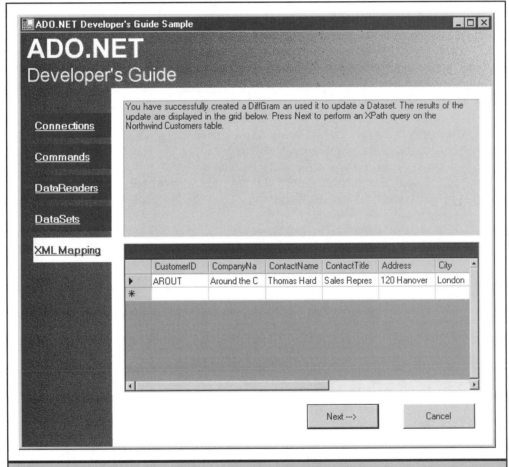

Figure 30-6.   *Sample DiffGram generated from a DataSet*

Querying the DataSet Using XPath and XSLT/L

The last example in this chapter illustrates the basics of how you can query the data contained in a DataSet using XPath queries. Just as SQL is the standard query language for relational databases, XPath is the standard query language for XML documents. Like SQL, the XPath query language is a very capable language that is not only used to retrieve data but is also used for expressions, as well as various mathematic functions. You can learn more about the specifications for the XPath language at www.w3c.org/TR/xpath. Because of the close relationship between XML and the DataSet, XPath can be used and can perform certain functions more conveniently than directly querying the DataSet. For instance, you can use an XPath query to navigate between the Tables and other objects in a DataSet more easily than iterating through the object collections in the DataSet.

In order to use an XPath query on a DataSet, the DataSet must first be converted into an XmlDataDocument. The results of an XPath query can be represented in the form of an XmlNodeList. The XML nodes in the XmlNodeList can then be cast as XmlElement nodes, and even converted back to DataRow objects, using the GetRowFromElement method of the XmlDataDocument. You can see how to extract data from a DataSet using an XPath query in the following code listing.

```
Private Sub XMLXPath(ByVal sServer As String, ByVal sDB As String)
    Cursor.Current = Cursors.WaitCursor
    ' Setup the  connection and command
    Dim cn As New SqlConnection("SERVER=" & sServer _
        & ";INTEGRATED SECURITY=True;DATABASE=" & sDB)
    Dim ds As New DataSet()
    ' Create a SQL Select statement
    Dim sSQL As String = "Select * from Customers"
    ' Create a DataAdapter
    Dim da As New SqlDataAdapter(sSQL, cn)
    Try
        ' Fill the DataSet
        da.Fill(ds, "Customers")
        ' Load the document with the DataSet
        Dim doc As New XmlDataDocument(ds)
        ' Use an XPath Query
        Dim nodes As XmlNodeList = doc.SelectNodes( _
            "//Customers[City=""Portland""]")
        lstResults.Items.Clear()
        lstResults.Items.Add("Customers in Portland")
        Dim node As XmlNode
        For Each node In nodes
            Dim dr As DataRow = doc.GetRowFromElement(node)
```

```
            lstResults.Items.Add(dr("City") + "   " _
                + dr("CompanyName"))
        Next
    Catch ex As Exception
        MessageBox.Show(ex.ToString())
    End Try
    Cursor.Current = Cursors.WaitCursor
End Sub
```

The C# version of the XMLXpath subroutine follows.

```csharp
private void XMLXPath(string sServer, string sDB)
{
    Cursor.Current = Cursors.WaitCursor;
    // Setup the  connection and command
    SqlConnection cn = new SqlConnection("SERVER=" + sServer
        + ";INTEGRATED SECURITY=True;DATABASE=" + sDB);
    DataSet ds = new DataSet();
    // Create a SQL Select statement
    string sSQL = "Select * from Customers";
    // Create a DataAdapter
    SqlDataAdapter da = new SqlDataAdapter(sSQL, cn);
    try
    {
        // Fill the DataSet with the selected records.
        da.Fill(ds,"Customers");
        // Load the document with the DataSet
        XmlDataDocument doc = new XmlDataDocument(ds);
        // Use an XPath Query
        XmlNodeList nodes = doc.SelectNodes(
            "//Customers[City=""Portland""]");
        lstResults.Items.Clear();
        lstResults.Items.Add("Customers in Portland");
        foreach(XmlNode node in nodes)
        {
            DataRow dr = doc.GetRowFromElement((XmlElement)node);
            lstResults.Items.Add(dr["City"] + "   "
                + dr["CompanyName"]);
        }
    }
    catch (Exception ex)
```

```
    {
        MessageBox.Show(ex.ToString());
    }
    Cursor.Current = Cursors.WaitCursor;
}
```

In the beginning of the XMLXPath subroutine, a SqlConnection object is created along with a new DataSet object. Then a SQL SELECT statement that retrieves all of the rows and columns from the Customers table in the Northwind database is created and passed in to the SqlDataAdapter.

Next, a Try-Catch block is used to first populate the DataSet using the SqlDataAdapter's Fill method, and then a new XmlDataDocument named doc is created by passing the DataSet object to the XmlDataDocument object's constructor. The new XML document will contain the schema and data that was in the ds DataSet object. After the XmlDataDocument has been created, you can then query the XmlDataDocument using an XPath query. The example shown in the XMLXPath subroutine then uses the XPath query to populate an XMLNodeList object named nodes. The XPath query is executed by passing the XPath query string to the XmlDataDocuments SelectNodes method. This particular XPath query selects the nodes in the Customers element where the City subelement contains a value of Portland. In the XPath syntax, elements are represented using just their name, whereas attribute names must be preceded by an @ symbol.

After the XPath query has been executed, the lstResults list box that will display the results is cleared, and the data in the node's XmlNodeList object is processed using a For Each loop. Inside the For Each loop, the GetRowFromElements method is used to convert the XML node elements back to a DataRow. Then the content of the DataRow Item array's City and CompanyName items are add to the lstResults list box You can see the output produced by the XMLXPath subroutine in Figure 30-7.

Summary

This chapter presented a brief primer on the XML technology. However, as you probably gathered from the examples in this chapter, XML is a huge topic that can't be coved in a single chapter. The examples presented in this chapter showed some of the most important aspects of how XML is deeply integrated with the ADO.NET Framework. The first examples illustrated the use of the XmlReader to read XML data streams returned from a SQL Server database. And the other examples presented several facets of the ADO.NET DataSet object's XML foundation.

For more information about the basics of XML, refer to www.w3c.org. For more information about SQL Server 2000's support for XML, see *SQL Server 2000 Developer's Guide* by Michael Otey and Paul Conte (Osborne/McGraw-Hill, 2001).

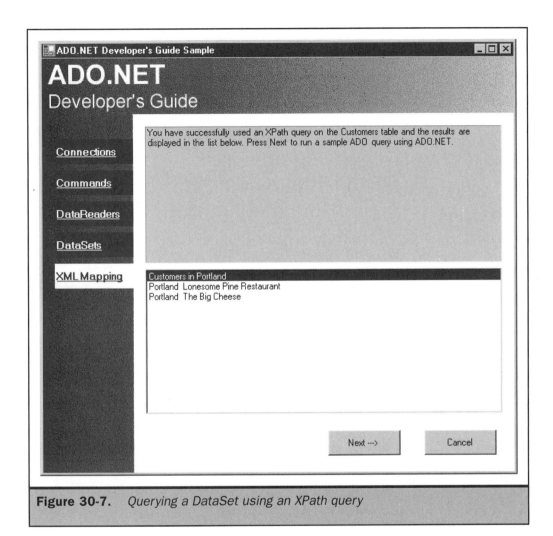

Figure 30-7.   *Querying a DataSet using an XPath query*

Chapter 31

Using ADO
from ADO.NET

A lthough ADO.NET is more capable than ADO, ADO.NET is also substantially different from ADO. Migrating your existing applications to ADO.NET is no small undertaking. There's no silver bullet that will quickly and painlessly convert all that ADO code into ADO.NET code. Although Microsoft does supply a migration wizard with Visual Studio.NET that's designed to migrate your existing COM applications to the .NET Framework, you only have to try to use it a couple of times before discovering that it leaves all of the heavy lifting to you. The reality is that if you have a significant number of COM-based ADO applications running, in all likelihood you're going to be keeping them for a while. Although rewriting applications may be quicker than writing them in the first place, a conversion from COM to .NET and ADO to ADO.NET definitely requires a full application rewrite. Most businesses already have projects underway that don't allow them to drop everything and rewrite their existing applications for the sake of taking advantage of new technology. One way of beginning to merge your existing code into the .NET Framework is by using the .NET Framework's COM interoperability functions to call COM-based ADO from .NET applications. In this chapter, you'll see how you can incorporate ADO into your new .NET applications. The first part of this chapter illustrates how to import the msado15.dll, which contains ADO, into your .NET application. The second part of this chapter shows how to use the ADO Recordset object. First, by populating and navigating through the recordset, and then by using an ADO Recordset object to load an ADO.NET DataSet. The chapter concludes by discussing some of the important ADO–ADO.NET coexistence issues that you need to be aware of when using ADO from the .NET Framework.

Importing ADO into the .NET Framework

Although ADO and ADO.NET are very different, they do have some overall similarities. They both use a Connection object to connect to the data source. They both issue commands to the database and are capable of executing stored procedures and retrieving resultsets. And they both provide mechanisms for navigating the returned results as well as binding them to the objects in the client application. For ADO, the underlying connection to the data source is made using an OLE DB Provider. The ADO.NET equivalent to this is the .NET Data Provider. The ADO Connection and Command objects are essentially equivalent to the ADO.NET OleDbConnection and OleDbCommand objects if you're using the .NET Framework Data Provider for OLE DB. In the ADO framework, resultsets are surfaced using the ADO Recordset object, which is closest to the ADO.NET DataSet. However, the new ADO.NET DataSet provides a host of functionality that isn't available in the ADO Recordset object. Using ADO from a .NET application bears a strong resemblance to using ADO.NET, and coding those ADO calls will definitely be familiar territory. The first step in using ADO for the .NET Framework is to import the msado15.dll, which contains the COM-based ADO functionality, into your .NET application as is described in the following section.

ADO.NET DATA
INTEGRATION

Referencing the msado15.dll in Visual Studio.NET

In order to use ADO from a .NET Framework application, you must first have a .NET class wrapper for the ADO COM library. .NET applications aren't able to directly call COM objects like ADO. Instead, .NET assemblies can only call other .NET assemblies. To call a COM object from a .NET application, you need to use the .NET System.Runtime .InteropServices namespace in your application. This namespace provides the classes required to interface with the COM objects. Fortunately, you don't need to do this manually for the ADO COM library. Microsoft has provided a COM InterOp assembly for the ADO msado15.dll called ADODB, which by default is located under the C:\Program Files \Microsoft.NET\Primary Interop folder.

 Note   *In spite of its name, the msado15.dll isn't ADO 1.5. All of the recent versions of ADO have been contained in the msado15.dll dynamic link library.*

In order to use this assembly in your application, you must first create a reference for it in your Visual Studio project. To add a reference to your Visual Studio.NET project, you must first open up the Project menu and then select the Add Reference option. The Add References dialog box shown in Figure 31-1 will be displayed.

To add a new reference for the ADODB assembly, scroll through the list of components until you see the ADODB component. Select the ADODB component from the list by clicking it then clicking Select. As you can see in Figure 31-1 the ADODB component name will be copied into the Selected Components list shown at the bottom of the Add Reference dialog box. When you've finished selecting components, clicking OK adds a reference to the selected components to your Visual Studio.NET project.

Manually Creating the COM InterOp Assemblies

If you can't locate the ADODB assembly on your system, or if you have other COM objects you've created that you want to make use of in your .NET applications, you can use the tlbimp (Type Library Importer) utility that Microsoft has provided with the .NET Framework. The tlbimp.exe program allows you to import COM DLLs into .NET assemblies. You can run the tlbimp.exe from the Visual Studio Command Console as follows:

```
tlbimp.exe "C:\Program Files\Common Files\System\ado\msado15.dll"
```

Running the tlbimp.exe program with this argument will result in the creation of the ADODB.DLL in the C:\Program Files\Microsoft.NET\Primary Interop folder. After creating the ADODB.DLL, you can then add a reference to the ADODB component using the steps described in the preceding section.

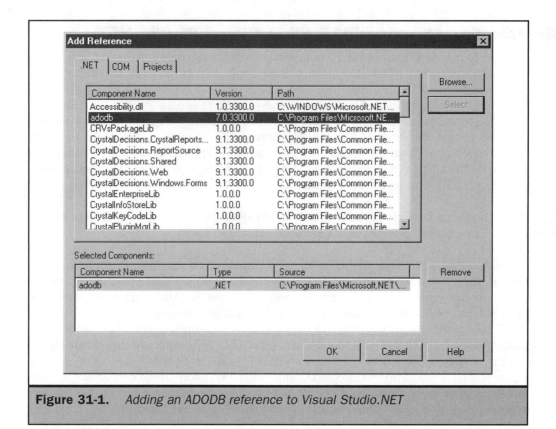

Figure 31-1. *Adding an ADODB reference to Visual Studio.NET*

Importing the ADODB DLL

After you've created a .NET assembly for the COM object you want to use in your .NET application, you can optionally import that assembly into your .NET application. Importing the assembly into the application isn't a requirement. However, doing so allows you to refer to the objects in your application without needing to use the fully qualified name. For instance, the ADODB component contains the Connection, Recordset, and Command objects. Without adding an import directive, you would need to reference each component using its fully qualified name: ADODB.Connection, ADODB.Recordset, and ADODB.Command. When an import directive is added to your project, you have the option to drop the ADODB qualifier and refer to the objects using their base name much like in standard ADO. In this case: Connection, Recordset, and Command.

To add an import directive for the ADODB.DLL assembly to a VB.NET project, you would add the following code to the declarations section of your source file:

```
Imports ADODB
```

To add an import directive for the ADODB assembly to a C# project, the code would appear as follows:

```
using ADODB;
```

Using an ADO Recordset

After adding an import directive to your code, you're ready to begin using the different ADO objects contained in the ADODB assembly. The first thing that you'll probably want to do is to retrieve data from the data source and populate an ADO Recordset object. The Recordset is the primary ADO object that's used to retrieve data. The following ADORecordset subroutine illustrates opening an ADO Recordset object that selects those rows in the Customers table of the Northwind database where the Country column contains the value of Denmark:

```
Private Sub ADORecordset(ByVal sServer As String, _
ByVal sDB As String)
    Dim ADOcn As Connection = New ADODB.Connection()
    Dim ADOrs As Recordset = New ADODB.Recordset()
    Dim ADOfld As Field
    ADOcn.Open("PROVIDER=SQLOLEDB;DATA SOURCE=" & sServer _
        & ";INITIAL CATALOG=" & sDB & ";INTEGRATED SECURITY=SSPI;")
    ' Create a recordset
    Dim sSQL As String = "SELECT CustomerID, CompanyName, " _
        & "Country FROM Customers WHERE Country = 'Denmark'"
    ADOrs.Open(sSQL, ADOcn, _
        ADODB.CursorTypeEnum.adOpenForwardOnly, _
        ADODB.LockTypeEnum.adLockReadOnly, 0)
    'Setup column heading in the list
    lstResults.Items.Add(ADOrs.Fields("CustomerID").Name & vbTab _
        & ADOrs.Fields("CompanyName").Name & vbTab & vbTab _
        & ADOrs.Fields("Country").Name)
    ' The recordset can't be bound so read one row at a time
    Do Until ADOrs.EOF
        ' Add the Recordset fields to a list and get the next row
        lstResults.Items.Add(ADOrs.Fields("CustomerID").Value & _
            vbTab & vbTab & ADOrs.Fields("CompanyName").Value & _
            vbTab & vbTab & ADOrs.Fields("Country").Value)
        ADOrs.MoveNext()
    Loop
    ' Close the Recordset
```

```
      ADOrs.Close()
      ADOcn.Close()
End Sub
```

The C# version of the ADORecordset subroutine is shown here:

```
private void ADORecordset(string sServer, string sDB)
{
    ADODB.Connection ADOcn = new ADODB.Connection();
    ADODB.Recordset ADOrs = new ADODB.Recordset();
    ADOcn.Open("PROVIDER=SQLOLEDB;DATA SOURCE=" + sServer
        + ";INITIAL CATALOG=" + sDB + ";INTEGRATED SECURITY=SSPI;",
        "","",-1);
    // Create a recordset
    string sSQL = "SELECT CustomerID, CompanyName, Country "
        + "FROM Customers WHERE Country = 'Denmark'";
    ADOrs.Open(sSQL, ADOcn, ADODB.CursorTypeEnum.adOpenForwardOnly,
        ADODB.LockTypeEnum.adLockReadOnly, 0);
    // Setup column heading in the list
    lstResults.Items.Add(ADOrs.Fields["CustomerID"].Name + '\t'
        + ADOrs.Fields["CompanyName"].Name + '\t' + '\t'
        + ADOrs.Fields["Country"].Name);
    // The recordset can't be bound so read one row at a time
    while (!ADOrs.EOF)
    {
        // Add the Recordset fields to a list and get the next row
        lstResults.Items.Add(
            (string)ADOrs.Fields["CustomerID"].Value + '\t' +
            '\t' + (string)ADOrs.Fields["CompanyName"].Value +
            '\t' + '\t' + (string)ADOrs.Fields["Country"].Value);
        ADOrs.MoveNext();
    }
    // Close the Recordset
    ADOrs.Close();
    ADOcn.Close();
}
```

Note *In these examples, the sServer variable contains the name of a SQL Server system and the sDB variable contains the name of Northwind—setting the default database to the Northwind sample database included with SQL Server.*

At the beginning of this subroutine, you can see where instances of an ADO Connection and Recordset object named ADOcn and ADOrs are created. Like its name implies, the ADO Connection object is used to open a connection to the data source, whereas the ADO Recordset object is used to send a SQL select statement to the target database and hold the resultset that is returned. The Recordset object can provide navigation, data access, and update capabilities. Next, the ADOcn Connection object's Open method is used to initiate an active connection with the database system. The first parameter of the Open method takes an OLE DB connection string. In this case, the Provider keyword indicates that the OLE DB Provider for SQL Server will be used. The Data Source keyword specifies that the target database is identified by the sServer variable. The Initial Catalog keyword sets the default database to the database name contained in the sDB variable. Finally, the Integrated Security keyword indicates that Windows authentication will be used to connect to the target database. For more information about OLE connection strings, you can refer to Chapter 6.

Note *In C#, you need to explicitly define all of the parameters that are required by a given method. VB.NET does not have this requirement. That's why the Open method in the C# version of this code requires three extra parameters. In the case of the Connection object's Open method, these parameters are optionally used to pass in the user ID, password, and options flag. The user ID and password are passed in as empty strings; the options value of –1 in the fourth parameter indicates that the connection is opened synchronously.*

After a connection has been opened to the data source, a string variable named sSQL is assigned with a SQL Select statement that will retrieve the CustomerID, CompanyName, and Country column from the Customers table where the contents of the Country column contains the value of Denmark. Then the Open method of the ADOrs Recordset object is used to populate the Recordset object. The first parameter of the ADOrs Recordset object's Open method accepts the SQL statement that will be sent to the data source. The second parameter accepts the name of an active ADO Connection object—in this case, the ADOcn object that was just opened. The third and fourth parameters indicate the type of connection that will be opened. The value of CursorTypeEnum.adForwardOnly indicates that the Recordset object will use a forward-only cursor that provides high performance but is not scrollable. The value of LockTypeEnum.adLockReadOnly in the fourth parameter indicates that the Recordset will be read-only, so no updates are allowed. The value of 0 in the fourth parameter indicates that the type of command used in the first parameter is a SQL statement.

The next section of code outputs the contents of the ADOrs Recordset object to a .NET List Box named lstResults. An ADO Recordset object cannot be directly bound to a .NET data-aware interface component, so the contents of the Recordset must be manually parsed. First, the column headings of the columns retrieved in the Recordset object are written to the top line in the lstResults ListBox. You add items to the .NET Framework's List Box by invoking the Add method that's supplied by the Items collection of the lstResults List Box object. In this case, the List Box's Add method is passed a string parameter that concatenates the value contained in the Name property of each ADO Field object that's contained in the Fields collection. You should note that the name of each column is used as the index to identify the desired ADO Field object in the Fields collection. Tab characters are inserted into the string just to help the column heading line up better within the List Box.

Note *The .NET Framework does not provide support for using default properties. This means that when using ADO objects, you cannot use the Bang notation (e.g., ADOrs!CustomerID) that was supported by VB 6.0 and VC++. Instead, you need to explicitly define the properties you want to work with.*

Next, all of the row values in the Recordset are added to the List Box by setting up a looping structure that is repeated until the ADOrs.EOF property contains the value of True—indicating the end of the rows in the Recordset. In this instance, the List Box's Add method is passed a string parameter that concatenates the value contained in the Value property of each ADO Field object. Again, Tab characters are inserted just to help the results line up better in the List Box. Then the ADOrs Recordset object's MoveNext method is used to move the pointer to the next row in the resultset.

At the end of this subroutine, you can see that the ADOrs Recordset object and the ADOcn Connection object are explicitly closed using each respective object's Close method. Explicitly calling the Close method is an essential technique in .NET applications to ensure that the object resources are released.

Loading an ADO.NET DataSet from an ADO Recordset

One key step in migrating your ADO applications to ADO.NET is beginning to take advantage of the native ADO.NET objects. In addition to being able to use the native ADO objects such as the Recordset object from .NET applications, you can also create interfaces between these ADO objects and the native ADO.NET objects. The following example illustrates how you can load an ADO.NET DataSet from the data contained in an ADO Recordset object. This can be advantageous because the DataSet can be bound to other .NET interface objects like the DataGrid. In the following example, you can see how to open an ADO Recordset and then use the .NET DataAdapter's Fill method to populate a DataSet using the ADO Recordset. Filling a DataSet with the contents of an ADO object is a one-way operation. In other words, once you move the data from the ADO Recordset object into the ADO.NET DataSet object, the Recordset object is closed, and all of the data operations such as navigation and updates are performed using the DataSet object.

```
Private Sub ADOLoadDataSet(ByVal sServer As String, _
      ByVal sDB As String)
   Dim ADOcn As Connection = New ADODB.Connection()
   Dim ADOrs As Recordset = New ADODB.Recordset()
   ADOcn.Open("PROVIDER=SQLOLEDB;DATA SOURCE=" & sServer _
      & ";INITIAL CATALOG=" & sDB & ";INTEGRATED SECURITY=SSPI;")
   ' Create a recordset. Bear in mind that
   Dim sSQL As String = "SELECT * FROM Customers " & _
      "WHERE Country = 'USA'"
   ADOrs.Open(sSQL, ADOcn, CursorTypeEnum.adOpenForwardOnly, _
      LockTypeEnum.adLockReadOnly, 0)
   Dim da As New OleDbDataAdapter()
   Dim ds As New DataSet()
   ' Load the Recordset into a DataTable object
   ' Fill closes the Recordset upon completion
   da.Fill(ds, ADOrs, "ADOrsTable")
   ' Bind the DataTable to a grid
   grdResults.DataSource = ds.Tables("ADOrsTable")
   ADOcn.Close()
End Sub
```

The C# version of the ADOLoadDataset subroutine follows:

```
private void ADOLoadDataSet(string sServer, string sDB)
{
    ADODB.Connection ADOcn = new ADODB.Connection();
    ADODB.Recordset ADOrs = new ADODB.Recordset();
    string sSQL = "SELECT * FROM Customers WHERE Country = 'USA'";
    ADOcn.Open("PROVIDER=SQLOLEDB;DATA SOURCE=" + sServer
        + ";INITIAL CATALOG=" + sDB + ";INTEGRATED SECURITY=SSPI;",
        "","",-1);
    ADOrs.Open(sSQL,ADOcn,CursorTypeEnum.adOpenForwardOnly,
        LockTypeEnum.adLockReadOnly, 0);
    // Converts a Recordset into a DataTable object
    OleDbDataAdapter da = new OleDbDataAdapter();
    DataSet ds = new DataSet();
    da.Fill(ds, ADOrs, "ADOrsTable");
    // The recordset is implicitly closed and is unusable
    // Bind the DataTable to a grid
    grdResults.DataSource = ds.Tables["ADOrsTable"];
    ADOcn.Close();
}
```

At the beginning of the ADOLoadDataSet subroutine, you can see where an ADO Connection object named ADOcn and an ADORecordset object named ADOrs are created. Next, the ADOcn Connection object's Open method is used to initiate an active connection with the database system. The first parameter of the Open method uses an OLE DB connection string that sets the OLE DB Provider to SQLOLEDB, the SQL Server OLE DB Provider. The database server and default database are set to the values contained in the sServer and sDB variables, and the authentication method is set to use integrated Windows security.

Next, a SQL statement that retrieves all of the columns from the Customers table where the Country column contains the value USA is assigned to the sSQL variable. The sSQL variable is then passed as the first parameter of the ADOrs Recordset object's Open method. The remaining parameters specify that the ADOrs Recordset object will be forward-only and read-only.

After the ADOrs Recordset object is populated, the next two lines create an OleDbDataAdpater object and a DataSet object named da and ds, respectively. Then the OleDbDataAdapter's Fill method is used to create a new DataTable object within the DataSet. This overloaded instance of the OleDbDataAdpater's Fill method accepts three parameters. The first parameter identifies the DataSet that is the target of the Fill operation. The second parameter identifies the ADO Recordset object that is the data source. And the third parameter optionally names the DataTable object that will be created in the DataSet. In this example, a DataTable named ADOrsTable will be created in the ds DataSet based on the data in the ADOrs Recordset object. The Fill method implicitly closes the ADOrs Recordset object after it completes—making it impossible to use the Recordset object again unless it is explicitly reopened. Once the DataTable has been created, it's bound to a DataGrid object named grdResults and the ADOcn Connection object is closed.

| **Note** | *While the Recordset is closed following the completion of the OleDbDataAdapter's Fill, you can still post data changes back to the database from the DataSet via the DataAdapter.* |

Updating Data with an ADO Recordset Object

The previous examples illustrated how to retrieve data into a .NET application using the ADO Recordset object. However, the ADO Recordset object isn't restricted to being used in a read-only mode. In fact, it's completely capable of performing all of the same functionality from a .NET application as it is from a legacy COM application. In the next example, you'll see how you can create an updateable ADO Recordset object from a .NET application and use it to add rows to a table. Here, the Recordset object is opened using an updateable keyset cursor, which allows forward and backward scrolling, as well as bookmarking rows for direct navigation.

In order to run the following example, you need to create the department table using the following SQL:

```
CREATE TABLE [dbo].[Department] (
      [DepartmentID] [int] NOT NULL ,
      [DepartmentName] [char] (25)
) ON [PRIMARY]
```

The VB.NET code to update an ADO Recordset object follows:

```
Private Sub ADOUpdateRecordset(ByVal sServer As String, _
        ByVal sDB As String)
    Dim ADOcn As Connection = New ADODB.Connection()
    Dim ADOrs As Recordset = New ADODB.Recordset()
    Dim ADOfld As Field
    ADOcn.Open("PROVIDER=SQLOLEDB;DATA SOURCE=" & sServer _
        & ";INITIAL CATALOG=" & sDB & ";INTEGRATED SECURITY=SSPI;")
    ' Create a recordset
    Dim sSQL As String = "SELECT DepartmentID, DepartmentName" & _
        & "FROM Department"
    ADOrs.Open(sSQL, ADOcn, CursorTypeEnum.adOpenKeyset, _
        LockTypeEnum.adLockOptimistic, 0)
    Dim i As Integer
    For i = 1 To 10
        ' Create anew buffer
        ADOrs.AddNew()
        ' Set the column values
        ADOrs.Fields("DepartmentID").Value = i
        ADOrs.Fields("DepartmentName").Value = _
            "Department" & CStr(i)
        ' Add the row
        ADOrs.Update()
    Next
    ' Display the updated recordset in a grid
    Dim da As New OleDbDataAdapter()
    Dim ds As New DataSet()
    ' Load the Recordset into a DataTable object
    '  Fill closes the Recordset upon completion
    da.Fill(ds, ADOrs, "ADOrsTable")
    ' Bind the DataTable to a Grid
    grdResults.DataSource = ds.Tables("ADOrsTable")
    ADOcn.Close()
End Sub
```

The C# version of the ADOUpdateRecordset subroutine is shown here:

```csharp
private void ADOUpdateRecordset(string sServer, string sDB)
{
    ADODB.Connection ADOcn = new ADODB.Connection();
    ADODB.Recordset ADOrs = new ADODB.Recordset();
    ADOcn.Open("PROVIDER=SQLOLEDB;DATA SOURCE=" + sServer
        + ";INITIAL CATALOG=" + sDB + ";INTEGRATED SECURITY=SSPI;",
        "","",-1);
    // Create a recordset
    string sSQL = "SELECT DepartmentID, DepartmentName " +
        "FROM Department";
    // For C#, make sure you set up a client cursor
    ADOrs.CursorLocation = CursorLocationEnum.adUseClient;
    ADOrs.Open(sSQL, ADOcn, CursorTypeEnum.adOpenKeyset,
        LockTypeEnum.adLockOptimistic, -1);
    int i;
    for (i = 1; i <= 10; i++)
    {
        // Create a new buffer
        // C# requires you to supply the AddNew parameters
        ADOrs.AddNew("DepartmentID", i);
        ADOrs.Update("DepartmentName", "Department" + i);
    }
    // Display the updated recordset in a grid
    OleDbDataAdapter da = new OleDbDataAdapter();
    DataSet ds = new DataSet();
    // Load the Recordset into a DataTable object
    // Fill closes the Recordset upon completion
    da.Fill(ds, ADOrs, "ADOrsTable");
    // Bind the DataTable to a Grid
    grdResults.DataSource = ds.Tables["ADOrsTable"];
    // Close the ADO connection
    ADOcn.Close();
}
```

At the beginning of the ADOUpdateRecordset subroutine, you can see where the ADO Connection and Recordset objects named ADOcn and ADOrs are created. Next, the ADOcn Connection object's Open method is used to initiate a connection to the database system identified in the sServer variable that's passed into the beginning of this subroutine. From the connection string, you can see that this connection uses the SQL Server OLE DB Provider and the database contained in the sDB variable will be used as the initial catalog (aka. default database) and the connection is set to use integrated Windows security.

After a connection has been opened, the sSQL variable is assigned a SQL Select statement that will retrieve all the DepartmentID and DepartmentName columns from the Department table that was built earlier in this chapter.

Next, the ADOrs Recordset object's Open method is used to populate the Recordset object. As in the earlier examples, the first parameter contains the SQL statement that's sent to the target database; the second parameter contains an active ADO Connection object. In this case, note that the third parameter of the Recordset's Open method sets the Recordset's cursor type to CursorTypeEnum.adOpenKeyset. Unlike the forward-only cursor shown in the previous examples, the keyset cursor supports both resultset navigation and updating. The fourth parameter uses the LockTypeEnum.Optimistic value to set the locking type to optimistic—which essentially means that no lock is held on the data in the Recordset until immediately before any updates are sent to the database. These values in the third and forth parameters allow the ADO Recordset object to update the data in the Recordset, and those updates will be immediately propagated back to the data source. One key difference between the VB.NET routine and C# routine is that C# requires you to explicitly set the cursor location to a client cursor using the CursorLocation.adUseClient enumerator for the Recordset object's CursorLocation property.

Once the Recordset has been populated with a resultset from the target database, a For-Next loop is used to add 10 rows to the department table. The first operation within the For-Next loop is the invocation of the ADOrs Recordset object's AddNew method. The AddNew method essentially allocates a buffer within the Recordset object for a new row. Next, the Value property of the two Field objects contained in the ADOrs.Fields collection are assigned new values. For the sake of simplicity, this example assigns the DepartmentID column the value of the loop counter contained in variable i, and the string containing the name "Department" is concatenated with the value of the loop counter and assigned to the DepartmentName column. At the bottom of the For-Next loop, the ADOrs Recordset object's Update method is called to add the new row to the Recordset, which also results in the row being added to the data source.

Note   *C# doesn't allow the use of default parameters, so you need to explicitly define each of the parameters. In this example, the AddNew method of the C# ADOUpdateRecordset subroutine supplies the two optional parameters with the values used for the first column. Here, the string "DepartmentID" identifies the column name in the new Recordset buffer, and the value of variable i supplies the value for the column. Subsequent usage of the Update method supplies the remaining column values.*

The next section of code displays the updated Recordset object in a grid. First, an OleDbDataAdpater object and a DataSet object named da and ds are instantiated. Then the OleDbDataAdapter's Fill method is used to create a new DataTable object within the DataSet named ADOrsTable, using the data in the ADOrs Recordset object. The Fill method implicitly closes the ADOrs Recordset object after it completes. Once the DataTable has been created, it's bound to a DataGrid object named grdResults and the ADOcn Connection object is closed.

Using an ADO Command Object

The previous examples all illustrated using the ADO Recordset object; however, that's not the only ADO object that's supported within the .NET Framework. All of the ADO objects can be used. To round out the ADO examples, the following example illustrates using the ADODB assembly to invoke the ADO Command object. In this case, the ADO Command object will be used to execute a parameterized query that updates the data in the department table that was used in the earlier example. In this section of code, you'll see how to create an ADO Command object and add ADO Parameter objects to it, as well as how to set the Parameter object's attributes:

```
Private Sub ADOCommand(ByVal sServer As String, ByVal sDB As String)
    Dim ADOcn As Connection = New ADODB.Connection()
    Dim ADOrs As Recordset = New ADODB.Recordset()
    Dim ADOcmd As Command = New ADODB.Command()
    ADOcn.Open("PROVIDER=SQLOLEDB;DATA SOURCE=" & sServer _
        & ";INITIAL CATALOG=" & sDB & ";INTEGRATED SECURITY=SSPI;")
    With ADOcmd
        .ActiveConnection = ADOcn
        .CommandText = _
            "UPDATE department SET DepartmentName = ? " & _
            "WHERE DepartmentID = ?"
        .CreateParameter(, DataTypeEnum.adChar, _
            ParameterDirectionEnum.adParamInput, 25)
        .CreateParameter(, DataTypeEnum.adInteger, _
            ParameterDirectionEnum.adParamInput)
    End With
    Dim i As Integer
    For i = 1 To 10
        ADOcmd.Parameters(0).Value = "Updated DepartmentName:" & _
            CStr(i)
        ADOcmd.Parameters(1).Value = CStr(i)
        ADOcmd.Execute(, , -1)
    Next
    ADOrs.Open("SELECT * FROM department", ADOcn, _
        CursorTypeEnum.adOpenForwardOnly, _
        LockTypeEnum.adLockReadOnly, 0)
    ' Display the updated recordset in a grid
    Dim da As New OleDbDataAdapter()
    Dim ds As New DataSet()
    ' Load the Recordset into a DataTable object
    '  Fill closes the Recordset upon completion
```

```
    da.Fill(ds, ADOrs, "ADOrsTable")
    ' Bind the DataTable to a Grid
    grdResults.DataSource = ds.Tables("ADOrsTable")
    ADOcn.Close()
End Sub
```

The C# version of the ADOCommand subroutine follows:

```csharp
private void ADOCommand(string sServer, string sDB)
{
    ADODB.Connection ADOcn = new ADODB.Connection();
    ADODB.Recordset ADOrs = new ADODB.Recordset();
    ADODB.Command ADOcmd = new ADODB.Command();
    ADOcn.Open("PROVIDER=SQLOLEDB;DATA SOURCE=" + sServer +
        ";INITIAL CATALOG=" + sDB + ";INTEGRATED SECURITY=SSPI;",
        "","",-1);
    // Set the Command object properties
    ADOcmd.ActiveConnection = ADOcn;
    ADOcmd.CommandText =
        "UPDATE department SET DepartmentName = ? " +
        "WHERE DepartmentID = ?";
    ADOcmd.CreateParameter("", DataTypeEnum.adChar,
        ParameterDirectionEnum.adParamInput, 25 ,"");
    ADOcmd.CreateParameter("" , DataTypeEnum.adInteger,
        ParameterDirectionEnum.adParamInput, 4, 0);
    // Update 10 rows
    int i;
    object nRowsAffected;
    object o = Missing.Value;
    for (i = 1; i <= 10; i++)
    {
        ADOcmd.Parameters[0].Value = "Updated DepartmentName:" + i;
        ADOcmd.Parameters[1].Value = i;
        ADOcmd.Execute(out nRowsAffected, ref o, 1);
    }
    // Open a recordset
    ADOrs.Open("SELECT * FROM department", ADOcn,
        CursorTypeEnum.adOpenForwardOnly,
        LockTypeEnum.adLockReadOnly, 0);
    // Display the updated recordset in a grid
    OleDbDataAdapter da = new OleDbDataAdapter();
```

```
DataSet ds = new DataSet();
// Load the Recordset into a DataTable object
// Fill closes the Recordset upon completion
da.Fill(ds, ADOrs, "ADOrsTable");
// Bind the DataTable to a Grid
grdResults.DataSource = ds.Tables["ADOrsTable"];
// Close the ADO connection
ADOcn.Close();
}
```

At the top of the ADOCommand subroutine, you can see where the ADO Connection, Recordset, and Command objects named ADOcn, ADOrs, and ADOcmd are created. Next, the ADOcn Connection object's Open method is used to initiate a connection to the database system identified in the sServer variable. Like the earlier examples, this connection uses the SQL Server OLE DB Provider to connect to the database identified in the sDB variable using integrated security.

After a connection has been opened, the ADOcmd Command object's properties are assigned. The VB.NET version uses a With statement for this; the C# version, which doesn't support the With structure, uses simple assignment statements. First, the ActiveConnection property is set to the ADOcn Connection object. Next, the CommandText property is assigned a SQL Update statement. In this example, note that the Update statement is using two parameters indicated with the "?" character. The "?" is used as a parameter marker and will be substituted with the value in an associated Parameter object at runtime. Next, the ADOcmd.CreateParameter method is used to create two Parameter objects that are added to the ADOcmd Command object. The first parameter accepts a string that optionally names the parameter. The second parameter is used to identify the Parameter object's data type. The value of DataTypeEnum.adChar indicates a character value. The third parameter of the CreateParameter method specifies the direction of the parameter. In this case, the value of ParameterDirectionEnum.adParamInput shows that both Parameter objects will be input parameters. The fourth parameter shows the size of the parameter; the fifth parameter provides an optional default value.

Next, a For-Next loop is used to update the 10 rows in the department table that were added in an earlier example. With the For-Next loop, the first statement sets the first Parameter object, identified with an index of 0, to a new string value starting with the characters "Updated DepartmentName" concatenated with the loop counter. The second statement sets the Parameter object, identified with the index of 1, to the value of the loop counter. After values have been assigned to the Parameter objects, the ADOcmd .Execute method is called to actually perform the update. You might notice that the VB.NET version does some of the work for you by automatically handling the three

ADO.NET DATA INTEGRATION

optional parameters of the ADOcmd.Execute method, whereas the C# version requires that you explicitly provide variables for the parameters.

Note *In the previous C# examples, you saw how to use the various ADO functions that required optional parameters by explicitly supplying the parameter values in your code. Note that this example is different. In this case, the System.Reflection namespace is added to the Visual Studio.NET project and the Missing.Value member of that namespace is used to handle the optional parameter. In this C# code, an object named o is created and assigned the Missing.Value property. This allows the object to be passed to the ADO Execute method without explicitly assigning it a value. This technique allows C# code to work much more like VB.NET, which has the capability to supply default parameters.*

The last section of code then opens a Recordset object and uses the OleDbDataAdapter's Fill method to load a DataTable with the resultset from the Recordset. Then the DataTable is bound to a DataGrid named grdResults and displayed to the user, and the ADO Connection object is closed.

ADO and ADO.NET Coexistence Issues

As you've seen in the previous examples, the .NET Framework is fully capable of utilizing COM objects like the ADO object library. And, in fact, doing so is very much like using ADO from the earlier COM-based languages such as VB 6.0 and VC++. However, as you probably noted from some of the earlier examples, the usage isn't identical—especially if you're writing in C#. You need to look out for several differences, including the following:

- .NET languages such as VB.NET and C# can't use default properties.
- .NET languages require the use of parentheses when calling methods.
- C# explicitly requires you to supply values for all of the method parameters.
- Arguments passed to subroutines default to ByVal rather than ByRef.

Summary

Although ADO.NET is definitely the preferred method of accessing data using the .NET Framework, the difference between .NET applications and COM-based applications, and the difference between ADO.NET and ADO, combine to make migration a long-term process, thereby ensuring that ADO code will be around for a long time to come. In this chapter, you saw how you could use ADO with ADO.NET applications as one method to begin moving your existing ADO code to ADO.NET.

For more information about ADO, you can refer to the following resources:

- *SQL Server 2000 Developer's Guide*, Osborne McGraw Hill, Otey and Conte
- http://msdn.microsoft.com/library/default.asp?url=/library/en-us/ado270/htm/dasdkadooverview.asp

The
Complete
Reference

Part VII

Appendixes

Appendix A

System.Data
Namespace Reference

System.Data Namespace

The System.Data namespace contains classes that make up the ADO.NET architecture and allows you to efficiently manage data from multiple data sources. ADO.NET provides the tools to access and manipulate data in multiple-tier systems in an environment like the Internet, as well as two-tier, client/server–style applications, and even single-tier, desktop style applications.

At the heart of the ADO.NET architecture is the DataSet class, which can contain multiple DataTable objects. Each DataTable contains data from a single data source. The primary classes contained in the System.Data namespace follow:

Constraint Class   The Constraint class represents a rule that is used on DataColumn objects to maintain DataTable integrity.

ConstraintCollection Class   The ConstraintCollection class contains a collection of Constraint objects.

ConstraintException Class   The ConstraintException class contains the exception that is thrown when a constraint has been violated.

DataColumn Class   The DataColumn class contains the schema for a DataTable column.

DataColumnChangeEventArgs Class   The DataColumnChangeEventArgs class supplies the data for the ColumnChanging event when a DataTable column value changes.

DataColumnCollection Class   The DataColumnCollection class contains a collection of DataColumn objects.

DataException Class   The DataException class contains the exception that is thrown when an error is generated by ADO.NET components.

DataRelation Class   The DataRelation class parent/child relationship information used to relate two DataTable objects together.

DataRelationCollection Class   The DataRelationCollection class contains a collection of DataRelation objects.

DataRow Class   The DataRow class represents a DataTable row of data.

DataRowBuilder Class   The DataRowBuilder class supports the .NET infrastructure and is not used directly from your code.

DataRowChangeEventArgs Class   The DataRowChangeEventArgs class supplies the data for the RowChanged, RowChanging, OnRowDeleted, and OnRowDeleting events when a DataRow changes.

DataRowCollection Class   The DataRowCollection class contains a collection of DataRow objects.

DataRowView Class   The DataRowView class represents a Windows Form control that is a customized view of a DataRow object.

DataSet Class   The DataSet class is a set of DataTable objects. The cache of data in the DataSet is in-memory.

DataSysDescriptionAttribute Class   The DataSysDescriptionAttribute class allows you to attach a description to a property or event.

DataTable Class   The DataTable class represents a table of in-memory data.

DataTableCollection Class   The DataTableCollection class contains a collection of DataTable objects for a specific DataSet.

DataView Class   The DataView class contains a customized view of data in a DataTable.

DataViewManager Class   The DataViewManager class contains a DataViewSettingCollection object for each DataSet's DataTable.

DataViewSetting Class   The DataViewSetting class contains default settings for DataView objects that were created using the DataViewManager class.

DataViewSettingCollection Class   The DataViewSettingCollection class contains a collection of DataViewSetting objects.

DBConcurrencyException Class   The DBConcurrencyException class contains the exception that is thrown when the number of affected rows of a DataAdapter is zero when an updated operation is attempted.

DeletedRowInaccessibleException Class   The DeletedRowInaccessibleException class contains the exception that is thrown when a DataRow object has been deleted and an action is attempted against it.

DuplicateNameException Class   The DuplicateNameException class contains the exception that is thrown when an add operation is attempted to a DataSet-type object and a duplicate database name is found.

EvaluateException Class   The EvaluateException class contains the exception that is thrown when a DataColumn object's Expression property cannot be evaluated.

FillErrorEventArgs Class   The FillErrorEventArgs class supplies the data for the FillError event for the DbDataAdapter object.

ForeignKeyConstraint Class   The ForeignKeyConstraint class contains the rules for actions to perform when a column is updated or deleted.

InRowChangingEventException Class   The InRowChangingEventException class contains the exception that is thrown when calling the RowChanging event's EndEdit method.

InternalDataCollectionBase Class   The InternalDataCollectionBase class is the standard base class for deriving other collection classes.

InvalidConstraintException Class   The InvalidConstraintException class contains the exception that is thrown when a relation is incorrectly created or accessed.

InvalidExpressionException Class   The InvalidExpressionException class contains the exception that is thrown when a DataColumn object that contains an invalid expression is added to the DataColumnCollection.

MergeFailedEventArgs Class   The MergeFailedEventArgs class contains conflict data when a target and source DataRow have the same primary key information.

MissingPrimaryKeyException Class   The MissingPrimaryKeyException class contains the exception that is thrown when a row in a table with no primary key is accessed.

NoNullAllowedException Class   The NoNullAllowedException class contains the exception that is thrown when a column's AllowDBNull property is set to False and null is being inserted into the column.

PropertyCollection Class   The PropertyCollection class allows you to add custom properties to the DataColumn, DataSet, and DataTable objects.

ReadOnlyException Class   The ReadOnlyException class contains the exception that is thrown when a read-only column is attempting to be changed.

RowNotInTableException Class   The RowNotInTableException class contains the exception that is thrown when an action is attempted against a nonexistent DataRow in a DataTable.

StateChangeEventArgs Class   The StateChangeEventArgs class supplies the data for the state change event for the .NET provider.

StrongTypingException Class   The StrongTypingException class contains the exception that is thrown when a user accesses the DBNull property of a strong-typed DataSet.

SyntaxErrorException Class   The SyntaxErrorException class contains the exception that is thrown when a DataColumn object contains a syntax error in the Expression property.

TypedDataSetGenerator Class   The TypedDataSetGenerator class contains information for creating strong-type DataSets.

TypedDataSetGeneratorException Class   The TypedDataSetGeneratorException class contains the exception that is thrown when generating a strong-type DataSet and a name conflict occurs.

UniqueConstraint Class   The UniqueConstraint class is the rule stating that the primary key must be unique.

VersionNotFoundException Class   The VersionNotFoundException class contains the exception that is thrown when an attempt is made to retrieve the version information of a DataRow that does not exist.

DataColumnChangeEventHandler Delegate   The DataColumnChangeEventHandler delegate is the method that handles the ColumnChanging event.

DataRowChangeEventHandler Delegate   The DataRowChangeEventHandler delegate is the method that handles the RowChanging, RowChanged, RowDeleting, and RowDeleted events of the DataTable object.

FillErrorEventHandler Delegate   The FillErrorEventHandler delegate is the method that handles the FillError event.

MergeFailedEventHandler Delegate   The MergeFailedEventHandler delegate is the method that handles the MergeFailed event.

StateChangeEventHandler Delegate   The StateChangeEventHandler delegate is the method that handles the StateChange event.

AcceptRejectRule Enumeration   The AcceptRejectRule enumeration contains information about the actions that are used in the AcceptChanges or RejectChanges method. These actions are used on a DataTable with a ForeignKeyConstraint.

CommandBehavior Enumeration   The CommandBehavior enumeration contains information about the literals that are used by the ExecuteReader method.

CommandType Enumeration   The CommandType enumeration contains information about how a string command is understood.

ConnectionState Enumeration   The ConnectionState enumeration contains information about the literals that are used with the State property of the OleDbConnection and SqlConnection objects.

DataRowAction Enumeration   The DataRowAction enumeration contains information about the literals that are used by the DataRow object.

DataRowState Enumeration   The DataRowState enumeration contains information about the literals that are used with the RowState property of the DataRow object.

DataRowVersion Enumeration   The DataRowVersion enumeration contains information about the literals that are used to describe the version of the DataRow object.

DataViewRowState Enumeration   The DataViewRowState enumeration contains information about the literals that are used to describe the version of the data in the DataRow object.

DbType Enumeration   The DbType enumeration contains the data types that are used in the fields, properties, or parameters of the data provider.

IsolationLevel Enumeration   The IsolationLevel enumeration contains information about the literals that are used when a data provider performs a transaction.

KeyRestrictionBehavior Enumeration   The KeyRestrictionBehavior enumeration contains information about the literals that are used when a data provider performs a transaction.

MappingType Enumeration   The MappingType enumeration contains information about the literals that are used in the ColumnMapping property of the DataColumn object.

MissingMappingAction Enumeration   The MissingMappingAction enumeration contains information about the literals that are used when mapping is missing from a source table of column.

MissingSchemaAction Enumeration   The MissingSchemaAction enumeration contains information about the literals that are used when a DataTable or DataColumn object is missing and data is being added to a DataSet object.

ParameterDirection Enumeration   The ParameterDirection enumeration contains information about the literals that are used with the parameter direction of the OleDbParameter and SqlParameter objects.

PropertyAttributes Enumeration   The PropertyAttributes enumeration contains information about the attributes of a property.

Rule Enumeration   The Rule enumeration contains information about the literals that are used with ForeignKeyConstraint objects.

SchemaType Enumeration   The SchemaType enumeration contains information about the literals that are used with the FillSchema method.

SqlDbType Enumeration   The SqlDbType enumeration contains information about the SQL Server data types.

StatementType Enumeration   The StatementType enumeration contains information about the SQL queries used in these classes: OleDbRowUpdatedEventArgs, OleDbRowUpdatingEventArgs, SqlRowUpdatedEventArgs, and SqlRowUpdatingEventArgs.

UpdateRowSource Enumeration   The UpdateRowSource enumeration contains information about the literals that are used in the UpdatedRowSource property.

UpdateStatus Enumeration   The UpdateStatus enumeration contains information about the literals that are used on the remaining rows when an Update method is executed.

XmlReadMode Enumeration   The XmlReadMode enumeration contains information about how XML data is read into a DataSet.

XmlWriteMode Enumeration   The XmlWriteMode enumeration contains information about how XML data is read from a DataSet.

IColumnMapping Interface   The IColumnMapping interface is implemented in System.Data.Common.DataColumnMapping class. It relates a data source column with a DataSet column.

IColumnMappingCollection Interface   The IColumnMappingCollection interface is implemented in System.Data.Common.DataColumnMappingCollection class. It contains a collection of DataColumnMapping objects.

IDataAdapter Interface   The IDataAdapter interface allows an inherited class to implement a DataAdapter.

IDataParameter Interface   The IDataParameter interface represents parameters for Command objects and mappings to the DataSet. It allows an inherited class to implement a Parameter class.

IDataParameterCollection Interface   The IDataParameterCollection interface is a collection of parameters for Command objects and mappings to the DataSet. It allows an inherited class to implement a Parameter collection class.

IDataReader Interface   The IDataReader interface allows for reading forward-only streams of data rows from a data source.

IDataRecord Interface   The IDataRecord interface allows access to column values for rows for a DataReader.

IDbCommand Interface   The IDbCommand interface represents a SQL statement.

IDbConnection Interface   The IDbConnection interface represents a connection to a data source.

IDbDataAdapter Interface   The IDbDataAdapter interface is a set of properties used to fill the DataSet and update the data source.

IDbDataParameter Interface   The IDbDataParameter interface represents parameters for Command objects and mappings to the DataSet. Used by VB.NET data designers.

IDbTransaction Interface   The IDbTransaction interface represents a transaction to be performed against a data source.

ITableMapping Interface   The ITableMapping interface relates a source table to a table in a DataSet.

ITableMappingCollection Interface   The ITableMappingCollection interface contains a collection of DataTableMapping objects.

Constraint Class

The Constraint class represents a constraint that can be imposed on a DataColumn object. A constraint is a rule that is used to maintain the integrity of the data in the associated DataTable.

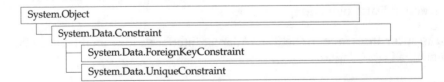

Constructor   Initializes a new instance of the Constraint class

```
protected Constraint();
// C# example
System.Data.DataTable dt = new System.Data.DataTable();
System.Data.Constraint con = dt.Constraints[0];
```

Constraint Class Properties

ConstraintName Property   Returns or sets the name of the Constraint.

```
public virtual string ConstraintName { get; set; }
```

ExtendedProperties Property   Returns a PropertyCollection of the user-defined custom properties for the Constraint object.

```
public PropertyCollection ExtendedProperties { get; }
```

Table Property   Returns the DataTable that this Constraint object applies to.

```
public abstract DataTable Table { get; }
```

_DataSet Property   The _DataSet property supports the .NET infrastructure and is not used directly from your code.

Constraint Class Methods

CheckStateForProperty Method   The CheckStateForProperty method supports the .NET infrastructure and is not used directly from your code.

SetDataSet Method   The SetDataSet method supports the .NET infrastructure and is not used directly from your code.

ToString Method   The ToString method returns the name of the Constraint object as a string.

```
public override string ToString();
```

Mutual Properties, Methods, and Events Included in the Constraint Class

The following lists the mutual properties, methods, and events that are included in the Constraint class.

Inherited from Object

Equals method

Finalize method

GetHashCode method

GetType method

MemberwiseClone method

ConstraintCollection Class

The ConstraintCollection class contains a collection of Constraint objects. You do not create a ConstraintCollection by calling a constructor. The ConstraintCollection is accessed through the DataTable.Constraints property.

```
System.Object
    System.Data.InternalDataCollectionBase
        System.Data.ConstraintCollection
```

ConstraintCollection Class Properties

Item Property   Overloaded. Returns the Constraint object found at the specified integer index or string parameter name.

```
public virtual Constraint this[int index] { get; }
public virtual Constraint this[string parmName] {get; }
```

List Property   Returns an ArrayList of Constraints in this collection.

```
protected override ArrayList List { get; }
```

ConstraintCollection Class Methods

Add Method   Overloaded. The first Add method adds the specified Constraint to the ConstraintCollection. The second Add method creates a UniqueConstraint and adds it to the ConstraintCollection using the specified name, DataColumn, and Boolean indicating whether the column is a primary key; then returns the added Constraint. The third Add method creates a ForeignKeyConstraint and adds it to the ConstraintCollection using the specified name, parent column, and child column; then returns the added Constraint. The fourth Add method creates a UniqueConstraint and adds it to the ConstraintCollection using the specified name, DataColumn array, and Boolean indicating whether the columns are a primary keys; then returns the added Constraint. The fifth Add method creates a ForeignKeyConstraint and adds it to the ConstraintCollection using the specified name, parent column array, and child column array; then returns the added Constraint.

```
public void Add(Constraint);
public virtual Constraint Add(string conName, DataColumn, bool);
public virtual Constraint Add(string conName, DataColumn primKey,
    DataColumn forgKey);
public virtual Constraint Add(string conName, DataColumn[], bool);
public virtual Constraint Add(string conName, DataColumn[] primKey,
    DataColumn[] forgKey);
```

AddRange Method   Adds an array of Constraint objects to the end of the ConstraintCollection.

```
public void AddRange(Constraint[]);
```

CanRemove Method   Returns a Boolean indicating whether the specified Constraint may be removed. True if the Constraint may be removed, otherwise an exception is thrown.

```
public bool CanRemove(Constraint);
```

Clear Method   Removes all the items from the ConstraintCollection.

```
public void Clear();
```

Contains Method   Returns True if the ConstraintCollection contains the specified Constraint name.

```
public bool Contains(string parmName);
```

IndexOf Method   Overloaded. The first IndexOf method returns the location of the specified Constraint object within the ConstraintCollection. The second IndexOf method returns the location of the Constraint object with the specified name.

```
public int IndexOf(Constraint);
public virtual int IndexOf(string);
```

OnCollectionChanged Method   Raises the CollectionChanged event, which invokes the event handler delegate.

```
protected virtual void OnCollectionChanged
    (CollectionChangeEventArgs);
```

Remove Method   Overloaded. The first Remove method removes the specified Constraint from the ConstraintCollection. The second Remove method removes the Constraint object from the collection that matches the specified name.

```
public void Remove(Constraint);
public void Remove(string);
```

RemoveAt Method   The RemoveAt method removes the Constraint object from the ConstraintCollection at the specified integer index. Throws an exception if the Constraint object does not exist in the collection at the specified location.

```
public void RemoveAt(int);
```

ConstraintCollection Class Events

CollectionChanged Event   Fires when a Constraint object is added or removed from the ConstraintCollection.

```
public event CollectionChangeEventHandler CollectionChanged;
```

Mutual Properties, Methods, and Events Included in the ConstraintCollection Class

The following lists the mutual properties, methods, and events that are included in the ConstraintCollection class.

Inherited from Object	Inherited from InternalDataCollectionBase
Equals method	Count property
Finalize method	IsReadOnly property
GetHashCode method	IsSynchronized property
GetType method	SyncRoot property
MemberwiseClone method	CopyTo method
ToString method	GetEnumerator method

ConstraintException Class

The ConstraintException class contains the exception that is thrown when a constraint has been violated.

```
System.Object
    └─ System.Exception
        └─ System.SystemException
            └─ System.Data.DataException
                └─ System.Data.ConstraintException
```

Constructor   Overloaded. The first constructor initializes a new instance of the ConstraintException class. The second constructor initializes a new instance of the ConstraintException class specifying an error message that explains the exception. The third constructor specifies serialization information and streaming context.

```
public ConstraintException();
public ConstraintException(string);
protected ConstraintException(SerializationInfo siEx,
    StreamingContext scEx);
// C# example
System.Data.ConstraintException conEx =
    new System.Data.ConstraintException();
System.Data.ConstraintException conEx2 =
```

```
    new System.Data.ConstraintException("constraint error");
System.Runtime.Serialization.SerializationInfo serInfo;
System.Runtime.Serialization.StreamingContext strmContext;
System.Data.ConstraintException conEx3 =
    new System.Data.ConstraintException(serInfo, strmContext);
```

Mutual Properties, Methods, and Events Included in the ConstraintException Class

The following lists the mutual properties, methods, and events that are included in the ConstraintException class.

Inherited from Exception	Inherited from Object
HelpLink property	Equals method
HResult property	Finalize method
InnerException property	GetHashCode method
Message property	GetType method
Source property	MemberwiseClone method
StackTrace property	
TargetSite property	
GetBaseException method	
GetObjectData method	
ToString method	

DataColumn Class

The DataColumn class contains the schema for a DataTable column.

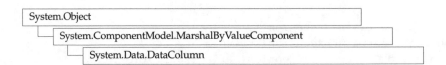

Constructor   Overloaded. The first constructor initializes a new instance of the DataColumn class with no default column name. The second constructor creates a DataColumn object with the specified string column name. The third constructor specifies the string column name and data type to use. The fourth constructor uses the specified string column name, data type, and expression. The fifth constructor uses the specified string column name, data type, expression, and MappingType value.

```
public DataColumn();
public DataColumn(string colName);
public DataColumn(string colName, System.Type dataType);
public DataColumn(string colName, System.Type dataType, string expr);
public DataColumn(string colName, System.Type dataType, string expr,
    MappingType);
// C# example
System.Data.DataColumn dc = new System.Data.DataColumn();
System.Data.DataColumn dc2 = new System.Data.DataColumn("Sales");
System.Data.DataColumn dc3 = new System.Data.DataColumn("Sales",
System.Type.GetType("System.Int32"));
System.Data.DataColumn dc4 = new System.Data.DataColumn("Sales",
    System.Type.GetType("System.Int32"), "Total * .5");
System.Data.DataColumn dc5 = new System.Data.DataColumn("Sales",
    System.Type.GetType("System.Int32"), "Total * .5",
    MappingType.Attribute);
```

DataColumn Class Properties

AllowDBNull Property   Returns or sets a Boolean indicating whether a null value is allowed.

```
public bool AllowDBNull { get; set; }
```

AutoIncrement Property   Returns or sets a Boolean indicating whether the column value will be automatically incremented when new rows are added. True will increment the value, False will not.

```
public bool AutoIncrement { get; set; }
```

AutoIncrementSeed Property   Returns or sets the starting value for the AutoIncrement property.

```
public long AutoIncrementSeed { get; set; }
```

AutoIncrementStep Property   Returns or sets the stepping value for the AutoIncrement property. The default value is 1.

```
public long AutoIncrementStep { get; set; }
```

Caption Property   Returns or sets a string for the caption of the column.

```
public string Caption { get; set; }
```

ColumnMapping Property   Returns or sets the MappingType value for the column.

```
public virtual MappingType ColumnMapping { get; set; }
```

ColumnName Property   Returns or sets a string for the column name of the column.

```
public string ColumnName { get; set; }
```

DataType Property   Returns or sets a Type object for the data type of the column.

```
public System.Type DataType { get; set; }
```

DefaultValue Property   Returns or sets the default value of the column.

```
public object DefaultValue { get; set; }
```

Expression Property   Returns or sets a string expression used to filter or calculate the value.

```
public string Expression { get; set; }
```

ExtendedProperties Property   Returns the PropertyCollection object that contains user-defined custom properties.

```
public PropertyCollection ExtendedProperties { get; }
```

MaxLength Property   Returns or sets a maximum length for the column.

```
public int MaxLength { get; set; }
```

Namespace Property   Returns or sets the namespace of the column.

```
public string Namespace { get; set; }
```

Ordinal Property   Returns an integer value indicating the ordinal position of the column in the DataColumnCollection. Returns –1 if the column does not exist in the DataColumnCollection.

```
public int Ordinal { get; }
```

Prefix Property   Returns or sets an XML prefix for the column's DataTable.

```
public string Prefix { get; set; }
```

ReadOnly Property   Returns or sets a Boolean indicating whether the column is read-only. True if column is read-only; otherwise it returns False.

```
public bool ReadOnly { get; set; }
```

Table Property   Returns the DataTable of the column.

```
public DataTable Table { get; }
```

Unique Property   Returns or sets a Boolean indicating whether the column value must be unique. True if column value must be unique; otherwise it returns False.

```
public bool Unique { get; set; }
```

DataColumn Class Methods

CheckNotAllowNull Method   The CheckNotAllowNull method supports the .NET infrastructure and is not used directly from your code.

CheckUnique Method   The CheckUnique method supports the .NET infrastructure and is not used directly from your code.

OnPropertyChanging Method   Raises the OnPropertyChanging event. The PropertyChangedEventArgs parameter contains the event data that is raised.

```
protected internal virtual void OnPropertyChanging
    (PropertyChangedEventArgs);
```

RaisePropertyChanging Method   Raises information that the specified column is about to change.

```
protected internal void RaisePropertyChanging(string);
```

ToString Method   Returns the string expression of the column.

```
public override string ToString();
```

Mutual Properties, Methods, and Events Included in the DataColumn Class

The following lists the mutual properties, methods, and events that are included in the DataColumn class.

Inherited from MarshalByValueComponent

Container property

DesignMode property

Events property

Site property

Dispose method

GetService method

Disposed event

Inherited from Object

Equals method

Finalize method

GetHashCode method

GetType method

MemberwiseClone method

DataColumnChangeEventArgs Class

The DataColumnChangeEventArgs class supplies the data for the ColumnChanging event when a DataTable column value changes.

```
System.Object
    System.EventArgs
        System.Data.DataColumnChangeEventArgs
```

Constructor   Initializes a new instance of the DataColumnChangeEventArgs class using the specified DataRow, DataColumn, and object.

```
public DataColumnChangeEventArgs(DataRow, DataColumn, object);
// C# example
System.Data.DataRow dr = new System.Data.DataTable().NewRow();
System.Data.DataColumn dc = new System.Data.DataColumn();
System.Data.DataColumnChangeEventArgs dccea = new
    System.Data.DataColumnChangeEventArgs(dr, dc, 4);
```

DataColumnChangeEventArgs Class Properties

Column Property   Returns the DataColumn that is changing.

```
public DataColumn Column { get; }
```

ProposedValue Property   Returns or sets the proposed new value for the DataColumn.

```
public object ProposedValue { get; set; }
```

Row Property   Returns the DataRow for the column that is changing.

```
public DataRow Row { get; }
```

Mutual Properties, Methods, and Events Included in the DataColumnChangeEventArgs Class

The following lists the mutual properties, methods, and events that are included in the DataColumnChangeEventArgs class.

Inherited from Object

Equals method

Finalize method

GetHashCode method

GetType mMethod

MemberwiseClone method

ToString method

DataColumnCollection Class

The DataColumnCollection class contains a collection of DataColumn objects. You do not create a DataColumnCollection by calling a constructor. The DataColumnCollection is accessed through the DataTable.Columns property.

```
System.Object
    └── System.Data.InternalDataCollectionBase
            └── System.Data.DataColumnCollection
```

DataColumnCollection Class Properties

Item Property   Overloaded. Returns the DataColumn object found at the specified integer index or string parameter name.

```
public virtual DataColumn this[int index] { get; }
public virtual DataColumn this[string parmName] {get; }
```

List Property   Returns an ArrayList of DataColumns in this collection.

```
protected override ArrayList List { get; }
```

DataColumnCollection Class Methods

Add Method   Overloaded. The first and second Add methods create and add the specified DataColumn to the DataColumnCollection. The third Add method creates and adds a DataColumn to the DataColumnCollection using the specified name and returns the added DataColumn. The fourth Add method creates and adds a DataColumn to the DataColumnCollection using the specified name and column type, and then returns the added DataColumn. The fifth Add method creates and adds a DataColumn to the DataColumnCollection using the specified name, column type, and expression, and then returns the added DataColumn.

```
public virtual DataColumn Add();
public void Add(DataColumn);
public virtual DataColumn Add(string colName);
public virtual DataColumn Add(string colName, System.Type);
public virtual DataColumn Add(string colName, System.Type,
    string exp);
```

AddRange Method   Adds an array of DataColumn objects to the end of the DataColumnCollection.

```
public void AddRange(DataColumn[]);
```

CanRemove Method   Returns a Boolean indicating whether the specified DataColumn may be removed. True if the DataColumn may be removed, otherwise an exception is thrown.

```
public bool CanRemove(DataColumn);
```

Clear Method   Removes all the items from the DataColumnCollection.

```
public void Clear();
```

Contains Method   Returns True if the DataColumnCollection contains the specified DataColumn name.

```
public bool Contains(string parmName);
```

IndexOf Method   Overloaded. The first IndexOf method returns the location of the specified DataColumn object within the DataColumnCollection. The second IndexOf method returns the location of the DataColumn object with the specified name.

```
public virtual int IndexOf(DataColumn);
public int IndexOf(string);
```

OnCollectionChanged Method   Raises the CollectionChanged event, which invokes the event handler delegate.

```
protected virtual void OnCollectionChanged
    (CollectionChangeEventArgs);
```

OnCollectionChanging Method   Raises the CollectionChanging event, which invokes the event handler delegate.

```
protected internal virtual void OnCollectionChanging
    (CollectionChangeEventArgs);
```

Remove Method   Overloaded. The first Remove method removes the specified DataColumn from the DataColumnCollection. The second Remove method removes the DataColumn object from the collection that matches the specified name.

```
public void Remove(DataColumn);
public void Remove(string);
```

RemoveAt Method   The RemoveAt method removes the DataColumn object from the DataColumnCollection at the specified integer index. Throws an exception if the DataColumn object does not exist in the collection at the specified location.

```
public void RemoveAt(int);
```

DataColumnCollection Class Events

CollectionChanged Event   Fires when a DataColumn object is added or removed from the DataColumnCollection.

```
public event CollectionChangeEventHandler CollectionChanged;
```

Mutual Properties, Methods, and Events Included in the DataColumnCollection Class

The following lists the mutual properties, methods, and events that are included in the DataColumnCollection class.

Inherited from Object	Inherited from InternalDataCollectionBase
Equals method	Count property
Finalize method	IsReadOnly property
GetHashCode method	IsSynchronized property
GetType method	SyncRoot property
MemberwiseClone method	CopyTo method
ToString method	GetEnumerator method

DataException Class

The DataException class contains the exception that is thrown when an error is generated by ADO.NET components.

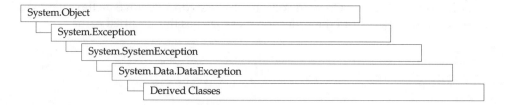

Constructor   Overloaded. The first constructor initializes a new instance of the DataException class. The second constructor initializes a new instance of the DataException class specifying an error message that explains the exception. The third constructor specifies serialization information and streaming context. The fourth constructor specifies an error message that explains the exception and an inner exception.

```
public DataException();
public DataException(string);
protected DataException(SerializationInfo siEx,
    StreamingContext scEx);
public DataException(string, Exception);
// C# example
System.Data.DataException deEx =
    new System.Data.DataException();
```

```
System.Data.DataException deEx2 =
    new System.Data.DataException("data error");
System.Runtime.Serialization.SerializationInfo serInfo;
System.Runtime.Serialization.StreamingContext strmContext;
System.Data.DataException deEx3 =
    new System.Data.DataException(serInfo, strmContext);
```

Mutual Properties, Methods, and Events Included in the DataException Class

The following lists the mutual properties, methods, and events that are included in the DataException class.

Inherited from Exception

HelpLink property

HResult property

InnerException property

Message property

Source property

StackTrace property

TargetSite property

GetBaseException method

GetObjectData method

ToString method

Inherited from Object

Equals method

Finalize method

GetHashCode method

GetType method

MemberwiseClone method

DataRelation Class

The DataRelation class parent/child relationship information used to relate two DataTable objects together.

System.Object
System.Data.DataRelation

Constructor   Overloaded. The first constructor initializes an instance of the DataRelation class using the specified string name and parent/child columns. The second constructor specifies a string name and parent/child column arrays. The third constructor specifies a string name, parent column, child column, and Boolean indicating whether to also create constraints. True will create the constraints. The fourth constructor creates a DataRelation using the specified string name, parent column array, child column array, and Boolean indicating whether to also create constraints. True will create the constraints. The fifth constructor uses the specified string name, parent table, child table, parent column array, child column array, and Boolean indicating whether the relationships are nested.

```
public DataRelation(string relName, DataColumn colParent,
    DataColumn colChild);
public DataRelation(string relName, DataColumn[] colParent,
    DataColumn[] colChild);
public DataRelation(string relName, DataColumn colParent,
    DataColumn colChild, bool);
public DataRelation(string relName, DataColumn[] colParent,
    DataColumn[] colChild, bool);
public DataRelation(string relName, string tblParentName,
    string tblChildName, string[] colParentName,
    string[] colChildName, bool);
// C# example
System.Data.DataColumn dcParent = new System.Data.DataColumn();
System.Data.DataColumn dcChild = new System.Data.DataColumn();
System.Data.DataColumn dcParents = new System.Data.DataColumn();
System.Data.DataColumn dcChilds = new System.Data.DataColumn();
string[] sColParents = new string[1];
string[] sColChilds = new string[1];
sColParents[0] = "Sales"; sColChilds[0] = "ShipToSales";
System.Data.DataRelation drel = new System.Data.DataRelation
    ("CustId", dcParent, dcChild);
System.Data.DataRelation drel2 = new System.Data.DataRelation
    ("CustId", dcParents, dcChilds);
System.Data.DataRelation drel3 = new System.Data.DataRelation
    ("CustId", dcParent, dcChild, true);
System.Data.DataRelation drel4 = new System.Data.DataRelation
    ("CustId", dcParents, dcChilds, true);
System.Data.DataRelation drel5 = new System.Data.DataRelation
    ("CustId", "Customer", "ShipTo", sColParents, sColChilds, true);
```

DataRelation Class Properties

ChildColumns Property   Returns an array of DataColumn objects for this relation.

```
public virtual DataColumn[] ChildColumns { get; }
```

ChildKeyConstraint Property   Returns the ForeignKeyConstraint.

```
public virtual ForeignKeyConstraint ChildKeyConstraint { get; }
```

ChildTable Property   Returns the child DataTable object.

```
public virtual DataTable ChildTable { get; }
```

DataSet Property   Returns the DataSet object for this relation.

```
public virtual DataSet DataSet { get; }
```

ExtendedProperties Property   Returns the PropertyCollection object that contains user-defined custom properties.

```
public PropertyCollection ExtendedProperties { get; }
```

Nested Property   Returns or sets a Boolean value indicating whether the objects in the DataRelation are nested. True if they are nested; otherwise it returns False.

```
public virtual bool Nested { get; set; }
```

ParentColumns Property   Returns an array of DataColumn objects for this relation.

```
public virtual DataColumn[] ParentColumns { get; }
```

ParentKeyConstraint Property   Returns the UniqueConstraint.

```
public virtual UniqueConstraint ParentKeyConstraint { get; }
```

ParentTable Property   Returns the parent DataTable of the relationship.

```
public virtual DataTable ParentTable { get; }
```

RelationName Property   Returns or sets a string for the DataRelation.

```
public virtual string RelationName { get; set; }
```

DataRelation Class Methods

CheckStateForProperty Method   Checks the validity of the DataRelation object.

```
protected void CheckStateForProperty();
```

OnPropertyChanging Method   The OnPropertyChanging method supports the .NET infrastructure and is not used directly from your code.

RaisePropertyChanging Method   The RaisePropertyChanging method supports the .NET infrastructure and is not used directly from your code.

ToString Method   Returns the string name of the DataRelation.

```
public override string ToString();
```

Mutual Properties, Methods, and Events Included in the DataRelation Class

The following lists the mutual properties, methods, and events that are included in the DataRelation class.

Inherited from Object

Equals method

Finalize method

GetHashCode method

GetType method

MemberwiseClone method

DataRelationCollection Class

The DataRelationCollection class contains a collection of DataRelation objects.

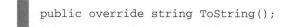

```
System.Object
  └── System.Data.InternalDataCollectionBase
        └── System.Data.DataRelationCollection
```

Constructor   Initializes a new instance of the DataRelationCollection class.

```
protected DataRelationCollection();
// C# example
System.Data.DataSet ds = new System.Data.DataSet();
System.Data.DataRelationCollection drelColl = ds.Relations;
```

DataRelationCollection Class Properties

Item Property   Overloaded. Returns the DataRelation object found at the specified integer index or string parameter name.

```
public abstract DataRelation this[int index] { get; }
public abstract DataRelation this[string parmName] {get; }
```

DataRelationCollection Class Methods

Add Method   Overloaded. The first Add method creates and adds the specified DataRelation to the DataRelationCollection. The second Add method creates and adds a DataRelation to the DataRelationCollection using the specified parent column and child column. The third Add method creates and adds a DataRelation using the specified parent column array and child column array. The fourth Add method creates and adds a DataRelation using the specified string name, parent column, and child column. The fifth Add method creates and adds a DataRelation using the specified string name, parent column array, and child column array. The sixth Add method creates and adds a DataRelation using the specified string name, parent column, child column, and Boolean indicating whether to also create constraints. True will create the constraints. The seventh Add method creates and adds a DataRelation using the specified string name, parent column array, child column array, and Boolean indicating whether to also create constraints. True will create the constraints.

```
public void Add(DataRelation);
public virtual DataRelation Add(DataColumn parentCol,
    DataColumn childCol);
public virtual DataRelation Add(DataColumn[] parentCols,
    DataColumn[] childCols);
public virtual DataRelation Add(string relName, DataColumn parentCol,
    DataColumn childCol);
public virtual DataRelation Add(string relName,
    DataColumn[] parentCols, DataColumn[] childCols);
public virtual DataRelation Add(string relName, DataColumn parentCol,
    DataColumn childCol, bool);
public virtual DataRelation Add(string relName,
    DataColumn[] parentCols, DataColumn[] childCols, bool);
```

AddCore Method   Verifies the specified DataRelation.

```
protected virtual void AddCore(DataRelation);
```

AddRange Method   Adds an array of DataRelation objects to the end of the DataRelationCollection.

```
public virtual void AddRange(DataRelation[]);
```

CanRemove Method   Returns a Boolean indicating whether the specified DataRelation may be removed. True if the DataRelation may be removed, otherwise it returns False.

```
public virtual bool CanRemove(DataRelation);
```

Clear Method   Removes all the items from the DataRelationCollection.

```
public virtual void Clear();
```

Contains Method   Returns True if the DataRelationCollection contains the specified DataRelation name.

```
public virtual bool Contains(string parmName);
```

GetDataSet Method   Returns the DataSet of this DataRelationCollection.

```
protected abstract DataSet GetDataSet();
```

IndexOf Method   Overloaded. The first IndexOf method returns the location of the specified DataRelation object within the DataRelationCollection. The second IndexOf method returns the location of the DataRelation object with the specified name.

```
public virtual int IndexOf(DataRelation);
public virtual int IndexOf(string);
```

OnCollectionChanged Method   Raises the CollectionChanged event, which invokes the event handler delegate.

```
protected virtual void OnCollectionChanged
    (CollectionChangeEventArgs);
```

OnCollectionChanging Method   Raises the CollectionChanging event, which invokes the event handler delegate.

```
protected internal virtual void OnCollectionChanging
    (CollectionChangeEventArgs);
```

Remove Method   Overloaded. The first Remove method removes the specified DataRelation from the DataRelationCollection. The second Remove method removes the DataRelation object from the collection that matches the specified name.

```
public void Remove(DataRelation);
public void Remove(string);
```

RemoveAt Method   The RemoveAt method removes the DataRelation object from the DataRelationCollection at the specified integer index. Throws an exception if the DataRelation object does not exist in the collection at the specified location.

```
public void RemoveAt(int);
```

RemoveCore Method   Verifies the specified DataRelation.

```
protected virtual void RemoveCore(DataRelation);
```

DataRelationCollection Class Events

CollectionChanged Event   Fires when a DataRelation object is added or removed from the DataRelationCollection.

```
public event CollectionChangeEventHandler CollectionChanged;
```

Mutual Properties, Methods, and Events
Included in the DataRelationCollection Class
The following lists the mutual properties, methods, and events that are included in the DataRelationCollection class.

Inherited from Object	Inherited from InternalDataCollectionBase
Equals Method	Count property
Finalize method	IsReadOnly property
GetHashCode method	IsSynchronized property
GetType method	List property
MemberwiseClone method	SyncRoot property
ToString method	CopyTo method
	GetEnumerator method

APPENDIXES

DataRow Class

The DataRow class represents a DataTable row of data. DataRow objects are created using the DataTable.NewRow method.

```
System.Object
    └──  System.Data.DataRow
```

DataRow Class Properties

HasErrors Property   Returns a Boolean indicating True if there are errors in the row; otherwise it returns False.

```
public bool HasErrors { get; }
```

Item Property   Overloaded. Returns or sets the data at the specified integer index, string column name, or DataColumn object.

```
public object this[string colName] { get; set; }
public object this[DataColumn] {get; set; }
public object this[int] { get; set; }
public object this[string colName, DataRowVersion] { get; }
public object this[DataColumn, DataRowVersion] { get; }
public object this[int, DataRowVersion] { get; }
```

ItemArray Property   Returns or sets the values for the row.

```
public object[] ItemArray { get; set; }
```

RowError Property   Returns or sets the text error description for the row.

```
public string RowError { get; set; }
```

RowState Property   Returns the current DataRowState value for the row.

```
public DataRowState RowState { get; }
```

Table Property   Returns the DataTable of the row.

```
public DataTable Table { get; }
```

DataRow Class Methods

AcceptChanges Method   Changes made to the row are committed.

```
public void AcceptChanges();
```

BeginEdit Method   Puts a DataRow into edit mode.

```
public void BeginEdit();
```

CancelEdit Method   Cancels a DataRow from edit mode.

```
public void CancelEdit();
```

ClearErrors Method   Clears any error that exist for a row.

```
public void ClearErrors();
```

Delete Method   Deletes a DataRow.

```
public void Delete();
```

EndEdit Method   Ends a DataRow from edit mode.

```
public void EndEdit();
```

GetChildRows Method   Overloaded. The first method returns an array of DataRow objects that are child rows of the specified DataRelation. The second method returns an array of DataRow objects that are child rows of the specified string relation name. The third method returns an array of DataRow objects that are child rows of the specified DataRelation object and DataRowVersion value. The fourth method returns an array of DataRow objects that are child rows of the specified string relation name and DataRowVersion value.

```
public DataRow[] GetChildRows(DataRelation);
public DataRow[] GetChildRows(string relName);
public DataRow[] GetChildRows(DataRelation, DataRowVersion);
public DataRow[] GetChildRows(string relName, DataRowVersion);
```

GetColumnError Method   Overloaded. Returns a string text description of any column errors for the specified integer index, string column name, or DataColumn object.

```
public string GetColumnError(DataColumn);
public string GetColumnError(int colIndex);
public string GetColumnError(string colName);
```

GetColumnsInError Method   Returns an array of DataColumn objects that contain errors.

```
public DataColumn[] GetColumnsInError ();
```

GetParentRow Method   Overloaded. The first method returns a DataRow object that is the parent row of the specified DataRelation. The second method returns a DataRow object that is the parent row of the specified string relation name. The third method returns a DataRow object that is the parent row of the specified DataRelation object and DataRowVersion value. The fourth method returns a DataRow object that is the parent row of the specified string relation name and DataRowVersion value.

```
public DataRow GetParentRow(DataRelation);
public DataRow GetParentRow(string relName);
public DataRow GetParentRow(DataRelation, DataRowVersion);
public DataRow GetParentRow(string relName, DataRowVersion);
```

GetParentRows Method   Overloaded. The first method returns an array of DataRow objects that are parent rows of the specified DataRelation. The second method returns an array of DataRow objects that are parent rows of the specified string relation name. The third method returns an array of DataRow objects that are parent rows of the specified DataRelation object and DataRowVersion value. The fourth method returns an array of DataRow objects that are parent rows of the specified string relation name and DataRowVersion value.

```
public DataRow[] GetParentRows(DataRelation);
public DataRow[] GetParentRows(string relName);
public DataRow[] GetParentRows(DataRelation, DataRowVersion);
public DataRow[] GetParentRows(string relName, DataRowVersion);
```

HasVersion Method Returns a Boolean indicating whether the DataRow has the specified version. True indicates that the DataRow has the version; otherwise it returns False.

```
public bool HasVersion(DataRowVersion);
```

IsNull Method Overloaded. The first method returns a Boolean indicating whether the specified DataColumn contains a null. The second checks for null at the specified column integer index. The third checks for a null in the specified column name value. The fourth method uses the specified DataColumn and DataRowVersion. True indicates that the parameter is null. False indicates that it's not null.

```
public bool IsNull(DataColumn);
public bool IsNull(int colIndex);
public bool IsNull(string colName);
public bool IsNull(DataColumn, DataRowVersion);
```

RejectChanges Method Rejects any changes made to the data row.

```
public void RejectChanges();
```

SetColumnError Method Overloaded. Sets the specified string text with error description for the specified DataColumn, column integer index, or column name.

```
public void SetColumnError(DataColumn, string errText);
public void SetColumnError(int colIndex, string errText);
public void SetColumnError(string colName, string errText);
```

SetNull Method Sets the value of the specified column to null.

```
protected void SetNull(DataColumn);
```

SetParentRow Method Overloaded. Changes the current parent row to the specified parent row or parent row and relation.

```
public void SetParentRow(DataRow);
public void SetParentRow(DataRow, DataRelation);
```

Mutual Properties, Methods, and Events Included in the DataRow Class

The following lists the mutual properties, methods, and events that are included in the DataRow class.

Inherited from Object

Equals method

Finalize method

GetHashCode method

GetType method

MemberwiseClone method

ToString method

DataRowBuilder Class

The DataRowBuilder supports the .NET infrastructure and is not used directly from your code

DataRowChangeEventArgs Class

The DataRowChangeEventArgs class supplies the data for the RowChanged, RowChanging, OnRowDeleted, and OnRowDeleting events when a DataRow changes.

```
System.Object
    System.EventArgs
        System.Data.DataRowChangeEventArgs
```

Constructor   Initializes a new instance of the DataRowChangeEventArgs class using the specified DataRow and DataRowAction.

```
public DataRowChangeEventArgs(DataRow, DataRowAction);
// C# example
System.Data.DataRow dr = new System.Data.DataTable().NewRow();
System.Data.DataRowChangeEventArgs drcea = new
    System.Data.DataRowChangeEventArgs(dr, DataRowAction.Add);
```

DataRowChangeEventArgs Class Properties

Action Property   Returns the action that has occurred.

```
public DataRowAction Action { get; }
```

Row Property   Returns the DataRow for the action that has occurred.

```
public DataRow Row { get; }
```

Mutual Properties, Methods, and Events Included in the DataRowChangeEventArgs Class

The following lists the mutual properties, methods, and events that are included in the DataRowChangeEventArgs class.

Inherited from Object

Equals method

Finalize method

GetHashCode method

GetType method

MemberwiseClone method

ToString method

DataRowCollection Class

The DataRowCollection class contains a collection of DataRow objects. You do not create a DataRowCollection by calling a constructor.

```
System.Object
    System.Data.InternalDataCollectionBase
        System.Data.DataRowCollection
```

DataRowCollection Class Properties

Item Property   Returns the DataRow object found at the specified integer index.

```
public DataRow this[int index] { get; }
```

List Property   Returns an ArrayList of DataRows in this collection.

```
protected override ArrayList List { get; }
```

DataRowCollection Class Methods

Add Method   Overloaded. The first Add method creates and adds the specified DataRow to the DataRowCollection. The second Add method creates and adds a DataRow to the DataRowCollection using the specified values.

```
public void Add(DataRow);
public virtual DataRow Add(object[]);
```

Clear Method   Removes all the items from the DataRowCollection.

```
public void Clear();
```

Contains Method   Overloaded. Returns True if the primary key column contains the specified value or values.

```
public bool Contains(object);
public bool Contains(object[]);
```

Find Method   Overloaded. Returns a DataRow that contains the specified value or values.

```
public DataRow Find(object);
public DataRow Find(object[]);
```

InsertAt Method   Inserts into the DataRowCollection the specified DataRow at the specified location.

```
public void InsertAt(DataRow, int loc);
```

Remove Method   Removes the specified DataRow from the DataRowCollection.

```
public void Remove(DataRow);
```

RemoveAt Method   Removes the DataRow object from the DataRowCollection at the specified integer index.

```
public void RemoveAt(int);
```

Mutual Properties, Methods, and Events Included in the DataRowCollection Class

The following lists the mutual properties, methods, and events that are included in the DataRowCollection class.

Inherited from Object	Inherited from InternalDataCollectionBase
Equals method	Count property
Finalize method	IsReadOnly property
GetHashCode method	IsSynchronized property
GetType method	SyncRoot property
MemberwiseClone method	CopyTo method
ToString method	GetEnumerator method

DataRowView Class

The DataRowView class represents a Windows Form control that is a customized view of a DataRow object.

```
System.Object
    └── System.Data.DataRowView
```

DataRowView Class Properties

DataView Property   Returns the DataView object for this DataRowView.

```
public DataView DataView {get; }
```

IsEdit Property   Returns True if the DataView is in edit mode; otherwise it returns False.

```
public bool IsEdit { get; }
```

IsNew Property   Returns True if the DataView is new; otherwise it returns False.

```
public bool IsNew { get; }
```

Item Property   Overloaded. Returns or sets the object found at the specified integer index or string parameter name.

```
public object this[int index] { get; set; }
public object this[string parmName] { get; set; }
```

Row Property   Returns the current DataRow for the DataRowView.

```
public DataRow Row { get; }
```

RowVersion Property   Returns the current DataRowVersion for the DataRow.

```
public DataRowVersion RowVersion { get; }
```

System.ComponentModel.IDataErrorInfo.Error Property   Returns the exception error for the current DataRowView.

```
string IDataErrorInfo.Error { get; }
```

System.ComponentModel.IDataErrorInfo.Item Property   Returns the exception error source for the current DataRowView.

```
string IDataErrorInfo.this[string colName] { get; }
```

DataRowView Class Methods

BeginEdit Method   Puts a DataRowView into edit mode.

```
public void BeginEdit();
```

CancelEdit Method   Cancels a DataRowView from edit mode.

```
public void CancelEdit();
```

CreateChildView Method   Overloaded. Creates and returns a DataView object of the child DataTable using the specified DataRelation or data relation name.

```
public DataView CreateChildView(DataRelation);
public DataView CreateChildView(string relName);
```

Delete Method   Deletes a row.

```
public void Delete();
```

EndEdit Method   Ends a DataRowView from edit mode.

```
public void EndEdit();
```

Equals Method   Determines the equality of two object instances.

```
public override bool Equals(object);
```

GetHashCode Method   Returns 32-bit signed integer hash code for this DataRowView.

```
public override int GetHashCode();
```

ICustomTypeDescriptor.GetAttributes Method   The ICustomTypeDescriptor .GetAttributes method supports the .NET infrastructure and is not used directly from your code.

ICustomTypeDescriptor.GetClassName Method   The ICustomTypeDescriptor .GetClassName method supports the .NET infrastructure and is not used directly from your code.

ICustomTypeDescriptor.GetComponentName Method   The ICustomTypeDescriptor.GetComponentName method supports the .NET infrastructure and is not used directly from your code.

ICustomTypeDescriptor.GetConverter Method   The ICustomTypeDescriptor .GetConverter method supports the .NET infrastructure and is not used directly from your code.

ICustomTypeDescriptor.GetDefaultEvent Method   The ICustomTypeDescriptor .GetDefaultEvent method supports the .NET infrastructure and is not used directly from your code.

ICustomTypeDescriptor.GetDefaultProperty Method   The ICustomTypeDescriptor .GetDefaultProperty method supports the .NET infrastructure and is not used directly from your code.

ICustomTypeDescriptor.GetEditor Method   The ICustomTypeDescriptor .GetEditor method supports the .NET infrastructure and is not used directly from your code.

ICustomTypeDescriptor.GetEvents Method   The ICustomTypeDescriptor .GetEvents method supports the .NET infrastructure and is not used directly from your code.

ICustomTypeDescriptor.GetProperties Method   The ICustomTypeDescriptor .GetProperties method supports the .NET infrastructure and is not used directly from your code.

ICustomTypeDescriptor.GetPropertyOwner Method   The ICustomTypeDescriptor .GetPropertyOwner method supports the .NET infrastructure and is not used directly from your code.

Mutual Properties, Methods, and Events Included in the DataRowView Class

The following lists the mutual properties, methods, and events that are included in the DataRowView class.

Inherited from Object

Finalize method

GetType method

MemberwiseClone method

ToString method

DataSet Class

The DataSet class is a set of DataTable objects. The cache of data in the DataSet is in-memory.

```
System.Object
    └── System.ComponentModel.MarshalByValueComponent
            └── System.Data.DataSet
```

Constructor   Overloaded. The first constructor initializes a new instance of the DataSet class. The second constructor initializes a new instance of the DataSet class specifying s string name for the DataSet. The third constructor specifies serialization information and streaming context.

```
public DataSet();
public DataSet(string dsName);
```

```
protected DataSet(SerializationInfo siDS, StreamingContext scDS);
// C# example
System.Data.DataSet ds = new System.Data.DataSet();
System.Data.DataSet ds2 = new System.Data.DataSet("CustomerInfo");
System.Runtime.Serialization.SerializationInfo serInfo;
System.Runtime.Serialization.StreamingContext strmContext;
System.Data.DataSet ds3 =
    new System.Data.DataSet(serInfo, strmContext);
```

DataSet Class Properties

CaseSensitive Property   Returns or sets a Boolean indicating whether string comparison within the DataTable are case sensitive. True if the strings are case sensitive, otherwise it returns False.

```
public bool CaseSensitive { get; set; }
```

DataSetName Property   Returns or sets a string value for the current DataSet name.

```
public string DataSetName { get; set; }
```

DefaultViewManager Property   Returns a DataViewManager object that allows filtering and searching of data in the DataSet.

```
public DataViewManager DefaultViewManager { get; }
```

EnforceConstraints Property   Returns or sets a Boolean indicating whether constraints are enforced. True if are enforced, otherwise it returns False.

```
public bool EnforceConstraints { get; set; }
```

ExtendedProperties Property   Returns a PropertyCollection of the user-defined custom properties.

```
public PropertyCollection ExtendedProperties { get; }
```

HasErrors Property   Returns a Boolean indicating True if there are errors in the rows of the tables of the DataSet, otherwise it returns False.

```
public bool HasErrors { get; }
```

Locale Property   Returns or sets CultureInfo data about the user's machine locale.

```
public System.Globalization.CultureInfo Locale { get; set; }
```

Namespace Property   Returns or sets the namespace for the DataSet as a string.

```
public string Namespace { get; set; }
```

Prefix Property   Returns or sets an XML prefix for the DataSet namespace.

```
public string Prefix { get; set; }
```

Relations Property   Returns the DataRelationCollection that contains the linked tables for this DataSet.

```
public DataRelationCollection Relations { get; }
```

Site Property   Returns or sets the ISite interface for this DataSet.

```
public override System.ComponentModel.ISite Site { get; set; }
```

System.ComponentModel.IListSource.ContainsListCollection Property
Returns True if the collection contains IList objects, otherwise returns False.

```
bool IListSource.ContainsListCollection { get; }
```

Tables Property   Returns the DataTableCollection that contains the tables for this DataSet.

```
public DataTableCollection Tables { get; }
```

DataSet Class Methods

AcceptChanges Method   Changes made to the row are committed.

```
public void AcceptChanges();
```

BeginInit Method   The BeginInit method supports the .NET infrastructure and is not used directly from your code.

Clear Method   Removes all the rows from the DataSet.

```
public void Clear();
```

Clone Method   Copies the structure of the current DataSet to a new DataSet and returns it.

```
public virtual DataSet Clone();
```

Copy Method   Copies the structure and data of the current DataSet to a new DataSet and returns it.

```
public DataSet Copy();
```

EndInit Method   The EndInit method supports the .NET infrastructure and is not used directly from your code.

GetChanges Method   Overloaded. Returns a filtered copy of the current DataSet that contains only changed information. The second method is filtered further by the specified DataRowState value.

```
public DataSet GetChanges();
public DataSet GetChanges(DataRowState);
```

GetSchemaSerializable Method   The GetSchemaSerializable method supports the .NET infrastructure and is not used directly from your code.

GetSerializationData Method   The GetSerializationData method supports the .NET infrastructure and is not used directly from your code.

GetXml Method   Returns a string of the DataSet data as XML.

```
public string GetXml();
```

GetXmlSchema Method   Returns a string of the DataSet primary schema as XML.

```
public string GetXmlSChema();
```

HasChanges Method   Overloaded. Returns a Boolean indicating whether the DataSet has been changed. The second method is filtered by the DataRowState value. True if the DataSet has been changed; otherwise it returns False.

```
public bool HasChanges();
public bool HasChanges(DataRowState);
```

IListSource.GetList Method   The IListSource.GetList method supports the .NET infrastructure and is not used directly from your code.

InferXmlSchema Method   Overloaded. Infers into the DataSet the specified Stream, file, TextReader, or XmlRead and excludes the specified string array of namespace URIs.

```
public void InferXmlSchema(System.IO.Stream, string[] nsURI);
public void InferXmlSchema(string file, string[] nsURI);
public void InferXmlSchema(System.IO.TextReader, string[] nsURI);
public void InferXmlSchema(System.Xml.XmlReader, string[] nsURI);
```

ISerializable.GetObjectData Method   The ISerializable.GetObjectData method supports the .NET infrastructure and is not used directly from your code.

IXmlSerializable.GetSchema Method   The IXmlSerializable.GetSchema method supports the .NET infrastructure and is not used directly from your code.

IXmlSerializable.ReadXml Method   The IXmlSerializable.ReadXml method supports the .NET infrastructure and is not used directly from your code.

IXmlSerializable.WriteXml Method   The IXmlSerializable.WriteXml method supports the .NET infrastructure and is not used directly from your code.

Merge Method   Overloaded. The first Merge method merges the specified DataRow array into the DataSet. The second method merges the specified DataSet into the current DataSet. The third method specifies a DataTable to merge. The fourth method merges a DataSet into the current DataSet and specifies a Boolean indicating whether to preserve the current DataSet information. True to preserve the current DataSet, else False. The fifth method merges the specified DataRow array into the current DataSet, and specifies a Boolean indicating whether to preserve the current DataSet information and MissingSchemaAction value. The sixth method merges the specified DataSet into the current DataSet and specifies a Boolean indicating whether to preserve the current DataSet information and MissingSchemaAction value. The seventh method merges the specified DataTable into the current DataSet and specifies a Boolean indicating whether to preserve the current DataSet information and MissingSchemaAction value.

```
public void Merge(DataRow[]);
public void Merge(DataSet);
public void Merge(DataTable);
public void Merge(DataSet, bool);
public void Merge(DataRow[], bool, MissingSchemaAction);
public void Merge(DataSet, bool, MissingSchemaAction);
public void Merge(DataTable, bool, MissingSchemaAction);
```

OnPropertyChanging Method   Raises the OnPropertyChanging event. The PropertyChangedEventArgs parameter contains the event data that is raised.

```
protected internal virtual void OnPropertyChanging
    (PropertyChangedEventArgs);
```

OnRemoveRelation Method   Specifies the DataRelation to remove.

```
protected virtual void OnRemoveRelation(DataRelation);
```

OnRemoveTable Method   Specifies the DataTable to remove.

```
protected virtual void OnRemoveTable(DataTable);
```

RaisePropertyChanging Method   Raises information that the specified column is about to change.

```
protected internal void RaisePropertyChanging(string);
```

ReadXml Method   Overloaded. The first ReadXml method reads the specified Stream into the DataSet. The second method reads the specified file into the current DataSet. The third method specifies a TextReader object to read. The fourth method reads an XmlReader object into the current DataSet. The fifth method reads the specified Stream into the current DataSet using the specified XmlReadMode value. The sixth method reads the specified file into the current DataSet using the specified XmlReadMode value. The seventh method reads the specified TextReader into the current DataSet using the specified XmlReadMode value. The eighth method reads the specified XmlReader into the current DataSet using the specified XmlReadMode value.

```
public XmlReadMode ReadXml(System.IO.Stream);
public XmlReadMode ReadXml(string file);
public XmlReadMode ReadXml(System.IO.TextReader);
```

```
public XmlReadMode ReadXml(System.Xml.XmlReader);
public XmlReadMode ReadXml(System.IO.Stream, XmlReadMode);
public XmlReadMode ReadXml(string file, XmlReadMode);
public XmlReadMode ReadXml(System.IO.TextReader, XmlReadMode);
public XmlReadMode ReadXml(System.Xml.XmlReader, XmlReadMode);
```

ReadXmlSchema Method　　Overloaded. The first ReadXmlSchema method reads the specified Stream schema into the DataSet. The second method reads the specified file schema into the current DataSet. The third method specifies a TextReader object to read. The fourth method reads an XmlReader object schema into the current DataSet.

```
public void ReadXmlSchema(System.IO.Stream);
public void ReadXmlSchema(string file);
public void ReadXmlSchema(System.IO.TextReader);
public void ReadXmlSchema(System.Xml.XmlReader);
```

ReadXmlSerializable Method　　The ReadXmlSerializable method supports the .NET infrastructure and is not used directly from your code.

RejectChanges Method　　Changes made to the row are rolled back.

```
public virtual void RejectChanges();
```

Reset Method　　Resets a DataSet to its original state.

```
public virtual void Reset();
```

ShouldSerializeRelations Method　　Returns a Boolean indicating whether the DataSet's Relation property should persist. True if the property should persist; otherwise it returns False.

```
protected virtual bool ShouldSerializeRelations();
```

ShouldSerializeTables Method　　Returns a Boolean indicating whether the DataSet's Tables property should persist. True if the property should persist; otherwise it returns False.

```
protected virtual bool ShouldSerializeTables();
```

WriteXml Method　　Overloaded. The first WriteXml method writes data from the DataSet into the specified Stream. The second method writes from the DataSet into the specified file. The third method writes to the specified TextWriter object. The fourth method writes the current DataSet into an XmlWriter object. The fifth method writes the current DataSet into the specified Stream using the specified XmlWriteMode value. The sixth method writes the current DataSet into the specified file using the specified XmlWriteMode value. The seventh method writes the current DataSet into the specified TextWriter using the specified XmlWriteMode value. The eighth method writes the current DataSet into the specified XmlWriter using the specified XmlWriteMode value.

```
public XmlWriteMode WriteXml(System.IO.Stream);
public XmlWriteMode WriteXml(string file);
public XmlWriteMode WriteXml(System.IO.TextWriter);
public XmlWriteMode WriteXml(System.Xml.XmlWriter);
public XmlWriteMode WriteXml(System.IO.Stream, XmlWriteMode);
public XmlWriteMode WriteXml(string file, XmlWriteMode);
public XmlWriteMode WriteXml(System.IO.TextWriter, XmlWriteMode);
public XmlWriteMode WriteXml(System.Xml.XmlWriter, XmlWriteMode);
```

WriteXmlSchema Method   Overloaded. The first WriteXmlSchema method writes the DataSet schema into the specified Stream. The second method writes the current DataSet schema into the specified file. The third method specifies to write to a TextWriter object. The fourth method writes the current DataSet schema into an XmlWriter object.

```
public void WriteXmlSchema(System.IO.Stream);
public void WriteXmlSchema(string file);
public void WriteXmlSchema(System.IO.TextWriter);
public void WriteXmlSchema(System.Xml.XmlWriter);
```

DataSet Class Events

MergeFailed Event   Fires when the primary key value for a target and source DataRow are the same and constraints are enforced.

```
public event MergeFailedEventHandler MergeFailed;
```

Mutual Properties, Methods, and Events Included in the DataSet Class

The following lists the mutual properties, methods, and events that are included in the DataSet class.

Inherited from MarshalByValueComponent	Inherited from Object
Container property	Equals method
DesignMode property	Finalize method

Inherited from MarshalByValueComponent	Inherited from Object
Events property	GetHashCode method
Dispose method	GetType method
GetService method	MemberwiseClone method
Disposed event	ToString method

DataSysDescriptionAttribute Class

The DataSysDescriptionAttribute class allows you to attach a description to a property or event.

```
System.Object
    System.Attribute
        System.ComponentModel.DescriptionAttribute
            System.Data.DataSysDescriptionAttribute
```

Constructor   Initializes a new instance of the DataSysDescriptionAttribute class.

```
public DataSysDescriptionAttribute(string descText);
// C# example
System.Data.DataSysDescriptionAttribute dsda = new
    System.Data.DataSysDescriptionAttribute("North Sales Region");
```

DataSysDescriptionAttribute Class Properties

Description Property   Returns the description text.

```
public override string Description {get; }
```

Mutual Properties, Methods, and Events Included in the DataSysDescriptionAttribute Class

The following lists the mutual properties, methods, and events that are included in the DataSysDescriptionAttribute class.

Inherited from Object	Inherited from Attribute
Equals method	TypeId property
Finalize method	GetHashCode method

Inherited from Object	**Inherited from Attribute**
GetType method	IsDefaultAttribute method
MemberwiseClone method	Match method
ToString method	

Inherited from DescriptionAttribute

DescriptionValue property

DataTable Class

The DataTable class represents an in-memory data table that's part of the DataSet.

```
System.Object
    System.ComponentModel.MarshalByValueComponent
        System.Data.DataTable
```

Constructor   Overloaded. The first constructor initializes a new instance of the DataTable class. The second constructor initializes a new instance of the DataTable class specifying s string name for the DataTable. The third constructor specifies serialization information and streaming context.

```
public DataTable();
public DataTable(string dtName);
protected DataTable(SerializationInfo siDT, StreamingContext scDT);
// C# example
System.Data.DataTable dt = new System.Data.DataTable();
System.Data.DataTable dt2 = new System.Data.DataTable("Customers");
System.Runtime.Serialization.SerializationInfo serInfo;
System.Runtime.Serialization.StreamingContext strmContext;
System.Data.DataTable dt3 =
    new System.Data.DataTable(serInfo, strmContext);
```

DataTable Class Properties

CaseSensitive Property   Returns or sets a Boolean indicating whether string comparisons within the DataTable are case sensitive. True if the strings are case sensitive, otherwise it returns False.

```
public bool CaseSensitive { get; set; }
```

APPENDIXES

ChildRelations Property   Returns a DataRelationCollection that contains the child relations for this table.

```
public DataRelationCollection ChildRelations { get; }
```

Columns Property   Returns a DataColumnCollection that contains the columns for this table.

```
public DataColumnCollection Columns { get; }
```

Constraints Property   Returns a ConstraintCollection that contains the constraints for this table.

```
public ConstraintCollection Constraints { get; }
```

DataSet Property   Returns the DataSet for this table.

```
public DataSet DataSet { get; }
```

DefaultView Property   Returns a DataView object that is a customized view of the table.

```
public DataView DefaultView { get; }
```

DisplayExpression Property   Returns or sets a string expression used to display to the user about this table.

```
public string DisplayExpression { get; set; }
```

ExtendedProperties Property   Returns a PropertyCollection of the user-defined custom properties.

```
public PropertyCollection ExtendedProperties { get; }
```

HasErrors Property   Returns a Boolean indicating True if there are errors in the rows of the tables of the DataSet, otherwise it returns False.

```
public bool HasErrors { get; }
```

Locale Property   Returns or sets CultureInfo data about the user's machine locale.

```
public System.Globalization.CultureInfo Locale { get; set; }
```

MinimumCapacity Property   Returns or sets the starting number of rows for this table. Default value is 25.

```
public int MinimumCapacity { get; set; }
```

Namespace Property   Returns or sets the namespace for the DataTable as a string.

```
public string Namespace { get; set; }
```

ParentRelations Property   Returns a DataRelationCollection that contains the parent relations for this table.

```
public DataRelationCollection ParentRelations { get; }
```

Prefix Property   Returns or sets an XML prefix for the DataTable namespace.

```
public string Prefix { get; set; }
```

PrimaryKey Property   Returns or sets an array of DataColumns that is used as the primary key for the table.

```
public DataColumn[] PrimaryKey { get; set; }
```

Rows Property   Returns a DataRowCollection that contains the rows for this table.

```
public DataRowCollection Rows { get; }
```

Site Property   Returns or sets the ISite interface for this DataSet.

```
public override System.ComponentModel.ISite Site { get; set; }
```

System.ComponentModel.IListSource.ContainsListCollection Property
Returns True if the collection contains IList objects, otherwise returns False.

```
bool IListSource.ContainsListCollection { get; }
```

APPENDIXES

TableName Property   Returns or sets the DataTable name as a string.

```
public string TableName { get; set; }
```

DataTable Class Methods

AcceptChanges Method   Changes made to the table are committed.

```
public void AcceptChanges();
```

BeginInit Method   Used at runtime to initialize a DataTable that is used on a form.

```
public void BeginInit();
```

BeginLoadData Method   Suspends notifications while the data is loading.

```
public void BeginLoadData();
```

Clear Method   Removes all the data from the DataTable.

```
public void Clear();
```

Clone Method   Copies the structure and constraints of the current DataTable to a new DataTable and returns it.

```
public virtual DataTable Clone();
```

Compute Method   Computes the current rows using the specified string expression and filter.

```
public object Compute(string expr, string filter);
```

Copy Method   Copies the structure and data of the current DataTable to a new DataTable and returns it.

```
public DataTable Copy();
```

EndInit Method   Used at runtime to end initialization of a DataTable that is used on a form.

```
public void EndInit();
```

EndLoadData Method   Ends suspension of notifications while the data is loading.

```
public void EndLoadData();
```

GetChanges Method   Overloaded. Returns a filtered copy of the current DataTable that contains only changed information. The second method is filtered further by the specified DataRowState value.

```
public DataSet GetChanges();
public DataSet GetChanges(DataRowState);
```

GetErrors Method   Returns an array of DataRow objects that contain errors.

```
public DataRow[] GetErrors();
```

GetRowType Method   The GetRowType method supports the .NET infrastructure and is not used directly from your code.

IListSource.GetList Method   The IListSource.GetList method supports the .NET infrastructure and is not used directly from your code.

ImportRow Method   Imports the specified DataRow into the table.

```
public void ImportRow(DataRow);
```

ISerializable.GetObjectData Method   The ISerializable.GetObjectData method supports the .NET infrastructure and is not used directly from your code.

LoadDataRow Method   Uses the specified object array values to find and update a DataRow or create a new row if no matching row exists. The specified Boolean indicates whether changes are accepted. True if changes are accepted; otherwise it returns False.

```
public DataRow LoadDataRow(object[], bool);
```

NewRow Method   Creates a new DataRow in the table.

```
public DataRow NewRow();
```

APPENDIXES

NewRowArray Method   The NewRowArray method supports the .NET infrastructure and is not used directly from your code.

NewRowFromBuilder Method   Creates a new row in the table from an existing row using the specified DataRowBuilder.

```
protected virtual DataRow NewRowFromBuilder(DataRowBuilder);
```

OnColumnChanged Method   Raises the ColumnChanged event, which invokes the event handler delegate.

```
protected virtual void OnColumnChanged(DataColumnChangeEventArgs);
```

OnColumnChanging Method   Raises the ColumnChanging event, which invokes the event handler delegate.

```
protected virtual void OnColumnChanging(DataColumnChangeEventArgs);
```

OnPropertyChanging Method   Raises the OnPropertyChanging event. The PropertyChangedEventArgs parameter contains the event data that is raised.

```
protected internal virtual void OnPropertyChanging
    (PropertyChangedEventArgs);
```

OnRemoveColumn Method   Specifies the DataColumn to remove.

```
protected internal virtual void OnRemoveColumn(DataColumn);
```

OnRowChanged Method   Raises the RowChanged event, which invokes the event handler delegate.

```
protected virtual void OnRowChanged(DataRowChangeEventArgs);
```

OnRowChanging Method   Raises the RowChanging event, which invokes the event handler delegate.

```
protected virtual void OnRowChanging(DataRowChangeEventArgs);
```

OnRowDeleted Method   Raises the RowDeleted event, which invokes the event handler delegate.

```
protected virtual void OnRowDeleted(DataRowChangeEventArgs);
```

OnRowDeleting Method   Raises the RowDeleting event, which invokes the event handler delegate.

```
protected virtual void OnRowDeleting(DataRowChangeEventArgs);
```

RejectChanges Method   Rolls back any changes made to the data table.

```
public void RejectChanges();
```

Reset Method   Resets a DataTable to its original state.

```
public virtual void Reset();
```

Select Method   Overloaded. The first method returns an array of all DataRow objects. The second method returns an array of all DataRow objects that conform to the specified string expression filter. The third method returns an array of all DataRow objects that conform to the specified string expression filter and sort order. The fourth method returns an array of all DataRow objects that conform to the specified string expression filter and sort order and match the DataViewRowState value.

```
public DataRow[] Select();
public DataRow[] Select(string expr);
public DataRow[] Select(string expr, string srt);
public DataRow[] Select(string expr, string srt, DataViewRowState);
```

ToString Method   Returns the name of the DataTable object as a string.

```
public override string ToString();
```

DataTable Class Events

ColumnChanged Event   Fires when a DataColumn object has been changed.

```
public event DataColumnChangeEventHandler ColumnChanged;
```

ColumnChanging Event   Fires when a DataColumn object is being changed.

```
public event DataColumnChangeEventHandler ColumnChanging;
```

APPENDIXES

RowChanged Event   Fires when a DataRow object has been changed.

```
public event DataRowChangeEventHandler RowChanged;
```

RowChanging Event   Fires when a DataRow object is being changed.

```
public event DataRowChangeEventHandler RowChanging;
```

RowDeleted Event   Fires when a DataRow object has been deleted.

```
public event DataRowChangeEventHandler RowDeleted;
```

RowDeleting Event   Fires when a DataRow object is being deleted.

```
public event DataRowChangeEventHandler RowDeleting;
```

Mutual Properties, Methods, and Events Included in the DataTable Class

The following lists the mutual properties, methods, and events that are included in the DataTable class.

Inherited from MarshalByValueComponent	Inherited from Object
Container property	Equals method
DesignMode property	Finalize method
Events property	GetHashCode method
Dispose method	GetType method
GetService method	MemberwiseClone method
Disposed event	

DataTableCollection Class

The DataTableCollection class contains a collection of DataTable objects. You do not create a DataTableCollection by calling a constructor. The DataTableCollection is accessed through the DataSet.Tables property.

```
System.Object
    System.Data.InternalDataCollectionBase
        System.Data.DataTableCollection
```

DataTableCollection Class Properties

Item Property   Overloaded. Returns the DataTable object found at the specified integer index or string parameter name.

```
public DataTable this[int index] { get; }
public DataTable this[string parmName] { get; }
```

List Property   Returns an ArrayList of DataTables in this collection.

```
protected override ArrayList List { get; }
```

DataTableCollection Class Methods

Add Method   Overloaded. The first and second Add methods create and add the specified DataTable to the DataTableCollection. The third Add method creates and adds a DataTable to the DataTableCollection using the specified name and returns the added DataTable.

```
public virtual DataTable Add();
public virtual void Add(DataTable);
public virtual DataTable Add(string tblName);
```

AddRange Method   Adds an array of DataTable objects to the end of the DataTableCollection.

```
public void AddRange(DataTable[]);
```

CanRemove Method   Returns a Boolean indicating whether the specified DataTable may be removed. True if the DataTable may be removed, otherwise it returns False.

```
public bool CanRemove(DataTable);
```

Clear Method   Removes all the items from the DataTableCollection.

```
public void Clear();
```

Contains Method   Returns True if the DataTableCollection contains the specified DataTable name.

```
public bool Contains(string parmName);
```

IndexOf Method   Overloaded. The first IndexOf method returns the location of the specified DataTable object within the DataTableCollection. The second IndexOf method returns the location of the DataTable object with the specified name.

```
public virtual int IndexOf(DataTable);
public virtual int IndexOf(string);
```

OnCollectionChanged Method   Raises the CollectionChanged event, which invokes the event handler delegate.

```
protected virtual void OnCollectionChanged
    (CollectionChangeEventArgs);
```

OnCollectionChanging Method   Raises the CollectionChanging event, which invokes the event handler delegate.

```
protected internal virtual void OnCollectionChanging
    (CollectionChangeEventArgs);
```

Remove Method   Overloaded. The first Remove method removes the specified DataTable from the DataTableCollection. The second Remove method removes the DataTable object from the collection that matches the specified name.

```
public void Remove(DataTable);
public void Remove(string);
```

RemoveAt Method   The RemoveAt method removes the DataTable object from the DataTableCollection at the specified integer index. Throws an exception if the DataTable object does not exist in the collection at the specified location.

```
public void RemoveAt(int);
```

DataTableCollection Class Events

CollectionChanged Event   Fires when a DataTable object is added or removed from the DataTableCollection.

```
public event CollectionChangeEventHandler CollectionChanged;
```

CollectionChanging Event   Fires when a DataTable object is being added or removed from the DataTableCollection.

```
public event CollectionChangeEventHandler CollectionChanging;
```

Mutual Properties, Methods, and Events
Included in the DataTableCollection Class

The following lists the mutual properties, methods, and events that are included in the DataTableCollection class.

Inherited from Object	Inherited from InternalDataCollectionBase
Equals method	Count property
Finalize method	IsReadOnly property
GetHashCode method	IsSynchronized property
GetType method	SyncRoot property
MemberwiseClone method	CopyTo method
ToString method	GetEnumerator method

DataView Class

The DataView class contains a customized view of data in a DataTable.

```
System.Object
   └─ System.ComponentModel.MarshalByValueComponent
         └─ System.Data.DataView
```

Constructor   Overloaded. The first constructor initializes a new instance of the DataView class. The second constructor initializes a new instance of the DataView class specifying a DataTable. The third constructor specifies a DataTable, string row filter, string sort, and DataViewRowState value.

```
public DataView();
public DataView(DataTable);
public DataView(DataTable, string filter, string srt,
    DataViewRowState);
// C# example
System.Data.DataTable dt = new System.Data.DataTable();
System.Data.DataView dv = new System.Data.DataView();
System.Data.DataView dv2 = new System.Data.DataView(dt);
System.Data.DataView dv3 = new System.Data.DataView(dt,
    "City = 'Portland'", "CustID DESC", DataViewRowState.Added);
```

DataView Class Properties

AllowDelete Property   Returns or sets a Boolean indicating whether deletes are allowed. True if deletes are allowed; otherwise it returns False.

```
public bool AllowDelete { get; set; }
```

AllowEdit Property   Returns or sets a Boolean indicating whether edits are allowed. True if edits are allowed; otherwise it returns False.

```
public bool AllowEdit { get; set; }
```

AllowNew Property   Returns or sets a Boolean indicating whether new rows may be added. True if new rows may be added; otherwise it returns False.

```
public bool AllowNew { get; set; }
```

ApplyDefaultSort Property   Returns or sets a Boolean indicating whether the default sort should be used. True if default sort is to be used; otherwise it returns False.

```
public bool ApplyDefaultSort { get; set; }
```

Count Property   Returns the number of records in the DataView.

```
public int Count { get; }
```

DataViewManager Property   Returns the DataViewManager object that this DataView belongs to.

```
public DataViewManager DataViewManager { get; }
```

IsOpen Property   Returns a Boolean indicating whether the data source is open. True if the data source is open; otherwise it returns False.

```
protected bool IsOpen { get; }
```

Item Property   Returns the row found at the specified integer index.

```
public DataRowView this[int index] { get; }
```

RowFilter Property   Returns or sets a string expression used to filter the view.

```
public virtual string RowFilter { get; set; }
```

RowStateFilter Property   Returns or sets a DataViewRowState value to indicate the filtering used for the view.

```
public DataViewRowState RowStateFilter { get; set; }
```

Sort Property   Returns or sets a string that contains the sort order.

```
public string Sort { get; set; }
```

System.Collections.ICollection.IsSynchronized Property   The System .Collections.ICollection.IsSynchronized property supports the .NET infrastructure and is not used directly from your code.

System.Collections.ICollection.SyncRoot Property   The System.Collections .ICollection.SyncRoot property supports the .NET infrastructure and is not used directly from your code.

System.Collections.IList.IsFixedSize Property   The System.Collections.IList .IsFixedSize property supports the .NET infrastructure and is not used directly from your code.

System.Collections.IList.IsReadOnly Property   The System.Collections.IList .IsReadOnly property supports the .NET infrastructure and is not used directly from your code.

System.Collections.IList.Item Property   Implements the System.Collections .IList.Item interface to return or set the item at the specified location in the collection.

```
object IList.this[int index] { get; set; }
```

System.ComponentModel.IBindingList.AllowEdit Property   The System .ComponentModel.IBindingList.AllowEdit property supports the .NET infrastructure and is not used directly from your code.

System.ComponentModel.IBindingList.AllowNew Property   The System .ComponentModel.IBindingList.AllowNew property supports the .NET infrastructure and is not used directly from your code.

APPENDIXES

System.ComponentModel.IBindingList.AllowRemove Property   The System
.ComponentModel.IBindingList.AllowRemove property supports the .NET infrastructure
and is not used directly from your code.

System.ComponentModel.IBindingList.IsSorted Property   The System
.ComponentModel.IBindingList.IsSorted property supports the .NET infrastructure
and is not used directly from your code.

System.ComponentModel.IBindingList.SortDirection Property   The System
.ComponentModel.IBindingList.SortDirection property supports the .NET infrastructure
and is not used directly from your code.

System.ComponentModel.IBindingList.SortProperty Property   The System
.ComponentModel.IBindingList.SortProperty property supports the .NET infrastructure
and is not used directly from your code.

**System.ComponentModel.IBindingList.SupportsChangeNotification
Property**   The System.ComponentModel.IBindingList.SupportsChangeNotification
property supports the .NET infrastructure and is not used directly from your code.

System.ComponentModel.IBindingList.SupportsSearching Property   The
System.ComponentModel.IBindingList.SupportsSearching property supports
the .NET infrastructure and is not used directly from your code.

System.ComponentModel.IBindingList.SupportsSorting Property   The
System.ComponentModel.IBindingList.SupportsSorting property supports
the .NET infrastructure and is not used directly from your code.

Table Property   Returns the DataTable used for this view.

```
public DataTable Table { get; }
```

DataView Class Methods

AddNew Method   Adds a new row to the view.

```
public virtual DataRowView AddNew();
```

BeginInit Method   Used at runtime to initialize a DataView that is used on a form.

```
public void BeginInit();
```

Close Method   Closes the DataView object.

```
protected void Close();
```

ColumnCollectionChanged Method   Fires when the DataColumnCollection object changes.

```
protected virtual void ColumnCollectionChanged(object,
    CollectionChangeEventArgs);
```

CopyTo Method   Copies items into the specified array starting at the specified integer index. Only used for Web Forms.

```
public void CopyTo(Array, int);
```

Delete Method   Deletes a row at the specified integer index.

```
public void Delete(int);
```

Dispose Method   Overloaded. Overridden. Disposes the resources used by the DataView. If the Boolean is set to True in the first method, it will dispose of both managed and unmanaged resources, False releases only unmanaged resources. The second method releases all the resources used by the object.

```
protected override void Dispose(bool);
public void Dispose();
```

EndInit Method   Used at runtime to end initialization of a DataTable that is used on a form.

```
public void EndInit();
```

Find Method   Overloaded. Finds the specified row or array of rows in the DataView object and returns its integer index location.

```
public int Find(object);
public int Find(object[]);
```

FindRows Method   Overloaded. Returns an array of DataRowView objects that match the specified object or object array.

```
public DataRowView[] Find(object);
public DataRowView[] Find(object[]);
```

GetEnumerator Method   Returns an IEnumerator object for this collection.

```
public System.Collections.IEnumerator GetEnumerator();
```

IBindingList.AddIndex Method   The IBindingList.AddIndex method supports the .NET infrastructure and is not used directly from your code.

IBindingList.AddNew Method   The IBindingList.AddNew method supports the .NET infrastructure and is not used directly from your code.

IBindingList.ApplySort Method   The IBindingList.ApplySort method supports the .NET infrastructure and is not used directly from your code.

IBindingList.Find Method   The IBindingList.Find method supports the .NET infrastructure and is not used directly from your code.

IBindingList.RemoveIndex Method   The IBindingList.RemoveIndex method supports the .NET infrastructure and is not used directly from your code.

IBindingList.RemoveSort Method   The IBindingList.RemoveSort method supports the .NET infrastructure and is not used directly from your code.

IList.Add Method   The IList.Add method supports the .NET infrastructure and is not used directly from your code.

IList.Clear Method   The IList.Clear method supports the .NET infrastructure and is not used directly from your code.

IList.Contains Method   The IList.Contains method supports the .NET infrastructure and is not used directly from your code.

IList.IndexOf Method   The IList.IndexOf method supports the .NET infrastructure and is not used directly from your code.

IList.Insert Method   The IList.Insert method supports the .NET infrastructure and is not used directly from your code.

IList.Remove Method   The IList.Remove method supports the .NET infrastructure and is not used directly from your code.

IList.RemoveAt Method   The IList.RemoveAt method supports the .NET infrastructure and is not used directly from your code.

IndexListChanged Method   Fires when the DataView has been changed.

```
protected virtual void IndexListChanged(object,
    ListChangedEventArgs);
```

ITypedList.GetItemProperties Method   The ITypedList.GetItemProperties method supports the .NET infrastructure and is not used directly from your code.

ITypedList.GetListName Method   The ITypedList.GetListName method supports the .NET infrastructure and is not used directly from your code.

OnListChanged Method   Raises the ListChanged event, which invokes the event handler delegate.

```
protected virtual void OnListChanged(ListChangedEventArgs);
```

Open Method   Opens the DataView object.

```
protected void Open();
```

Reset Method   Reserved. Internal use only.

UpdateIndex Method   Reserved. Internal use only.

DataView Class Events

ListChanged Event   Fires when a DataView object is changed.

```
public event ListChangedEventHandler ListChanged;
```

Mutual Properties, Methods, and Events Included in the DataView Class
The following lists the mutual properties, methods, and events that are included in the DataView class.

Inherited from MarshalByValueComponent	Inherited from Object
Container property	Equals method
DesignMode property	Finalize method
Events property	GetHashCode method
Site property	GetType method

Inherited from MarshalByValueComponent	**Inherited from Object**
Dispose method	MemberwiseClone method
GetService method	ToString method
Disposed event	

DataViewManager Class

The DataViewManager class contains a DataViewSettingCollection object for each DataSet's DataTable.

```
System.Object
    System.ComponentModel.MarshalByValueComponent
        System.Data.DataViewManager
```

Constructor   Overloaded. The first constructor initializes a new instance of the DataViewManager class. The second constructor initializes a new instance of the DataViewManager class for the specified DataSet.

```
public DataViewManager();
public DataViewManager(DataSet);
// C# example
System.Data.DataSet ds = new System.Data.DataSet();
System.Data.DataViewManager dvm = new System.Data.DataViewManager();
System.Data.DataViewManager dvm2 = new
    System.Data.DataViewManager(ds);
```

DataViewManager Class Properties

DataSet Property   Returns or sets the DataSet object.

```
public DataSet DataSet { get; set; }
```

DataViewSettingCollectionString Property   Returns or sets a string used for code persistence.

```
public string DataViewSettingCollectionString { get; set; }
```

DataViewSettings Property   For each DataTable in the DataSet, returns a DataViewSettingCollection object.

```
public DataViewSettingCollection DataViewSettings { get; }
```

System.Collections.ICollection.Count Property   The System.Collections
.ICollection.Count property supports the .NET infrastructure and is not used
directly from your code.

System.Collections.ICollection.IsSynchronized Property   The System
.Collections.ICollection.IsSynchronized property supports the .NET infrastructure
and is not used directly from your code.

System.Collections.ICollection.SyncRoot Property   The System.Collections
.ICollection.SyncRoot property supports the .NET infrastructure and is not used
directly from your code.

System.Collections.IList.IsFixedSize Property   The System.Collections.IList
.IsFixedSize property supports the .NET infrastructure and is not used directly from
your code.

System.Collections.IList.IsReadOnly Property   The System.Collections.IList
.IsReadOnly property supports the .NET infrastructure and is not used directly from
your code.

System.Collections.IList.Item Property   Implements the System.Collections
.IList.Item interface to return or set the item at the specified location in the collection.

```
object IList.this[int index] { get; set; }
```

System.ComponentModel.IBindingList.AllowEdit Property   The System
.ComponentModel.IBindingList.AllowEdit property supports the .NET infrastructure
and is not used directly from your code.

System.ComponentModel.IBindingList.AllowNew Property   The System
.ComponentModel.IBindingList.AllowNew property supports the .NET infrastructure
and is not used directly from your code.

System.ComponentModel.IBindingList.AllowRemove Property   The System
.ComponentModel.IBindingList.AllowRemove property supports the .NET infrastructure
and is not used directly from your code.

System.ComponentModel.IBindingList.IsSorted Property   The System
.ComponentModel.IBindingList.IsSorted property supports the .NET infrastructure
and is not used directly from your code.

APPENDIXES

System.ComponentModel.IBindingList.SortDirection Property   The System .ComponentModel.IBindingList.SortDirection property supports the .NET infrastructure and is not used directly from your code.

System.ComponentModel.IBindingList.SortProperty Property   The System .ComponentModel.IBindingList.SortProperty property supports the .NET infrastructure and is not used directly from your code.

System.ComponentModel.IBindingList.SupportsChangeNotification Property   The System.ComponentModel.IBindingList.SupportsChangeNotification property supports the .NET infrastructure and is not used directly from your code.

System.ComponentModel.IBindingList.SupportsSearching Property   The System.ComponentModel.IBindingList.SupportsSearching property supports the .NET infrastructure and is not used directly from your code.

System.ComponentModel.IBindingList.SupportsSorting Property   The System.ComponentModel.IBindingList.SupportsSorting property supports the .NET infrastructure and is not used directly from your code.

DataViewManager Class Methods

CreateDataView Method   Creates and returns a DataView object for the specified DataTable.

```
public DataView CreateDataView(DataTable);
```

IBindingList.AddIndex Method   The IBindingList.AddIndex method supports the .NET infrastructure and is not used directly from your code.

IBindingList.AddNew Method   The IBindingList.AddNew method supports the .NET infrastructure and is not used directly from your code.

IBindingList.ApplySort Method   The IBindingList.ApplySort method supports the .NET infrastructure and is not used directly from your code.

IBindingList.Find Method   The IBindingList.Find method supports the .NET infrastructure and is not used directly from your code.

IBindingList.RemoveIndex Method   The IBindingList.RemoveIndex method supports the .NET infrastructure and is not used directly from your code.

IBindingList.RemoveSort Method   The IBindingList.RemoveSort method supports the .NET infrastructure and is not used directly from your code.

ICollection.CopyTo Method The ICollection.CopyTo method supports the .NET infrastructure and is not used directly from your code.

IEnumerable.GetEnumerator Method The IEnumerable.GetEnumerator method supports the .NET infrastructure and is not used directly from your code.

IList.Add Method The IList.Add method supports the .NET infrastructure and is not used directly from your code.

IList.Clear Method The IList.Clear method supports the .NET infrastructure and is not used directly from your code.

IList.Contains Method The IList.Contains method supports the .NET infrastructure and is not used directly from your code.

IList.IndexOf Method The IList.IndexOf method supports the .NET infrastructure and is not used directly from your code.

IList.Insert Method The IList.Insert method supports the .NET infrastructure and is not used directly from your code.

IList.Remove Method The IList.Remove method supports the .NET infrastructure and is not used directly from your code.

IList.RemoveAt Method The IList.RemoveAt method supports the .NET infrastructure and is not used directly from your code.

ITypedList.GetItemProperties Method The ITypedList.GetItemProperties method supports the .NET infrastructure and is not used directly from your code.

ITypedList.GetListName Method The ITypedList.GetListName method supports the .NET infrastructure and is not used directly from your code.

OnListChanged Method Raises the ListChanged event, which invokes the event handler delegate.

```
protected virtual void OnListChanged(ListChangedEventArgs);
```

RelationCollectionChanged Method Raises the CollectionChanged event, which invokes the event handler delegate.

```
protected virtual void RelationCollectionChanged(object,
    CollectionChangeEventArgs);
```

TableCollectionChanged Event   Raises the CollectionChanged event, which invokes the event handler delegate.

```
protected virtual void TableCollectionChanged(object,
    CollectionChangeEventArgs);
```

DataViewManager Class Events

ListChanged Event   Fires when a DataView object is changed.

```
public event ListChangedEventHandler ListChanged;
```

Mutual Properties, Methods, and Events Included in the DataViewManager Class

The following lists the mutual properties, methods, and events that are included in the DataViewManager class.

Inherited from MarshalByValueComponent	Inherited from Object
Container property	Equals method
DesignMode property	Finalize method
Events property	GetHashCode method
Site property	GetType method
Dispose method	MemberwiseClone method
GetService method	ToString method
Disposed event	

DataViewSetting Class

The DataViewSetting class contains default settings for DataView objects that were created using the DataViewManager class.

```
System.Object
    System.Data.DataViewSetting
```

DataViewSetting Class Properties

ApplyDefaultSort Property   Returns or sets a Boolean to indicate the use of default sort. A return value of true indicates the default sort is used; otherwise it returns False.

```
public bool ApplyDefaultSort {get; set; }
```

DataViewManager Property   Returns the DataViewManager object.

```
public DataViewManager DataViewManager { get; }
```

RowFilter Property   Returns or sets a string that contains the filters to apply.

```
public string RowFilter { get; set; }
```

RowStateFilter Property   Returns or sets the DataViewRowState value indicating which rows to display.

```
public DataViewRowState RowStateFilter { get; set; }
```

Sort Property   Returns or sets a string that contains the sort.

```
public string Sort { get; set; }
```

Table Property   Returns the DataTable.

```
public DataTable Table { get; }
```

Mutual Properties, Methods, and Events Included in the DataViewSetting Class

The following lists the mutual properties, methods, and events that are included in the DataViewSetting class.

Inherited from Object

Equals method

Finalize method

GetHashCode method

GetType method

MemberwiseClone method

ToString method

DataViewSettingCollection Class

The DataViewSettingCollection class contains a collection of DataViewSetting objects. You do not create a DataViewSettingCollection by calling a constructor.

System.Object
System.Data.DataViewSettingCollection

DataViewSettingCollection Class Properties

Count Property Returns the number of items in this collection.

```
public virtual int Count { get; }
```

IsReadOnly Property Returns a Boolean of True, indicating that the collection is read-only.

```
public bool IsReadOnly { get; }
```

IsSynchronized Property Returns a Boolean of False, indicating that the access to the collection is synchronized.

```
public bool IsSynchronized { get; }
```

Item Property Overloaded. Returns the specified DataTable object or the DataTable object found at the specified integer index or string table name.

```
public virtual DataViewSetting this[DataTable] { get; set; }
public virtual DataViewSetting this[int index] { get; set; }
public virtual DataViewSetting this[string tblName] {get; }
```

SyncRoot Property Returns an object used to synchronize the collection.

```
public object SyncRoot { get; }
```

DataViewSettingCollection Class Methods

CopyTo Method Copies the objects in the DataViewSettingCollection to the specified array and sets the starting index of the array to the specified integer.

```
public void CopyTo(array, int);
```

GetEnumerator Method   Returns an IEnumerator object for this collection.

```
public System.Collections.IEnumerator GetEnumerator();
```

Mutual Properties, Methods, and Events
Included in the DataViewSettingCollection Class

The following lists the mutual properties, methods, and events that are included in the DataViewSettingCollection class.

Inherited from Object

Equals method

Finalize method

GetHashCode method

GetType method

MemberwiseClone method

ToString method

DBConcurrencyException Class

The DBConcurrencyException class contains the exception that is thrown when the number of affected rows of a DataAdapter is zero when an updated operation is attempted.

```
System.Object
    System.Exception
        System.SystemException
            System.Data.DBConcurrencyException
```

Constructor   Overloaded. The first constructor initializes a new instance of the DBConcurrencyException class and sets any fields to their default value. The second constructor specifies an error message that explains the exception. The third constructor specifies an error message that explains the exception and a reference to an inner exception.

```
public DBConcurrencyException();
public DBConcurrencyException(string);
public DBConcurrencyException(string, Exception);
// C# example
System.Data.DBConcurrencyException dbcEx = new
    System.Data.DBConcurrencyException();
System.Data.DBConcurrencyException dbcEx2 = new
```

```
        System.Data.DBConcurrencyException("DBconcur error");
    System.Exception DBex = new System.Exception();
    System.Data.DBConcurrencyException dbcEx3 = new
        System.Data.DBConcurrencyException("DBconcur error", DBex);
```

DBConcurrencyException Class Properties

Row Property   Returns or sets the value of the DataRow.

```
public DataRow Row { get; set; }
```

DBConcurrencyException Class Methods

GetObjectData Method   Sets the SerializationInfo object with information about the error. The StreamingContext contains the source and destination for the serialization information.

```
public override void GetObjectData(
    System.Runtime.Serialization.SerializationInfo sInfo,
    System.Runtime.Serialization.StreamingContext sContext);
```

Mutual Properties, Methods, and Events Included in the DBConcurrencyException Class

The following lists the mutual properties, methods, and events that are included in the DBConcurrencyException class.

Inherited from Exception	Inherited from Object
HelpLink property	Equals method
HResult property	Finalize method
InnerException property	GetHashCode method
Message property	GetType method
Source property	MemberwiseClone method
StackTrace property	
TargetSite property	
GetBaseException method	
ToString method	

DeletedRowInaccessibleException Class

The DeletedRowInaccessibleException class contains the exception that is thrown when a DataRow object has been deleted and an action is attempted against it.

```
System.Object
    └── System.Exception
            └── System.SystemException
                    └── System.Data.DataException
                            └── System.Data.DeletedRowInaccessibleException
```

Constructor   Overloaded. The first constructor initializes a new instance of the DeletedRowInaccessibleException class. The second constructor initializes a new instance of the DeletedRowInaccessibleException class specifying an error message that explains the exception. The third constructor specifies serialization information and streaming context.

```
public DeletedRowInaccessibleException();
public DeletedRowInaccessibleException(string);
protected DeletedRowInaccessibleException(SerializationInfo siEx,
    StreamingContext scEx);
// C# example
System.Data.DeletedRowInaccessibleException delrEx =
    new System.Data.DeletedRowInaccessibleException();
System.Data.DeletedRowInaccessibleException delrEx2 =
    new System.Data.DeletedRowInaccessibleException("delRow error");
System.Runtime.Serialization.SerializationInfo serInfo;
System.Runtime.Serialization.StreamingContext strmContext;
System.Data.DeletedRowInaccessibleException delrEx3 =
    new System.Data.DeletedRowInaccessibleException(serInfo,
    strmContext);
```

Mutual Properties, Methods, and Events Included in the DeletedRowInaccessibleException Class

The following lists the mutual properties, methods, and events that are included in the DeletedRowInaccessibleException class.

Inherited from Exception	Inherited from Object
HelpLink property	Equals method
HResult property	Finalize method
InnerException property	GetHashCode method

Inherited from Exception	Inherited from Object
Message property	GetType method
Source property	MemberwiseClone method
StackTrace property	
TargetSite property	
GetBaseException method	
GetObjectData method	
ToString method	

DuplicateNameException Class

The DuplicateNameException class contains the exception that is thrown when an add operation is attempted to a DataSet-type object and a duplicate database name is found.

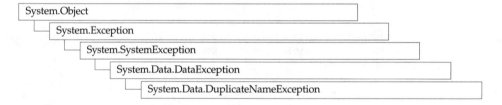

Constructor Overloaded. The first constructor initializes a new instance of the DuplicateNameException class. The second constructor initializes a new instance of the DuplicateNameException class specifying an error message that explains the exception. The third constructor specifies serialization information and streaming context.

```
public DuplicateNameException();
public DuplicateNameException(string);
protected DuplicateNameException(SerializationInfo siEx,
    StreamingContext scEx);
// C# example
System.Data.DuplicateNameException dupEx =
    new System.Data.DuplicateNameException();
System.Data.DuplicateNameException dupEx2 =
    new System.Data.DuplicateNameException("dupName error");
System.Runtime.Serialization.SerializationInfo serInfo;
System.Runtime.Serialization.StreamingContext strmContext;
System.Data.DuplicateNameException dupEx3 =
    new System.Data.DuplicateNameException(serInfo, strmContext);
```

Mutual Properties, Methods, and Events Included in the DuplicateNameException Class

The following lists the mutual properties, methods, and events that are included in the DuplicateNameException class.

Inherited from Exception	**Inherited from Object**
HelpLink property	Equals method
Hresult property	Finalize method
InnerException property	GetHashCode method
Message property	GetType method
Source property	MemberwiseClone method
StackTrace property	
TargetSite property	
GetBaseException method	
GetObjectData method	
ToString method	

EvaluateException Class

The EvaluateException class contains the exception that is thrown when a DataColumn object's Expression property cannot be evaluated.

```
System.Object
  └── System.Exception
        └── System.SystemException
              └── System.Data.DataException
                    └── System.Data.InvalidExpressionException
                          └── System.Data.EvaluateException
```

Constructor   Overloaded. The first constructor initializes a new instance of the EvaluateException class. The second constructor initializes a new instance of the EvaluateException class specifying an error message that explains the exception. The third constructor specifies serialization information and streaming context.

```
public EvaluateException();
public EvaluateException(string);
```

```
protected EvaluateException(SerializationInfo siEx,
    StreamingContext scEx);
// C# example
System.Data.EvaluateException evlEx =
    new System.Data.EvaluateException();
System.Data.EvaluateException evlEx2 =
    new System.Data.EvaluateException("eval error");
System.Runtime.Serialization.SerializationInfo serInfo;
System.Runtime.Serialization.StreamingContext strmContext;
System.Data.EvaluateException evlEx3 =
    new System.Data.EvaluateException(serInfo, strmContext);
```

Mutual Properties, Methods, and Events Included in the EvaluateException Class

The following lists the mutual properties, methods, and events that are included in the EvaluateException class.

Inherited from Exception	Inherited from Object
HelpLink property	Equals method
HResult property	Finalize method
InnerException property	GetHashCode method
Message property	GetType method
Source property	MemberwiseClone method
StackTrace property	
TargetSite property	
GetBaseException method	
GetObjectData method	
ToString method	

FillErrorEventArgs Class

The FillErrorEventArgs class supplies the data for the FillError event for the DbDataAdapter object.

```
System.Object
  └── System.EventArgs
        └── System.Data.FillErrorEventArgs
```

Constructor   Initializes a new instance of the FillErrorEventArgs class for the specified DataTable and object values being updated.

```
public FillErrorEventArgs(DataTable, object[]);
// C# example
System.Data.DataTable dt = new System.Data.DataTable();
string[] sArgs = new string[2];
sArgs[0] = "First error"; sArgs[1] = "Second error";
System.Data.FillErrorEventArgs feea = new
    System.Data.FillErrorEventArgs(dt, sArgs);
```

FillErrorEventArgs Class Properties

Continue Property   Returns or sets a Boolean indicating whether the action should continue. True if the action should continue and False to stop fill action.

```
public bool Continue { get; set; }
```

DataTable Property   Returns the DataTable that is being updated.

```
public DataTable DataTable { get; }
```

Errors Property   Returns or sets the exception error that is being handled by this event.

```
public Exception Errors { get; set; }
```

Values Property   Returns the values for the row being updated.

```
public object[] Values { get; }
```

Mutual Properties, Methods, and Events Included in the FillErrorEventArgs Class

The following lists the mutual properties, methods, and events that are included in the FillErrorEventArgs class.

Inherited from Object

Equals method

Finalize method

Inherited from Object

GetHashCode method

GetType method

MemberwiseClone method

ToString method

ForeignKeyConstraint Class

The ForeignKeyConstraint class contains the rules for actions to perform when a column is updated or deleted.

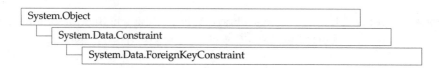

Constructor   Overloaded. The first constructor initializes an instance of the ForeignKeyConstraint class using the specified parent and child columns. The second constructor specifies parent and child column arrays. The third constructor specifies a string name, parent column, and child column. The fourth constructor creates a ForeignKeyConstraint using the specified string name, parent column array, and child column array. The fifth constructor uses the specified string name, parent table name, parent column name array, child column name array, and Rule objects for accept, delete, and update.

```
public ForeignKeyConstraint(DataColumn dcParent, DataColumn dcChild);
public ForeignKeyConstraint(DataColumn[] dcParents,
    DataColumn[] dcChilds);
public ForeignKeyConstraint(string fkeyName, DataColumn dcParent,
    DataColumn dcChild);
public ForeignKeyConstraint(string fkeyName, DataColumn[] dcParents,
    DataColumn[] dcChilds);
public ForeignKeyConstraint(string fkeyName, string tblParentName,
    string[] colParentName, string[] colChildName,
    AcceptRejectRule accRule, Rule delRule, Rule updRule);
// C# example
System.Data.DataColumn dcParent = new System.Data.DataColumn();
System.Data.DataColumn dcChild = new System.Data.DataColumn();
System.Data.DataColumn dcParents = new System.Data.DataColumn();
System.Data.DataColumn dcChilds = new System.Data.DataColumn();
string[] sColParents = new string[1];
string[] sColChilds = new string[1];
sColParents[0] = "Sales"; sColChilds[0] = "ShipToSales";
System.Data.ForeignKeyConstraint fkey = new
```

```
    System.Data.ForeignKeyConstraint(dcParent, dcChild);
System.Data.ForeignKeyConstraint fkey2 = new
    System.Data.ForeignKeyConstraint(dcParents, dcChilds);
System.Data.ForeignKeyConstraint fkey3 = new
    System.Data.ForeignKeyConstraint("CustIdKey", dcParent, dcChild);
System.Data.ForeignKeyConstraint fkey4 = new
    System.Data.ForeignKeyConstraint("CustIdKey", dcParents,
    dcChilds);
System.Data.ForeignKeyConstraint fkey5 = new
    System.Data.ForeignKeyConstraint("CustIdKey", "Customer",
    sColParents, sColChilds, AcceptRejectRule.Cascade,
    Rule.SetDefault, Rule.None);
```

ForeignKeyConstraint Class Properties

AcceptRejectRule Property   Returns or sets the AcceptRejectRule value that should take place when the AcceptChanges event is fired.

```
public virtual AcceptRejectRule AcceptRejectRule { get; set; }
```

Columns Property   Returns an array of DataColumn objects that are child columns for this constraint.

```
public virtual DataColumn[] Columns { get; }
```

DeleteRule Property   Returns or sets the Rule value that should take place when a row is deleted.

```
public virtual Rule DeleteRule { get; set; }
```

RelatedColumns Property   Returns an array of DataColumn objects that are parent columns for this constraint.

```
public virtual DataColumn[] RelatedColumns { get; }
```

RelatedTable Property   Returns the parent table.

```
public virtual DataTable RelatedTable { get; }
```

Table Property   Returns the child table.

```
public override DataTable Table { get; }
```

UpdateRule Property   Returns or sets the Rule value that should take place when a row is updated.

```
public virtual Rule UpdateRule { get; set; }
```

ForeignKeyConstraint Class Methods

Equals Method   Determines the equality of two object instances.

```
public override bool Equals(object);
```

GetHashCode Method   Returns 32-bit signed integer hash code for this DataRowView.

```
public override int GetHashCode();
```

Mutual Properties, Methods, and Events Included in the ForeignKeyConstraint Class

The following lists the mutual properties, methods, and events that are included in the ForeignKeyConstraint class.

Inherited from Constraint	Inherited from Object
ConstraintName property	Finalize method
ExtendedProperties property	GetType method
ToString method	MemberwiseClone method

InRowChangingEventException Class

The InRowChangingEventException class contains the exception that is thrown when calling the RowChanging event's EndEdit method.

System.Object
  System.Exception
    System.SystemException
      System.Data.DataException
        System.Data.InRowChangingEventException

Constructor   Overloaded. The first constructor initializes a new instance of the InRowChangingEventException class. The second constructor initializes a new instance of the InRowChangingEventException class specifying an error message that explains the exception. The third constructor specifies serialization information and streaming context.

```
public InRowChangingEventException();
public InRowChangingEventException(string);
protected InRowChangingEventException(SerializationInfo siEx,
    StreamingContext scEx);
// C# example
System.Data.InRowChangingEventException irceEx =
    new System.Data.InRowChangingEventException();
System.Data.InRowChangingEventException irceEx2 =
    new System.Data.InRowChangingEventException("row change error");
System.Runtime.Serialization.SerializationInfo serInfo;
System.Runtime.Serialization.StreamingContext strmContext;
System.Data.InRowChangingEventException irceEx3 =
    new System.Data.InRowChangingEventException(serInfo,
    strmContext);
```

Mutual Properties, Methods, and Events Included in the InRowChangingEventException Class

The following lists the mutual properties, methods, and events that are included in the InRowChangingEventException class.

Inherited from Exception	Inherited from Object
HelpLink property	Equals method
HResult property	Finalize method
InnerException property	GetHashCode method
Message property	GetType method
Source property	MemberwiseClone method
StackTrace property	
TargetSite property	
GetBaseException method	
GetObjectData method	
ToString method	

InternalDataCollectionBase Class

The InternalDataCollectionBase class is the standard base class for deriving other collection classes.

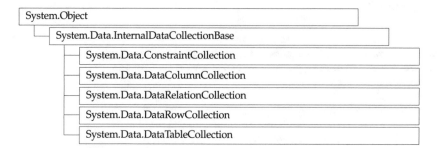

Constructor Initializes a new instance of the InternalDataCollectionBase class.

```
public InternalDataCollectionBase();
// C# example
System.Data.InternalDataCollectionBase idcb = new
    System.Data.InternalDataCollectionBase();
```

InternalDataCollectionBase Class Properties

Count Property Returns the number of items in this collection.

```
public virtual int Count { get; }
```

IsReadOnly Property Returns a Boolean indicating whether the collection is read-only. True if collection is read-only; otherwise it returns False.

```
public bool IsReadOnly { get; }
```

IsSynchronized Property Returns a Boolean indicating whether the collection is synchronized. True if collection is synchronized; otherwise it returns False.

```
public bool IsSynchronized { get; }
```

List Property Returns an ArrayList of items in this collection.

```
protected virtual ArrayList List { get; }
```

SyncRoot Property   Returns an object used to synchronize the collection.

```
public object SyncRoot { get; }
```

InternalDataCollectionBase Class Methods

CopyTo Method   Copies the objects in the InternalDataCollectionBase to the specified array and sets the starting index of the array to the specified integer.

```
public void CopyTo(array, int);
```

GetEnumerator Method   Returns an IEnumerator object for this collection.

```
public System.Collections.IEnumerator GetEnumerator();
```

Mutual Properties, Methods, and Events Included in the InternalDataCollectionBase Class

The following lists the mutual properties, methods, and events that are included in the InternalDataCollectionBase class.

Inherited from Object

Equals method

Finalize method

GetHashCode method

GetType method

MemberwiseClone method

ToString method

InvalidConstraintException Class

The InvalidConstraintException class contains the exception that is thrown when a relation is incorrectly created or accessed.

Constructor Overloaded. The first constructor initializes a new instance of the InvalidConstraintException class. The second constructor initializes a new instance of the InvalidConstraintException class specifying an error message that explains the exception. The third constructor specifies serialization information and streaming context.

```
public InvalidConstraintException();
public InvalidConstraintException(string);
protected InvalidConstraintException(SerializationInfo siEx,
    StreamingContext scEx);
// C# example
System.Data.InvalidConstraintException icEx =
    new System.Data.InvalidConstraintException();
System.Data.InvalidConstraintException icEx2 =
    new System.Data.InvalidConstraintException("inv con error");
System.Runtime.Serialization.SerializationInfo serInfo;
System.Runtime.Serialization.StreamingContext strmContext;
System.Data.InvalidConstraintException icEx3 =
    new System.Data.InvalidConstraintException(serInfo,
strmContext);
```

Mutual Properties, Methods, and Events Included in the InvalidConstraintException Class

The following lists the mutual properties, methods, and events that are included in the InvalidConstraintException class.

Inherited from Exception

HelpLink property

HResult property

InnerException property

Message property

Source property

StackTrace property

TargetSite property

GetBaseException method

GetObjectData method

ToString method

Inherited from Object

Equals method

Finalize method

GetHashCode method

GetType method

MemberwiseClone method

InvalidExpressionException Class

The InvalidExpressionException class contains the exception that is thrown when a DataColumn object that contains an invalid expression is added to the DataColumnCollection.

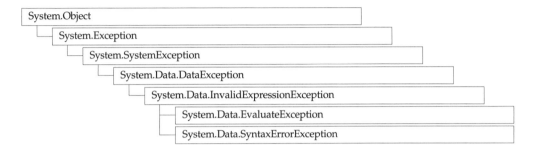

Constructor   Overloaded. The first constructor initializes a new instance of the InvalidExpressionException class. The second constructor initializes a new instance of the InvalidExpressionException class specifying an error message that explains the exception. The third constructor specifies serialization information and streaming context.

```
public InvalidExpressionException();
public InvalidExpressionException(string);
protected InvalidExpressionException(SerializationInfo siEx,
    StreamingContext scEx);
// C# example
System.Data.InvalidExpressionException ieEx =
    new System.Data.InvalidExpressionException();
System.Data.InvalidExpressionException ieEx2 =
    new System.Data.InvalidExpressionException("inv expr error");
System.Runtime.Serialization.SerializationInfo serInfo;
System.Runtime.Serialization.StreamingContext strmContext;
System.Data.InvalidExpressionException ieEx3 =
    new System.Data.InvalidExpressionException(serInfo,
strmContext);
```

Mutual Properties, Methods, and Events Included in the InvalidExpressionException Class

The following lists the mutual properties, methods, and events that are included in the InvalidExpressionException class.

Inherited from Exception	Inherited from Object
HelpLink property	Equals method
HResult property	Finalize method
InnerException property	GetHashCode method
Message property	GetType method
Source property	MemberwiseClone method
StackTrace property	
TargetSite property	
GetBaseException method	
GetObjectData method	
ToString method	

MergeFailedEventArgs Class

The MergeFailedEventArgs class contains conflict data when a target and source DataRow have the same primary key information.

```
System.Object
   └── System.EventArgs
          └── System.Data.MergeFailedEventArgs
```

Constructor   Initializes a new instance of the MergeFailedEventArgs class for the specified DataTable and a string describing the clash.

```
public MergeFailedEventArgs(DataTable, string);
// C# example
System.Data.DataTable dt = new System.Data.DataTable();
System.Data.MergeFailedEventArgs mfea = new
    System.Data.MergeFailedEventArgs(dt, "merge failed");
```

MergeFailedEventArgs Class Properties

Conflict Property   Returns a string describing the clash.

```
public string Conflict { get; }
```

Table Property   Returns the DataTable.

```
public DataTable Table { get; }
```

Mutual Properties, Methods, and Events
Included in the MergeFailedEventArgs Class

The following lists the mutual properties, methods, and events that are included in the MergeFailedEventArgs class.

Inherited from Object

Equals method

Finalize method

GetHashCode method

GetType method

MemberwiseClone method

ToString method

MissingPrimaryKeyException Class

The MissingPrimaryKeyException class contains the exception that is thrown when a row in a table with no primary key is accessed.

```
System.Object
    System.Exception
        System.SystemException
            System.Data.DataException
                System.Data.MissingPrimaryKeyException
```

Constructor   Overloaded. The first constructor initializes a new instance of the MissingPrimaryKeyException class. The second constructor initializes a new instance of the MissingPrimaryKeyException class specifying an error message that explains the exception. The third constructor specifies serialization information and streaming context.

```
public MissingPrimaryKeyException();
public MissingPrimaryKeyException(string);
protected MissingPrimaryKeyException(SerializationInfo siEx,
    StreamingContext scEx);
// C# example
System.Data.MissingPrimaryKeyException mpkEx =
    new System.Data.MissingPrimaryKeyException();
System.Data.MissingPrimaryKeyException mpkEx2 =
```

```
        new System.Data.MissingPrimaryKeyException("prim key error");
System.Runtime.Serialization.SerializationInfo serInfo;
System.Runtime.Serialization.StreamingContext strmContext;
System.Data.MissingPrimaryKeyException mpkEx3 =
        new System.Data.MissingPrimaryKeyException(serInfo, strmContext);
```

Mutual Properties, Methods, and Events Included in the MissingPrimaryKeyException Class

The following lists the mutual properties, methods, and events that are included in the MissingPrimaryKeyException class.

Inherited from Exception	Inherited from Object
HelpLink property	Equals method
HResult property	Finalize method
InnerException property	GetHashCode method
Message property	GetType method
Source property	MemberwiseClone method
StackTrace property	
TargetSite property	
GetBaseException method	
GetObjectData method	
ToString method	

NoNullAllowedException Class

The NoNullAllowedException class contains the exception that is thrown when a column's AllowDBNull property is set to False and null is being inserted into the column.

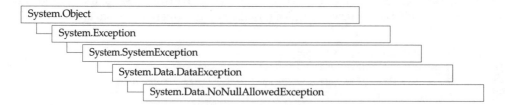

Constructor Overloaded. The first constructor initializes a new instance of the NoNullAllowedException class. The second constructor initializes a new instance of the NoNullAllowedException class specifying an error message that explains the exception. The third constructor specifies serialization information and streaming context.

```
public NoNullAllowedException();
public NoNullAllowedException(string);
protected NoNullAllowedException(SerializationInfo siEx,
    StreamingContext scEx);
// C# example
System.Data.NoNullAllowedException nnaEx =
    new System.Data.NoNullAllowedException();
System.Data.NoNullAllowedException nnaEx2 =
    new System.Data.NoNullAllowedException("no null error");
System.Runtime.Serialization.SerializationInfo serInfo;
System.Runtime.Serialization.StreamingContext strmContext;
System.Data.NoNullAllowedException nnaEx3 =
    new System.Data.NoNullAllowedException(serInfo, strmContext);
```

Mutual Properties, Methods, and Events Included in the NoNullAllowedException Class

The following lists the mutual properties, methods, and events that are included in the NoNullAllowedException class.

Inherited from Exception	Inherited from Object
HelpLink property	Equals method
HResult property	Finalize method
InnerException property	GetHashCode method
Message property	GetType method
Source property	MemberwiseClone method
StackTrace property	
TargetSite property	
GetBaseException method	
GetObjectData method	
ToString method	

APPENDIXES

PropertyCollection Class

The PropertyCollection class allows you to add custom properties to the DataColumn, DataSet, and DataTable objects.

```
System.Object
    System.Collections.Hashtable
        System.Data.PropertyCollection
```

Constructor   Initializes a new instance of the PropertyCollection class.

```
public PropertyCollection();
// C# example
System.Data.PropertyCollection propColl = new
    System.Data.PropertyCollection();
```

Mutual Properties, Methods, and Events Included in the PropertyCollection Class

The following lists the mutual properties, methods, and events that are included in the PropertyCollection class.

Inherited from Hashtable	Inherited from Object
comparer property	Equals method
Count property	Finalize method
hcp property	GetHashCode method
IsFixedSize property	GetType method
IsReadOnly property	MemberwiseClone method
IsSynchronized property	ToString method
Item property	
Keys property	
SyncRoot property	
Values property	
Add method	
Clear method	
Clone method	
Contains method	

Inherited from Hashtable	**Inherited from Object**
ContainsKeys method	
ContainsValue method	
CopyTo method	
GetEnumerator method	
GetHash method	
GetObjectData method	
KeyEquals method	
OnDeserialization method	
Remove method	

ReadOnlyException Class

The ReadOnlyException class contains the exception that is thrown when a read-only column is attempting to be changed.

```
System.Object
    System.Exception
        System.SystemException
            System.Data.DataException
                System.Data.ReadOnlyException
```

Constructor   Overloaded. The first constructor initializes a new instance of the ReadOnlyException class. The second constructor initializes a new instance of the ReadOnlyException class specifying an error message that explains the exception. The third constructor specifies serialization information and streaming context.

```
public ReadOnlyException();
public ReadOnlyException(string);
protected ReadOnlyException(SerializationInfo siEx,
    StreamingContext scEx);
// C# example
System.Data.ReadOnlyException roEx =
    new System.Data.ReadOnlyException();
System.Data.ReadOnlyException roEx2 =
    new System.Data.ReadOnlyException("read only error");
System.Runtime.Serialization.SerializationInfo serInfo;
System.Runtime.Serialization.StreamingContext strmContext;
```

```
System.Data.ReadOnlyException roEx3 =
    new System.Data.ReadOnlyException(serInfo, strmContext);
```

Mutual Properties, Methods, and Events
Included in the ReadOnlyException Class

The following lists the mutual properties, methods, and events that are included in the ReadOnlyException class.

Inherited from Exception	Inherited from Object
HelpLink property	Equals method
HResult property	Finalize method
InnerException property	GetHashCode method
Message property	GetType method
Source property	MemberwiseClone method
StackTrace property	
TargetSite property	
GetBaseException method	
GetObjectData method	
ToString method	

RowNotInTableException Class

The RowNotInTableException class contains the exception that is thrown when an action is attempted against a nonexistent DataRow in a DataTable.

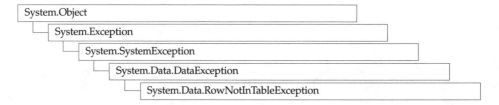

Constructor   Overloaded. The first constructor initializes a new instance of the RowNotInTableException class. The second constructor initializes a new instance of the RowNotInTableException class specifying an error message that explains the exception. The third constructor specifies serialization information and streaming context.

```
public RowNotInTableException();
public RowNotInTableException(string);
protected RowNotInTableException(SerializationInfo siEx,
    StreamingContext scEx);
// C# example
System.Data.RowNotInTableException rnitEx =
    new System.Data.RowNotInTableException();
System.Data.RowNotInTableException rnitEx2 =
    new System.Data.RowNotInTableException("no row error");
System.Runtime.Serialization.SerializationInfo serInfo;
System.Runtime.Serialization.StreamingContext strmContext;
System.Data.RowNotInTableException sqlEx3 =
    new System.Data.RowNotInTableException(serInfo, strmContext);
```

Mutual Properties, Methods, and Events Included in the RowNotInTableException Class

The following lists the mutual properties, methods, and events that are included in the RowNotInTableException class.

Inherited from Exception	Inherited from Object
HelpLink property	Equals method
HResult property	Finalize method
InnerException property	GetHashCode method
Message property	GetType method
Source property	MemberwiseClone method
StackTrace property	
TargetSite property	
GetBaseException method	
GetObjectData method	
ToString method	

StateChangeEventArgs Class

The StateChangeEventArgs class supplies the data for the state change event for the .NET provider.

```
System.Object
    └─ System.EventArgs
        └─ System.Data.StateChangeEventArgs
```

Constructor   Initializes a new instance of the StateChangeEventArgs class using the specified original state and current state.

```
public StateChangeEventArgs(ConnectionState origState,
    ConnectionState currState);
// C# example
System.Data.StateChangeEventArgs scea = new
    System.Data.StateChangeEventArgs(ConnectionState.Open,
    ConnectionState.Broken);
```

StateChangeEventArgs Class Properties

CurrentState Property   Returns the current connection state.

```
public ConnectionState CurrentState { get; }
```

OriginalState Property   Returns the original connection state.

```
public ConnectionState OriginalState { get; }
```

Mutual Properties, Methods, and Events Included in the StateChangeEventArgs Class

The following lists the mutual properties, methods, and events that are included in the StateChangeEventArgs class.

Inherited from Object

Equals method

Finalize method

GetHashCode method

GetType method

MemberwiseClone method

ToString method

StrongTypingException Class

The StrongTypingException class contains the exception that is thrown when a user accesses the DBNull property of a strong-typed DataSet.

```
System.Object
    System.Exception
        System.SystemException
            System.Data.DataException
                System.Data.StrongTypingException
```

Constructor   Overloaded. The first constructor initializes a new instance of the StrongTypingException class. The second constructor specifies serialization information and streaming context. The third constructor specifies an error message that explains the exception and an inner exception.

```
public StrongTypingException();
protected StrongTypingException(SerializationInfo siEx,
    StreamingContext scEx);
public StrongTypingException(string, Exception);
// C# example
System.Data.StrongTypingException stEx =
    new System.Data.StrongTypingException();
System.Exception STex = new System.Exception();
System.Data.StrongTypingException stEx2 =
    new System.Data.StrongTypingException("strong type error", STex);
System.Runtime.Serialization.SerializationInfo serInfo;
System.Runtime.Serialization.StreamingContext strmContext;
System.Data.StrongTypingException stEx3 =
    new System.Data.StrongTypingException(serInfo, strmContext);
```

Mutual Properties, Methods, and Events Included in the StrongTypingException Class

The following lists the mutual properties, methods, and events that are included in the StrongTypingException class.

Inherited from Exception	**Inherited from Object**
HelpLink property	Equals method
HResult property	Finalize method
InnerException property	GetHashCode method
Message property	GetType method
Source property	MemberwiseClone method
StackTrace property	
TargetSite property	
GetBaseException method	

Inherited from Exception	Inherited from Object
GetObjectData method	
ToString method	

SyntaxErrorException Class

The SyntaxErrorException class contains the exception that is thrown when a DataColumn object contains a syntax error in the Expression property.

```
System.Object
    System.Exception
        System.SystemException
            System.Data.DataException
                System.Data.InvalidExpressionException
                    System.Data.SyntaxErrorException
```

Constructor   Overloaded. The first constructor initializes a new instance of the SyntaxErrorException class. The second constructor initializes a new instance of the SyntaxErrorException class specifying an error message that explains the exception. The third constructor specifies serialization information and streaming context.

```
public SyntaxErrorException();
public SyntaxErrorException(string);
protected SyntaxErrorException(SerializationInfo siEx,
    StreamingContext scEx);
// C# example
System.Data.SyntaxErrorException seEx =
    new System.Data.SyntaxErrorException();
System.Data.SyntaxErrorException seEx2 =
    new System.Data.SyntaxErrorException("syntax error");
System.Runtime.Serialization.SerializationInfo serInfo;
System.Runtime.Serialization.StreamingContext strmContext;
System.Data.SyntaxErrorException seEx3 =
    new System.Data.SyntaxErrorException(serInfo, strmContext);
```

Mutual Properties, Methods, and Events Included in the SyntaxErrorException Class

The following lists the mutual properties, methods, and events that are included in the SyntaxErrorException class.

Inherited from Exception	**Inherited from Object**
HelpLink property	Equals method
HResult property	Finalize method
InnerException property	GetHashCode method
Message property	GetType method
Source property	MemberwiseClone method
StackTrace property	
TargetSite property	
GetBaseException method	
GetObjectData method	
ToString method	

TypedDataSetGenerator Class

The TypedDataSetGenerator class contains information for creating strong-type DataSets.

System.Object
System.Data.TypedDataSetGenerator

Constructor   Initializes a new instance of the TypedDataSetGenerator class.

```
public TypedDataSetGenerator();
// C# example
System.Data.TypedDataSetGenerator tdsg = new
    System.Data.TypedDataSetGenerator();
```

TypedDataSetGenerator Class Methods

Generate Method   Creates a strong-typed DataSet using the specified DataSet, CodeNameSpace, and CodeGenerator interface.

```
public static void Generate(DataSet, System.CodeDom.CodeNamespace,
    System.CodeDom.Compiler.ICodeGenerator);
```

GenerateIdName Method   Returns a typed DataSet name as a string value using the specified string name and CodeGenerator interface.

```
public static string GenerateIdName(string,
    System.CodeDom.Compiler.ICodeGenerator);
```

Mutual Properties, Methods, and Events Included in the TypedDataSetGenerator Class

The following lists the mutual properties, methods, and events that are included in the TypedDataSetGeneratorException class.

Inherited from Object

Equals method

Finalize method

GetHashCode method

GetType method

MemberwiseClone method

ToString method

TypedDataSetGeneratorException Class

The TypedDataSetGeneratorException class contains the exception that is thrown when generating a strong-type DataSet and a name conflict occurs.

```
System.Object
    └── System.Exception
            └── System.SystemException
                    └── System.Data.DataException
                            └── System.Data.TypedDataSetGeneratorException
```

Constructor   Overloaded. The first constructor initializes a new instance of the TypedDataSetGeneratorException class. The second constructor initializes a new instance of the TypedDataSetGeneratorException class specifying an ArrayList of exceptions. The third constructor specifies serialization information and streaming context.

```
public TypedDataSetGeneratorException();
public TypedDataSetGeneratorException(ArrayList);
protected TypedDataSetGeneratorException(SerializationInfo siEx,
```

```
        StreamingContext scEx);
// C# example
System.Data.TypedDataSetGeneratorException tdsgEx =
    new System.Data.TypedDataSetGeneratorException ();
System.Collections.ArrayList al = new System.Collections.ArrayList();
al.Add("Typed DS"); al.Add("Generator error");
System.Data.TypedDataSetGeneratorException tdsgEx2 =
    new System.Data.TypedDataSetGeneratorException (al);
System.Runtime.Serialization.SerializationInfo serInfo;
System.Runtime.Serialization.StreamingContext strmContext;
System.Data.TypedDataSetGeneratorException tdsgEx3 =
    new System.Data.TypedDataSetGeneratorException (serInfo,
    strmContext);
```

TypedDataSetGeneratorException Class Properties

ErrorList Property   Returns an arraylist of generated errors.

```
public ArrayList ErrorList { get; }
```

TypedDataSetGeneratorException Class Methods

GetObjectData Method   Sets the SerializationInfo with information about the error.
The StreamingContext contains the source and destination for the serialization information.

```
public override void GetObjectData(
    System.Runtime.Serialization.SerializationInfo sInfo,
    System.Runtime.Serialization.StreamingContext sContext);
```

Mutual Properties, Methods, and Events Included in the TypedDataSetGeneratorException Class

The following lists the mutual properties, methods, and events that are included in the
TypedDataSetGeneratorException class.

Inherited from Exception	Inherited from Object
HelpLink property	Equals method
HResult property	Finalize method
InnerException property	GetHashCode method

Inherited from Exception

Message property

Source property

StackTrace property

TargetSite property

GetBaseException method

ToString method

Inherited from Object

GetType method

MemberwiseClone method

UniqueConstraint Class

The UniqueConstraint class is the rule stating that the primary key must be unique.

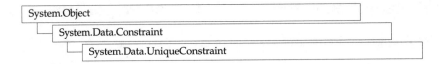

Constructor   Overloaded. The first constructor initializes an instance of the UniqueConstraint class using the specified data column. The second constructor specifies a data column array. The third constructor initializes an instance of the UniqueConstraint class using the specified data column and Boolean indicating whether the constraint is a primary key. True designates the constraint as a primary key. The fourth constructor specifies a data column array and Boolean indicating whether the constraint is a primary key. True designates the constraint as a primary key. The fifth constructor specifies a string constraint name and data column. The sixth constructor creates a UniqueConstraint using the specified string constraint name and data column array. The seventh constructor initializes an instance of the UniqueConstraint class using the specified string constraint name, data column, and Boolean indicating whether the constraint is a primary key. True designates the constraint as a primary key. The eighth constructor specifies a string constraint name, data column array, and Boolean indicating whether the constraint is a primary key. True designates the constraint as a primary key. The ninth constructor specifies a string constraint name, string column name array, and Boolean indicating whether the constraint is a primary key. True designates the constraint as a primary key.

```
public UniqueConstraint(DataColumn);
public UniqueConstraint(DataColumn[]);
public UniqueConstraint(DataColumn, bool primKey);
public UniqueConstraint(DataColumn[], bool primKey);
public UniqueConstraint(string uniName, DataColumn);
public UniqueConstraint(string uniName, DataColumn[]);
```

```
public UniqueConstraint(string uniName, DataColumn, bool primKey);
public UniqueConstraint(string uniName, DataColumn[], bool primKey);
public UniqueConstraint(string uniName, string[] colName,
    bool primKey);
// C# example
System.Data.DataColumn dcol = new System.Data.DataColumn();
System.Data.DataColumn dcols = new System.Data.DataColumn();
string[] colNames = new string[2];
colNames[0] = "CustId"; colNames[1] = "CustName";
System.Data.UniqueConstraint uCon = new
    System.Data.UniqueConstraint(dcol);
System.Data.UniqueConstraint uCon2 = new
    System.Data.UniqueConstraint(dcols);
System.Data.UniqueConstraint uCon3 = new
    System.Data.UniqueConstraint(dcol, true);
System.Data.UniqueConstraint uCon4 = new
    System.Data.UniqueConstraint(dcols, true);
System.Data.UniqueConstraint uCon5 = new
    System.Data.UniqueConstraint("uCon", dcol);
System.Data.UniqueConstraint uCon6 = new
    System.Data.UniqueConstraint("uCon", dcols);
System.Data.UniqueConstraint uCon7 = new
    System.Data.UniqueConstraint("uCon", dcol, true);
System.Data.UniqueConstraint uCon8 = new
    System.Data.UniqueConstraint("uCon", dcols, true);
System.Data.UniqueConstraint uCon9 = new
    System.Data.UniqueConstraint("uCon", colNames, true);
```

UniqueConstraint Class Properties

Columns Property   Returns an array of DataColumn objects that are child columns for this constraint.

```
public virtual DataColumn[] Columns { get; }
```

IsPrimaryKey Property   Returns True if this constraint is on the primary key; otherwise it returns False.

```
public bool IsPrimaryKey { get; }
```

Table Property   Returns the table.

```
public override DataTable Table { get; }
```

UniqueConstraint Class Methods

Equals Method   Determines the equality of two object instances.

```
public override bool Equals(object);
```

GetHashCode Method   Returns 32-bit signed integer hash code for this DataRowView.

```
public override int GetHashCode();
```

Mutual Properties, Methods, and Events Included in the UniqueConstraint Class

The following lists the mutual properties, methods, and events that are included in the UniqueConstraint class.

Inherited from Constraint	Inherited from Object
ConstraintName property	Finalize method
ExtendedProperties property	GetType method
ToString method	MemberwiseClone method

VersionNotFoundException Class

The VersionNotFoundException class contains the exception that is thrown when an attempt is made to retrieve the version information of a DataRow that does not exist.

```
System.Object
    System.Exception
        System.SystemException
            System.Data.DataException
                System.Data.VersionNotFoundException
```

Constructor   Overloaded. The first constructor initializes a new instance of the VersionNotFoundException class. The second constructor initializes a new instance of the VersionNotFoundException class specifying an error message that explains the exception. The third constructor specifies serialization information and streaming context.

```
public VersionNotFoundException();
public VersionNotFoundException(string);
```

```
protected VersionNotFoundException(SerializationInfo siEx,
    StreamingContext scEx);
// C# example
System.Data.VersionNotFoundException vnfEx =
    new System.Data.VersionNotFoundException();
System.Data.VersionNotFoundException vnfEx2 =
    new System.Data.VersionNotFoundException("version error");
System.Runtime.Serialization.SerializationInfo serInfo;
System.Runtime.Serialization.StreamingContext strmContext;
System.Data.VersionNotFoundException vnfEx3 =
    new System.Data.VersionNotFoundException(serInfo, strmContext);
```

Mutual Properties, Methods, and Events Included in the VersionNotFoundException Class

The following lists the mutual properties, methods, and events that are included in the VersionNotFoundException class.

Inherited from Exception	Inherited from Object
HelpLink property	Equals method
HResult property	Finalize method
InnerException property	GetHashCode method
Message property	GetType method
Source property	MemberwiseClone method
StackTrace property	
TargetSite property	
GetBaseException method	
GetObjectData method	
ToString method	

DataColumnChangeEventHandler Delegate

The DataColumnChangeEventHandler delegate is the method that handles the ColumnChanging event. The first parameter, object, indicates the source of the event to handle. The second parameter is a DataColumnChangeEventArgs object that contains the event information.

```
public delegate void DataColumnChangeEventHandler(object,
    DataColumnChangeEventArgs);
```

DataRowChangeEventHandler Delegate

The DataRowChangeEventHandler delegate is the method that handles the RowChanging, RowChanged, RowDeleting, and RowDeleted events of the DataTable object. The first parameter, object, indicates the source of the event to handle. The second parameter is a DataRowChangeEventArgs object that contains the event information.

```
public delegate void DataRowChangeEventHandler(object,
    DataRowChangeEventArgs);
```

FillErrorEventHandler Delegate

The FillErrorEventHandler delegate is the method that handles the FillError event. The first parameter, object, indicates the source of the event to handle. The second parameter is a FillErrorEventArgs object that contains the event information.

```
public delegate void FillErrorEventHandler(object,
    FillErrorEventArgs);
```

MergeFailedEventHandler Delegate

The MergeFailedEventHandler delegate is the method that handles the MergeFailed event. The first parameter, object, indicates the source of the event to handle. The second parameter is a MergeFailedEventArgs object that contains the event information.

```
public delegate void MergeFailedEventHandler(object,
    MergeFailedEventArgs);
```

StateChangeEventHandler Delegate

The StateChangeEventHandler delegate is the method that handles the StateChange event. The first parameter, object, indicates the source of the event to handle. The second parameter is a StateChangeEventArgs object that contains the event information.

```
public delegate void StateChangeEventHandler(object,
    StateChangeEventArgs);
```

AcceptRejectRule Enumeration

The AcceptRejectRule enumeration contains information about the actions that are used in AcceptChanges or RejectChanges method. These actions are used on a DataTable with a ForeignKeyConstraint.

Cascade	Changes cascade through the DataTable and the relationship.
None	No cascade takes place.

CommandBehavior Enumeration

The CommandBehavior enumeration contains information about the literals that are used by the ExecuteReader method. You may use a bitwise combination of these values.

Name	Description	Value
CloseConnection	Close the Connection object when the DataReader object is closed.	32
Default	A query may return multiple results.	0
KeyInfo	Returns column and primary key information.	4
SchemaOnly	Returns column information only.	2
SequentialAccess	Query results are read sequentially.	16
SingleResult	Only one result is returned from the query.	1
SingleRow	Only a single row is returned from the query.	8

CommandType Enumeration

The CommandType enumeration contains information about how a string command is understood.

Text	Default. A SQL statement to execute.
StoredProcedure	The name of a stored procedure to execute.
TableDirect	The name of the table to be accessed.

ConnectionState Enumeration

The ConnectionState enumeration contains information about the literals that are used with the State property of the OleDbConnection and SqlConnection objects. You may use a bitwise combination of these values.

Name	Description	Value
Broken	A previously opened connection is now broken.	16
Closed	The current connection is not open.	0

Name	Description	Value
Connecting	The connection object is attempting to connect to the data source.	2
Executing	The connection object is currently executing a command.	4
Fetching	The connection object is currently fetching data.	8
Open	The current connection is open.	1

DataRowAction Enumeration

The DataRowAction enumeration contains information about the literals that are used by the DataRow object. You may use a bitwise combination of these values.

Name	Description	Value
Add	The row has been added to the DataTable.	16
Change	The DataTable row has changed.	2
Commit	The changes to the DataTable rows have been committed.	8
Delete	The row was deleted from the DataTable.	1
Nothing	The DataTable row has not changed.	0
Rollback	The latest changes to the DataTable rows have been rolled back.	4

DataRowState Enumeration

The DataRowState enumeration contains information about the literals that are used with the RowState property of the DataRow object. You may use a bitwise combination of these values.

Name	Description	Value
Added	The row has been added to the DataRowCollection. AcceptChanges has been called.	4
Deleted	The row was deleted.	8

Name	Description	Value
Detached	The row has been created. The row has not been added to the DataRowCollection.	1
Modified	The row has been changed. AcceptChanges has not been called.	16
Unchanged	The row has not changed.	2

DataRowVersion Enumeration

The DataRowVersion enumeration contains information about the literals that are used to describe the version of the DataRow object.

Current	Row contains current values.
Default	Row is versioned according to the DataRowState.
Original	Row contains its original values.
Proposed	Row contains proposed values.

DataViewRowState Enumeration

The DataViewRowState enumeration contains information about the literals that are used to describe the version of the data in the DataRow object. You may use a bitwise combination of these values.

Name	Description	Value
Added	This is a new row.	4
CurrentRows	These are the current rows.	22
Deleted	This is a deleted row.	8
ModifiedCurrent	This is the current version of the row. This row has been changed from the original.	16
ModifiedOriginal	This is the original version of the row.	32
None	No row.	0
OriginalRows	These are the original rows.	42
Unchanged	This is an unchanged row.	2

DbType Enumeration

The DbType enumeration contains the data types that are used in the fields, properties, or parameters of the data provider.

AnsiString	Variable-length stream of 1 to 8,000 characters. Non-Unicode.
AnsiStringFixedLength	Fixed-length stream of characters. Non-Unicode.
Binary	Variable-length stream of binary data. 1 to 8,000 bytes.
Boolean	Values of True or False.
Byte	8-bit unsigned integer. Value range 0 to 255.
Currency	Value range –922,337,203,685,477.5808 to 922,337,203,685,477.5807. Accuracy to ten-thousandth of unit.
Date	Value range January 1, 1753, to December 31, 9999. Accuracy to 3.33 milliseconds.
DateTime	Represents date and time values.
Decimal	Value range 1.0×10^{-28} to approximately 7.9×10^{28}. Significant digits of 28 to 29.
Double	Floating point type. Value range approximately 5.0×10^{-324} to 1.7×10^{308} Precision of 15 to 16 digits.
Guid	Globally unique identifier.
Int16	Signed 16-bit integer. Value range –32,768 to 32,767.
Int32	Signed 32-bit integer. Value range –2,147,483,648 to 2,147,483,647.
Int64	Signed 64-bit integer. Value range –9,223,372,036,854,775,808 to 9,223,372,036,854,775,807.
Object	General type.
SByte	Signed 8-bit integer. Value range –128 to 127.
Single	Floating point type. Value range approximately 1.5×10^{-45} to 3.4×10^{38}. Precision of 7 digits.
String	String of characters. Unicode.
StringFixedLength	Fixed-length stream of characters. Unicode.
Time	Value range January 1, 1753 to December 31, 9999. Accuracy to 3.33 milliseconds.

Uint16	Unsigned 16-bit integer. Value range 0 to 65,535.
Uint32	Unsigned 32-bit integer. Value range 0 to 4,294,967,295.
Uint64	Unsigned 64-bit integer. Value range 0 to 18,446,744,073,709,551,615.
VarNumeric	Variable-length numeric value.

IsolationLevel Enumeration

The IsolationLevel enumeration contains information about the literals that are used when a data provider performs a transaction. You may use a bitwise combination of these values.

Name	Description	Value
Chaos	Cannot overwrite more highly isolated transactions that are pending.	16
ReadCommited	To avoid dirty reads, the shared locks are held during reading of data. May result in nonrepeatable read or phantom data is changed before the transaction ends.	4096
ReadUncommited	No exclusive locks are allowed and no shared locks are done. May result in a dirty read.	256
RepeatableRead	Locks are placed on the queried data. May result in phantom rows.	65536
Serializable	A range lock is placed on the rows in the DataSet.	1048576
Unspecified	The isolation level cannot be determined.	−1

KeyRestrictionBehavior Enumeration

The KeyRestrictionBehavior enumeration indicates whether a list of connection string parameters are allowed or not allowed. The connection string parameters are identified in the DBDataPermissionAttribute.KeyRestrictions property.

AllowOnly	Default. Only the connection string parameters that are identified are allowed.
PreventUsage	The connection string parameters that are identified are not allowed.

MappingType Enumeration

The MappingType enumeration contains information about the literals that are used in the ColumnMapping property of the DataColumn object.

Attribute	The DataColumn is mapped to an XML attribute.
Element	The DataColumn is mapped to an XML element.
Hidden	The DataColumn is mapped to an internal structure.
SimpleContent	The DataColumn is mapped to XMLText.

MissingMappingAction Enumeration

The MissingMappingAction enumeration contains information about the literals that are used when mapping is missing from a source table of columns.

Error	A SystemException error is generated.
Ignore	The column or table is ignored. Returns a null reference.
Passthrough	Default. The column or table is created and added to the DataSet.

MissingSchemaAction Enumeration

The MissingSchemaAction enumeration contains information about the literals that are used when a DataTable or DataColumn object is missing and data is being added to a DataSet object.

Add	Default. Will add the columns to complete the schema.
AddWithKey	Will add the columns and primary key information to complete the schema.
Error	A SystemException error is generated.
Ignore	The extra columns are ignored.

ParameterDirection Enumeration

The ParameterDirection enumeration contains information about the literals that are used with the parameter direction of the OleDbParameter and SqlParameter objects.

Input	Parameter is input only.
InputOutput	Parameter is both input and output.
Output	Parameter is output only.
ReturnValue	Parameter is a return value from an operation like a stored procedure.

PropertyAttributes Enumeration

The PropertyAttributes enumeration contains information about the attributes of a property. You may use a bitwise combination of these values.

Name	Description	Value
NonSupported	This property is not supported.	0
Optional	User does not need to supply a value for this property.	2
Read	This property may be read.	512
Required	User must supply a value for this property.	1
Write	This property may be written to.	1024

Rule Enumeration

The Rule enumeration contains information about the literals that are used with ForeignKeyConstraint objects.

Cascade	Default. Related rows are updated or deleted.
None	Related rows are not affected.
SetDefault	Related rows are set to their DefaultValue.
SetNull	Related rows are set to DBNull.

SchemaType Enumeration

The SchemaType enumeration contains information about the literals that are used with the FillSchema method.

| Mapped | Use any table or column mappings on the data. |
| Source | Ignore any table or column mappings. |

SqlDbType Enumeration

The SqlDbType enumeration contains information about the SQL Server data types.

BigInt	Int64 : Signed 64-bit integer. Value range –9,223,372,036,854,775,808 to 9,223,372,036,854,775,807.
Binary	An array of type Byte : Variable-length stream of binary data. 1 to 8,000 bytes.
Bit	Boolean : Values of 0,1, or null.
Char	String : Fixed-length stream of non-Unicode characters. Value range 1 and 8,000 characters
DateTime	DateTime : Value range January 1, 1753, to December 31, 9999. Accuracy to 3.33 milliseconds.
Decimal	Decimal : Value range 1.0×10^{-28} to approximately 7.9×10^{28}. Significant digits of 28 to 29.
Float	Double : Floating point type. Value range approximately 5.0×10^{-324} to 1.7×10^{308} Precision of 15 to 16 digits.
Image	An array of type Byte : Variable-length stream of binary data. Value range 0 to 2^{31} –1 (or 2,147,483,647) bytes.
Int	Int32 : Signed 32-bit integer. Value range –2,147,483,648 to 2,147,483,647.
Money	Decimal : Value range -2^{63} (or –922,337,203,685,477.5808) to 2^{63} –1 (or +922,337,203,685,477.5807). Accuracy to a ten-thousandth of a currency unit.
NChar	String : Fixed-length stream of Unicode characters. Value range 1 to 8,000 characters.
NText	String : Variable-length stream of Unicode characters. Value range 1 to 2^{30} –1 (or 1,073,741,823) characters.
NVarChar	String : Variable-length stream of Unicode characters. Value range 1 to 8,000 characters.
Real	Single : Floating point type. Value range –3.40E +38 to 3.40E +38.
SmallDateTime	DateTime : Value range January 1, 1900, to June 6, 2079. Accuracy of one minute.
SmallInt	Int16 : Signed 16-bit integer. Value range –32768 to 32767.

SmallMoney	Decimal : Value range –214,748.3648 to +214,748.3647. Accuracy to a ten-thousandth of a currency unit.
Text	String : Variable-length stream of non-Unicode characters. Value range 1 to $2^{31}-1$ (or 2,147,483,647) characters.
Timestamp	DateTime : Format *yyyymmddhhmmss*.
TinyInt	Byte : Unsigned 8-bit integer. Value range 0 to 255.
UniqueIdentifier	Guid : Globally unique identifier.
VarBinary	An array of type Byte : Variable-length stream of binary data. 1 to 8,000 bytes.
VarChar	String : Variable-length stream of non-Unicode characters. Value range 1 to 8,000 characters.
Variant	Object : General type.

StatementType Enumeration

The StatementType enumeration contains information about the SQL queries used in classes: OleDbRowUpdatedEventArgs, OleDbRowUpdatingEventArgs, SqlRowUpdatedEventArgs, and SqlRowUpdatingEventArgs.

Delete	This is a DELETE statement in a SQL query.
Insert	This is an INSERT statement in a SQL query.
Select	This is a SELECT statement in a SQL query.
Update	This is a UPDATE statement in a SQL query.

UpdateRowSource Enumeration

The UpdateRowSource enumeration contains information about the literals that are used in the UpdatedRowSource property.

Both	The first returned row and the output parameters are mapped to the DataSet at the changed row.
FirstReturnedRecord	The first returned row is mapped to the DataSet at the changed row.
None	Returned results are ignored.
OutputParameters	The output parameters are mapped to the DataSet at the changed row.

UpdateStatus Enumeration

The UpdateStatus enumeration contains information about the literals that are used on the remaining rows when an Update method is executed.

Continue	Default. The DataAdapter continues to process rows.
ErrorsOccurred	The Update should be treated as an error.
SkipAllRemainingRows	Stop processing rows, including current row.
SkipCurrentRow	The current row is not processed.

XmlReadMode Enumeration

The XmlReadMode enumeration contains information about how XML data is read into a DataSet.

Auto	Default; sets XmlReadMode to appropriate mode based on data or dataset schema
DiffGram	Reads a DiffGram and, like Merge, applies changes from the DiffGram to the DataSet
Fragment	Reads XML documents against a SQL Server instance
IgnoreSchema	Reads data into the DataSet schema, ignoring the inline schema
InferSchema	Uses schema inferred from the data, ignoring the inline schema
ReadSchema	Uses the inline schema

XmlWriteMode Enumeration

The XmlWriteMode enumeration contains information about how XML data is read from a DataSet.

DiffGram	Writes the DataSet as a DiffGram
IgnoreSchema	Writes DataSet contents as XML data
WriteSchema	Default; writes DataSet contents as XML data, including relational structure as inline schema

Appendix B

System.Data.Common
Namespace Reference

System.Data.Common Namespace

The System.Data.Common namespace contains the classes that are shared by the System.Data.OleDb and System.Data.SqlClient data providers. Many of these classes are used as base classes for the types defined by the System.Data.OleDb and System.Data.SqlClient data providers.

DataAdapter Class   The DataAdapter class represents a data connection and a set of data commands that are used to fill a DataSet and update the data source.

DataColumnMapping Class   The DataColumnMapping class contains generic column mapping, allowing you to use column names in a DataTable that are different than those in the data source.

DataColumnMappingCollection Class   The DataColumnMappingCollection class contains a collection of DataColumnMapping objects.

DataTableMapping Class   The DataTableMapping class describes the mapping relationship between queried data returned from a data source and a DataTable object.

DataTableMappingCollection Class   The DataTableMappingCollection class contains a collection of DataTableMapping objects.

DbDataAdapter Class   The DbDataAdapter class helps implement the IDbDataAdapter interface, which assists a class with implementing a DataAdapter.

DBDataPermission Class   The DBDataPermission class provides user security–level setting for data access with the System.Data.OleDb and System.Data.SqlClient data providers.

DBDataPermissionAttribute Class   The DBDataPermissionAttribute class relates a security action to a security permission attribute.

DbDataRecord Class   The DbDataRecord class supports the .NET infrastructure and is not used directly from your code.

DbEnumerator Class   The DbEnumerator class supports the .NET infrastructure and is not used directly from your code.

RowUpdatedEventArgs Class   The RowUpdatedEventArgs class supplies the System.Data.OleDb and System.Data.SqlClient data providers with the data for the RowUpdated event.

RowUpdatingEventArgs Class   The RowUpdatingEventArgs class supplies the System.Data.OleDb and System.Data.SqlClient data providers with the data for the RowUpdating event.

DataAdapter Class

The DataAdapter creates a DataSet and manages the data exchanges between the DataSet and the data source. The DataAdapter allows you to map commands to records so that you may manage the data in a DataSet at runtime. By mapping the Fill method, the data in the DataSet changes to match the data in the data source, and mapping the Update method changes the data in the data source to match the data in the DataSet.

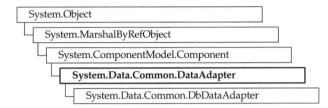

Constructor   Overloaded. The first constructor initializes a new instance of the DataAdapter class. The second constructor creates a new DataAdapter from an existing DataAdapter object; usually used in a clone scenario.

```
protected DataAdapter();
protected DataAdapter(DataAdapter);
// C# example
System.Data.Common.DataAdapter da = new
    System.Data.OleDb.OleDbDataAdapter();
System.Data.Common.DataAdapter da2 = new
    System.Data.OleDb.OleDbDataAdapter(da);
```

DataAdapter Class Properties

AcceptChangesDuringFill Property   Indicates whether the AcceptChanges function is called after a row is added to the DataTable.

```
public bool AcceptChangesDuringFill { get; set; }
```

ContinueUpdateOnError Property   Indicates whether to throw an exception if an error is encountered during an update operation. Set to True to continue without throwing an exception, False to throw an exception. Default is False.

```
public bool ContinueUpdateOnError { get; set; }
```

APPENDIXES

MissingMappingAction Property   Designates the action to take if the data coming in does not have a matching column or table.

```
public System.Data.MissingMappingAction MissingMappingAction
    { get; set; }
```

System.Data.MissingMappingAction enumeration:

Error   A SystemException error is generated.

Ignore   The column or table is ignored. Returns a null reference.

Passthrough   Default. The column or table is created and added to the DataSet.

MissingSchemaAction Property   Designates the action to take if the DataSet schema does not match the data coming in.

```
public System.Data.MissingSchemaAction MissingSchemaAction
    { get; set; }
```

System.Data.MissingSchemaAction enumeration:

Add   Default. Will add the columns to complete the schema.

AddWithKey   Will add the columns and primary key information to complete the schema.

Error   A SystemException error is generated.

Ignore   The extra columns are ignored.

System.Data.IDataAdapter.TableMappings Property   The System.Data.IData-Adapter.TableMappings property supports the .NET infrastructure and is not used directly from your code.

TableMappings Property   Returns a collection that contains the mapping between a DataTable and a source table.

```
public DataTableMappingCollection TableMappings { get; }
```

DataAdapter Class Methods

CloneInternals Method   Creates a copy of the DataAdapter instance. The commands and properties are cloned, but the connections for the commands are not cloned; they are shared, allowing the cloned DataAdapter to use the original connection.

```
protected virtual DataAdapter CloneInternals();
```

Note   *This method is now obsolete.*

CreateTableMappings Method   Creates a new DataTableMappingCollection object.

```
protected virtual DataTableMappingCollection CreateTableMappings();
```

Dispose Method   Overloaded. Overridden. Disposes the resources used by the DataAdapter. If the Boolean is set to True in the first overloaded method, it will dispose of both managed and unmanaged resources.

```
protected override void Dispose(bool);
public virtual void Dispose();
```

Fill Method   Sets the rows in the DataSet to match the rows in the data source and creates DataTable objects if they do not exist. Returns the number of affected rows in the DataSet.

```
public abstract int Fill(DataSet);
```

FillSchema Method   Creates a DataTable and adds it to the specified DataSet, configuring the schema to match the data source. Returns from the data source an array of DataTable objects that contain schema information.

```
public abstract DataTable[] FillSchema(System.Data.DataSet,
    System.Data.SchemaType);
```

System.Data.SchemaType enumeration:

Mapped   Use any table or column mappings on the data.

Source   Ignore any table or column mappings.

GetFillParameters Method   Returns an array of IDataParameter objects that contain the parameters set by the user when executing a SQL SELECT statement.

```
public abstract System.Data.IDataParameter[] GetFillParameters();
```

ShouldSerializeTableMappings Method   Returns Boolean value indicating whether or not DataTableMappings exist.

```
protected virtual bool ShouldSerializeTableMappings();
```

Update Method   Executes to the data source the appropriate INSERT, UPDATE, or DELETE statement for each row in the specified DataSet. Returns the number of affected rows from the DataSet.

```
public abstract int Update(System.Data.DataSet);
```

Mutual Properties, Methods, and Events Included in the DataAdapter Class

The following lists the mutual properties, methods, and events that are included in the DataAdapter class.

Inherited from Component	Inherited from Object	Inherited from MarshalByRefObject
Container property	Equals method	CreateObjRef method
DesignMode property	Finalize method	GetLifetimeService method
Events property	GetHashCode method	InitializeLifetimeService method
Site property	GetType method	
Dispose method	MemberwiseClone method	
GetService method	ToString method	
Disposed event		

DataColumnMapping Class

The DataColumnMapping class allows you to use generic names for columns in a DataTable that are different than the column names in the data source. The DataAdapter uses this mapping to match the column names when the DataTables that are in the DataSet or data source are changed.

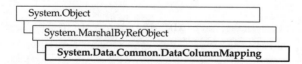

Constructor   Overloaded. Initializes a new instance of the DataColumnMapping class. The first constructor initializes all the fields to their default values. The second constructor specifies a case-sensitive data source column name to map from and a non-case-sensitive column name from a DataSet to map to.

```
public DataColumnMapping();
public DataColumnMapping(string sourceColumn, string datasetColumn);
// C# example
System.Data.Common.DataColumnMapping dcm = new
    System.Data.Common.DataColumnMapping();
System.Data.Common.DataColumnMapping dcm2 = new
    System.Data.Common.DataColumnMapping("CUSTID", "CustomerID");
```

DataColumnMapping Class Properties

DataSetColumn Property   Specifies the name of the column in the DataSet to map to. The column name in the DataSet is not case sensitive.

```
public string DataSetColumn { get; set; }
```

SourceColumn Property   Specifies the name of the column in the data source to map from. The column name in the data source is case sensitive.

```
public string SourceColumn { get; set; }
```

DataColumnMapping Class Methods

GetDataColumnBySchemaAction Method   Returns a DataColumn from the specified DataTable by searching the DataTable by the specified Type. If a DataColumn of the requested Type cannot be found in the DataTable, the action in the MissingSchemaAction parameter is performed. The returned DataColumn is given the name found in the DataSetColumn property.

```
public System.Data.DataColumn GetDataColumnBySchemaAction(
    System.Data.DataTable, System.Type,
    System.Data.MissingSchemaAction);
```

System.Data.MissingSchemaAction enumeration:

Add   Creates a DataColumn, but does not add it to the DataTable.

Error   An exception error is generated.

Ignore   Returns a null.

ICloneable.Clone Method   The ICloneable.Clone method supports the .NET infrastructure and is not used directly from your code.

```
object ICloneable.Clone();
```

ToString Method   Overridden. Returns the current SourceColumn name as a string.

```
public override string ToString();
```

Mutual Properties, Methods, and Events Included in the DataColumnMapping Class

The following lists the mutual properties, methods, and events that are included in the DataColumnMapping class.

Inherited from Object	Inherited from MarshalByRefObject
Equals method	CreateObjRef method
Finalize method	GetLifetimeService method
GetHashCode method	InitializeLifetimeService method
GetType method	
MemberwiseClone method	

DataColumnMappingCollection Class

The DataColumnMappingCollection class contains a collection of the DataColumnMapping objects.

```
┌─────────────────────────────────────────────────────┐
│ System.Object                                        │
│  ┌───────────────────────────────────────────────┐  │
│  │ System.MarshalByRefObject                     │  │
│  │  ┌─────────────────────────────────────────┐  │  │
│  │  │ System.Data.Common.DataColumnMappingCollection │  │
│  │  └─────────────────────────────────────────┘  │  │
│  └───────────────────────────────────────────────┘  │
└─────────────────────────────────────────────────────┘
```

Constructor   Creates a DataColumnMappingCollection object and initializes all the fields to their default values.

```
public DataColumnMappingCollection();
// C# example
System.Data.Common.DataColumnMappingCollection dcmCol = new
    System.Data.Common.DataColumnMappingCollection();
```

DataColumnMappingCollection Class Properties

Count Property   Returns the number of items in this collection.

```
public int Count { get; }
```

Item Property   Overloaded. Returns or sets the DataColumnMapping object found at the specified integer index or string source column name.

```
public DataColumnMapping this[int index] { get; set; }
public DataColumnMapping this[string sourceColumn] {get; set; }
```

System.Collections.ICollection.IsSynchronized Property   The System .Collections.ICollection.IsSynchronized property supports the .NET infrastructure and is not used directly from your code.

System.Collections.ICollection.SyncRoot Property   The System.Collections .ICollection.SyncRoot property supports the .NET infrastructure and is not used directly from your code.

System.Collections.IList.IsFixedSize Property   The System.Collections.IList .IsFixedSize property supports the .NET infrastructure and is not used directly from your code.

System.Collections.IList.IsReadOnly Property   The System.Collections.IList .IsReadOnly property supports the .NET infrastructure and is not used directly from your code.

System.Collections.IList.Item Property   Implements the System.Collections .IList.Item interface to return or set the item at the specified location in the collection.

```
object IList.this[int index] { get; set; }
```

System.Data.IColumnMappingCollection.Item Property   Implements the System.Data.IColumnMappingCollection.Item interface to return or set the item at the specified location in the collection.

```
object IColumnMappingCollection.this[string index] { get; set; }
```

DataColumnMappingCollection Class Methods

Add Method   Overloaded. The first Add method adds the specified Object to the DataColumnMappingCollection and returns the index of the added Object. The second Add method adds column mapping to the collection specifying the case-sensitive source column name to map to in the first parameter, and the non-case-sensitive DataSet column name to map to in the second parameter. The second Add method returns the DataColumnMapping object that was added.

```
public int Add(Object);
public DataColumnMapping Add(string sourceColumn,
    string datasetColumn);
```

AddRange Method   Adds an array of DataColumnMapping objects to the end of the DataColumnMappingCollection.

```
public void AddRange(DataColumnMapping[]);
```

Clear Method   Removes all the items from the DataColumnMappingCollection.

```
public void Clear();
```

Contains Method   Overloaded. The first Contains method returns True if the DataColumnMappingCollection contains the specified Object. The second Contains method returns True if the collection contains a DataColumnMapping object with the specified case-sensitive source column name.

```
public bool Contains(Object);
public bool Contains(string sourceColumn);
```

CopyTo Method   Copies the objects in the DataColumnMappingCollection to the specified array and sets the starting index of the array to the specified integer.

```
public void CopyTo(array, int);
```

GetByDataSetColumn Method   Returns the DataColumnMapping object with the specified non-case-sensitive DataSet column name.

```
public DataColumnMapping GetByDataSetColumn(string datasetColumn);
```

GetColumnMappingBySchemaAction Method   Returns a DataColumnMapping from the specified DataColumnMappingCollection by searching the collection by the specified case-sensitive source column name. If a DataColumnMapping of the requested source column name cannot be found in the collection, the action in the MissingMappingAction parameter is performed.

```
public static DataColumnMapping GetDataColumnMappingBySchemaAction(
    DataColumnMappingCollection, string sourceColumn,
    System.Data.MissingMappingAction);
```

System.Data.MissingMappingAction enumeration:

Passthrough   Creates a DataColumnMapping object and sets both the source
                 column name and the DataSet name with the specified source column
                 name. The created DataColumnMapping is not added to the collection.

Error   An exception error is generated.

Ignore   Returns a null.

GetEnumerator Method   The GetEnumerator method supports the .NET infrastructure and is not used directly from your code.

```
public IEnumerator GetEnumerator();
```

IColumnMappingCollection.Add Method   The IColumnMappingCollection.Add method supports the .NET infrastructure and is not used directly from your code.

```
IColumnMapping IColumnMappingCollection.Add(string srcColName,
    string datasetColName);
```

IColumnMappingCollection.GetByDataSetColumn Method   The IColumnMappingCollection.GetByDataSetColumn method supports the .NET infrastructure and is not used directly from your code.

```
IColumnMapping IColumnMappingCollection.GetByDataSetColumn(
    string datasetColName);
```

IndexOf Method   Overloaded. The first IndexOf method returns the location of the specified Object of type DataColumnMapping within the DataColumnMappingCollection. The second IndexOf method returns the location of the DataColumnMapping object with the specified case-sensitive source column name.

```
public int IndexOf(Object);
public int IndexOf(string sourceColumn);
```

IndexOfDataSetColumn Method   Returns the location of the DataColumnMapping object within the DataColumnMappingCollection with the specified non-case-sensitive DataSet column name. Returns –1 if the DataColumnMapping object does not exist in the collection.

```
public int IndexOfDataSetColumn(string datasetColumn);
```

Insert Method   Inserts a DataColumnMapping object into the DataColumnMappingCollection at the specified zero-based integer index.

```
public void Insert(int, object);
```

Remove Method   Removes an object that is of type DataColumnMapping from the DataColumnMappingCollection. Throws a SystemException if the specified object is not of type DataColumnMapping or the specified object does not exist in the collection.

```
public void Remove(object);
```

RemoveAt Method   Overloaded. The first RemoveAt method removes the DataColumnMapping object from the DataColumnMappingCollection at the specified zero-based integer index. The second RemoveAt method removes the DataColumnMapping object from the collection that matches the specified case-sensitive source column name. Both methods throw an IndexOutOfRangeException if the DataColumnMapping object does not exist in the collection at the specified location.

```
public void RemoveAt(int);
public void RemoveAt(string sourceColumn);
```

Mutual Properties, Methods, and Events Included in the DataColumnMappingCollection Class

The following lists the mutual properties, methods, and events that are included in the DataColumnMappingCollection class.

Inherited from Object	Inherited from MarshalByRefObject
Equals method	CreateObjRef method
Finalize method	GetLifetimeService method
GetHashCode method	InitializeLifetimeService method
GetType method	
MemberwiseClone method	
ToString method	

DataTableMapping Class

The DataTableMapping class provides a mapping relationship between a source table and a DataTable. The DataTableMapping name may be passed to a DataAdapter to populate a DataSet in place of the DataTable name.

```
System.Object
   └── System.MarshalByRefObject
          └── System.Data.Common.DataTableMapping
```

Constructor   Overloaded. Initializes a new instance of the DataTableMapping class. The first constructor initializes all the fields to their default values. The second constructor specifies a case-sensitive source table name from a data source and a table name from a DataSet to map to. The third constructor specifies a case-sensitive source table name from a data source and a table name from a DataSet to map to, and includes mapping the columns in the specified DataColumnMapping array.

```
public DataTableMapping();
public DataTableMapping(string sourceTable, string datasetTable);
public DataTableMapping(string sourceTable, string datasetTable,
    DataColumnMapping[]);
// C# example
System.Data.Common.DataTableMapping dtm = new
    System.Data.Common.DataTableMapping();
System.Data.Common.DataTableMapping dtm2 = new
    System.Data.Common.DataTableMapping("CUSTOMERS",
    "DataCustomers");
System.Data.Common.DataColumnMapping[] dcm3 = {};
System.Data.Common.DataTableMapping dtm3 = new
    System.Data.Common.DataTableMapping("CUSTOMERS",
    "DataCustomers", dcm3);
```

DataTableMapping Class Properties

ColumnMappings Property   Returns the DataColumnMappingCollection object for this DataTable.

```
public DataColumnMappingCollection ColumnMappings { get; }
```

DataSetTable Property   Returns or sets the table name from a DataSet object.

```
public string DataSetTable { get; set; }
```

SourceTable Property   Returns or sets the case-sensitive source table name from a data source.

```
public string SourceTable { get; set; }
```

System.Data.ITableMapping.ColumnMappings Property   The System.Data .ITableMapping.ColumnMappings property supports the .NET infrastructure and is not used directly from your code.

DataTableMapping Class Methods

GetColumnMappingBySchemaAction Method   Returns a DataColumn from the specified DataTable searching by the specified DataColumn name. If a DataColumn of the requested DataColumn name cannot be found in the DataTable, the action in the MissingMappingAction parameter is performed.

```
public DataColumnMapping GetColumnBySchemaAction(
    string sourceColumn, System.Data.MissingMappingAction);
```

System.Data.MissingMappingAction enumeration:

Error	A SystemException error is generated.
Ignore	The column or table is ignored. Returns a null reference.
Passthrough	The column or table is created and added to the DataSet.

GetDataTableBySchemaAction Method   Returns the current DataTable from the specified DataSet. If the DataTable does not exist, the action in the MissingSchema-Action parameter is performed.

```
public System.Data.DataTable GetDataTableBySchemaAction(
    System.Data.DataSet, System.Data.MissingSchemaAction);
```

System.Data.MissingSchemaAction enumeration:

Add	Default. Will add the columns to complete the schema.
AddWithKey	Will add the columns and primary key information to complete the schema.
Error	A SystemException error is generated.
Ignore	The extra columns are ignored.

ICloneable.Clone Method   The ICloneable.Clone method supports the .NET infrastructure and is not used directly from your code.

```
object ICloneable.Clone();
```

ToString Method   Returns the current SourceTable name as a string.

```
public override string ToString();
```

Mutual Properties, Methods, and Events Included in the DataTableMapping Class

The following lists the mutual properties, methods, and events that are included in the DataTableMapping class.

Inherited from Object	Inherited from MarshalByRefObject
Equals method	CreateObjRef method
Finalize method	GetLifetimeService method
GetHashCode method	InitializeLifetimeService method
GetType method	
MemberwiseClone method	

DataTableMappingCollection Class

The DataTableMappingCollection class contains a collection of the DataTableMapping objects.

```
System.Object
  └── System.MarshalByRefObject
        └── System.Data.Common.DataTableMappingCollection
```

Constructor   Creates a DataTableMappingCollection object and initializes all the fields to their default values.

```
public DataTableMappingCollection();
// C# example
System.Data.Common.DataTableMappingCollection dtmCol = new
    System.Data.Common.DataTableMappingCollection();
```

APPENDIXES

DataTableMappingCollection Class Properties

Count Property   Returns the number of items in this collection.

```
public int Count { get; }
```

Item Property   Overloaded. Returns or sets the DataTableMapping object found at the specified integer index or string source table name.

```
public DataTableMapping this[int index] { get; set; }
public DataTableMapping this[string sourceTable] {get; set; }
```

System.Collections.ICollection.IsSynchronized Property   The System.Collections .ICollection.IsSynchronized property supports the .NET infrastructure and is not used directly from your code.

System.Collections.ICollection.SyncRoot Property   The System.Collections .ICollection.SyncRoot property supports the .NET infrastructure and is not used directly from your code.

System.Collections.IList.IsFixedSize Property   The System.Collections.IList .IsFixedSize property supports the .NET infrastructure and is not used directly from your code.

System.Collections.IList.IsReadOnly Property   The System.Collections.IList .IsReadOnly property supports the .NET infrastructure and is not used directly from your code.

System.Collections.IList.Item Property   Implements the System.Collections.IList .Item interface to return or set the item at the specified location in the collection.

```
object IList.this[int index] { get; set; }
```

System.Data.ITableMappingCollection.Item Property   Implements the System .Data.ITableMappingCollection.Item interface to return or set the item at the specified location in the collection.

```
object ITableMappingCollection.this[string index] { get; set; }
```

DataTableMappingCollection Class Methods

Add Method   Overloaded. The first Add method adds the specified Object to the DataTableMappingCollection and returns the index of the added Object. The second Add method adds table mapping to the collection specifying the case-sensitive source table name to map to in the first parameter, and the non-case-sensitive DataSet table name to map to in the second parameter. The second Add method returns the DataTableMapping object that was added.

```
public int Add(Object);
public DataTableMapping Add(string sourceTable,string datasetTable);
```

AddRange Method   Adds an array of DataTableMapping objects to the end of the DataTableMappingCollection.

```
public void AddRange(DataTableMapping[]);
```

Clear Method   Removes all the items from the DataTableMappingCollection.

```
public void Clear();
```

Contains Method   Overloaded. The first Contains method returns True if the DataTableMappingCollection contains the specified Object. The second Contains method returns True if the collection contains a DataTableMapping object with the specified case-sensitive source table name.

```
public bool Contains(Object);
public bool Contains(string sourceTable);
```

CopyTo Method   Copies the objects in the DataTableMappingCollection to the specified array and sets the starting index of the array to the specified integer.

```
public void CopyTo(array, int);
```

GetByDataSetTable Method   Returns the DataTableMapping object with the specified non-case-sensitive DataSet table name.

```
public DataTableMapping GetByDataSetTable(string datasetTable);
```

GetEnumerator Method   The GetEnumerator method supports the .NET infrastructure and is not used directly from your code.

```
public IEnumerator GetEnumerator();
```

GetTableMappingBySchemaAction Method   Returns a DataTableMapping from the specified DataTableMappingCollection by searching the collection by the specified case-sensitive source table name. Also assigns the specified non-case-sensitive name to the DataSet table. If a DataTableMapping of the requested source table name cannot be found in the collection, the action in the MissingMappingAction parameter is performed.

```
public static DataTableMapping GetTableMappingBySchemaAction(
    DataTableMappingCollection, string sourceTable,
    string datasetTable, System.Data.MissingMappingAction);
```

System.Data.MissingMappingAction enumeration:

Passthrough	Creates a DataTableMapping object and sets the source table name to the specified sourceTable string and the DataSet name with the specified datasetTable string. The created DataTableMapping is not added to the collection.
Error	An exception error is generated. The datasetTable parameter is ignored.
Ignore	Returns a null. The datasetTable parameter is ignored.

IndexOf Method   Overloaded. The first IndexOf method returns the location of the specified Object of type DataTableMapping within the DataTableMappingCollection. The second IndexOf method returns the location of the DataTableMapping object with the specified case-sensitive source table name.

```
public int IndexOf(Object);
public int IndexOf(string sourceTable);
```

IndexOfDataSetTable Method   Returns the location of the DataTableMapping object within the DataTableMappingCollection with the specified non-case-sensitive DataSet table name. Returns –1 if the DataTableMapping object does not exist in the collection.

```
public int IndexOfDataSetTable(string datasetTable);
```

Insert Method   Inserts a DataTableMapping object into the DataTableMappingCollection at the specified zero-based integer index.

```
public void Insert(int, object);
```

ITableMappingCollection.Add Method   The ITableMappingCollection.Add method supports the .NET infrastructure and is not used directly from your code.

```
ITableMapping ITableMappingCollection.Add(string srcTabName,
    string datasetTabName);
```

ITableMappingCollection.GetByDataSetTable Method   The ITableMappingCollection .GetByDataSetTable method supports the .NET infrastructure and is not used directly from your code.

```
ITableMapping ITableMappingCollection.GetByDataSetTable(
    string datasetTabName);
```

Remove Method   Removes an object that is of type DataTableMapping from the DataTableMappingCollection. Throws a SystemException if the specified object is not of type DataTableMapping or the specified object does not exist in the collection.

```
public void Remove(object);
```

RemoveAt Method   Overloaded. The first RemoveAt method removes the DataTableMapping object from the DataTableMappingCollection at the specified zero-based integer index. The second RemoveAt method removes the DataTableMapping object from the collection that matches the specified case-sensitive source table name. Both methods throw an IndexOutOfRangeException if the DataTableMapping object does not exist in the collection at the specified location.

```
public void RemoveAt(int);
public void RemoveAt(string sourceTable);
```

Mutual Properties, Methods, and Events Included in the DataTableMappingCollection Class

The following lists the mutual properties, methods, and events that are included in the DataTableMappingCollection class.

Inherited from Object	Inherited from MarshalByRefObject
Equals method	CreateObjRef method
Finalize method	GetLifetimeService method
GetHashCode method	InitializeLifetimeService method
GetType method	
MemberwiseClone method	
ToString method	

DbDataAdapter Class

The DbDataAdapter class inherits from the DataAdapter class and assists a class in the implementation of a DataAdapter through the IDbDataAdapter interface. The inherited DbDataAdapter class would be designed for use with a relational database and must implement the inherited members. You would then define additional members to allow provider-specific functionality.

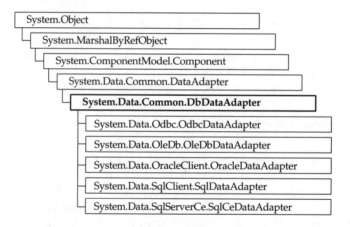

Constructor   Overloaded. The first constructor initializes a new instance of the DbDataAdapter class. The second constructor creates a new DbDataAdapter from an existing DbDataAdapter object; usually used in a clone scenario.

```
protected DbDataAdapter();
protected DbDataAdapter(DbDataAdapter);
// C# example
System.Data.Common.DbDataAdapter dbda;
```

DbDataAdapter Class Fields

DefaultSourceTableName Field   Contains the default name used by the DataAdapter object when an application adds a table mapping and the application does not specify a DataTable name.

```
public const string DefaultSourceTableName;
```

DbDataAdapter Class Methods

CreateRowUpdatedEvent Method   Returns a new instance of the RowUpdated-EventArgs class. The first parameter of the CreateRowUpdatedEvent method is the DataRow that is used to update the data source. The second parameter, IDbCommand, represents the SQL statement that is executed during the Update; and the third parameter, StatementType, specifies whether the command is a SELECT, INSERT, UPDATE, or DELETE statement. The fourth parameter is the DataTableMapping object.

```
protected abstract RowUpdatedEventArgs CreateRowUpdatedEvent(
    System.Data.DataRow, System.Data.IDbCommand,
    System.Data.StatementType, DataTableMapping);
```

CreateRowUpdatingEvent Method   Returns a new instance of the RowUpdatingEventArgs class. The first parameter of the CreateRowUpdatingEvent method is the DataRow that is used to update the data source. The second parameter, IDbCommand, represents the SQL statement that is executed during the Update; and the third parameter, StatementType, specifies whether the command is a SELECT, INSERT, UPDATE, or DELETE statement. The fourth parameter is the DataTableMapping object.

```
protected abstract RowUpdatingEventArgs CreateRowUpdatingEvent(
    System.Data.DataRow, System.Data.IDbCommand,
    System.Data.StatementType, DataTableMapping);
```

Dispose Method   Overloaded. Overridden. Disposes the resources used by the DataAdapter. If the Boolean is set to True in the first overloaded method, it will dispose of both managed and unmanaged resources.

```
protected override void Dispose(bool);
public virtual void Dispose();
```

Fill Method   Overloaded. Sets rows in the DataSet to match the rows in the data source using the specified parameters. Returns the number of affected rows. The first method synchronizes the data and creates a DataTable named Table. The second method synchronizes the data in the specified DataTable. The third method synchronizes the data using the specified DataSet and source table. The fourth method synchronizes the data using the specified DataTable and IDataReader object. An IDataReader allows reading of forward-only streams. The fifth method synchronizes the data using the specified DataTable. The fifth method allows you to specify an IDbCommand object, which is the SQL statement used to retrieve rows from the data source and the command behavior that will take place. The sixth method synchronizes the data using the specified DataSet and source table, starting at the specified zero-based record and continuing for the specified maximum records. The seventh method synchronizes the data using the specified DataSet, source table for mapping, and IDataReader object. The seventh method starts at the specified zero-based record and continues for the specified maximum records. The eighth method synchronizes the data using the specified DataSet and source table, starting at the specified zero-based record and continuing for the specified maximum records. The eighth method allows you to specify an IDbCommand object, which is the SQL statement used to retrieve rows from the data source and the command behavior that will take place.

```
public override int Fill(System.Data.DataSet);
public int Fill(System.Data.DataTable);
public int Fill(System.Data.DataSet, string sourceTable);
protected virtual int Fill(System.Data.DataTable,
    System.Data.IDataReader);
protected virtual int Fill(System.Data.DataTable,
    System.Data.IDbCommand, System.Data.CommandBehavior);
public int Fill(System.Data.DataSet, int startRecord, int maxRecords,
    string sourceTable);
protected virtual int Fill(System.Data.DataSet, string sourceTable,
    System.Data.IDataReader, int startRecord, int maxRecords);
protected virtual int Fill(System.Data.DataSet, int startRecord,
    int maxRecords, string sourceTable, System.Data.IDbCommand,
    System.Data.CommandBehavior);
```

System.Data.CommandBehavior enumeration:

CloseConnection	Close the Connection object when the DataReader object is closed.
KeyInfo	Returns column and primary key information.
SchemaOnly	Returns column information only.
SequentialAccess	Query results are read sequentially.
SingleResult	Only one result is returned from the query.
SingleRow	Only a single row is returned from the query.

FillSchema Method   Overloaded. Adds a DataTable to a DataSet configuring the schema to match the data source. Returns from the data source a DataTable object or an array of DataTable objects that contain schema information. The first method configures the specified DataTable based on the specified SchemaType. The second method configures the specified DataTable based on the specified SchemaType and allows you to specify an IDbCommand object, which is the SQL statement used to retrieve rows from the data source and the command behavior that will take place. The third method configures the specified DataSet based on the specified SchemaType. The fourth method configures the specified DataSet based on the specified SchemaType and source table for mapping. The fifth method configures the specified DataSet DataTable based on the specified SchemaType and source table for mapping. The fifth method also allows you to specify an IDbCommand object, which is the SQL statement used to retrieve rows from the data source and the command behavior that will take place.

```
public System.Data.DataTable FillSchema(System.Data.DataTable,
    System.Data.SchemaType);
protected virtual System.Data.DataTable FillSchema(
    System.Data.DataTable, System.Data.SchemaType,
    System.Data.IDbCommand, System.Data.CommandBehavior);
public override System.Data.DataTable[] FillSchema(
    System.Data.DataSet, System.Data.SchemaType);
public System.Data.DataTable[] FillSchema(System.Data.DataSet,
    System.Data.SchemaType, string sourceTable);
protected virtual System.Data.DataTable[] FillSchema(
    System.Data.DataTable, System.Data.SchemaType,
    System.Data.IDbCommand, string sourceTable,
    System.Data.CommandBehavior);
```

System.Data.SchemaType enumeration:

Mapped	Use any table or column mappings on the data.
Source	Ignore any table or column mappings.

System.Data.CommandBehavior enumeration:

CloseConnection	Close the Connection object when the DataReader object is closed.
KeyInfo	Returns column and primary key information.
SchemaOnly	Returns column information only.
SequentialAccess	Query results are read sequentially.
SingleResult	Only one result is returned from the query.
SingleRow	Only a single row is returned from the query.

GetFillParameters Method   Returns an array of IDataParameter objects that contain the parameters set by the user when executing a SQL SELECT statement.

```
public override System.Data.IDataParameter[] GetFillParameters();
```

ICloneable.Clone Method

 Note   *This method is now obsolete.*

The ICloneable.Clone method supports the .NET infrastructure and is not used directly from your code.

```
object ICloneable.Clone();
```

OnFillError Method   Raises the FillError event. The FillErrorEventArgs parameter contains the event data that is raised.

```
protected virtual void OnFillError(System.Data.FillErrorEventArgs);
```

OnRowUpdated Method   Raises the RowUpdated event. The RowUpdatedEventArgs parameter contains the event data that is raised.

```
protected abstract void OnRowUpdated(RowUpdatedEventArgs);
```

OnRowUpdating Method   Raises the RowUpdating event. The RowUpdating EventArgs parameter contains the event data that is raised.

```
protected abstract void OnRowUpdating(RowUpdatingEventArgs);
```

Update Method   Overloaded. Executes the appropriate INSERT, UPDATE, or DELETE statement for each row in the specified parameter object. Returns the number of affected rows.

```
public int Update(System.Data.DataRow[]);
public override int Update(System.Data.DataSet);
public int Update(System.Data.DataTable);
protected virtual int Update(System.Data.DataRow[],
    DataTableMapping);
public int Update(System.Data.DataSet, string sourceTable);
```

DbDataAdapter Class Events

FillError Event   Fires when an error occurs during a Fill operation. The FillError EventHandler designates the event that will handle the error.

```
public event System.Data.FillErrorEventHandler FillError;
```

Mutual Properties, Methods, and Events Included in the DbDataAdapter Class

The following lists the mutual properties, methods, and events that are included in the DbDataAdapter class.

Inherited from Component	Inherited from Object	Inherited from MarshalByRefObject
Container property	Equals method	CreateObjRef method
DesignMode property	Finalize method	GetLifetimeService method
Events property	GetHashCode method	InitializeLifetimeService method
Site property	GetType method	
Dispose method	MemberwiseClone method	
GetService method	ToString method	
Disposed event		

The following also lists the properties, methods, and events inherited from the DataAdapter class.

Inherited from DataAdapter

AcceptChangesDuringFill property

ContinueUpdateOnError property

MissingMappingAction property

MissingSchemaAction property

TableMappings property

CloneInternals method

CreateTableMappings method

ShouldSerializeTableMappings method

DBDataPermission Class

The DBDataPermission class provides the ability for the data provider to ascertain that a user has the adequate security level to access data.

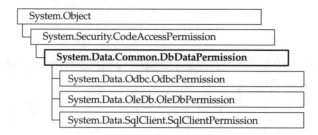

Constructor   Overloaded. Initializes a new instance of the DBDataPermission class. The second constructor creates a new DBDataPermission class from an existing DBDataPermission class; usually used in a clone scenario. The third constructor creates a DBDataPermission class with the specified custom permission attributes. The fourth constructor specifies whether a user should have all access or no access. The fifth constructor checks for all access or no access and a blank password.

```
protected DBDataPermission();
protected DBDataPermission(DBDataPermission);
protected DBDataPermission(DBDataPermissionAttribute);
protected DBDataPermission(
    System.Security.Permissions.PermissionState);
protected DBDataPermission(
    System.Security.Permissions.PermissionState,
    bool allowBlankPassword);
// C# example
System.Data.Common.DBDataPermission dbdp =
    new System.Data.OleDb.OleDbPermission();
System.Data.Common.DBDataPermission dbdp2 =
    new System.Data.OleDb.OleDbPermission(dbdp);
System.Data.Common.DBDataPermission dbdp3 =
    new System.Data.OleDb.OleDbPermission(
    DBDataPermissionAttribute.KeyRestrictions);
System.Data.Common.DBDataPermission dbdp4 =
    new System.Data.OleDb.OleDbPermission(
    System.Security.Permissions.PermissionState.None);
System.Data.Common.DBDataPermission dbdp5 =
    new System.Data.OleDb.OleDbPermission(
    System.Security.Permissions.PermissionState.None, true);
```

System.Security.Permissions.PermissionState enumeration:

None	Indicates no access to the resource
Unrestricted	Indicates full access to the resource

DBDataPermission Class Properties

AllowBlankPassword Property   Returns or sets a Boolean indicating whether a blank password is allowed.

```
public bool AllowBlankPassword { get; set; }
```

DBDataPermission Class Methods

Add Method   Adds to the state of the permission the specified access for the specified connection string.

```
public virtual void Add(string conn, string restrict,
    System.Data.KeyRestrictionBehavior);
```

System.Data.KeyRestrictionBehavior enumeration:

AllowOnly	Default. Only the connection string parameters that are identified are allowed.
PreventUsage	The connection string parameters that are identified are not allowed.

Clear Method   Removes permissions added using the Add method.

```
protected void Clear();
```

Copy Method   Returns a copy of the current security permission object, IPermission, with the same access to resources as the original object. The IPermission object describes the functions of the object.

```
public override System.Security.IPermission Copy();
```

CreateInstance Method   Creates a new DataPermission object.

```
protected virtual DBDataPermission CreateInstance();
```

FromXml Method   Builds a security object with the specified XML security-encoded state.

```
public override void FromXml(System.Security.SecurityElement);
```

Intersect Method   Returns a security permission object, IPermission, that intersects the current permission object with the specified permission object. A request that passes both original permission objects will be allowed to pass the intersection. An IPermission object describes the functions of the object.

```
public override System.Security.IPermission Intersect(
    System.Security.IPermission);
```

IsSubsetOf Method   Returns True if the current security permission object is a subset of the specified permission object. The IPermission object describes the functions of the object.

```
public override bool IsSubsetOf(System.Security.IPermission);
```

IsUnrestricted Method   Returns True if a security permission object can be represented as unrestricted. Because this is a binary representation, it will always return True.

```
public bool IsUnrestricted();
```

ToXml Method   Returns an XML security encoding of the current security object with its current state information.

```
public override System.Security.SecurityElement ToXml();
```

Union Method   Returns a security permission object that joins the current permission object with the specified permission object. A request that passes either permission object will pass the union. An IPermission object describes the functions of the object.

```
public override System.Security.IPermission Union(
    System.Security.IPermission);
```

Mutual Properties, Methods, and Events Included in the DBDataPermission Class

The following lists the mutual properties, methods, and events that are included in the DBDataPermission class.

Inherited from CodeAccessPermission	Inherited from Object
Assert method	Equals method
Demand method	Finalize method
Deny method	GetHashCode method
PermitOnly method	GetType method
ToString method	MemberwiseClone method

DBDataPermissionAttribute Class

The DBDataPermissionAttribute class relates a security action to a security permission attribute.

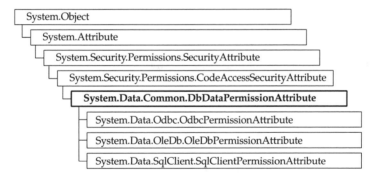

```
System.Object
  System.Attribute
    System.Security.Permissions.SecurityAttribute
      System.Security.Permissions.CodeAccessSecurityAttribute
        System.Data.Common.DbDataPermissionAttribute
          System.Data.Odbc.OdbcPermissionAttribute
          System.Data.OleDb.OleDbPermissionAttribute
          System.Data.SqlClient.SqlClientPermissionAttribute
```

Constructor   Initializes a new instance of the DBDataPermissionAttribute class.

```
protected DBDataPermissionAttribute(
    System.Security.Permissions.SecurityAction);
// C# example
System.Data.Common.DBDataPermissionAttribute dbdpa =
    new System.Data.OleDb.OleDbPermissionAttribute(
    System.Security.Permissions.SecurityAction.LinkDemand);
```

System.Security.Permissions.SecurityAction enumeration:

Assert	Allows security to bypass code permission check.
Demand	Performs security check for enforcing restrictions on calling code.
Deny	Prevents access to the resource specified.
InheritanceDemand	Checks for granted permissions for inherited class.
LinkDemand	Checks for granted permission for immediate caller.
PermitOnly	Allows access only to the resource specified.
RequestMinimum	Requests the minimum permissions for code.
RequestOptional	Requests the optional permissions.
RequestRefuse	Request permissions not be granted to calling code.

DBDataPermissionAttribute Class Properties

AllowBlankPassword Property   Returns or sets a Boolean indicating whether a blank password is allowed.

```
public bool AllowBlankPassword { get; set; }
```

ConnectionString Property   Returns or sets the permitted connection string.

```
public string ConnectionString { get; set; }
```

KeyRestrictionBehavior Property   Returns or sets the allowed connection string parameter values.

```
public System.Data.KeyRestrictionBehavior KeyRestrictionBehavior
    { get; set; }
```

System.Data.KeyRestrictionBehavior enumeration:

AllowOnly	Default. Only the connection string parameters that are identified are allowed.
PreventUsage	The connection string parameters that are identified are not allowed.

KeyRestrictions Property   Returns or sets the connection string parameter restrictions.

```
public string KeyRestrictions { get; set; }
```

Mutual Properties, Methods, and Events Included in the DBDataPermissionAttribute Class

The following lists the mutual properties, methods, and events that are included in the DBDataPermissionAttribute class.

Inherited from Attribute	Inherited from Object	Inherited from SecurityAttribute
TypeId property	Equals method	Action property
GetHashCode method	Finalize method	Unrestricted property
IsDefaultAttribute method	GetType method	CreatePermission method
Match method	MemberwiseClone method	
	ToString method	

DbDataRecord Class

The DbDataRecord class provides data binding support for the DbEnumerator class and implements the IDataRecord and ICustomTypeDescriptor classes.

DbDataRecord Class Properties

FieldCount Property   Returns the number of fields in the current record.

```
public virtual int FieldCount {get; }
```

Item Property   Overloaded. Returns the object found at the specified integer index or string parameter name.

```
public object this[string] { get; }
public object this[int] { get; }
```

DbDataRecord Class Methods

GetBoolean Method   Returns the column specified by the integer as a Boolean.

```
public virtual bool GetBoolean(int);
```

GetByte Method   Returns the column specified by the integer as a byte.

```
public virtual byte GetByte(int);
```

GetBytes Method   Returns the value of the column specified by the integer starting at the point in the srcDataIndex. Copies the information into the buffer, starting at the point in the bufferIndex for a length of the specified length integer.

```
public virtual long GetBytes (int i, long srcDataIndex,
    byte[] buffer, int bufferIndex, int length);
```

GetChar Method   Returns the column specified by the integer as a character.

```
public virtual char GetChar(int);
```

GetChars Method   Returns the value of the column specified by the integer starting at the point in the srcDataIndex. Copies the information into the buffer, starting at the point in the bufferIndex for a length of the specified length integer.

```
public virtual long GetChars (int i, long srcDataIndex,
    char[] buffer, int bufferIndex, int length);
```

GetData Method   The GetData method supports the .NET infrastructure and is not used directly from your code.

```
public virtual IDataReader GetData(int);
```

GetDataTypeName Method   Returns the name of the back-end data type for the column specified by the integer.

```
public virtual string GetDataTypeName(int);
```

GetDateTime Method   Returns the column specified by the integer as a DateTime object. No conversion is performed.

```
public virtual DateTime GetDateTime(int);
```

GetDecimal Method   Returns the column specified by the integer as a decimal.

```
public virtual decimal GetDecimal(int);
```

GetDouble Method   Returns the column specified by the integer as a double.

```
public virtual double GetDouble(int);
```

GetFieldType Method   Returns the column specified by the integer as a System.Type.

```
public virtual System.Type GetFieldType(int);
```

GetFloat Method   Returns the column specified by the integer as a floating point number.

```
public virtual float GetFloat(int);
```

GetGuid Method   Returns the column specified by the integer as a System.Guid.

```
public virtual System.Guid GetGuid(int);
```

GetInt16 Method   Returns the column specified by the integer as a 16-bit signed integer.

```
public virtual short GetInt16(int);
```

GetInt32 Method   Returns the column specified by the integer as a 32-bit signed integer.

```
public virtual int GetInt32(int);
```

GetInt64 Method   Returns the column specified by the integer as a 64-bit signed integer.

```
public virtual long GetInt64(int);
```

GetName Method   Returns the name of the column specified by the integer.

```
public virtual string GetName(int);
```

GetOrdinal Method   Returns the ordinal of the column specified by the column name.

```
public virtual int GetOrdinal(string name);
```

GetString Method   Returns the column specified by the integer as a string.

```
public virtual string GetString(int);
```

GetValue Method   Returns the column specified by the integer in its native format.

```
public virtual object GetValue(int);
```

GetValues Method   Returns the field attributes for the current record.

```
public virtual int GetValues(object[] values);
```

ICustomTypeDescriptor.GetAttributes Method   The ICustomTypeDescriptor
.GetAttributes method supports the .NET infrastructure and is not used directly from
your code.

```
AttributeCollection ICustomTypeDescriptor.GetAttributes();
```

ICustomTypeDescriptor.GetClassName Method   The
ICustomTypeDescriptor.GetClassName method supports the .NET infrastructure and
is not used directly from your code.

```
string ICustomTypeDescriptor.GetClassName();
```

ICustomTypeDescriptor.GetComponentName Method   The ICustomType
Descriptor.GetComponentName method supports the .NET infrastructure and is not
used directly from your code.

```
string ICustomTypeDescriptor.GetComponentName();
```

ICustomTypeDescriptor.GetConverter Method   The ICustomTypeDescriptor
.GetConverter method supports the .NET infrastructure and is not used directly from
your code.

```
TypeConverter ICustomTypeDescriptor.GetConverter();
```

ICustomTypeDescriptor.GetDefaultEvent Method   The ICustomTypeDescriptor
.GetDefaultEvent method supports the .NET infrastructure and is not used directly
from your code.

```
EventDescriptor ICustomTypeDescriptor.GetDefaultEvent();
```

ICustomTypeDescriptor.GetDefaultProperty Method   The ICustomTypeDescriptor
.GetDefaultProperty method supports the .NET infrastructure and is not used directly
from your code.

```
PropertyDescriptor ICustomTypeDescriptor.GetDefaultDescriptor();
```

ICustomTypeDescriptor.GetEditor Method   The ICustomTypeDescriptor.GetEditor
method supports the .NET infrastructure and is not used directly from your code.

```
object ICustomTypeDescriptor.GetEditor(Type editorbasetype);
```

ICustomTypeDescriptor.GetEvents Method   The ICustomTypeDescriptor.Get-
Events method supports the .NET infrastructure and is not used directly from
your code.

```
EventDescriptorCollection ICustomTypeDescriptor.GetEvents();
EventDescriptorCollection ICustomTypeDescriptor.GetEvents(
    Attribute[] attributes);
```

ICustomTypeDescriptor.GetProperties Method   The ICustomTypeDescriptor
.GetProperties method supports the .NET infrastructure and is not used directly from
your code.

```
PropertyDescriptorCollection ICustomTypeDescriptor.GetProperties();
PropertyDescriptorCollection ICustomTypeDescriptor.GetProperties(
    Attribute[] attributes);
```

ICustomTypeDescriptor.GetPropertyOwner Method   The ICustomTypeDescriptor
.GetPropertyOwner method supports the .NET infrastructure and is not used directly
from your code.

```
object ICustomTypeDescriptor.GetPropertyOwner(
    PropertyDescriptor propdesc);
```

APPENDIXES

IsDBNull Method   Returns True if the specified column contains DBNull, else returns False.

```
public virtual bool IsDBNull(int);
```

Mutual Properties, Methods, and Events Included in the DbDataRecord Class

The following lists the mutual properties, methods, and events that are included in the DbDataRecord class.

Inherited from Object

Equals method

Finalize method

GetHashCode method

GetType method

MemberwiseClone method

ToString method

DbEnumerator Class

The DbEnumerator class is implemented by the .NET Framework data providers for data binding support. Supports a simple iteration over a collection by exposing the GetEnumerator method.

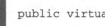

System.Object
System.Data.Common.DbDataEnumerator

Constructor   Overloaded. Initializes a new instance of the DbEnumerator class using the specified DataReader. The second constructor specifies the DataReader and whether to close the DataReader after iterating through its data.

```
public DbEnumerator(IDataReader);
public DbEnumerator(IDataReader, bool);
// C# example
System.Data.SqlClient.SqlConnection sqlCn = new
    System.Data.SqlClient.SqlConnection(
    "server=TECA4;uid=sa;pwd=;database=NW2");
System.Data.SqlClient.SqlCommand sqlCmd = new
```

```
    System.Data.SqlClient.SqlCommand("SELECT * FROM Shippers",sqlCn);
sqlCn.Open();
System.Data.SqlClient.SqlDataReader dr = sqlCmd.ExecuteReader();
System.Data.IDataReader iDR = dr;
DbEnumerator dbE = new DbEnumerator(iDR);
DbEnumerator dbE = new DbEnumerator(iDR, True);
```

DbEnumerator Class Properties

Current Property   Returns the current element of the collection.

```
public object Current { get; }
```

DbEnumerator Class Methods

MoveNext Method   Moves the enumerator to the next element of the collection and returns True if successful. Returns False if unsuccessful.

```
public virtual bool MoveNext();
```

Reset Method   Moves the enumerator to before the first element in the collection.

```
public virtual void Reset();
```

Mutual Properties, Methods, and Events Included in the DbEnumerator Class

The following lists the mutual properties, methods, and events that are included in the DbEnumerator class.

Inherited from Object

Equals method

Finalize method

GetHashCode method

GetType method

MemberwiseClone method

ToString method

RowUpdatedEventArgs Class

The RowUpdatedEventArgs class supplies the .NET Framework data providers with the data for the RowUpdated event.

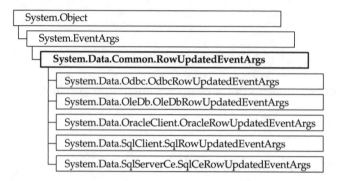

Constructor   Initializes a new instance of the RowUpdatedEventArgs class using the specified DataRow, the IDbCommand, and the StatementType. The IDbCommand represents the SQL statement that was executed, and the StatementType specifies whether the command was a SELECT, INSERT, UPDATE, or DELETE statement. Also uses the mapped tables specified.

```
protected RowUpdatedEventArgs(System.Data.DataRow,
    System.Data.IDbCommand, System.Data.StatementType,
    DataTableMapping);
// C# example
System.Data.DataRow dr = new System.Data.DataTable().NewRow();
System.Data.OleDb.OleDbCommand cmd = new
    System.Data.OleDb.OleDbCommand("SELECT * from Customers");
System.Data.Common.DataTableMapping dtm = new
    System.Data.Common.DataTableMapping();
System.Data.Common.RowUpdatedEventArgs ruea = new
    System.Data.OleDb.OleDbRowUpdatedEventArgs(dr, cmd,
    System.Data.StatementType.Select, dtm);
```

RowUpdatedEventArgs Class Properties

Command Property   Returns the SQL statement, IDbCommand, that was executed when Update was called.

```
public System.Data.IDbCommand Command { get; }
```

Errors Property   Contains the exception errors generated when a command was executed.

```
public System.Exception Errors { get; set; }
```

RecordsAffected Property   Returns the number of rows affected by an INSERT, CHANGE, or DELETE SQL statement. Returns 0 if no rows were affected or the SQL statement failed. Returns –1 if the SQL statement is a SELECT statement.

```
public int RecordsAffected { get; }
```

Row Property   Returns the DataRow used with an Update command.

```
public System.Data.DataRow Row {get; }
```

StatementType Property   Returns the type of SQL statement, StatementType, that was executed. The StatementType specifies whether the command is a SELECT, INSERT, UPDATE, or DELETE statement.

```
public System.Data.StatementType StatementType { get; }
```

Status Property   Returns or sets the UpdateStatus value for a command. The UpdateStatus specifies the actions to take on rows during an Update.

```
public System.Data.UpdateStatus Status { get; set; }
```

System.Data.UpdateStatus enumeration:

Continue	Default. The DataAdapter continues to process rows.
ErrorsOccurred	The Update should be treated as an error.
SkipAllRemainingRows	Stop processing rows, including current row.
SkipCurrentRow	The current row is not processed.

TableMapping Property   Returns the DataTableMapping used with an Update command.

```
public DataTableMapping TableMapping { get; }
```

Mutual Properties, Methods, and Events Included in the RowUpdatedEventArgs Class

The following lists the mutual properties, methods, and events that are included in the RowUpdatedEventArgs class.

Inherited from Object

Equals method

Finalize method

GetHashCode method

GetType method

MemberwiseClone method

ToString method

RowUpdatingEventArgs Class

The RowUpdatingEventArgs class supplies the .NET Framework data providers with the data for the RowUpdating event.

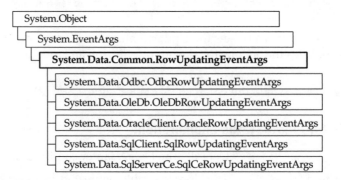

Constructor   Initializes a new instance of the RowUpdatedEventArgs class using the specified DataRow, the IDbCommand, and the StatementType. The IDbCommand represents the SQL statement that will be executed and the StatementType specifies whether the command is a SELECT, INSERT, UPDATE, or DELETE statement.

```
protected RowUpdatingEventArgs(System.Data.DataRow,
    System.Data.IDbCommand, System.Data.StatementType,
    DataTableMapping);
// C# example
System.Data.DataRow dr = new System.Data.DataTable().NewRow();
System.Data.OleDb.OleDbCommand cmd = new
```

```
    System.Data.OleDb.OleDbCommand("SELECT * from Customers");
System.Data.Common.DataTableMapping dtm = new
    System.Data.Common.DataTableMapping();
System.Data.Common.RowUpdatingEventArgs ruea = new
    System.Data.OleDb.OleDbRowUpdatingEventArgs(dr, cmd,
    System.Data.StatementType.Select, dtm);
```

RowUpdatingEventArgs Class Properties

Command Property   Returns or sets the SQL statement, IDbCommand, that will be executed when Update is called.

```
public System.Data.IDbCommand Command { get; set; }
```

Errors Property   Contains the exception errors generated when a command is executed.

```
public System.Exception Errors { get; set; }
```

Row Property   Returns the DataRow that will be used with an Update command.

```
public System.Data.DataRow Row {get; }
```

StatementType Property   Returns the type of SQL statement, StatementType, that will be executed. The StatementType specifies whether the command is a SELECT, INSERT, UPDATE, or DELETE statement.

```
public System.Data.StatementType StatementType { get; }
```

Status Property   Returns or sets the UpdateStatus value for a command. The UpdateStatus specifies the actions to take on rows during an Update.

```
public System.Data.UpdateStatus Status { get; set; }
```

System.Data.UpdateStatus enumeration:

Continue	Default. The DataAdapter continues to process rows.
ErrorsOccurred	The Update should be treated as an error.
SkipAllRemainingRows	Stop processing rows, including current row.
SkipCurrentRow	The current row is not processed.

TableMapping Property   Returns the DataTableMapping that will be used with an Update command.

```
public DataTableMapping TableMapping { get; }
```

Mutual Properties, Methods, and Events Included in the RowUpdatingEventArgs Class

The following lists the mutual properties, methods, and events that are included in the RowUpdatingEventArgs class.

Inherited from Object

Equals method

Finalize method

GetHashCode method

GetType method

MemberwiseClone method

ToString method

The Complete Reference

Appendix C

System.Data.Odbc Namespace Reference

System.Data.Odbc Namespace

The System.Data.Odbc namespace contains classes that comprise the ODBC .NET Data Provider, which are a group of classes that are used to access native ODBC drivers.

OdbcCommand Class   The OdbcCommand class represents a stored procedure or SQL statement to implement at a data source.

OdbcCommandBuilder Class   The OdbcCommandBuilder class allows for automatic generation of single table commands.

OdbcConnection Class   The OdbcConnection class represents a connection to an ODBC data source name.

OdbcDataAdapter Class   The OdbcDataAdapter class represents a database connection and a set of commands that are used to fill a DataSet and update a data source.

OdbcDataReader Class   The OdbcDataReader class allows for reading forward-only streams of data rows from a data source.

OdbcError Class   The OdbcError class contains information regarding errors returned by the data source.

OdbcErrorCollection Class   The OdbcErrorCollection class contains a collection of OdbcError objects.

OdbcException Class   The OdbcException class represents the exception that is thrown when an error is returned by the ODBC data source.

OdbcInfoMessageEventArgs Class   The OdbcInfoMessageEventArgs class supplies information for the InfoMessage event.

OdbcParameter Class   The OdbcParameter class represents a parameter for the OdbcCommand object. It may also be used for the OdbcCommand object's mapping to the DataSet column.

OdbcParameterCollection Class   The OdbcParameterCollection class is a collection of OdbcParameter classes and their related mapping information for DataSet columns.

OdbcPermission Class   The OdbcPermission class provides user security level setting for data access with the ODBC data providers.

OdbcPermissionAttribute Class   The OdbcPermissionAttribute class relates a security action to a security permission attribute.

OdbcRowUpdatedEventArgs Class   The OdbcRowUpdatedEventArgs class supplies the information for the RowUpdated event.

OdbcRowUpdatingEventArgs Class   The OdbcRowUpdatingEventArgs class supplies the information for the RowUpdating event.

OdbcTransaction Class   The OdbcTransaction class represents a SQL transaction to implement at a data source.

OdbcInfoMessageEventHandler Delegate   The OdbcInfoMessageEventHandler delegate is the method that handles the InfoMessage event of the OdbcConnection object.

OdbcRowUpdatedEventHandler Delegate   The OdbcRowUpdatedEventHandler delegate is the method that handles the RowUpdatedEvent of the OdbcDataAdapter object.

OdbcRowUpdatingEventHandler Delegate   The OdbcRowUpdatingEventHandler delegate is the method that handles the RowUpdatingEvent of the OdbcDataAdapter object.

OdbcType Enumeration   The OdbcType enumeration contains the data types that are used in the fields, properties, or parameters of the namespace objects.

OdbcCommand Class

The OdbcCommand class represents a stored procedure or SQL statement to implement at a data source. A new instance of the OdbcCommand will set the read/write properties to their initial values.

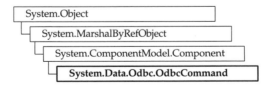

Constructor   Overloaded. Initializes a new instance of the OdbcCommand class. The first constructor initializes all the fields to their default value. The second constructor specifies the text of a query to execute. The third constructor specifies the text of the query to execute through the specified OdbcConnection. The fourth constructor specifies the text of the query to execute through the specified OdbcConnection as reflected through the specified OdbcTransaction object.

```
public OdbcCommand();
public OdbcCommand(string cmdText);
public OdbcCommand(string cmdText, OdbcConnection);
public OdbcCommand(string cmdText, OdbcConnection, OdbcTransaction);
// C# example
System.Data.Odbc.OdbcCommand odbcCmd = new
    System.Data.Odbc.OdbcCommand();
System.Data.Odbc.OdbcCommand odbcCmd2 = new
    System.Data.Odbc.OdbcCommand("SELECT * FROM Customers");
System.Data.Odbc.OdbcConnection odbcConn = new
    System.Data.Odbc.OdbcConnection();
System.Data.Odbc.OdbcCommand odbcCmd3 = new
    System.Data.Odbc.OdbcCommand("SELECT * FROM Customers",
    odbcConn);
System.Data.Odbc.OdbcTransaction odbcTrans =
    odbcConn.BeginTransaction();
System.Data.Odbc.OdbcCommand odbcCmd4 = new
    System.Data.Odbc.OdbcCommand("SELECT * FROM Customers",
    odbcConn, odbcTrans);
```

OdbcCommand Class Properties

CommandText Property   Returns or sets the SQL statement query text or stored procedure to execute.

```
public string CommandText { get; set; }
```

CommandTimeout Property   Returns or sets the wait time in seconds before an attempted command is terminated and an error is generated. Default wait time is 30 seconds.

```
public int CommandTimeout { get; set; }
```

CommandType Property   Designates what type of command this object is.

```
public System.Data.CommandType CommandType { get; set; }
```

System.Data.CommandType enumeration:

Text	Default. A SQL statement to execute.
StoredProcedure	The name of a stored procedure to execute.
TableDirect	The name of the table to be accessed.

Connection Property   Returns or sets the OdbcConnection object for this OdbcCommand object.

```
public OdbcConnection Connection { get; set; }
```

DesignTimeVisible Property   Returns or sets a Boolean value specifying whether the OdbcCommand object should be visible. The default value is False.

```
public bool DesignTimeVisible { get; set; }
```

Parameters Property   Returns the OdbcParameterCollection, which designates the parameters for a stored procedure or SQL statement for this OdbcCommand object.

```
public OdbcParametersCollection Parameters { get; }
```

Transaction Property   Returns or sets the OdbcTransaction that the OdbcCommand implements.

```
public OdbcTransaction Transaction { get; set; }
```

UpdatedRowSource Property   Returns or sets how the results of a command are applied to a DataSet when the Update method is used. If the command is automatically generated, the default result is None; otherwise, the default result is Both.

```
public System.Data.UpdateRowSource UpdatedRowSource { get; set; }
```

System.Data.UpdateRowSource enumeration:

Both	The first returned row and the output parameters are mapped to the DataSet at the changed row.
FirstReturnedRecord	The first returned row is mapped to the DataSet at the changed row.
None	Returned results are ignored.
OutputParameters	The output parameters are mapped to the DataSet at the changed row.

OdbcCommand Class Methods

Cancel Method   A cancellation of the execution of the OdbcCommand is attempted. No exception is generated, even if the attempt to cancel the OdbcCommand failed.

```
public void Cancel();
```

CreateParameter Method   Creates a new OdbcParameter object.

```
public OdbcParameter CreateParameter();
```

Dispose Method   Overloaded. Overridden. Disposes the resources used by the OdbcCommand. If the Boolean is set to True in the first method, it will dispose of both managed and unmanaged resources; False releases only unmanaged resources. The second method releases all the resources used by the object.

```
protected override void Dispose(bool);
public void Dispose();
```

ExecuteNonQuery Method   Used for catalog operations or to execute an UPDATE, INSERT, or DELETE SQL statement to a database. Returns the number of affected rows.

```
public int ExecuteNonQuery();
```

ExecuteReader Method   Overloaded. Returns an OdbcDataReader object after executing a SQL statement using the Connection object. The second method returns the OdbcDataReader object based on the specified CommandBehavior.

```
public OdbcDataReader ExecuteReader();
public OdbcDataReader ExecuteReader(System.Data.CommandBehavior);
```

System.Data.CommandBehavior enumeration:

CloseConnection	The Connection object is closed when the DataReader object is closed.
Default	Sets no CommandBehavior flags. Same as using ExecuteReader.
KeyInfo	Returns column and primary key information.

System.Data.CommandBehavior enumeration:

SchemaOnly	Returns column information only. Database state not affected.
SequentialAccess	Enables the DataReader to return data as a stream. You need to use GetBytes or GetChars to start the reading of data at a specified location.
SingleResult	Returns a single resultset.
SingleRow	Returns a single row of data.

ExecuteScalar Method   Returns a single value represented in the first column of the first row of a resultset.

```
public object ExecuteScalar();
```

ICloneable.Clone Method   The ICloneable.Clone method supports the .NET infrastructure and is not used directly from your code.

```
object ICloneable.Clone();
```

IDbCommand.CreateParameter Method   The IDbCommand.CreateParameter method supports the .NET infrastructure and is not used directly from your code.

```
IDbDataParameter IDbCommand.CreateParameter();
```

IDbCommand.ExecuteReader Method   The IDbCommand.ExecuteReader method supports the .NET infrastructure and is not used directly from your code.

```
IDbDataReader IDbCommand.ExecuteReader();
IDbDataReader IDbCommand.ExecuteReader(System.Data.CommandBehavior);
```

Prepare Method   Creates a compiled version of this command object if the CommandType property is set to Text or StoredProcedure. You need to specify the data type of each parameter in the command statement before using the Prepare method. If the parameter has variable-length data, then you also need to specify the maximum Size of the data.

```
public void Prepare();
```

ResetCommandTimeout Method   Resets the CommandTimeout property to its default of 30 seconds.

```
public void ResetCommandTimeout();
```

Mutual Properties, Methods, and Events Included in the OdbcCommand Class

The following lists the mutual properties, methods, and events that are included in the OdbcCommand class.

Inherited from Component	Inherited from Object	Inherited from MarshalByRefObject
Container property	Equals method	CreateObjRef method
DesignMode property	Finalize method	GetLifetimeService method
Events property	GetHashCode method	InitializeLifetimeService method
Site property	GetType method	
Dispose method	MemberwiseClone method	
GetService method	ToString method	
Disposed event		

OdbcCommandBuilder Class

The OdbcCommandBuilder class is used to automatically generate SQL statements for updates of single tables. An OdbcDataAdapter object does not generate the required SQL statements automatically to synchronize the changes made to a DataSet with the data source, therefore an OdbcCommandBuilder is needed to automatically generate the SQL statements and synchronize the data.

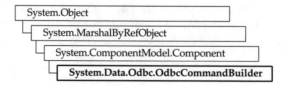

Constructor   Overloaded. Initializes a new instance of the OdbcCommandBuilder class. The second constructor specifies the associated OdbcDataAdapter. The OdbcCommandBuilder object will register itself as a listener to the OdbcDataAdapter's RowUpdating events.

```
public OdbcCommandBuilder();
public OdbcCommandBuilder(OdbcDataAdapter);
// C# example
System.Data.Odbc.OdbcCommandBuilder odbcCmdBldr = new
    System.Data.Odbc.OdbcCommandBuilder();
System.Data.Odbc.OdbcDataAdapter odbcDA = new
    System.Data.Odbc.OdbcDataAdapter();
System.Data.Odbc.OdbcCommandBuilder odbcCmdBldr2 = new
    System.Data.Odbc.OdbcCommandBuilder(odbcDA);
```

OdbcCommandBuilder Class Properties

DataAdapter Property   Returns or sets the OdbcDataAdapter object that SQL statements are automatically generated for.

```
public OdbcDataAdapter DataAdapter { get; set; }
```

QuotePrefix Property   Returns or sets the beginning character(s) to use as delimiters when database object names contain characters such as spaces and commas. The default value is an empty string.

```
public string QuotePrefix { get; set; }
```

QuoteSuffix Property   Returns or sets the ending character(s) to use as delimiters when database object names contain characters such as spaces and commas. The default value is an empty string.

```
public string QuoteSuffix { get; set; }
```

OdbcCommandBuilder Class Methods

DeriveParameters Method   Fills the Parameters collection of the specified OdbcCommand object with parameter information for the stored procedure of the specified OdbcCommand object.

```
public static void DeriveParameters(OdbcCommand);
```

Dispose Method   Overloaded. Overridden. Disposes the resources used by the OdbcCommandBuilder. If the Boolean is set to True in the first method, it will dispose of both managed and unmanaged resources; False releases only unmanaged resources. The second method releases all the resources used by the object.

```
protected override void Dispose(bool);
public void Dispose();
```

GetDeleteCommand Method   Returns the automatically generated OdbcCommand object for performing deletions.

```
public OdbcCommand GetDeleteCommand();
```

GetInsertCommand Method   Returns the automatically generated OdbcCommand object for performing inserts.

```
public OdbcCommand GetInsertCommand();
```

GetUpdateCommand Method   Returns the automatically generated OdbcCommand object for performing updates.

```
public OdbcCommand GetUpdateCommand();
```

RefreshSchema Method   Refreshes the database schema information. Should be used when the SELECT statement of the OdbcCommandBuilder object changes.

```
public void RefreshSchema();
```

Mutual Properties, Methods, and Events Included in the OdbcCommandBuilder Class

The following lists the mutual properties, methods, and events that are included in the OdbcCommandBuilder class.

Inherited from Component	Inherited from Object	Inherited from MarshalByRefObject
Container property	Equals method	CreateObjRef method

Inherited from Component	Inherited from Object	Inherited from MarshalByRefObject
DesignMode property	Finalize method	GetLifetimeService method
Events property	GetHashCode method	InitializeLifetimeService method
Site property	GetType method	
Dispose method	MemberwiseClone method	
GetService method	ToString method	
Disposed event		

OdbcConnection Class

The OdbcConnection class represents a connection to a data source.

Note   *If an OdbcConnection object goes out of scope, the object is not closed. You need to explicitly call Close or Dispose in order to close the open connection.*

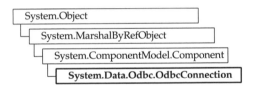

Constructor   Overloaded. Initializes a new instance of the OdbcConnection class. The first constructor initializes all the fields to their default values. The second constructor specifies the connection string to use to open the connection.

```
public OdbcConnection();
public OdbcConnection(string connString);
// C# example
System.Data.Odbc.OdbcConnection odbcConn = new
    System.Data.Odbc.OdbcConnection();
System.Data.Odbc.OdbcConnection odbcConn2 = new
    System.Data.Odbc.OdbcConnection("DRIVER={SQL Server};
    SERVER=MyServer;UID=myID;PWD=MyPwd;DATABASE=Northwind");
```

OdbcConnection Class Properties

ConnectionString Property   Returns or sets the connection string that is used to open the connection to the data source.

```
public string ConnectionString { get; set; }
```

ConnectionTimeout Property   Returns wait time in seconds before an attempted connection is terminated and an error generated. Default wait time is 15 seconds.

```
public int ConnectionTimeout { get; }
```

Database Property   Returns the name of the database that will be used when a connection is opened. The default database name is an empty string.

```
public string Database { get; }
```

DataSource Property   Returns the location and the filename of the data source to use. The default value is an empty string.

```
public string DataSource { get; }
```

Driver Property   Returns the name of the ODBC driver used for the current connection.

```
public string Driver { get; }
```

ServerVersion Property   Returns the version of the server that the client is connected to. The version string that is returned is in the form ##.##.#### (*major version . minor version . release build*).

```
public string ServerVersion { get; }
```

State Property   Returns a bitwise value indicating the ConnectionState value of the current connection. The default value is Closed.

```
public System.Data.ConnectionState State { get; }
```

System.Data.ConnectionState enumeration:

Broken	A previously opened connection is now broken.
Closed	The current connection is not open.
Connecting	The Connection object is attempting to connect to the data source.
Executing	The Connection object is currently executing a command.
Fetching	The Connection object is currently fetching data.
Open	The current connection is open.

OdbcConnection Class Methods

BeginTransaction Method   Overloaded. Begins a transaction to the database and returns an object that represents that transaction. The second method specifies the IsolationLevel for the transaction.

```
public OdbcTransaction BeginTransaction();
public OdbcTransaction BeginTransaction(System.Data.IsolationLevel);
```

System.Data.IsolationLevel enumeration:

Chaos	Cannot overwrite more highly isolated transactions that are pending.
ReadCommited	To avoid dirty reads, the shared locks are held during reading of data. May result in non-repeatable read or phantom data if data is changed before the transaction ends.
ReadUncommited	No exclusive locks are allowed and no shared locks are done. May result in a dirty read.
RepeatableRead	Locks are placed on the queried data. May result in phantom rows.
Serializable	A range lock is placed on the rows in the DataSet.
Unspecified	The isolation level cannot be determined.

ChangeDatabase Method   Changes the database name for the open OdbcConnection object. The database name parameter cannot be a blank string or null value. Throws an exception if the database name is not valid or the connection is not open.

```
public void ChangeDatabase(string databaseName);
```

Close Method   Closes the connection to the data source and rolls back any pending transactions. No exception is generated if an application calls the Close method more than once.

```
public void Close();
```

CreateCommand Method   Creates and returns an OdbcCommand object.

```
public OdbcCommand CreateCommand();
```

Dispose Method   Overloaded. Overridden. Disposes the resources used by the OdbcConnection object. If the Boolean is set to True in the first method, it will dispose of both managed and unmanaged resources; False releases only unmanaged resources. The second method releases all the resources used by the object.

```
protected override void Dispose(bool);
public void Dispose();
```

EnlistDistributedTransaction Method   Registers the specified transaction as a distributed transaction.

```
public void EnlistDistributedTransaction(ITransaction);
```

ICloneable.Clone Method   The ICloneable.Clone method supports the .NET infrastructure and is not used directly from your code.

```
object ICloneable.Clone();
```

IDbConnection.BeginTransaction Method   The IDbConnection.BeginTransaction method supports the .NET infrastructure and is not used directly from your code.

```
IDbTransaction IDbConnection.BeginTransaction();
IDbTransaction IDbConnection.BeginTransaction(
    System.Data.IsolationLevel);
```

IDbConnection.CreateCommand Method   The IDbConnection.CreateCommand method supports the .NET infrastructure and is not used directly from your code.

```
IDbCommand IDbConnection.CreateCommand();
```

Open Method   Opens a connection to a database from the connection pool. If a connection from the connection pool is not available, this will create a new connection to the data source.

```
public void Open();
```

ReleaseObjectPool Method   Clears the OdbcConnection object pool when the OLE DB provider is released.

```
public static void ReleaseObjectPool();
```

OdbcConnection Class Events

InfoMessage Event   Fires when the provider sends a warning or informational message to the event handler.

```
public event OdbcInfoMessageEventHandler InfoMessage;
```

StateChange Event   Fires when the state of the connection changes.

```
public event StateChangeEventHandler StateChange;
```

Mutual Properties, Methods, and Events Included in the OdbcConnection Class

The following lists the mutual properties, methods, and events that are included in the OdbcConnection class.

Inherited from Component	Inherited from Object	Inherited from MarshalByRefObject
Container property	Equals method	CreateObjRef method
DesignMode property	Finalize method	GetLifetimeService method
Events property	GetHashCode method	InitializeLifetimeService method
Site property	GetType method	

Inherited from Component	**Inherited from Object**	**Inherited from MarshalByRefObject**
Dispose method	MemberwiseClone method	
GetService method	ToString method	
Disposed event		

OdbcDataAdapter Class

The OdbcDataAdapter class represents a database connection and a set of commands that are used to fill a DataSet and update a data source. The OdbcDataAdapter class uses the Fill method to fill the DataSet with information from the data source, and it uses the Update method to move changed information from the DataSet back to the data source.

```
System.Object
    System.MarshalByRefObject
        System.ComponentModel.Component
            System.DataCommon.DataAdapter
                System.DataCommon.DbDataAdapter
                    System.Data.Odbc.OdbcDataAdapter
```

Constructor   Overloaded. Initializes a new instance of the OdbcDataAdapter class. The first constructor creates a new object where all property values are set to their default values. The second constructor specifies a SELECT statement or stored procedure, OdbcCommand, to use as the SelectCommand property. The third constructor specifies a string that is a SELECT statement or stored procedure and an OdbcConnection to open and use. The fourth constructor specifies a string that is a SELECT statement or stored procedure and a connection string.

```
public OdbcDataAdapter();
public OdbcDataAdpapter(OdbcCommand);
public OdbcDataAdapter(string selectCmdText, OdbcConnection);
public OdbcDataAdapter(string selectCmdText, string selectConnStr);
// C# example
System.Data.Odbc.OdbcDataAdapter odbcDA = new
    System.Data.Odbc.OdbcDataAdapter();
System.Data.Odbc.OdbcCommand odbcCmd = new
    System.Data.Odbc.OdbcCommand();
System.Data.Odbc.OdbcDataAdapter odbcDA2 = new
```

```
            System.Data.Odbc.OdbcDataAdapter(odbcCmd);
    System.Data.Odbc.OdbcConnection odbcConn = new
        System.Data.Odbc.OdbcConnection();
    System.Data.Odbc.OdbcDataAdapter odbcDA3 = new
        System.Data.Odbc.OdbcDataAdapter("SELECT * FROM Customers",
        odbcConn);
    System.Data.Odbc.OdbcDataAdapter odbcDA4 = new
        System.Data.Odbc.OdbcDataAdapter("SELECT * FROM Customers",
        "DRIVER={SQL Server};SERVER=MyServer;UID=myID;PWD=MyPwd;" +
        "DATABASE=Northwind");
```

OdbcDataAdapter Class Properties

DeleteCommand Property   Returns or sets the SQL statement or stored procedure used for deleting records from the data source.

```
public new OdbcCommand DeleteCommand { get; set; }
```

InsertCommand Property   Returns or sets the SQL statement or stored procedure used for inserting records into the data source.

```
public new OdbcCommand InsertCommand { get; set; }
```

SelectCommand Property   Returns or sets the SQL statement or stored procedure used for selecting records from the data source.

```
public new OdbcCommand SelectCommand { get; set; }
```

UpdateCommand Property   Returns or sets the SQL statement or stored procedure used for updating records in the data source.

```
public new OdbcCommand UpdateCommand { get; set; }
```

OdbcDataAdapter Class Methods

CreateRowUpdatedEvent Method   Overrides System.Data.Common.DbData-Adapter.CreateRowUpdatedEvent. Returns a new instance of the RowUpdatedEventArgs object. The first parameter of the CreateRowUpdatedEvent method is the DataRow that is used to update the data source. The second parameter, IDbCommand, represents the SQL statement that is executed during the update; and the third parameter, StatementType, specifies whether the command is a SELECT, INSERT, UPDATE, or DELETE statement. The fourth parameter is the DataTableMapping object.

```
protected override RowUpdatedEventArgs CreateRowUpdatedEvent(
    System.Data.DataRow, System.Data.IDbCommand,
    System.Data.StatementType, System.Data.Common.DataTableMapping);
```

CreateRowUpdatingEvent Method　Overrides System.Data.Common.DbData-Adapter.CreateRowUpdatingEvent. Returns a new instance of the RowUpdatingEventArgs class. The first parameter of the CreateRowUpdatingEvent method is the DataRow that is used to update the data source. The second parameter, IDbCommand, represents the SQL statement that is executed during the Update; and the third parameter, StatementType, specifies whether the command is a SELECT, INSERT, UPDATE, or DELETE statement. The fourth parameter is the DataTableMapping object.

```
protected override RowUpdatingEventArgs CreateRowUpdatingEvent(
    System.Data.DataRow, System.Data.IDbCommand,
    System.Data.StatementType, System.Data.Common.DataTableMapping);
```

Dispose Method　Overloaded. Overridden. Disposes the resources used by the DataAdapter. If the Boolean is set to True in the first overloaded method, it will dispose of both managed and unmanaged resources.

```
protected override void Dispose(bool);
public virtual void Dispose();
```

ICloneable.Clone Method　The ICloneable.Clone method supports the .NET infrastructure and is not used directly from your code.

```
object ICloneable.Clone();
```

OnRowUpdated Method　Raises the RowUpdated event. The RowUpdatedEventArgs parameter contains the event data that is raised.

```
protected override void OnRowUpdated(RowUpdatedEventArgs);
```

OnRowUpdating Method　Raises the RowUpdating event. The RowUpdatingEventArgs parameter contains the event data that is raised.

```
protected override void OnRowUpdating(RowUpdatingEventArgs);
```

OdbcDataAdapter Class Events

RowUpdated Event   Fires after an Update command is executed against a data source.

```
public event OdbcRowUpdatedEventHandler RowUpdated;
```

RowUpdating Event   Fires before an Update command is executed against a data source.

```
public event OdbcRowUpdatingEventHandler RowUpdating;
```

Mutual Properties, Methods, and Events Included in the OdbcDataAdapter Class

The following lists the mutual properties, methods, and events that are included in the OdbcDataAdapter class.

Inherited from Component	Inherited from Object	Inherited from MarshalByRefObject
Container property	Equals method	CreateObjRef method
DesignMode property	Finalize method	GetLifetimeService method
Events property	GetHashCode method	InitializeLifetimeService method
Site property	GetType method	
Dispose method	MemberwiseClone method	
GetService method	ToString method	
Disposed event		

Inherited from DataAdapter	Inherited from DbDataAdapter
AcceptChangesDuringFill property	Fill method

Inherited from DataAdapter	Inherited from DbDataAdapter
ContinueUpdateOnError property	FillSchema method
MissingMappingAction property	GetFillParameters method
MissingSchemaAction property	OnFillError method
TableMappings property	Update method
CloneInternals method	FillError event
CreateTableMappings method	
ShouldSerializeTableMappings method	

OdbcDataReader Class

The OdbcDataReader class allows for reading forward-only streams of data rows from a data source. You do not create an OdbcDataReader by calling a constructor, but rather by calling the ExecuteReader method of an OdbcCommand object. The OdbcConnection object that is associated with the OdbcDataReader is used exclusively by the OdbcDataReader, therefore only the Close operation may be performed on the OdbcConnection.

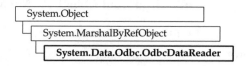

OdbcDataReader Class Properties

Depth Property   Returns an integer designating the depth of the current row's nesting.

```
public int Depth { get; }
```

FieldCount Property   Returns the number of columns (or fields) in the current row. The default value for the FieldCount property is –1.

```
public int FieldCount { get; }
```

HasRows Property   Returns a Boolean designating whether the OdbcDataReader contains rows. Returns True if the data reader has rows, False if it does not.

```
public bool HasRows { get; }
```

IsClosed Property   Returns a Boolean designating whether the OdbcDataReader is opened or closed. Returns True if the data reader is closed, False if it is open.

```
public bool IsClosed { get; }
```

Item Property   Overloaded. Returns the object found at the specified column ordinal or string column name.

```
public object this[int index] { get; }
public object this[string colName] {get; }
```

RecordsAffected Property   Returns the number of rows affected by a changed, inserted, or deleted action.

```
public int RecordsAffected { get; }
```

OdbcDataReader Class Methods

Close Method   Closes an open OdbcDataReader object.

```
public void Close();
```

Finalize Method   Frees object resources and performs cleanup functions before object is deleted. Finalizers in C# and C++ use the destructor syntax.

```
~OdbcDataReader();
```

GetBoolean Method   Returns the value in the specified zero-based column ordinal as a Boolean. The data to be retrieved must already be in the form of a Boolean, or an exception is generated. Call IsNull before calling this method.

```
public virtual bool GetBoolean(int colOrdinal);
```

GetByte Method   Returns the value in the specified zero-based column ordinal as a byte. The data to be retrieved must already be in the form of a byte or an exception is generated. Call IsNull before calling this method.

```
public virtual bool GetByte(int colOrdinal);
```

GetBytes Method   Reads a stream of bytes from the specified zero-based column ordinal starting at the specified column offset. The bytes are placed into the specified byte buffer starting at the specified byte buffer offset for a length of the specified buffer length. The GetBytes method returns the actual number of bytes that were read. The data to be retrieved must already be in the form of a byte array or an exception is generated.

```
public virtual long GetBytes(int colOrdinal, long colOffset,
    byte[] buffer, int bufferOffset, int bufferLength);
```

GetChar Method   Returns the value in the specified zero-based column ordinal as a character. The data to be retrieved must already be in the form of a character, or an exception is generated. Call IsNull before calling this method.

```
public virtual char GetChar(int colOrdinal);
```

GetChars Method   Reads a stream of characters from the specified zero-based column ordinal starting at the specified column offset. The characters are placed into the specified character buffer starting at the specified character buffer offset for a length of the specified buffer length. Returns the actual number of characters that were read. The data to be retrieved must already be in the form of a character array or an exception is generated.

```
public virtual long GetChars(int colOrdinal, long colOffset, char[]
    buffer, int bufferOffset, int bufferLength);
```

GetData Method   The GetData method supports the .NET infrastructure and is not used directly from your code.

GetDataTypeName Method   The GetDataTypeName method supports the .NET infrastructure and is not used directly from your code.

GetDate Method   Returns the value in the specified zero-based column ordinal as a DateTime object.

```
public DateTime GetDate (int colOrdinal);
```

GetDateTime Method   Returns the value in the specified zero-based column ordinal as a DateTime object. The data to be retrieved must already be in the form of a DateTime object, or an exception is generated. Call IsNull before calling this method.

```
public virtual DateTime GetDateTime(int colOrdinal);
```

GetDecimal Method   Returns the value in the specified zero-based column ordinal as a decimal. The data to be retrieved must already be in the form of a decimal or an exception is generated. Call IsNull before calling this method.

```
public virtual decimal GetDecimal(int colOrdinal);
```

GetDouble Method   Returns the value in the specified zero-based column ordinal as a double-precision floating point number. The data to be retrieved must already be in the form of a double, or an exception is generated. Call IsNull before calling this method.

```
public virtual double GetDouble(int colOrdinal);
```

GetFieldType Method   Returns the data type of the object in the specified zero-based column ordinal.

```
public virtual Type GetFieldType(int colOrdinal);
```

GetFloat Method   Returns the value in the specified zero-based column ordinal as a single-precision floating point number. The data to be retrieved must already be in the form of a float, or an exception is generated. Call IsNull before calling this method.

```
public virtual float GetFloat(int colOrdinal);
```

GetGuid Method   Returns the value in the specified zero-based column ordinal as a globally unique identifier (GUID). The data to be retrieved must already be in the form of a GUID, or an exception is generated. Call IsNull before calling this method.

```
public virtual Guid GetGuid(int colOrdinal);
```

GetInt16 Method   Returns the value in the specified zero-based column ordinal as a 16-bit signed integer. The data to be retrieved must already be in the form of a short, or an exception is generated. Call IsNull before calling this method.

```
public virtual short GetInt16(int colOrdinal);
```

GetInt32 Method   Returns the value in the specified zero-based column ordinal as a 32-bit signed integer. The data to be retrieved must already be in the form of an integer, or an exception is generated. Call IsNull before calling this method.

```
public virtual int GetInt32(int colOrdinal);
```

GetInt64 Method   Returns the value in the specified zero-based column ordinal as a 64-bit signed integer. The data to be retrieved must already be in the form of a long, or an exception is generated. Call IsNull before calling this method.

```
public virtual long GetInt64(int colOrdinal);
```

GetName Method   Returns the name of the column in the specified zero-based column ordinal as a string.

```
public virtual string GetName(int colOrdinal);
```

GetOrdinal Method   Returns the zero-based column ordinal value of the specified column name.

```
public virtual int GetOrdinal(string colName);
```

GetSchemaTable Method   Returns a DataTable object that contains the metadata for the columns in the current OdbcDataReader object.

```
public virtual System.Data.DataTable GetSchemaTable();
```

GetString Method   Returns the value in the specified zero-based column ordinal as a string. The data to be retrieved must already be in the form of a string or an exception is generated. Call IsNull before calling this method.

```
public virtual string GetString(int colOrdinal);
```

GetTime Method   Returns the value in the specified zero-based column ordinal as a TimeSpan object.

```
public TimeSpan GetTime(int colOrdinal);
```

GetValue Method   Returns the value in the specified zero-based column ordinal in its native form.

```
public virtual object GetValue(int colOrdinal);
```

GetValues Method   Fills the specified object array with the column attributes of the current row. Returns the number of objects in the object array.

```
public virtual int GetValues(object[] cols);
```

IDisposable.Dispose Method   The IDisposable.Dispose method supports the .NET infrastructure and is not used directly from your code.

```
void IDisposable.Dispose();
```

IEnumerable.GetEnumerator Method   The IEnumerable.GetEnumerator method supports the .NET infrastructure and is not used directly from your code.

```
IEnumerator IEnumerable.GetEnumerator();
```

IsDBNull Method   Returns a Boolean indicating whether the value in the specified zero-based column ordinal exists. True if the value is DBNull; otherwise, the method returns False.

```
public virtual bool IsDBNull(int colOrdinal);
```

NextResult Method   Moves to the next rresultset. Used when multiple resultsets were generated by a batch SQL statement. Returns True if there are more resultsets; otherwise, the method returns False.

```
public virtual bool NextResult();
```

Read Method   Moves to the next record in the OdbcDataReader object. Default position is prior to the first record, so use Read to begin processing data. Returns True if there are more rows; otherwise, the method returns False.

```
public virtual bool Read();
```

Mutual Properties, Methods, and Events Included in the OdbcDataReader Class

The following lists the mutual properties, methods, and events that are included in the OdbcDataReader class.

Inherited from Object	**Inherited from MarshalByRefObject**
Equals method	CreateObjRef method
GetHashCode method	GetLifetimeService method
GetType method	InitializeLifetimeService method
MemberwiseClone method	
ToString method	

OdbcError Class

The OdbcError class contains information regarding errors returned by the data source. You do not create an OdbcError instance by calling a constructor. The creation and management of the OdbcError class is done by the OdbcDataAdapter and OdbcErrorCollection classes.

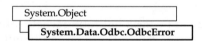

```
System.Object
    System.Data.Odbc.OdbcError
```

OdbcError Class Properties

Message Property   Contains a brief description of the error.

```
public string Message { get; }
```

NativeError Property   Contains the error information that is specifically related to the database.

```
public int NativeError { get; }
```

Source Property   Contains the name of the ODBC driver that produced the error.

```
public string Source { get; }
```

SQLState Property   Contains a five-character code that identifies the error source.

```
public string SQLState { get; }
```

OdbcError Class Methods

ToString Method   Returns the full text of the error.

```
public override string ToString();
```

Mutual Properties, Methods, and Events Included in the OdbcError Class

The following lists the mutual properties, methods, and events that are included in the OdbcError class.

Inherited from Object

Equals method

Finalize method

GetHashCode method

GetType method

MemberwiseClone method

OdbcErrorCollection Class

The OdbcErrorCollection class contains a collection of OdbcError objects. You do not create an OdbcErrorCollection by calling a constructor. The OdbcErrorCollection is created by the OdbcException class and will always contain at least one instance of the OdbcError class.

```
System.Object
    System.Data.Odbc.OdbcErrorCollection
```

OdbcErrorCollection Class Properties

Count Property   Returns the number of items in this collection.

```
public int Count { get; }
```

Item Property   Returns the OdbcError object found at the specified zero-based index.

```
public OdbcError this[int index] { get; }
```

OdbcErrorCollection Class Methods

CopyTo Method   Copies the objects in the OdbcErrorCollection to the specified array, and sets the starting index of the array to the specified integer.

```
public void CopyTo(Array arr, int index);
```

GetEnumerator Method   The GetEnumerator method supports the .NET infrastructure and is not used directly from your code.

Mutual Properties, Methods, and Events Included in the OdbcErrorCollection Class

The following lists the mutual properties, methods, and events that are included in the OdbcErrorCollection class.

Inherited from Object

Equals method

Finalize method

GetHashCode method

GetType method

MemberwiseClone method

ToString method

OdbcException Class

The OdbcException class represents the exception that is thrown when an error is returned by the ODBC data source. You do not create an OdbcException by calling a constructor. The OdbcException is created when the OdbcDataAdapter encounters an unhandled error.

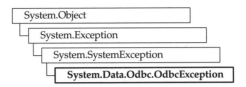

OdbcException Class Properties

Errors Property   Contains the OdbcErrorCollection object.

```
public OdbcErrorCollection Errors { get; }
```

Message Property   Contains the text description for the error.

```
public override string Message { get; }
```

Source Property   Contains the name of the ODBC driver that produced the error.

```
public override string Source { get; }
```

OdbcException Class Methods

GetObjectData Method   Overrides the Exception.GetObjectData method and returns information about the exception into the SerializationInfo parameter.

```
public override void GetObjectData(
    System.Runtime.Serialization.SerializationInfo,
    System.Runtime.Serialization.StreamingContext);
```

Mutual Properties, Methods, and Events Included in the OdbcException Class

The following lists the mutual properties, methods, and events that are included in the OdbcException class.

Inherited from Exception	Inherited from Object
HelpLink property	Equals method

Inherited from Exception	Inherited from Object
HResult property	Finalize method
InnerException property	GetHashCode method
StackTrace property	GetType method
TargetSite property	MemberwiseClone method
GetBaseException method	
ToString method	

OdbcInfoMessageEventArgs Class

The OdbcInfoMessageEventArgs class supplies information for the InfoMessage event. You do not create an OdbcInfoMessageEventArgs by calling a constructor, but it is a parameter of the OdbcInfoMessageEventHandler.

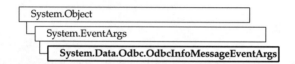

OdbcInfoMessageEventArgs Class Properties

Errors Property   Contains the OdbcErrorCollection sent from the data source.

```
public OdbcErrorCollection Errors { get; }
```

Message Property   Contains the text description for the error.

```
public string Message { get; }
```

OdbcInfoMessageEventArgs Class Methods

ToString Method   Returns the InfoMessage event text.

```
public override string ToString();
```

Mutual Properties, Methods, and Events included in the OdbcInfoMessageEventArgs Class

The following lists the mutual properties, methods, and events that are included in the OdbcInfoMessageEventArgs class.

Inherited from Object

Equals method

Finalize method

GetHashCode method

GetType method

MemberwiseClone method

OdbcParameter Class

The OdbcParameter class is a parameter for the OdbcCommand object. May also be used for the OdbcCommand object's mapping to the DataSet column. The parameters for the OdbcCommand class are not case sensitive.

```
System.Object
    System.MarshallByRefObject
        System.Data.Odbc.OdbcParameter
```

Constructor   Overloaded. Initializes a new instance of the OdbcParameter class. The first constructor creates a new object using the default property values. The second constructor specifies the parameter name and value type. The third constructor specifies the parameter name and data type. The fourth constructor specifies the parameter name, data type, and parameter size. The fifth constructor specifies the parameter name, data type, parameter size, and source column name. The sixth constructor sets all of the properties of the OdbcParameter object at the time it is created with the specified values.

```
public OdbcParameter();
public OdbcParameter(string parmName, object parmValue);
public OdbcParameter(string parmName, OdbcType parmType);
public OdbcParameter(string parmName, OdbcType parmType,
    int parmSize);
```

```
public OdbcParameter(string parmName, OdbcType parmType,
    int parmSize, string srcColumn);
public OdbcParameter(string parmName, OdbcType parmType,
    int parmSize, ParameterDirection parmDir, bool isNullable,
    byte parmPrecision, byte parmScale, string srcColumn,
    DataRowVersion srcVersion, object parmValue);
// C# example
System.Data.Odbc.OdbcParameter odbcParm = new
    System.Data.Odbc.OdbcParameter();
System.Data.Odbc.OdbcParameter odbcParm2 = new
    System.Data.Odbc.OdbcParameter("CustomerName", odbcParm);
System.Data.Odbc.OdbcParameter odbcParm3 = new
    System.Data.Odbc.OdbcParameter("CustomerName",
    System.Data.Odbc.OdbcType.Text);
System.Data.Odbc.OdbcParameter odbcParm4 = new
    System.Data.Odbc.OdbcParameter("CustomerName",
    System.Data.Odbc.OdbcType.Text, 25);
System.Data.Odbc.OdbcParameter odbcParm5 = new
    System.Data.Odbc.OdbcParameter("CustomerName",
    System.Data.Odbc.OdbcType.Text, 25, "CustName");
System.Data.Odbc.OdbcParameter odbcParm6 = new
    System.Data.Odbc.OdbcParameter("CustomerName",
    System.Data.Odbc.OdbcType.Text, 25,
    System.Data.ParameterDirection.Input, true, 0, 0, "CustName",
    System.Data.DataRowVersion.Current, odbcParm);
```

OdbcParameter Class Properties

DbType Property   Returns or sets the DbType for the parameter. Default DbType
is String.

```
public System.Data.DbType DbType { get; set; }
```

System.Data.DbType enumeration:

AnsiString	Variable-length stream of 1 to 8,000 characters. Non-Unicode.
AnsiStringFixedLength	Fixed-length stream of characters. Non-Unicode.
Binary	Variable-length stream of binary data. 1 to 8,000 bytes.

System.Data.DbType enumeration:

Boolean	Values of True or False.
Byte	8-bit unsigned integer. Value range 0 to 255.
Currency	Value range —922,337,203,685,477.5808 to 922,337,203,685,477.5807. Accuracy to ten-thousandth of unit.
Date	Value range January 1, 1753, to December 31, 9999. Accuracy to 3.33 milliseconds.
DateTime	Represents date and time values.
Decimal	Value range 1.0×10^{-28} to approx 7.9×10^{28}. Significant digits of 28 to 29.
Double	Floating point type. Value range approx 5.0×10^{-324} to 1.7×10^{308}. Precision of 15 to 16 digits.
Guid	Globally unique identifier.
Int16	Signed 16-bit integer. Value range –32,768 to 32,767.
Int32	Signed 32-bit integer. Value range –2,147,483,648 to 2,147,483,647.
Int64	Signed 64-bit integer. Value range –9,223,372,036,854,775,808 to 9,223,372,036,854,775,807.
Object	General type.
SByte	Signed 8-bit integer. Value range –128 to 127.
Single	Floating point type. Value range approx 1.5×10^{-45} to 3.4×10^{38}. Precision of 7 digits.
String	String of characters. Unicode.
StringFixedLength	Fixed-length stream of characters. Unicode.
Time	Value range January 1, 1753 to December 31, 9999. Accuracy to 3.33 milliseconds.
Uint16	Unsigned 16-bit integer. Value range 0 to 65,535.
Uint32	Unsigned 32-bit integer. Value range 0 to 4,294,967,295.

Uint64	Unsigned 64-bit integer. Value range 0 to 18,446,744,073,709,551,615.

Direction Property   Returns or sets the directional aspect of the parameter. The default value is Input.

```
public System.Data.ParameterDirection Direction { get; set; }
```

System.Data.ParameterDirection enumeration:

Input	Parameter is input only.
InputOutput	Parameter is both input and output.
Output	Parameter is output only.
ReturnValue	Parameter is a return value from an operation like a stored procedure.

IsNullable Property   Returns or sets a Boolean indicating whether the parameter accepts null values. True indicates nulls are accepted. The default value is False.

```
public bool IsNullable { get; set; }
```

OdbcType Property   Returns or sets the OdbcType for the parameter. Setting the DbType property changes the OdbcType property to the corresponding data type. The default OdbcType is Nchar.

```
public OdbcType OdbcType { get; set; }
```

ParameterName Property   Returns or sets the name of the OdbcParameter. The default value is an empty string.

```
public string ParameterName { get; set; }
```

Precision Property   Returns or sets the maximum number of digits to use. The default value is 0.

```
public byte Precision { get; set; }
```

Scale Property   Returns or sets the number of decimal places to use. The default value is 0.

```
public byte Scale { get; set; }
```

Size Property   Returns or sets the maximum bytes of data for the column. Used for binary and string column types. The default value is derived from the parameter type.

```
public int Size { get; set; }
```

SourceColumn Property   Returns or sets the name of the source column that is mapped to the DataSet. The default value is an empty string.

```
public string SourceColumn { get; set; }
```

SourceVersion Property   Returns or sets the DataRowVersion to use. The default value is Current.

```
public System.Data.DataRowVersion SourceVersion { get; set; }
```

System.Data.DataRowVersion enumeration:

Current	Row contains current values.
Default	Row is versioned according to the DataRowState.
Original	Row contains its original values.
Proposed	Row contains proposed values.

Value Property   Returns or sets the value of the parameter. The default value is Null.

```
public object Value { get; set; }
```

OdbcParameter Class Methods

ICloneable.Clone Method   The ICloneable.Clone method supports the .NET infrastructure and is not used directly from your code.

```
object ICloneable.Clone();
```

ToString Method   Returns the ParameterName in a string.

```
public override string ToString();
```

Mutual Properties, Methods, and Events Included in the OdbcParameter Class

The following lists the mutual properties, methods, and events that are included in the OdbcParameter class.

Inherited from Object	Inherited from MarshalByRefObject
Equals method	CreateObjRef method
Finalize method	GetLifetimeService method
GetHashCode method	InitializeLifetimeService method
GetType method	
MemberwiseClone method	

OdbcParameterCollection Class

The OdbcParameterCollection class is a collection of OdbcParameter objects for an OdbcCommand object and their related mapping information for DataSet columns. You do not create an OdbcParameterCollection by calling a constructor, but rather it is accessed through the OdbcCommand object.

```
System.Object
  System.MarshallByRefObject
    System.Data.Odbc.OdbcParameterCollection
```

OdbcParameterCollection Class Properties

Count Property   Returns the number of items in this collection.

```
public int Count { get; }
```

Item Property   Overloaded. Returns or sets the OdbcParameter object found at the specified integer index or string parameter name.

```
public OdbcParameter this[int index] { get; set; }
public OdbcParameter this[string parmName] {get; set; }
```

OdbcParameterCollection Class Methods

Add Method   Overloaded. The first Add method adds the specified object to the OdbcCommand's OdbcParameterCollection and returns the index of the added object. The second Add method adds the specified OdbcParameter to the OdbcCommand's OdbcParameterCollection and returns the added OdbcParameter. The third Add method adds the specified object to the OdbcParameterCollection using the specified parameter name and returns the added OdbcParameter. The fourth Add method adds an OdbcParameter to the OdbcParameterCollection using the specified parameter name and data type and returns the added OdbcParameter. The fifth Add method adds an OdbcParameter to the OdbcParameterCollection using the specified parameter name, data type, and parameter size, and returns the added OdbcParameter. The sixth Add method adds an OdbcParameter to the OdbcParameterCollection using the specified parameter name, data type, parameter size, and column source name, and returns the added OdbcParameter.

```
public int Add(object);
public OdbcParameter Add(OdbcParameter);
public OdbcParameter Add(string parmName, object);
public OdbcParameter Add(string parmName, OdbcType);
public OdbcParameter Add(string parmName, OdbcType, int parmSize);
public OdbcParameter Add(string parmName, OdbcType, int parmSize,
    string sourceColumn);
```

Clear Method   Removes all the items from the OdbcParameterCollection.

```
public void Clear();
```

Contains Method   Overloaded. The first Contains method returns True if the OdbcParameterCollection contains the specified object. The second Contains method returns True if the collection contains an OdbcParameter object with the specified parameter name.

```
public bool Contains(Object);
public bool Contains(string parmName);
```

CopyTo Method   Copies the objects in the OdbcParameterCollection to the specified array and sets the starting index of the array to the specified integer.

```
public void CopyTo(array, int);
```

GetEnumerator Method   The GetEnumerator method supports the .NET infrastructure and is not used directly from your code.

IndexOf Method   Overloaded. The first IndexOf method returns the location of the specified object of type OdbcParameter within the OdbcParameterCollection. The second IndexOf method returns the location of the OdbcParameter object with the specified parameter name.

```
public int IndexOf(Object);
public int IndexOf(string parmName);
```

Insert Method   Inserts an OdbcParameter object into the OdbcParameterCollection at the specified zero-based integer index.

```
public void Insert(int, object);
```

Remove Method   Removes an object that is of type OdbcParameter from the OdbcParameterCollection. Throws a SystemException if the specified object is not of type OdbcParameter or the specified object does not exist in the collection.

```
public void Remove(object);
```

RemoveAt Method   Overloaded. The first RemoveAt method removes the OdbcParameter object from the OdbcParameterCollection at the specified zero-based integer index. The second RemoveAt method removes the OdbcParameter object from the collection that matches the specified parameter name. Both methods throw an exception if the OdbcParameter object does not exist in the collection at the specified location.

```
public void RemoveAt(int);
public void RemoveAt(string parmName);
```

Mutual Properties, Methods, and Events Included in the OdbcParameterCollection Class

The following lists the mutual properties, methods, and events that are included in the OdbcParameterCollection class.

Inherited from Object	Inherited from MarshalByRefObject
Equals method	CreateObjRef method

Inherited from Object	Inherited from MarshalByRefObject
Finalize method	GetLifetimeService method
GetHashCode method	InitializeLifetimeService method
GetType method	
MemberwiseClone method	
ToString method	

OdbcPermission Class

The OdbcPermission class provides user security level setting to access an ODBC data source with the ODBC data provider.

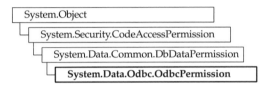

```
System.Object
    System.Security.CodeAccessPermission
        System.Data.Common.DbDataPermission
            System.Data.Odbc.OdbcPermission
```

Constructor   Overloaded. Initializes a new instance of the DBDataPermission class. The first constructor creates a new OdbcPermission object using the default values. The second constructor specifies whether a user should have all access or no access. The third constructor checks for all access or no access and whether a blank password is allowed.

Note   *The first constructor and the third constructor for this class are now obsolete.*

```
public OdbcPermission();
public OdbcPermission(
    System.Security.Permissions.PermissionState);
public OdbcPermission(
    System.Security.Permissions.PermissionState,
    bool allowBlankPassword);
// C# example
System.Data.Odbc.OdbcPermission odbcP = new
    System.Data.Odbc.OdbcPermission();
System.Data.Odbc.OdbcPermission odbcP2 = new
    System.Data.Odbc.OdbcPermission(
    System.Security.Permissions.PermissionState.None);
```

APPENDIXES

```
System.Data.Odbc.OdbcPermission odbcP3 = new
    System.Data.Odbc.OdbcPermission(
    System.Security.Permissions.PermissionState.None, true);
```

System.Security.Permissions.PermissionState enumeration:

None   Indicates no access to the resource

Unrestricted   Indicates full access to the resource

OdbcPermission Class Methods

Add Method   Adds to the state of the permission the specified access for the specified connection string.

```
public virtual void Add(string conn, string restrict,
    System.Data.KeyRestrictionBehavior);
```

System.Data.KeyRestrictionBehavior enumeration :

AllowOnly   Default. Only the connection string parameters that are
                        identified are allowed.

PreventUsage   The connection string parameters that are identified are
                        not allowed.

Copy Method   Returns a copy of the current security permission object, IPermission, with the same access to resources as the original object. The IPermission object describes the functions of the object.

```
public override System.Security.IPermission Copy();
```

Mutual Properties, Methods, and Events Included in the OdbcPermission Class

The following lists the mutual properties, methods, and events that are included in the OdbcPermission class.

Inherited from DBDataPermission	Inherited from CodeAccessPermission	Inherited from Object
AllowBlankPassword property	Assert method	Equals method
Clear method	Demand method	Finalize method
CreateInstance method	Deny method	GetHashCode method
FromXml method	PermitOnly method	GetType method
Intersect method	ToString method	MemberwiseClone method
IsSubsetOf method		
IsUnrestricted method		
ToXml method		
Union method		

OdbcPermissionAttribute Class

The OdbcPermissionAttribute class relates a security action to a security permission attribute.

```
System.Object
  └ System.Attribute
      └ System.Security.Permissions.SecurityAttribute
          └ System.Security.Permissions.CodeAccessSecurityAttribute
              └ System.DataCommon.DbDataPermissionAttribute
                  └ System.Data.Odbc.OdbcPermissionAttribute
```

Constructor   Initializes a new instance of the OdbcPermissionAttribute class.

```
public OdbcPermissionAttribute(
    System.Security.Permissions.SecurityAction);
// C# example
System.Data.Odbc.OdbcPermissionAttribute odbcPA = new
    System.Data.Odbc.OdbcPermissionAttribute(
    System.Security.Permissions.SecurityAction.LinkDemand);
```

System.Security.Permissions.SecurityAction enumeration:

Assert	Allows security to bypass code permission check
Demand	Performs security check for enforcing restrictions on calling code
Deny	Prevents access to the resource specified
InheritanceDemand	Checks for granted permissions for inherited class
LinkDemand	Checks for granted permission for immediate caller
PermitOnly	Allows access only to the resource specified
RequestMinimum	Requests the minimum permissions for code
RequestOptional	Requests the optional permissions
RequestRefuse	Requests permissions not be granted to calling code

OdbcPermission Class Methods

CreatePermission Method Returns an OdbcPermission object that contains the current attribute properties.

```
public override System.Security.IPermission CreatePermission();
```

Mutual Properties, Methods, and Events Included in the OdbcPermissionAttribute Class

The following lists the mutual properties, methods, and events that are included in the OdbcPermissionAttribute class.

Inherited from Attribute	Inherited from Object
TypeId property	Equals method
GetHashCode method	Finalize method
IsDefaultAttribute method	GetType method
Match method	MemberwiseClone method
	ToString method

Inherited from SecurityAttribute	Inherited from DBDataPermission
Action property	AllowBlankPassword property
Unrestricted property	ConnectionString property
	KeyRestrictionBehavior property
	KeyRestrictions property

OdbcRowUpdatedEventArgs Class

The OdbcRowUpdatedEventArgs class supplies the information for the RowUpdated event that is raised when an update to a row has been completed.

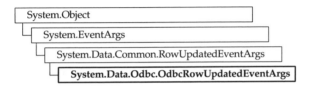

```
System.Object
  └ System.EventArgs
      └ System.Data.Common.RowUpdatedEventArgs
          └ System.Data.Odbc.OdbcRowUpdatedEventArgs
```

Constructor   Initializes a new instance of the OdbcRowUpdatedEventArgs class using the specified DataRow, the IDbCommand, the StatementType, and the DataTableMapping. The IDbCommand represents the SQL statement that was executed, and the StatementType specifies whether the command was a SELECT, INSERT, UPDATE, or DELETE statement. The DataTableMapping object describes the mapped relationship of the source table and the DataTable.

```
public OdbcRowUpdatedEventArgs(System.Data.DataRow,
    System.Data.IDbCommand, System.Data.StatementType,
    System.Data.Common.DataTableMapping);
// C# example
System.Data.DataRow dr = new System.Data.DataTable().NewRow();
System.Data.Odbc.OdbcCommand cmd = new
    System.Data.Odbc.OdbcCommand("SELECT * FROM Customers");
System.Data.Common.DataTableMapping dtm = new
    System.Data.Common.DataTableMapping();
System.Data.Common.RowUpdatedEventArgs ruea = new
    System.Data.Odbc.OdbcRowUpdatedEventArgs(dr, cmd,
    System.Data.StatementType.Select, dtm);
```

OdbcRowUpdatedEventArgs Class Properties

Command Property   Returns the OdbcCommand that was executed when Update was called.

```
public new OdbcCommand Command { get; }
```

Mutual Properties, Methods, and Events Included in the OdbcRowUpdatedEventArgs Class

The following lists the mutual properties, methods, and events that are included in the OdbcRowUpdatedEventArgs class.

Inherited from RowUpdatedEventArgs	Inherited from Object
Errors property	Equals method
RecordsAffected property	Finalize method
Row property	GetHashCode method
StatementType property	GetType method
Status property	MemberwiseClone method
TableMapping property	ToString method

OdbcRowUpdatingEventArgs Class

The OdbcRowUpdatingEventArgs class supplies the information for the RowUpdating event that is raised when an update to a row is about to take place.

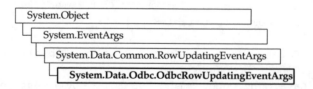

Constructor   Initializes a new instance of the OdbcRowUpdatingEventArgs class using the specified DataRow, the IDbCommand, the StatementType, and the DataTableMapping. The IDbCommand represents the SQL statement that will be executed, and the StatementType specifies whether the command is a SELECT, INSERT,

UPDATE, or DELETE statement. The DataTableMapping object describes the mapped relationship of the source table and the DataTable.

```
public OdbcRowUpdatingEventArgs(System.Data.DataRow,
    System.Data.IDbCommand, System.Data.StatementType,
    System.Data.Common.DataTableMapping);
// C# example
System.Data.DataRow dr = new System.Data.DataTable().NewRow();
System.Data.Odbc.OdbcCommand cmd = new
    System.Data.Odbc.OdbcCommand("SELECT * FROM Customers");
System.Data.Common.DataTableMapping dtm = new
    System.Data.Common.DataTableMapping();
System.Data.Common.RowUpdatingEventArgs ruea = new
    System.Data.Odbc.OdbcRowUpdatedEventArgs(dr, cmd,
    System.Data.StatementType.Select, dtm);
```

OdbcRowUpdatingEventArgs Class Properties

Command Property   Returns or sets the OdbcCommand that will be executed when Update is called.

```
public new OdbcCommand Command { get; set; }
```

Mutual Properties, Methods, and Events Included in the OdbcRowUpdatingEventArgs Class

The following lists the mutual properties, methods, and events that are included in the OdbcRowUpdatingEventArgs class.

Inherited from RowUpdatedEventArgs	Inherited from Object
Errors property	Equals method
Row property	Finalize method
StatementType property	GetHashCode method
Status property	GetType method
TableMapping property	MemberwiseClone method
	ToString method

OdbcTransaction Class

The OdbcTransaction class represents a SQL transaction to implement at a data source. You do not create an OdbcTransaction object by calling a constructor, but rather by calling the BeginTransaction method of an OdbcConnection object.

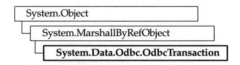

OdbcTransaction Class Properties

Connection Property   Returns the OdbcConnection object associated with this OdbcTransaction.

```
public OdbcConnection Connection { get; }
```

IsolationLevel Property   Returns the isolation level for this OdbcTransaction object. The default value is ReadCommited.

```
public System.Data.IsolationLevel IsolationLevel { get; }
```

System.Data.IsolationLevel enumeration:

Chaos	Cannot overwrite more highly isolated transactions that are pending.
ReadCommited	To avoid dirty reads, the shared locks are held during reading of data. May result in non-repeatable read or phantom data is changed before the transaction ends.
ReadUncommited	No exclusive locks are allowed, and no shared locks are done. May result in a dirty read.
RepeatableRead	Locks are placed on the queried data. May result in phantom rows.
Serializable	A range lock is placed on the rows in the DataSet.
Unspecified	The isolation level cannot be determined.

OdbcTransaction Class Methods

Commit Method   Commits the transaction to the database. Throws an exception if there is an error committing the transaction or the connection is broken.

```
public void Commit();
```

IDisposable.Dispose Method   The IDisposable.Dispose method supports the .NET infrastructure and is not used directly from your code.

```
void IDisposable.Dispose();
```

Rollback Method   Rolls back a transaction that is in a pending state. Throws an exception if the transaction has already been committed or the connection is broken.

```
public void Rollback();
```

Mutual Properties, Methods, and Events Included in the OdbcTransaction Class

The following lists the mutual properties, methods, and events that are included in the OdbcTransaction class.

Inherited from Object	Inherited from MarshalByRefObject
Equals method	CreateObjRef method
Finalize method	GetLifetimeService method
GetHashCode method	InitializeLifetimeService method
GetType method	
MemberwiseClone method	
ToString method	

OdbcInfoMessageEventHandler Delegate

The OdbcInfoMessageEventHandler delegate is the method that handles the InfoMessage event of the OdbcConnection object. The first parameter, object, indicates the source of the event to handle. The second parameter is an OdbcInfoMessageEventArgs object that contains the event information.

```
public delegate void OdbcInfoMessageEventHandler(object,
    OdbcRowUpdatedEventArgs):
```

OdbcRowUpdatedEventHandler Delegate

The OdbcRowUpdatedEventHandler delegate is the method that handles the RowUpdatedEvent of the OdbcDataAdpapter object. The first parameter, object, indicates the source of the event to handle. The second parameter is an OdbcRowUpdatedEventArgs object that contains the event information.

```
public delegate void OdbcRowUpdatedEventHandler(object,
    OdbcRowUpdatedEventArgs);
```

OdbcRowUpdatingEventHandler Delegate

The OdbcRowUpdatingEventHandler delegate is the method that handles the RowUpdatingEvent of the OdbcDataAdapter object. The first parameter, object, indicates the source of the event to handle. The second parameter is an OdbcRowUpdatingEventArgs object that contains the event information.

```
public delegate void OdbcRowUpdatingEventHandler(object,
    OdbcRowUpdatingEventArgs);
```

OdbcType Enumeration

The OdbcType enumeration contains the data types that are used in the fields, properties, or parameters of the namespace objects. The following table shows the OdbcTypes mapped to the OLE DB data types and the .NET Framework data types.

System.Data.OdbcType enumeration:

System.Data.OdbcType	ODBC Data Type	.NET Framework Type
BigInt	SQL_BIGINT	Int64
Binary	SQL_BINARY	An array of type Byte
Bit	SQL_BIT	Boolean
Char	SQL_CHAR	String
Date	SQL_TYPE_DATE	DateTime
DateTime	SQL_TYPE_TIMESTAMP	DateTime
Decimal	SQL_DECIMAL	Decimal
Double	SQL_DOUBLE	Double
Image	SQL_LONGVARBINARY	An array of type Byte

System.Data.OdbcType enumeration:

System.Data.OdbcType	ODBC Data Type	.NET Framework Type
Int	SQL_INTEGER	Int32
Nchar	SQL_WCHAR	String
Ntext	SQL_WLONGVARCHAR	String
Numeric	SQL_NUMERIC	Decimal
NVarChar	SQL_WVARCHAR	String
Real	SQL_REAL	Single
SmallDateTime	SQL_TYPE_TIMESTAMP	DateTime
SmallInt	SQL_SMALLINT	Int16
Text	SQL_LONGVARCHAR	String
Time	SQL_TYPE_TIME	DateTime
Timestamp	SQL_BINARY	An array of type Byte
TinyInt	SQL_TINYINT	Byte
UniqueIdentifier	SQL_GUID	Guid
VarBinary	SQL_VARBINARY	An array of type Byte
VarChar	SQL_CHAR	String

Appendix D

System.Data.OleDb
Namespace Reference

System.Data.OleDb Namespace

The System.Data.OleDb namespace contains classes that comprise the OLE DB .NET data provider, which are a group of classes that are used to access a data source.

OleDbCommand Class The OleDbCommand class represents a stored procedure or SQL statement to implement at a data source.

OleDbCommandBuilder Class The OleDbCommandBuilder class allows for automatic generation of single table commands.

OleDbConnection Class The OleDbConnection class represents a connection to a data source.

OleDbDataAdapter Class The OleDbDataAdapter class represents a database connection and a set of commands that are used to fill a DataSet and update a data source.

OleDbDataReader Class The OleDbDataReader class allows for reading forward-only streams of data rows from a data source.

OleDbError Class The OleDbError class contains information regarding errors returned by the data source.

OleDbErrorCollection Class The OleDbErrorCollection class contains a collection of OleDbError objects.

OleDbException Class The OleDbException class represents the exception that is thrown when an error is returned by the OLE DB data source.

OleDbInfoMessageEventArgs Class The OleDbInfoMessageEventArgs class supplies information for the InfoMessage event.

OleDbParameter Class The OleDbParameter class is a parameter for the OleDbCommand object. May also be used for the OleDbCommand object's mapping to the DataSet column.

OleDbParameterCollection Class The OleDbParameterCollection class is a collection of OleDbParameter classes and their related mapping information for DataSet columns.

OleDbPermission Class The OleDbPermission class provides user security level setting for data access with the OLE DB data providers.

OleDbPermissionAttribute Class The OleDbPermissionAttribute class relates a security action to a security permission attribute.

OleDbRowUpdatedEventArgs Class   The OleDbRowUpdatedEventArgs class supplies the information for the RowUpdated event.

OleDbRowUpdatingEventArgs Class   The OleDbRowUpdatingEventArgs class supplies the information for the RowUpdating event.

OleDbSchemaGuid Class   The OleDbSchemaGuid class returns the type of schema table from the method GetOleDbSchemaTable.

OleDbTransaction Class   The OleDbTransaction class represents a SQL transaction to implement at a data source.

OleDbInfoMessageEventHandler Delegate   The OleDbInfoMessageEventHandler delegate is the method that handles the InfoMessage event of the OleDbConnection object.

OleDbRowUpdatedEventHandler Delegate   The OleDbRowUpdatedEventHandler delegate is the method that handles the RowUpdatedEvent of the OleDbDataAdapter object.

OleDbRowUpdatingEventHandler Delegate   The OleDbRowUpdatingEventHandler delegate is the method that handles the RowUpdatingEvent of the OleDbDataAdapter object.

OleDbLiteral Enumeration   The OleDbLiteral enumeration contains information about the literals that are used in the text commands and database objects.

OleDbType Enumeration   The OleDbType enumeration contains the data types that are used in the fields, properties, or parameters of the namespace objects.

OleDbCommand Class

The OleDbCommand class represents a stored procedure or SQL statement to implement at a data source. A new instance of the OleDbCommand will set the read/write properties to their initial values.

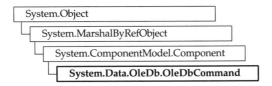

Constructor   Overloaded. Initializes a new instance of the OleDbCommand class. The first constructor initializes all the fields to their default values. The second constructor specifies the text of a query to execute. The third constructor specifies the text of the query to execute through the specified OleDbConnection. The fourth constructor specifies the text of the query to execute through the specified OleDbConnection as reflected through the specified OleDbTransaction object.

```
public OleDbCommand();
public OleDbCommand(string cmdText);
public OleDbCommand(string cmdText, OleDbConnection);
public OleDbCommand(string cmdText, OleDbConnection,
    OleDbTransaction); // C# example
System.Data.OleDb.OleDbCommand oledbCmd = new
    System.Data.OleDb.OleDbCommand();
System.Data.OleDb.OleDbCommand oledbCmd2 = new
    System.Data.OleDb.OleDbCommand("SELECT * FROM Customers");
System.Data.OleDb.OleDbConnection oledbConn = new
    System.Data.OleDb.OleDbConnection();
System.Data.OleDb.OleDbCommand oledbCmd3 = new
    System.Data.OleDb.OleDbCommand("SELECT * FROM Customers",
    oledbConn);
System.Data.OleDb.OleDbTransaction oledbTrans =
    oledbConn.BeginTransaction();
System.Data.OleDb.OleDbCommand oledbCmd4 = new
    System.Data.OleDb.OleDbCommand("SELECT * FROM Customers",
    oledbConn, oledbTrans);
```

OleDbCommand Class Properties

CommandText Property   Returns or sets the SQL statement query text or stored procedure to execute.

```
public string CommandText { get; set; }
```

CommandTimeout Property   Returns or sets the wait time in seconds before an attempted command is terminated and an error is generated. Default wait time is 30 seconds.

```
public int CommandTimeout { get; set; }
```

CommandType Property   Designates what type of command this object is.

```
public System.Data.CommandType CommandType { get; set; }
```

System.Data.CommandType enumeration:

Text	Default. An SQL statement to execute
StoredProcedure	The name of a stored procedure to execute
TableDirect	The name of the table to be accessed

Connection Property   Returns or sets the OleDbConnection object for this OleDbCommand object.

```
public OleDbConnection Connection { get; set; }
```

DesignTimeVisible Property   Returns or sets a Boolean value specifying whether the OleDbCommand object should be visible. The default value is False.

```
public bool DesignTimeVisible { get; set; }
```

Parameters Property   Returns the OleDbParameterCollection, which designates the parameters for a stored procedure or SQL statement for this OleDbCommand object.

```
public OleDbParametersCollection Parameters { get; }
```

Transaction Property   Returns or sets the OleDbTransaction that the OleDbCommand implements.

```
public OleDbTransaction Transaction { get; set; }
```

UpdatedRowSource Property   Returns or sets how the results of a command are applied to a DataSet when the Update method is used. If the command is automatically generated, the default result is None; otherwise the default result is Both.

```
public System.Data.UpdateRowSource UpdatedRowSource { get; set; }
```

System.Data.UpdateRowSource enumeration:

Both	The first returned row and the output parameters are mapped to the DataSet at the changed row.
FirstReturnedRecord	The first returned row is mapped to the DataSet at the changed row.
None	Returned results are ignored.
OutputParameters	The output parameters are mapped to the DataSet at the changed row.

OleDbCommand Class Methods

Cancel Method   A cancellation of the execution of the OleDbCommand is attempted. No exception is generated, even if the attempt to cancel the OleDbCommand failed.

```
protected void Cancel();
```

CreateParameter Method   Creates a new OleDbParameter object.

```
protected OleDbParameter CreateParameter();
```

Dispose Method   Overloaded. Overridden. Disposes the resources used by the OleDbCommand. If the Boolean is set to True in the first method, it will dispose of both managed and unmanaged resources; False releases only unmanaged resources. The second method releases all the resources used by the object.

```
protected override void Dispose(bool);
public void Dispose();
```

ExecuteNonQuery Method   Used for catalog operations or to execute an UPDATE, INSERT, or DELETE SQL statement to a database without using a DataSet. Returns the number of affected rows.

```
public int ExecuteNonQuery();
```

ExecuteReader Method   Overloaded. Returns an OleDbDataReader object after sending the CommandText to the Connection object. The second method returns the OleDbDataReader object based on the specified CommandBehavior.

```
public OleDbDataReader ExecuteReader();
public OleDbDataReader ExecuteReader(System.Data.CommandBehavior);
```

System.Data.CommandBehavior enumeration:

CloseConnection	The Connection object is closed when the DataReader object is closed.
Default	Sets no CommandBehavior flags. Same as using ExecuteReader().

System.Data.CommandBehavior enumeration:

KeyInfo	Returns column and primary key information.
SchemaOnly	Returns column information only. Database state not affected.
SequentialAccess	Enables the DataReader to return data as a stream. You need to use GetBytes or GetChars to start the reading of data at a specified location.
SingleResult	Returns a single resultset.
SingleRow	Returns a single row of data.

ExecuteScalar Method   Returns a single value represented in the first column of the first row of a resultset.

```
public object ExecuteScalar();
```

ICloneable.Clone Method   The ICloneable.Clone method supports the .NET infrastructure and is not used directly from your code.

IDbCommand.CreateParameter Method   The IDbCommand.CreateParameter method supports the .NET infrastructure and is not used directly from your code.

IDbCommand.ExecuteReader Method   Overloaded. The IDbCommand.ExecuteReader method supports the .NET infrastructure and is not used directly from your code.

Prepare Method   Creates a compiled version of this command object if the CommandType is set to Text or StoredProcedure. You need to specify the data type of each parameter in the command statement before using the Prepare method. If the parameter has variable-length data, you also need to specify the maximum size of the data.

```
public void Prepare();
```

ResetCommandTimeout Method   Resets the CommandTimeout property to its default setting of 30 seconds.

```
public void ResetCommandTimeout();
```

APPENDIXES

Mutual Properties, Methods, and Events Included in the OleDbCommand Class

The following lists the mutual properties, methods, and events that are included in the OleDbCommand class.

Inherited from Component	Inherited from Object	Inherited from MarshalByRefObject
Container property	Equals method	CreateObjRef method
DesignMode property	Finalize method	GetLifetimeService method
Events property	GetHashCode method	InitializeLifetimeService method
Site property	GetType method	
Dispose method	MemberwiseClone method	
GetService method	ToString method	
Disposed event		

OleDbCommandBuilder Class

The OleDbCommandBuilder class is used to automatically generate SQL statements for updates of single tables. An OleDbDataAdapter object does not generate the required SQL statements automatically to synchronize the changes made to a DataSet with the data source, therefore an OleDbCommandBuilder is needed to automatically generate the SQL statements and synchronize the data.

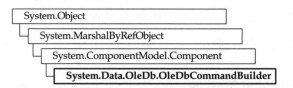

```
System.Object
    System.MarshalByRefObject
        System.ComponentModel.Component
            System.Data.OleDb.OleDbCommandBuilder
```

Constructor   Overloaded. Initializes a new instance of the OleDbCommandBuilder class. The second constructor specifies the associated OleDbDataAdapter. The OleDbCommandBuilder object will register itself as a listener to the OleDbDataAdapter's RowUpdating events.

```
public OleDbCommandBuilder();
public OleDbCommandBuilder(OleDbDataAdapter);
// C# example
```

```
System.Data.OleDb.OleDbCommandBuilder oledbCmdBldr = new
    System.Data.OleDb.OleDbCommandBuilder();
System.Data.OleDb.OleDbDataAdapter oledbDA = new
    System.Data.OleDb.OleDbDataAdapter();
System.Data.OleDb.OleDbCommandBuilder oledbCmdBldr2 = new
    System.Data.OleDb.OleDbCommandBuilder(oledbDA);
```

OleDbCommandBuilder Class Properties

DataAdapter Property   Returns or sets the OleDbDataAdapter object that SQL statements are automatically generated for.

```
public OleDbDataAdapter DataAdapter { get; set; }
```

QuotePrefix Property   Returns or sets the beginning character(s) to use as delimiters when database object names contain characters such as spaces and commas. The default value is an empty string.

```
public string QuotePrefix { get; set; }
```

QuoteSuffix Property   Returns or sets the ending character(s) to use as delimiters when database object names contain characters such as spaces and commas. The default value is an empty string.

```
public string QuoteSuffix { get; set; }
```

OleDbCommandBuilder Class Methods

DeriveParameters Method   Fills the Parameters collection of the specified OleDbCommand object with parameter information for the stored procedure of the same specified OleDbCommand object.

```
public static void DeriveParameters(OleDbCommand);
```

Dispose Method   Overloaded. Overridden. Disposes the resources used by the OleDbCommandBuilder. If the Boolean is set to True in the first method, it will dispose of both managed and unmanaged resources, False releases only unmanaged resources. The second method releases all the resources used by the object.

```
protected override void Dispose(bool);
public void Dispose();
```

APPENDIXES

GetDeleteCommand Method Returns the automatically generated OleDbCommand object for performing deletions.

```
public OleDbCommand GetDeleteCommand();
```

GetInsertCommand Method Returns the automatically generated OleDbCommand object for performing inserts.

```
public OleDbCommand GetInsertCommand();
```

GetUpdateCommand Method Returns the automatically generated OleDbCommand object for performing updates.

```
public OleDbCommand GetUpdateCommand();
```

RefreshSchema Method Refreshes the database schema information. Should be used when the SELECT statement of the OleDbCommandBuilder object changes.

```
public void RefreshSchema();
```

Mutual Properties, Methods, and Events Included in the OleDbCommandBuilder Class

The following lists the mutual properties, methods, and events that are included in the OleDbCommandBuilder class.

Inherited from Component	Inherited from Object	Inherited from MarshalByRefObject
Container property	Equals method	CreateObjRef method
DesignMode property	GetHashCode method	GetLifetimeService method
Events property	GetType method	InitializeLifetimeService method
Site property	MemberwiseClone method	
Dispose method	ToString method	
Finalize method		

Inherited from Component	Inherited from Object	Inherited from MarshalByRefObject

GetService method

Disposed event

OleDbConnection Class

The OleDbConnection class represents a connection to a data source.

 If an OleDbConnection object goes out of scope, the object is not closed. You need to explicitly call Close or Dispose in order to close the open connection.

```
System.Object
  System.MarshalByRefObject
    System.ComponentModel.Component
      System.Data.OleDb.OleDbConnection
```

Constructor   Overloaded. Initializes a new instance of the OleDbConnection class. The first constructor initializes all the fields to their default values. The second constructor specifies the connection string to use to open the connection.

```
public OleDbConnection();
public OleDbConnection(string connString);
// C# example
System.Data.OleDb.OleDbConnection oledbConn = new
    System.Data.OleDb.OleDbConnection();
System.Data.OleDb.OleDbConnection oledbConn2 = new
    System.Data.OleDb.OleDbConnection("PROVIDER=SQLOLEDB;
    DATA SOURCE=localhost;INTEGRATED SECURITY=SSPI;
    CONNECT TIMEOUT=30");
```

OleDbConnection Class Properties

ConnectionString Property   Returns or sets the connection string that is used to open the connection to the data source.

```
public string ConnectionString { get; set; }
```

ConnectionTimeout Property   Returns wait time in seconds before an attempted connection is terminated and an error is generated. Default wait time is 15 seconds.

```
public int ConnectionTimeout { get; }
```

Database Property   Returns the name of the database that will be used when a connection is opened. Default database name is an empty string.

```
public string Database { get; }
```

DataSource Property   Returns the location and the file name of the data source to use. The default value is an empty string.

```
public string DataSource { get; }
```

Provider Property   Returns the name of the OLE DB provider that is specified in the "Provider=" section of the connection string. Default provider name is an empty string.

```
public string Provider { get; }
```

ServerVersion Property   Returns the version of the server that the client is connected to. The version string that is returned is in the form ##.##.#### (major version.minor version.release build).

```
public string ServerVersion { get; }
```

State Property   Returns the bitwise ConnectionState value of the connection. The default value is Closed.

```
public System.Data.ConnectionState State { get; }
```

System.Data.ConnectionState enumeration:

Broken	A previously opened connection is now broken.
Closed	The current connection is not open.
Connecting	The connection object is attempting to connect to the data source.
Executing	The connection object is currently executing a command.
Fetching	The connection object is currently fetching data.
Open	The current connection is open.

OleDbConnection Class Methods

BeginTransaction Method   Overloaded. Begins a transaction to the database and returns an object that represents that transaction. The second method specifies the IsolationLevel for the transaction.

```
public OleDbTransaction BeginTransaction();
public OleDbTransaction
    BeginTransaction(System.Data.IsolationLevel);
```

System.Data.IsolationLevel enumeration:

Chaos	Cannot overwrite more highly isolated transactions that are pending.
ReadCommited	To avoid dirty reads, the shared locks are held during reading of data. May result in nonrepeatable read or phantom data is data is changed before the transaction ends.
ReadUncommited	No exclusive locks are allowed and no shared locks are done. May result in a dirty read.
RepeatableRead	Locks are placed on the queried data. May result in phantom rows.
Serializable	A range lock is placed on the rows in the DataSet.
Unspecified	The isolation level cannot be determined.

ChangeDatabase Method   Changes the database name for the open OleDbConnection object. The database name parameter cannot be a blank string or null value. Throws an exception if the database name is not valid or the connection is not open.

```
public void ChangeDatabase(string databaseName);
```

Close Method   Closes the connection to the data source and rolls back any pending transactions. No exception is generated if an application calls Close more than once.

```
public void Close();
```

CreateCommand Method   Creates and returns an OleDbCommand object.

```
public OleDbCommand CreateCommand();
```

Dispose Method   Overloaded. Overridden. Disposes the resources used by the OleDbConnection object. If the Boolean is set to True in the first method, it will dispose of both managed and unmanaged resources; False releases only unmanaged resources. The second method releases all the resources used by the object.

```
protected override void Dispose(bool);
public void Dispose();
```

GetOleDbSchemaTable Method   Returns a DataTable that contains the specified Guid schema table information. The specified restrictions are applied before the DataTable is returned.

```
public DataTable GetOleDbSchemaTable(System.Guid schema, object[] restrictions);
```

EnlistedDistributedTransaction Method   Registers the specified transaction as a distributed transaction.

```
public void EnlistDistributedTransaction(ITransaction);
```

ICloneable.Clone Method   The ICloneable.Clone method supports the .NET infrastructure and is not used directly from your code.

IDbConnection.BeginTransaction Method   Overloaded. The IDbConnection.BeginTransaction method supports the .NET infrastructure and is not used directly from your code.

IDbConnection.CreateCommand Method   The IDbConnection.CreateCommand method supports the .NET infrastructure and is not used directly from your code.

Open Method   Opens a connection to a database from the connection pool. If a connection from the connection pool is not available, this will create a new connection to the data source.

```
public void Open();
```

ReleaseObjectPool Method   Clears the OleDbConnection object pool when the OLE DB provider is released.

```
public static void ReleaseObjectPool();
```

OleDbConnection Class Events

InfoMessage Event Fires when the provider sends a warning or informational message to the event handler.

```
public event OleDbInfoMessageEventHandler InfoMessage;
```

StateChange Event Fires when the state of the connection changes.

```
public event StateChangeEventHandler StateChange;
```

Mutual Properties, Methods, and Events Included in the OleDbConnection Class

The following lists the mutual properties, methods, and events that are included in the OleDbConnection class.

Inherited from Component	Inherited from Object	Inherited from MarshalByRefObject
Container property	Equals method	CreateObjRef method
DesignMode property	GetHashCode method	GetLifetimeService method
Events property	GetType method	InitializeLifetimeService method
Site property	MemberwiseClone method	
Dispose method	ToString method	
Finalize method		
GetService method		
Disposed event		

OleDbDataAdapter Class

The OleDbDataAdapter class represents a database connection and a set of commands that are used to fill a DataSet and update a data source. The OleDbDataAdapter class uses the Fill method to fill the DataSet with information from the data source and the Update method to move changed information from the DataSet back to the data source.

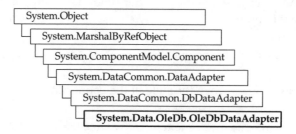

Constructor   Overloaded. Initializes a new instance of the OleDbDataAdapter class. The second constructor specifies a SELECT statement or stored procedure, OleDbCommand, to use as the SelectCommand property. The third constructor specifies a string that is a SELECT statement or stored procedure and an OleDbConnection to open and use. The fourth constructor specifies a string that is a SELECT statement or stored procedure and a connection string.

```
public OleDbDataAdapter();
public OleDbDataAdapter(OleDbCommand);
public OleDbDataAdapter(string selectCmdText, OleDbConnection);
public OleDbDataAdapter(string selectCmdText, string selectConnStr);
// C# example
System.Data.OleDb.OleDbDataAdapter oledbDA = new
    System.Data.OleDb.OleDbDataAdapter();
System.Data.OleDb.OleDbCommand oledbCmd = new
    System.Data.OleDb.OleDbCommand();
System.Data.OleDb.OleDbDataAdapter oledbDA2 = new
    System.Data.OleDb.OleDbDataAdapter(oledbCmd);
System.Data.OleDb.OleDbConnection oledbConn = new
    System.Data.OleDb.OleDbConnection();
System.Data.OleDb.OleDbDataAdapter oledbDA3 = new
    System.Data.OleDb.OleDbDataAdapter("SELECT * FROM Customers",
    oledbConn);
System.Data.OleDb.OleDbDataAdapter oledbDA2 = new
    System.Data.OleDb.OleDbDataAdapter("SELECT * FROM Customers",
    "PROVIDER=SQLOLEDB;DATA SOURCE=LOCALHOST;INTEGRATED
    SECURITY=SSPI;CONNECT TIMEOUT=30");
```

OleDbDataAdapter Class Properties

DeleteCommand Property   Returns or sets the SQL statement or stored procedure used for deleting records from the data source.

```
public new OleDbCommand DeleteCommand { get; set; }
```

InsertCommand Property   Returns or sets the SQL statement or stored procedure used for inserting records into the data source.

```
public new OleDbCommand InsertCommand { get; set; }
```

SelectCommand Property   Returns or sets the SQL statement or stored procedure used for selecting records from the data source.

```
public new OleDbCommand SelectCommand { get; set; }
```

UpdateCommand Property   Returns or sets the SQL statement or stored procedure used for updating records in the data source.

```
public new OleDbCommand UpdateCommand { get; set; }
```

OleDbDataAdapter Class Methods

CreateRowUpdatedEvent Method   Overrides System.Data.Common.DbDataAdapter. CreateRowUpdatedEvent. Returns a new instance of the RowUpdatedEventArgs class. The first parameter of the CreateRowUpdatedEvent method is the DataRow that is used to update the data source. The second parameter, IDbCommand, represents the SQL statement that is executed during the Update and the third parameter, StatementType, specifies whether the command is a SELECT, INSERT, UPDATE, or DELETE statement. The fourth parameter is the DataTableMapping object.

```
protected override RowUpdatedEventArgs CreateRowUpdatedEvent(
    System.Data.DataRow, System.Data.IDbCommand,
    System.Data.StatementType,
    System.Data.Common.DataTableMapping);
```

CreateRowUpdatingEvent Method   Overrides System.Data.Common.DbDataAdapter. CreateRowUpdatingEvent. Returns a new instance of the RowUpdatingEventArgs class. The first parameter of the CreateRowUpdatingEvent method is the DataRow that is used to update the data source. The second parameter, IDbCommand, represents the SQL statement that is executed during the Update, and the third parameter, StatementType, specifies whether the command is a SELECT, INSERT, UPDATE, or DELETE statement. The fourth parameter is the DataTableMapping object.

APPENDIXES

```
protected override RowUpdatingEventArgs CreateRowUpdatingEvent(
    System.Data.DataRow, System.Data.IDbCommand,
    System.Data.StatementType, System.Data.Common.DataTableMapping);
```

Dispose Method   Overloaded. Overridden. Disposes the resources used by the OleDbDataAdapter object. If the Boolean is set to True in the first method, it will dispose of both managed and unmanaged resources; False releases only unmanaged resources. The second method releases all the resources used by the object.

```
protected override void Dispose(bool);
public void Dispose();
```

Fill Method   Overloaded. Sets rows in the DataTable to match the rows in an ADO Recordset or Record object using the specified parameters. Returns the number of rows successfully refreshed in the DataTable. The first method specifies the DataTable to refresh and the ADO recordset or record to use. The second method specifies the DataSet to refresh, ADO recordset or record, and the source table to use for table mappings.

```
public int Fill(System.Data.DataTable, object adoRS);
public int Fill(System.Data.DataSet, object adoRS, string sourceTable);
```

ICloneable.Clone Method   The ICloneable.Clone method supports the .NET infrastructure and is not used directly from your code.

OnRowUpdated Method   Raises the RowUpdated event. The RowUpdatedEventArgs parameter contains the event data that is raised.

```
protected override void OnRowUpdated(RowUpdatedEventArgs);
```

OnRowUpdating Method   Raises the RowUpdating event. The RowUpdatingEventArgs parameter contains the event data that is raised.

```
protected override void OnRowUpdating(RowUpdatingEventArgs);
```

OleDbDataAdapter Class Events

RowUpdated Event   Fires after an Update command is executed against a data source.

```
public event OleDbRowUpdatedEventHandler RowUpdated;
```

RowUpdating Event   Fires before an Update command is executed against a data source.

```
public event OleDbRowUpdatingEventHandler RowUpdating;
```

Mutual Properties, Methods, and Events Included in the OleDbDataAdapter Class

The following lists the mutual properties, methods, and events that are included in the OleDbDataAdapter class.

Inherited from Component	Inherited from Object	Inherited from MarshalByRefObject
Container property	Equals method	CreateObjRef method
DesignMode property	GetHashCode method	GetLifetimeService method
Events property	GetType method	InitializeLifetimeService method
Site property	MemberwiseClone method	
Dispose method	ToString method	
Finalize method		
GetService method		
Disposed event		

Inherited from DataAdapter	Inherited from DbDataAdapter
AcceptChangesDuringFill property	Dispose method
ContinueUpdateOnError property	Fill method
MissingMappingAction property	FillSchema method
MissingSchemaAction property	GetFillParameters method
TableMappings property	OnFillError method
CloneInternals method	Update method
CreateTableMappings method	FillError event
ShouldSerializeTableMappings method	

OleDbDataReader Class

The OleDbDataReader class allows for reading forward-only streams of data rows from a data source. You do not create an OleDbDataReader by calling a constructor, but rather by calling the ExecuteReader method of an OleDbCommand object. The OleDbConnection object that is associated with the OleDbDataReader is used exclusively by the OleDbDataReader, therefore only the Close operation may be performed on the OleDbConnection.

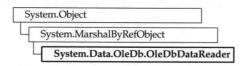

```
System.Object
    System.MarshalByRefObject
        System.Data.OleDb.OleDbDataReader
```

OleDbDataReader Class Properties

Depth Property   Returns an integer designating the depth of the current row's nesting.

```
public int Depth { get; }
```

FieldCount Property   Returns the number of columns (or fields) in the current row. Default FieldCount is –1.

```
public int FieldCount { get; }
```

IsClosed Property   Returns a Boolean designating whether the OleDbDataReader is opened or closed. True if the data reader is closed; False if it is open.

```
public bool IsClosed { get; }
```

Item Property   Overloaded. Returns the object found at the specified column ordinal or string column name.

```
public object this[int index] { get; }
public object this[string colName] {get; }
```

RecordsAffected Property   Returns the number of rows affected by a changed, inserted, or deleted action.

```
public int RecordsAffected { get; }
```

OleDbDataReader Class Methods

Close Method   Closes an open OleDbDataReader object.

```
public void Close();
```

Finalize Method   Frees the OleDbDataReader resources before the object is deleted. Finalizers in C# and C++ use the destructor syntax.

```
~OleDbDataReader();
```

GetBoolean Method   Returns the value in the specified zero-based column ordinal as a Boolean. The data to be retrieved must already be in the form of a Boolean or an exception is generated. Call IsNull before calling this method.

```
public bool GetBoolean(int colOrdinal);
```

GetByte Method   Returns the value in the specified zero-based column ordinal as a byte. The data to be retrieved must already be in the form of a byte or an exception is generated. Call IsNull before calling this method.

```
public bool GetByte(int colOrdinal);
```

GetBytes Method   Reads a stream of bytes from the specified zero-based column ordinal starting at the specified column offset and it places the bytes into the specified byte buffer, starting at the specified byte buffer offset for a length of the specified buffer length. Returns the actual number of bytes that were read. The data to be retrieved must already be in the form of a byte array or an exception is generated.

```
public long GetBytes(int colOrdinal, long colOffset, byte[] buffer, int
    bufferOffset, int bufferLength);
```

GetChar Method   Returns the value in the specified zero-based column ordinal as a character. The data to be retrieved must already be in the form of a character or an exception is generated. Call IsNull before calling this method.

```
public char GetChar(int colOrdinal);
```

GetChars Method   Reads a stream of characters from the specified zero-based column ordinal starting at the specified column offset, and places the characters into the specified character buffer starting at the specified character buffer offset for a length of the specified buffer length. Returns the actual number of characters that were read. The data to be retrieved must already be in the form of a character array or an exception is generated.

```
public long GetChars(int colOrdinal, long colOffset, char[] buffer, int
    bufferOffset, int bufferLength);
```

GetData Method   The GetData method supports the .NET infrastructure and is not used directly from your code.

GetDataTypeName Method   Returns the name of the data type in the specified zero-based column ordinal as a string.

```
public string GetDataTypeName(int colOrdinal);
```

GetDateTime Method   Returns the value in the specified zero-based column ordinal as a DateTime object. The data to be retrieved must already be in the form of a DateTime object or an exception is generated. Call IsNull before calling this method.

```
public DateTime GetDateTime(int colOrdinal);
```

GetDecimal Method   Returns the value in the specified zero-based column ordinal as a decimal. The data to be retrieved must already be in the form of a decimal or an exception is generated. Call IsNull before calling this method.

```
public decimal GetDecimal(int colOrdinal);
```

GetDouble Method   Returns the value in the specified zero-based column ordinal as a double-precision floating point number. The data to be retrieved must already be in the form of a double or an exception is generated. Call IsNull before calling this method.

```
public double GetDouble(int colOrdinal);
```

GetFieldType Method   Returns the data type of the object in the specified zero-based column ordinal.

```
public Type GetFieldType(int colOrdinal);
```

GetFloat Method   Returns the value in the specified zero-based column ordinal as a single-precision floating point number. The data to be retrieved must already be in the form of a float or an exception is generated. Call IsNull before calling this method.

```
public float GetFloat(int colOrdinal);
```

GetGuid Method   Returns the value in the specified zero-based column ordinal as a globally unique identifier (GUID). The data to be retrieved must already be in the form of a Guid or an exception is generated. Call IsNull before calling this method.

```
public Guid GetGuid(int colOrdinal);
```

GetInt16 Method   Returns the value in the specified zero-based column ordinal as a 16-bit signed integer. The data to be retrieved must already be in the form of a short or an exception is generated. Call IsNull before calling this method.

```
public short GetInt16(int colOrdinal);
```

GetInt32 Method   Returns the value in the specified zero-based column ordinal as a 32-bit signed integer. The data to be retrieved must already be in the form of an integer or an exception is generated. Call IsNull before calling this method.

```
public int GetInt32(int colOrdinal);
```

GetInt64 Method   Returns the value in the specified zero-based column ordinal as a 64-bit signed integer. The data to be retrieved must already be in the form of a long or an exception is generated. Call IsNull before calling this method.

```
public long GetInt64(int colOrdinal);
```

GetName Method   Returns the name of the column in the specified zero-based column ordinal as a string.

```
public string GetName(int colOrdinal);
```

GetOrdinal Method   Returns the zero-based column ordinal value of the specified column name.

```
public int GetOrdinal(string colName);
```

GetSchemaTable Method   Returns a DataTable object that contains the metadata for the columns in the current OleDbDataReader object.

```
public System.Data.DataTable GetSchemaTable();
```

GetString Method Returns the value in the specified zero-based column ordinal as a string. The data to be retrieved must already be in the form of a string or an exception is generated. Call IsNull before calling this method.

```
public string GetString(int colOrdinal);
```

GetTimeSpan Method Returns the value in the specified zero-based column ordinal as a TimeSpan object. The data to be retrieved must already be in the form of a TimeSpan or an exception is generated. Call IsNull before calling this method.

```
public TimeSpan GetTimeSpan(int colOrdinal);
```

GetValue Method Returns the value in the specified zero-based column ordinal in its native form.

```
public object GetValue(int colOrdinal);
```

GetValues Method Fills the specified object array with the column attributes of the current row. Returns the number of objects in the object array.

```
public int GetValues(object[] cols);
```

IDataRecord.GetData Method The IDataRecord.GetData method supports the .NET infrastructure and is not used directly from your code.

IDisposable.Dispose Method The IDisposable.Dispose method supports the .NET infrastructure and is not used directly from your code.

IEnumerator.GetEnumerator Method The IEnumerator.GetEnumerator method supports the .NET infrastructure and is not used directly from your code.

IsDBNull Method Returns a bool indicating whether the value in the specified zero-based column ordinal exists. True if the value is DBNull, else False.

```
public bool IsDBNull(int colOrdinal);
```

NextResult Method Moves to the next resultset. Used when multiple resultsets are generated by a batch SQL statement. Returns True if there are more resultsets, else False.

```
public bool NextResult();
```

Read Method   Moves to the next record in the OleDbDataReader object. Default position is prior to the first record, so use Read to begin processing data. Returns True if there are more rows, else False.

```
public bool Read();
```

Mutual Properties, Methods, and Events Included in the OleDbDataReader Class

The following lists the mutual properties, methods, and events that are included in the OleDbDataReader class.

Inherited from Object	Inherited from MarshalByRefObject
Equals method	CreateObjRef method
GetHashCode method	GetLifetimeService method
GetType method	InitializeLifetimeService method
MemberwiseClone method	
ToString method	

OleDbError Class

The OleDbError class contains information regarding errors returned by the data source. You do not create an OleDbError instance by calling a constructor. The creation and management of the OleDbError class is done by the OleDbErrorCollection class.

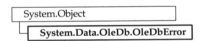

```
System.Object
    System.Data.OleDb.OleDbError
```

OleDbError Class Properties

Message Property   Contains a brief description of the error.

```
public string Message { get; }
```

NativeError Property   Contains the error information that is specifically related to the database.

```
public int NativeError { get; }
```

APPENDIXES

Source Property   Contains the name of the data provider that produced the error.

```
public string Source { get; }
```

SQLState Property   Contains a five-character code that identifies the error source.

```
public string SQLState { get; }
```

OleDbError Class Methods

ToString Method   Returns the full text of the error.

```
public override string ToString();
```

Mutual Properties, Methods, and Events Included in the OleDbError Class

The following lists the mutual properties, methods, and events that are included in the OleDbError class.

Inherited from Object

Equals method

Finalize method

GetHashCode method

GetType method

MemberwiseClone method

OleDbErrorCollection Class

The OleDbErrorCollection class contains a collection of OleDbError objects. You do not create an OleDbErrorCollection by calling a constructor. The OleDbErrorCollection is created by the OleDbException class and will always contain at least one instance of the OleDbError class.

```
System.Object
    System.Data.OleDb.OleDbErrorCollection
```

OleDbErrorCollection Class Properties

Count Property   Returns the number of items in this collection.

```
public int Count { get; }
```

Item Property   Returns the OleDbError object found at the specified zero-based index.

```
public OleDbError this[int index] { get; }
```

OleDbErrorCollection Class Methods

CopyTo Method   Copies the objects in the OleDbErrorCollection to the specified array and sets the starting index of the array to the specified integer.

```
public void CopyTo(Array arr, int index);
```

GetEnumerator Method   The GetEnumerator method supports the .NET infrastructure and is not used directly from your code.

Mutual Properties, Methods, and Events Included in the OleDbErrorCollection Class

The following lists the mutual properties, methods, and events that are included in the OleDbErrorCollection class.

Inherited from Object

Equals method

Finalize method

GetHashCode method

GetType method

MemberwiseClone method

ToString method

OleDbException Class

The OleDbException class represents the exception that is thrown when an error is returned by the OLE DB data source. You do not create an OleDbException by calling a constructor. The OleDbException is created when the OLE DB data provider encounters an error created by the server.

```
┌─────────────────────────────────────────────────────┐
│ System.Object                                       │
│  └─┌──────────────────────────────────────────────┐ │
│    │ System.Exception                             │ │
│    │  └─┌───────────────────────────────────────┐ │ │
│    │    │ System.SystemException                │ │ │
│    │    │  └─┌────────────────────────────────┐ │ │ │
│    │    │    │ System.RunTime.InteropServices.ExternalException │ │ │
│    │    │    │  └─┌─────────────────────────┐ │ │ │ │
│    │    │    │    │ System.Data.OleDb.OleDbException │ │ │ │
```

OleDbException Class Properties

ErrorCode Property   Contains the HRESULT for the error.

```
public override int ErrorCode { get; }
```

Errors Property   Contains the OleDbErrorCollection object.

```
public OleDbErrorCollection Errors { get; }
```

Message Property   Contains the text description for the error.

```
public override string Message { get; }
```

Source Property   Contains the name of the data provider that produced the error.

```
public override string Source { get; }
```

OleDbException Class Methods

GetObjectData Method   Overrides the Exception.GetObjectData, which sets the SerializationInfo with information about the error. The StreamingContext contains the source and destination for the serialization information.

```
public override void
    GetObjectData(System.Runtime.Serialization.SerializationInfo sInfo,
    System.Runtime.Serialization.StreamingContext sContext);
```

Mutual Properties, Methods, and Events Included in the OleDbException Class

The following lists the mutual properties, methods, and events that are included in the OleDbException class.

Inherited from Exception	Inherited from Object
HelpLink property	Equals method
HResult property	Finalize method
InnerException property	GetHashCode method
StackTrace property	GetType method
TargetSite property	MemberwiseClone method
GetBaseException method	
ToString method	

OleDbInfoMessageEventArgs Class

The OleDbInfoMessageEventArgs class supplies information for the InfoMessage event. You do not create an OleDbInfoMessageEventArgs by calling a constructor, but it is a parameter of the OleDbInfoMessageEventHandler.

```
System.Object
  └─ System.EventArgs
       └─ System.Data.OleDb.OleDbInfoMessageEventArgs
```

OleDbInfoMessageEventArgs Class Properties

ErrorCode Property   Contains the HRESULT for the source of the error.

```
public int ErrorCode { get; }
```

Errors Property   Contains the OleDbErrorCollection sent from the data source.

```
public OleDbErrorCollection Errors { get; }
```

Message Property   Contains the text description for the error sent from the data source.

```
public string Message { get; }
```

Source Property   Contains the name of the object that produced the error.

```
public string Source { get; }
```

OleDbInfoMessageEventArgs Class Methods

ToString Method   Returns the InfoMessage event text.

```
public override string ToString();
```

Mutual Properties, Methods, and Events Included in the OleDbInfoMessageEventArgs Class

The following lists the mutual properties, methods, and events that are included in the OleDbInfoMessageEventArgs class.

Inherited from Object

Equals method

Finalize method

GetHashCode method

GetType method

MemberwiseClone method

OleDbParameter Class

The OleDbParameter class is a parameter for the OleDbCommand object. May also be used for the OleDbCommand object's mapping to the DataSet column. The parameters for the OleDbCommand class are not case sensitive.

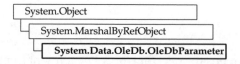

Constructor   Overloaded. Initializes a new instance of the OleDbParameter class. The second constructor specifies the parameter name and value type. The third constructor specifies the parameter name and data type. The fourth constructor specifies the parameter name, data type, and parameter size. The fifth constructor specifies the parameter name, data type, parameter size, and source column name. The sixth constructor sets all of the properties of the OleDbParameter object at the time it is created with the specified values.

```
public OleDbParameter();
public OleDbParameter(string parmName, object parmValue);
public OleDbParameter(string parmName, OleDbType parmType);
public OleDbParameter(string parmName, OleDbType parmType,
    int parmSize);
public OleDbParameter(string parmName, OleDbType parmType,
    int parmSize, string srcColumn);
public OleDbParameter(string parmName, OleDbType parmType,
    int parmSize, ParameterDirection parmDir, bool isNullable,
    byte parmPrecision, byte parmScale, string srcColumn,
    DataRowVersion srcVersion, object parmValue);
// C# example
System.Data.OleDb.OleDbParameter oledbParm = new
    System.Data.OleDb.OleDbParameter();
System.Data.OleDb.OleDbParameter oledbParm2 = new
    System.Data.OleDb.OleDbParameter("CustomerName", oledbParm);
System.Data.OleDb.OleDbParameter oledbParm3 = new
    System.Data.OleDb.OleDbParameter("CustomerName",
    System.Data.OleDb.OleDbType.BSTR);
System.Data.OleDb.OleDbParameter oledbParm4 = new
    System.Data.OleDb.OleDbParameter("CustomerName",
    System.Data.OleDb.OleDbType.BSTR, 25);
System.Data.OleDb.OleDbParameter oledbParm5 = new
    System.Data.OleDb.OleDbParameter("CustomerName",
    System.Data.OleDb.OleDbType.BSTR, 25, "CUSTNAME");
System.Data.OleDb.OleDbParameter oledbParm6 = new
    System.Data.OleDb.OleDbParameter("CustomerName",
    System.Data.OleDb.OleDbType.BSTR, 25,
    System.Data.ParameterDirection.Input, true, 0, 0, "CUSTNAME",
    System.Data.DataRowVersion.Current, oledbParm);
```

OleDbParameter Class Properties

DbType Property   Returns or sets the DbType for the parameter. Default DbType is string.

```
public System.Data.DbType DbType { get; set; }
```

System.Data.DbType enumeration:

AnsiString	Variable-length stream of 1 to 8,000 characters. Non-Unicode.
AnsiStringFixedLength	Fixed-length stream of characters. Non-Unicode.
Binary	Variable-length stream of binary data. 1 to 8,000 bytes.
Boolean	Values of True or False.
Byte	8-bit unsigned integer. Value range 0 to 255.
Currency	Value range −922,337,203,685,477.5808 to 922,337,203,685,477.5807. Accuracy to ten-thousandth of unit.
Date	Value range January 1, 1753, to December 31, 9999. Accuracy to 3.33 milliseconds.
DateTime	Represents date and time values.
Decimal	Value range 1.0×10^{-28} to approx 7.9×10^{28}. Significant digits of 28 to 29.
Double	Floating point type. Value range approx 5.0×10^{-324} to 1.7×10^{308}. Precision of 15 to 16 digits.
Guid	Globally unique identifier.
Int16	Signed 16-bit integer. Value range −32,768 to 32,767.
Int32	Signed 32-bit integer. Value range −2,147,483,648 to 2,147,483,647.
Int64	Signed 64-bit integer. Value range −9,223,372,036,854,775,808 to 9,223,372,036,854,775,807.
Object	General type.
SByte	Signed 8-bit integer. Value range −128 to 127.
Single	Floating point type. Value range approx 1.5×10^{-45} to 3.4×10^{38}. Precision of 7 digits.
String	String of characters. Unicode.
StringFixedLength	Fixed-length stream of characters. Unicode.
Time	Value range January 1, 1753, to December 31, 9999. Accuracy to 3.33 milliseconds.
Uint16	Unsigned 16-bit integer. Value range 0 to 65,535.
Uint32	Unsigned 32-bit integer. Value range 0 to 4,294,967,295.
Uint64	Unsigned 64-bit integer. Value range 0 to 18,446,744,073,709,551,615.

Direction Property   Returns or sets the directional aspect of the parameter.

```
public System.Data.ParameterDirection Direction { get; set; }
```

System.Data.ParameterDirection enumeration:

Input	Parameter is input only.
InputOutput	Parameter is both input and output.
Output	Parameter is output only.
ReturnValue	Parameter is a return value from an operation like a stored procedure.

IsNullable Property   Returns or sets a bool indicating whether the parameter accepts null values. True indicates nulls are accepted. The default value is False.

```
public bool IsNullable { get; set; }
```

OleDbType Property   Returns or sets the OleDbType for the parameter. Setting the DbType property changes the OleDbType property to the corresponding data type. The default OleDbType is VarWChar.

```
public OleDbType OleDbType { get; set; }
```

ParameterName Property   Returns or sets the name of the OleDbParameter. The default value is an empty string.

```
public string Parameter { get; set; }
```

Precision Property   Returns or sets the maximum number of digits to use. The default value is 0.

```
public byte Precision { get; set; }
```

Scale Property   Returns or sets the number of decimal places to use. The default value is 0.

```
public byte Scale { get; set; }
```

APPENDIXES

Size Property   Returns or sets the maximum bytes of data for the column. Used for binary and string column types. The default value is derived from the parameter type.

```
public int Size { get; set; }
```

SourceColumn Property   Returns or sets the name of the source column that is mapped to the DataSet. The default value is an empty string.

```
public string SourceColumn { get; set; }
```

SourceVersion Property   Returns or sets the DataRowVersion to use.

```
public System.Data.DataRowVersion SourceVersion { get; set; }
```

System.Data.DataRowVersion enumeration:

Current	Row contains current values.
Default	Row is versioned according to the DataRowState.
Original	Row contains its original values.
Proposed	Row contains proposed values.

Value Property   Returns or sets the value of the parameter.

```
public object Value { get; set; }
```

OleDbParameter Class Methods

ICloneable.Clone Method   The ICloneable.Clone method supports the .NET infrastructure and is not used directly from your code.

ToString Method   Returns the ParameterName in a string.

```
public override string ToString();
```

Mutual Properties, Methods, and Events Included in the OleDbParameter Class

The following lists the mutual properties, methods, and events that are included in the OleDbParameter class.

Inherited from Object	**Inherited from MarshalByRefObject**
Equals method	CreateObjRef method
Finalize method	GetLifetimeService method
GetHashCode method	InitializeLifetimeService method
GetType method	
MemberwiseClone method	

OleDbParameterCollection Class

The OleDbParameterCollection class is a collection of OleDbParameter classes and their related mapping information for DataSet columns. You do not create an OleDbParameterCollection by calling a constructor, but rather it is accessed through the OleDbCommand object.

```
System.Object
    System.MarshalByRefObject
        System.Data.OleDb.OleDbParameterCollection
```

OleDbParameterCollection Class Properties

Count Property   Returns the number of items in this collection.

```
public int Count { get; }
```

Item Property   Overloaded. Returns or sets the OleDbParameter object found at the specified integer index or string source column name.

```
public OleDbParameter this[int index] { get; set; }
public OleDbParameter this[string sourceColumn] {get; set; }
```

OleDbParameterCollection Class Methods

Add Method   Overloaded. The first Add method adds the specified object to the OleDbCommand's OleDbParameterCollection and returns the index of the added object. The second Add method adds the specified OleDbParameter to the OleDbCommand's OleDbParameterCollection and returns the added OleDbParameter. The third method adds an OleDbParameter to the collection using the specified parameter name and value. The fourth method adds the parameter object to the collection using the specified parameter name and OleDbType. The fifth method uses the parameter name, OleDbType, and column length integer to add the OleDbParameter to the collection. The sixth method adds the OleDbParameter object to the OleDbParameterCollection using the specified parameter name, OleDbType, column length, and source column.

```
public int Add(object);
public OleDbParameter Add(OleDbParameter);
public OleDbParameter Add(string parmName, object);
public OleDbParameter Add(string parmName, OleDbType);
public OleDbParameter Add(string parmName, OleDbType, int colLen);
public OleDbParameter Add(string parmName, OleDbType, int colLen,
    string srcCol);
```

Clear Method   Removes all the items from the OleDbParameterCollection.

```
public void Clear();
```

Contains Method   Overloaded. The first Contains method returns True if the OleDbParameterCollection contains the specified Object. The second Contains method returns True if the collection contains an OleDbParameter object with the specified parameter name.

```
public bool Contains(Object);
public bool Contains(string parmName);
```

CopyTo Method   Copies the objects in the OleDbParameterCollection to the specified array and sets the starting index of the array to the specified integer.

```
public void CopyTo(array, int);
```

GetEnumerator Method   The GetEnumerator method supports the .NET infrastructure and is not used directly from your code.

IndexOf Method   Overloaded. The first IndexOf method returns the location of the specified Object of type OleDbParameter within the OleDbParameterCollection. The second IndexOf method returns the location of the OleDbParameter object with the specified parameter name.

```
public int IndexOf(Object);
public int IndexOf(string parmName);
```

Insert Method   Inserts an OleDbParameter object into the OleDbParameterCollection at the specified zero-based integer index.

```
public void Insert(int, object);
```

Remove Method   Removes an object that is of type OleDbParameter from the OleDbParameterCollection. Throws a SystemException if the specified object is not of type OleDbParameter or the specified object does not exist in the collection.

```
public void Remove(object);
```

RemoveAt Method   Overloaded. The first RemoveAt method removes the OleDbParameter object from the OleDbParameterCollection at the specified zero-based integer index. The second RemoveAt method removes the OleDbParameter object from the collection that matches the specified parameter name. Both methods throw an exception if the OleDbParameter object does not exist in the collection at the specified location.

```
public void RemoveAt(int);
public void RemoveAt(string parmName);
```

Mutual Properties, Methods, and Events Included in the OleDbParameterCollection Class

The following lists the mutual properties, methods, and events that are included in the OleDbParameterCollection class.

Inherited from Object	Inherited from MarshalByRefObject
Equals method	CreateObjRef method
Finalize method	GetLifetimeService method
GetHashCode method	InitializeLifetimeService method
GetType method	
MemberwiseClone method	
ToString method	

OleDbPermission Class

The OleDbPermission class provides user security level setting to access an OLE DB data source with the OLE DB data provider.

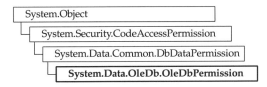

```
System.Object
    System.Security.CodeAccessPermission
        System.Data.Common.DbDataPermission
            System.Data.OleDb.OleDbPermission
```

Constructor   Overloaded. Initializes a new instance of the OleDbDataPermission class. The second constructor specifies whether a user should have all access or no access. The third constructor checks for all access or no access and whether a blank password is allowed.

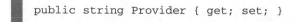 **Note**   *The first constructor and the third constructor for this class are now obsolete.*

```
public OleDbPermission();
public OleDbPermission(
    System.Security.Permissions.PermissionState);
public OleDbPermission(
    System.Security.Permissions.PermissionState,
    bool allowBlankPassword);
// C# example
System.Data.OleDb.OleDbPermission oledbP =
    new System.Data.OleDb.OleDbPermission();
System.Data.OleDb.OleDbPermission oledbP =
    new System.Data.OleDb.OleDbPermission(
    System.Security.Permissions.PermissionState.None);
System.Data.OleDb.OleDbPermission oledbP =
    new System.Data.OleDb.OleDbPermission(
    System.Security.Permissions.PermissionState.None, true);
```

System.Security.Permissions.PermissionState enumeration:

None	Indicates no access to the resource
Unrestricted	Indicates full access to the resource

OleDbPermission Class Properties

Provider Property   Returns or sets a list of providers allowed. The list is comma-delimited.

```
public string Provider { get; set; }
```

OleDbPermission Class Methods

Copy Method   Returns a copy of the current security permission object, IPermission, with the same access to resources as the original object. The IPermission object describes the functions of the object.

```
public override System.Security.IPermission Copy();
```

FromXml Method Populates the OleDbPermission object with the specified XML security-encoded state.

```
public override void FromXml(System.Security.SecurityElement);
```

Intersect Method Returns a security permission object, IPermission, that intersects the current OleDbPermission object with the specified permission object. A request that passes both original permission objects will be allowed to pass the intersection. An IPermission object describes the functions of the object.

```
public override System.Security.IPermission Intersect(
    System.Security.IPermission);
```

ToXml Method Returns an XML security encoding of the current OleDbPermission object with its current state information.

```
public override System.Security.SecurityElement ToXml();
```

Union Method Returns a security permission object that joins the current OleDbPermission object with the specified permission object. A request that passes either permission object will pass the union. An IPermission object describes the functions of the object.

```
public override System.Security.IPermission Union(
    System.Security.IPermission);
```

Mutual Properties, Methods, and Events Included in the OleDbPermission Class

The following lists the mutual properties, methods, and events that are included in the OleDbPermission class.

Inherited from DBDataPermission	Inherited from CodeAccessPermission	Inherited from Object
AllowBlankPassword property	Assert method	Equals method
Add method	Demand method	Finalize method
Clear method	Deny method	GetHashCode method
CreateInstance method	PermitOnly method	GetType method

Inherited from DBDataPermission	Inherited from CodeAccessPermission	Inherited from Object
IsSubsetOf method	ToString method	MemberwiseClone method
IsUnrestricted method		

OleDbPermissionAttribute Class

The OleDbPermissionAttribute class relates a security action to a security permission attribute.

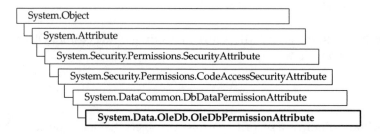

Constructor   Initializes a new instance of the OleDbPermissionAttribute class.

```
public OleDbPermissionAttribute(
    System.Security.Permissions.SecurityAction);
// C# example
System.Data.OleDb.OleDbPermissionAttribute oledbPA =
    new System.Data.OleDb.OleDbPermissionAttribute(
    System.Security.Permissions.SecurityAction.LinkDemand);
```

System.Security.Permissions.SecurityAction enumeration:

Assert	Allows security to bypass code permission check
Demand	Performs security check for enforcing restrictions on calling code
Deny	Prevents access to the resource specified
InheritanceDemand	Checks for granted permissions for inherited class
LinkDemand	Checks for granted permission for immediate caller
PermitOnly	Allows access only to the resource specified
RequestMinimum	Requests the minimum permissions for code

System.Security.Permissions.SecurityAction enumeration:

RequestOptional	Requests the optional permissions
RequestRefuse	Request permissions not be granted to calling code

OleDbPermissionAttribute Class Properties

Provider Property   Returns or sets a list of providers allowed. The list is comma-delimited.

```
public string Provider { get; set; }
```

OleDbPermission Class Methods

CreatePermission Method   Returns an OleDbPermission object that contains the current attribute properties.

```
public override System.Security.IPermission CreatePermission();
```

Mutual Properties, Methods, and Events Included in the OleDbPermissionAttribute Class

The following lists the mutual properties, methods, and events that are included in the OleDbPermissionAttribute class.

Inherited from Attribute	Inherited from Object
TypeId property	Equals method
GetHashCode method	Finalize method
IsDefaultAttribute method	GetType method
Match method	MemberwiseClone method
	ToString method

Inherited from SecurityAttribute	Inherited from DBDataPermission
Action property	AllowBlankPassword property
Unrestricted property	ConnectionString property
	KeyRestrictionBehavior property
	KeyRestrictions property

APPENDIXES

OleDbRowUpdatedEventArgs Class

The OleDbRowUpdatedEventArgs class supplies the information for the RowUpdated event that is raised when an Update to a row has been completed.

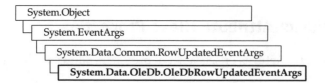

Constructor Initializes a new instance of the OleDbRowUpdatedEventArgs class using the specified DataRow, the IDbCommand, the StatementType, and the DataTableMapping. The IDbCommand represents the SQL statement that was executed and the StatementType specifies whether the command was a SELECT, INSERT, UPDATE, or DELETE statement. The DataTableMapping object describes the mapped relationship of the source table and the DataTable.

```
public OleDbRowUpdatedEventArgs(System.Data.DataRow,
    System.Data.IDbCommand, System.Data.StatementType,
    System.Data.Common.DataTableMapping);
// C# example
System.Data.DataRow dr = new System.Data.DataTable().NewRow();
System.Data.OleDb.OleDbCommand cmd = new
    System.Data.OleDb.OleDbCommand("SELECT * FROM Customers");
System.Data.Common.DataTableMapping dtm = new
    System.Data.Common.DataTableMapping();
System.Data.Common.RowUpdatedEventArgs ruea = new
    System.Data.OleDb.OleDbRowUpdatedEventArgs(dr, cmd,
    System.Data.StatementType.Select, dtm);
```

OleDbRowUpdatedEventArgs Class Properties

Command Property Returns the OleDbCommand that was executed when Update was called.

```
public new OleDbCommand Command { get; }
```

Mutual Properties, Methods, and Events Included in the OleDbRowUpdatedEventArgs Class

The following lists the mutual properties, methods, and events that are included in the OleDbRowUpdatedEventArgs class.

Inherited from RowUpdatedEventArgs	Inherited from Object
Errors property	Equals method
RecordsAffected property	Finalize method
Row property	GetHashCode method
StatementType property	GetType method
Status property	MemberwiseClone method
TableMapping property	ToString method

OleDbRowUpdatingEventArgs Class

The OleDbRowUpdatingEventArgs class supplies the information for the RowUpdating event that is raised when an Update to a row is about to take place.

```
System.Object
    System.EventArgs
        System.Data.Common.RowUpdatingEventArgs
            System.Data.OleDb.OleDbRowUpdatingEventArgs
```

Constructor   Initializes a new instance of the OleDbRowUpdatingEventArgs class using the specified DataRow, the IDbCommand, the StatementType, and the DataTableMapping. The IDbCommand represents the SQL statement that will be executed, and the StatementType specifies whether the command is a SELECT, INSERT, UPDATE, or DELETE statement. The DataTableMapping object describes the mapped relationship of the source table and the DataTable.

```
public OleDbRowUpdatingEventArgs(System.Data.DataRow,
    System.Data.IDbCommand, System.Data.StatementType,
    System.Data.Common.DataTableMapping);
// C# example
System.Data.DataRow dr = new System.Data.DataTable().NewRow();
System.Data.OleDb.OleDbCommand cmd = new
    System.Data.OleDb.OleDbCommand("SELECT * FROM Customers");
System.Data.Common.DataTableMapping dtm = new
    System.Data.Common.DataTableMapping();
System.Data.Common.RowUpdatingEventArgs ruea = new
    System.Data.OleDb.OleDbRowUpdatedEventArgs(dr, cmd,
    System.Data.StatementType.Select, dtm);
```

APPENDIXES

OleDbRowUpdatingEventArgs Class Properties

Command Property   Returns or sets the OleDbCommand that will be executed when Update is called.

```
public new OleDbCommand Command { get; set; }
```

Mutual Properties, Methods, and Events Included in the OleDbRowUpdatingEventArgs Class

The following lists the mutual properties, methods, and events that are included in the OleDbRowUpdatingEventArgs class.

Inherited from RowUpdatedEventArgs	Inherited from Object
Errors property	Equals method
Row property	Finalize method
StatementType property	GetHashCode method
Status property	GetType method
TableMapping property	MemberwiseClone method
	ToString method

OleDbSchemaGuid Class

The OleDbSchemaGuid class returns the type of schema table from the method GetOleDbSchemaTable. The fields in the OleDbSchemaGuid class are mapped to the OLE DB schema rowset.

```
System.Object
    System.Data.OleDb.OleDbSchemaGuid
```

Constructor   Initializes a new instance of the OleDbSchemaGuid class and initializes all the fields to their default values.

```
public OleDbSchemaGuid();
// C# example
System.Data.OleDb.OleDbSchemaGuid oledbS =
    new System.Data.OleDb.OleDbSchemaGuid();
```

OleDbSchemaGuid Class Fields

Assertions Field   Returns the assertions owned by a user that are defined in a catalog of a data source.

```
public static readonly Guid Assertions;
```

Catalogs Field   Returns the attributes of the catalogs available from the data source.

```
public static readonly Guid Catalogs;
```

Character_Sets Field   Returns the character sets that the user has access to.

```
public static readonly Guid Character_Sets;
```

Check_Constraints Field   Returns the check constraints that the user owns.

```
public static readonly Guid Check_Constraints;
```

Check_Constraints_By_Table Field   Returns the check constraints that the user owns.

```
public static readonly Guid Check_Constraints_By_Table;
```

Collations Field   Returns the character collations that the user has access to.

```
public static readonly Guid Collations;
```

Columns Field   Returns the columns of tables and views that the user has access to.

```
public static readonly Guid Columns;
```

Column_Domain_Usage Field   Returns the columns owned by a user that rely on a domain defined in the catalog.

```
public static readonly Guid Column_Domain_Usage;
```

Column_Privileges Field   Returns the privileges of table columns that are accessible to a user or granted by a user.

```
public static readonly Guid Column_Privileges;
```

Constraint_Column_Usage Field   Returns the columns used by constraints and assertions owned by a user. The constraints returned are referential constraints, unique constraints, or check constraints.

```
public static readonly Guid Constraint_Column_Usage;
```

Constraint_Table_Usage Field   Returns the tables used by constraints and assertions owned by a user. The constraints returned are referential constraints, unique constraints, or check constraints.

```
public static readonly Guid Constraint_Table_Usage;
```

DbInfoLiterals Field   Returns a list of literals used in text commands that are provider specific.

```
public static readonly Guid DbInfoLiterals;
```

Foreign_Keys Field   Returns the foreign key columns that a user has defined.

```
public static readonly Guid Foreign_Keys;
```

Indexes Field   Returns the indexes that the user owns.

```
public static readonly Guid Indexes;
```

Key_Column_Usage Field   Returns the columns that are constrained by keys by the user.

```
public static readonly Guid Key_Column_Usage;
```

Primary_Keys Field   Returns the primary key columns that a user has defined.

```
public static readonly Guid Primary_Keys;
```

Procedures Field   Returns the procedures that the user owns.

```
public static readonly Guid Procedures;
```

Procedure_Columns Field   Returns information about the columns of the rowsets that are returned by procedures.

```
public static readonly Guid Procedure_Columns;
```

Procedure_Parameters Field   Returns information about the return codes and parameters of procedures.

```
public static readonly Guid Procedure_Parameters;
```

Provider_Types Field   Returns the data types of the OLE DB provider.

```
public static readonly Guid Provider_Types;
```

Referential_Constraints Field   Returns the referential constraints that the user owns.

```
public static readonly Guid Referential_Constraints;
```

Schemata Field   Returns the schema objects that the user owns.

```
public static readonly Guid Schemata;
```

Sql_Languages Field   Returns the SQL-specific processing information that is defined in the catalog.

```
public static readonly Guid Sql_Languages;
```

Statistics Field   Returns the statistics that the user owns.

```
public static readonly Guid Statistics;
```

Tables Field   Returns the tables and views that are available to a user.

```
public static readonly Guid Tables;
```

Tables_Info Field   Returns the tables and views that are available to a user.

```
public static readonly Guid Tables_Info;
```

Table_Constraints Field   Returns the table constraints that the user owns.

```
public static readonly Guid Table_Constraints;
```

Table_Privileges Field   Returns the privileges of tables that are accessible to a user or granted by a user.

```
public static readonly Guid Table_Privileges;
```

Table_Statistics Field   Contains the available statistics for the tables in the OLE DB provider.

```
public static readonly Guid Table_Statistics;
```

Translations Field   Returns the character translations that the user has access to.

```
public static readonly Guid Translations;
```

Trustee Field   Contains the trustees that are defined in the data source.

```
public static readonly Guid Trustee;
```

Usage_Privileges Field   Returns the USAGE privileges on objects in the catalog that are accessible to a user or granted by a user.

```
public static readonly Guid Usage_Privileges;
```

Views Field   Returns the views that are available to a user.

```
public static readonly Guid Views;
```

View_Column_Usage Field   Returns the columns owned by a user that rely on viewed tables.

```
public static readonly Guid View_Column_Usage;
```

View_Table_Usage Field   Returns the tables owned by a user that rely on viewed tables.

```
public static readonly Guid View_Table_Usage;
```

Mutual Properties, Methods, and Events Included in the OleDbSchemaGuid Class

The following lists the mutual properties, methods, and events that are included in the OleDbSchemaGuid class.

Inherited from Object

Equals method

Finalize method

GetHashCode method

GetType method

MemberwiseClone method

ToString method

OleDbTransaction Class

The OleDbTransaction class represents a SQL transaction to implement at a data source. You do not create an OleDbTransaction object by calling a constructor, but rather by calling the BeginTransaction method of an OleDbConnection object.

```
System.Object
    System.MarshalByRefObject
        System.Data.OleDb.OleDBTransaction
```

OleDbTransaction Class Properties

Connection Property   Returns the OleDbConnection object associated with this OleDbTransaction.

```
public OleDbConnection Connection { get; }
```

IsolationLevel Property   Returns the isolation level for this OleDbTransaction object. The default value is ReadCommited.

```
public System.Data.IsolationLevel IsolationLevel { get; }
```

System.Data.IsolationLevel enumeration:

Chaos	Cannot overwrite more highly isolated transactions that are pending.
ReadCommited	To avoid dirty reads, the shared locks are held during reading of data. May result in nonrepeatable read or phantom rows.Data is changed before the transaction ends.
ReadUncommited	No exclusive locks are allowed and no shared locks are done. May result in a dirty read.
RepeatableRead	Locks are placed on the queried data. May result in phantom rows.
Serializable	A range lock is placed on the rows in the DataSet.
Unspecified	The isolation level cannot be determined.

OleDbTransaction Class Methods

Begin Method Overloaded. Begins a nested transaction to the database and returns an object that represents that transaction. The second method specifies the IsolationLevel for the transaction.

```
public OleDbTransaction Begin();
public OleDbTransaction Begin(System.Data.IsolationLevel);
```

System.Data.IsolationLevel enumeration:

Chaos	Cannot overwrite more highly isolated transactions that are pending.
ReadCommited	To avoid dirty reads, the shared locks are held during reading of data. May result in nonrepeatable read or phantom rows. Data is changed before the transaction ends.
ReadUncommited	No exclusive locks are allowed and no shared locks are done. May result in a dirty read.
RepeatableRead	Locks are placed on the queried data. May result in phantom rows.
Serializable	A range lock is placed on the rows in the DataSet.
Unspecified	The isolation level cannot be determined.

Commit Method   Commits the transaction to the database. Throws an exception if there is an error committing the transaction or the connection is broken.

```
public void Commit();
```

Finalize Method   Frees the OleDbTransaction resources before the object is deleted. Finalizers in C# and C++ use the destructor syntax.

```
~OleDbTransaction();
```

IDisposable.Dispose Method   The IDisposable.Dispose method supports the .NET infrastructure and is not used directly from your code.

Rollback Method   Rolls back a transaction that is in a pending state. Throws an exception if the transaction has already been committed or the connection is broken.

```
public void Rollback();
```

Mutual Properties, Methods, and Events Included in the OleDbTransaction Class

The following lists the mutual properties, methods, and events that are included in the OleDbTransaction class.

Inherited from Object

Equals method

GetHashCode method

GetType method

MemberwiseClone method

ToString method

Inherited from MarshalByRefObject

CreateObjRef method

GetLifetimeService method

InitializeLifetimeService method

OleDbInfoMessageEventHandler Delegate

The OleDbInfoMessageEventHandler delegate is the method that handles the InfoMessage event of the OleDbConnection object. The first parameter, object, indicates the source of the event to handle. The second parameter is an OleDbInfoMessageEventArgs object that contains the event information.

```
public delegate void OleDbInfoMessageEventHandler(object,
OleDbInfoMessageEventArgs);
```

APPENDIXES

OleDbRowUpdatedEventHandler Delegate

The OleDbRowUpdatedEventHandler delegate is the method that handles
the RowUpdatedEvent of the OleDbDataAdapter object. The first parameter,
object, indicates the source of the event to handle. The second parameter is an
OleDbRowUpdatedEventArgs object that contains the event information.

```
public delegate void OleDbRowUpdatedEventHandler(object,
    OleDbRowUpdatedEventArgs);
```

OleDbRowUpdatingEventHandler Delegate

The OleDbRowUpdatingEventHandler delegate is the method that handles
the RowUpdatingEvent of the OleDbDataAdapter object. The first parameter,
object, indicates the source of the event to handle. The second parameter is an
OleDbRowUpdatingEventArgs object that contains the event information.

```
public delegate void OleDbRowUpdatingEventHandler(object,
    OleDbRowUpdatingEventArgs);
```

OleDbLiteral Enumeration

The OleDbLiteral enumeration contains information about the literals that are used
in the text commands and database objects.

System.Data.OleDbLiteral enumeration:

Binary_Literal	Binary literal in a text command. Maps to DBLITERAL_BINARY_LITERAL.
Catalog_Name	Catalog name in a text command. Maps to DBLITERAL_CATALOG_NAME.
Catalog_Separator	Character that separates the catalog name from the rest of the text command. Maps to DBLITERAL_CATALOG_SEPARATOR.
Char_Literal	Character literal in a text command. Maps to DBLITERAL_CHAR_LITERAL.
Column_Alias	Column alias in a text command. Maps to DBLITERAL_COLUMN_ALIAS.
Column_Name	Column name in a text command. Maps to DBLITERAL_COLUMN_NAME.

System.Data.OleDbLiteral enumeration:

Correlation_Name	Table alias in a text command. Maps to DBLITERAL_CORRELATION_NAME.
Cube_Name	Name of the cube in a schema. If the provider does not support schemas, this is the catalog name.
Cursor_Name	Cursor name in a text command. Maps to DBLITERAL_CURSOR_NAME.
Dimension_Name	Name of the dimension. One row exists for each cube/dimension combination, if dimension is a part of multiple cubes.
Escape_Percent_Prefix	Character used to escape the character returned for the DBLITERAL_LIKE_PERCENT literal. Maps to DBLITERAL_ESCAPE_PERCENT_PREFIX.
Escape_Percent_Suffix	Escape character used to suffix the character returned for the DBLITERAL_LIKE_PERCENT literal. Maps to DBLITERAL_ESCAPE_PERCENT_SUFFIX.
Escape_Underscore_Prefix	Character used to escape the character returned for the DBLITERAL_LIKE_UNDERSCORE literal. Maps to DBLITERAL_ESCAPE_UNDERSCORE_PREFIX.
Escape_Underscore_Suffix	Character used to escape the character returned for the DBLITERAL_LIKE_UNDERSCORE literal. Maps to DBLITERAL_ESCAPE_UNDERSCORE_SUFFIX.
Hierarchy_Name	Name of the hierarchy. Current column contains a null value, if dimension does not contain a hierarchy or contains only one hierarchy.
Index_Name	Index name used in a text command. Maps to DBLITERAL_INDEX_NAME.
Invalid	Invalid value. Maps to DBLITERAL_INVALID.
Level_Name	Name of the cube for the current level.
Like_Percent	Character used in a LIKE clause. Maps to DBLITERAL_LIKE_PERCENT.
Like_Underscore	Character used in a LIKE clause to match just one character. Maps to DBLITERAL_LIKE_UNDERSCORE.
Member_Name	Name of the member.

System.Data.OleDbLiteral enumeration:

Procedure_Name	Procedure name in a text command. Maps to DBLITERAL_PROCEDURE_NAME.
Property_Name	Name of the property.
Quote_Prefix	Character used in a text command as the opening quote. Maps to DBLITERAL_QUOTE_PREFIX.
Quote_Suffix	Character used in a text command as the closing quote. Maps to DBLITERAL_QUOTE_SUFFIX.
Schema_Name	Schema name in a text command. Maps to DBLITERAL_SCHEMA_NAME.
Schema_Separator	Character that separates the schema name from the rest of the text command. Maps to DBLITERAL_SCHEMA_SEPARATOR.
Table_Name	Table name used in a text command. Maps to DBLITERAL_TABLE_NAME.
Text_Command	Text command. Maps to DBLITERAL_TEXT_COMMAND.
User_Name	User name in a text command. Maps to DBLITERAL_USER_NAME.
View_Name	View name in a text command. Maps to DBLITERAL_VIEW_NAME.

OleDbType Enumeration

The OleDbType enumeration contains the data types that are used in the fields, properties, or parameters of the namespace objects. The following table shows the OleDbTypes mapped to the OLE DB data types and the .NET Framework data types.

System.Data.OleDbType enumeration:

System.Data.OleDbType	OLE DB Data Type	.NET Framework Type
BigInt	DBTYPE_I8	Int64
Binary	DBTYPE_BYTES	An array of type Byte
Boolean	DBTYPE_BOOL	Boolean
BSTR	DBTYPE_BSTR	String
Char	DBTYPE_STR	String

System.Data.OleDbType enumeration:

System.Data.OleDbType	OLE DB Data Type	.NET Framework Type
Currency	DBTYPE_CY	Decimal
Date	DBTYPE_DATE	DateTime
DBDate	DBTYPE_DBDATE	DateTime
DBTime	DBTYPE_DBTIME	TimeSpan
DBTimeStamp	DBTYPE_DBTIMESTAMP	DateTime
Decimal	DBTYPE_DECIMAL	Decimal
Double	DBTYPE_R8	Double
Empty	DBTYPE_EMPTY	Empty
Error	DBTYPE_ERROR	Exception
Filetime	DBTYPE_FILETIME	DateTime
Guid	DBTYPE_GUID	Guid
IDispatch	DBTYPE_IDISPATCH	Object
Integer	DBTYPE_I4	Int32
IUnknown	DBTYPE_UNKNOWN	Object
LongVarBinary	n/a	An array of type Byte
LongVarChar	n/a	String
LongVarWChar	n/a	String
Numeric	DBTYPE_NUMERIC	Decimal
PropVariant	DBTYPE_PROP_VARIANT	Object
Single	DBTYPE_R4	Single
SmallInt	DBTYPE_I2	Int16
TinyInt	DBTYPE_I1	SByte
UnsignedBigInt	DBTYPE_UI8	UInt64
UnsignedInt	DBTYPE_UI4	UInt32
UnsignedSmallInt	DBTYPE_UI2	UInt16
UnsignedTinyInt	DBTYPE_UI1	Byte
VarBinary	n/a	An array of type Byte

System.Data.OleDbType enumeration:

System.Data.OleDbType	OLE DB Data Type	.NET Framework Type
VarChar	n/a	String
Variant	May contain numeric, string, binary, date, empty, or null values	Object
VarNumeric	n/a	Decimal
VarWChar	n/a	String
WChar	DBTYPE_WSTR	String

Appendix E

System.Data.OracleClient
Namespace Reference

System.Data.OracleClient Namespace

The System.Data.OracleClient namespace contains classes that comprise the Oracle .NET Data Provider, which are a group of classes that are used to access an Oracle database using the Oracle Call Interface (OCI) that is provided by Oracle Client software.

OracleBFile Class   The OracleBFile class represents an object that is designed to work with the Oracle BFILE data type.

OracleCommand Class   The OracleCommand class represents a stored procedure or SQL statement to implement at a data source.

OracleCommandBuilder Class   The OracleCommandBuilder class allows for automatic generation of single table commands.

OracleConnection Class   The OracleConnection class represents a connection to an Oracle data source name.

OracleDataAdapter Class   The OracleDataAdapter class represents a database connection and a set of commands that are used to fill a DataSet and update a data source.

OracleDataReader Class   The OracleDataReader class allows for reading forward-only streams of data rows from a data source.

OracleException Class   The OracleException class represents the exception that is thrown when an error is returned by the Oracle data source.

OracleInfoMessageEventArgs Class   The OracleInfoMessageEventArgs class supplies information for the InfoMessage event.

OracleLob Class   The OracleLob class represents Oracle's Large Object Binary (LOB) data type.

OracleParameter Class   The OracleParameter class represents a parameter for the OracleCommand object. It may also be used for the OracleCommand object's mapping to the DataSet column.

OracleParameterCollection Class   The OracleParameterCollection class is a collection of OracleParameter classes and their related mapping information for DataSet columns.

OraclePermission Class   The OraclePermission class provides user security level setting for Oracle database access with the .NET Framework for Oracle Data Provider.

OraclePermissionAttribute Class   The OraclePermissionAttribute class relates a security action to a security permission attribute.

OracleRowUpdatedEventArgs Class   The OracleRowUpdatedEventArgs class supplies the information for the RowUpdated event.

OracleRowUpdatingEventArgs Class   The OracleRowUpdatingEventArgs class supplies the information for the RowUpdating event.

OracleTransaction Class   The OracleTransaction class represents a transaction to implement at a data source.

OracleInfoMessageEventHandler Delegate   The OracleInfoMessageEventHandler delegate is the method that handles the InfoMessage event of the OracleConnection object.

OracleRowUpdatedEventHandler Delegate   The OracleRowUpdatedEventHandler delegate is the method that handles the RowUpdated event of the OracleDataAdapter object.

OracleRowUpdatingEventHandler Delegate   The OracleRowUpdatingEventHandler delegate is the method that handles the RowUpdating event of the OracleDataAdapter object.

OracleBinary Structure   The OracleBinary structure contains a variable-length binary stream.

OracleBoolean Structure   The OracleBoolean structure contains the result of a comparison operation performed on Oracle data types. It does not map to an Oracle Boolean data type.

OracleDateTime Structure   The OracleDateTime structure contains date and time data ranging in value from January 1, 4712 B.C. to December 31, 4712 A.D.

OracleMonthSpan Structure   The OracleMonthSpan structure contains a time interval in months. Maps to the INTERVAL_YEAR_TO_MONTH data type (Oracle 9i or later).

OracleNumber Structure   The OracleNumber structure contains fixed precision and scale numeric data ranging in value from $-10^{38} - 1$ to $10^{38} - 1$.

OracleString Structure   The OracleString structure contains a variable-length character stream.

OracleTimeSpan Structure   The OracleTimeSpan structure contains a time interval. It maps to the INTERVAL_DAY_TO_SECOND data type (Oracle 9i or later).

OracleLobOpenMode Enumeration   The OracleLobOpenMode enumeration contains the options for opening an OracleLob object.

OracleType Enumeration   The OracleType enumeration contains the data types that are used in the OracleParameter objects.

OracleBFile Class

The OracleBFile class represents an Oracle BFILE data type. A BFILE data type is a read-only binary file that is physically stored in the operating system rather than the server. BFILE data types have a maximum size of; 4GB and differ from LOB data type objects in that they support server-side chunking, they contain unstructured data; and when you perform a copy operation on a BFILE data type, only the reference locator to the file is copied, not the data. You do not create an OracleBFile by calling a constructor, but rather it is accessed through the OracleDataReader object's GetOracleBFile method.

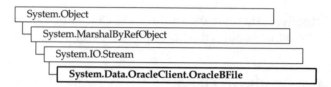

OracleBFile Class Fields

The following lists the constant fields used in the OracleBFile class.

Null field	`public static readonly OracleBFile Null;`

OracleBFile Class Properties

CanRead Property   Returns a Boolean indicating whether the BFILE can be read. False indicates that the BFILE is closed. True indicates that the BFILE may be read or it is null.

```
public override bool CanRead { get; }
```

CanSeek Property   Returns a Boolean indicating whether the forward and backward seek operations may be performed on the BFILE. False indicates that the BFILE is closed. True indicates that the BFILE may be read or it is null.

```
public override bool CanSeek { get; }
```

CanWrite Property   Returns a Boolean indicating whether the BFILE supports write operations. False is always returned because BFILE objects are read-only.

```
public override bool CanWrite { get; }
```

Connection Property   Returns the OracleConnection object associated with this OracleBFile.

```
public OracleConnection Connection { get; }
```

DirectoryName Property   Returns the DIRECTORY object associated with this OracleBFile.

```
public string DirectoryName { get; }
```

FileExists Property   Returns a Boolean indicating whether a physical file containing BFILE data exists in the operating system. True if the file exists; otherwise, False.

```
public bool FileExists { get; }
```

FileName Property   Returns the name of the BFILE in a string.

```
public string FileName { get; }
```

IsNull Property   Returns a Boolean indicating whether the OracleBFile object is a null stream. True if the OracleBFile is null; otherwise, False.

```
public virtual bool IsNull { get; }
```

Length Property   Returns a long value indicating the length of the physical file in bytes of the associated OracleBFile object.

```
public override long Length { get; }
```

Position Property   Returns or sets a long value indicating the current read position in the OracleBFile object.

```
public override long Position { get; set; }
```

Value Property   Returns a byte array that contains the OracleBFile binary data.

```
public object Value { get; }
```

OracleBFile Class Methods

Clone Method   Returns an object that is a copy of the OracleBFile object and is associated with the same physical file.

```
public virtual object Clone();
```

CopyTo Method   Overloaded. The first CopyTo method copies the entire OracleBFile to the specified OracleLob object. The second method copies the OracleBFile to the OracleLob object at the specified offset. The third method copies the OracleBFile to the OracleLob object starting in the indicated source location and outputting to the indicated destination location for the specified length of bytes.

```
public long CopyTo(OracleLob);
public long CopyTo(OracleLob, long offSet);
public long CopyTo(long srcOffset, OracleLob, long destOffset,
    long count);
```

Dispose Method   Disposes the resources used by the OracleBFile.

```
public virtual void Dispose();
```

Flush Method   Currently not supported.

```
public override void Flush();
```

Read Method   Reads the specified number of bytes into the byte array indicated, starting at the specified offset.

```
public override int Read(byte[], int offset, int count);
```

Seek Method   Sets the position in the OracleBFile to the specified offset position relative to the specified original position and returns the new current position in the OracleBFile.

```
public override long Seek(long offset, System.IO.SeekOrigin);
```

System.IO.SeekOrigin enumeration:

Begin	Indicates the beginning of the stream
Current	Indicates the current position in the stream
End	Indicates the end of the stream

SetFileName Method   Associates an OracleBFile object to a physical file in the operating system.

```
public void SetFileName(string directory, string file);
```

SetLength Method   Currently not supported.

```
public override void SetLength(long);
```

Write Method   Currently not supported.

```
public override void Write(byte[], int offset, int count);
```

Mutual Properties, Methods, and Events Included in the OracleBFile Class

The following lists the mutual properties, methods, and events that are included in the OracleBFile class.

Inherited from Stream	Inherited from Object	Inherited from MarshalByRefObject
BeginRead method	Equals method	CreateObjRef method
BeginWrite method	Finalize method	GetLifetimeService method
Close method	GetHashCode method	InitializeLifetimeService method
CreateWaitHandle method	GetType method	
EndRead method	MemberwiseClone method	
EndWrite method	ToString method	
ReadByte method		
WriteByte method		

OracleCommand Class

The OracleCommand class represents a stored procedure or SQL statement to implement at a data source. A new instance of the OracleCommand will set the read/write properties to their initial values.

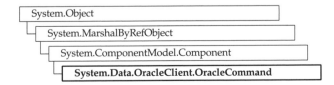

APPENDIXES

Constructor   Overloaded. Initializes a new instance of the OracleCommand class. The first constructor initializes all the fields to their default values. The second constructor specifies the text of a query to execute. The third constructor specifies the text of the query to execute through the specified OracleConnection. The fourth constructor specifies the text of the query to execute through the specified OracleConnection as reflected through the specified OracleTransaction object.

```
public OracleCommand();
public OracleCommand(string cmdText);
public OracleCommand(string cmdText, OracleConnection);
public OracleCommand(string cmdText, OracleConnection,
    OracleTransaction);
// C# example
System.Data.OracleClient.OracleCommand OracleCmd = new
    System.Data.OracleClient.OracleCommand();
System.Data.OracleClient.OracleCommand OracleCmd2 = new
    System.Data.OracleClient.OracleCommand(
    "SELECT * FROM Customers");
System.Data.OracleClient.OracleConnection OracleConn = new
    System.Data.OracleClient.OracleConnection();
System.Data.OracleClient.OracleCommand OracleCmd3 = new
    System.Data.OracleClient.OracleCommand(
    "SELECT * FROM Customers", OracleConn);
System.Data.OracleClient.OracleTransaction OracleTrans =
    OracleConn.BeginTransaction();
System.Data.OracleClient.OracleCommand OracleCmd4 = new
    System.Data.OracleClient.OracleCommand(
    "SELECT * FROM Customers", OracleConn, OracleTrans);
```

OracleCommand Class Properties

CommandText Property   Returns or sets the SQL statement query text or stored procedure to execute.

```
public virtual string CommandText { get; set; }
```

CommandType Property   Designates what type of command this object is.

```
public virtual System.Data.CommandType CommandType { get; set; }
```

System.Data.CommandType enumeration:

Text	Default. A SQL statement to execute
StoredProcedure	The name of a stored procedure to execute
TableDirect	The name of the table to be accessed

Connection Property   Returns or sets the OracleConnection object for this OracleCommand object.

```
public OracleConnection Connection { get; set; }
```

DesignTimeVisible Property   Returns or sets a Boolean value specifying whether the OracleCommand object should be visible. The default value is False.

```
public bool DesignTimeVisible { get; set; }
```

Parameters Property   Returns the OracleParameterCollection, which designates the parameters for a stored procedure or SQL statement for this OracleCommand object.

```
public OracleParametersCollection Parameters { get; }
```

Transaction Property   Returns or sets the OracleTransaction that the OracleCommand implements.

```
public OracleTransaction Transaction { get; set; }
```

UpdatedRowSource Property   Returns or sets how the results of a command are applied to a DataSet when the Update method is used. If the command is automatically generated, the default result is None; otherwise; the default result is Both.

```
public virtual System.Data.UpdateRowSource UpdatedRowSource
    { get; set; }
```

System.Data.UpdateRowSource enumeration:

Both	The first returned row and the output parameters are mapped to the DataSet at the changed row.
FirstReturnedRecord	The first returned row is mapped to the DataSet at the changed row.
None	Returned results are ignored.
OutputParameters	The output parameters are mapped to the DataSet at the changed row.

OracleCommand Class Methods

Cancel Method   A cancellation of the execution of the OracleCommand is attempted. No exception is generated, even if the attempt to cancel the OracleCommand failed.

```
public virtual void Cancel();
```

Clone Method   Returns an OracleCommand object that is a copy of the current object.

```
public virtual object Clone();
```

CreateParameter Method   Creates a new OracleParameter object.

```
public OracleParameter CreateParameter();
```

ExecuteNonQuery Method   Used for catalog operations or to execute an UPDATE, INSERT, or DELETE SQL statement to a database. Returns the number of affected rows.

```
public virtual int ExecuteNonQuery();
```

ExecuteOracleNonQuery Method   Used for catalog operations or to execute an UPDATE, INSERT, or DELETE SQL statement to a database. Returns the number of rows affected and the row ID as an output parameter.

```
public int ExecuteOracleNonQuery(out OracleString rowid);
```

ExecuteOracleScalar Method   Returns the first column of the first row in the resultset as an Oracle data type after executing the query.

```
public object ExecuteOracleScalar();
```

ExecuteReader Method   Overloaded. Returns an OracleDataReader object after executing a SQL statement using the Connection object. The second method returns the OracleDataReader object based on the specified CommandBehavior.

```
public OracleDataReader ExecuteReader();
public OracleDataReader ExecuteReader(System.Data.CommandBehavior);
```

System.Data.CommandBehavior enumeration:

CloseConnection	The Connection object is closed when the DataReader object is closed.
Default	Sets no CommandBehavior flags. Same as using ExecuteReader.
KeyInfo	Returns column and primary key information.
SchemaOnly	Returns column information only. Database state not affected.

System.Data.CommandBehavior enumeration:

SequentialAccess	Enables the DataReader to return data as a stream. You need to use GetBytes or GetChars to start the reading of data at a specified location.
SingleResult	Returns a single resultset.
SingleRow	Returns a single row of data.

ExecuteOracleScalar Method   Returns the first column of the first row in the resultset as a .NET Framework data type after executing the query.

```
public virtual object ExecuteScalar();
```

IDbCommand.CreateParameter Method   The IDbCommand.CreateParameter method supports the .NET infrastructure and is not used directly from your code.

IDbCommand.ExecuteReader Method   The IDbCommand.ExecuteReader method supports the .NET infrastructure and is not used directly from your code.

Prepare Method   Creates a compiled version of this command object if the CommandType property is set to Text or StoredProcedure. You need to specify the data type of each parameter in the command statement before using the Prepare method. If the parameter has variable-length data, you also need to specify the maximum Size of the data.

```
public virtual void Prepare();
```

Mutual Properties, Methods, and Events Included in the OracleCommand Class

The following lists the mutual properties, methods, and events that are included in the OracleCommand class.

Inherited from Component	Inherited from Object	Inherited from MarshalByRefObject
Container property	Equals method	CreateObjRef method
DesignMode property	Finalize method	GetLifetimeService method
Events property	GetHashCode method	InitializeLifetimeService method
Site property	GetType method	

Inherited from Component	Inherited from Object	Inherited from MarshalByRefObject
Dispose method	MemberwiseClone method	
GetService method	ToString method	
Disposed event		

OracleCommandBuilder Class

The OracleCommandBuilder class is used to automatically generate SQL statements for updates of single tables. An OracleDataAdapter object does not generate the required SQL statements automatically to synchronize the changes made to a DataSet with the data source; therefore, an OracleCommandBuilder is needed to automatically generate the SQL statements and synchronize the data.

```
System.Object
    System.MarshalByRefObject
        System.ComponentModel.Component
            System.Data.OracleClient.OracleCommandBuilder
```

Constructor   Overloaded. Initializes a new instance of the OracleCommandBuilder class. The second constructor specifies the associated OracleDataAdapter. The OracleCommandBuilder object will register itself as a listener to the OracleDataAdapter's RowUpdating events.

```
public OracleCommandBuilder();
public OracleCommandBuilder(OracleDataAdapter);
// C# example
System.Data.OracleClient.OracleCommandBuilder OracleCmdBldr = new
    System.Data.OracleClient.OracleCommandBuilder();
System.Data.OracleClient.OracleDataAdapter OracleDA = new
    System.Data.OracleClient.OracleDataAdapter();
System.Data.OracleClient.OracleCommandBuilder OracleCmdBldr2 = new
    System.Data.OracleClient.OracleCommandBuilder(OracleDA);
```

OracleCommandBuilder Class Properties

DataAdapter Property   Returns or sets the OracleDataAdapter object that SQL statements are automatically generated for.

```
public OracleDataAdapter DataAdapter { get; set; }
```

QuotePrefix Property   Returns or sets the beginning character(s) to use as delimiters when database object names contain characters such as spaces and commas. The default value is an empty string.

```
public string QuotePrefix { get; set; }
```

QuoteSuffix Property   Returns or sets the ending character(s) to use as delimiters when database object names contain characters such as spaces and commas. The default value is an empty string.

```
public string QuoteSuffix { get; set; }
```

OracleCommandBuilder Class Methods

DeriveParameters Method   Fills the Parameters collection of the specified OracleCommand object with parameter information for the stored procedure of the specified OracleCommand object.

```
public static void DeriveParameters(OracleCommand);
```

Dispose Method   Overloaded. Overridden. Disposes the resources used by the OracleCommandBuilder. If the Boolean is set to True in the first method, it will dispose of both managed and unmanaged resources; False releases only unmanaged resources. The second method releases all the resources used by the object.

```
protected override void Dispose(bool);
public void Dispose();
```

GetDeleteCommand Method   Returns the automatically generated OracleCommand object for performing deletions.

```
public OracleCommand GetDeleteCommand();
```

GetInsertCommand Method   Returns the automatically generated OracleCommand object for performing inserts.

```
public OracleCommand GetInsertCommand();
```

GetUpdateCommand Method   Returns the automatically generated OracleCommand object for performing updates.

```
public OracleCommand GetUpdateCommand();
```

RefreshSchema Method   Refreshes the database schema information. Should be used when the SELECT statement of the OracleCommandBuilder object changes.

```
public void RefreshSchema();
```

Mutual Properties, Methods, and Events Included in the OracleCommandBuilder Class

The following lists the mutual properties, methods, and events that are included in the OracleCommandBuilder class.

Inherited from Component	Inherited from Object	Inherited from MarshalByRefObject
Container property	Equals method	CreateObjRef method
DesignMode property	Finalize method	GetLifetimeService method
Events property	GetHashCode method	InitializeLifetimeService method
Site property	GetType method	
Dispose method	MemberwiseClone method	
GetService method	ToString method	
Disposed event		

OracleConnection Class

The OracleConnection class represents a connection to a data source.

```
System.Object
  System.MarshalByRefObject
    System.ComponentModel.Component
      System.Data.OracleClient.OracleConnection
```

Constructor   Overloaded. Initializes a new instance of the OracleConnection class. The first constructor initializes all the fields to their default values. The second constructor specifies the connection string to use to open the connection.

```
public OracleConnection();
public OracleConnection(string connString);
// C# example
```

```
System.Data.OracleClient.OracleConnection OracleConn = new
    System.Data.OracleClient.OracleConnection();
System.Data.OracleClient.OracleConnection OracleConn2 = new
    System.Data.OracleClient.OracleConnection("DRIVER={SQL Server};
    SERVER=MyServer;UID=myID;PWD=MyPwd;DATABASE=Northwind");
```

OracleConnection Class Properties

ConnectionString Property   Returns or sets the connection string that is used to open the connection to the data source.

```
public virtual string ConnectionString { get; set; }
```

DataSource Property   Returns the name of the Oracle server to connect to.

```
public string DataSource { get; }
```

ServerVersion Property   Returns the version of the server that the client is connected to. The version string that is returned is in Oracle version format.

```
public string ServerVersion { get; }
```

State Property   Returns a bitwise value indicating the ConnectionState value of the current connection. The default value is Closed.

```
public virtual System.Data.ConnectionState State { get; }
```

System.Data.ConnectionState enumeration:

Broken	A previously opened connection is now broken.
Closed	The current connection is not open.
Connecting	The Connection object is attempting to connect to the data source.
Executing	The Connection object is currently executing a command.
Fetching	The Connection object is currently fetching data.
Open	The current connection is open.

APPENDIXES

OracleConnection Class Methods

BeginTransaction Method   Overloaded. Begins a transaction to the database and returns an object that represents that transaction. The second method specifies the IsolationLevel for the transaction.

```
public OracleTransaction BeginTransaction();
public OracleTransaction BeginTransaction(
    System.Data.IsolationLevel);
```

System.Data.IsolationLevel enumeration:

Chaos	Cannot overwrite more highly isolated transactions that are pending.
ReadCommited	To avoid dirty reads, the shared locks are held during reading of data. May result in nonrepeatable read or phantom data being changed before the transaction ends.
ReadUncommited	No exclusive locks are allowed and no shared locks are done. May result in a dirty read.
RepeatableRead	Locks are placed on the queried data. May result in phantom rows.
Serializable	A range lock is placed on the rows in the DataSet.
Unspecified	The isolation level cannot be determined.

Close Method   Closes the connection to the data source and rolls back any pending transactions. No exception is generated if an application calls the Close method more than once.

```
public virtual void Close();
```

CreateCommand Method   Creates and returns an OracleCommand object.

```
public OracleCommand CreateCommand();
```

Dispose Method   Overloaded. Overridden. Disposes the resources used by the OracleConnection object. If the Boolean is set to True in the first method, it will dispose of both managed and unmanaged resources; False releases only unmanaged resources. The second method releases all the resources used by the object.

```
protected override void Dispose(bool);
public void Dispose();
```

EnlistDistributedTransaction Method   Registers the specified transaction as a distributed transaction.

```
public void EnlistDistributedTransaction(ITransaction);
```

ICloneable.Clone Method   The ICloneable.Clone method supports the .NET infrastructure and is not used directly from your code.

IDbConnection.BeginTransaction Method   The IDbConnection.BeginTransaction method supports the .NET infrastructure and is not used directly from your code.

IDbConnection.ChangeDatabase Method   The IDbConnection.ChangeDatabase method supports the .NET infrastructure and is not used directly from your code.

IDbConnection.CreateCommand Method   The IDbConnection.CreateCommand method supports the .NET infrastructure and is not used directly from your code.

Open Method   Opens a connection to a database from the connection pool. If a connection from the connection pool is not available, it will create a new connection to the data source.

```
public virtual void Open();
```

OracleConnection Class Events

InfoMessage Event   Fires when the provider sends a warning or informational message to the event handler.

```
public event OracleInfoMessageEventHandler InfoMessage;
```

StateChange Event   Fires when the state of the connection changes.

```
public event StateChangeEventHandler StateChange;
```

Mutual Properties, Methods, and Events Included in the OracleConnection Class

The following lists the mutual properties, methods, and events that are included in the OracleConnection class.

Inherited from Component	Inherited from Object	Inherited from MarshalByRefObject
Container property	Equals method	CreateObjRef method

Inherited from Component	Inherited from Object	Inherited from MarshalByRefObject
DesignMode property	GetHashCode method	GetLifetimeService method
Events property	GetType method	InitializeLifetimeService method
Site property	MemberwiseClone method	
Dispose method	ToString method	
Finalize method		
GetService method		
Disposed event		

OracleDataAdapter Class

The OracleDataAdapter class represents a database connection and a set of commands that are used to fill a DataSet and update a data source. The OracleDataAdapter class uses the Fill method to fill the DataSet with information from the data source, and uses the Update method to move changed information from the DataSet back to the data source.

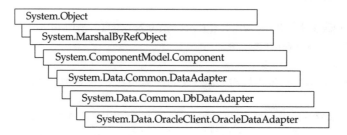

Constructor   Overloaded. Initializes a new instance of the OracleDataAdapter class. The first constructor creates a new object where all property values are set to their default values. The second constructor specifies a SELECT statement or stored procedure, OracleCommand, to use as the SelectCommand property. The third constructor specifies a string that is a SELECT statement or stored procedure and an OracleConnection to open and use. The fourth constructor specifies a string that is a SELECT statement or stored procedure and a connection string.

```
public OracleDataAdapter();
public OracleDataAdapter(OracleCommand);
public OracleDataAdapter(string selectCmdText, OracleConnection);
```

```
public OracleDataAdapter(string selectCmdText, string selectCnStr);
// C# example
System.Data.OracleClient.OracleDataAdapter OracleDA = new
    System.Data.OracleClient.OracleDataAdapter();
System.Data.OracleClient.OracleCommand OracleCmd = new
    System.Data.OracleClient.OracleCommand();
System.Data.OracleClient.OracleDataAdapter OracleDA2 = new
    System.Data.OracleClient.OracleDataAdapter(OracleCmd);
System.Data.OracleClient.OracleConnection OracleConn = new
    System.Data.OracleClient.OracleConnection();
System.Data.OracleClient.OracleDataAdapter OracleDA3 = new
    System.Data.OracleClient.OracleDataAdapter(
    "SELECT * FROM Customers", OracleConn);
System.Data.OracleClient.OracleDataAdapter OracleDA4 = new
    System.Data.OracleClient.OracleDataAdapter(
    "SELECT * FROM Customers",
    "DRIVER={SQL Server};SERVER=MyServer;UID=myID;PWD=MyPwd;
    DATABASE=Northwind");
```

OracleDataAdapter Class Properties

DeleteCommand Property   Returns or sets the SQL statement or stored procedure used for deleting records from the data source.

```
public new OracleCommand DeleteCommand { get; set; }
```

InsertCommand Property   Returns or sets the SQL statement or stored procedure used for inserting records into the data source.

```
public new OracleCommand InsertCommand { get; set; }
```

SelectCommand Property   Returns or sets the SQL statement or stored procedure used for selecting records from the data source.

```
public new OracleCommand SelectCommand { get; set; }
```

UpdateCommand Property   Returns or sets the SQL statement or stored procedure used for updating records in the data source.

```
public new OracleCommand UpdateCommand { get; set; }
```

OracleDataAdapter Class Methods

CreateRowUpdatedEvent Method Overrides System.Data.Common. DbDataAdapter.CreateRowUpdatedEvent. Returns a new instance of the RowUpdatedEventArgs object. The first parameter of the CreateRowUpdatedEvent method is the DataRow that is used to update the data source. The second parameter, IDbCommand, represents the SQL statement that is executed during the update; and the third parameter, StatementType, specifies whether the command is a SELECT, INSERT, UPDATE, or DELETE statement. The fourth parameter is the DataTableMapping object.

```
protected override RowUpdatedEventArgs CreateRowUpdatedEvent(
    System.Data.DataRow, System.Data.IDbCommand,
    System.Data.StatementType, System.Data.Common.DataTableMapping);
```

CreateRowUpdatingEvent Method Overrides System.Data.Common .DbDataAdapter.CreateRowUpdatingEvent. Returns a new instance of the RowUpdatingEventArgs class. The first parameter of the CreateRowUpdatingEvent method is the DataRow that is used to update the data source. The second parameter, IDbCommand, represents the SQL statement that is executed during the Update; and the third parameter, StatementType, specifies whether the command is a SELECT, INSERT, UPDATE, or DELETE statement. The fourth parameter is the DataTableMapping object.

```
protected override RowUpdatingEventArgs CreateRowUpdatingEvent(
    System.Data.DataRow, System.Data.IDbCommand,
    System.Data.StatementType, System.Data.Common.DataTableMapping);
```

OnRowUpdated Method Raises the RowUpdated event. The RowUpdatedEventArgs parameter contains the event data that is raised.

```
protected override void OnRowUpdated(RowUpdatedEventArgs);
```

OnRowUpdating Method Raises the RowUpdating event. The RowUpdatingEventArgs parameter contains the event data that is raised.

```
protected override void OnRowUpdating(RowUpdatingEventArgs);
```

OracleDataAdapter Class Events

RowUpdated Event Fires after an Update command is executed against a data source.

```
public event OracleRowUpdatedEventHandler RowUpdated;
```

RowUpdating Event   Fires before an Update command is executed against a data source.

```
public event OracleRowUpdatingEventHandler RowUpdating;
```

Mutual Properties, Methods, and Events Included in the OracleDataAdapter Class

The following lists the mutual properties, methods, and events that are included in the OracleDataAdapter class.

Inherited from Component	Inherited from Object	Inherited from MarshalByRefObject
Container property	Equals method	CreateObjRef method
DesignMode property	GetHashCode method	GetLifetimeService method
Events property	GetType method	InitializeLifetimeService method
Site property	MemberwiseClone method	
Dispose method	ToString method	
Finalize method		
GetService method		
Disposed event		

Inherited from DataAdapter	Inherited from DbDataAdapter
AcceptChangesDuringFill property	Dispose method
ContinueUpdateOnError property	Fill method
MissingMappingAction property	FillSchema method
MissingSchemaAction property	GetFillParameters method
TableMappings property	OnFillError method
CloneInternals method	Update method
CreateTableMappings method	FillError event
ShouldSerializeTableMappings method	

OracleDataReader Class

The OracleDataReader class allows for reading forward-only streams of data rows from a data source. You do not create an OracleDataReader by calling a constructor, but rather by calling the ExecuteReader method of an OracleCommand object. The OracleConnection object that is associated with the OracleDataReader is used exclusively by the OracleDataReader; therefore, only the Close operation may be performed on the OracleConnection.

```
System.Object
    System.EventArgs
        System.Data.OracleClient.OracleDataReader
```

OracleDataReader Class Properties

Depth Property   Returns an integer designating the depth of the current row's nesting.

```
public virtual int Depth { get; }
```

FieldCount Property   Returns the number of columns (or fields) in the current row. The default value for the FieldCount property is –1.

```
public virtual int FieldCount { get; }
```

HasRows Property   Returns a Boolean designating whether the OracleDataReader contains rows. True if the data reader has rows; False if it does not.

```
public bool HasRows { get; }
```

IsClosed Property   Returns a Boolean designating whether the OracleDataReader is opened or closed. True if the data reader is closed; False if it is open.

```
public virtual bool IsClosed { get; }
```

Item Property   Overloaded. Returns the object found at the specified column ordinal or string column name.

```
public virtual object this[int index] { get; }
public virtual object this[string colName] {get; }
```

RecordsAffected Property   Returns the number of rows affected by a changed, inserted, or deleted action.

```
public virtual int RecordsAffected { get; }
```

OracleDataReader Class Methods

Close Method   Closes an open OracleDataReader object.

```
public virtual void Close();
```

Dispose Method   Disposes the resources used by the OracleDataReader object.

```
protected virtual void Dispose();
```

GetBoolean Method   Returns the value in the specified zero-based column ordinal as a Boolean. The data to be retrieved must already be in the form of a Boolean or an exception is generated. Call IsDBNull before calling this method.

```
public virtual bool GetBoolean(int colOrdinal);
```

GetByte Method   Returns the value in the specified zero-based column ordinal as a byte. The data to be retrieved must already be in the form of a byte or an exception is generated. Call IsDBNull before calling this method.

```
public virtual bool GetByte(int colOrdinal);
```

GetBytes Method   Reads a stream of bytes from the specified zero-based column ordinal starting at the specified column offset. The bytes are placed into the specified byte buffer starting at the specified byte buffer offset for a length of the specified buffer length. The GetBytes method returns the actual number of bytes that were read. The data to be retrieved must already be in the form of a byte array or an exception is generated.

```
public virtual long GetBytes(int colOrdinal, long colOffset,
    byte[] buffer, int bufferOffset, int bufferLength);
```

GetChar Method   Returns the value in the specified zero-based column ordinal as a character. The data to be retrieved must already be in the form of a character or an exception is generated. Call IsDBNull before calling this method.

```
public virtual char GetChar(int colOrdinal);
```

GetChars Method   Reads a stream of characters from the specified zero-based column ordinal starting at the specified column offset. The characters are placed into the specified character buffer starting at the specified character buffer offset for a length of the specified buffer length. Returns the actual number of characters that were read.

The data to be retrieved must already be in the form of a character array or an exception is generated.

```
public virtual long GetChars(int colOrdinal, long colOffset,
    char[] buffer, int bufferOffset, int bufferLength);
```

GetData Method   Currently not supported.

GetDataTypeName Method   Returns the name of the data type in the specified zero-based column ordinal as a string.

```
public virtual string GetDataTypeName(int colOrdinal);
```

GetDateTime Method   Returns the value in the specified zero-based column ordinal as a DateTime object. The data to be retrieved must already be in the form of a DateTime object or an exception is generated. Call IsDBNull before calling this method.

```
public virtual DateTime GetDateTime(int colOrdinal);
```

GetDecimal Method   Returns the value in the specified zero-based column ordinal as a decimal. The data to be retrieved must already be in the form of a decimal or an exception is generated. Call IsDBNull before calling this method.

```
public virtual decimal GetDecimal(int colOrdinal);
```

GetDouble Method   Returns the value in the specified zero-based column ordinal as a double-precision floating point number. The data to be retrieved must already be in the form of a double or an exception is generated. Call IsDBNull before calling this method.

```
public virtual double GetDouble(int colOrdinal);
```

GetFieldType Method   Returns the data type of the object in the specified zero-based column ordinal.

```
public virtual Type GetFieldType(int colOrdinal);
```

GetFloat Method   Returns the value in the specified zero-based column ordinal as a single-precision floating point number. The data to be retrieved must already be in the form of a float or an exception is generated. Call IsDBNull before calling this method.

```
public virtual float GetFloat(int colOrdinal);
```

GetGuid Method Returns the value in the specified zero-based column ordinal as a globally unique identifier (GUID). The data to be retrieved must already be in the form of a Guid or an exception is generated. Call IsDBNull before calling this method.

```
public virtual Guid GetGuid(int colOrdinal);
```

GetInt16 Method Returns the value in the specified zero-based column ordinal as a 16-bit signed integer. The data to be retrieved must already be in the form of a short or an exception is generated. Call IsDBNull before calling this method.

```
public virtual short GetInt16(int colOrdinal);
```

GetInt32 Method Returns the value in the specified zero-based column ordinal as a 32-bit signed integer. The data to be retrieved must already be in the form of an integer or an exception is generated. Call IsDBNull before calling this method.

```
public virtual int GetInt32(int colOrdinal);
```

GetInt64 Method Returns the value in the specified zero-based column ordinal as a 64-bit signed integer. The data to be retrieved must already be in the form of a long or an exception is generated. Call IsDBNull before calling this method.

```
public virtual long GetInt64(int colOrdinal);
```

GetName Method Returns the name of the column in the specified zero-based column ordinal as a string.

```
public virtual string GetName(int colOrdinal);
```

GetOracleBFile Method Returns the value in the specified zero-based column ordinal as an OracleBFile object. Call IsDBNull before calling this method.

```
public OracleBFile GetOracleBFile(int colOrdinal);
```

GetOracleBinary Method Returns the value in the specified zero-based column ordinal as an OracleBinary object. Call IsDBNull before calling this method.

```
public OracleBinary GetOracleBinary(int colOrdinal);
```

GetOracleDateTime Method Returns the value in the specified zero-based column ordinal as an OracleDateTime object. Call IsDBNull before calling this method.

```
public OracleDateTime GetOracleDateTime(int colOrdinal);
```

GetOracleLob Method Returns the value in the specified zero-based column ordinal as an OracleLob object. Call IsDBNull before calling this method.

```
public OracleLob GetOracleLob(int colOrdinal);
```

GetOracleMonthSpan Method Returns the value in the specified zero-based column ordinal as an OracleMonthSpan object. Call IsDBNull before calling this method.

```
public OracleMonthSpan GetOracleMonthSpan(int colOrdinal);
```

GetOracleNumber Method Returns the value in the specified zero-based column ordinal as an OracleNumber. Call IsDBNull before calling this method.

```
public OracleNumber GetOracleNumber(int colOrdinal);
```

GetOracleString Method Returns the value in the specified zero-based column ordinal as an OracleString. Call IsDBNull before calling this method.

```
public OracleString GetOracleString(int colOrdinal);
```

GetOracleTimeSpan Method Returns the value in the specified zero-based column ordinal as an OracleTimeSpan object. Call IsDBNull before calling this method.

```
public OracleTimeSpan GetOracleTimeSpan(int colOrdinal);
```

GetOracleValue Method Returns the value in the specified zero-based column ordinal in its Oracle form. Returns DBNull if column is null.

```
public object GetOracleValue(int colOrdinal);
```

GetOracleValues Method Fills the specified object array with the column attributes of the current row. Returns the number of objects in the object array.

```
public int GetOracleValues(object[] cols);
```

GetOrdinal Method Returns the zero-based column ordinal value of the specified column name.

```
public virtual int GetOrdinal(string colName);
```

GetSchemaTable Method Returns a DataTable object that contains the metadata for the columns in the current OracleDataReader object.

```
public virtual System.Data.DataTable GetSchemaTable();
```

GetString Method   Returns the value in the specified zero-based column ordinal as a string. The data to be retrieved must already be in the form of a string or an exception is generated. Call IsDBNull before calling this method.

```
public virtual string GetString(int colOrdinal);
```

GetTimeSpan Method   Returns the value in the specified zero-based column ordinal in the form of System.TimeSpan.

```
public System.TimeSpan GetTimeSpan(int colOrdinal);
```

GetValue Method   Returns the value in the specified zero-based column ordinal in its native form.

```
public virtual object GetValue(int colOrdinal);
```

GetValues Method   Fills the specified object array with the column attributes of the current row. Returns the number of objects in the object array.

```
public virtual int GetValues(object[] cols);
```

IEnumerator.GetEnumerator Method   The IEnumerator.GetEnumerator method supports the .NET infrastructure and is not used directly from your code.

IsDBNull Method   Returns a Boolean indicating whether the value in the specified zero-based column ordinal exists. True if the value is DBNull; otherwise, the method returns False.

```
public virtual bool IsDBNull(int colOrdinal);
```

NextResult Method   Moves to the next resultset. Used when multiple resultsets were generated by a batch SQL statement. Returns True if there are more resultsets; otherwise, the method returns False.

```
public virtual bool NextResult();
```

Read Method   Moves to the next record in the OracleDataReader object. Default position is prior to the first record, so use Read to begin processing data. Returns True if there are more rows; otherwise, the method returns False.

```
public virtual bool Read();
```

Mutual Properties, Methods, and Events Included in the OracleDataReader Class

The following lists the mutual properties, methods, and events that are included in the OracleDataReader class.

Inherited from Object	**Inherited from MarshalByRefObject**
Equals method	CreateObjRef method
Finalize method	GetLifetimeService method
GetHashCode method	InitializeLifetimeService method
GetType method	
MemberwiseClone method	
ToString method	

OracleException Class

The OracleException class represents the exception that is thrown when an error is returned by the Oracle data source. You do not create an OracleException by calling a constructor. The OracleException is created when the OracleDataAdapter encounters an unhandled error.

```
System.Object
    System.Exception
        System.SystemException
            System.Data.OracleClient.OracleException
```

OracleException Class Properties

Code Property   Contains an integer representing the code portion of the error that was generated.

```
public int Code { get; }
```

Message Property   Contains the full text description for the error that was sent from the database.

```
public override string Message { get; }
```

Mutual Properties, Methods, and Events Included in the OracleException Class

The following lists the mutual properties, methods, and events that are included in the OracleException class.

Inherited from Exception

HelpLink property

HResult property

InnerException property

StackTrace property

TargetSite property

GetBaseException method

GetObjectData method

ToString method

Inherited from Object

Equals method

Finalize method

GetHashCode method

GetType method

MemberwiseClone method

OracleInfoMessageEventArgs Class

The OracleInfoMessageEventArgs class supplies information for the InfoMessage event. You do not create an OracleInfoMessageEventArgs class by calling a constructor, but is a parameter of the OracleInfoMessageEventHandler.

```
System.Object
    System.EventArgs
        System.Data.OracleClient.OracleInfoMessageEventArgs
```

OracleInfoMessageEventArgs Class Properties

Code Property   Contains an integer representing the code portion of the error that was generated.

```
public int Code { get; }
```

Message Property   Contains the full text description for the error that was sent from the database.

```
public string Message { get; }
```

Source Property   Returns a string that contains the name of the object that generated the error.

```
public string Source { get; }
```

OracleInfoMessageEventArgs Class Methods

ToString Method   Returns the InfoMessage event in a string.

```
public override string ToString();
```

Mutual Properties, Methods, and Events Included in the OracleInfoMessageEventArgs Class

The following lists the mutual properties, methods, and events that are included in the OracleInfoMessageEventArgs class.

Inherited from Object

Equals method

Finalize method

GetHashCode method

GetType method

MemberwiseClone method

OracleLob Class

The OracleLob class represents an Oracle LOB (Large Object Binary) data type. An OracleLob is stored in the database rather than a physically stored file in the operating system, and it is read-write capable. The following lists the accepted OracleLob types:

Blob	Oracle BLOB data type. Binary data. Maximum size is 4GB. Maps to a byte array type.
Clob	Oracle CLOB data type. Server default character data. Maximum size is 4GB. Maps to a String type.
NClob	Oracle NCLOB data type. National character set data. Maximum size is 4GB. Maps to a String type.

You do not create an OracleLob by calling a constructor, but rather it is accessed through the OracleDataReader object's GetOracleLob method.

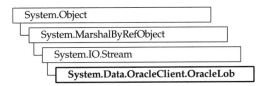

OracleLob Class Fields

The following lists the constant fields used in the OracleLob class.

Null field   `public static readonly OracleLob Null;`

OracleLob Class Properties

CanRead Property   Returns a Boolean indicating whether the LOB stream can be read. False indicates that the LOB is closed. True indicates that the LOB stream may be read.

```
public override bool CanRead { get; }
```

CanSeek Property   Returns a Boolean indicating whether the forward and backward seek operations may be performed on the LOB stream. False indicates that the LOB is closed. True indicates that the LOB stream may be read or it is null.

```
public override bool CanSeek { get; }
```

CanWrite Property   Returns a Boolean. False is returned if the LOB stream is closed; otherwise, True is returned regardless of whether the LOB stream may be written to or not.

```
public override bool CanWrite { get; }
```

ChunkSize Property   Contains the minimum number of bytes to receive or send to the server during a read or write operation.

```
public int ChunkSize { get; }
```

Connection Property   Returns the OracleConnection object associated with this OracleLob.

```
public OracleConnection Connection { get; }
```

IsBatched Property   Contains a Boolean indicating whether the BeginBatch method has been called. True if the method has been called; otherwise, False.

```
public bool IsBatched { get; }
```

IsNull Property   Returns a Boolean indicating whether the OracleLob object is a null stream. True if the OracleLob is null; otherwise, False.

```
public virtual bool IsNull { get; }
```

IsTemporary Property   Returns a Boolean indicating whether the OracleLob object is temporary. True if the OracleLob is temporary; otherwise, False.

```
public bool IsTemporary { get; }
```

Length Property   Returns a long value indicating the length of the OracleLob object in bytes.

```
public override long Length { get; }
```

LobType Property   Returns the OracleType LOB data type contained in the OracleLob object.

```
public OracleType LobType { get; }
```

Position Property   Returns or sets a long value indicating the current position in the OracleLob object.

```
public override long Position { get; set; }
```

Value Property   Returns a byte array that contains the OracleLob data if the LobType is Blob. Returns a String that contains the OracleLob data if the LobType is Clob or NClob.

```
public object Value { get; }
```

OracleLob Class Methods

Append Method   Appends data to the current LOB from the specified LOB.

```
public void Append(OracleLob);
```

BeginBatch Method Overloaded. While multiple write operations are being performed, this method prevents server-side triggers from being fired. The second method also specifies an OracleLobOpenMode option.

```
public void BeginBatch();
public void BeginBatch(OracleLobOpenMode);
```

Clone Method Returns an object that is a copy of the OracleLob object and associated with the same LOB data type.

```
public virtual object Clone();
```

Close Method Closes an open OracleLob object.

```
public override void Close();
```

CopyTo Method Overloaded. The first CopyTo method copies the current OracleLob to the specified OracleLob object. The second method copies the current OracleLob to the OracleLob object at the specified offset. The third method copies the current OracleLob to the OracleLob object starting in the indicated source location and outputting to the indicated destination location for the specified length of bytes.

```
public long CopyTo(OracleLob);
public long CopyTo(OracleLob, long offSet);
public long CopyTo(long srcOffset, OracleLob, long destOffset,
    long count);
```

Dispose Method Disposes the resources used by the OracleLob.

```
public virtual void Dispose();
```

EndBatch Method Resumes firing of server-side triggers while performing multiple write operations.

```
public void EndBatch();
```

Erase Method Overloaded. Clears the OracleLob of data and returns the number of bytes erased. The second method erases data from the OracleLob beginning at the specified offset for the specified number of bytes.

```
public long Erase();
public long Erase(long offset, long count);
```

Flush Method   Currently not supported.

```
public override void Flush();
```

Read Method   Reads the specified number of bytes into the byte array indicated, starting at the specified offset.

```
public override int Read(byte[], int offset, int count);
```

Seek Method   Sets the position in the OracleLob to the specified offset position relative to the specified original position and returns the new current position in the OracleLob.

```
public override long Seek(long offset, System.IO.SeekOrigin);
```

System.IO.SeekOriginenumeration:

Begin	Indicates the beginning of the stream
Current	Indicates the current position in the stream
End	Indicates the end of the stream

SetLength Method   Resets the length of the OracleLob to the specified lesser value. Clob and NClob types must use an even number.

```
public override void SetLength(long);
```

Write Method   Writes the specified byte array buffer to the current OracleLob starting at the offset for the length of count specified.

```
public override void Write(byte[], int offset, int count);
```

Mutual Properties, Methods, and Events Included in the OracleBFile Class

The following lists the mutual properties, methods, and events that are included in the OracleBFile class.

Inherited from Stream	Inherited from Object	Inherited from MarshalByRefObject
BeginRead method	Equals method	CreateObjRef method
BeginWrite method	Finalize method	GetLifetimeService method

Inherited from Stream	Inherited from Object	Inherited from MarshalByRefObject
CreateWaitHandle method	GetHashCode method	InitializeLifetimeService method
EndRead method	GetType method	
EndWrite method	MemberwiseClone method	
ReadByte method	ToString method	
WriteByte method		

OracleParameter Class

The OracleParameter class is a parameter for the OracleCommand object. May also be used for the OracleCommand object's mapping to the DataSet column. The parameters for the OracleCommand class are not case sensitive.

```
System.Object
    System.MarshalByRefObject
        System.Data.OracleClient.OracleParameter
```

Constructor   Overloaded. Initializes a new instance of the OracleParameter class. The first constructor creates a new object using the default property values. The second constructor specifies the parameter name and value type. The third constructor specifies the parameter name and data type. The fourth constructor specifies the parameter name, data type, and parameter size. The fifth constructor specifies the parameter name, data type, parameter size, and source column name. The sixth constructor sets all of the properties of the OracleParameter object at the time it is created with the specified values.

```
public OracleParameter();
public OracleParameter(string parmName, object parmValue);
public OracleParameter(string parmName, OracleType parmType);
public OracleParameter(string parmName, OracleType parmType,
    int parmSize);
public OracleParameter(string parmName, OracleType parmType,
    int parmSize, string srcColumn);
public OracleParameter(string parmName, OracleType parmType,
    int parmSize, ParameterDirection parmDir, bool isNullable,
    byte parmPrecision, byte parmScale, string srcColumn,
    DataRowVersion srcVersion, object parmValue);
// C# example
System.Data.OracleClient.OracleParameter OracleParm = new
```

```
         System.Data.OracleClient.OracleParameter();
System.Data.OracleClient.OracleParameter OracleParm2 = new
    System.Data.OracleClient.OracleParameter("CustomerName",
    OracleParm);
System.Data.OracleClient.OracleParameter OracleParm3 = new
    System.Data.OracleClient.OracleParameter("CustomerName",
    System.Data.OracleClient.OracleType.Text);
System.Data.OracleClient.OracleParameter OracleParm4 = new
    System.Data.OracleClient.OracleParameter("CustomerName",
    System.Data.OracleClient.OracleType.Text, 25);
System.Data.OracleClient.OracleParameter OracleParm5 = new
    System.Data.OracleClient.OracleParameter("CustomerName",
    System.Data.OracleClient.OracleType.Text, 25, "CustName");
System.Data.OracleClient.OracleParameter OracleParm6 = new
    System.Data.OracleClient.OracleParameter("CustomerName",
    System.Data.OracleClient.OracleType.Text, 25,
    System.Data.ParameterDirection.Input, true, 0, 0, "CustName",
    System.Data.DataRowVersion.Current, OracleParm);
```

OracleParameter Class Properties

DbType Property Returns or sets the DbType for the parameter. Default DbType is string.

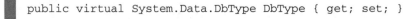

```
public virtual System.Data.DbType DbType { get; set; }
```

System.Data.DbType enumeration:

AnsiString	Variable-length stream of 1 to 8000 characters. Non-Unicode.
AnsiStringFixedLength	Fixed-length stream of characters. Non-Unicode.
Binary	Variable-length stream of binary data. 1 to 8,000 bytes.
Boolean	Values of True or False.
Byte	8-bit unsigned integer. Value range 0 to 255.
Currency	Value range –922,337,203,685,477.5808 to 922,337,203,685,477.5807. Accuracy to ten-thousandth of unit.
Date	Value range January 1, 1753, to December 31, 9999. Accuracy to 3.33 milliseconds.
DateTime	Represents date and time values.

System.Data.DbType enumeration:

Decimal	Value range 1.0×10^{-28} to approximately 7.9×10^{28}. Significant digits of 28 to 29.
Double	Floating point type. Value range approximately 5.0×10^{-324} to 1.7×10^{308}. Precision of 15 to 16 digits.
Guid	Globally unique identifier.
Int16	Signed 16-bit integer. Value range –32,768 to 32,767.
Int32	Signed 32-bit integer. Value range –2,147,483,648 to 2,147,483,647.
Int64	Signed 64-bit integer. Value range –9,223,372,036,854,775,808 to 9,223,372,036,854,775,807.
Object	General type.
SByte	Signed 8-bit integer. Value range –128 to 127.
Single	Floating point type. Value range approximately 1.5×10^{-45} to 3.4×10^{38}. Precision of 7 digits.
String	String of characters. Unicode.
StringFixedLength	Fixed-length stream of characters. Unicode.
Time	Value range January 1, 1753, to December 31, 9999. Accuracy to 3.33 milliseconds.
Uint16	Unsigned 16-bit integer. Value range 0 to 65,535.
Uint32	Unsigned 32-bit integer. Value range 0 to 4,294,967,295.
Uint64	Unsigned 64-bit integer. Value range 0 to 18,446,744,073,709,551,615.

Direction Property   Returns or sets the directional aspect of the parameter. The default value is Input.

```
public virtual System.Data.ParameterDirection Direction {get; set;}
```

System.Data.ParameterDirection enumeration:

Input	Parameter is input only.
InputOutput	Parameter is both input and output.
Output	Parameter is output only.
ReturnValue	Parameter is a return value from an operation like a stored procedure.

IsNullable Property   Returns or sets a Boolean indicating whether the parameter accepts null values. True indicates nulls are accepted. The default value is False.

```
public virtual bool IsNullable { get; set; }
```

Offset Property   Returns or sets the offset value for the Value property. The default value is 0. This property is used for client-side chunking of string and binary data.

```
public int Offset { get; set; }
```

OracleType Property   Returns or sets the OracleType for the parameter. Setting the DbType property changes the OracleType property to the corresponding data type. The default OracleType is Nchar.

```
public OracleType OracleType { get; set; }
```

ParameterName Property   Returns or sets the name of the OracleParameter. The default value is an empty string.

```
public virtual string ParameterName { get; set; }
```

Precision Property   Returns or sets the maximum number of digits to use. The default value is 0.

```
public virtual byte Precision { get; set; }
```

Scale Property   Returns or sets the number of decimal places to use. The default value is 0.

```
public virtual byte Scale { get; set; }
```

Size Property   Returns or sets the maximum bytes of data for the column. Used for binary and string column types. The default value is derived from the parameter type.

```
public virtual int Size { get; set; }
```

SourceColumn Property   Returns or sets the name of the source column that is mapped to the DataSet. The default value is an empty string.

```
public virtual string SourceColumn { get; set; }
```

SourceVersion Property Returns or sets the DataRowVersion to use. The default value is Current.

```
public virtual System.Data.DataRowVersion SourceVersion {get; set;}
```

System.Data.DataRowVersion enumeration:

Current	Row contains current values.
Default	Row is versioned according to the DataRowState.
Original	Row contains its original values.
Proposed	Row contains proposed values.

Value Property Returns or sets the value of the parameter. The default value is null.

```
public virtual object Value { get; set; }
```

OracleParameter Class Methods

ICloneable.Clone Method The ICloneable.Clone method supports the .NET infrastructure and is not used directly from your code.

ToString Method Returns the ParameterName in a string.

```
public override string ToString();
```

Mutual Properties, Methods, and Events Included in the OracleParameter Class

The following lists the mutual properties, methods, and events that are included in the OracleParameter class.

Inherited from Object	Inherited from MarshalByRefObject
Equals method	CreateObjRef method
Finalize method	GetLifetimeService method
GetHashCode method	InitializeLifetimeService method
GetType method	
MemberwiseClone method	

OracleParameterCollection Class

The OracleParameterCollection class is a collection of OracleParameter objects for an OracleCommand object and their related mapping information for DataSet columns.

```
System.Object
    System.MarshalByRefObject
        System.Data.OracleClient.OracleParameterCollection
```

Constructor   Initializes a new instance of the OracleParameterCollection class.

```
public OracleParameterCollection();
// C# example
System.Data.OracleClient.OracleParameterCollection OraclePCol = new
    System.Data.OracleClient.OracleParameterCollection();
```

OracleParameterCollection Class Properties

Count Property   Returns the number of items in this collection.

```
public virtual int Count { get; }
```

IsFixedSize Property   Returns a Boolean indicating whether the OracleParameterCol-lection object is a fixed size. True if the OracleParameterCollection is a fixed size; otherwise, False. Default value is False.

```
public virtual bool IsFixedSize { get; }
```

IsReadOnly Property   Returns a Boolean indicating whether the OracleParameterCol-lection object is read-only. True if the OracleParameterCollection is read-only; otherwise, False. Default value is False.

```
public virtual bool IsReadOnly { get; }
```

IsSynchronized Property   Returns a Boolean indicating whether the OracleParameterCollection object is thread safe. Always returns False.

```
public virtual bool IsSynchronized { get; }
```

Item Property   Overloaded. Returns or sets the OracleParameter object found at the specified integer index or string parameter name.

```
public OracleParameter this[int index] { get; set; }
public OracleParameter this[string parmName] {get; set; }
```

SyncRoot Property   Returns an object that is used to synchronize access to the OracleParameterCollection.

```
public virtual object SyncRoot { get; }
```

OracleParameterCollection Class Methods

Add Method   Overloaded. The first Add method adds the specified object to the OracleCommand's OracleParameterCollection and returns the index of the added object. The second Add method adds the specified OracleParameter to the OracleCommand's OracleParameterCollection and returns the added OracleParameter. The third Add method adds the specified object to the OracleParameterCollection using the specified parameter name and returns the added OracleParameter. The fourth Add method adds an OracleParameter to the OracleParameterCollection using the specified parameter name and data type and returns the added OracleParameter. The fifth Add method adds an OracleParameter to the OracleParameterCollection using the specified parameter name, data type, and parameter size and returns the added OracleParameter. The sixth Add method adds an OracleParameter to the OracleParameterCollection using the specified parameter name, data type, parameter size, and column source name and returns the added OracleParameter.

```
public int Add(object);
public OracleParameter Add(OracleParameter);
public OracleParameter Add(string parmName, object);
public OracleParameter Add(string parmName, OracleType);
public OracleParameter Add(string parmName, OracleType,
    int parmSize);
public OracleParameter Add(string parmName, OracleType,
    int parmSize, string sourceColumn);
```

Clear Method   Removes all the items from the OracleParameterCollection.

```
public void Clear();
```

Contains Method   Overloaded. The first Contains method returns True if the OracleParameterCollection contains the specified Object. The second Contains method returns True if the collection contains an OracleParameter object with the specified parameter name.

```
public bool Contains(Object);
public bool Contains(string parmName);
```

CopyTo Method   Copies the objects in the OracleParameterCollection to the specified array and sets the starting index of the array to the specified integer.

```
public void CopyTo(array, int);
```

GetEnumerator Method   The GetEnumerator method supports the .NET infrastructure and is not used directly from your code.

IndexOf Method   Overloaded. The first IndexOf method returns the location of the specified Object of type OracleParameter within the OracleParameterCollection. The second IndexOf method returns the location of the OracleParameter object with the specified parameter name.

```
public int IndexOf(Object);
public int IndexOf(string parmName);
```

Insert Method   Inserts an OracleParameter object into the OracleParameterCollection at the specified zero-based integer index.

```
public void Insert(int, object);
```

Remove Method   Removes an object that is of type OracleParameter from the OracleParameterCollection. Throws a SystemException if the specified object is not of type OracleParameter or the specified object does not exist in the collection.

```
public void Remove(object);
```

RemoveAt Method   Overloaded. The first RemoveAt method removes the OracleParameter object from the OracleParameterCollection at the specified zero-based integer index. The second RemoveAt method removes the OracleParameter object from the collection that matches the specified parameter name. Both methods throw an exception if the OracleParameter object does not exist in the collection at the specified location.

```
public void RemoveAt(int);
public void RemoveAt(string parmName);
```

Mutual Properties, Methods, and Events Included in the OracleParameterCollection Class

The following lists the mutual properties, methods, and events that are included in the OracleParameterCollection class.

Inherited from Object	**Inherited from MarshalByRefObject**
Equals method	CreateObjRef method
Finalize method	GetLifetimeService method
GetHashCode method	InitializeLifetimeService method
GetType method	

Inherited from Object

MemberwiseClone method

ToString method

Inherited from MarshalByRefObject

OraclePermission Class

The OraclePermission class provides user security level setting to access an Oracle data source with the .NET Framework for Oracle Data Provider.

```
System.Object
    System.Security.CodeAccessPermission
        System.Data.OracleClient.OraclePermission
```

Constructor   Overloaded. Initializes a new instance of the OraclePermission class specifying whether a user should have all access or no access.

```
public OraclePermission(
    System.Security.Permissions.PermissionState);
// C# example
System.Data.OracleClient.OraclePermission OraclePerm = new
    System.Data.OracleClient.OraclePermission(
    System.Security.Permissions.PermissionState.None);
```

System.Security.Permissions.PermissionState enumeration:

None   Indicates no access to the resource

Unrestricted   Indicates full access to the resource

OraclePermission Class Properties

AllowBlankPassword Property   Returns or sets a Boolean indicating whether a blank password is allowed.

```
public bool AllowBlankPassword { get; set; }
```

OraclePermission Class Methods

Copy Method   Returns a copy of the current security permission object, IPermission, with the same access to resources as the original object. The IPermission object describes the functions of the object.

```
public override System.Security.IPermission Copy();
```

FromXml Method   Populates the OraclePermission object with the specified XML security-encoded state.

```
public override void FromXml(System.Security.SecurityElement);
```

Intersect Method   Returns a security permission object, IPermission, that intersects the current OraclePermission object with the specified permission object. A request that passes both original permission objects will be allowed to pass the intersection. An IPermission object describes the functions of the object.

```
public override System.Security.IPermission Intersect(
    System.Security.IPermission);
```

IsSubsetOf Method   Returns True if the current OraclePermission object is a subset of the specified permission object. The IPermission object describes the functions of the object.

```
public override bool IsSubsetOf(System.Security.IPermission);
```

IsUnrestricted Method   Returns True if a security permission object can be represented as unrestricted. Because this is a binary representation, it will always return True.

```
public virtual bool IsUnrestricted();
```

ToXml Method   Returns an XML security encoding of the current OraclePermission object with its current state information.

```
public override System.Security.SecurityElement ToXml();
```

Union Method   Returns a security permission object that joins the current OraclePermission object with the specified permission object. A request that passes either permission object will pass the union. An IPermission object describes the functions of the object.

```
public override System.Security.IPermission Union(
    System.Security.IPermission);
```

Mutual Properties, Methods, and Events
Included in the OraclePermission Class

The following lists the mutual properties, methods, and events that are included in the OraclePermission class.

Inherited from CodeAccessPermission	Inherited from Object
Assert method	Equals method
Demand method	Finalize method
Deny method	GetHashCode method
PermitOnly method	GetType method
ToString method	MemberwiseClone method

OraclePermissionAttribute Class

The OraclePermissionAttribute class relates a security action to a security permission attribute.

```
System.Object
    System.Attribute
        System.Security.Permissions.SecurityAttribute
            System.Security.Permissions.CodeAccessSecurityAttribute
                System.Data.OracleClient.OraclePermissionAttribute
```

Constructor   Initializes a new instance of the OraclePermissionAttribute class.

```
public OraclePermissionAttribute(
    System.Security.Permissions.SecurityAction);
// C# example
System.Data.OracleClient.OraclePermissionAttribute OraclePA = new
    System.Data.OracleClient.OraclePermissionAttribute(
    System.Security.Permissions.SecurityAction.LinkDemand);
```

System.Security.Permissions.SecurityAction enumeration:

Assert	Allows security to bypass code permission check
Demand	Performs security check for enforcing restrictions on calling code
Deny	Prevents access to the resource specified
InheritanceDemand	Checks for granted permissions for inherited class
LinkDemand	Checks for granted permission for immediate caller
PermitOnly	Allows access only to the resource specified

APPENDIXES

System.Security.Permissions.SecurityAction enumeration:

RequestMinimum   Requests the minimum permissions for code

RequestOptional   Requests the optional permissions

RequestRefuse   Request permissions not be granted to calling code

OraclePermissionAttribute Class Properties

AllowBlankPassword Property   Returns or sets a Boolean indicating whether a blank password is allowed.

```
public bool AllowBlankPassword { get; set; }
```

OraclePermissionAttribute Class Methods

CreatePermission Method   Returns an OraclePermission object that contains the current attribute properties.

```
public override System.Security.IPermission CreatePermission();
```

Mutual Properties, Methods, and Events Included in the OraclePermissionAttribute Class

The following lists the mutual properties, methods, and events that are included in the OraclePermissionAttribute class.

Inherited from Attribute	Inherited from Object	Inherited from SecurityAttribute
TypeId property	Equals method	Action property
GetHashCode method	Finalize method	Unrestricted property
IsDefaultAttribute method	GetType method	
Match method	MemberwiseClone method	
	ToString method	

OracleRowUpdatedEventArgs Class

The OracleRowUpdatedEventArgs class supplies the information for the RowUpdated event that is raised when an update to a row has been completed.

```
System.Object
    System.EventArgs
        System.Data.Common.RowUpdatedEventArgs
            System.Data.OracleClient.OracleRowUpdatedEventArgs
```

Constructor   Initializes a new instance of the OracleRowUpdatedEventArgs class using the specified DataRow, the IDbCommand, the StatementType, and the DataTableMapping. The IDbCommand represents the SQL statement that was executed, and the StatementType specifies whether the command was a SELECT, INSERT, UPDATE, or DELETE statement. The DataTableMapping object describes the mapped relationship of the source table and the DataTable.

```
public OracleRowUpdatedEventArgs(System.Data.DataRow,
    System.Data.IDbCommand, System.Data.StatementType,
    System.Data.Common.DataTableMapping);
// C# example
System.Data.DataRow dr = new System.Data.DataTable().NewRow();
System.Data.OracleClient.OracleCommand cmd = new
    System.Data.OracleClient.OracleCommand(
    "SELECT * FROM Customers");
System.Data.Common.DataTableMapping dtm = new
    System.Data.Common.DataTableMapping();
System.Data.Common.RowUpdatedEventArgs ruea = new
    System.Data.OracleClient.OracleRowUpdatedEventArgs(dr, cmd,
    System.Data.StatementType.Select, dtm);
```

OracleRowUpdatedEventArgs Class Properties

Command Property   Returns the OracleCommand that was executed when Update was called.

```
public new OracleCommand Command { get; }
```

Mutual Properties, Methods, and Events Included in the OracleRowUpdatedEventArgs Class

The following lists the mutual properties, methods, and events that are included in the OracleRowUpdatedEventArgs class.

Inherited from RowUpdatedEventArgs	Inherited from Object
Errors property	Equals method
RecordsAffected property	Finalize method
Row property	GetHashCode method

Inherited from RowUpdatedEventArgs	Inherited from Object
StatementType property	GetType method
Status property	MemberwiseClone method
TableMapping property	ToString method

OracleRowUpdatingEventArgs Class

The OracleRowUpdatingEventArgs class supplies the information for the RowUpdating event that is raised when an update to a row is about to take place.

```
System.Object
  System.EventArgs
    System.Data.Common.RowUpdatingEventArgs
      System.Data.OracleClient.OracleRowUpdatingEventArgs
```

Constructor   Initializes a new instance of the OracleRowUpdatingEventArgs class using the specified DataRow, the IDbCommand, the StatementType, and the DataTableMapping. The IDbCommand represents the SQL statement that will be executed, and the StatementType specifies whether the command is a SELECT, INSERT, UPDATE, or DELETE statement. The DataTableMapping object describes the mapped relationship of the source table and the DataTable.

```
public OracleRowUpdatingEventArgs(System.Data.DataRow,
    System.Data.IDbCommand, System.Data.StatementType,
    System.Data.Common.DataTableMapping);
// C# example
System.Data.DataRow dr = new System.Data.DataTable().NewRow();
System.Data.OracleClient.OracleCommand cmd = new
    System.Data.OracleClient.OracleCommand(
    "SELECT * FROM Customers");
System.Data.Common.DataTableMapping dtm = new
    System.Data.Common.DataTableMapping();
System.Data.Common.RowUpdatingEventArgs ruea = new
    System.Data.OracleClient.OracleRowUpdatedEventArgs(dr, cmd,
    System.Data.StatementType.Select, dtm);
```

OracleRowUpdatingEventArgs Class Properties

Command Property   Returns or sets the OracleCommand that will be executed when Update is called.

```
public new OracleCommand Command { get; set; }
```

Mutual Properties, Methods, and Events Included in the OracleRowUpdatingEventArgs Class

The following lists the mutual properties, methods, and events that are included in the OracleRowUpdatingEventArgs class.

Inherited from RowUpdatingEventArgs	Inherited from Object
Errors property	Equals method
Row property	Finalize method
StatementType property	GetHashCode method
Status property	GetType method
TableMapping property	MemberwiseClone method
	ToString method

OracleTransaction Class

The OracleTransaction class represents a transaction to implement at a data source. You do not create an OracleTransaction object by calling a constructor, but rather by calling the BeginTransaction method of an OracleConnection object.

```
System.Object
    System.EventArgs
        System.Data.OracleClient.OracleTransaction
```

OracleTransaction Class Properties

Connection Property   Returns the OracleConnection object associated with this OracleTransaction.

```
public OracleConnection Connection { get; }
```

IsolationLevel Property   Returns the isolation level for this OracleTransaction object. The default value is ReadCommited.

```
public virtual System.Data.IsolationLevel IsolationLevel { get; }
```

System.Data.IsolationLevel enumeration:

Chaos	Cannot overwrite more highly isolated transactions that are pending.
ReadCommited	To avoid dirty reads, the shared locks are held during reading of data. May result in nonrepeatable read or phantom data being changed before the transaction ends.

System.Data.IsolationLevel enumeration:

ReadUncommited	No exclusive locks are allowed and no shared locks are done. May result in a dirty read.
RepeatableRead	Locks are placed on the queried data. May result in phantom rows.
Serializable	A range lock is placed on the rows in the DataSet.
Unspecified	The isolation level cannot be determined.

OracleTransaction Class Methods

Commit Method Commits the transaction to the database. Throws an exception if there is an error committing the transaction or the connection is broken.

```
public virtual void Commit();
```

Dispose Method Disposes the resources used by the OracleTransaction.

```
public virtual void Dispose();
```

Rollback Method Rolls back a transaction that is in a pending state. Throws an exception if the transaction has already been committed or the connection is broken.

```
public virtual void Rollback();
```

Mutual Properties, Methods, and Events Included in the OracleTransaction Class

The following lists the mutual properties, methods, and events that are included in the OracleTransaction class.

Inherited from Object	**Inherited from MarshalByRefObject**
Equals method	CreateObjRef method
Finalize method	GetLifetimeService method
GetHashCode method	InitializeLifetimeService method
GetType method	
MemberwiseClone method	
ToString method	

OracleInfoMessageEventHandler Delegate

The OracleInfoMessageEventHandler delegate is the method that handles the InfoMessage event of the OracleConnection object. The first parameter, object, indicates the source of the event to handle. The second parameter is an OracleInfoMessageEventArgs object that contains the event information.

```
public delegate void OracleInfoMessageEventHandler(object,
    OracleInfoMessageEventArgs);
```

OracleRowUpdatedEventHandler Delegate

The OracleRowUpdatedEventHandler delegate is the method that handles the RowUpdatedEvent of the OracleDataAdapter object. The first parameter, object, indicates the source of the event to handle. The second parameter is an OracleRowUpdatedEventArgs object that contains the event information.

```
public delegate void OracleRowUpdatedEventHandler(object,
    OracleRowUpdatedEventArgs);
```

OracleRowUpdatingEventHandler Delegate

The OracleRowUpdatingEventHandler delegate is the method that handles the RowUpdatingEvent of the OracleDataAdapter object. The first parameter, object, indicates the source of the event to handle. The second parameter is an OracleRowUpdatingEventArgs object that contains the event information.

```
public delegate void OracleRowUpdatingEventHandler(object,
    OracleRowUpdatingEventArgs);
```

OracleLobOpenMode Enumeration

The OracleLobOpenMode enumeration indicates whether an OracleLob object should be opened in read-only mode or read-write mode.

OracleLobOpenMode enumeration:

ReadOnly	LOB is opened for read-only access.
ReadWrite	LOB is opened for read-write access.

OracleType Enumeration

The OracleType enumeration contains the data types that are used in the fields, properties, or parameters of the namespace objects. The following table shows the

OracleTypes mapped to the Oracle data types, the OracleClient object, and the .NET Framework data types.

OracleType enumeration:

OracleType	Oracle Data Type	OracleClient Object	.NET Framework Type
BFile	BFILE	OracleBFile	
Blob	BLOB	OracleLob	
Byte			Byte
Char	CHAR	OracleString	String
Clob	CLOB	OracleLob	
Cursor	REF_CURSOR		
DateTime	DATE	OracleDateTime	DateTime
Double		OracleNumber	Double
Float		OracleNumber	Single
Int16		OracleNumber	Int16
Int32		OracleNumber	Int32
IntervalDayToSecond	INTERVAL_DAY_TO_SECOND (Oracle9i or later)	OracleTimeSpan	TimeSpan
IntervalYearToMonth	INTERVAL_YEAR_TO_MONTH (Oracle9i or later)	OracleMonthSpan	Int32
LongRaw	LONGRAW	OracleBinary	Byte[]
LongVarChar	LONG	OracleString	String
NChar	NCHAR	OracleString	String
NClob	NCLOB	OracleLob	
Number	NUMBER	OracleNumber	Decimal
NVarChar	NVARCHAR2	OracleString	String
Raw	RAW	OracleBinary	Byte[]
RowId	ROWID	OracleString	String
SByte			SByte
TimeStamp	TIMESTAMP	OracleDateTime	DateTime
TimestampLocal	TIMESTAMP_WITH_LOCAL_TIMEZONE (Oracle9i or later)	OracleDateTime	DateTime
TimestampWithTZ	TIMESTAMP_WITH_TIMEZONE (Oracle9i or later)	OracleDateTime	DateTime
UInt16		OracleNumber	UInt16
UInt32		OracleNumber	UInt32
VarChar	VARCHAR2	OracleString	String

Appendix F

System.Data.SqlClient
Namespace Reference

System.Data.SqlClient Namespace

The System.Data.SqlClient namespace contains classes that comprise the SQL Server .NET data provider, which are a group of classes that are used to access a SQL Server data source.

SqlClientPermission Class   The SqlClientPermission class provides user security level setting for data access with the SQL Server data providers.

SqlClientPermissionAttribute Class   The SqlClientPermissionAttribute class relates a security action to a security permission attribute.

SqlCommand Class   The SqlCommand class represents a stored procedure or T-SQL statement to implement at a data source.

SqlCommandBuilder Class   The SqlCommandBuilder class allows for automatic generation of single table commands.

SqlConnection Class   The SqlConnection class represents a connection to a SQL Server data source.

SqlDataAdapter Class   The SqlDataAdapter class represents a database connection and a set of commands that are used to fill a DataSet and update a data source.

SqlDataReader Class   The SqlDataReader class allows for reading forward-only streams of data rows from a data source.

SQLDebugging Class   The SQLDebugging class supports the .NET infrastructure and is not used directly from your code.

SqlError Class   The SqlError class contains information regarding errors returned by the data source.

SqlErrorCollection Class   The SqlErrorCollection class contains a collection of SqlError objects.

SqlException Class   The SqlException class represents the exception that is thrown when an error is returned by the SQL Server data source.

SqlInfoMessageEventArgs Class   The SqlInfoMessageEventArgs class supplies information for the InfoMessage event.

SqlParameter Class   The SqlParameter class represents a parameter for the SqlCommand object. May also be used for the SqlCommand object's mapping to the DataSet column.

SqlParameterCollection Class   The SqlParameterCollection class is a collection of SqlParameter classes and their related mapping information for DataSet columns.

SqlRowUpdatedEventArgs Class   The SqlRowUpdatedEventArgs class supplies the information for the RowUpdated event.

SqlRowUpdatingEventArgs Class   The SqlRowUpdatingEventArgs class supplies the information for the RowUpdating event.

SqlTransaction Class   The SqlTransaction class represents a T-SQL transaction to implement at a data source.

SqlInfoMessageEventHandler Delegate   The SqlInfoMessageEventHandler delegate is the method that handles the InfoMessage event of the SqlConnection object.

SqlRowUpdatedEventHandler Delegate   The SqlRowUpdatedEventHandler delegate is the method that handles the RowUpdatedEvent of the SqlDataAdapter object.

SqlRowUpdatingEventHandler Delegate   The SqlRowUpdatingEventHandler delegate is the method that handles the RowUpdatingEvent of the SqlDataAdapter object.

SqlClientPermission Class

The SqlClientPermission class provides user security level setting to access n SQL Server data source with the SQL Server data provider.

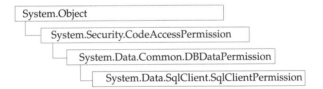

Constructor   Overloaded. Initializes a new instance of the SqlClientPermission class. The second constructor specifies whether a user should have all access or no access. The third constructor checks for all access or no access and whether a blank password is allowed.

Note   *The first constructor and the third constructor for this class are now obsolete.*

```
public SqlClientPermission();
public SqlClientPermission(
    System.Security.Permissions.PermissionState);
```

```
public SqlClientPermission(
    System.Security.Permissions.PermissionState,
    bool allowBlankPassword);
// C# example
System.Data.SqlClient.SqlClientPermission SqlP =
    new System.Data.SqlClient.SqlClientPermission();
System.Data.SqlClient.SqlClientPermission SqlP2 =
    new System.Data.SqlClient.SqlClientPermission(
    System.Security.Permissions.PermissionState.None);
System.Data.SqlClient.SqlClientPermission SqlP3 =
    new System.Data.SqlClient.SqlClientPermission(
    System.Security.Permissions.PermissionState.None, true);
```

System.Security.Permissions.PermissionState enumeration:

None   Indicates no access to the resource

Unrestricted   Indicates full access to the resource

SqlClientPermission Class Methods

Add Method   Adds to the state of the permission the specified access for the specified connection string.

```
public override void Add(string conn, string restrict,
    System.Data.KeyRestrictionBehavior);
```

System.Data.KeyRestrictionBehavior enumeration:

AllowOnly   Default. Only the connection string parameters that are
                identified are allowed.

PreventUsage   The connection string parameters that are identified are
                not allowed.

Copy Method   Returns a copy of the current security permission object, IPermission, with the same access to resources as the original object. The IPermission object describes the functions of the object.

```
public override System.Security.IPermission Copy();
```

Mutual Properties, Methods, Events Included in the SqlClientPermission Class

The following lists the mutual properties, methods, and events that are included in the SqlClientPermission class.

Inherited from DBDataPermission	Inherited from CodeAccessPermission	Inherited from Object
AllowBlankPassword property	Assert method	Equals method
Clear method	Demand method	Finalize method
CreateInstance method	Deny method	GetHashCode method
FromXml method	PermitOnly method	GetType method
Intersect method	ToString method	MemberwiseClone method
IsSubsetOf method		
IsUnrestricted method		
ToXml method		
Union method		

SqlClientPermissionAttribute Class

The SqlClientPermissionAttribute class relates a security action to a security permission attribute.

```
System.Object
    System.Attribute
        System.Security.Permissions.SecurityArrtibute
            System.Security.Permissions.CodeAccessSecurityAttribute
                System.Data.Common.DBDataPermissionAttribute
                    System.Data.SqlClient.SqlClientPermissionAttribute
```

Constructor   Initializes a new instance of the SqlClientPermissionAttribute class.

```
public SqlClientPermissionAttribute(
    System.Security.Permissions.SecurityAction);
// C# example
```

```
System.Data.SqlClient.SqlClientPermissionAttribute SqlPA =
    new System.Data.SqlClient.SqlClientPermissionAttribute(
    System.Security.Permissions.SecurityAction.LinkDemand);
```

System.Security.Permissions.SecurityAction enumeration:

Assert	Allows security to bypass code permission check
Demand	Performs security check for enforcing restrictions on calling code
Deny	Prevents access to the resource specified
InheritanceDemand	Checks for granted permissions for inherited class
LinkDemand	Checks for granted permission for immediate caller
PermitOnly	Allows access only to the resource specified
RequestMinimum	Requests the minimum permissions for code
RequestOptional	Requests the optional permissions
RequestRefuse	Request permissions not be granted to calling code

SqlClientPermission Class Methods

CreatePermission Method   Returns a SqlClientPermission object that contains the current attribute properties.

```
public override System.Security.IPermission CreatePermission();
```

Mutual Properties, Methods, Events Included in the SqlClientPermissionAttribute Class

The following lists the mutual properties, methods, and events that are included in the SqlClientPermissionAttribute class.

Inherited from Attribute	Inherited from Object
TypeId property	Equals method
GetHashCode method	Finalize method
IsDefaultAttribute method	GetType method
Match method	MemberwiseClone method
	ToString method

Inherited from SecurityAttribute	**Inherited from DBDataPermission**
Action property	AllowBlankPassword property
Unrestricted property	ConnectionString property
	KeyRestrictionBehavior property
	KeyRestrictions property

SqlCommand Class

The SqlCommand class represents a stored procedure or T-SQL statement to implement at a data source. A new instance of the SqlCommand will set the read/write properties to their initial values.

```
System.Object
    System.MarshalByRefObject
        System.ComponentModel.Component
            System.Data.SqlClient.SqlCommand
```

Constructor   Overloaded. Initializes a new instance of the SqlCommand class. The first constructor initializes all the fields to their default values. The second constructor specifies the text of a query to execute. The third constructor specifies the text of the query to execute through the specified SqlConnection. The fourth constructor specifies the text of the query to execute through the specified SqlConnection as reflected through the specified SqlTransaction object.

```
public SqlCommand();
public SqlCommand(string cmdText);
public SqlCommand(string cmdText, SqlConnection);
public SqlCommand(string cmdText, SqlConnection, SqlTransaction);
// C# example
System.Data.SqlClient.SqlCommand SqlCmd = new
    System.Data.SqlClient.SqlCommand();
System.Data.SqlClient.SqlCommand SqlCmd2 = new
    System.Data.SqlClient.SqlCommand("SELECT * FROM Customers");
System.Data.SqlClient.SqlConnection SqlConn = new
    System.Data.SqlClient.SqlConnection();
System.Data.SqlClient.SqlCommand SqlCmd3 = new
    System.Data.SqlClient.SqlCommand("SELECT * FROM Customers",
    SqlConn);
System.Data.SqlClient.SqlTransaction SqlTrans =
```

```
        SqlConn.BeginTransaction();
    System.Data.SqlClient.SqlCommand SqlCmd4 = new
        System.Data.SqlClient.SqlCommand("SELECT * FROM Customers",
        SqlConn, SqlTrans);
```

SqlCommand Class Properties

CommandText Property   Returns or sets the T-SQL statement query text or stored procedure to execute.

```
public string CommandText { get; set; }
```

CommandTimeout Property   Returns or sets the wait time in seconds before an attempted command is terminated and an error generated. Default wait time is 30 seconds.

```
public int CommandTimeout { get; set; }
```

CommandType Property   Designates what type of command this object is. The default CommandType is Text.

```
public System.Data.CommandType CommandType { get; set; }
```

System.Data.CommandType enumeration:

Text	Default; n SQL statement to execute
StoredProcedure	The name of a stored procedure to execute
TableDirect	The name of the table to be accessed

Connection Property   Returns or sets the SqlConnection object for this SqlCommand object.

```
public SqlConnection Connection { get; set; }
```

DesignTimeVisible Property   Returns or sets a Boolean value specifying whether the SqlCommand object should be visible. The default value is False.

```
public bool DesignTimeVisible { get; set; }
```

Parameters Property Returns the SqlParameterCollection, which designates the parameters for a stored procedure or T-SQL statement for this SqlCommand object.

```
public SqlParametersCollection Parameters { get; }
```

System.Data.IDbCommand.Connection Property The System.Data.IDbCommand.Connection property supports the .NET infrastructure and is not used directly from your code.

System.Data.IDbCommand.Parameters Property The System.Data.IDbCommand.Parameters property supports the .NET infrastructure and is not used directly from your code.

System.Data.IDbCommand.Transaction Property The System.Data.IDbCommand.Transaction property supports the .NET infrastructure and is not used directly from your code.

Transaction Property Returns or sets the SqlTransaction that the SqlCommand implements.

```
public SqlTransaction Transaction { get; set; }
```

UpdatedRowSource Property Returns or sets how the results of a command are applied to a DataSet when the Update method is used. If the command is automatically generated, the default result is None; otherwise the default result is Both.

```
public System.Data.UpdateRowSource UpdatedRowSource { get; set; }
```

System.Data.UpdateRowSource enumeration:

Both	The first returned row and the output parameters are mapped to the DataSet at the changed row.
FirstReturnedRecord	The first returned row is mapped to the DataSet at the changed row.
None	Returned results are ignored.
OutputParameters	The output parameters are mapped to the DataSet at the changed row.

SqlCommand Class Methods

Cancel Method   A cancellation of the execution of the SqlCommand is attempted. No exception is generated, even if the attempt to cancel the SqlCommand failed.

```
public void Cancel();
```

CreateParameter Method   Creates a new SqlParameter object.

```
public SqlParameter CreateParameter();
```

ExecuteNonQuery Method   Used for catalog operations or to execute an UPDATE, INSERT, or DELETE T-SQL statement to a database. Returns the number of affected rows.

```
public int ExecuteNonQuery();
```

ExecuteReader Method   Overloaded. Returns a SqlDataReader object after executing a SQL statement using the Connection object. The second method returns the SqlDataReader object based on the specified CommandBehavior.

```
public SqlDataReader ExecuteReader();
public SqlDataReader ExecuteReader(System.Data.CommandBehavior);
```

System.Data.CommandBehavior enumeration:

CloseConnection	The Connection object is closed when the DataReader object is closed.
Default	Sets no CommandBehavior flags. Same as using ExecuteReader().
KeyInfo	Returns column and primary key information.
SchemaOnly	Returns column information only. Database state not affected.
SequentialAccess	Enables the DataReader to return data as a stream. You need to use GetBytes or GetChars to start the reading of data at a specified location.
SingleResult	Returns a single resultset.
SingleRow	Returns a single row of data.

ExecuteScalar Method   Returns a single value represented in the first column of the first row of a resultset.

```
public object ExecuteScalar();
```

ExecuteXmlReader Method   Returns an XmlReader object after sending the CommandText to the Connection object.

```
public System.Xml.XmlReader ExecuteXmlReader();
```

ICloneable.Clone Method   The ICloneable.Clone method supports the .NET infrastructure and is not used directly from your code.

IDbCommand.CreateParameter Method   The IDbCommand.CreateParameter method supports the .NET infrastructure and is not used directly from your code.

IDbCommand.ExecuteReader Method   The IDbCommand.ExecuteReader method supports the .NET infrastructure and is not used directly from your code.

IDisposable.Dispose Method   The IDisposable.Dispose method supports the .NET infrastructure and is not used directly from your code.

Prepare Method   Creates a compiled version of this command object if the CommandType property is set to Text or StoredProcedure. You need to specify the data type of each parameter in the command statement before using the Prepare method. If the parameter has variable length data, you also need to specify the maximum Size of the data.

```
public void Prepare();
```

ResetCommandTimeout Method   Resets the CommandTimeout property to its default setting of 30 seconds.

```
public void ResetCommandTimeout();
```

Mutual Properties, Methods, Events Included in the SqlCommand Class

The following lists the mutual properties, methods, and events that are included in the SqlCommand class.

Inherited from Component	Inherited from Object	Inherited from MarshalByRefObject
Container property	Equals method	CreateObjRef method
DesignMode property	GetHashCode method	GetLifetimeService method

APPENDIXES

Inherited from Component	Inherited from Object	Inherited from MarshalByRefObject
Events property	GetType method	InitializeLifetimeService method
Site property	MemberwiseClone method	
Dispose method	ToString method	
Finalize method		
GetService method		
Disposed event		

SqlCommandBuilder Class

The SqlCommandBuilder class is used to automatically generate T-SQL statements for updates of single tables. A SqlDataAdapter object does not generate the required SQL statements automatically to synchronize the changes made to a DataSet with the data source, therefore a SqlCommandBuilder is needed to automatically generate the SQL statements and synchronize the data.

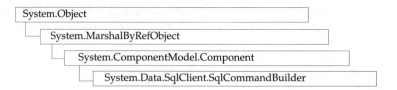

Constructor   Overloaded. Initializes a new instance of the SqlCommandBuilder class. The second constructor specifies the associated SqlDataAdapter. The SqlCommandBuilder object will register itself as a listener to the SqlDataAdapter's RowUpdating events.

```
public SqlCommandBuilder();
public SqlCommandBuilder(SqlDataAdapter);
// C# example
System.Data.SqlClient.SqlCommandBuilder SqlCmdBldr = new
    System.Data.SqlClient.SqlCommandBuilder();
System.Data.SqlClient.SqlDataAdapter SqlDA = new
    System.Data.SqlClient.SqlDataAdapter();
System.Data.SqlClient.SqlCommandBuilder SqlCmdBldr2 = new
    System.Data.SqlClient.SqlCommandBuilder(SqlDA);
```

SqlCommandBuilder Class Properties

DataAdapter Property   Returns or sets the SqlDataAdapter object that T-SQL statements are automatically generated for.

```
public SqlDataAdapter DataAdapter { get; set; }
```

QuotePrefix Property   Returns or sets the beginning character(s) to use as delimiters when database object names contain characters such as spaces and commas. The default value is an empty string.

```
public string QuotePrefix { get; set; }
```

QuoteSuffix Property   Returns or sets the ending character(s) to use as delimiters when database object names contain characters such as spaces and commas. The default value is an empty string.

```
public string QuoteSuffix { get; set; }
```

SqlCommandBuilder Class Methods

DeriveParameters Method   Fills the Parameters collection of the specified SqlCommand object with parameter information for the stored procedure of the specified SqlCommand object.

```
public static void DeriveParameters(SqlCommand);
```

Dispose Method   Overloaded. Overridden. Disposes the resources used by the SqlCommandBuilder. If the Boolean is set to True in the first method, it will dispose of both managed and unmanaged resources; False releases only unmanaged resources. The second method releases all the resources used by the object.

```
protected override void Dispose(bool);
public void Dispose();
```

GetDeleteCommand Method   Returns the automatically generated SqlCommand object for performing deletions.

```
public SqlCommand GetDeleteCommand();
```

GetInsertCommand Method   Returns the automatically generated SqlCommand object for performing inserts.

```
public SqlCommand GetInsertCommand();
```

GetUpdateCommand Method   Returns the automatically generated SqlCommand object for performing updates.

```
public SqlCommand GetUpdateCommand();
```

RefreshSchema Method   Refreshes the database schema information. Should be used when the SELECT statement of the SqlCommandBuilder object changes.

```
public void RefreshSchema();
```

Mutual Properties, Methods, Events Included in the SqlCommandBuilder Class

The following lists the mutual properties, methods, and events that are included in the SqlCommandBuilder class.

Inherited from Component	Inherited from Object	Inherited from MarshalByRefObject
Container property	Equals method	CreateObjRef method
DesignMode property	GetHashCode method	GetLifetimeService method
Events property	GetType method	InitializeLifetimeService method
Site property	MemberwiseClone method	
Dispose method	ToString method	
Finalize method		
GetService method		
Disposed event		

SqlConnection Class

The SqlConnection class represents a connection to a data source.

Note   *If a SqlConnection object goes out of scope, the object is not closed. You need to explicitly call Close or Dispose in order to close the open connection.*

```
System.Object
    System.MarshalByRefObject
        System.ComponentModel.Component
            System.Data.SqlClient.SqlConnection
```

Constructor   Overloaded. Initializes a new instance of the SqlConnection class. The first constructor initializes all the fields to their default values. The second constructor specifies the connection string to use to open the connection.

```
public SqlConnection();
public SqlConnection(string connString);
// C# example
System.Data.SqlClient.SqlConnection SqlConn = new
    System.Data.SqlClient.SqlConnection();
System.Data.SqlClient.SqlConnection SqlConn2 = new
    System.Data.SqlClient.SqlConnection("USER ID=sa;" +
    "PASSWORD=Lr710j;data source= localhost;" +
    "CONNECT TIMEOUT=30");
```

SqlConnection Class Properties

ConnectionString Property   Returns or sets the connection string that is used to open the connection to the data source.

```
public string ConnectionString { get; set; }
```

ConnectionTimeout Property   Returns wait time in seconds before an attempted connection is terminated and an error generated. Default wait time is 15 seconds.

```
public int ConnectionTimeout { get; }
```

Database Property   Returns the name of the database that will be used when a connection is opened. Default database name is an empty string.

```
public string Database { get; }
```

APPENDIXES

DataSource Property   Returns the location and the filename of the data source to use. The default value is an empty string.

```
public string DataSource { get; }
```

PacketSize Property   Returns the size (in bytes) of the network packets that are used to communicate with SQL Server. The default packet size is 8,192. The PacketSize value ranges from 512 to 32,767 bytes.

```
public int PacketSize { get; }
```

ServerVersion Property   Returns the version of the server that the client is connected to. The version string that is returned is in the form ##.##.#### (major version.minor version.release build).

```
public string ServerVersion { get; }
```

State Property   Returns the bitwise ConnectionState value of the connection. The default value is Closed.

```
public System.Data.ConnectionState State { get; }
```

System.Data.ConnectionState enumeration:

Broken	A previously opened connection is now broken.
Closed	The current connection is not open.
Connecting	The connection object is attempting to connect to the data source.
Executing	The connection object is currently executing a command.
Fetching	The connection object is currently fetching data.
Open	The current connection is open.

WorkstationId Property   Returns a string that identifies the database client. If the database client was not specified, then it will return the client computer name.

```
public string WorkstationId { get; }
```

SqlConnection Class Methods

BeginTransaction Method   Overloaded. Begins a transaction to the database and returns an object that represents that transaction. The second method specifies the

IsolationLevel for the transaction. The third method begins the specified transaction to the database and returns an object that represents the new transaction. The fourth method begins the specified transaction to the database using the specified IsolationLevel for the transaction.

```
public SqlTransaction BeginTransaction();
public SqlTransaction BeginTransaction(System.Data.IsolationLevel);
public SqlTransaction BeginTransaction(string trans);
public SqlTransaction BeginTransaction(System.Data.IsolationLevel,
    string trans);
```

System.Data.IsolationLevel enumeration:

Chaos	Cannot overwrite more highly isolated transactions that are pending.
ReadCommited	To avoid dirty reads, the shared locks are held during reading of data. May result in nonrepeatable read or phantom data is changed before the transaction ends.
ReadUncommited	No exclusive locks are allowed and no shared locks are done. May result in a dirty read.
RepeatableRead	Locks are placed on the queried data. May result in phantom rows.
Serializable	A range lock is placed on the rows in the DataSet.
Unspecified	The isolation level cannot be determined.

ChangeDatabase Method   Changes the database name for the open SqlConnection object. The database name parameter cannot be a blank string or null value. Throws an exception if the database name is not valid or the connection is not open.

```
public void ChangeDatabase(string databaseName);
```

Close Method   Closes the connection to the data source and rolls back any pending transactions. No exception is generated if an application calls Close more than once.

```
public void Close();
```

CreateCommand Method   Creates and returns a SqlCommand object.

```
public SqlCommand CreateCommand();
```

APPENDIXES

Dispose Method   Overloaded. Overridden. Disposes the resources used by the SqlConnection object. If the Boolean is set to True in the first method, it will dispose of both managed and unmanaged resources; False releases only unmanaged resources. The second method releases all the resources used by the object.

```
protected override void Dispose(bool);
public void Dispose();
```

EnlistDistributedTransaction Method   Registers the specified transaction as a distributed transaction.

```
public void EnlistDistributedTransaction(ITransaction);
```

ICloneable.Clone Method   The ICloneable.Clone method supports the .NET infrastructure and is not used directly from your code.

IDbConnection.BeginTransaction Method   The IDbConnection.BeginTransaction method supports the .NET infrastructure and is not used directly from your code.

IDbConnection.CreateCommand Method   The IDbConnection.CreateCommand method supports the .NET infrastructure and is not used directly from your code.

IDisposable.Dispose Method   The IDisposable.Dispose method supports the .NET infrastructure and is not used directly from your code.

Open Method   Opens a connection to a database from the connection pool. If a connection from the connection pool is not available, it will create a new connection to the data source.

```
public void Open();
```

SqlConnection Class Events

InfoMessage Event   Fires when the provider sends a warning or informational message to the event handler.

```
public event SqlInfoMessageEventHandler InfoMessage;
```

StateChange Event   Fires when the state of the connection changes.

```
public event StateChangeEventHandler StateChange;
```

Mutual Properties, Methods, Events Included in the SqlConnection Class

The following lists the mutual properties, methods, and events that are included in the SqlConnection class.

Inherited from Component	Inherited from Object	Inherited from MarshalByRefObject
Container property	Equals method	CreateObjRef method
DesignMode property	GetHashCode method	GetLifetimeService method
Events property	GetType method	InitializeLifetimeService method
Site property	MemberwiseClone method	
Dispose method	ToString method	
Finalize method		
GetService method		
Disposed event		

SqlDataAdapter Class

The SqlDataAdapter class represents a database connection and a set of commands that are used to fill a DataSet and update a data source. The SqlDataAdapter class uses the Fill method to fill the DataSet with information from the data source and the Update method to move changed information from the DataSet back to the data source.

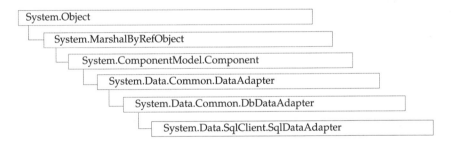

Constructor   Overloaded. Initializes a new instance of the SqlDataAdapter class. The first constructor creates a new object where all property values are set to their default values. The second constructor specifies a SELECT statement or stored procedure, SqlCommand, to use as the SelectCommand property. The third constructor specifies a string that is a SELECT statement or stored procedure and a SqlConnection to open and use. The fourth constructor specifies a string that is a SELECT statement or stored procedure and a connection string.

```
public SqlDataAdapter();
public SqlDataAdapter(SqlCommand);
public SqlDataAdapter(string selectCmdText, SqlConnection);
public SqlDataAdapter(string selectCmdText, string selectConnStr);
// C# example
System.Data.SqlClient.SqlDataAdapter SqlDA = new
    System.Data.SqlClient.SqlDataAdapter();
System.Data.SqlClient.SqlCommand SqlCmd = new
    System.Data.SqlClient.SqlCommand();
System.Data.SqlClient.SqlDataAdapter SqlDA2 = new
    System.Data.SqlClient.SqlDataAdapter(SqlCmd);
System.Data.SqlClient.SqlConnection SqlConn = new
    System.Data.SqlClient.SqlConnection();
System.Data.SqlClient.SqlDataAdapter SqlDA3 = new
    System.Data.SqlClient.SqlDataAdapter("SELECT * FROM Customers",
    SqlConn);
System.Data.SqlClient.SqlDataAdapter SqlDA4 = new
    System.Data.SqlClient.SqlDataAdapter("SELECT * FROM Customers",
    "DATA SOURCE=localhost;INTEGRATED SECURITY=SSPI;
    CONNECT TIMEOUT=30");
```

SqlDataAdapter Class Properties

DeleteCommand Property   Returns or sets the SQL statement or stored procedure used for deleting records from the data source.

```
public new SqlCommand DeleteCommand { get; set; }
```

InsertCommand Property   Returns or sets the SQL statement or stored procedure used for inserting records into the data source.

```
public new SqlCommand InsertCommand { get; set; }
```

SelectCommand Property   Returns or sets the SQL statement or stored procedure used for selecting records from the data source.

```
public new SqlCommand SelectCommand { get; set; }
```

UpdateCommand Property   Returns or sets the SQL statement or stored procedure used for updating records in the data source.

```
public new SqlCommand UpdateCommand { get; set; }
```

System.Data.IDbDataAdapter.DeleteCommand Method   The System.Data .IDbDataAdapter.DeleteCommand method supports the .NET infrastructure and is not used directly from your code.

System.Data.IDbDataAdapter.InsertCommand Method   The System.Data .IDbDataAdapter.InsertCommand method supports the .NET infrastructure and is not used directly from your code.

System.Data.IDbDataAdapter.SelectCommand Method   The System.Data .IDbDataAdapter.SelectCommand method supports the .NET infrastructure and is not used directly from your code.

System.Data.IDbDataAdapter.UpdateCommand Method   The System.Data .IDbDataAdapter.UpdateCommand method supports the .NET infrastructure and is not used directly from your code.

SqlDataAdapter Class Methods

CreateRowUpdatedEvent Method   Overrides System.Data.Common .DbDataAdapter.CreateRowUpdatedEvent. Returns a new instance of the RowUpdatedEventArgs class. The first parameter of the CreateRowUpdatedEvent method is the DataRow that is used to update the data source. The second parameter, IDbCommand, represents the SQL statement that is executed during the update and the third parameter, StatementType, specifies whether the command is a SELECT, INSERT, UPDATE, or DELETE statement. The fourth parameter is the DataTableMapping object.

```
protected override RowUpdatedEventArgs CreateRowUpdatedEvent(
    System.Data.DataRow, System.Data.IDbCommand,
    System.Data.StatementType, System.Data.Common.DataTableMapping);
```

CreateRowUpdatingEvent Method   Overrides System.Data.Common .DbDataAdapter.CreateRowUpdatingEvent. Returns a new instance of the RowUpdatingEventArgs class. The first parameter of the CreateRowUpdatingEvent method is the DataRow that is used to update the data source. The second parameter, IDbCommand, represents the SQL statement that is executed during the Update, and the third parameter, StatementType, specifies whether the command is a SELECT, INSERT, UPDATE, or DELETE statement. The fourth parameter is the DataTableMapping object.

```
protected override RowUpdatingEventArgs CreateRowUpdatingEvent(
    System.Data.DataRow, System.Data.IDbCommand,
    System.Data.StatementType,
    System.Data.Common.DataTableMapping);
```

Dispose Method   Overloaded. Overridden. Disposes the resources used by the DataAdapter. If the Boolean is set to True in the first overloaded method, it will dispose of both managed and unmanaged resources.

```
protected override void Dispose(bool);
public virtual void Dispose();
```

ICloneable.Clone Method   The ICloneable.Clone method supports the .NET infrastructure and is not used directly from your code.

```
object ICloneable.Clone();
```

OnRowUpdated Method   Raises the RowUpdated event. The RowUpdatedEventArgs parameter contains the event data that is raised.

```
protected override void OnRowUpdated(RowUpdatedEventArgs);
```

OnRowUpdating Method   Raises the RowUpdating event. The RowUpdatingEventArgs parameter contains the event data that is raised.

```
protected override void OnRowUpdating(RowUpdatingEventArgs);
```

SqlDataAdapter Class Events

RowUpdated Event   Fires after an Update command is executed against a data source.

```
public event SqlRowUpdatedEventHandler RowUpdated;
```

RowUpdating Event   Fires before an Update command is executed against a data source.

```
public event SqlRowUpdatingEventHandler RowUpdating;
```

Mutual Properties, Methods, Events Included in the SqlDataAdapter Class

The following lists the mutual properties, methods, and events that are included in the SqlDataAdapter class.

Inherited from Component	**Inherited from Object**	**Inherited from MarshalByRefObject**
Container property	Equals method	CreateObjRef method
DesignMode property	GetHashCode method	GetLifetimeService method
Events property	GetType method	InitializeLifetimeService method
Site property	MemberwiseClone method	
Dispose method	ToString method	
Finalize method		
GetService method		
Disposed event		

Inherited from DataAdapter	**Inherited from DbDataAdapter**
AcceptChangesDuringFill property	Fill method
ContinueUpdateOnError property	FillSchema method
MissingMappingAction property	GetFillParameters method
MissingSchemaAction property	OnFillError method
TableMappings property	Update method
CloneInternals method	FillError Event
CreateTableMappings method	
ShouldSerializeTableMappings method	

SqlDataReader Class

The SqlDataReader class allows for reading forward-only streams of data rows from a data source. You do not create a SqlDataReader by calling a constructor, but rather by calling the ExecuteReader method of a SqlCommand object. The SqlConnection object that is associated with the SqlDataReader is used exclusively by the SqlDataReader, therefore only the Close operation may be performed on the SqlConnection.

SqlDataReader Class Properties

Depth Property   Returns an integer designating the depth of the current row's nesting.

```
public int Depth { get; }
```

FieldCount Property   Returns the number of columns (or fields) in the current row. Default FieldCount is –1.

```
public int FieldCount { get; }
```

HasRows Property   Returns a Boolean designating whether the SqlDataReader contains rows. True if the data reader has rows, False if it does not.

```
public bool HasRows { get; }
```

IsClosed Property   Returns a Boolean designating whether the SqlDataReader is opened or closed. True if the data reader is closed, False if it is open.

```
public bool IsClosed { get; }
```

Item Property   Overloaded. Returns the object found at the specified column ordinal or string column name.

```
public object this[int index] { get; }
public object this[string colName] {get; }
```

RecordsAffected Property   Returns the number of rows affected by a changed, inserted, or deleted action.

```
public int RecordsAffected { get; }
```

SqlDataReader Class Methods

Close Method   Closes an open SqlDataReader object.

```
public virtual void Close();
```

GetBoolean Method   Returns the value in the specified zero-based column ordinal as a Boolean. The data to be retrieved must already be in the form of a Boolean or an exception is generated. Call IsNull before calling this method.

```
public virtual bool GetBoolean(int colOrdinal);
```

GetByte Method   Returns the value in the specified zero-based column ordinal as a byte. The data to be retrieved must already be in the form of a byte or an exception is generated. Call IsNull before calling this method.

```
public virtual bool GetByte(int colOrdinal);
```

GetBytes Method   Reads a stream of bytes from the specified zero-based column ordinal starting at the specified column offset. The bytes are placed into the specified byte buffer starting at the specified byte buffer offset for a length of the specified buffer length. Returns the actual number of bytes that were read. The data to be retrieved must already be in the form of a byte array or an exception is generated.

```
public virtual long GetBytes(int colOrdinal, long colOffset, byte[] buffer,
    int bufferOffset, int bufferLength);
```

GetChar Method   Returns the value in the specified zero-based column ordinal as a character. The data to be retrieved must already be in the form of a character or an exception is generated. Call IsNull before calling this method.

```
public virtual char GetChar(int colOrdinal);
```

GetChars Method   Reads a stream of characters from the specified zero-based column ordinal starting at the specified column offset. The characters are placed into the specified character buffer starting at the specified character buffer offset for a length of the specified buffer length. Returns the actual number of characters that were read. The data to be retrieved must already be in the form of a character array or an exception is generated.

```
public virtual long GetChars(int colOrdinal, long colOffset,
    char[] buffer, int bufferOffset, int bufferLength);
```

GetData Method   The GetData method supports the .NET infrastructure and is not used directly from your code.

GetDataTypeName Method Returns the name of the data type in the specified zero-based column ordinal as a string.

```
public virtual string GetDataTypeName(int colOrdinal);
```

GetDateTime Method Returns the value in the specified zero-based column ordinal as a DateTime object. The data to be retrieved must already be in the form of a DateTime object or an exception is generated. Call IsNull before calling this method.

```
public virtual DateTime GetDateTime(int colOrdinal);
```

GetDecimal Method Returns the value in the specified zero-based column ordinal as a decimal. The data to be retrieved must already be in the form of a decimal or an exception is generated. Call IsNull before calling this method.

```
public virtual decimal GetDecimal(int colOrdinal);
```

GetDouble Method Returns the value in the specified zero-based column ordinal as a double-precision floating point number. The data to be retrieved must already be in the form of a double or an exception is generated. Call IsNull before calling this method.

```
public virtual double GetDouble(int colOrdinal);
```

GetFieldType Method Returns the data type of the object in the specified zero-based column ordinal.

```
public virtual Type GetFieldType(int colOrdinal);
```

GetFloat Method Returns the value in the specified zero-based column ordinal as a single-precision floating point number. The data to be retrieved must already be in the form of a float or an exception is generated. Call IsNull before calling this method.

```
public virtual float GetFloat(int colOrdinal);
```

GetGuid Method Returns the value in the specified zero-based column ordinal as a globally unique identifier (GUID). The data to be retrieved must already be in the form of a Guid or an exception is generated. Call IsNull before calling this method.

```
public virtual Guid GetGuid(int colOrdinal);
```

GetInt16 Method   Returns the value in the specified zero-based column ordinal as a 16-bit signed integer. The data to be retrieved must already be in the form of a short or an exception is generated. Call IsNull before calling this method.

```
public virtual short GetInt16(int colOrdinal);
```

GetInt32 Method   Returns the value in the specified zero-based column ordinal as a 32-bit signed integer. The data to be retrieved must already be in the form of an integer or an exception is generated. Call IsNull before calling this method.

```
public virtual int GetInt32(int colOrdinal);
```

GetInt64 Method   Returns the value in the specified zero-based column ordinal as a 64-bit signed integer. The data to be retrieved must already be in the form of a long or an exception is generated. Call IsNull before calling this method.

```
public virtual long GetInt64(int colOrdinal);
```

GetName Method   Returns the name of the column in the specified zero-based column ordinal as a string.

```
public virtual string GetName(int colOrdinal);
```

GetOrdinal Method   Returns the zero-based column ordinal value of the specified column name.

```
public virtual int GetOrdinal(string colName);
```

GetSchemaTable Method   Returns a DataTable object that contains the metadata for the columns in the current SqlDataReader object.

```
public virtual System.Data.DataTable GetSchemaTable();
```

GetSqlBinary Method   Returns the value in the specified zero-based column ordinal as a SqlBinary. The data to be retrieved must already be in the form of a binary structure or an exception is generated.

```
public SqlBinary GetSqlBinary(int colOrdinal);
```

GetSqlBoolean Method   Returns the value in the specified zero-based column ordinal as a SqlBoolean. The data to be retrieved must already be in the form of a Boolean or an exception is generated.

```
public SqlBoolean GetSqlBoolean(int colOrdinal);
```

GetSqlByte Method   Returns the value in the specified zero-based column ordinal as a SqlByte. The data to be retrieved must already be in the form of a byte or an exception is generated.

```
public SqlByte GetSqlByte(int colOrdinal);
```

GetSqlDateTime Method   Returns the value in the specified zero-based column ordinal as a SqlDateTime object. The data to be retrieved must already be in the form of a DateTime object or an exception is generated.

```
public SqlDateTime GetSqlDateTime(int colOrdinal);
```

GetSqlDecimal Method   Returns the value in the specified zero-based column ordinal as a SqlDecimal. The data to be retrieved must already be in the form of a decimal or an exception is generated.

```
public SqlDecimal GetSqlDecimal(int colOrdinal);
```

GetSqlDouble Method   Returns the value in the specified zero-based column ordinal as a SqlDouble. The data to be retrieved must already be in the form of a double-precision floating point or an exception is generated.

```
public SqlDouble GetSqlDouble(int colOrdinal);
```

GetSqlGuid Method   Returns the value in the specified zero-based column ordinal as a SqlGuid. The data to be retrieved must already be in the form of a globally unique identifier (GUID) or an exception is generated.

```
public SqlGuid GetSqlGuid(int colOrdinal);
```

GetSqlInt16 Method   Returns the value in the specified zero-based column ordinal as a SqlInt16. The data to be retrieved must already be in the form of a 16-bit signed integer or an exception is generated.

```
public SqlInt16 GetSqlInt16(int colOrdinal);
```

GetSqlInt32 Method   Returns the value in the specified zero-based column ordinal as a SqlInt32. The data to be retrieved must already be in the form of a 32-bit signed integer or an exception is generated.

```
public SqlInt32 GetSqlInt32(int colOrdinal);
```

GetSqlInt64 Method   Returns the value in the specified zero-based column ordinal as a SqlInt64. The data to be retrieved must already be in the form of a 64-bit signed integer or an exception is generated.

```
public SqlInt64 GetSqlInt64(int colOrdinal);
```

GetSqlMoney Method   Returns the value in the specified zero-based column ordinal as a SqlMoney. The data to be retrieved must already be in the form of a decimal or an exception is generated.

```
public SqlMoney GetSqlMoney(int colOrdinal);
```

GetSqlSingle Method   Returns the value in the specified zero-based column ordinal as a SqlSingle. The data to be retrieved must already be in the form of a single-precision floating point or an exception is generated.

```
public SqlSingle GetSqlSingle(int colOrdinal);
```

GetSqlString Method   Returns the value in the specified zero-based column ordinal as a SqlString. The data to be retrieved must already be in the form of a string or an exception is generated.

```
public SqlString GetSqlString(int colOrdinal);
```

GetSqlValue Method   Returns the value in the specified zero-based column ordinal in its native SQL Server form. The returned object contains a System.Data.SqlDbType variant.

```
public object GetSqlValue(int colOrdinal);
```

GetSqlValues Method   Fills the specified object array with the column attributes of the current row. Returns the number of objects in the object array.

```
public int GetSqlValues(object[] cols);
```

GetString Method   Returns the value in the specified zero-based column ordinal as a string. The data to be retrieved must already be in the form of a string or an exception is generated. Call IsNull before calling this method.

```
public virtual string GetString(int colOrdinal);
```

GetValue Method   Returns the value in the specified zero-based column ordinal in its native form.

```
public virtual object GetValue(int colOrdinal);
```

GetValues Method   Fills the specified object array with the column attributes of the current row. Returns the number of objects in the object array.

```
public virtual int GetValues(object[] cols);
```

IDisposable.Dispose Method   The IDisposable.Dispose method supports the .NET infrastructure and is not used directly from your code.

IEnumerator.GetEnumerator Method   The IEnumerator.GetEnumerator method supports the .NET infrastructure and is not used directly from your code.

IsDBNull Method   Returns a Boolean indicating whether the value in the specified zero-based column ordinal exists. True if the value is DBNull, else False.

```
public virtual bool IsDBNull(int colOrdinal);
```

NextResult Method   Moves to the next resultset. Used when multiple resultsets were generated by a batch SQL statement. Returns True if there are more resultsets, else False.

```
public virtual bool NextResult();
```

Read Method   Moves to the next record in the SqlDataReader object. Default position is prior to the first record, so use Read to begin processing data. Returns True if there are more rows, else False.

```
public virtual bool Read();
```

Mutual Properties, Methods, Events Included in the SqlDataReader Class

The following lists the mutual properties, methods, and events that are included in the SqlDataReader class.

Inherited from Object	Inherited from MarshalByRefObject
Equals method	CreateObjRef method
Finalize method	GetLifetimeService method
GetHashCode method	InitializeLifetimeService method
GetType method	
MemberwiseClone method	
ToString method	

SQLDebugging Class

The SQLDebugging class supports the .NET infrastructure and is not used directly from your code.

SqlError Class

The SqlError class contains information regarding errors returned by the data source. You do not create a SqlError instance by calling a constructor. The creation and management of the SqlError class is done by the SqlErrorCollection class.

```
System.Object
    System.Data.SqlClient.SqlError
```

SqlError Class Properties

Class Property   Contains a byte value from 1 to 25 indicating an error severity level. Default value is 0.

```
public byte Class { get; }
```

LineNumber Property   Contains the one-based line number of the stored procedure or T-SQL statement of the error.

```
public int LineNumber { get; }
```

Message Property   Contains a brief description of the error.

```
public string Message { get; }
```

Number Property   Contains a number identifier of the error.

```
public int Number { get; }
```

Procedure Property   Contains the name of the RPC or stored procedure that produced the error.

```
public string Procedure { get; }
```

Server Property   Contains the name of the SQL Server that produced the error.

```
public string Server { get; }
```

Source Property   Contains the name of the data provider that produced the error.

```
public string Source { get; }
```

State Property   Contains numeric code from SQL Server that identifies the error.

```
public byte State { get; }
```

SqlError Class Methods

ToString Method   Returns the full text of the error.

```
public override string ToString();
```

Mutual Properties, Methods, Events Included in the SqlError Class

The following lists the mutual properties, methods, and events that are included in the SqlError class.

Inherited from Object

Equals method

Finalize method

Inherited from Object

GetHashCode method

GetType method

MemberwiseClone method

SqlErrorCollection Class

The SqlErrorCollection class contains a collection of SqlError objects. You do not create a SqlErrorCollection by calling a constructor. The SqlErrorCollection is created by the SqlException class and will always contain at least one instance of the SqlError class.

```
System.Object
    System.Data.SqlClient.SqlErrorCollection
```

SqlErrorCollection Class Properties

Count Property   Returns the number of items in this collection.

```
public int Count { get; }
```

Item Property   Returns the SqlError object found at the specified zero-based index.

```
public SqlError this[int index] { get; }
```

System.Collections.ICollection.IsSynchronized Property   Contains a Boolean indicating whether the data source and the collection are synchronized.

```
bool ICollection.IsSynchronized { get; }
```

System.Collections.ICollection.SyncRoot Property   Returns an object that is used to synchronize the collection.

```
object ICollection.SyncRoot { get; }
```

SqlErrorCollection Class Methods

CopyTo Method   Copies the objects in the SqlErrorCollection to the specified array and sets the starting index of the array to the specified integer.

```
public void CopyTo(Array arr, int index);
```

GetEnumerator Method   The GetEnumerator method supports the .NET infrastructure and is not used directly from your code.

Mutual Properties, Methods, Events Included in the SqlErrorCollection Class

The following lists the mutual properties, methods, and events that are included in the SqlErrorCollection class.

Inherited from Object

Equals method

Finalize method

GetHashCode method

GetType method

MemberwiseClone method

ToString method

SqlException Class

The SqlException class represents the exception that is thrown when an error is returned by the SQL Server data source. You do not create a SqlException by calling a constructor. The SqlException is created when the SQL Server data provider encounters an error created by the server.

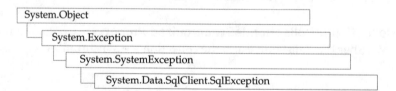

```
System.Object

   System.Exception

      System.SystemException

         System.Data.SqlClient.SqlException
```

SqlException Class Properties

Class Property   Contains a byte value from 1 to 25 indicating an error severity level. Default value is 0.

```
public byte Class { get; }
```

Errors Property   Contains the SqlErrorCollection object.

```
public SqlErrorCollection Errors { get; }
```

LineNumber Property   Contains the one-based line number of the stored procedure or T-SQL statement of the error.

```
public int LineNumber { get; }
```

Message Property   Contains a brief description of the error.

```
public override string Message { get; }
```

Number Property   Contains a number identifier of the error.

```
public int Number { get; }
```

Procedure Property   Contains the name of the RPC or stored procedure that produced the error.

```
public string Procedure { get; }
```

Server Property   Contains the name of the SQL Server that produced the error.

```
public string Server { get; }
```

Source Property   Contains the name of the data provider that produced the error.

```
public override string Source { get; }
```

State Property   Contains numeric code from SQL Server that identifies the error.

```
public byte State { get; }
```

SqlException Class Methods

GetObjectData Method   Overrides the Exception.GetObjectData, which sets the SerializationInfo with information about the error. The StreamingContext contains the source and destination for the serialization information.

```
public override void GetObjectData(
    System.Runtime.Serialization.SerializationInfo sInfo,
    System.Runtime.Serialization.StreamingContext sContext);
```

Mutual Properties, Methods, Events Included in the SqlException Class

The following lists the mutual properties, methods, and events that are included in the SqlException class.

Inherited from Exception	Inherited from Object
HelpLink property	Equals method
HResult property	Finalize method
InnerException property	GetHashCode method
StackTrace property	GetType method
TargetSite property	MemberwiseClone method
GetBaseException method	
ToString method	

SqlInfoMessageEventArgs Class

The SqlInfoMessageEventArgs class supplies information for the InfoMessage event. You do not create a SqlInfoMessageEventArgs by calling a constructor, but it is a parameter of the SqlInfoMessageEventHandler.

```
System.Object
    System.EventArgs
        System.Data.SqlClient.SqlInfoMessageEventArgs
```

SqlInfoMessageEventArgs Class Properties

Errors Property   Contains the SqlErrorCollection sent from the data source.

```
public SqlErrorCollection Errors { get; }
```

Message Property   Contains the text description for the error sent from the data source.

```
public string Message { get; }
```

Source Property   Contains the name of the object that produced the error.

```
public string Source { get; }
```

SqlInfoMessageEventArgs Class Methods

ToString Method   Returns the InfoMessage event text.

```
public override string ToString();
```

Mutual Properties, Methods, Events Included in the SqlInfoMessageEventArgs Class

The following lists the mutual properties, methods, and events that are included in the SqlInfoMessageEventArgs class.

Inherited from Object

Equals method

Finalize method

GetHashCode method

GetType method

MemberwiseClone method

SqlParameter Class

The SqlParameter class is a parameter for the SqlCommand object. May also be used for the SqlCommand object's mapping to the DataSet column. The parameters for the SqlCommand class are not case sensitive.

```
System.Object
     System.MarshalByRefObject
          System.Data.SqlClient.SqlParameter
```

Constructor   Overloaded. Initializes a new instance of the SqlParameter class. The first constructor creates a new object using the default property values. The second constructor specifies the parameter name and value type. The third constructor specifies the parameter name and data type. The fourth constructor specifies the parameter name, data type, and parameter size. The fifth constructor specifies the parameter name, data type, parameter size, and source column name. The sixth constructor sets all of the properties of the SqlParameter object at the time it is created with the specified values.

```
public SqlParameter();
public SqlParameter(string parmName, object parmValue);
public SqlParameter(string parmName, SqlType parmType);
```

```
public SqlParameter(string parmName, SqlType parmType,
    int parmSize);
public SqlParameter(string parmName, SqlType parmType,
    int parmSize, string srcColumn);
public SqlParameter(string parmName, SqlType parmType,
    int parmSize, ParameterDirection parmDir, bool isNullable,
    byte parmPrecision, byte parmScale, string srcColumn,
    DataRowVersion srcVersion, object parmValue);
// C# example
System.Data.SqlClient.SqlParameter SqlParm = new
    System.Data.SqlClient.SqlParameter();
System.Data.SqlClient.SqlParameter SqlParm2 = new
    System.Data.SqlClient.SqlParameter("@CustomerName", SqlParm);
System.Data.SqlClient.SqlParameter SqlParm3 = new
    System.Data.SqlClient.SqlParameter("@CustomerName",
    System.Data.SqlClient.SqlType.VarChar);
System.Data.SqlClient.SqlParameter SqlParm4 = new
    System.Data.SqlClient.SqlParameter("@CustomerName",
    System.Data.SqlClient.SqlType.VarChar, 25);
System.Data.SqlClient.SqlParameter SqlParm5 = new
    System.Data.SqlClient.SqlParameter("@CustomerName",
    System.Data.SqlClient.SqlType.VarChar, 25, "CustName");
System.Data.SqlClient.SqlParameter SqlParm6 = new
    System.Data.SqlClient.SqlParameter("@CustomerName",
    System.Data.SqlClient.SqlType.VarChar, 25,
    System.Data.ParameterDirection.Input, true, 0, 0, "CustName",
    System.Data.DataRowVersion.Current, SqlParm);
```

SqlParameter Class Properties

DbType Property   Returns or sets the DbType for the parameter. Default DbType is string.

```
public System.Data.DbType DbType { get; set; }
```

System.Data.DbType enumeration:

AnsiString	Variable length stream of 1 to 8,000 characters Non-Unicode
AnsiStringFixedLength	Fixed length stream of characters. Non-Unicode
Binary	Variable length stream of binary data. 1 to 8,000 bytes
Boolean	Values of True or False

System.Data.DbType enumeration:

Byte	8-bit unsigned integer. Value range 0 to 255.
Currency	Value range −922,337,203,685,477.5808 to 922,337,203,685,477.5807. Accuracy to ten-thousandth of unit.
Date	Value range January 1, 1753 to December 31, 9999. Accuracy to 3.33 milliseconds.
DateTime	Represents date and time values.
Decimal	Value range 1.0×10^{-28} to approx 7.9×10^{28}. Significant digits of 28 to 29.
Double	Floating point type. Value range approx 5.0×10^{-324} to 1.7×10^{308} Precision of 15 to 16 digits.
Guid	Globally unique identifier.
Int16	Signed 16-bit integer. Value range −32,768 to 32,767.
Int32	Signed 32-bit integer. Value range −2,147,483,648 to 2,147,483,647.
Int64	Signed 64-bit integer. Value range −9,223,372,036,854,775,808 to 9,223,372,036,854,775,807.
Object	General type.
SByte	Signed 8-bit integer. Value range −128 to 127.
Single	Floating point type. Value range approx 1.5×10^{-45} to 3.4×10^{38} Precision of 7 digits.
String	String of characters. Unicode.
StringFixedLength	Fixed length stream of characters. Unicode.
Time	Value range January 1, 1753 to December 31, 9999. Accuracy to 3.33 milliseconds.
Uint16	Unsigned 16-bit integer. Value range 0 to 65,535.
Uint32	Unsigned 32-bit integer. Value range 0 to 4,294,967,295.
Uint64	Unsigned 64-bit integer. Value range 0 to 18,446,744,073,709,551,615.

APPENDIXES

Direction Property   Returns or sets the directional aspect of the parameter.

```
public System.Data.ParameterDirection Direction { get; set; }
```

System.Data.ParameterDirection enumeration:

Input	Parameter is input only.
InputOutput	Parameter is both input and output.
Output	Parameter is output only.
ReturnValue	Parameter is a return value from an operation like a stored procedure.

IsNullable Property   Returns or sets a Boolean indicating whether the parameter accepts null values. True indicates nulls are accepted. The default value is False.

```
public bool IsNullable { get; set; }
```

Offset Property   Returns or sets the number of bytes for binary parameter types or the number characters for string types. The default value is 0.

```
public int Offset { get; set; }
```

ParameterName Property   Returns or sets the name of the SqlParameter. The default value is an empty string.

```
public string Parameter { get; set; }
```

Precision Property   Returns or sets the maximum number if digits to use. The default value is 0.

```
public byte Precision { get; set; }
```

Scale Property   Returns or sets the number of decimal places to use. The default value is 0.

```
public byte Scale { get; set; }
```

Size Property   Returns or sets the maximum bytes of data for the column. Used for binary and string column types. The default value is derived from the parameter type.

```
public int Size { get; set; }
```

SourceColumn Property Returns or sets the name of the source column that is mapped to the DataSet. The default value is an empty string.

```
public string SourceColumn { get; set; }
```

SourceVersion Property Returns or sets the DataRowVersion to use. The default value is Current.

```
public System.Data.DataRowVersion SourceVersion { get; set; }
```

System.Data.DataRowVersion enumeration:

Current	Row contains current values.
Default	Row is versioned according to the DataRowState.
Original	Row contains its original values.
Proposed	Row contains proposed values.

SqlDbType Property Returns or sets the SqlDbType for the parameter. Setting the DbType property changes the SqlDbType property to the corresponding data type. The default SqlDbType is n VarChar.

```
public SqlDbType SqlDbType { get; set; }
```

Value Property Returns or sets the value of the parameter. The default value is null.

```
public object Value { get; set; }
```

SqlParameter Class Methods

ICloneable.Clone Method The ICloneable.Clone method supports the .NET infrastructure and is not used directly from your code.

ToString Method Returns the ParameterName in a string.

```
public override string ToString();
```

Mutual Properties, Methods, Events Included in the SqlParameter Class

The following lists the mutual properties, methods, and events that are included in the SqlParameter class.

Inherited from Object	Inherited from MarshalByRefObject
Equals method	CreateObjRef method
Finalize method	GetLifetimeService method
GetHashCode method	InitializeLifetimeService method
GetType method	
MemberwiseClone method	

SqlParameterCollection Class

The SqlParameterCollection class is a collection of SqlParameter objects and their related mapping information for DataSet columns. You do not create a SqlParameterCollection by calling a constructor, but rather it is accessed through the SqlCommand object.

```
System.Object
    System.MarshalByRefObject
        System.Data.SqlClient.SqlParameterCollection
```

SqlParameterCollection Class Properties

Count Property   Returns the number of items in this collection.

```
public int Count { get; }
```

Item Property   Overloaded. Returns or sets the SqlParameter object found at the specified integer index or string parameter name.

```
public SqlParameter this[int index] { get; set; }
public SqlParameter this[string parmName] {get; set; }
```

System.Collections.ICollection.IsSynchronized Property   The System.Collections.ICollection.IsSynchronized property supports the .NET infrastructure and is not used directly from your code.

System.Collections.ICollection.SyncRoot Property   The System.Collections .ICollection.SyncRoot property supports the .NET infrastructure and is not used directly from your code.

System.Collections.IList.IsFixedSize Property   The System.Collections.IList .IsFixedSize property supports the .NET infrastructure and is not used directly from your code.

System.Collections.IList.IsReadOnly Property   The System.Collections.IList .IsReadOnly property supports the .NET infrastructure and is not used directly from your code.

System.Collections.IList.Item Property   Implements the System.Collections.IList .Item interface to return or set the item at the specified location in the collection.

```
object IList.this[int index] { get; set; }
```

System.Data.IDataParameterCollection.Item Property   Returns or sets the indexer for the SqlParameterCollection.

```
object IDataParameterCollection.this[int index] { get; set; }
```

SqlParameterCollection Class Methods

Add Method   Overloaded. The first Add method adds the specified object to the SqlParameterCollection and returns the index of the added object. The second Add method adds the specified SqlParameter to the SqlCommand object and returns the added SqlParameter. The third Add method adds the specified object to the SqlParameterCollection using the specified parameter name and returns the added SqlParameter. The fourth Add method adds a SqlParameter to the SqlParameterCollection using the specified parameter name and data type and returns the added SqlParameter. The fifth Add method adds a SqlParameter to the SqlParameterCollection using the specified parameter name, data type, and parameter size and returns the added SqlParameter. The sixth Add method adds a SqlParameter to the SqlParameterCollection using the specified parameter name, data type, parameter size, and column source name and returns the added SqlParameter.

```
public int Add(object);
public SqlParameter Add(SqlParameter);
public SqlParameter Add(string parmName, object);
public SqlParameter Add(string parmName, SqlDbType);
```

```
public SqlParameter Add(string parmName, SqlDbType, int parmSize);
public SqlParameter Add(string parmName, SqlDbType, int parmSize,
    string sourceColumn);
```

Clear Method   Removes all the items from the SqlParameterCollection.

```
public void Clear();
```

Contains Method   Overloaded. The first Contains method returns True if the SqlParameterCollection contains the specified Object. The second Contains method returns True if the collection contains a SqlParameter object with the specified parameter name.

```
public bool Contains(Object);
public bool Contains(string parmName);
```

CopyTo Method   Copies the objects in the SqlParameterCollection to the specified array and sets the starting index of the array to the specified integer.

```
public void CopyTo(array, int);
```

GetEnumerator Method   The GetEnumerator method supports the .NET infrastructure and is not used directly from your code.

IndexOf Method   Overloaded. The first IndexOf method returns the location of the specified Object of type SqlParameter within the SqlParameterCollection. The second IndexOf method returns the location of the SqlParameter object with the specified parameter name.

```
public int IndexOf(Object);
public int IndexOf(string parmName);
```

Insert Method   Inserts a SqlParameter object into the SqlParameterCollection at the specified zero-based integer index.

```
public void Insert(int, object);
```

Remove Method   Removes an object that is of type SqlParameter from the SqlParameterCollection. Throws a SystemException if the specified object is not of type SqlParameter or the specified object does not exist in the collection.

```
public void Remove(object);
```

RemoveAt Method   Overloaded. The first RemoveAt method removes the SqlParameter object from the SqlParameterCollection at the specified zero-based integer index. The second RemoveAt method removes the SqlParameter object from the collection that matches the specified parameter name. Both methods throw an exception if the SqlParameter object does not exist in the collection at the specified location.

```
public void RemoveAt(int);
public void RemoveAt(string parmName);
```

Mutual Properties, Methods, Events Included in the SqlParameterCollection Class

The following lists the mutual properties, methods, and events that are included in the SqlParameterCollection class.

Inherited from Object	Inherited from MarshalByRefObject
Equals method	CreateObjRef method
Finalize method	GetLifetimeService method
GetHashCode method	InitializeLifetimeService method
GetType method	
MemberwiseClone method	
ToString method	

SqlRowUpdatedEventArgs Class

The SqlRowUpdatedEventArgs class supplies the information for the RowUpdated event that is raised when an update to a row has been completed.

```
System.Object
    └── System.EventArgs
            └── SystemData.Common.RowUpdatedEventArgs
                    └── System.Data.SqlClient.SqlRowUpdatedEventArgs
```

Constructor   Initializes a new instance of the SqlRowUpdatedEventArgs class using the specified DataRow, the IDbCommand, the StatementType, and the DataTableMapping. The IDbCommand represents the SQL statement that was executed and the StatementType specifies whether the command was a SELECT, INSERT, UPDATE, or DELETE statement. The DataTableMapping object describes the mapped relationship of the source table and the DataTable.

```
public SqlRowUpdatedEventArgs(System.Data.DataRow,
    System.Data.IDbCommand, System.Data.StatementType,
    System.Data.Common.DataTableMapping);
// C# example
System.Data.DataRow dr = new System.Data.DataTable().NewRow();
System.Data.SqlClient.SqlCommand cmd = new
    System.Data.SqlClient.SqlCommand("SELECT * FROM Customers");
System.Data.Common.DataTableMapping dtm = new
    System.Data.Common.DataTableMapping();
System.Data.Common.RowUpdatedEventArgs ruea = new
    System.Data.SqlClient.SqlRowUpdatedEventArgs(dr, cmd,
    System.Data.StatementType.Select, dtm);
```

SqlRowUpdatedEventArgs Class Properties

Command Property   Returns the SqlCommand that was executed when Update was called.

```
public new SqlCommand Command { get; }
```

Mutual Properties, Methods, Events Included in the SqlRowUpdatedEventArgs Class

The following lists the mutual properties, methods, and events that are included in the SqlRowUpdatedEventArgs class.

Inherited from RowUpdatedEventArgs	Inherited from Object
Errors property	Equals method
RecordsAffected property	Finalize method
Row property	GetHashCode method
StatementType property	GetType method
Status property	MemberwiseClone method
TableMapping property	ToString method

SqlRowUpdatingEventArgs Class

The SqlRowUpdatingEventArgs class supplies the information for the RowUpdating event that is raised when an update to a row is about to take place.

```
System.Object
    System.EventArgs
        System.Data.Common.RowUpdatingEventArgs
            System.Data.SqlClient.SqlRowUpdatingEventArgs
```

Constructor   Initializes a new instance of the SqlRowUpdatingEventArgs class using the specified DataRow, the IDbCommand, the StatementType, and the DataTableMapping. The IDbCommand represents the SQL statement that will be executed and the StatementType specifies whether the command is a SELECT, INSERT, UPDATE, or DELETE statement. The DataTableMapping object describes the mapped relationship of the source table and the DataTable.

```
public SqlRowUpdatingEventArgs(System.Data.DataRow,
    System.Data.IDbCommand, System.Data.StatementType,
    System.Data.Common.DataTableMapping);
// C# example
System.Data.DataRow dr = new System.Data.DataTable().NewRow();
System.Data.SqlClient.SqlCommand cmd = new
    System.Data.SqlClient.SqlCommand("SELECT * FROM Customers");
System.Data.Common.DataTableMapping dtm = new
    System.Data.Common.DataTableMapping();
System.Data.Common.RowUpdatingEventArgs ruea = new
    System.Data.SqlClient.SqlRowUpdatedEventArgs(dr, cmd,
    System.Data.StatementType.Select, dtm);
```

SqlRowUpdatingEventArgs Class Properties

Command Property   Returns or sets the SqlCommand that will be executed when Update is called.

```
public new SqlCommand Command { get; set; }
```

APPENDIXES

Mutual Properties, Methods, Events Included in the SqlRowUpdatingEventArgs Class

The following lists the mutual properties, methods, and events that are included in the SqlRowUpdatingEventArgs class.

Inherited from RowUpdatingEventArgs	Inherited from Object
Errors property	Equals method
Row property	Finalize method
StatementType property	GetHashCode method
Status property	GetType method
TableMapping property	MemberwiseClone method
	ToString method

SqlTransaction Class

The SqlTransaction class represents a SQL transaction to implement at a data source. You do not create a SqlTransaction object by calling a constructor, but rather by calling the BeginTransaction method of a SqlConnection object.

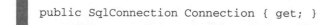

```
System.Object
    System.MarshalByRefObject
        System.Data.SqlClient.SqlTransaction
```

SqlTransaction Class Properties

Connection Property   Returns the SqlConnection object associated with this SqlTransaction.

```
public SqlConnection Connection { get; }
```

IsolationLevel Property   Returns the isolation level for this SqlTransaction object. The default value is ReadCommited.

```
public System.Data.IsolationLevel IsolationLevel { get; }
```

System.Data.IsolationLevel enumeration:

Chaos   Cannot overwrite more highly isolated transactions that are pending.

System.Data.IsolationLevel enumeration:

ReadCommited	To avoid dirty reads, the shared locks are held during reading of data. May result in nonrepeatable read or phantom data is changed before the transaction ends.
ReadUncommited	No exclusive locks are allowed and no shared locks are done. May result in a dirty read.
RepeatableRead	Locks are placed on the queried data. May result in phantom rows.
Serializable	A range lock is placed on the rows in the DataSet.
Unspecified	The isolation level cannot be determined.

System.Data.IDbTransaction.Connection Method   The System.Data.IDbTransaction.Connection method supports the .NET infrastructure and is not used directly from your code.

SqlTransaction Class Methods

Commit Method   Commits the transaction to the database. Throws an exception if there is an error committing the transaction or the connection is broken.

```
public void Commit();
```

Dispose Method   Overloaded. Disposes the resources used by the SqlTransaction object. The second method specifies a Boolean. Specifying True disposes managed and unmanaged resources; False disposes only unmanaged resources.

```
protected virtual void Dispose();
protected virtual void Dispose(bool);
```

Rollback Method   Overloaded. Rolls back a transaction that is in a pending state. The second method specifies a transaction name or savepoint to roll back to. Throws an exception if the transaction has already been committed or the connection is broken.

```
public void Rollback();
public void RollBack(string transName);
```

Save Method   Creates a savepoint with the specified name.

```
public void Save(string savePointName);
```

Mutual Properties, Methods, Events Included in the SqlTransaction Class

The following lists the mutual properties, methods, and events that are included in the SqlTransaction class.

Inherited from Object	Inherited from MarshalByRefObject
Equals method	CreateObjRef method
Finalize method	GetLifetimeService method
GetHashCode method	InitializeLifetimeService method
GetType method	
MemberwiseClone method	
ToString method	

SqlInfoMessageEventHandler Delegate

The SqlInfoMessageEventHandler delegate is the method that handles the InfoMessage event of the SqlConnection object. The first parameter, object, indicates the source of the event to handle. The second parameter is a SqlInfoMessageEventArgs object that contains the event information.

```
public delegate void SqlInfoMessageEventHandler(object,
    SqlInfoMessageEventArgs);
```

SqlRowUpdatedEventHandler Delegate

The SqlRowUpdatedEventHandler delegate is the method that handles the RowUpdatedEvent of the SqlDataAdapter object. The first parameter, object, indicates the source of the event to handle. The second parameter is a SqlRowUpdatedEventArgs object that contains the event information.

```
public delegate void SqlRowUpdatedEventHandler(object,
    SqlRowUpdatedEventArgs);
```

SqlRowUpdatingEventHandler Delegate

The SqlRowUpdatingEventHandler delegate is the method that handles the RowUpdatingEvent of the SqlDataAdapter object. The first parameter, object, indicates the source of the event to handle. The second parameter is a SqlRowUpdatingEventArgs object that contains the event information.

```
public delegate void SqlRowUpdatingEventHandler(object,
    SqlRowUpdatingEventArgs);
```

Index

J

X

INTERNATIONAL CONTACT INFORMATION

AUSTRALIA
McGraw-Hill Book Company Australia Pty. Ltd.
TEL +61-2-9900-1800
FAX +61-2-9878-8881
http://www.mcgraw-hill.com.au
books-it_sydney@mcgraw-hill.com

CANADA
McGraw-Hill Ryerson Ltd.
TEL +905-430-5000
FAX +905-430-5020
http://www.mcgraw-hill.ca

GREECE, MIDDLE EAST, & AFRICA
(Excluding South Africa)
McGraw-Hill Hellas
TEL +30-210-6560-990
TEL +30-210-6560-993
TEL +30-210-6560-994
FAX +30-210-6545-525

MEXICO (Also serving Latin America)
McGraw-Hill Interamericana Editores S.A. de C.V.
TEL +525-117-1583
FAX +525-117-1589
http://www.mcgraw-hill.com.mx
fernando_castellanos@mcgraw-hill.com

SINGAPORE (Serving Asia)
McGraw-Hill Book Company
TEL +65-863-1580
FAX +65-862-3354
http://www.mcgraw-hill.com.sg
mghasia@mcgraw-hill.com

SOUTH AFRICA
McGraw-Hill South Africa
TEL +27-11-622-7512
FAX +27-11-622-9045
robyn_swanepoel@mcgraw-hill.com

SPAIN
McGraw-Hill/Interamericana de España, S.A.U.
TEL +34-91-180-3000
FAX +34-91-372-8513
http://www.mcgraw-hill.es
professional@mcgraw-hill.es

UNITED KINGDOM, NORTHERN, EASTERN, & CENTRAL EUROPE
McGraw-Hill Education Europe
TEL +44-1-628-502500
FAX +44-1-628-770224
http://www.mcgraw-hill.co.uk
computing_europe@mcgraw-hill.com

ALL OTHER INQUIRIES Contact:
Osborne/McGraw-Hill
TEL +1-510-549-6600
FAX +1-510-883-7600
http://www.osborne.com
omg_international@mcgraw-hill.com